MW01627329

SIENA

THE RISE OF PAINTING
1300–1350

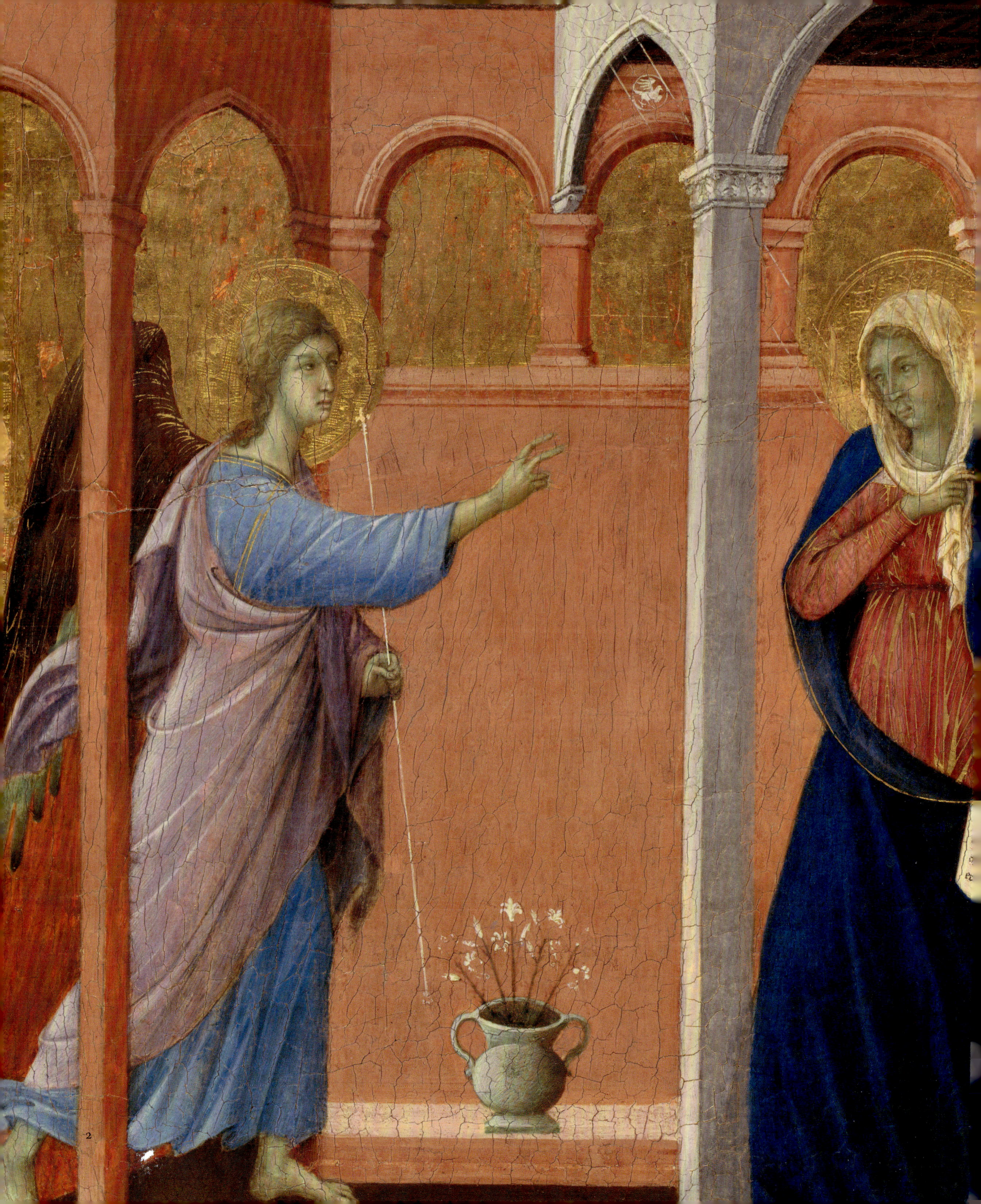

2

SIENA

THE RISE OF PAINTING
1300–1350

Edited by
JOANNA CANNON

with
Caroline Campbell and Stephan Wolohojian

NATIONAL GALLERY GLOBAL, LONDON
DISTRIBUTED BY YALE UNIVERSITY PRESS

CONTENTS

SIENESE CONTEMPORARIES

SIENA AND THE WIDER WORLD

DIRECTORS' FOREWORD

In 1897 the Lithuanian-born American art critic and historian Bernard Berenson succumbed to the attraction of the art of medieval Siena, 'then, as always, sorceress and queen among Italian cities' (Berenson 1930, p. 143). The superlative narrative skills of the city's artists, the material splendour and exquisiteness of their productions – whether in stone, paint, gold or enamel – invested Siena's art with an irresistible aesthetic charm. British writers and poets in the same period were drawn to the spiritual qualities they saw in the works of Duccio ('the flower from whose seed all Sienese art sprang', to stick with 'BB'; Berenson 1930, p. 143), the Lorenzetti brothers and Simone Martini, and highlighted their depth of feeling and the 'dreamy enchantment' they engendered (Stevenson 1894). Today's critics recognise a compellingly modern sensibility in their work, a fascinating embeddedness in the culture, faith, economy and practices of the city, and a profound influence on Italian and European art in the fourteenth and fifteenth centuries.

Siena: The Rise of Painting, 1300–1350 is the first major exhibition to be held on Sienese trecento art at The Metropolitan Museum of Art in New York and at the National Gallery in London. It brings together an impressive group of paintings by the principal painters of the period, including an unprecedented gathering outside of Siena of panels from Duccio's *Maestà*, as well as Pietro Lorenzetti's recently restored Pieve Polyptych from Arezzo, and superb examples of sculpture, goldsmiths' work and textiles. In addition to the works in our own collections, we have been able to count on many extraordinarily generous loans from churches, museums and private collections across Europe and the USA. We wish to express our gratitude to King Charles III, to the bishops, deans and priests, as well as the museum directors, curators and collectors who have accepted to be parted from their precious works for the duration of the exhibitions. We are grateful, too, to the two Mayors of Siena who during the preparation of this project have shown unstinting support for it.

The exhibition has been conceived by Professor Joanna Cannon of the Courtauld Institute of Art and Caroline Campbell at the National Gallery, London, working very closely with Stephan Wolohojian at The Metropolitan Museum of Art. It has been long in gestation and Joanna has meanwhile become Professor Emerita and Stephan and Caroline have taken on significant new responsibilities as the John Pope-Hennessy Curator in Charge of the Department of European Paintings at the Met in 2021 and Director of the National Gallery of Ireland in 2022, respectively. We are grateful for all their continued commitment to this endeavour. Numerous other scholars have contributed knowledge and insights to the catalogue and to them, too, we say thank you.

In New York, many friends of The Met showed their support for this monumental exhibition, and we gratefully acknowledge the generosity of Laura and John Arnold, a gift in memory of Regina Jaglom Wachter, The Huo Family Foundation, The Richard and Natalie Jacoff Foundation, the Robert Lehman Foundation, Trevor and Alexis Traina, the Malcolm Hewitt Wiener Foundation and the Horace W. Goldsmith Foundation. All of these partners made important investments in this exhibition that helped to bring it to fruition. We thank them and all those at The Metropolitan Museum of Art who have allowed us to realise this presentation.

At the National Gallery, we would like to express our gratitude to the Lead Philanthropic Supporter of the exhibition, The Huo Family Foundation, and to its Lead

Sponsor, Intesa Sanpaolo. We would also like to thank Gregory Annenberg Weingarten for his ongoing support of the Gallery's exhibition programme through GRoW@ Annenberg Foundation, and Cockayne – Grants for the Arts: a donor-advised fund held at The London Community Foundation. Lastly, we would like to thank Peggy Czyzak-Dannenbaum, The Vaseppi Trust, Laura Lindsay, Sam Fogg, The Hutton Foundation, Fabrizio Moretti, Elizabeth and Daniel Peltz, Marco Voena, Count and Countess Emilio Voli, Richard Deutsch and Graciela Fairclough, and the other individual donors who have helped to make this exhibition possible.

GABRIELE FINALDI
Director, The National Gallery

MAX HOLLEIN
Marina Kellen French Director and CEO,
The Metropolitan Museum of Art

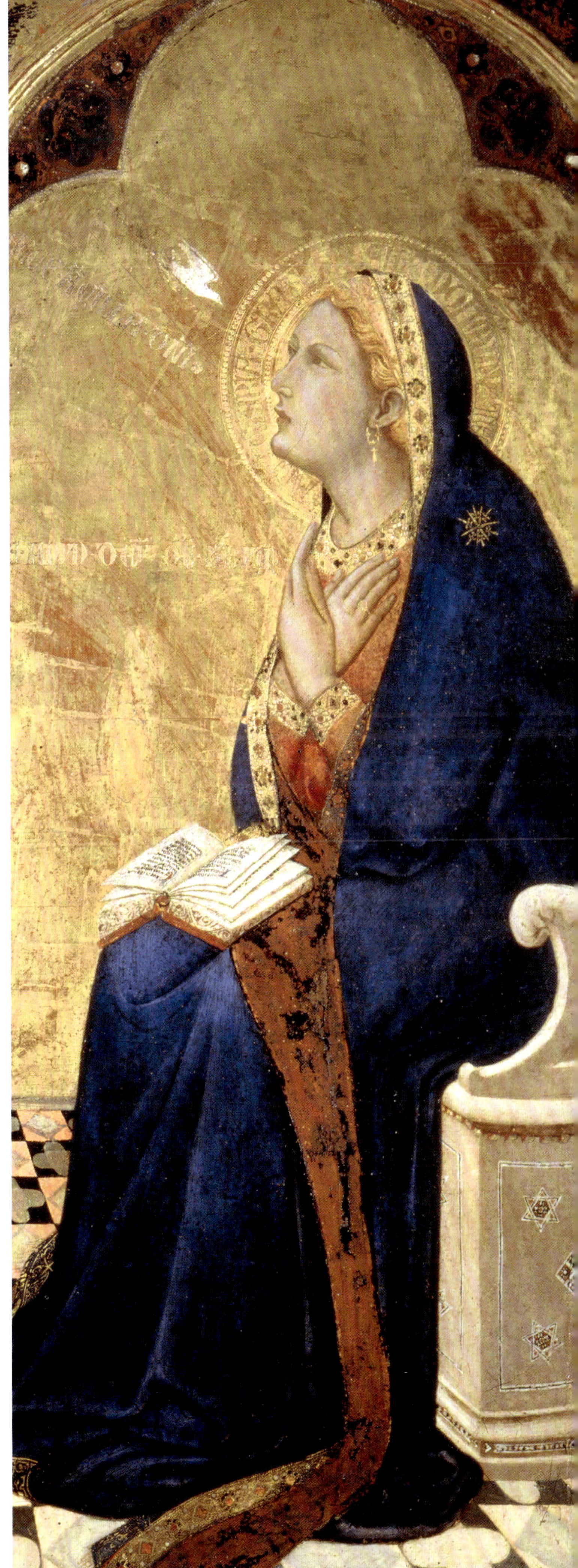

CURATORS' INTRODUCTION

The importance of Siena for the history of Western European art is undeniable, but its significance has been all too often overshadowed by its neighbour Florence. At the start of the fourteenth century, spurred on by competitiveness and curiosity, the leading Sienese painters pushed the boundaries of what painting could be. They created an art of sophistication and experiment, worthy of the closest attention. They developed an artistic language that was locally distinctive and, at the same time, internationally connected: their works contributed decisively to the development of European painting.

The exhibition *Siena: The Rise of Painting, 1300–1350* celebrates the achievements of four remarkable painters, Duccio di Buoninsegna, Simone Martini and Pietro and Ambrogio Lorenzetti, and considers them together with some of the sculptors and goldsmiths who were their Sienese contemporaries. Because large fresco programmes and complex altarpieces are not transportable for temporary display, this project focuses on more portable paintings, to explore the travels of artists, objects and ideas. Within the pages of this book and at its partner exhibition we hope for many fruitful encounters: encounters between works by different artists, in a range of media, from diverse countries and cultures; encounters between ensembles separated for centuries; encounters between these objects and the readers and exhibition visitors already enthralled by Sienese art, as well as those experiencing these artworks for the first time.

Collegial exchange and generous collaboration have been at the heart of the preparation of this project. The first idea for the show began to be shaped by Caroline Campbell and Joanna Cannon at a lunch on the Strand – appropriately halfway between the Courtauld Institute and the National Gallery – more than a decade ago. These conversations led to fruitful discussions with our friend Stephan Wolohojian at The Metropolitan Museum of Art. It has been a joy for the three of us to plan and deliver this exhibition together. The project has benefited infinitely from the more recent incorporation of Laura Llewellyn, Francesca Marzullo and Imogen Tedbury into the curatorial team. Imogen's PhD, an AHRC collaborative doctoral award held between the National Gallery and the Courtauld Institute, was a crucial element of the research that has shaped this exhibition.

The planning of both exhibition and publication has led to many rewarding meetings among curators, scholars, editors, administrators, institutions and enthusiasts. First, we wish to gratefully acknowledge the ongoing support and exceptional commitment shown by the Directors of the National Gallery, Metropolitan Museum of Art and Courtauld Institute, Gabriele Finaldi, Max Hollein, Mark Hallett and Deborah Swallow. The practical work of bringing this exhibition together would have been impossible without our dedicated colleagues in the exhibitions and collections teams at the National Gallery and The Met. We would like to acknowledge the key contributions of Quincy Houghton, Deputy Director for Exhibitions at The Met, and her colleagues Gillian Fruh, Zoe Tippl and Elsie Alonso, as well as Andrea Bayer, Deputy Director for Collections and Administration, together with, at the National Gallery, Jane Knowles, Director of Public Engagement and Christine Riding, Director of Collections and Research, with Sunnifa Hope, Phoebe Newman, Giulia Segreto and Nicholas Flory.

We also wish to recognise the wide-ranging achievements of our curatorial predecessors at the National Gallery and The Met: Keith Christiansen, Dillian Gordon and Luke Syson. Dillian's contributions to *Art in the Making: Italian*

Painting before 1400 (1989) and her catalogue of the National Gallery's collection of *The Italian Paintings before 1400* (2011), have been foundational for this exhibition and book. We have been inspired by Keith's lifelong enthusiasm for and commitment to Sienese painting, as a scholar and curator.

Most work in this field at our institutions has long been imbued with the spirit of collaboration, between colleagues in conservation, curatorial and scientific research. We are particularly indebted to the expertise of current National Gallery and Metropolitan Museum conservators and scientists, including Paul Ackroyd, Rachel Billinge, Jill Dunkerton, Lynn Harrison, Catherine Higgitt, Helen Howard, Larry Keith, Kristina Mandy, Marta Melchiorre Di Crescenzo, Britta New, David Peggie and Marika Spring at the National Gallery; Alan Miller, Kristen Holder, Charlotte Hale and Dorothy Mahon at The Met. In this spirit, we also wish to thank former National Gallery and Met colleagues, including George Bisacca, David Bomford, Michael Gallagher, Jo Kirby, Ashok Roy and Martin Wyld. We also extend our thanks to the Research Forum at the Courtauld for hosting three workshops on Sienese art in preparation for this publication, and to all those who contributed to them.

So many people have played key roles in the making of this exhibition, and we warmly thank you all (please see p. 311). There are some exceptional collaborators in Siena and Tuscany to whom we owe particular debts. Stefano Casciu has cast a benign and enthusiastic eye over our project since at least 2016, alongside his colleagues in the State Museums of Tuscany. The successive Rectors of the Opera della Metropolitana, Guido Pratesi and Giovanni Minnucci, together with the indefatigable Silvia Verdoliva, have been staunch and generous supporters, together with Don Enrico Grassini and his remarkable team at the Archdiocese of Siena, particularly Laura Ponticelli and Federico Nassi. Our thanks are also due to Axel Hémery, Director of the newly autonomous Pinacoteca Nazionale, for his backing. In Siena we are very grateful to Archbishop Lojudice, Mayor Fabio, Mayor De Mossi and Massimo Castellani for their strong advocacy. In Arezzo we have benefited from the constant support of Mayor Ghinelli and Marjorie Layden; Archbishops Fontana and Migliavacca and their team, including Serena Nocentini; Don Alvaro Bardelli and the parish of the Pieve; the extraordinary colleagues at RICERCA, led by the much-missed Isabella Droandi; and the generosity of Doug and Pam Walters. We also wish to acknowledge the essential role of the Soprintendenza of Siena, Arezzo and Grosseto, now led by Gabriele Nannetti.

We are also indebted to our exceptional collaborators at the Opificio delle Pietre Dure (OPD) in Florence. Its art historians, conservators and scientists embraced our proposal to work together – thanks to the openness of the Opera della Metropolitana in Siena – on a technical study of the *Maestà* panels that have remained in Siena, and we look forward to the joint publication of this material. At the OPD we wish to thank especially Emanuela Daffra, Soprintendente, Sandra Rossi, Director of Wall Painting and Easel Painting, Cecilia Frosinini, former Director of Wall Painting and Easel Painting, Roberto Bellucci and Ciro Castelli.

We are very grateful to the team of authors and editors who have contributed their time, knowledge, ideas and professionalism so generously and enthusiastically to the creation of this publication. We would particularly like to thank Flora Allen, who has project edited the book with great patience and skill, as well as Diana Adell and Laura Lappin.

This project has benefited from the loan of extraordinary objects, many of which have never left the institutions that keep them, which has made it possible to reunite works dispersed through international collections in more recent times. We are deeply indebted to all those who have enabled us to study these great objects and share them with our audiences. Through the interruptions and disruption caused by the global pandemic, and the many other challenges such ambitious projects present, we have been most grateful for your unwavering generosity and support.

CAROLINE CAMPBELL
JOANNA CANNON
LAURA LLEWELLYN
IMOGEN TEDBURY
STEPHAN WOLOHOJIAN

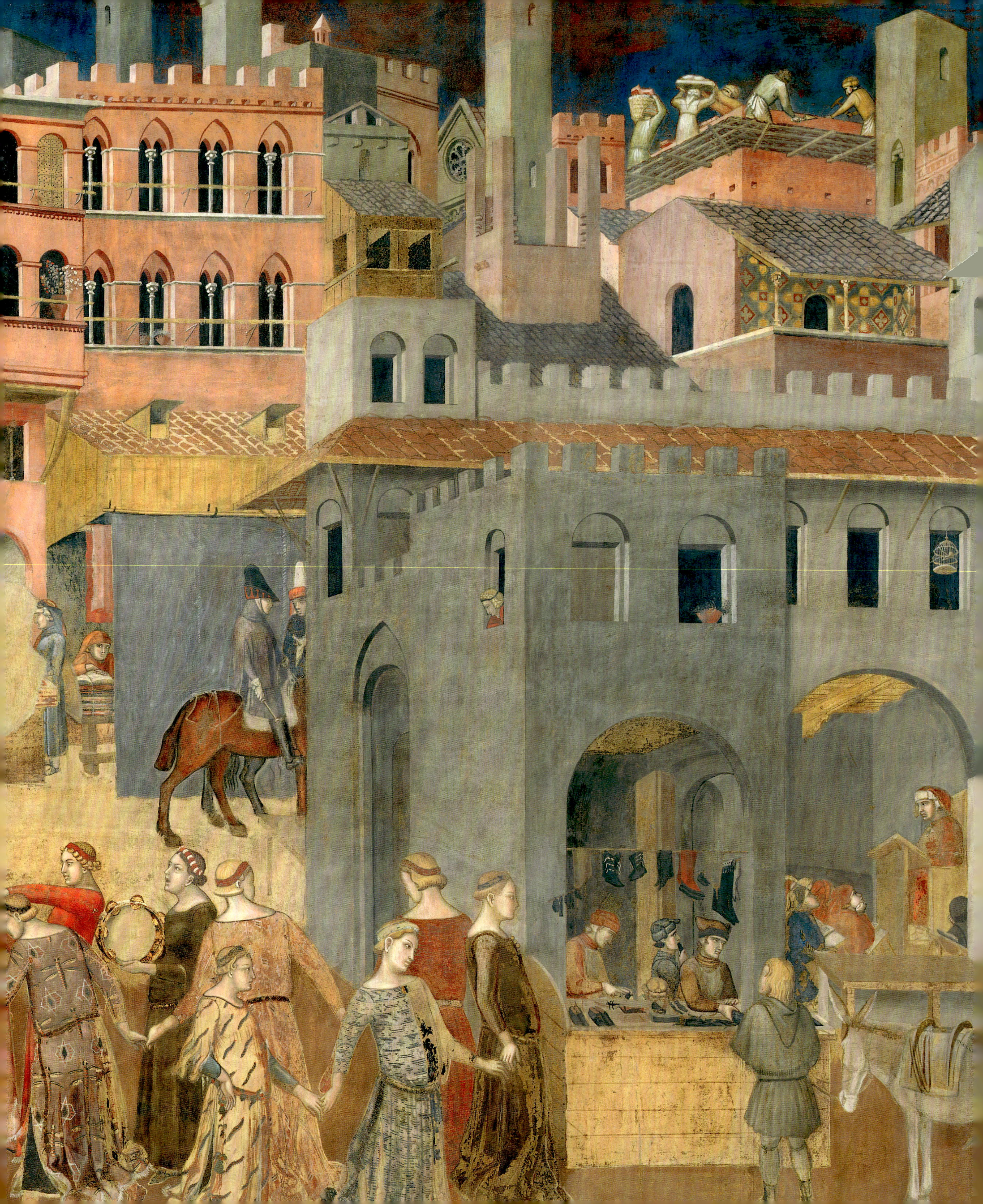

SIENA: MYTH AND REALITY

Caroline Campbell

Inscribed on the 1250 city seal of Siena is a striking request for the Virgin Mary's intercession: 'May the Virgin preserve Siena the ancient, whose loveliness she seals'.[1] It is remarkable that more than seven hundred and fifty years later, having endured many trials and setbacks – not least the underwhelming assessment of Giorgio Vasari, loyal Medici servant and proud Aretine – much of the loveliness of 'Siena the ancient' survives. The primary purpose of this book, and the exhibition it accompanies, is to jointly acknowledge and probe the achievement of Siena's trecento artists – in painting, sculpture and metalwork – as well as to study the impact that their stylistic and storytelling innovations had on successive generations of artists within Siena, more widely in central Italy and north of the Alps.

Key to Siena's collective identity was the sense that the city was under the personal protection of the Virgin Mary. On 4 September 1260 Siena inflicted what seemed a miraculous victory over the much greater forces of its Florentine enemies at Montaperti, less than 10 miles from the city. The chronicle attributed to Paolo di Tommaso Montauri, dating to the later fifteenth century, records her intervention. The night before the battle, Siena's mayor, Buonaguida, is said to have made his way to the cathedral, where he laid the keys of the city 'at the feet of the Queen and Emperor of Everlasting Life', where the *Madonna of the Large Eyes* was displayed (fig. 2) until the installation of Duccio's *Maestà* on the high altar on 6 June 1311. The Virgin is said to have cast her mantle over the Sienese soldiers at Montaperti, and over the city itself, as a symbol of her divine favour.[2]

The cult of Mary was a highly important element of medieval theology and identity, but there was something particularly all-encompassing about Siena's relationship with the Virgin. Not only was she found in countless images, small, large and of varying quality, in shrines, churches and religious foundations across the city, but also her connection to Siena was visibly proclaimed on every important site, sacred and secular, including the two principal city gates; the cathedral, centre of sacred power; the Palazzo Pubblico, hub of the Sienese state; and the hospital of Santa Maria della Scala.[3]

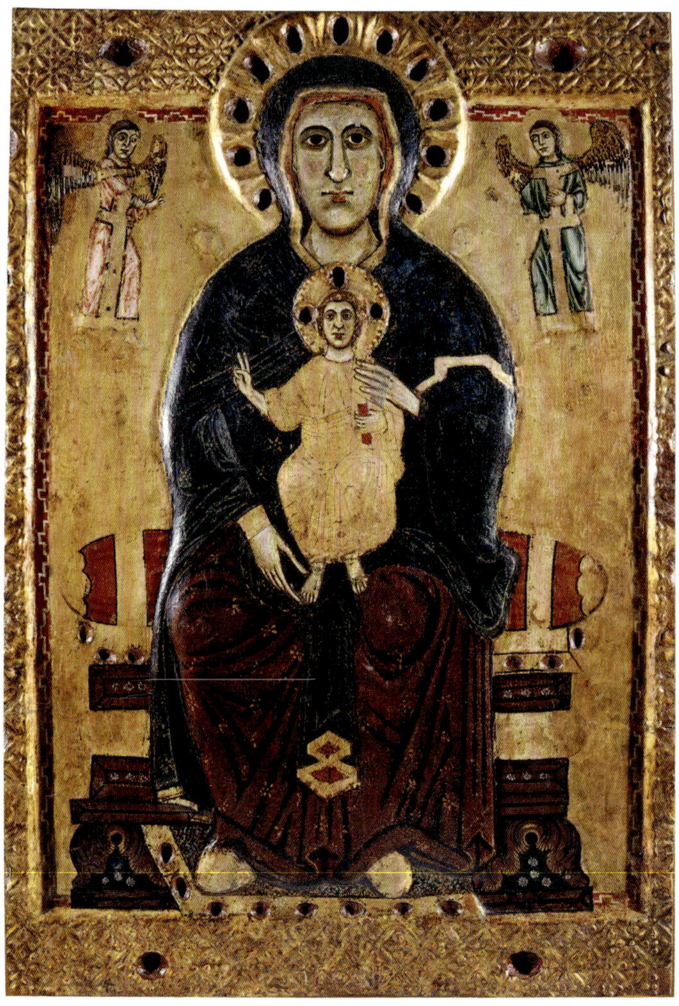

FIG. 1 (P. 10)
Ambrogio Lorenzetti
(documented 1319; died 1348/9)
The Effects of Good Government in the City (detail), 1338
Fresco
Palazzo Pubblico, Siena

FIG. 2
Master of Tressa
(active first quarter of the thirteenth century)
The Madonna of the Large Eyes, about 1215
Tempera on panel, 97 × 67 cm
Museo dell'Opera della Metropolitana, Siena

Veneration of the Virgin played a significant part in civic ritual. From at least 1200, Siena was one of the first places in Europe where the Feast of the Assumption of the Virgin – still a crucial date in the Roman Catholic liturgical calendar – was celebrated publicly.[4] Every year, on 14 August, the eve of the feast, the people of Siena climbed to the cathedral in their *contrade* (neighbourhood associations), to renew their individual and collective vow to Mary.[5] In 1310 the celebrated horse race, the Palio, was run for the first occasion in association with this event. From around this time, it became common practice on the Feast of the Assumption for those towns and territories under Siena's control to renew their own vows of allegiance to the Virgin's city,[6] thus eliding the secular and sacred powers of the Sienese state and its authority beyond Siena itself.

For all their Marian devotion, the people and rulers of medieval Siena were careful to spread their net for protection more widely. Four early Christian saints were particularly venerated in the city, and appear in countless altarpieces. To each a chapel was dedicated in the cathedral. Ansanus, Sabinus and Crescentius were all early Christian martyrs, while the soldier saint Victor was credited for a Sienese victory on his feast day. In addition, medieval Siena increasingly mythologised and celebrated the city's pre-Christian origins. The Sienese believed that they were descended from Remus, a hero of pre-Latin Rome. A further tradition credited the Senones, who participated in the Sack of Rome, with the city's origins. Many other central and northern Italian city states melded pagan and Christian stories in their foundation myths, although few did this as early or as persistently as Siena.

Siena's civic politics also fitted into a pattern seen in other prosperous cities on the Italian peninsula. The *comune* of Siena had been established (like those of Florence, Bologna and Ferrara) following the death of Countess Matilda of Tuscany in 1115 and the subsequent diminution of seigneurial power in the region. In spite of their apparently independent status, the townspeople were not immune from involvement in the lengthy pan-European struggle between the forces of the Pope (the Guelphs) and the Holy Roman Emperor (the Ghibellines). To begin with, Siena sided with the emperor, while Florence, its long-term rival, supported the papacy.

This abiding conflict represented an existential threat to Siena's material wealth. During the thirteenth century the young city state was established as one of Europe's principal banking centres. Its bankers offered bills of exchange and money transfer services across Western Europe. This was facilitated by the regular presence of Sienese merchants at the trade fairs in Champagne, Flanders and London. Montaperti, for all its lasting significance for the image and mythology of Siena,[7] was both economically and politically damaging for the small and reasonably vulnerable state. Siena's destruction of the Florentine forces led to the city being excommunicated by the Pope, making it impossible for its merchants to trade with the apostolic see, or for its bankers to lend money to the papacy. Following Siena's defeat by Florentine forces at Colle di Val d'Elsa in 1269, the Sienese had little choice, in practical terms, but to align themselves with the Guelph faction, in order to preserve their financial and commercial interests.

'IL BUON GOVERNO'

From 1287 to 1355, almost all the period covered by this exhibition, the city was under the rule of the 'Nine Governors and Defenders of the Comune and People of Siena', more commonly known as the Council of the Nine (the *Nove*), or 'il Buon Governo'. They were selected every two months from a group of Siena's male citizens.[8] Each member of the Nine held the chairmanship of the group for one week of their two-month rule. During this time, they lived together in the Palazzo Pubblico, sleeping and sharing meals in designated rooms. Many were merchants or bankers; some belonged to named noble houses (the *casati*). Judges, notaries and doctors were excluded from their number. From 1304 they could not be under 30 years of age. Most owned property outside the city. For the privilege of serving, members of the Nine had to wait another 20 months before becoming eligible for office again. This ensured that over a five-year period several hundred people had experience of playing a leading role in the affairs of the state.

The Nine controlled the selection of election of the city's general council, of its highest financial officials (the four *Provveditori di Biccherna*), and of the Consul of the Knights. They also oversaw the lists of names from whom their successors were drawn, even following the introduction of selection by lot, in 1318. They and their relatives took on most of the lesser offices of church, of locality and of state in Siena, so that their web of influence and connections spread across the city.[9] It was, however, for more than sixty years, a remarkably stable form of government, one that permitted Siena to exercise some power and influence beyond its boundaries, to hold a certain prestige and to become an important trading centre.

In addition, the Nine provided an environment that encouraged artistic experimentation, and the evolution of art forms that transformed the development of painting not just in Siena, or in central Italy, but across Western Europe. Their government also supported the structures that make a city liveable, including major civic and religious buildings, roads, reliable fresh water supplies, walls and drainage systems. The well-governed, morally righteous state was reflected back in the private buildings that surrounded its headquarters.

EXPERIENCING SIENA

Siena owed its wealth, and partly its identity, to its situation on the via Francigena or Romea (fig. 3). This was one of the most ancient and well-travelled pilgrimage routes connecting northern Europe to Rome, first reliably documented by Abbot Sigeric on his journey from Canterbury to the 'Eternal City' in 990.[10] Siena, 145 miles north of Rome, was one of the major stops on the central Italian leg of this voyage, which most medieval travellers would have undertaken on foot. Well into

FIG. 3
A panoramic view of Siena including the Cathedral and Piazza del Campo

FIG. 4
The Palazzo Pubblico from the top of the Piazza del Campo

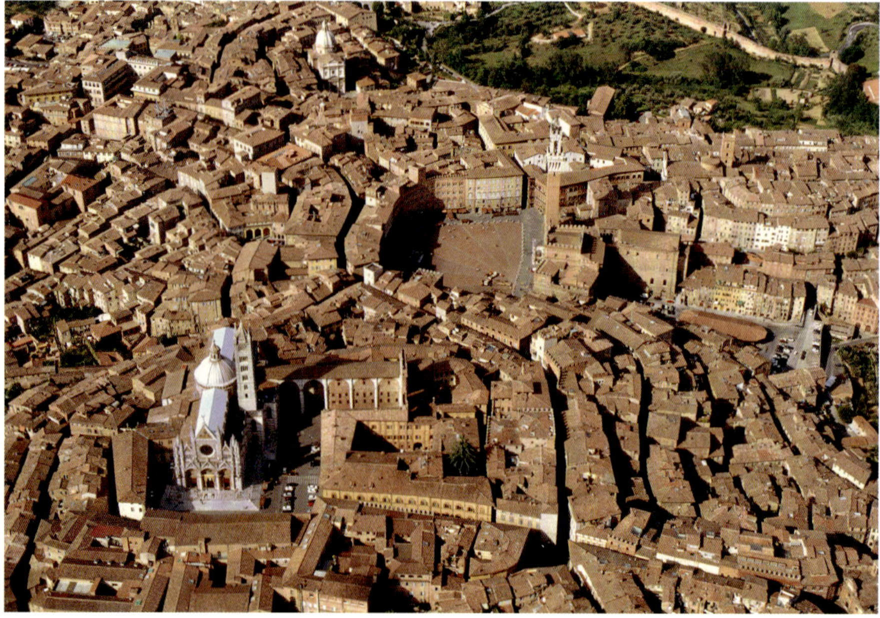

the fifteenth century the Sienese state continued to invest in the maintenance and safety of the road, called the 'Strada Romana' in the city. Traffic along the via Francigena provided custom for Siena's shops and hostelries.

The shape of medieval Siena, divided into the *terzi* (thirds) of Camollia, San Martino and the city itself, straddling three hills, was indebted to that of the road, which runs for approximately a mile and a half through the city, connecting the main gates of the Porta Camollia at the north, and the Porta Romana, or Nuova, at the south. Described by Fabrizio Nevola as an 'undulating visual tunnel',[11] from 1241 the Strada Romana was the first of Siena's thoroughfares to be paved in brick. It was maintained by the *Viarii* (officials of the street), and was protected by regulations that prevented private owners from damaging public property.[12]

In the fourteenth and fifteenth centuries the city's principal luxury traders – bankers, goldsmiths and cloth merchants – were strongly encouraged to set up shop on the Strada. Siena's goldsmiths, whose work was sold and used throughout Europe, benefited from commissions received from lay pilgrims and churchmen either on their way to or returning from Rome. The Loggia della Mercanzia, the meeting place for the corporation of Siena's guilds, was placed at the city's most important crossroads, the Croce del Travaglio: 'because of the Strada, all foreigners pass [here] ... whichever direction they enter Siena from.'[13]

Just below the Loggia stands the Campo, where the major roads leading to and from Siena came together. One of the more memorable parts of any visit to Siena remains the experience of walking down the inclining brick surface of this piazza, roughly in the shape of a shell, to the Palazzo Pubblico.[14] The conception of this magnificent building, an enduring model for city halls across Europe over many centuries, dates to the 1280s, when Siena's government decided to bring the offices of state and the residence of the state officials together in one place. This structure combined the offices of Customs, the Mint and the Council, along with the residence of the Podestà (the official responsible for the maintenance of law and order). It also housed the Nine, when in office.

THE PALAZZO PUBBLICO

The edifice that began to rise at the base of the Campo in 1297 was an imposing tower-block structure intended to convey the solidity and power of the Sienese state itself (fig. 4). The ground-floor facade, consisting of the typically Sienese architectural form of a shallow arch within a pointed arc, was faced in stone. The remainder of the building was covered in brick and crowned by battlements. The two side wings, constructed between 1307 and 1310, housed the Podestà (on the left) and the Council of the

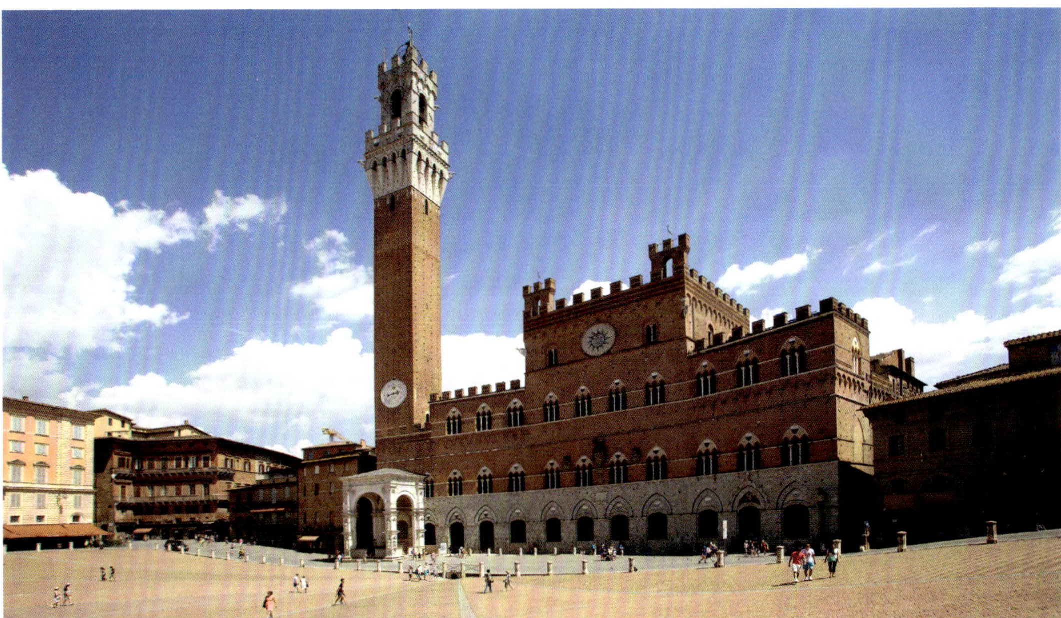

Nine (on the right). At the left rises the brick tower (Torre del Mangia) completed in 1348, just before the catastrophe of the Black Death, topped with a belfry of travertine marble.[15]

Although the building still seems strongly medieval in character, it has evolved significantly over the centuries. Much of the internal organisation and decoration has changed. We can both lament what has been destroyed, as well as celebrate what remains, on the palace's walls and in other places (including the Simone Martini polyptych reconstituted for the first time in this exhibition, see figs 75–9).[16] The most extraordinary elements are still to be found in two adjoining rooms on the first floor of the palace.

The left-hand wall as you enter the Great Council Chamber, now known as the Sala del Mappamondo, is still dominated by Simone's dazzling *Maestà* (see fig. 65), painted directly onto the wall.[17] This Queen of Heaven also enjoys explicit dominion over favoured parts of the terrestrial world. She sits under a canopy decorated with the arms of the royal house of Anjou, the people of Siena (represented by a lion) and the city itself, shown by its arms (or *balzana*). The words of Christ and his mother, reflecting on the responsibilities of government, were intended as direct messages to the councillors who met here.[18]

Next door, the Nine gathered in a much smaller room. Here survives one of the most exceptional visualisations of the mechanisms of government and its moral purpose ever made. Over a period of 16 months, from February 1338 to May 1339, Ambrogio Lorenzetti and his workshop frescoed its walls with scenes of good and bad government. The cycle consists of representations of the Vices and Virtues related to the practice of government, and depictions of rural and urban life under exemplary and problematic regimes (see figs 1 and 140).[19]

THE CATHEDRAL

Towering above Siena, a brisk 10-minute walk up the hill from the Campo, is the great cathedral church, a harmony in coloured marble, built and maintained to the honour of the Virgin Mary (fig. 5). On 9 June 1311 Duccio's *Maestà*, a work of exceptional innovation, commissioned to stand on the high altar, was processed to its prestigious location in triumph.[20] Duccio's double-sided altarpiece, one of the largest and most ambitious ever made, was central to the daily sacramental veneration of Christ and Mary in the cathedral. The building itself, the most significant structure in the city, bears witness to Siena's resilience, as well as to moments of collective trauma. The ambitious planned fourteenth-century extensions to the cathedral, which involved reorienting it by 90 degrees and constructing a new five-bay nave, were left incomplete because of the Black

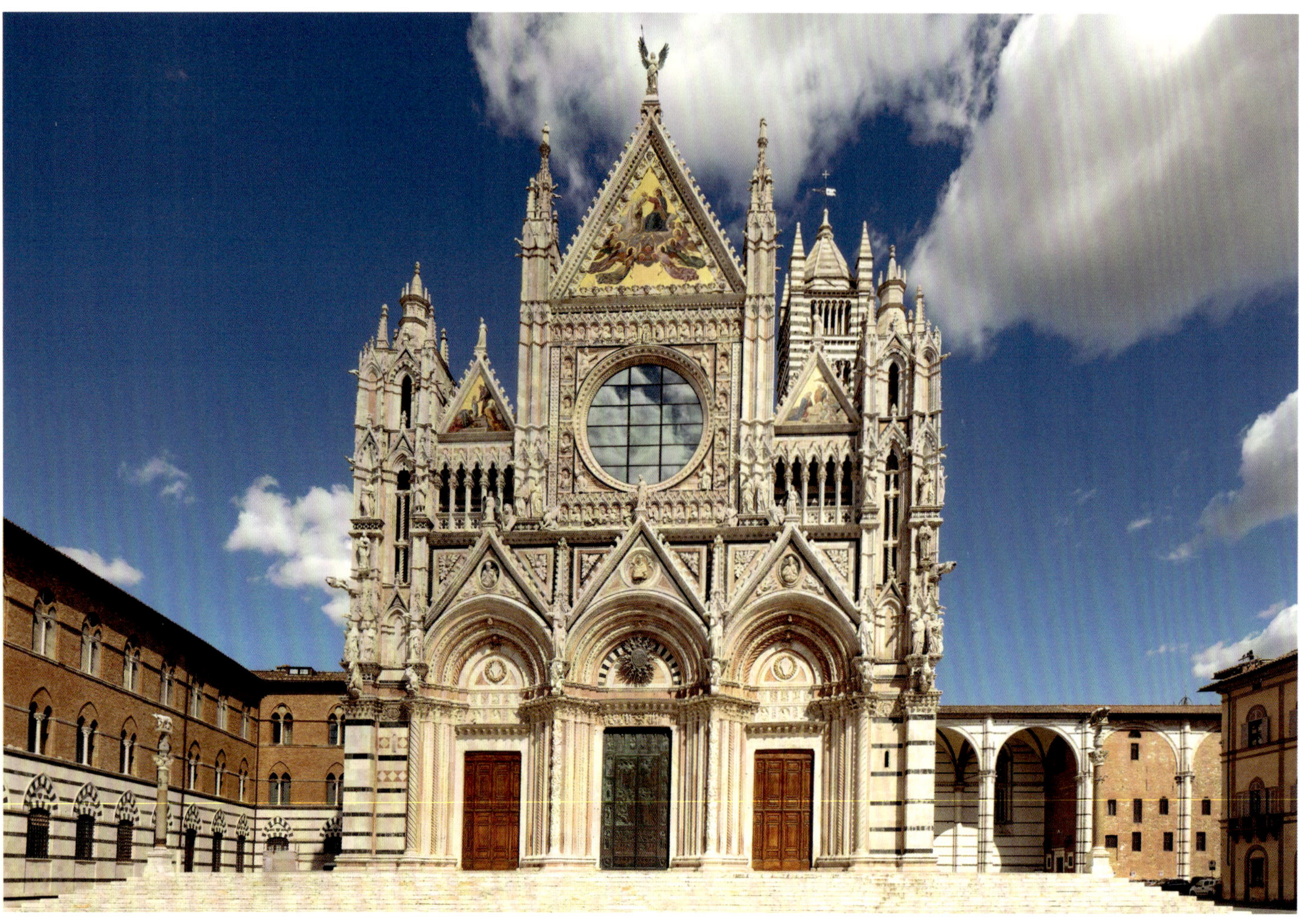

FIG. 5
Siena Cathedral

Death. Today, only the remains of the South Vaults (the current Museo dell'Opera della Metropolitana) and the outside walls, including the magnificent incomplete facade, remain.[21]

Visiting the current building is extraordinarily moving. It is a place where one is left in no doubt of the power of the Virgin Mary and the Christian faith to shape lives. This would have been more palpable in the early fourteenth century. Even taking account of the major building work that was omnipresent during this and the previous century, every visit to the cathedral – not only on the eve of the Assumption – would have been a performative experience. Climbing the great steps, probably for many recalling the Virgin Mary's own visit to the temple in Jerusalem with her parents, brought close the facade. Here, architecture works in harmony with a sea of sculptures, many by the hand of Giovanni Pisano. The dazzling cathedral interior, with its dome, vaulted choir, magnificent green-and-white-striped marble nave, and stained glass, is the work of many artists, including Duccio and Giovanni's father Nicola.[22] He, his assistants and son also created the remarkable octagonal pulpit, originally situated in the choir, from which the scriptures were read and sermons were preached.

These structures would have been key to the experience of the fourteenth-century visitor. Yet others, made for the cathedral, have been removed from their original home. All of the five principal altarpieces, on the high altar and the four chapels of Siena's patronal saints, have left their intended locations.[23] Duccio's great *Maestà* has perhaps suffered most. It was dismembered in the eighteenth century, and although the majority of its elements remain in Siena, the other parts are now divided between museums in New York, London, Washington DC, Madrid and Fort Worth. A major aspiration of the exhibition this volume accompanies has been to reconstitute the back predella of the *Maestà* for the first time in almost two hundred and fifty years (see figs 23–30).[24]

Across the square from the cathedral is the imposing front of Santa Maria della Scala (Our Lady of the Stairs). From the twelfth century this hospital was administered by a confraternity of lay people, headed by a rector, who managed its resources to care for the sick, pilgrims, the poor, and abandoned infants (foundlings). For much of the period that concerns this book, the hospital was the third major patron of art and architecture in the city, after the *comune* and the cathedral.[25] Most significant, in terms of the wider city and the story of this exhibition, were the frescoes of the life of the Virgin (completed by 1335), principally by the Lorenzetti brothers and Simone Martini, which adorned the front of the hospital overlooking the cathedral square until 1720.[26]

The destruction of the Santa Maria della Scala frescoes is one of the saddest losses to Siena's architectural fabric. We can only imagine how these paintings worked in conjunction with the sculpted front of the cathedral, with its three-dimensional representations of the prophets, sibyls and ancestors of Christ. Together they would have given the Sienese people, even without entering a church, the clearest visualisation of their city's intimate connection to the sacred stories of Christ and his mother.

* * *

The environment in which the artists of trecento Siena evolved gave rise to the constraints and conventions that shaped their lives and work, as well as their connections with other artistic, religious and economic centres. Here, the wider ambition and chauvinistic pride of the city state that forged them – 'Siena the ancient' – has been evoked to provide a context for the more detailed studies of particular artists and their artworks that follow. These elucidate the truly exceptional spirit of innovation that characterised the artistic production of Siena in the early fourteenth century, and which – diffused across Italy, and northern and eastern Europe – made a lasting impact on the evolution of European painting, sculpture, metalwork and the wider arts.

This essay is indebted to the deep scholarship and wise counsel of Joanna Cannon, and to many conversations and discussions with Joanna, Stephan Wolohojian, Imogen Tedbury and Laura Llewellyn. I would also like to thank Nicholas Flory for his assistance, and to acknowledge and thank all who participated in the Siena study days organised by Joanna at the Courtauld Institute of Art, under the aegis of the Courtauld Research Forum, in 2019.

1. 'Salvet Virgo Senam veterem quam signat amenam.' Seals – which are still in ceremonial use today – were used throughout Europe to authenticate and verify official documents ratified by rulers, towns, institutions, clerics and prestigious individuals.
2. White 1979, p. 95; Norman 1999b, p. 3.
3. For Marian devotion in Siena, see Hook 1979, pp. 124–33; for street shrines, see Leoncini 1994.
4. Cecchini 1983, p. 331.
5. Campbell 2005, pp. 436–7.
6. Syson 2007–8, p. 81.
7. For a recent account, see Franco 2021.
8. It is worth mentioning that between 1290 and 1292 the governmental system changed twice: from the 'Eighteen' to the 'Six', before reverting to the Nine. See Waley 1991, p. xxiii, for a chronology.
9. William Bowsky has characterised them as representative of the more numerous and individually less powerful, rather than the less numerous but individually more powerful. In contrast, Daniel Waley has emphasised that the Republic of Siena was an oligarchy that favoured the few rather than a 'popular' regime. See Bowsky 1981; Waley 1991.
10. Ortenberg 1990.
11. Nevola 2000, p. 35.
12. See ibid., pp. 27–8, and references in nn. 28–30.
13. Hansen 1993, p. 15.
14. For a wonderfully evocative rendering of a Sienese brick pavement, see Duccio's *Temptation of Christ on the Mountain*, fig. 24 (Frick Collection, New York).
15. Brandi 1983.
16. See Llewellyn, pp. 117–19, in the present volume; Christiansen 1994.
17. See Capron, p. 102, in the present volume.
18. Norman 2006.
19. See Wolohojian, p. 128, in the present volume. For fuller references see, in particular, Starn 1987; Starn and Partridge 1993, pp. 11–55; Boucheron 2018.
20. See Cannon, p. 25, in the present volume.
21. For an introduction to the cathedral (and to the contesting views on its construction and authorship of the major architectural elements), see Carli 1979; Pietramellara 1980; Van der Ploeg 1993; Haas and von Winterfeld 2006, especially pp. 271–96, pp. 736–836, docs 33–345; Butzek 2006 (the latter two are exceptionally thorough accounts, and to the author of this essay, compelling). Good English language summaries of the debates are found in Benton 1995 and Gordon 2011, pp. 178–9, and references in nn. 36–65.
22. For Nicola Pisano, see Testi Cristiani 1987.
23. For a summary, see Van Os 1984, pp. 77–89, 143. Pietro Lorenzetti's *Birth of the Virgin* (see fig. 40), for the chapel of San Savino, has only travelled to the Museo dell'Opera of Santa Maria. Simone Martini's *Annunciation*, made for the altar of Saint Ansanus, and Ambrogio Lorenzetti's *Presentation in the Temple* for the chapel of San Crescenzio, are now in the Gallerie degli Uffizi, Florence, while the remaining fragments of Bartolomeo Bulgarini's altarpiece for the chapel of San Vittore are now in Copenhagen, Frankfurt, Harvard and Paris.
24. See Cannon, p. 25, and Tedbury, pp. 46–51, in the present volume, for references and more information.
25. Morandi and Cairola 1975. See Williamson, pp. 184–9, in the present volume, regarding a mid-fourteenth-century reliquary commissioned by its rector.
26. Maginnis 1988.

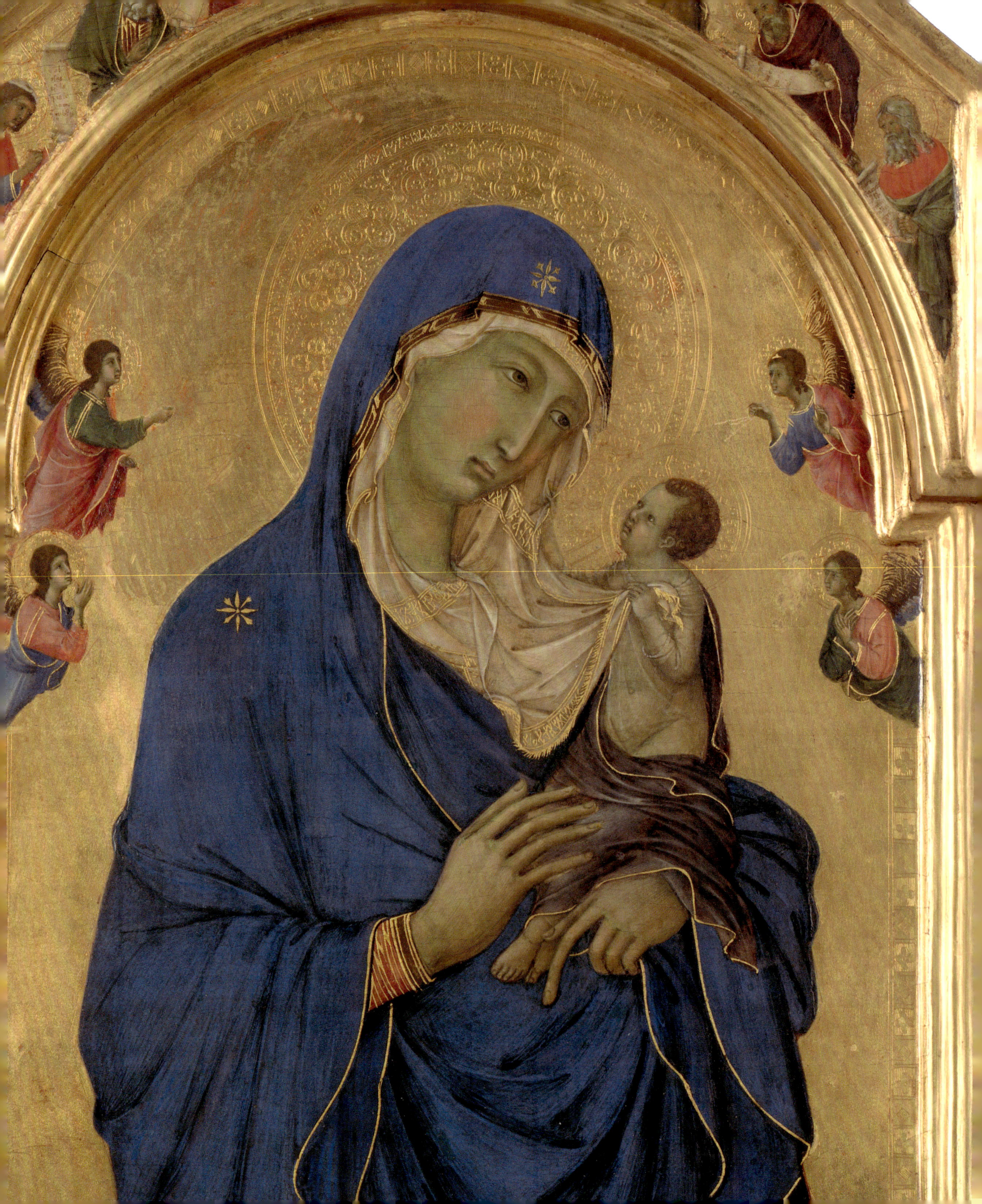

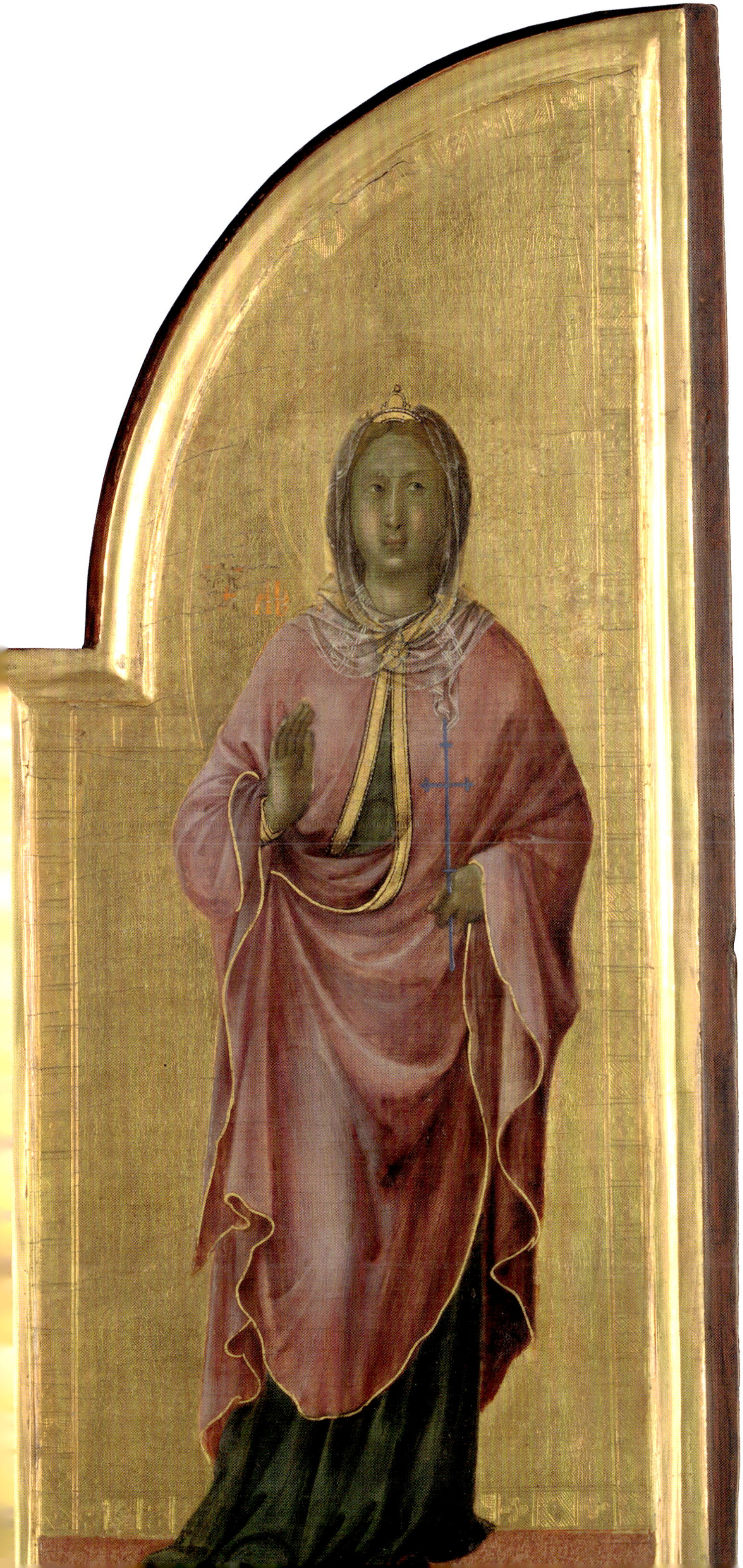

DUCCIO OF SIENA

On 15 April 1285 four representatives of a lay confraternity dedicated to the Virgin Mary, based in the Dominican Church of Santa Maria Novella in Florence, agreed a contract with 'Duccio, of the late Buoninsegna, painter from Siena' and provided him with 'a certain large panel' on which he was to paint, 'a most beautiful picture to the honour and glory of the blessed and glorious Virgin Mary'.[1] In addition to the images of the Virgin and of her son, other figures were to be included 'according to the wishes and pleasures of the commissioners'. They placed significant emphasis on the beauty of the panel, declaring that no payment would be forthcoming if the panel 'is not beautifully painted and if it is not embellished according to [their] wishes and desires'. The resulting work was, indeed, very beautifully painted and ornamented (fig. 6). Now generally known as the *Rucellai Madonna*, this huge work (450 × 290 cm) vies for dominance with two other great panel paintings of the Virgin and Child enthroned: Cimabue's *Santa Trinita Madonna* and Giotto's *Ognissanti Madonna*, all three displayed in the same room of the Gallerie degli Uffizi in Florence.[2] The laymen commissioning this work evidently had the highest standards and wished to keep a firm grip on the appearance and contents of an image before which they sang praises to the Virgin every evening. Their investment confirms the growing status of panel paintings, and the beauty that might be expected of them.

Their choice of a painter from Siena is striking.[3] Perhaps the leading Florentine painter of the day, Cimabue, was not available. Links between the Dominican-based confraternity and its Sienese counterpart, which already owned a large painting of the *Virgin and Child enthroned* executed by Guido da Siena in about 1275–80 (see fig. 12), may have played a part.[4] The reputation of 'Duccio of Siena' must have been high to secure such a prestigious Florentine commission. Nevertheless, over the centuries the link between painting and artist was forgotten and the work was long considered to be a masterpiece by Cimabue. The contract of 1285 was rediscovered in 1790, but the attribution to Cimabue was hard to dislodge. It was only in the 1930s that the connection between contract and painting was at last widely accepted.[5] This prioritising of a Florentine painter over one from Siena belongs with the long-running undervaluing of Sienese contributions to the history of art, characteristic of writing dominated over many centuries by a Florentine version of the past that is only gradually being revisited.[6] The presence of a major Sienese painting in Florence in the later thirteenth century is a forerunner of the appreciation that Florentine patrons showed for artists from Siena in subsequent decades, notably: Ugolino di Nerio's high altarpieces for Santa Maria Novella and for the Franciscan Church of Santa Croce;[7] several works by the Lorenzetti brothers – products of longer stays in Florence – including Ambrogio's Saint Nicholas scenes (see fig. 89) and triptych for

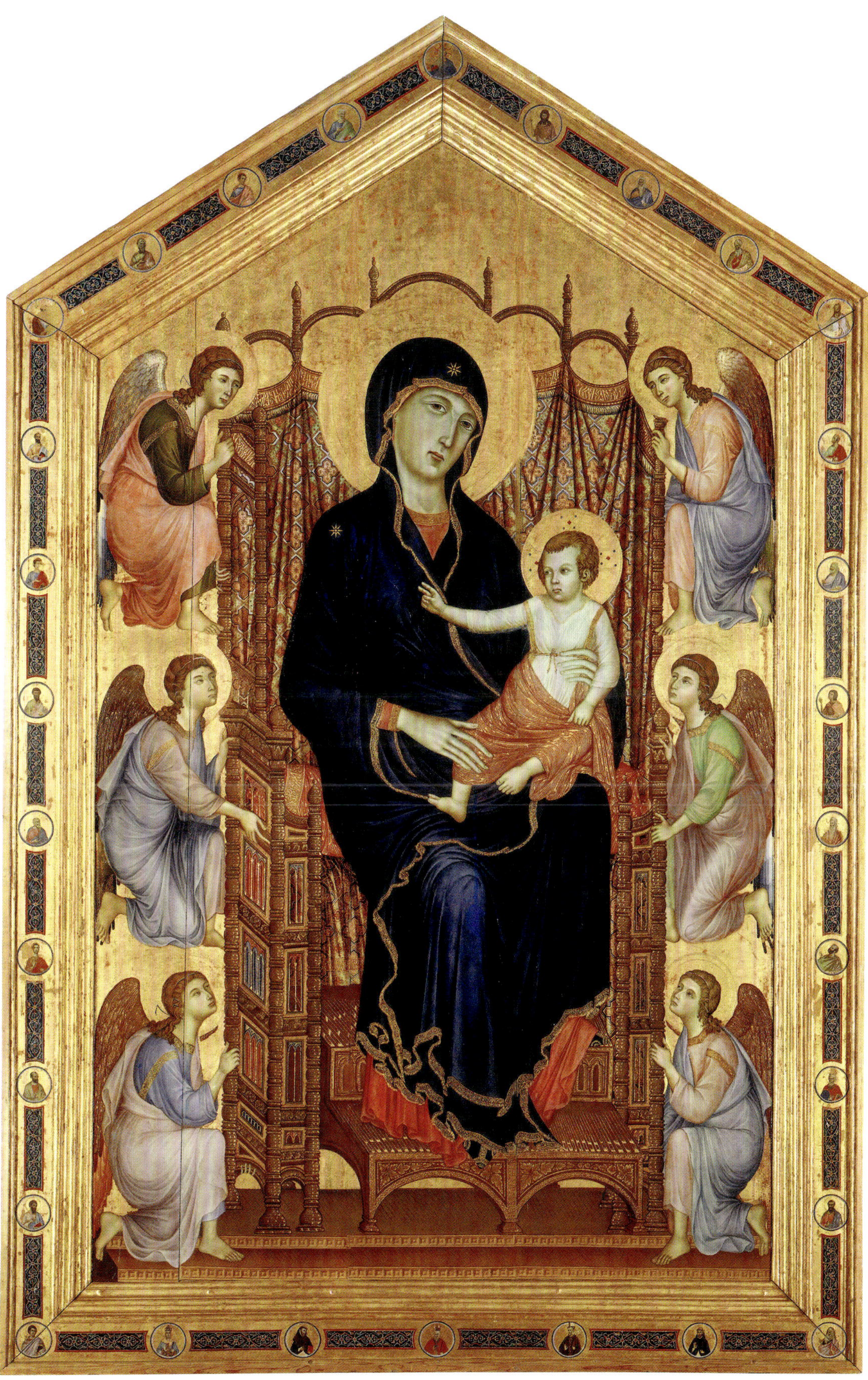

FIG. 6
Duccio (documented 1278; died 1319)
The Rucellai Madonna, 1285
Tempera on panel, 450 × 290 cm
Gallerie degli Uffizi, Florence

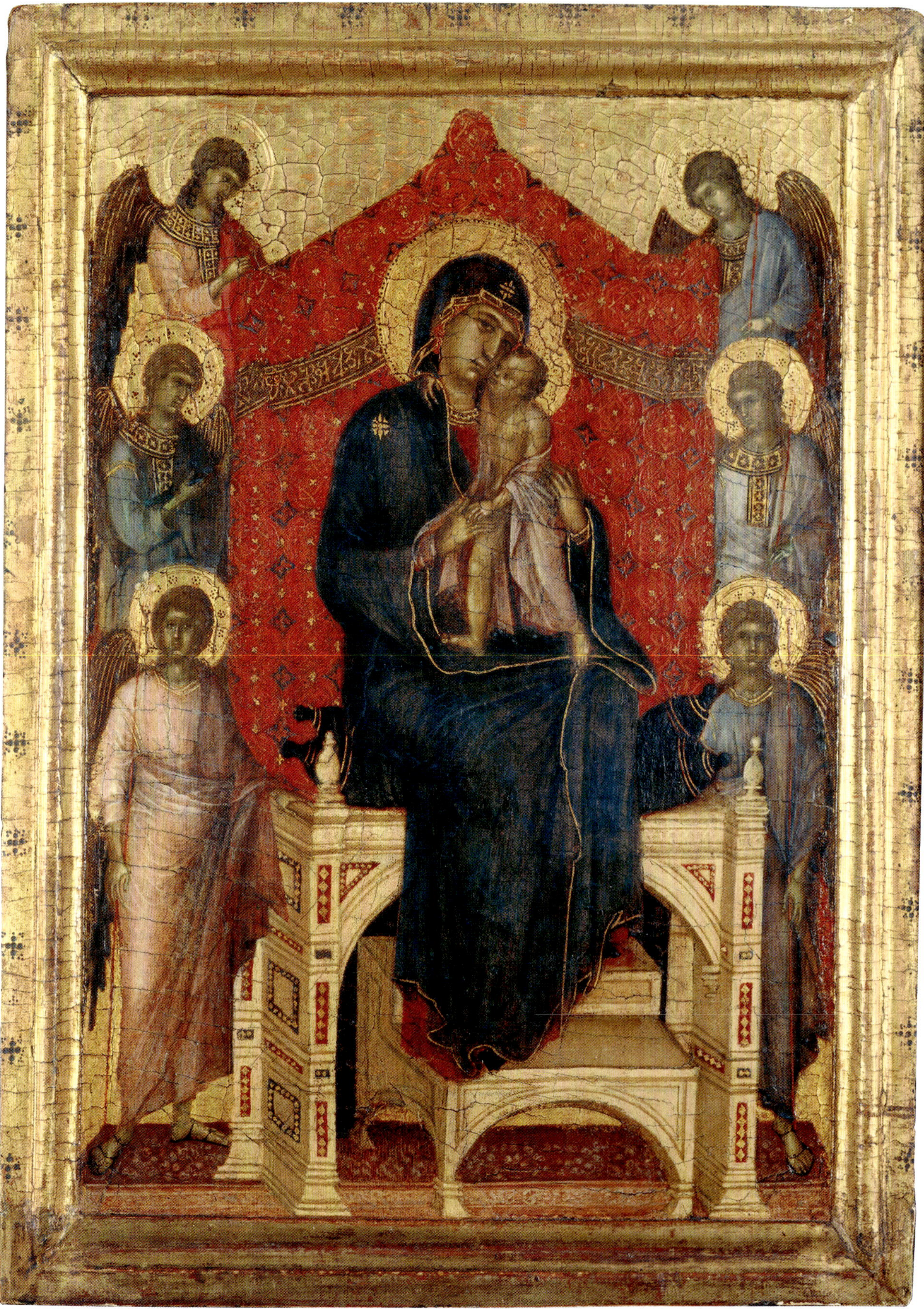

San Procolo (see fig. 91), and Pietro's panel of the Beata Umiltà (all now Gallerie degli Uffizi, Florence).[8] A Sienese sculptor, Tino di Camaino, also received important Florentine commissions: funerary monuments for Gastone della Torre, patriarch of Aquileia, in Santa Croce (1318–21), for Bishop Antonio d'Orso in the cathedral (1320–1), and, in 1322, works for the Florentine baptistery.[9]

Apart from the *Rucellai Madonna* only one other surviving work is documented as being by Duccio: the *Maestà* for the high altar of Siena Cathedral, his only signed work, a supreme piece that marks a crucial step in the establishment of independent paintings as a leading form of artwork in Western Europe (see figs 8, 9). Around these two documented works a small group of exquisite paintings has been assembled, with varying consensus, as being by Duccio (including figs 7, 17, 18, 31, 32), with a considerably larger number of works attributed to his assistants, followers and other Sienese painters working in Duccio's manner (see figs 205, 206).[10] Among the works generally attributed to Duccio himself, the *Virgin and Child enthroned with Angels* in the Kunstmuseum, Bern (fig. 7), exemplifies the artist's ability to work on an intimate scale so very different from his two monumental documented works: the *Rucellai Madonna* is more than 12 times wider and 14 times taller than the Bern panel, which would scarcely cover the right hand of the Rucellai Virgin.

The following chapter begins by focusing on Duccio's *Maestà*. It then steps back to consider briefly the artist's predecessors in Siena, and discusses a few of the works attributed to Duccio earlier in his career. *JC*

1. Satkowski 2000, pp. 49–53. See also Hueck 1990.
2. The *Rucellai Madonna* is the largest of the three: the *Santa Trinita Madonna* (about 1285) measures 385 × 223 cm (inv. 8343); the *Ognissanti Madonna* (about 1302–3) measures 355 × 229.5 cm (inv. 8344). The name 'Rucellai' relates to the chapel in which the painting was kept from the late seventeenth century until 1940. See Hueck 1990, pp. 33–4.
3. Two excellent surveys of Sienese painting of the period, from different standpoints, are Norman 1999b and Maginnis 2001. For shorter introductions, see Norman 2003; Hyman 2022.
4. Cannon 2013, pp. 79–86.
5. Stubblebine 1979, vol. 1, pp. 22–7.
6. Maginnis 2000, pp. 13–16, 24–9, 233–4; in greater depth Maginnis 1997 and Maginnis 2001. Crucial steps in this re-evaluation have been the comprehensive conservation in 1952–8 of the main panels of the *Maestà* (Brandi 1959), and of the *Rucellai Madonna* in 1988–9 (*La Maestà di Duccio restaurata* 1990). Further conservation work was carried out on the smaller Museo dell'Opera della Metropolitana panels of the *Maestà* in 1964 (four of the front gable panels) and 2001–3 (rear gables and predella): see Siena 2003–4, pp. 208, 216.
7. Ugolino di Nerio's high altarpiece for Santa Maria Novella (around 1320) is now lost, while the one for Santa Croce is now divided between various collections, including the National Gallery, London, the Gemäldegalerie, Berlin and The Metropolitan Museum of Art, New York (see figs 48 and 50).
8. Pietro Lorenzetti, *Beata Umiltà and Scenes from her Life*, about 1330–5 (inv. 6120–6, 6129–31, 8347).
9. For these Sienese artists working in Florence, see Gardner von Teuffel, Cooper and De Marchi, Marzullo and Wolohojian in the present volume.
10. For differing views of Duccio's career and oeuvre, and works by his circle, see Stubblebine 1979; White 1979; Deuchler 1984; Satkowski 2000; Siena 2003–4. These works are fundamental resources throughout the present section of this volume.

FIG. 7
Duccio (documented 1278; died 1319)
The Virgin and Child enthroned with Angels, about 1290–5
Tempera on poplar, 31.5 × 23.3 cm (with original frame)
Kunstmuseum Bern, Legacy of Adolf von Stürler, Versailles, 1902 (G 0873)

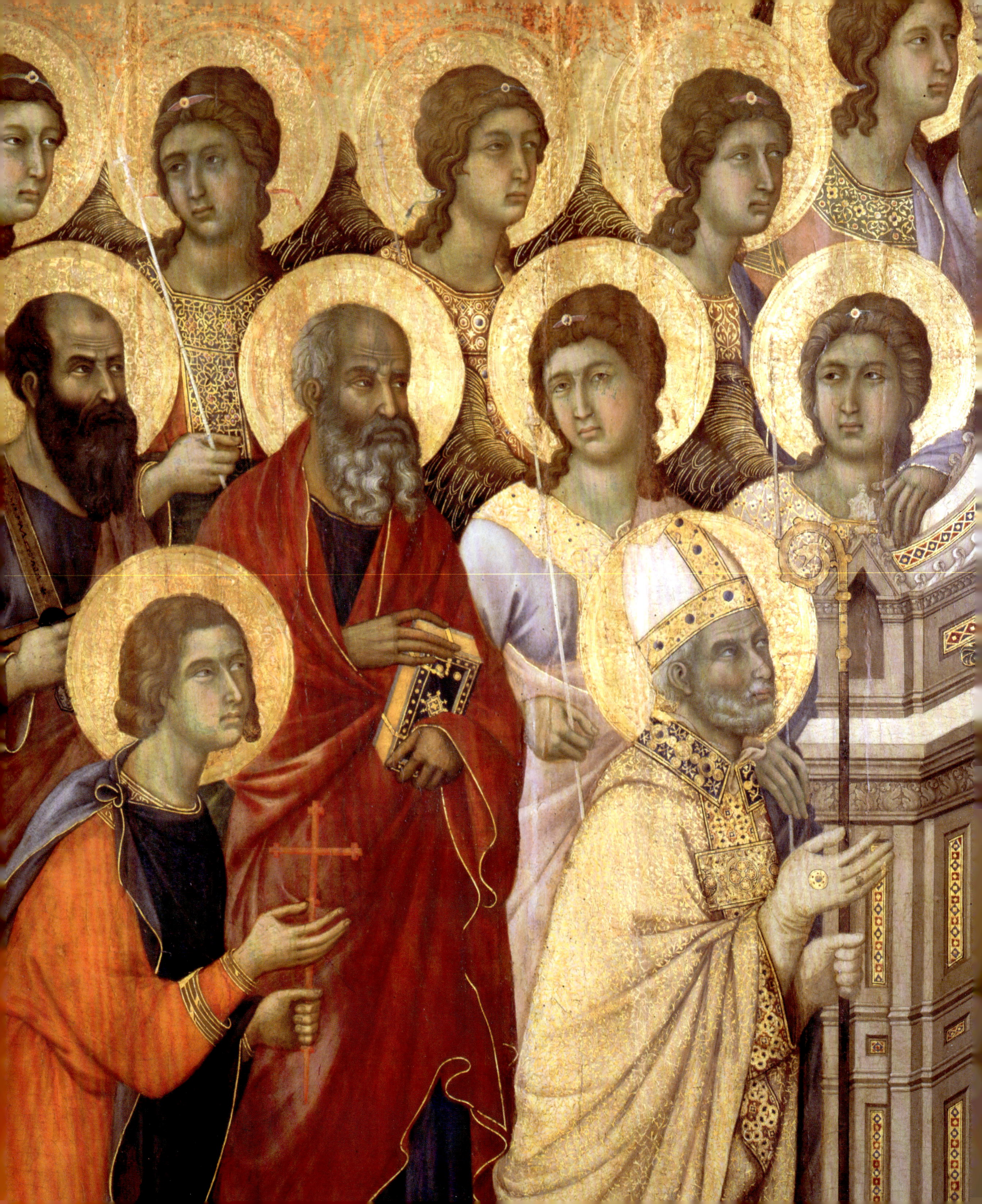

DUCCIO'S *MAESTÀ* FOR THE CATHEDRAL OF SIENA AND THE PRESTIGE OF SIENESE PAINTING

Joanna Cannon

When the governing officials of Siena, the *Nove* (Council of the Nine), met in the council chamber of their newly built palazzo on 28 November 1310 to discuss the income and expenditure of the *Opera del Duomo* (cathedral works), they considered ways to reduce costs.[1] A project to be urged on to completion as swiftly as possible was the 'new and great panel ['nova et magna tabula'] of the blessed and glorious Mary ever Virgin', already underway in October 1308, and destined for the high altar of the cathedral.[2] The wishes of the *Nove* must have prevailed, for on 9 June 1311 a group of the *comune*'s musicians – trumpeters and players of shawms and kettledrums – were paid for greeting the panel of the Virgin Mary ('una rinchontrata che feciero de la tavola de la Vergine Maria').[3] According to later chronicles (of varying reliability),[4] this 'rinchontrata' involved a procession escorting the painting from Duccio's workshop to the cathedral and included the bishop and clergy of Siena, civic leaders and officials, and the people of the city. In honouring the Queen of Heaven, also regarded as the protectress of the city of Siena, this painting expressed the overlapping sacred and secular spheres of the Virgin's majesty.[5] The term *Maestà* – majesty – had already been applied to earlier images, including one painted by Duccio in 1302 for 'the altar in the house of the *Nove*' which no longer exists, but underlines the intertwining of governmental and ecclesiastical functions in Siena.[6] Although *Maestà* can refer to any image of the Virgin enthroned, it is now associated specifically with this work, and with Duccio, the painter who signed it.

In 1506, after serving for almost two centuries as the high altarpiece of Siena Cathedral, the *Maestà* was moved to a side chapel.[7] In 1777 it was sawn in half through the thickness of the panel, separating the front and back main faces, which were then returned to the cathedral.[8] In 1886 the two principal sections were moved to the adjacent offices of the *Opera del Duomo* where they remain to this day, together with the surviving panels of the upper tier and some of those from the predella (step-like base). Other predella panels, and angel pinnacles, are widely dispersed: the *Maestà* is now in thirty-three separate pieces, scattered through ten collections in five different countries.[9]

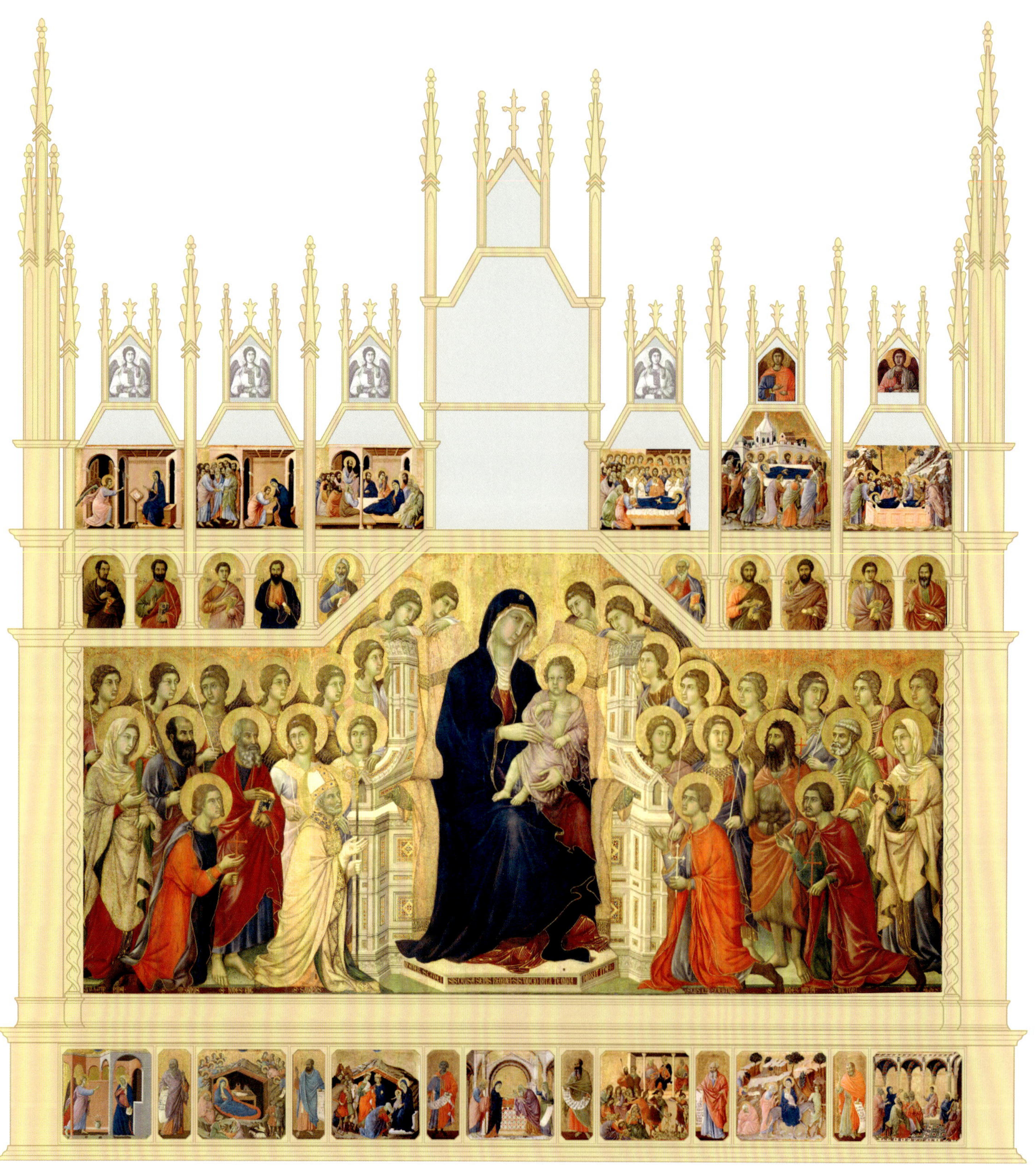

FIG. 8
Photomontage and reconstruction of the front face of Duccio's *Maestà* for Siena Cathedral (about 1308–11)

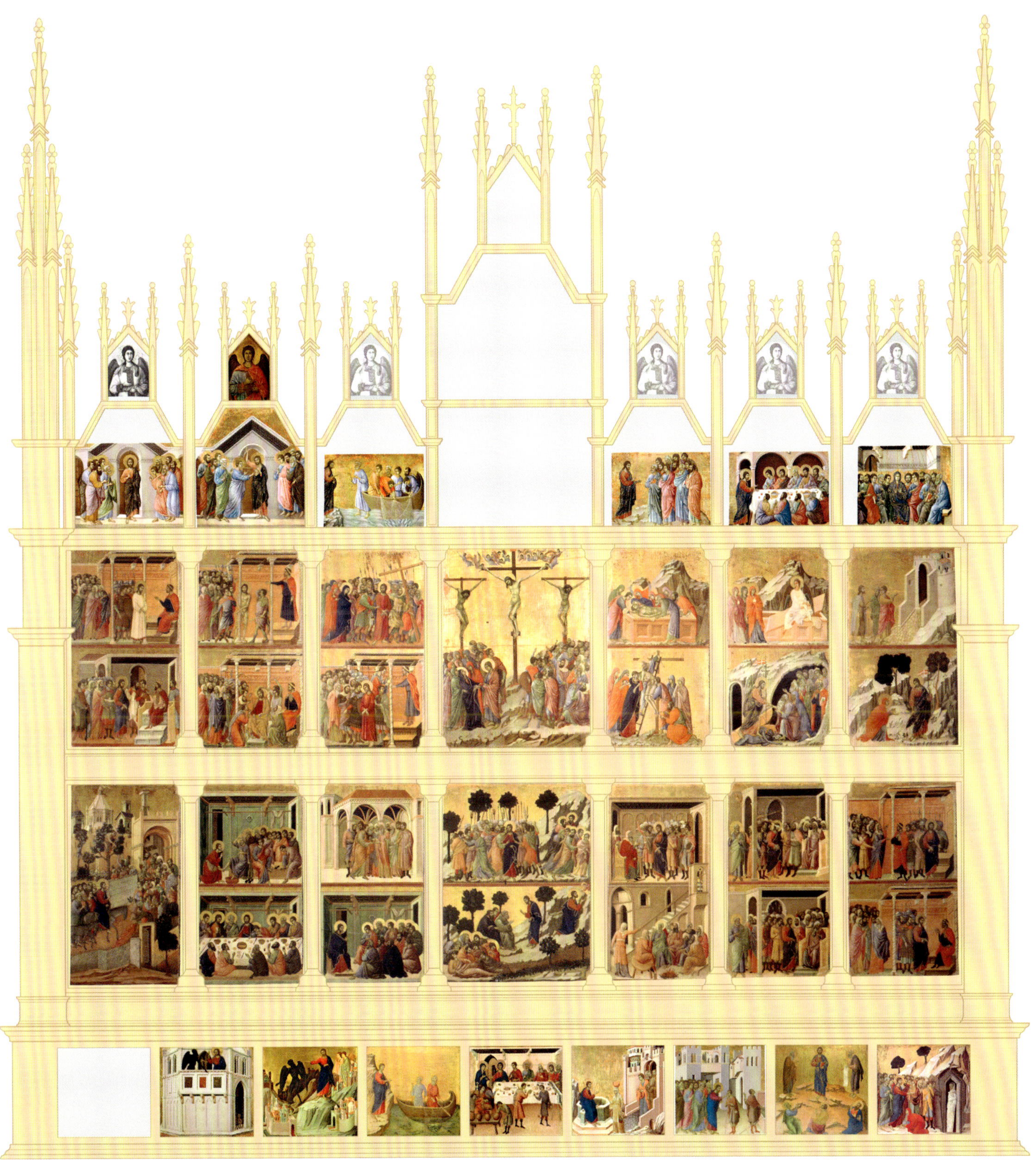

FIG. 9
Photomontage and reconstruction of the back face of Duccio's *Maestà* for Siena Cathedral (about 1308–11)

P. 24
Detail of Saint John the Evangelist, Saint Ansanus, Saint Sabinus and angels in Duccio's *Maestà* (fig. 8)

Much thought and ingenuity has gone into efforts to establish the original appearance of the painting and its integral framing.[10] A reconstruction helps to visualise the original setting of the surviving pieces, but inevitably presents the known and some aspects of the unknown without clear distinction (figs 8, 9).[11] Some elements are certain: an overall size of approximately 5 m square; fully painted and gilded on both sides – a most unusual, although not exceptional, feature for a panel painting at this date;[12] an upper tier crowned with pinnacles; colonettes framing each vertically arranged pair of scenes on the main rear panel; a substantial projecting predella.

Other elements have been persuasively proposed: large framing buttresses at either end to secure the structure; the existence of two scenes at the centre of the upper tiers on both faces of the altarpiece (now lost); the sequence of the predella and upper tier scenes. Still others remain uncertain or unknown: the size and shape of pinnacles and finials, and the extent to which, reaching up from the top of the altarpiece, they emphasised the kinship between the great Sienese altarpiece and the decorative language of Gothic architecture (as seen in the cathedral facade) and – at small scale – in goldsmiths' work and Gothic ivories (see figs 5, 47, 144, 173, 174).

A SINGULAR ARTIST?

At a time when the majority of paintings were unsigned, and the authors of many works are now unknown, the name of Duccio on the *Maestà* could hardly be more conspicuous. Placed on the Virgin's footstool, in an act of homage and supplication, the inscription speaks, through the four kneeling patron saints of Siena – one bishop and three laymen – on behalf of the whole city state and then, explicitly, for a single one of its citizens: 'Holy Mother of God, be thou the cause of peace for Siena, and of life for Duccio because he painted thee thus.'[13] The high status of the artist, and of the work for which he was responsible, within the civic and religious life of Siena, are forcefully proclaimed.

Only one painter is named in the inscription, and in the surviving documents, but he cannot have worked alone.[14] The construction of the large, elaborate wooden structure was a task for carpenters, while the laying of a smooth gessoed surface, the spreading of red bole on areas to be gilded and the grinding of pigments were activities that could be carried out by members of the workshop.[15] A work of the scale and ambition of the *Maestà* posed particular challenges in its planning and making. The act of painting, whether scene by scene, element by element or layer by layer, might be executed by more than one artist, requiring Duccio to find ways to ensure, as far as possible, stylistic unity. One method was for him to take advantage of the considerable repetitions within the cycle, executing an exemplar of a figure or setting that could be followed, to the best of their ability, by others. For example, the setting for Christ beaten before Caiaphas (fig. 11), with its three doorways and coffered ceiling, is rendered crisply and precisely, with careful attention to depth-creating lighting and recession. The architecture is repeated in the lower scene of Christ before Caiaphas, but close comparison reveals a less assured hand: the shading and tapering of the underside of the central arch, and of the mouldings supporting it, are less well understood, and the moulding supporting the left side of the left-hand arch does not align with the corresponding moulding on the right, and is abruptly cut off at the outer corner. However, the figure painting in the two scenes is of a closely comparable, uniformly high quality, confirming that different elements of a single scene might easily have been shared between different hands.

Besides the artists working under Duccio's direction there must have been other contributors: clerical advisers for the content of the altarpiece whose requirements and recommendations Duccio needed to take into account. Ruggero da Casole, Dominican Bishop of Siena from 1307 to 1316, has been proposed as the 'intellectual and theological driving force' behind the making of the *Maestà*.[16] Although not named in the inscription on the Virgin's footstool, Ruggero may, in a sense, be represented in the altarpiece: a bishop saint, Sabinus, one of the patrons of Siena, vested in cloth of gold, kneels in the place of honour immediately to the Virgin's right (see p. 24).

The *Maestà* shows Duccio's talent for planning, control and precision, from the meticulous detailing of the folds of a figured silk[17] to the complexities of orchestrating the Passion Cycle. The *Maestà* also reveals the painter's flexibility. Even after the main lines of planning had been established, and the gilded areas surrounding the background of every scene had been laid down, considerable alterations might occasionally still be made, as in the addition of the two angels to the *Temptation of Christ on the Mountain* in the rear predella,[18] or the change to the tomb in the *Raising of Lazarus* from horizontal sarcophagus to vertical cave (see figs 24, 30).[19] Duccio possessed a notable combination of the ability to plan, controlling a group of painters, and to improvise, following his own evolving preferences.[20] For both reasons the inclusion of his name, by itself on the *Maestà*, is justified for this singular artist.

EXPERIENCING THE *MAESTÀ*

Encountering a small individual panel from Duccio's *Maestà*, isolated at eye level on a well-lit gallery wall (for example fig. 28 or 215), can be an intense and rewarding experience.[21] But how might a layperson have experienced the *Maestà* in the decades following its creation?[22] Entering Siena Cathedral while a service was in progress – the recitation of the hours (communal prayers), seven times in the day, or the celebration of Mass – the visitor would first hear, and then see, the canons (cathedral clergy) seated in their stalls within the marble parapet that formed the hexagonal choir enclosure below the cathedral dome. Raised above the clergy, to the east of the enclosure, set on the high altar was Duccio's *Maestà*, by far the largest painted altarpiece known to exist in Europe at the time.[23]

The centre of the altarpiece was (and still is) dominated by the Virgin and Child, a little over life size, framed by the splayed sides of their marble and mosaic-encrusted throne, and attended by 10 richly vested saints and 20 angels, with 10 half-length apostles in the arcaded gallery above. For the viewer standing outside the choir enclosure, the canons would be seen to join the members of the heavenly court in their devotions to the Virgin. Both groups were arranged symmetrically and, in their own ways, hierarchically.

When Mass was celebrated at the high altar, the officiating priest ascended the altar steps and, raising his eyes, was rewarded with a close view of the Virgin and Child and, if he raised his eyes further, the central crowning scenes probably comprising the Virgin's Assumption to heaven and her Coronation, set within a narrative cycle of her last days, death and burial. Lowering his eyes towards the altar

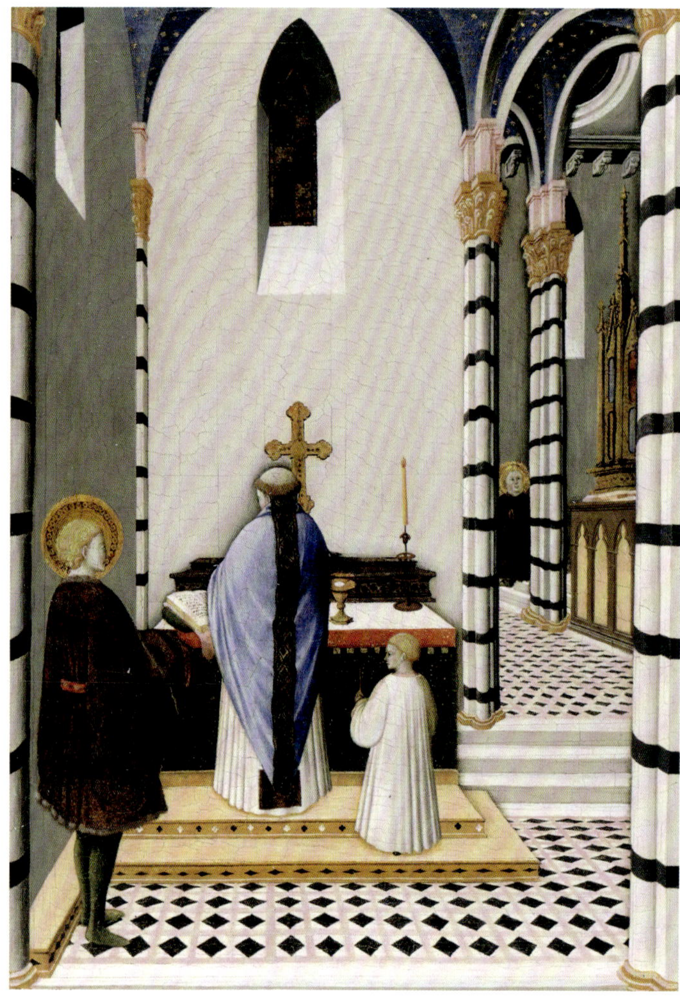

FIG. 10
Master of the Osservanza
(Sano di Pietro [1405–1481] ?)
Mass of Saint Anthony Abbot,
about 1435
Tempera on poplar, 46.8 × 33.4 cm
Staatliche Museen zu Berlin,
Gemäldegalerie (63)

the celebrant saw, beyond the missal, chalice, altar cross and candles, the predella that supported the main altarpiece and projected from it. This provided a horizontal zone presenting narratives of Christ's birth and early life from the Annunciation to Christ teaching in the Temple, with, at the centre, appropriately, the high priest receiving the Christ Child over the high altar of the temple.

A painting of about 1435, attributed to the Osservanza Master (now often identified with the young Sano di Pietro), gives an impression of the eastern parts of the cathedral in the later fourteenth century (fig. 10).[24] This scene from the life of Saint Anthony Abbot, part of a larger altarpiece, shows the holy man twice: in the foreground he witnesses a formal part of the liturgy – the celebration of Mass at a side altar – while in the background he is shown again, hands joined in prayer, in an act of private devotion, kneeling at the steps leading to the rear of the high altar. Between the striped piers we glimpse the side of the altar and, standing upon it, the side buttress of the altarpiece. The kneeling devotee looks towards the back of Duccio's *Maestà*, illustrating the access that a layperson might have had to those images in a private, non-liturgical, moment – an access confirmed by the provision, in 1339, of a candle for the benefit of the faithful praying at the back of the altarpiece.[25]

The story of the Passion was told on the reverse of the main panel through 26 scenes, starting at bottom left with the Entry into Jerusalem, occupying a double-height field, and ending at top right with the two disciples who encounter Christ on the road to Emmaus. The narrative is arranged in two main tiers. At the centre of the upper register the Crucifixion takes up a wider double-height scene. Above the main panel the central crowning scenes, now lost, probably represented Christ's Resurrection and Ascension[26] with, in the flanking gables, Christ's appearances after the Resurrection, and the descent of the Holy Spirit at Pentecost. Below the main panel, on the predella, were events from Christ's ministry, from the Temptations to the Raising of Lazarus. These formed the narrative link with the infancy cycle on the front predella. The central Crucifixion, with extensive gold background, signalled from a distance the heart of the narrative, and the double-height Entry into Jerusalem clearly marked its start, even if, at crowded moments, the devotee was not able to begin viewing at this point.

Whereas the single large-scale field of the main image of the front of the altarpiece functioned powerfully when viewed from a distance, the events in the small-scale scenes of the reverse could only be seen in detail when approached from close by. To engage fully with one sequence of events within the overall narrative a devotee needed to stand close to an altarpiece that was almost 5 m wide, and in order to connect with the full range of scenes they would have been obliged to move between at least three viewing positions. In experiencing the front and rear faces of the *Maestà*, stillness and movement thus played out in different ways. The unified, balanced composition of the front face, depicting the Virgin with her heavenly court, provided the still centre for the congregants' devotions, whereas the Passion Cycle offered numerous scenes full of incident, detail and figures in action. The movements of the clergy performing the liturgy before the front of the *Maestà* were predictable and often liturgically choreographed, but people viewing the Passion narratives might, on the contrary, move unpredictably, drawn by the power of individual points of focus, and sometimes pausing in a particular place for lengthy contemplation.[27]

SEQUENCE, SIMULTANEITY AND THE POWER OF DETAIL

The cluster of scenes showing, most unusually, all three of Saint Peter's denials, together with Christ's appearances before the religious authorities during the night following his betrayal and arrest, gave Duccio the opportunity to explore two aspects of narrative time – simultaneity and sequence – as articulated by architectural settings (fig. 11). The four gospels provided differing accounts of these events, allowing Duccio to select details from all four versions and to design a narrative that could draw the viewer in at many points. The first two scenes, narrated separately in the gospels, are shown here as simultaneous: as Christ is questioned by Annas, father-in-law of Caiaphas, the high priest (John 18:12–13), Peter, who has followed at a distance, reaches the high priest's palace, where he sits down among the attendants in the courtyard, warming himself by a fire (Mark 14:54, Luke 22:55, John 18:15, 18). A servant girl recognises him as one of Christ's followers, but Peter vehemently denies this.[28] Duccio combines these two events: at the same time as Christ is shown as isolated and threatened in the upper room, Peter is depicted as warm and in company directly below. Christ is denied by Peter, as he had foretold, at his very moment of need.[29] The architectural setting frames this simultaneity and leads the viewer's eye from the conspicuous figure of the servant girl in pink, at bottom left, her arm extending the line of the banisters, up to the interior of the palace, confirming that we are seeing simultaneous events at a single location.

This diagonal movement also leads towards the next pair of scenes to the right, where the same setting is used twice, confirming that each of these two events is taking place, sequentially, in the same location. The architecture of each of the two scenes is also used to frame simultaneous events: as Christ is interrogated by Caiaphas, who tears his robe in anger (lower scene), and blindfolded and beaten by the high priest's attendants (upper scene), Peter, placed in a narrow space outside the doorway (Matthew 26:71–5), denies Christ for a second and third time. The upwards movement of the staircase leading from the preceding scene implies that a 'correct' reading might start with the upper scene of the pair (as has been proposed), but the gospels do not agree on the sequence of events.[30] There are some indications that the lower scene comes first. Two of the gospels (Matthew and Mark) place the interrogation by Caiaphas (shown in the lower scene) before the blindfolding and beating (shown above).[31] After the Last Supper, Christ predicted that Peter would deny him three times before the cock crowed.[32] The crowing rooster at top left of the upper scene would thus seem to confirm that we see here Peter's third

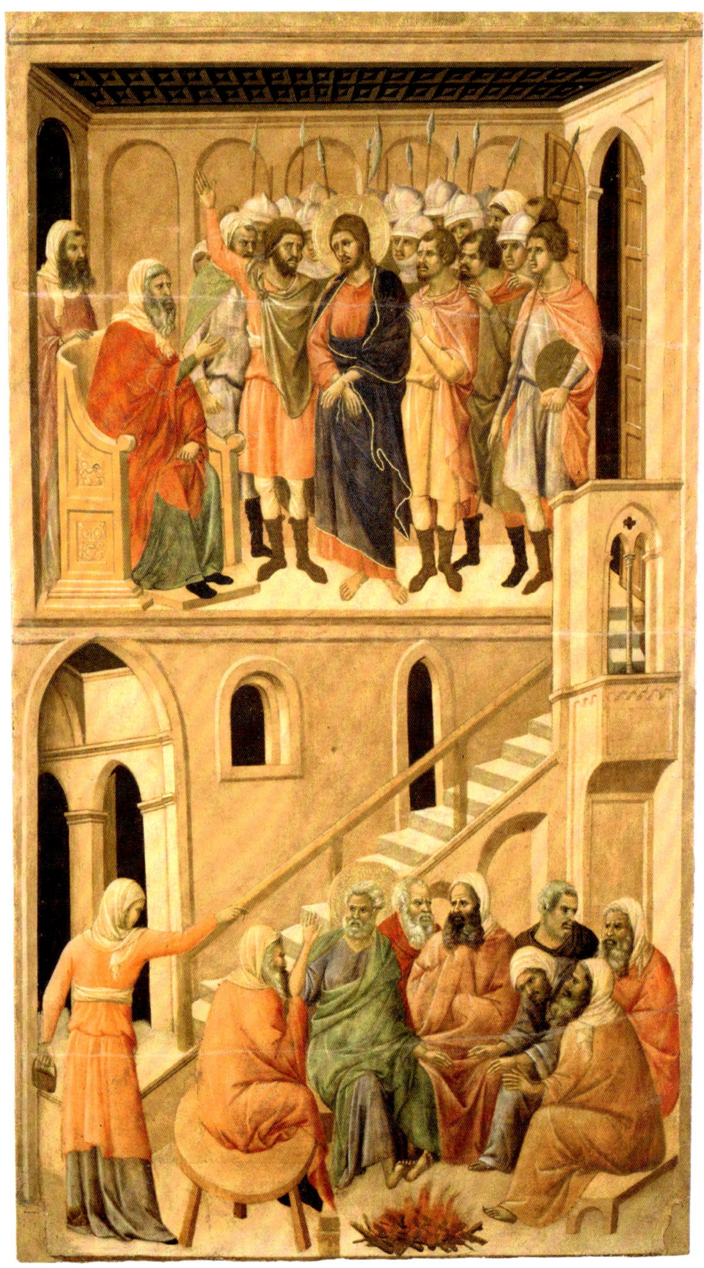

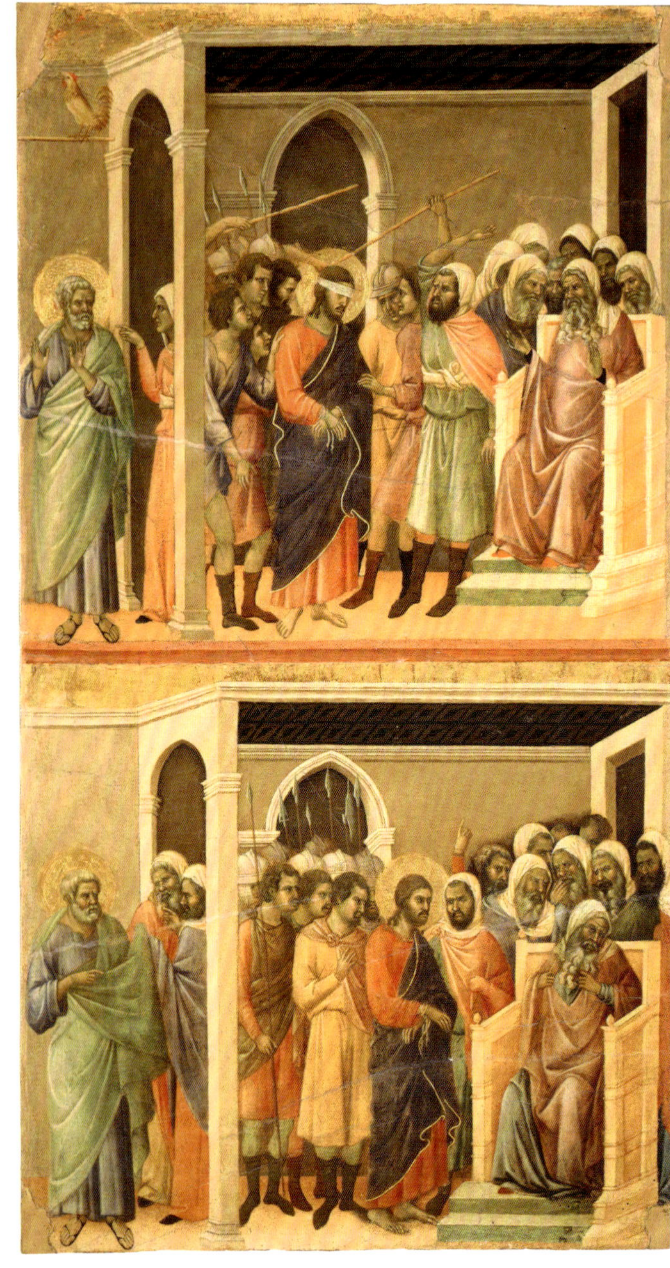

denial. However, Matthew's gospel (26:71–5) says that the second of Peter's denials was in response to the accusations of a different servant girl (as shown in the upper scene),[33] and that his third denial was provoked by 'bystanders' (as shown below). In Mark's version (14:66–72) the cock crows twice: once before the second denial (by a servant girl, as in the upper scene), and a second time immediately after an accusation by bystanders (as in the lower scene). By placing the cockerel in a prominent position, the artist allows the viewer to imagine the crowing resounding through both the upper and lower scenes. Rather than imposing a precise sequence for the reading of the two scenes, Duccio produces a compilation from the sources, creating a cumulative effect.

The use of simultaneity in these four scenes resonates with that found in the equivalent group in the lower left of the altarpiece. Judas receives the bribe for betraying Jesus (upper scene) at the same moment as Jesus addresses the remaining 11 apostles (lower scene).[34] A viewer could draw the comparison between Judas's betrayal, prepared for here, and shown explicitly in the central column of scenes, and Peter's denials

FIG. 11
Duccio (documented 1278; died 1319)
Maestà for Siena Cathedral, about 1308–11
Detail of back main panel:
Christ before Annas and Caiaphas,
and the Three Denials of Peter
Tempera on poplar
Museo dell'Opera della Metropolitana, Siena

(foretold by Christ during his sermon to the 11 apostles),[35] for which Peter subsequently repented with copious tears, setting an important model of contrition for penitents.[36]

The effect of Duccio's narratives, when experienced from close by, was to give viewers licence to navigate through these clusters of scenes in multiple ways.[37] One means of guiding the viewer was the artist's use of the power of detail to bring the faithful into the presence of Christ's Passion: the warmth of the fire, the balcony at the turn in the stairs protruding into the viewer's space (originally abutting the actual physical projection of the framing colonette; fig. 9), the way in which the semi-transparent knot on Christ's white blindfold (like his loincloth in the Crucifixion) catches the golden light.[38] Some of these details were taken from pre-existing imagery, some from direct observation, some from a combination of the two.[39] They do not, between them, mimic the visual experience of a single coherent credible world. Rather, whatever their source, the precision with which these details are rendered makes each of them a potential entry point, drawing the viewer into, and perhaps also through and beyond, the painted image.[40] The central role of detail in the practice of meditation is emphasised in the *Meditations on the Life of Christ*, the best-known and most widely translated of a range of devotional texts circulating in the later Middle Ages. The work was probably being composed, in nearby San Gimignano, in the same years as the *Maestà* was created.[41] The text was originally intended to aid the meditative practices of nuns, but was soon taken up by the laity as well. The reader is urged to focus on imagining vivid and precise details of the holy stories, augmenting the information available in the biblical text, in order to enter a contemplative state that leads towards the soul's union with God.[42]

Members of the clergy and laity, at many different levels of religious knowledge and commitment, could respond to Duccio's paintings. Besides instructing the viewer in key elements of the gospel narratives, these images provided much food for thought in several registers: moral, devotional and theological. Visual reward – the beauty of colour, shape, surface and texture – was surely keenly felt by many beholders of the *Maestà*. Some among them, well acquainted with the gospel stories and their depictions here, may also have prayed in the presence of these images with eyes closed, following the Passion narratives in imaginations well stocked with detail and fuelled by Duccio's inventions.

THE ROOTS OF AN UNPRECEDENTED WORK

Duccio's *Maestà* was unprecedented among panel paintings in its scale and design and contained many newly created elements, but it was also nourished by pre-existing productions, among them painting in Siena before Duccio, Duccio's own earlier works and the wealth of ideas to be found in the Basilica of San Francesco at Assisi.[43]

PAINTING IN SIENA BEFORE DUCCIO

The practice of high-quality panel painting was firmly established in Siena in the generation immediately preceding Duccio.[44] Initially, painters might come from other centres, most notably the Florentine artist Coppo di Marcovaldo, who signed the *Madonna del Bordone* for the church of the Servites in Siena in 1261.[45] Coppo's large-scale painting of

FIG. 12
Guido da Siena (active 1270s and 1280s)
The Virgin and Child enthroned with Christ and Angels, about 1275–80
(faces of the Virgin and Child, the Virgin's right hand and parts of the throne were repainted by a follower of Duccio, early fourteenth century)
Tempera on panel, 362 × 194 cm
(with post-medieval frame)
San Domenico, Siena

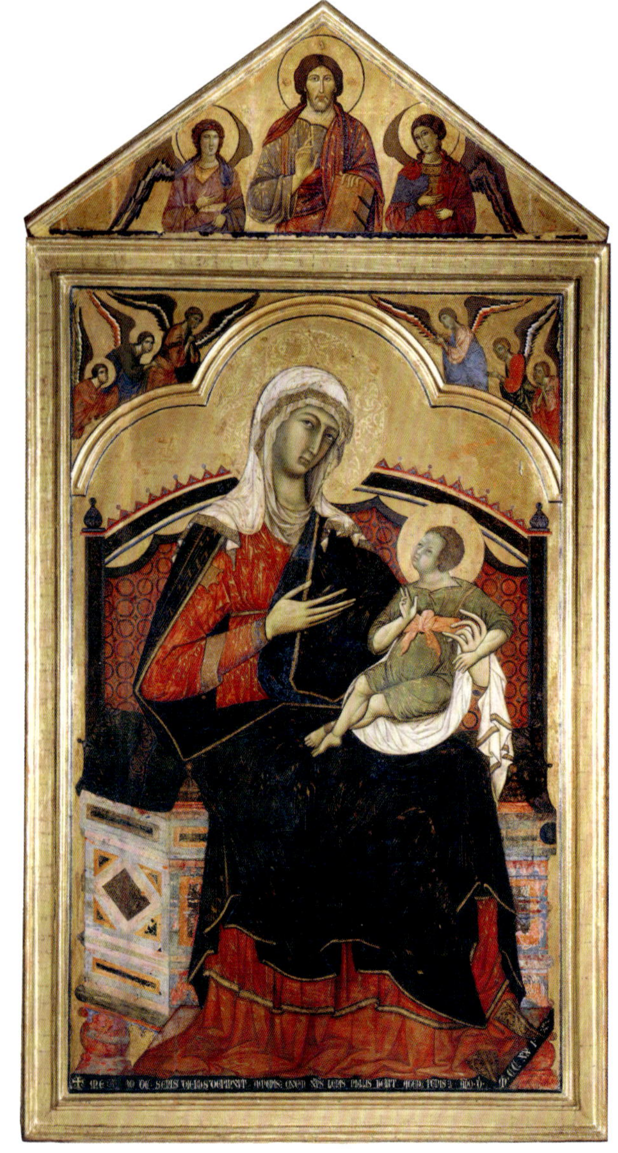

the Virgin and Child enthroned (220 × 125 cm) sparked the production of a series of imposing images of the regal Virgin, richly attired, seated on an elaborate throne and presenting her son to the faithful, created for churches within and beyond Siena (fig. 12).[46] Matching up existing paintings and documented artists can be a matter of fierce debate,[47] but it is clear that a considerable number of painters were active in Siena from the 1260s onwards, specialising (although not exclusively) in images of the Virgin and Child, and working in a distinctive manner that drew on Byzantine-inspired works by Pisan, Florentine, Lucchese and Umbrian artists.[48] Aspects of pose, dress and panel-painting technique owed a significant debt to the Byzantine tradition of half-length icons of the Virgin and Child.

A very fine, if damaged, example, probably dating from the thirteenth century and perhaps painted in Constantinople, survives in Siena (fig. 13). Recorded in the church of the Carmelite order in Siena in 1575, it was described as a long-standing focus of popular devotion.[49] Byzantine images of the Virgin repeated a small number of set types, named after the famous icons (most now lost) that they were thought to follow. The Carmelite painting is of the frequently repeated *Hodegetria* type, derived from an icon kept in the Hodegon monastery in Constantinople.[50] The Virgin looks at her son, supported, upright and blessing, on her left arm, and gestures towards him with her conspicuous, centrally placed, right hand. Her head and shoulders are covered by a gold-fringed blue shawl-like garment (a *maphorion*), her hair wrapped within a coif. The Child's tunic and mantle are densely decorated with strips of gold leaf applied to an adhesive (mordant) brushed on top of the paint surface, whose intricate pattern-making achieves multiple ends: describing the shape of folds, suggesting the fall of light and evoking divine radiance.[51] The Virgin's facial features are guided by established forms such as the elongated nose, the triangular shape at its bridge, its rounded tip and the pale lines running above the cheekbone from the prominent shadow beneath the eye. Within these accepted norms the painter has worked with freedom, using flowing brushwork layered over a greenish-brown initial layer to suggest the texture and shifting colours of skin. Rather than being gilded, the background and integral frame were simply painted in pale green, and the haloes in undecorated ochre, all originally covered by a gold and gilded silver revetment (now fragmentary), embossed with a pattern of roundels and Byzantine blossom, framing the painted figures.[52]

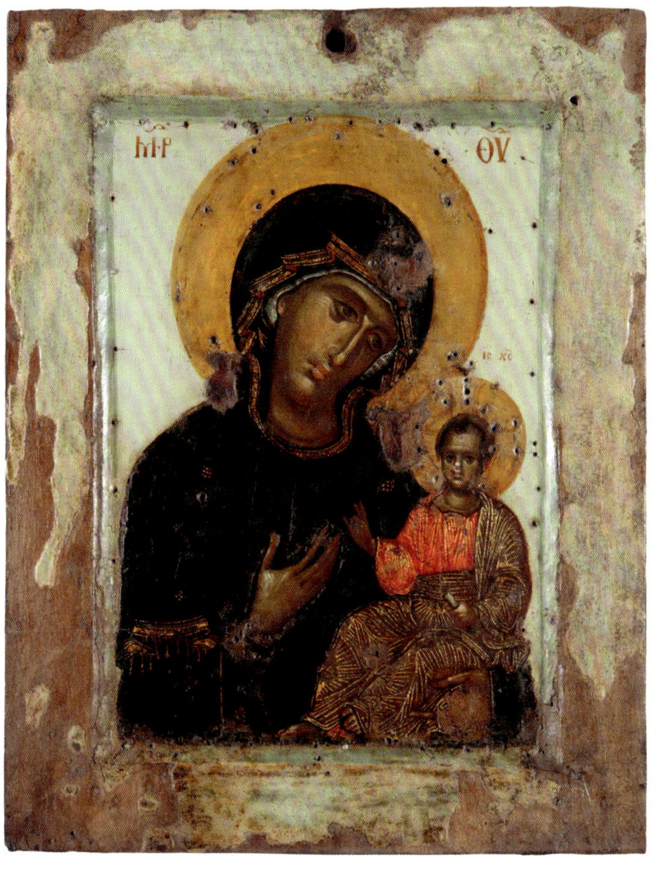

FIG. 13 *(left)*
Byzantine artist
The Virgin and Child ('La Madonna del Carmine'), thirteenth century
Tempera on panel, with embossed gold and gilded silver cover (not illustrated), 28 × 22 cm
(with integral frame)
From Chiesa di San Niccolò al Carmine, Siena. Kept at Museo Diocesano di San Bernardino, Siena

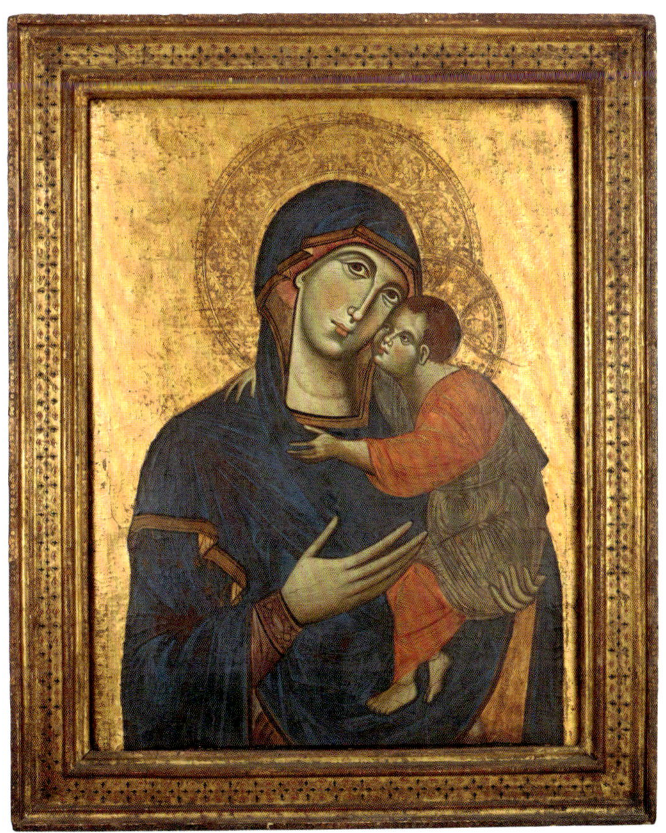

FIG. 14 *(below)*
Master of San Bernardino
(possibly Guido di Graziano)
The Virgin and Child, about 1265–80
Tempera on panel, 98.4 × 80.3 cm
(with modern frame)
Princeton University Art Museum, Princeton, NJ. Bequest of Dan Fellows Platt, Class of 1895 (Y19 62.48)

Sienese painters would generally have been more familiar with Italian versions of icons of the Virgin and Child than with the Byzantine originals. The *Virgin and Child* now in Princeton (fig. 14), attributed by some to the Master of San Bernardino and by others to Guido da Siena or Guido di Graziano, exemplifies the refinement and technical skill found in Sienese panel paintings around the time of the start of Duccio's career.[53] The Byzantine model followed here, probably at several removes, is a more intimate image of the Virgin interacting with her infant than the *Hodegetria* type. Now usually known as the *Eleousa* ('Compassionate Virgin' or 'Virgin of Tenderness'), it shows the Christ Child encircling the Virgin with his arms and pressing his cheek against hers.[54] The pose has a biblical source in the Song of Songs, 2:6, 'His left hand is under my head and his right hand shall embrace me', suggesting, to the informed viewer, Christ and the Virgin not only as mother and son, but also as Christ with his bride, the Church.[55] The Virgin looks out at the viewer, indicating the Christ Child with her conspicuously elongated right hand, as in the *Hodegetria* type. Like the Byzantine Carmelite Virgin, the flesh painting of the Princeton Virgin builds from an initial dark layer to paler detailing in pink and red with white highlights. In the Sienese painting the base layer is green rather than brown, and the upper layers are built up with numerous fine brushstrokes, running in parallel to shape forms and create a dense surface, over which are laid strongly defined facial features. The use of multiple thin parallel brushstrokes laid over green earth underpainting, left visible in places to form areas of shadow, continued to be characteristic of the flesh painting of Sienese painters of future generations. Although there was continuity of basic techniques of painting in egg tempera,[56] there was a change in the final effect. In Duccio's

FIG. 15
Master of the Clarisse (possibly Rinaldo da Siena [documented 1274–81])
The Virgin and Child with the Annunciation, Crucifixion and Scenes from the Last Judgement, about 1270–80
Tempera on panel (walnut?), 31.4 × 19.5 cm (with integral frame)
The National Gallery, London. Acquired with the assistance of the Art Fund (with a contribution from the Wolfson Foundation), 1998 (NG6571)

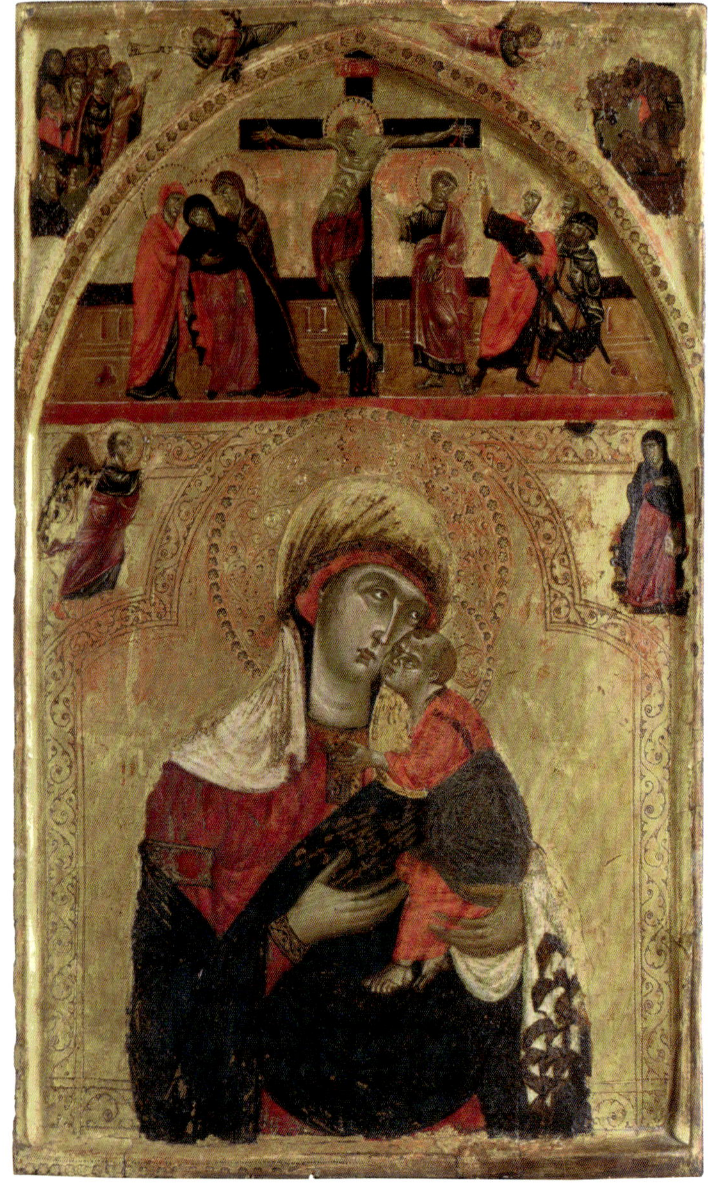

paintings the tonal range is much less emphatic than in the works of his predecessors, creating a gently modulated effect, and features are laid in more softly, avoiding pattern-making schemata. In Duccio's later works some cross-hatching of brushstrokes is also introduced (see fig. 31 and pp. 18–19).

Another version of the *Eleousa* type is the panel attributed to the Master of the Clarisse, possibly identifiable as Rinaldo da Siena, in the National Gallery, London (fig. 15).[57] The Princeton and National Gallery paintings are by different Sienese artists, both probably working before, during and after the 1270s. In both cases draperies were embellished with gold leaf (much of which is lost, leaving only the underlying sticky mordant visible),[58] but the London Virgin's garments are arranged differently, and she wears, over her red coif, a short white veil of a type introduced to Siena in Coppo di Marcovaldo's *Madonna del Bordone*. The gilding of the London panel is tooled in three ways: a freehand incised heart-shaped pattern in the Virgin's halo; a single point used to stipple parts of the burnished gilded surface, combining with the smooth, reflective, untooled areas to create a foliate pattern in the borders of the main panel; and a selection of shaped ('motif') punches (in this case a five-petalled rosette, and a simple ring punch) decorating the rim of the Virgin's halo and the surviving parts of the frame.[59] These three basic approaches continued to be employed by successive generations, with increasingly sophisticated use of motif punches, contributing to the great visual appeal of panel paintings by Sienese artists (see p. 100).[60]

Despite its small size, the London panel offers its viewer a guide to the history of salvation: the Annunciation, marking the incarnation of Christ; the Crucifixion, showing his suffering for the redemption of mankind; and the Last Judgement, at which the saved and damned are visible, summoned by trumpeting angels to a Judging Christ presumably once presiding in a crowning (gabled?) part of the painting, now lost. These three small scenes demonstrate proficiency in painting narratives with movement and emotion. Several elements, including the Virgin swooning at the foot of the Cross, are indebted to the Siena Cathedral pulpit, made by Nicola Pisano and his associates between 1265 and 1268 (see fig. 33). The pulpit proved a rich source of inspiration for other Sienese painters of successive generations, including Duccio.[61] It has been proposed that Rinaldo da Siena also contributed to the Passion Cycle

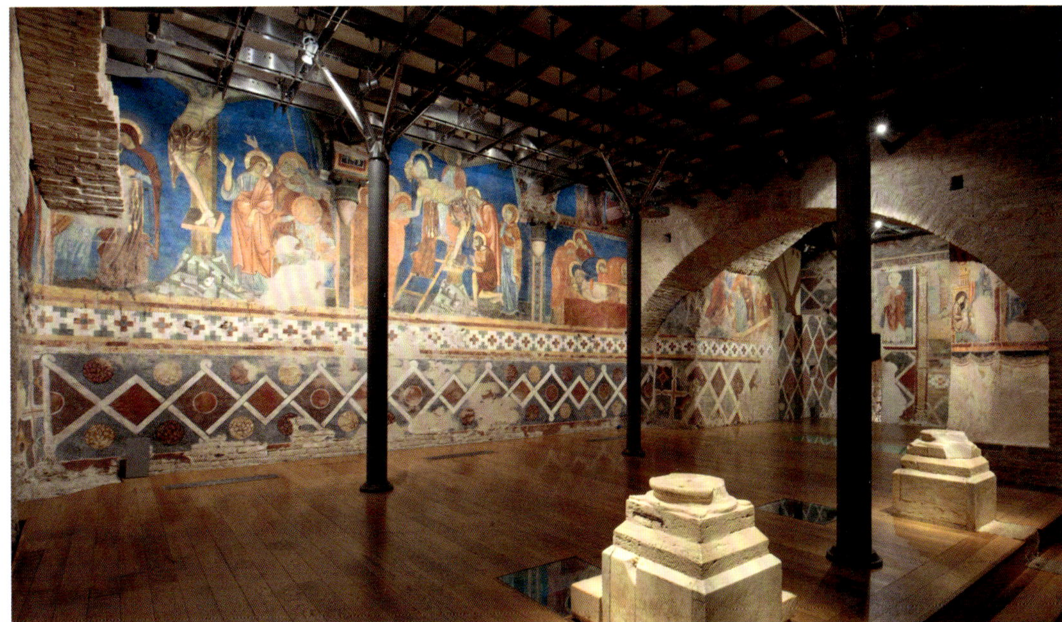

FIG. 16
Siena Cathedral 'crypt' (atrium), showing murals of the *Crucifixion*, *Deposition* and *Entombment*, about 1270–80

painted on the walls of the 'crypt' beneath the east end of Siena Cathedral, probably in the 1270s (fig. 16). These murals, together with cycles from the Old Testament and the Nativity and Childhood of Christ, works of high quality, evidently executed by several different artists, were rediscovered in 1999 in an area that served, in the thirteenth century, as the entrance to the cathedral for those approaching from the centre of town.[62] This discovery has added significantly to our awareness that painters in Siena worked on large-scale mural cycles in the later thirteenth century. The plans made in 1308 to construct the new baptistery up against this zone, blocking the doorways, may have been a factor in deciding to provide, in compensation, extensive narratives on Duccio's *Maestà*.[63]

In 1278 Rinaldo was paid for decorating the cover of a *Biccherna* book: a register containing the half-year accounts of the state treasury of Siena. The wooden panel from the binding still exists (Gemäldegalerie, Berlin, M 580), and shows the current treasurer, a monk from the Cistercian abbey of San Galgano, checking piles of coins, sorted into different denominations, against an open ledger.[64] From 1257 onwards several Sienese artists are recorded as painting *Biccherna* book covers, generally with the image of the state treasurer (often a monk or friar) and the coats of arms of the four supervisors (*quattro provveditori*), underlining the regard in which painted decoration was already held by the government of Siena.[65]

DUCCIO BEFORE THE *MAESTÀ*

The earliest documentary mentions of Duccio relate to payments for civic commissions: decorating 12 coffers in which the documents of the *comune* were kept (1278) and painting a *Biccherna* cover (1279).[66] Duccio was paid for painting six more *Biccherna* covers in the decade between 1285 and 1295, well into the period of his success as a painter (sadly, none of these survive).[67] Two small-scale paintings of the Virgin and Child enthroned, generally attributed to Duccio, help us to trace the artist's path from the *Rucellai Madonna* commissioned in 1285 (see fig. 6), through the lost *Maestà* of 1302, painted by Duccio for an altar in the residence of the *Nove*,[68] to the front face of the *Maestà*, completed in 1311 (fig. 8).[69] The Bern Madonna (see fig. 7) is likely to have been made in the years following the *Rucellai Madonna*.[70] The Crucifixion triptych in the Royal Collection (fig. 17), probably painted shortly before the cathedral *Maestà*, includes, on the left wing, an image of the Virgin and Child enthroned thought to reflect, in part, the lost *Maestà* of 1302.[71]

The Bern Madonna combines the full-length Virgin and Child enthroned, flanked by angels, more usually found at this time in large-scale images,[72] with the embrace of the *Eleousa* type, normally depicted – as we have seen – in half-length devotional panels (figs 14, 15). Despite the formality of

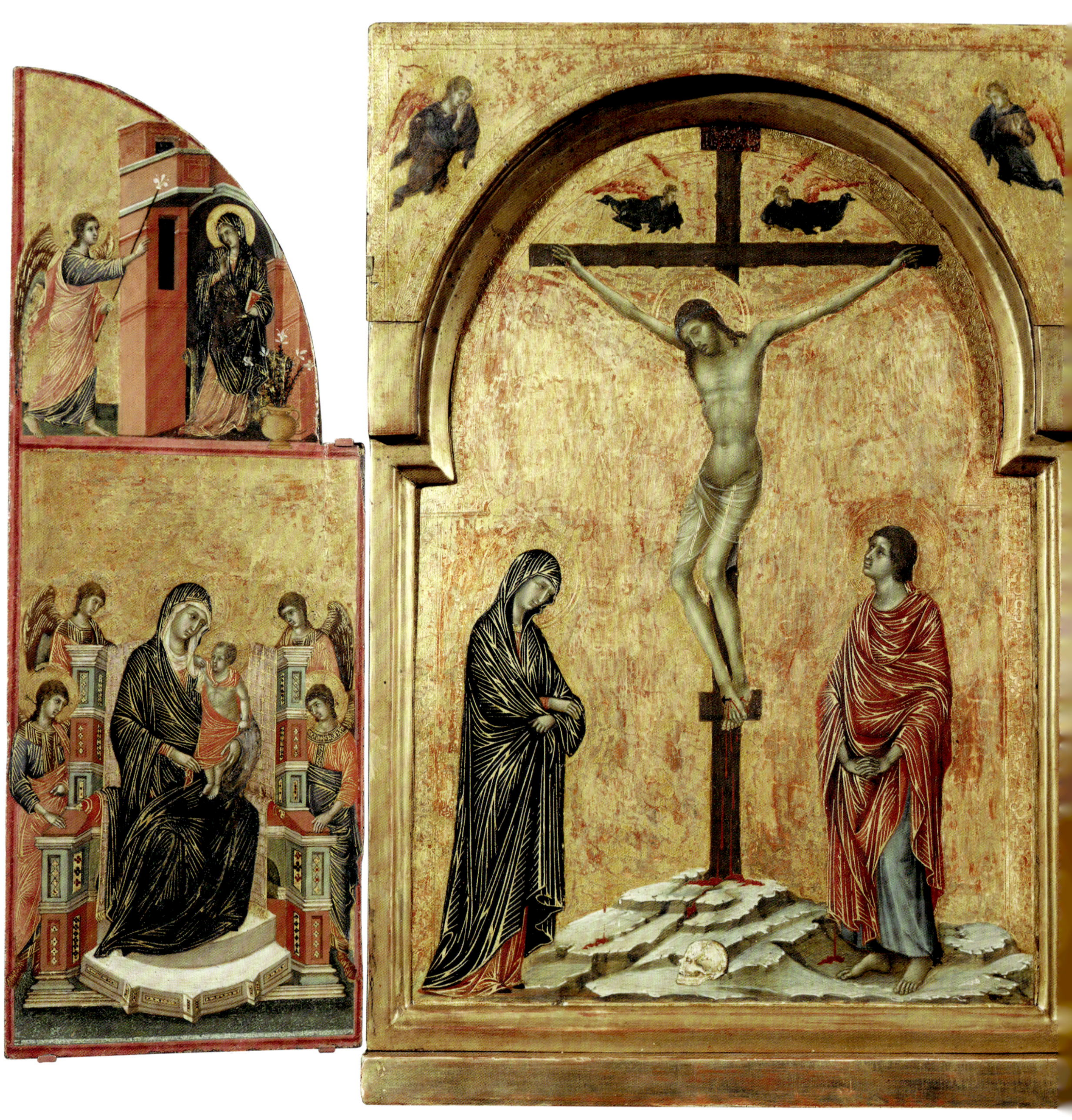

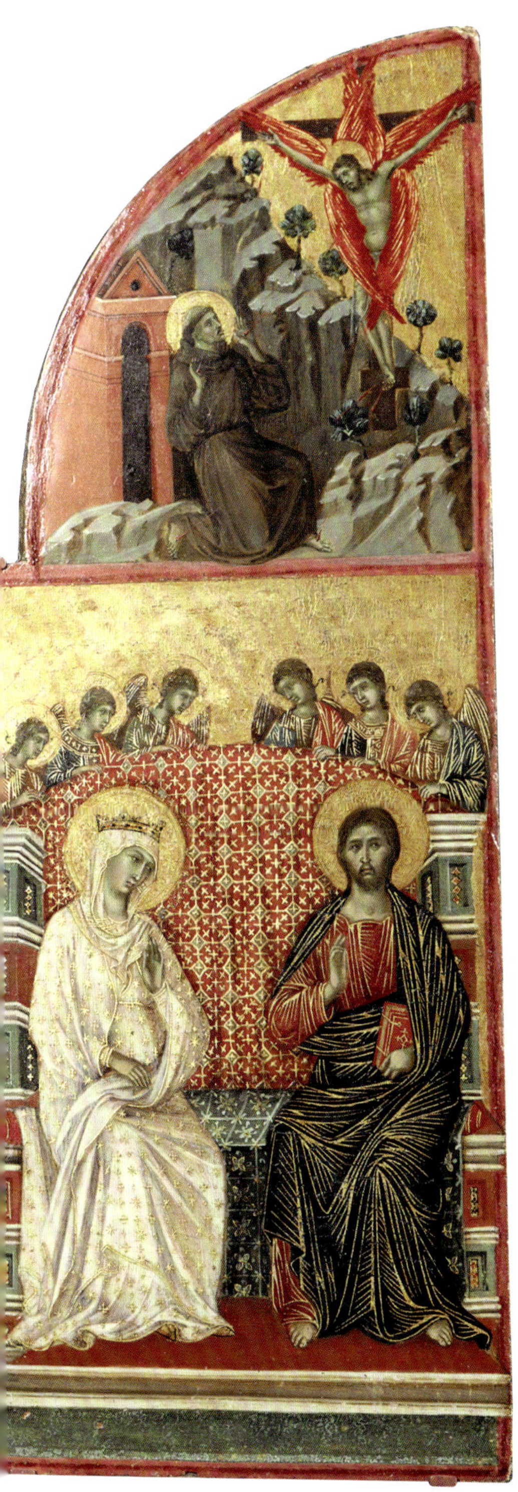

FIG. 17
Duccio (documented 1278; died 1319)
Triptych with the Crucifixion and Other Scenes,
about 1302–8
Tempera on panel, 44.9 × 31.4 cm (central panel);
44.8 × 16.9 cm (left wing); 44.8 × 17.1 cm (right wing);
13.9 × 34.9 cm (spandrel)
The Royal Collection / HM King Charles III (RCIN 400095)

enthronement, Duccio rekindles the intimacy of the *Eleousa* type. The insistent gesture of the Virgin's right hand is reimagined as a tender contact in which the Child's curving fingers stroke the back of his mother's hand.[73] Holding the Child protectively to her, the Virgin's gaze requires the viewer's attention. The Royal Collection painting shows a different relationship, suited to the larger-scale semi-public image it probably reflects: the Virgin looks across and downwards, towards her son; the Child stands up firmly and confidently. The draperies of many of the figures are lavishly ornamented with mordant gilding, a device used much more sparingly in the Siena Cathedral *Maestà* to denote states of transcendence.

The Bern throne, its left side splayed outwards to indicate recession and depth, resembles the general structure of the throne and, in particular, the separate footstool, in works by Cimabue.[74] The thrones on the left and right wings of the Royal Collection triptych (fig. 17) anticipate the front of the *Maestà* (fig. 8) in several respects: they have an (almost) symmetrical centralised recession;[75] the textile covering on the throne back leaves the projecting wings visible; the footstool on the left wing is solid and curved (although not yet polygonal); and the angels are tucked behind the throne arms, or leaning over its curved back. The representation of marble with gilded and coloured mosaic inlay, its recession so precisely rendered and glitteringly exploited on the throne of the cathedral *Maestà*, is already introduced in the Bern Madonna, and further explored in the triptych.

At Bern, as in Byzantium, and in the Princeton panel, the Virgin's hair is covered in the traditional coif (figs 13, 14). The dark tonality of the angels' faces also recalls Byzantium, and awareness of contemporary Byzantine art is suggested by their bulky lower bodies and elongated proportions.[76] The

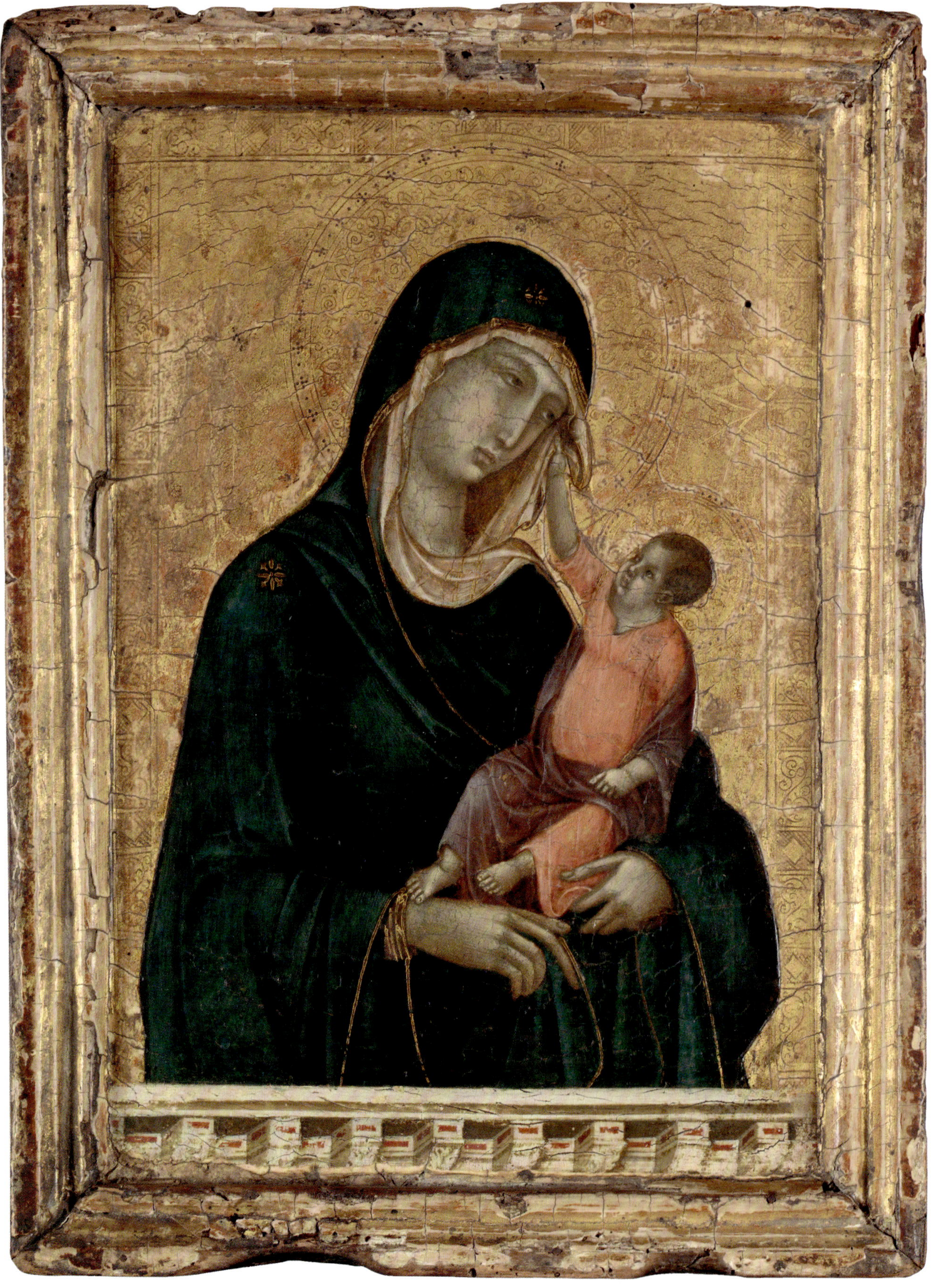

FIG. 18
Duccio (documented 1278; died 1319)
The Virgin and Child, about 1290–1300
Tempera on poplar, 27.9 × 21 cm (with engaged frame)
The Metropolitan Museum of Art, New York. Purchase, Rogers Fund, Walter and Leonore Annenberg and The Annenberg Foundation Gift, Lila Acheson Wallace Gift, Annette de la Renta Gift, Harris Brisbane Dick, Fletcher, Louis V. Bell, and Dodge Funds, Joseph Pulitzer Bequest, several members of The Chairman's Council Gifts, Elaine L. Rosenberg and Stephenson Family Foundation Gifts, 2003 Benefit Fund, and other gifts and funds from various donors, 2004 (2004.442)

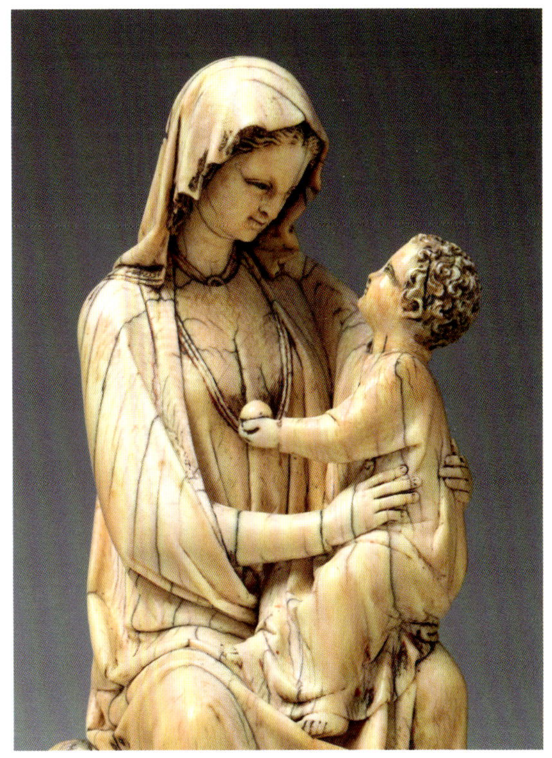

Royal Collection figures have much paler skin, the coif has been replaced by a fine white veil and the enthroned Virgin on the right wing wears a contemporary crown.[77] The change from coif to veil in Duccio's Virgins seems to have happened around 1300.[78] An early surviving example is the exquisite small half-length Virgin and Child often referred to as the *Stoclet Madonna*, now in The Metropolitan Museum of Art, New York (fig. 18).[79] The dark blue *maphorion* is retained, but under it Duccio paints a short white free-flowing veil that forms an undulating frame for the Virgin's face and is related to the veils of Gothic Virgins as seen in northern European painting and three-dimensional arts such as the Parisian ivory of about 1260–80, also in The Metropolitan Museum (fig. 19). The ivory Christ Child reaches up to catch hold of his mother's veil, in a playful gesture familiar from everyday life, as the Virgin bends her head down to look, with a smile, at her child.[80]

Duccio's Virgin does not smile. On the contrary, it may be that the Child scoops up the edge of his mother's veil so as to wipe a tear from the Virgin's eye.[81] Her pensive, melancholy expression can be paralleled in Byzantine images that suggest the Virgin's foreknowledge of the Crucifixion.[82] Her sorrowful face is particularly powerfully portrayed in a magnificent (if damaged) mosaic in the South Gallery of Hagia Sophia, Istanbul, representing the *Deesis* ('entreaty'), in which the Virgin and Saint John the Baptist intercede with Christ on behalf of mankind (fig. 20).[83] There are notable visual similarities in the depiction of skin: Duccio's subtle use of a bluish-green underlayer, overlaid with fine strokes of pale and darker pink, resembles the mosaicist's extraordinarily accomplished use of rows of mosaic tesserae of various hues to produce an effect of colour that blends in the eye of the beholder.[84] The Hagia Sophia *Deesis* is

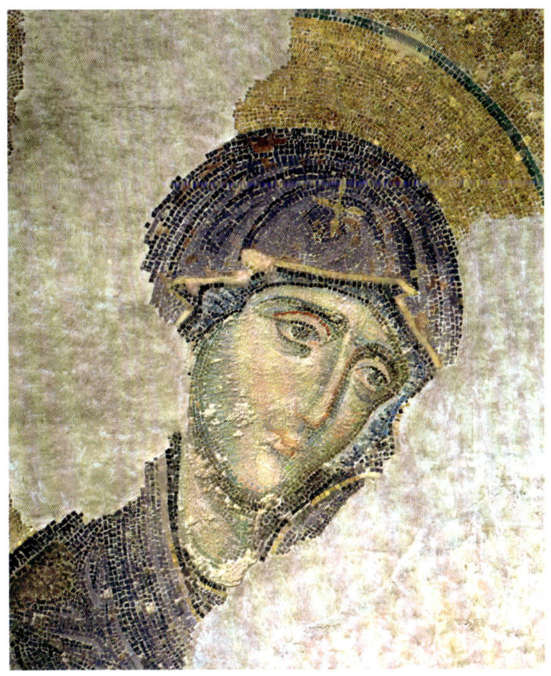

FIG. 19
Detail of the Virgin and Child in fig. 170

FIG. 20
Byzantine (Constantinopolitan?) artist
Deesis (detail of Virgin's head), after 1261 (?)
Mosaic
Hagia Sophia, South Gallery, Istanbul

FIG. 21
Duccio (documented 1278; died 1319)
Maestà for Siena Cathedral, about 1308–11
Detail of front main panel: Saints John the Baptist, Peter, Agnes, Crescentius and Victor
Tempera on panel
Museo dell'Opera della Metropolitana, Siena

FIG. 22
Master Honoré (documented 1289–1312)
Equity and Felony, leaf from *Laurent d'Orléans, La Somme le Roi*, about 1290–5
Tempera and ink on parchment, 15 × 10 cm
The Syndics of the Fitzwilliam Museum, University of Cambridge (MS 192)

generally dated in the years following the Byzantine recovery of Constantinople after the Latin occupation of 1204–61, but the relative chronology of these two works is uncertain, and the nature of any connection between the art of the mosaicist at work in Constantinople and that of the painter in Siena is unclear.[85]

A generation after Duccio, Pietro Lorenzetti's Altenburg Diptych (see fig. 106) demonstrates how the Virgin's sorrowful gaze, as she holds her son in the left wing of the diptych, might look towards his future, as the Man of Sorrows, shown in the right wing. The Virgin's veil in Duccio's painting may constitute a further reference to the Crucifixion: devotional texts describe how the Virgin covered her son's nakedness with her veil as he approached the Cross.[86] More joyfully, some texts also say that at his birth Mary, obliged to improvise, wrapped the infant in her veil.[87] One of Duccio's great gifts was the ability to draw on disparate sources to create a fully resolved work. Within this coherent piece were different strands that a viewer could choose to follow: they might warm to the depiction of a child's natural behaviour, admire the masterful handling of the fabric of the veil,[88] meditate on the sorrows of the Passion, or ponder the shifting direction and meaning of the Virgin's gaze.

The marble parapet behind which the New York Madonna appears to stand, forming an intermediate zone between the eternal world of the painted Virgin and Child, the physical mouldings of the frame and the present world of the devotee, resembles the fictive cornices framing the frescoes in the Upper Church of San Francesco, Assisi, especially those in the apse.[89] The murals of Assisi provided a wealth of ideas on which Duccio could draw at different times in his career. Duccio's Bern Madonna owes a debt to Cimabue's Virgin and Child enthroned in the Lower Church of San Francesco (painted about 1280),[90] while his Christ and Virgin enthroned in the Royal Collection triptych shows awareness of Cimabue's Christ and Virgin enthroned in the apse of the Upper Church (also about 1280).[91] Cimabue's Assisi cycle of the Last Days, Dormition (Death), Assumption and Heavenly Enthronement of the Virgin is a forerunner of certain choices made for the Virgin cycle in the upper tier of the front face of Duccio's *Maestà*.[92] Cimabue's two very large Crucifixion frescoes in the transepts of the Upper Church (about 1279–82) introduced the image of the crowded Crucifixion, thronged with onlookers exhibiting a range of strong emotions, that was to prove so popular.[93] Duccio's versions of these two compositions, as seen in the *Maestà* and in the Crucifixion triptych in the Museum of Fine Arts, Boston (see figs 35, 32), were instrumental in the diffusion of the type.[94] Very little in Duccio's oeuvre prepares us for his mastery of narrative cycles in the *Maestà*, but the Royal Collection triptych (see fig. 17) demonstrates his capacity to frame figures in arrested movement within a coherent architectural setting (the Annunciation), and to place them within an expressively rocky landscape (the Stigmatisation of Saint Francis), and points, again, towards Assisi. The *Stigmatisation* in the Saint Francis cycle of the Upper Church nave (about 1290–6) is the evident source for Duccio's saint and his setting.[95]

By around 1300 an artist employed at or visiting Assisi could see recent works by painters from Umbria, Rome, Pisa, Florence and other parts of Tuscany, as well as, in the transepts of the Upper Church, paintings and stained glass by artists from northern Europe.[96] Northern art also reached central Italy in three-dimensional form. As Sarah M. Guérin discusses in the present volume (pp. 216–23), Duccio's depiction of the body of the crucified Christ in his

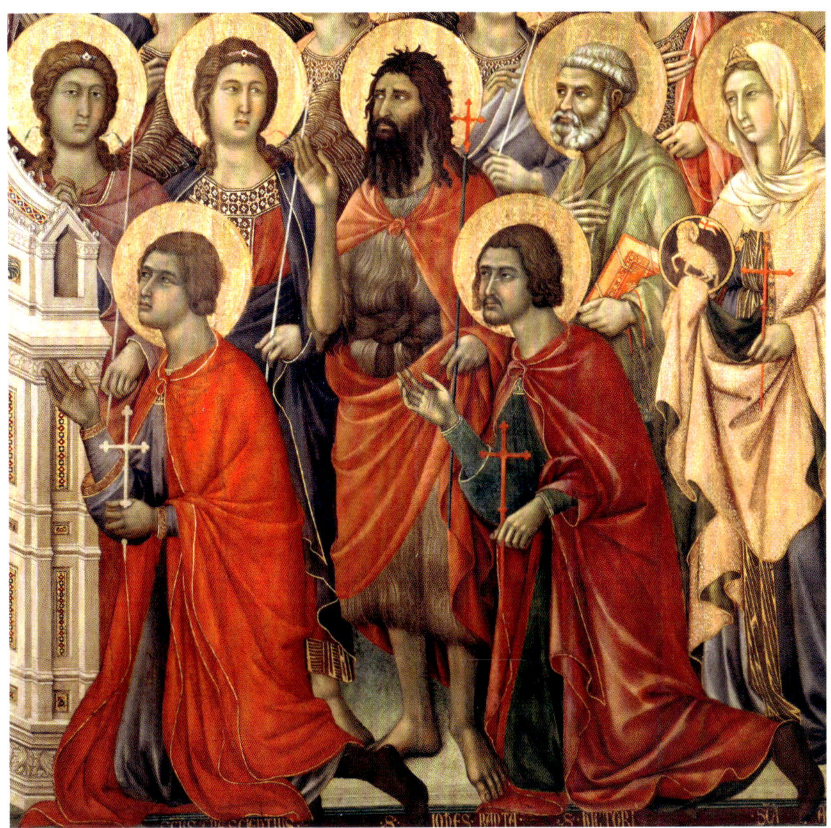

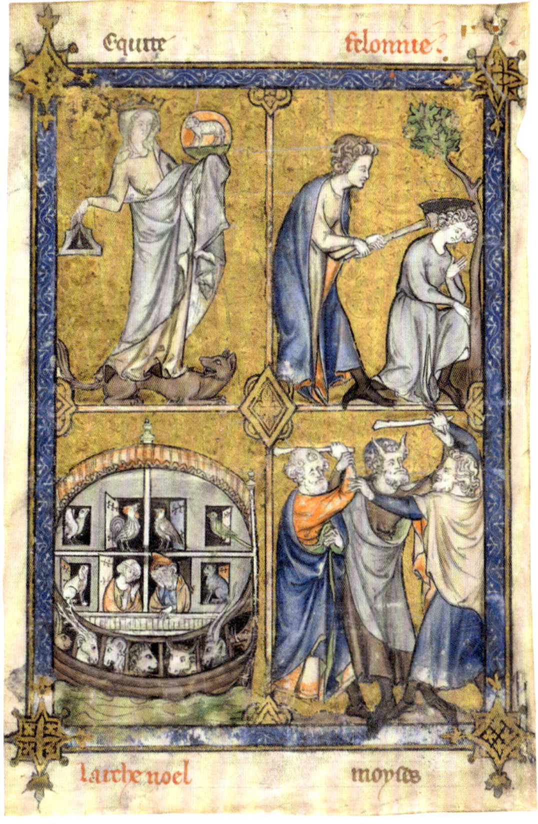

Maestà may have been made with knowledge of the Christ on a magnificent ivory in papal possession, the Saint Sulpice Triptych, made in Paris in about 1300 (see fig. 174).[97] Further comparison has been made between the Virgin in this triptych, with her prominent irregular drapery folds and meandering hem, and saints Catherine and Agnes on the front of the *Maestà* (fig. 21).[98] The bold sculptural folds that Duccio used, so popular in Parisian-inflected Gothic art, may have been known to him from a variety of sources: not only three-dimensional works but also paintings such as the manuscript illuminations of the pre-eminent Parisian painter Master Honoré as seen in, for instance, *La Somme le Roi* (fig. 22).[99] Honoré's work provides superb examples of painterly colour-modelled draperies, a technique explored in France and England in the later thirteenth century, and in Italy by Pietro Cavallini and Giotto.[100] Duccio may have drawn on several of these sources in refining his capacity to model draperies and imply the presence of the bodies beneath them, creating the appearance of shadow and highlight through carefully modulated tonal variation, achieved by the addition of white pigment to the principal hue.[101] On the front of the *Maestà*, Agnes's tunic and the garments of, for example, the kneeling patron saints Crescentius and Victor (fig. 21) showcase Duccio's mastery of colour-modelled drapery in red, purple, grey, green and blue. The mantles of saints Catherine and Agnes epitomise a different skill: Duccio's remarkable ability – discussed by Lisa Monnas in the present volume (pp. 198–215) – to depict the complex surfaces of figured silks (see fig. 151).

The roots of Duccio's *Maestà* were many and varied. The artist looked both within Siena and beyond, drawing on long-established forms and recent innovations. The 'new and great panel of the blessed and glorious Mary ever Virgin', as the government of the *Nove* called it, elevated the prestige of Sienese painting. 'Prestige' can also be invoked in this context in its earlier meaning: 'a conjuring trick or illusion'. Out of pigments, gold leaf and a wooden framework, Duccio conjured up the illusion of credible worlds, combining close observation of the visible world – the here and now – with the imaginative visualisation of the biblical past and the beauty of celestial eternity.

I am indebted to Dillian Gordon for her very careful reading of my text.

1. Satkowski 2000, pp. 77–9.
2. Ibid., pp. 69–72. Fundamental resources throughout this chapter are the excellent concise discussion of the *Maestà*, Gordon 2011, pp. 174–87; Bellosi 1999 (extensively illustrated); Ragionieri in Siena 2003–4, cat. 32, pp. 208–18. See also Stubblebine 1979; White 1979; Deuchler 1984.
3. Satkowski 2000, pp. 80–1; Siena 2003–4, p. 513.
4. Lucidly assessed in Satkowski 2000, pp. 97–108.
5. For an introduction to these overlapping spheres in relation to art, see Cannon 2000a.
6. Satkowski 2000, p. 67.
7. Gordon 2011, p. 177.
8. For the date of 1777, see ibid., p. 184, n. 24. The main panel was first sawn into seven vertical sections, each of which was then sawn through the thickness of the panel, separating the front and rear faces (severely damaging the Virgin's face when the saw slipped). The seven sections of each side of the main panel were then reassembled, forming two independent main panels. Stubblebine 1979, vol. 1, pp. 35–6; Satkowski 2000, p. 138.
9. Stubblebine 1979, vol. 1, pp. 35–7. Tucker 2008 corrects the previously accepted date of 1878 to 1886.
10. For surveys of reconstructions of Duccio's *Maestà*, see Stubblebine 1979, vol. 1, p. 37, vol. 2, figs 518–93; Deuchler 1984, pp. 73–8. John White's reconstruction (White 1973b; White 1979, pp. 80–95, 201–8) is now generally accepted, with certain modifications, for which see Gordon 2011, p. 177. See also Gardner von Teuffel 1979; Gardner von Teuffel, pp. 68–77, in the present volume.
11. For examples, see the works cited above, n. 10.
12. Israëls 2020.
13. 'MATER S[AN]C[T]A DEI SIS CAUSA SIENA REQUIEI. SIS DUCIO VITA TE QUIA PINXIT ITA': Donato 2003, p. 30. For the relation between Duccio's name and the Virgin's (hidden) foot above it, see Cannon 2010, pp. 28–31.
14. Proposals range from attribution of individual scenes to nine different artists (Stubblebine 1979, vol. 1, pp. 39–45, vol. 2, figs 590, 591) to a coherent workshop, under Duccio's supervision, working collaboratively, even within a single scene, and systematically from top to bottom of the altarpiece (White 1979, pp. 102–19).
15. An indispensable guide to the materials and techniques of Sienese panel paintings is London 1989–90. For transcription and translation of, and commentary on, Cennino Cennini's essential text of around 1400, see Broecke 2015.
16. Gordon 2011, p. 182, p. 187, n. 97. See also Seiler 2002, pp. 268–9; Gordon 2009, p. 21.
17. See Monnas, pp. 198–215, in the present volume.
18. Gordon 2009. See also Tedbury, pp. 254–69, in the present volume.
19. Wilkins Sullivan 1988.
20. For an analysis of Duccio's gradual process of changes to the figures and architecture of the predella Annunciation, see Gordon 2011, pp. 157–60.
21. Eloquently evoked in Matar 2019, pp. 4–8.
22. The following paragraphs draw on the reconstruction by Struchholz 1995, subsequent proposals in Butzek 2006 and Israëls 2008, and the summary in Gordon 2011, pp. 178–9. For the liturgy of Siena Cathedral, see Argenziano 2000; D'Accone 1997.
23. The Westminster Retable (96 × 333 cm), probably installed on the high altar of Westminster Abbey in the 1260s, is a very rare surviving example of a north European panel painting of the time designed to stand on top of an altar. See Binski and Massing 2009, especially pp. 18–20.
24. The east end of the cathedral within which the *Maestà* was initially installed was rebuilt later in the century, the high altar was moved further to the east in 1375, and the *Maestà* was reinstalled on it by 1382. Sano di Pietro's painting is a simplified version of that setting. For bibliography, see Gordon 2011, p. 186, n. 64, and the ground plan on p. 295, fig. 10.
25. Ibid., p. 179, pp. 185–6, n. 63.
26. Ibid., p. 176.
27. For a lucid introduction to art and contemplation in Siena, see Bacci 2009.
28. Matthew 26:69–70, Mark 14:66–8, Luke 22:56–7, John 18:17.
29. Matthew 26:30–5, Mark 14:26–31, Luke 22:31–4, John 13:36–8.
30. Several proposals for a single narrative order in the Passion Cycle have been made, including some elaborate conclusions about the zigzagging direction of the 'reading'. These risk conflating the planning of the cycle with the experience of viewing it. See Deuchler 1984, pp. 58–63, especially p. 60, diagrams 58–62. See also Stubblebine 1979, vol. 1, pp. 57–61; White 1979, pp. 124–31; Norman 1995a, pp. 73–5; Bellosi 1999, p. 124; Gordon 2011, p. 183, n. 8. Unlike most writers, Deuchler considers that the upper denial precedes the lower one.
31. Matthew 26:59–66, 67–8, Mark 14:55–64, 65. Luke says that the beating took place prior to Christ being brought before a meeting of the high priests, the following morning. John does not mention the beating. Visual logic might suggest that the upper scene comes first: Caiaphas tears his robe in the lower scene, but it appears to be undamaged in the upper scene.
32. See above, n. 29.
33. Mark (14:66–70) says it was the same maidservant who provoked the first and second denials, but differences between their garments show that here Duccio is closer to Matthew's account.
34. This version of events accords with John's gospel (13:26–30) in which Judas leaves to betray Jesus just before Jesus begins his discourse to the remaining apostles. In the other three gospels Judas goes to take the bribe before the Last Supper (Matthew 26:14–16, Mark 14:10–11, Luke 22:1–6).
35. John 13:36–8.
36. For the significance of the juxtaposition of Peter and Judas in other contexts, see Robson 2004; Bolgia 2022, especially pp. 163–70.
37. For multiple potential pathways in journeying through a medieval text, see Carruthers 2010.
38. Christ's blindfold is clearly illustrated in Bellosi 1999, p. 182.
39. Figures warming themselves before a fire are a common feature of medieval calendar illustrations for December, January or, more usually, February; the construction of the protruding balcony may be indebted to Giotto's Arena Chapel *Annunciation* (about 1303–5); golden light shining through a translucent loincloth is found in Cimabue's Crucifix for Santa Croce, Florence (about 1280), and Giotto's Crucifix for Santa Maria Novella, Florence (about 1288–90).
40. For darkened doorways in the *Maestà* and an important discussion of 'a realm beyond the material surface of the painting', see Rosser 2012.
41. Composed sometime before about 1304 and, at the latest, 1314. See Cooper 2021; Tóth 2021.
42. For example, in the Meditations on the Passion at Matins: 'enlarge on the scenes more fully. And so notice every detail as if you were present', Taney, Miller and Stallings-Taney 2000, p. 239. See Karnes 2011, pp. 166–78. For links between the text and two earlier works of art in Siena, see Cannon 2021.
43. The following sections focus principally on works displayed in the exhibition this volume accompanies. Other important forerunners are omitted, including images of the Virgin and Child (or an individual saint) flanked by scenes or by half-length saints, notably Duccio's own polyptychs. For predecessors of various elements of the overall design, see Seiler 2002, especially p. 251; Gordon 2011, p. 180. For a concise overview of the varied roots and functions of double-sided large-scale works of art, see Israëls 2020. For the design, function and patronage of multi-image Life of Christ panels from around Europe, both before and after the *Maestà*, see Seiler 2002, pp. 258–63; Ransom 2021; Zöschg 2022; Derbes and Neff 2023.
44. For fundamental surveys giving the wider context for the small selection of works in the following paragraphs, see Stubblebine 1964; Bellosi 1991a and 1991b; Maginnis 2001; Siena 2003–4; Boskovits 2021.
45. For the *Madonna del Bordone* in its political, civic and devotional contexts, see Corrie 1990; Mina 2000; Corrie 1996; Cannon 2010, pp. 10–16.

46. Cannon 2013, pp. 79–83; Boskovits 2021, pp. 482–5. Derbes 1989 argues that Sienese paintings reached the Levant in the thirteenth century.
47. Stubblebine 1964; Bellosi 1991a and 1991b; Maginnis 2002; Bellosi 2003–4a.
48. Belting 1994, especially chapter 17.
49. Siena 1979, pp. 104–5; Folda 2015, pp. 143–5, 262, 333–4, nn. 37, 40–2. See also Cannon 1987, pp. 20–1; Belting 1994, p. 341.
50. Ševčenko 1991.
51. Hills 1987, pp. 25–8. For the technique, see Folda 2015, especially pp. 250, 262.
52. Siena 1979, p. 104, fig. 88. Also illustrated in Cannon 1987, pl. 4d. For comparable Byzantine revetments, see Grabar 1975, especially pp. 35–7, figs 26–30; Durand 2004. The Virgin's right hand, a major point of intercession and devotion, was also covered in silver gilt, and a crown was subsequently added to her head.
53. Stubblebine 1964, pp. 77–9; Boskovits 2021, pp. 477–8 (who considers Guido da Siena and Guido di Graziano to be one and the same). See also Bellosi 1991a, p. 7; Maginnis 2002, pp. 472–3, 480; Giorgi 2003–4, p. 61. The frame in which the panel is displayed is not original.
54. Ševčenko 1991.
55. Schmidt in Siena 2003–4, cat. 27, pp. 184–6.
56. See London 1989–90, especially pp. 26–9.
57. Gordon 2011, pp. 348–55, with detailed illustrations. See also Boskovits 2021, pp. 549–50.
58. The metal leaf of the London Virgin is composed of a gold and silver alloy. Gordon 2011, p. 350.
59. The tooling of the haloes of the Princeton Virgin and Child has been remade. See Maginnis 2002, pp. 472–3.
60. London 1989–90, especially pp. 24–6. The fundamental study is Skaug 1994.
61. Seidel 2012, vol. 1, pp. 392–3.
62. Guerrini and Seidel 2003; Bagnoli 2003.
63. Israëls 2020, pp. 92–3; Butzek 2006, p. 32; Israëls 2008, p. 132; De Marchi 2016.
64. Becchis and Pierini 2002, p. 63; Pierini in Rome 2002, pp. 124–5; Boskovits 2021, pp. 545–6.
65. Maginnis 2001, pp. 275–86; Rome 2002. For communal payments to Sienese painters, see Maginnis 2001, pp. 123–35.
66. Becchis and Pierini 2002, p. 63; Siena 2003–4, p. 507. Satkowski 2000, p. 48, gives the year for the *Biccherna* cover as 1278.
67. Satkowski 2000, pp. 54–7, 60, 63; Siena 2003–4, pp. 508–11.
68. Satkowski 2000, p. 67; Maginnis 2001, pp. 127–8.
69. For a variety of views on Duccio's works discussed in this section, all with further bibliography, see Stubblebine 1979; White 1979; Deuchler 1984; Siena 2003–4.
70. Schmidt in Siena 2003–4, cat. 27, pp. 184–7, with further bibliography.
71. For the Crucifixion triptych in the Royal Collection, see Cannon and Pemberton-Pigott 2002; Bellosi in Siena 2003–4, cat. 29, pp. 192–7. Works by several of Duccio's followers are very likely to reflect the lost work of 1302. For reconstructions, see Brandi 1951, pp. 141–2; Stubblebine 1972.
72. For small-scale versions of large-scale images of the enthroned Virgin, see Schmidt 2005a, pp. 169–92.
73. Perhaps touching her ring finger with his, in a further reference to the bridal significance of the image type, mentioned on p. 35.
74. Closely comparable to the Virgin's throne in Cimabue's mural in the transept of the Lower Church of San Francesco at Assisi; see Poeschke 1985, pl. 93. See also the small panel of the *Virgin and Child enthroned*, attributed to Cimabue, in the National Gallery, London (inv. NG6583), Gordon 2011, pp. 32–41. Note that in the Bern Madonna the base of the left side of the throne and the left front leg of the footstool are modern reinstatements of an area of loss.
75. For adjustments to the handling of recession in relation to the viewing angle of the triptych wings, see Cannon and Pemberton-Pigott 2002, pp. 12–14.
76. For an introduction to contemporary Byzantine art, see Lowden 1997, chapter 10, especially pp. 392–7.
77. See the discussion of the Virgin's garments in Monnas, pp. 198–215, in the present volume. For contemporary crowns, see Seidel 2007, pp. 84–92.
78. Key images attributed to Duccio using the coif, from around the time of the *Rucellai Madonna*, are the *Crevole Madonna* (Museo dell'Opera della Metropolitana, Siena, inv. 37) and the *Madonna of the Franciscans* (Pinacoteca nazionale di Siena, inv. 20). For the Virgin's changing head coverings, see Monnas 2024 (forthcoming b).
79. Christiansen 2007; Christiansen 2008.
80. The Child's head is a nineteenth-century replacement. For the smile of French Gothic sculpture and its limited diffusion in Italy, see Seidel 2007, especially pp. 46–56.
81. John White suggests that the Christ Child in Duccio's *Crevole Madonna* reaches up to wipe a tear from the Virgin's eye, and proposes that a gesture of this kind, referring to the Virgin's sorrow at her foreknowledge of the Crucifixion, could also have inspired a passage in the *Meditations on the Life of Christ* in which the son comforts his tearful mother after his pain at the circumcision. See White 1979, pp. 23–4, fig. 1; Taney, Miller and Stallings-Taney 2000, pp. 30–1. For the Christ Child comforting his mother in Sienese painting, see also Shorr 1954, pp. 116–17, 120–2.
82. Belting 1994, pp. 281–90; Vassilaki and Tsironis 2000–1, especially pp. 460–1.
83. Lowden 1997, pp. 388–92; Cormack 2000–1, pp. 118–23.
84. The artist would have painted the Virgin's face on the wet plaster of the setting bed before laying the mosaic cubes.
85. For Duccio's relationship with contemporary Byzantine art, see also Belting 1994, pp. 370–6.
86. Derbes 1996, pp. 149–50; Taney, Miller and Stallings-Taney 2000, p. 252.
87. Taney, Miller and Stallings-Taney 2000, p. 25.
88. Evocatively discussed in Hills 2018, pp. 79–87.
89. See, for example, Poeschke 1985, pls 69, 76, 95, 144, 145; Bellosi 2003–4b, p. 134, figs 37–9; Christiansen 2008, pp. 50–2 and figs 40–2.
90. For Cimabue at Assisi, with excellent illustrations, see Bellosi 1998, pp. 147–245. For dating, see Cooper and Robson 2013, p. 86. For the significance of Cimabue's fresco for Duccio's *Madonna of the Franciscans*, see Schmidt 2000, pp. 38–9; Cannon 2010, pp. 9–10.
91. Cannon and Pemberton-Pigott 2002, p. 11; Poeschke 1985, pl. 69.
92. Poeschke 1985, pp. 71–3, pls 65–71; Bellosi 1998, pp. 206–13; Bellosi 2003–4b, pp. 140–1.
93. Bellosi 1998, pp. 148–9, 183–93; Bellosi 2003–4b, pp. 138–41.
94. See Cannon, pp. 52–9, in the present volume.
95. Cannon and Pemberton-Pigott 2002, p. 11; Poeschke 1985, pl. 177.
96. Bellosi 1988b; Romano 2001, pp. 49–76; Binski 2002.
97. A comparison made in Deuchler 1984, p. 183, which Guérin shows might have been the fruit of a direct connection.
98. Deuchler 1984, p. 183.
99. Fitzwilliam Museum, Cambridge, MS 192. See Panayotova in Cambridge 2016, cat. 49, pp. 210–11. See also a leaf from the same manuscript (Fitzwilliam Museum, Cambridge, MS 368), ibid., cat. 62, pp. 239–40.
100. Morgan 2016, pp. 225–6, with further bibliography. The use of colour modelling was already developing in some sections of the Psalter-Hours of Isabelle of France (Fitzwilliam Museum, Cambridge, MS 300) and its sister manuscript the Psalter of Saint Louis (Bibliothèque nationale de France, Paris, MS lat. 10525), both produced about 1265–70. Panayotova in Cambridge 2016, cat. 61, pp. 238–9. For the use of colour modelling in the Westminster Retable and its possible relation to French thirteenth-century panel painting (of which virtually nothing survives), see Binski and Massing 2009, especially pp. 16–44, 241–58.
101. Sometimes more than one hue was used to achieve the desired tonal range, depending on the particular properties of different pigments. For example, in fig. 31 Saint Aurea's mantle is painted with red lake and azurite, with white lead, her tunic with green earth, modelled with azurite and black. Gordon 2011, p. 193. For an excellent introduction to the handling of colour in illuminated manuscripts, see Panayotova 2016a and 2016b.

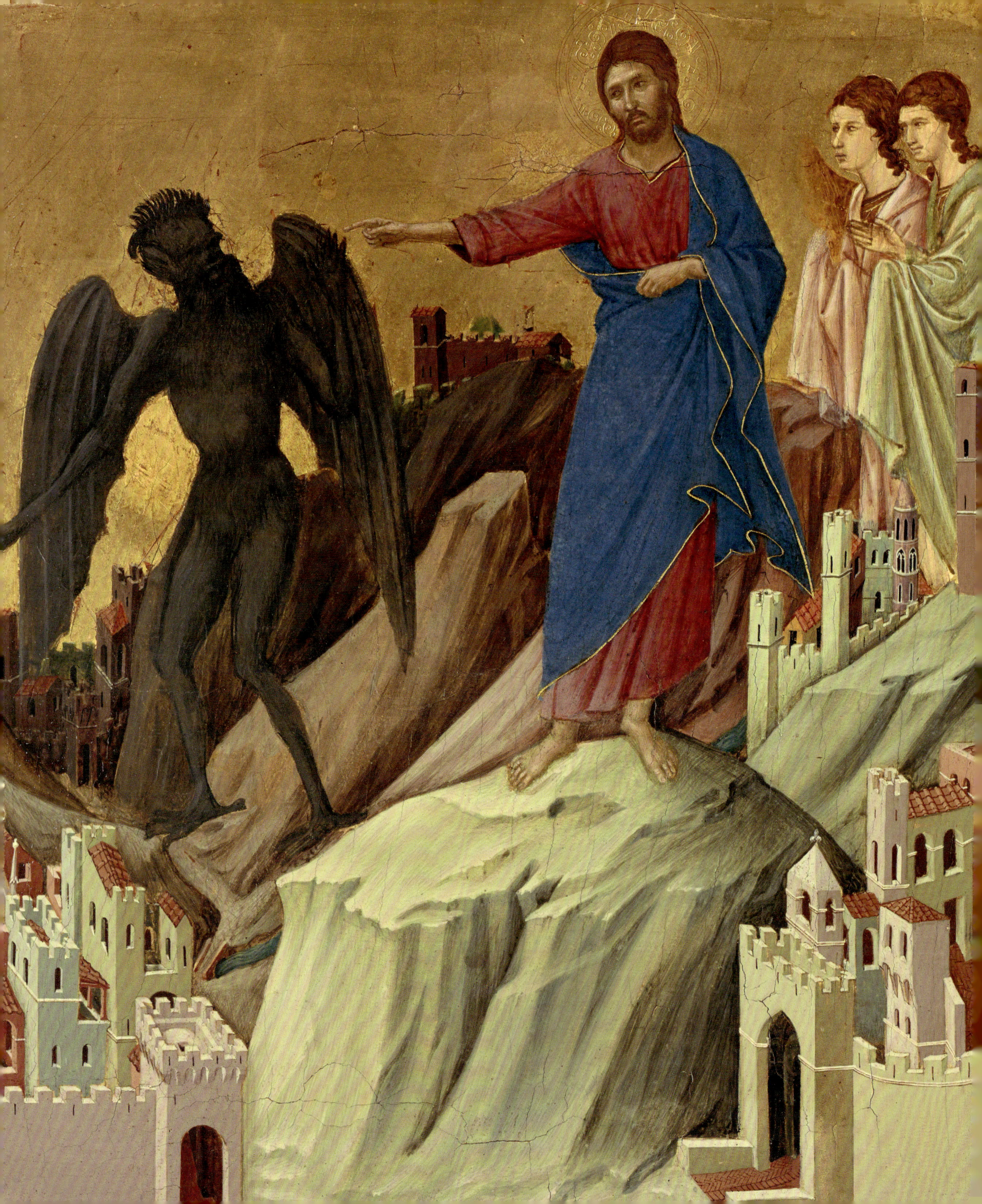

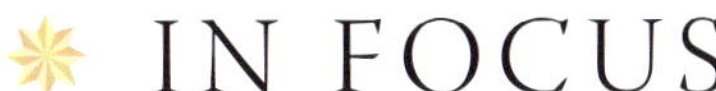

The Back Predella of Duccio's *Maestà*

Imogen Tedbury

The predella of Duccio's *Maestà* is the earliest surviving narrative predella (base of an altarpiece).[1] These structures were usually made from one or several long planks of wood, painted with individual images of saints or biblical figures – or, from the early fourteenth century onwards, scenes illustrating the gospels or lives of the saints. None of the documents relating to the commission of the *Maestà* specifically mention its predella, possibly because it had not been planned at the time the agreements were drawn up.[2] It was probably an early form of 'box predella', wider and deeper than the main panel, and providing structural support to the upper parts (see fig. 9).[3] The full width of the predella consisted of a single board on the front and back, perhaps braced by smaller sections set at right angles across the 'box'.[4] The production of an altarpiece on the scale of the *Maestà* may have shared certain characteristics with the production of frescoes, such as the use of ladders. Duccio and his assistants are likely to have worked downwards, from the upper to the lower parts, to avoid damaging areas they had already completed. They may have worked on both sides of the *Maestà* concurrently or focused on individual sections for a period of time.[5] Either way, the back predella scenes would have been among the last to be completed, and they represent some of Duccio's most confident, sensitive and radical designs. While the front predella had seven scenes, illustrating episodes from Christ's infancy and early life, interspersed with individual figures of Old Testament prophets, the back predella had no framing figures but almost certainly comprised nine events from Christ's public life as a teacher, minister and performer of miracles.[6]

Eight of these scenes from the back predella are known today. A study of the panels' woodgrain and carpentry confirms their original order, painted on a single broad plank of wood and widened with small additions attached with nails and glue at the top and the bottom. Each scene was once individually framed with attached mouldings similar to those that survive on *The Transfiguration* (fig. 29).[7] The varying treatments these panels have received while in the possession of different owners have resulted in some inconsistencies in their appearance and condition. The six panels now held outside Siena

Detail of FIG. 24

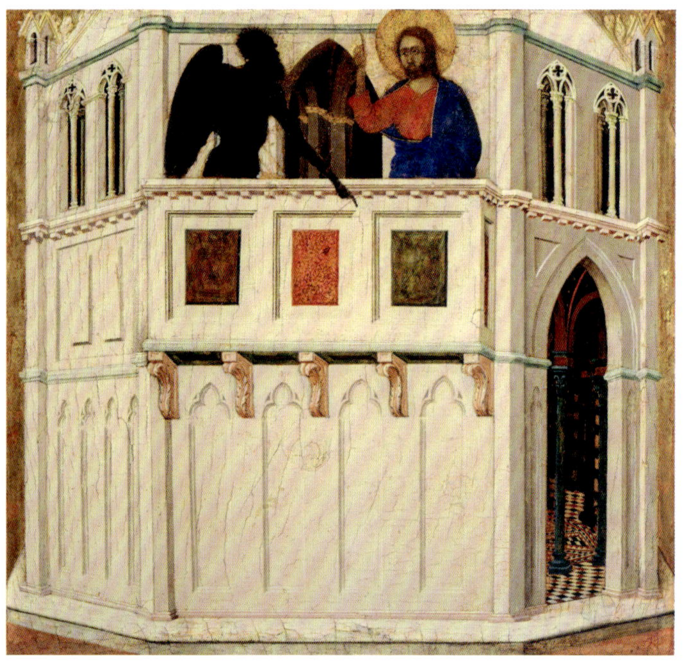

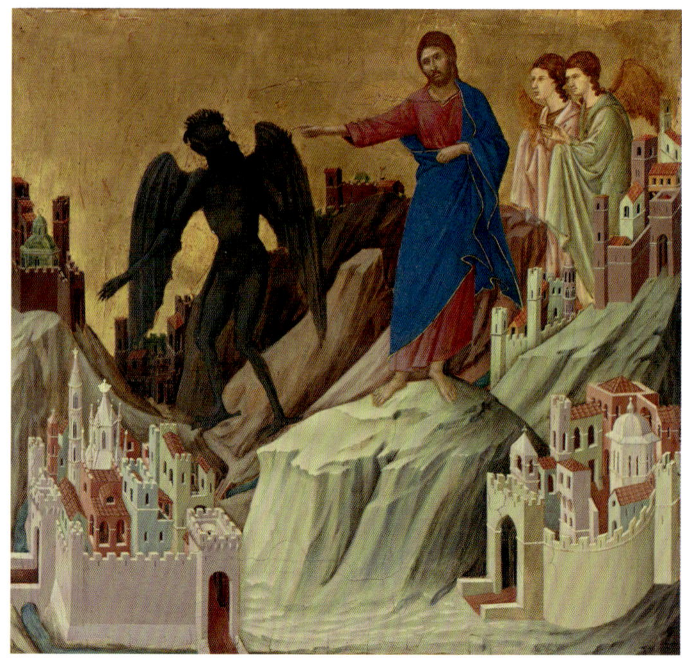

FIG. 23
Duccio (documented 1278; died 1319)
The Temptation of Christ on the Temple, about 1308–11
Tempera on poplar, 48 × 50 cm
Museo dell'Opera della Metropolitana, Siena

FIG. 24
Duccio (documented 1278; died 1319)
The Temptation of Christ on the Mountain, about 1308–11
Tempera on poplar, 43.2 × 46 cm
The Frick Collection, New York, Purchase 1927

probably entered private hands in the last decades of the eighteenth century, after the *Maestà*'s dismemberment (see p. 25). At least four of them belonged to the same private collection in Colle di Val d'Elsa and remained together until 1927.[8] It has been a significant ambition of the exhibition this volume accompanies to reunite the eight surviving panels from the back predella for the first time in some 250 years.

The ministry scenes on the back predella bridge the gap between Christ's early life, represented on the front predella, and his Passion, on the back of the main panel. The scenes suggest Duccio's thorough knowledge of Byzantine iconography, leading to speculation that he may have used a particular manuscript, now lost to us, as his source.[9] The cycle is certainly a fuller account of the ministry than any painted by others of Duccio's generation.[10] The Transfiguration, for example, was not a liturgical feast in the Latin Church, and its representation was relatively rare in Italy at this date.[11] The choice of scenes was probably guided by the *Maestà*'s clerical advisers (see p. 29). Located on the back of the *Maestà*, a little above eye level for someone kneeling at the back of the altarpiece, the scenes of the ministry cycle would have been the most visible for close inspection by a layperson.

One scene from the back predella is lost, almost certainly the first. Several ideas have been put forward for its subject. The Baptism of Christ, a notable absence among surviving elements of the *Maestà*, is perhaps the most likely candidate.[12] Alternatively, as the second and third scenes represent two of Christ's three temptations, the first scene might have represented the Temptation in the Wilderness. All three temptations are included on a fourteenth-century panel in Pienza, which copies other elements of the *Maestà*.[13] Rather more doubtful is the suggestion that a painting of an unusual episode, *Saint John the Baptist bearing Witness* (about 1310–30; Museum of Fine Arts, Budapest), might be identified as the missing panel.[14] Transferred from wood to canvas, it is in poor condition today, but was attributed to Duccio by Giovanni Battista Cavalcaselle, who saw the painting when it may have been in a better state.[15] An extension of the cycle beyond nine episodes has also been proposed. In the unlikely event that the box-ends of the predella's structure were painted, there might be as many as three missing scenes, with the first and last forming the box-ends.[16] The matter remains unresolved, although a narrative scheme as comprehensive as that of the *Maestà* would surely have included Christ's Baptism somewhere in its conception.

The extraordinary variety of the surviving scenes can only be appreciated fully when they are seen together. Their varying terrain, architectural

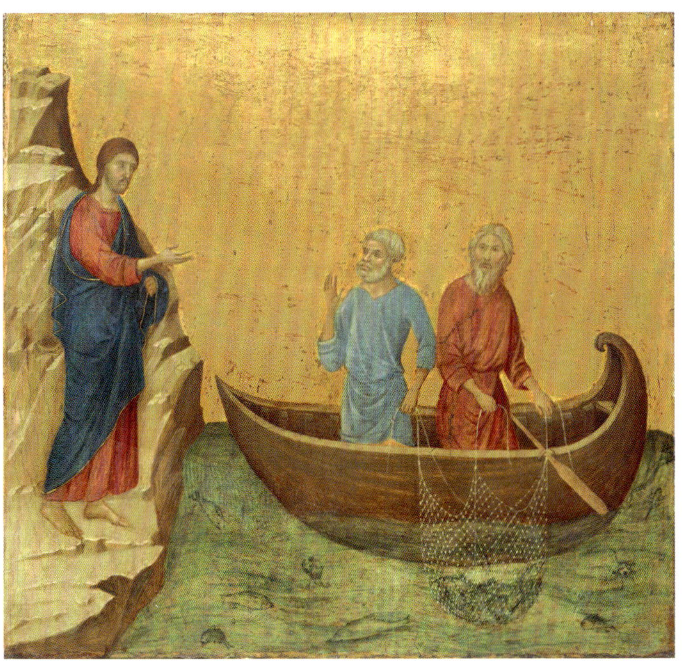

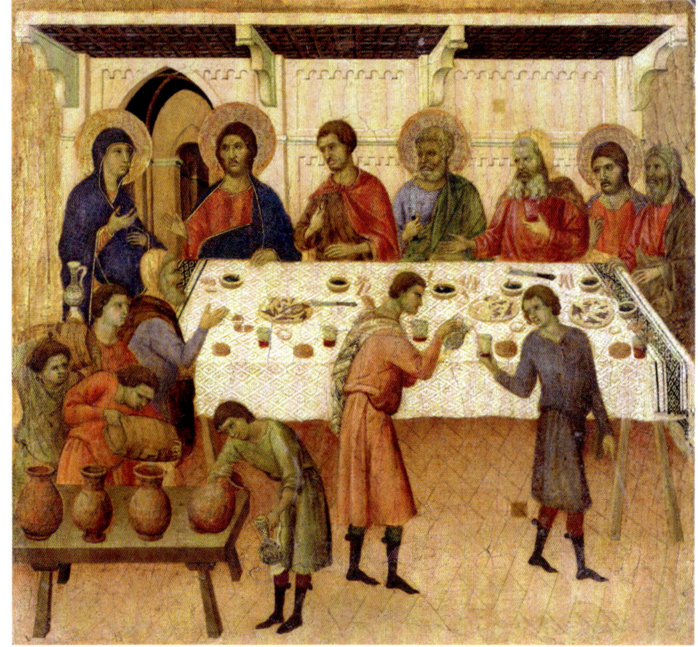

structures and vivid gold skies undulating across their shared horizon assist the viewer in finding connections between episodes. In the damaged *Temptation of Christ on the Temple* (fig. 23), Christ and the devil converse on the balcony of a polygonal building, seen in a close-up view that fills the picture frame. This exterior evokes Romanesque baptisteries at Florence and Pisa, while the black-and-white interior, teasingly glimpsed through the doorway, may have prompted a connection to Siena's striped cathedral. In the *Temptation of Christ on the Mountain* (fig. 24), Christ and the devil pick their way between hilltops populated with miniature cities. The architecture and topography of Siena itself are again suggested by the terracotta roofs, castellated towers and herringbone tiled paving, while the steep drop on the left falls away like the hills around Siena's cathedral complex.[17] The populated mountains of the *Temptation* rise to a barren peak in *The Calling of the Apostles Peter and Andrew* (fig. 25), a marine painting of sorts, in which the transparent waters of the lake reveal their living contents. The centrally positioned *Wedding at Cana* presents the only interior view, with figures seated around a table laid for the feast (fig. 26). The bustle of the wedding is conveyed by the open doorway behind, through which we can imagine guests and servants hurrying. Outside again in the adjacent scene, Christ perches on the edge of the green porphyry well as he converses with the Samaritan woman, watched over by the disciples who linger at the city gates. The city's rosy towers and high terraces with panelled shutters recur in the next episode's street scene. There, the man born blind stands, newly sighted and transfixed by his vision of Christ in the following scene, *The Transfiguration* (fig. 29).[18] Christ stands shimmering in his striated robes on the unforgiving, open plain of a high mountain, which glows slightly pink in Christ's light, emphasising the strangeness of the event witnessed by the disciples, who express their surprise and fear with raised hands. In the final scene the rocks rise with pointed peaks that mimic the pediment of Lazarus's tomb. The colourful crowd of onlookers packed onto a small outcrop witnesses the miraculous – though pungent – resurrection of the man silhouetted in the dark entrance, still wrapped in his white shroud.

Infrared examination reveals Duccio's characteristic underdrawing, achieved with a liquid medium and a brush, as well as compositional changes undertaken during the production process. Some of these changes – such as the late addition of the angels in the *Temptation of Christ on the Mountain*, or the adaption of Lazarus's tomb from an experimental horizontal sarcophagus to a more traditional, vertical opening in the

FIG. 25
Duccio (documented 1278; died 1319)
The Calling of the Apostles Peter and Andrew, about 1308–11
Tempera on poplar, 43.3 × 46.2 cm
National Gallery of Art, Washington, Samuel H. Kress Collection (1939.1.141)

FIG. 26
Duccio (documented 1278; died 1319)
The Wedding at Cana, about 1308–11
Tempera on poplar, 43.5 × 46.5 cm
Museo dell'Opera della Metropolitana, Siena

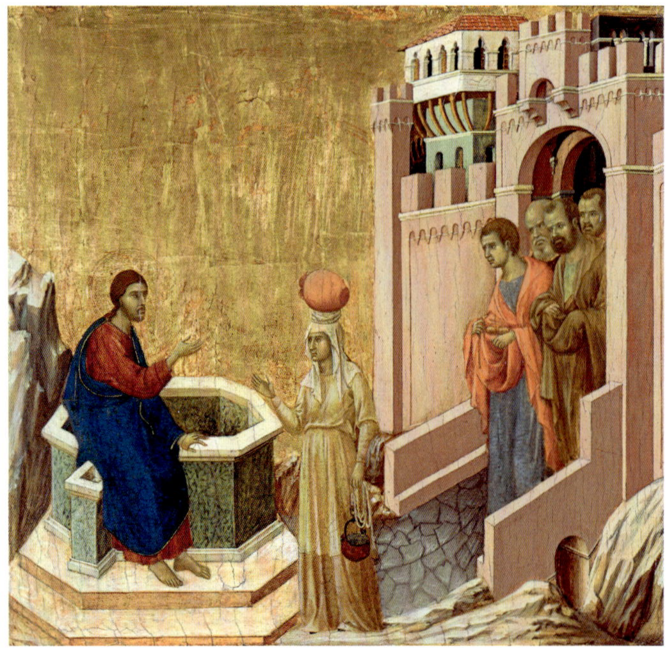

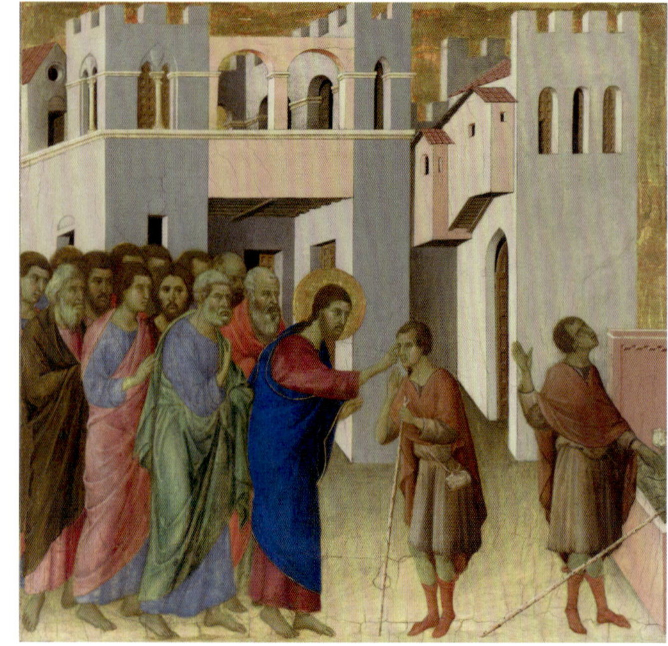

FIG. 27
Duccio (documented 1278; died 1319)
Christ and the Woman of Samaria, about 1308–11
Tempera on poplar, 43.5 × 46 cm
Museo Nacional Thyssen-Bornemisza, Madrid (133 [1971.7])

FIG. 28
Duccio (documented 1278; died 1319)
The Healing of the Man born Blind, about 1308–11
Tempera on poplar, 45.1 × 46.7 cm
The National Gallery, London. Bought, 1883 (NG1140)

FIG. 29
Duccio (documented 1278; died 1319)
The Transfiguration, about 1308–11
Tempera on poplar, 48.5 × 51.4 cm (with engaged frame)
The National Gallery, London. Presented by R.H. Wilson, 1891 (NG1330)

FIG. 30
Duccio (documented 1278; died 1319)
The Raising of Lazarus, about 1308–11
Tempera on poplar, transferred to cork, 43.5 × 46.4 cm
Kimbell Art Museum, Fort Worth, Texas (APx 1975.01)

rocks – may suggest the influence of a theological adviser tempering Duccio's bolder iconographical innovations.[19] While Duccio's personal oversight of these designs is not questioned, there has been considerable discussion of the involvement of other artists in the execution of his designs for the back predella. It is sometimes possible to discern their hands at work in addition to that of Duccio himself. In *The Healing of the Man born Blind* (fig. 28), Duccio seems to have been responsible for the design and some execution, with another painter, perhaps Simone Martini, responsible for painting the buildings, occasionally departing from Duccio's architectural underdrawing.[20]

The complex spatial devices used to represent architecture across the back predella also bear comparison to the subsequent works of Pietro Lorenzetti.[21] However, this does not necessarily indicate Pietro's involvement in these passages. Rather, the comparison attests to the long shadow that the *Maestà* cast on artists like Simone and the Lorenzetti brothers, who almost certainly began their careers working with Duccio in his workshop. Among the countless remarkable innovations of the *Maestà*, Duccio's radical approach to narrative would go on to inspire the next generation of extraordinary artists working in Siena and beyond.

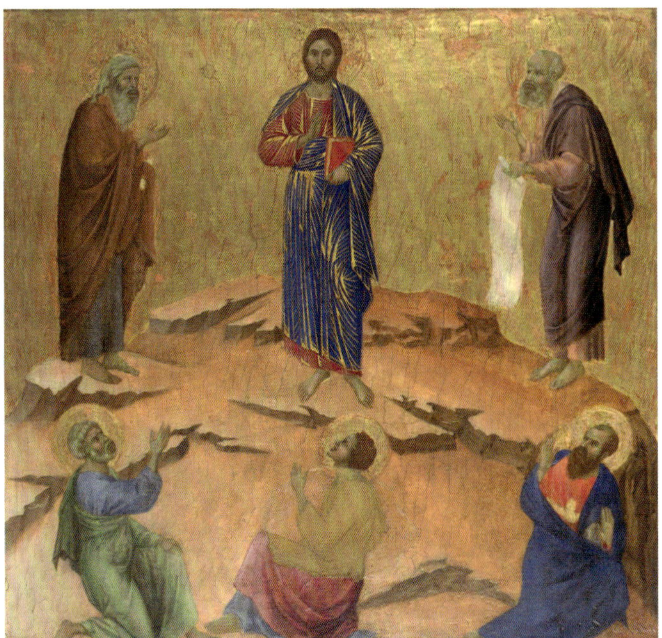

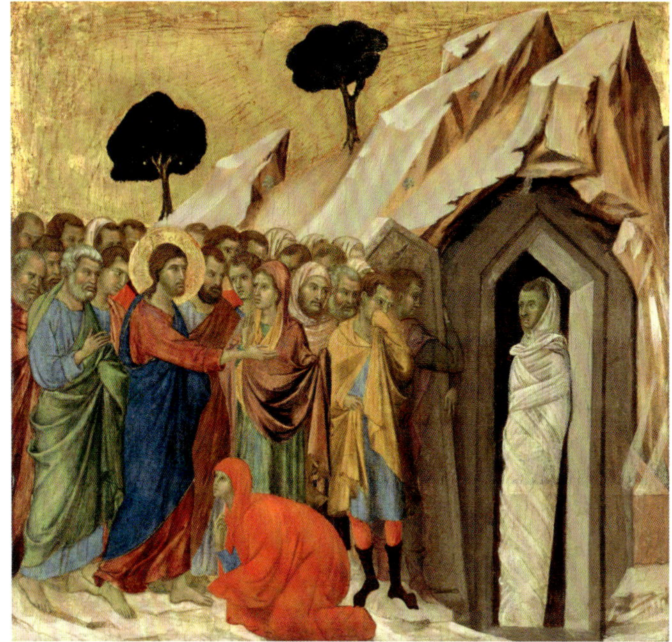

The OPD's 2024 technical investigation of the *Maestà* was still underway when this volume went to print; in anticipation of these results, this text remains indebted to John White's earlier study (1979). Especial thanks to Joanna Cannon for her guidance in the preparation of this contribution.

1. Two known earlier works – Cimabue's altarpiece for Santa Chiara in Pisa commissioned in 1301 (modern-style date) and Duccio's altarpiece for the Palazzo Pubblico in Siena (1302) – have not survived. If these paintings had predellas, they would probably have had half-length figures not narrative scenes.
2. The predella may have developed during production, as a solution to narrative or structural issues. White 1979, p. 82. For the documents, see Satkowski 2000.
3. An inventory of 1423 lists separate hanging draperies for the predella and the main panel, which would not have been required if these sections were the same width. Satkowski 2000, pp. 110–11. It is likely that the predella projected a little forward of the main panel, as in Simone Martini's Saint Louis of Toulouse Altarpiece (fig. 67), which took various elements of the *Maestà* as its model.
4. London 1989–90, pp. 69, 86.
5. White 1979, pp. 96, 106–7, 119, argues that the working sequence began with the rear pinnacle panels, followed by the front pinnacle scenes and the main rear panel, during which time the main front panel was begun, followed by the front predella, and, finally, the rear predella.
6. Stubblebine 1979, vol. 1, pp. 52–4, White 1979, p. 86, and Gordon 2011, p. 176, all agree on a predella nine scenes wide, although earlier scholars had different ideas. DeWald 1955 and Brandi 1959, p. 9, followed Weigelt's reconstruction of 10 scenes: Weigelt 1911, pp. 93–7. Lusini 1912, pp. 70–5, proposed 11 scenes, with two of these on the frame's lateral pillars.
7. The front predella was framed slightly differently, with all four corners of each scene and figure cut across diagonally. These original framing elements survive on all the front predella fragments in Washington DC (*Isaiah*, *The Nativity*, *Ezekiel*) and in Siena (*The Adoration of the Magi*, *Solomon*, *The Presentation in the Temple*, *Malachi*, *The Massacre of the Innocents*, *Jeremiah*, *The Dream of Joseph*, *Flight into Egypt*, *Hosea*, and *The Teaching in the Temple*).
8. *The Temptation of Christ on the Mountain*, *The Calling of Saints Peter and Andrew*, *Christ and the Woman of Samaria* and *The Raising of Lazarus* were lent by the brothers Giuseppe and Marziale Dini to an exhibition in Colle di Val d'Elsa in 1879. The dealer and Pre-Raphaelite painter Charles Fairfax Murray bought these four panels for Robert Henry Benson (see Tedbury, pp. 261–2, in the present volume). *The Healing of the Man born Blind* was sold by Murray to the National Gallery in 1883, acquired from 'Fagnano', probably the Bandini Piccolomini villa. *The Transfiguration* was given to the National Gallery by its owner R.H. Wilson in 1891; it is unknown where Wilson acquired this painting. With thanks to Paul Tucker.
9. Stubblebine 1979, vol. 1, p. 49.
10. White 1979, p. 102.
11. Two rare examples of the subject are the fresco in the Upper Church of San Francesco, Assisi, and a canvas painting attributed to Guido da Siena (about 1270; Pinacoteca nazionale di Siena, inv. 8). See Gordon 2011, pp. 170–2.
12. Bellosi 1998, p. 18, and White 1979, p. 86, consider this most likely.
13. Stubblebine 1979, vol. 1, p. 49.
14. Inv. 6. Boskovits 1982; Boskovits and Padovani 1990, p. 76. Schmidt 2002a, pp. 53–4, notes differences in the haloes and observes that Christ's clothing is inconsistent with his representation elsewhere on the *Maestà*, but Boskovits 2016, pp. 81–102, considers these differences negligible.
15. Crowe and Cavalcaselle 1864–6, vol. 2 (1864), p. 52.
16. Stubblebine 1979, vol. 1, p. 49; Wilkins Sullivan 1985, p. 35. These hypothetical side panels are not compatible with the external buttresses proposed by Gardner von Teuffel 1979, pp. 36–45, as necessary – and influential – structural elements. See also Gardner von Teuffel, pp. 68–77, in the present volume.
17. The Campo (Siena's main square) is paved with terracotta tiles arranged in a herringbone pattern. For Siena's paved brick thoroughfares, see Campbell, p. 14, in the present volume.
18. White 1979, p. 122, noted this connection between the scenes, which explains Duccio's innovation in painting the blind man standing upright, unlike earlier representations.
19. For these changes, see Gordon 2009; Wilkins Sullivan 1988. For the adviser, see Cannon, p. 29, in the present volume.
20. Gordon 2011, p. 168.
21. Stubblebine 1979, vol. 1, pp. 32, 41, also identifies the hands of Ugolino di Nerio, Segna di Bonaventura, Simone Martini, Pietro Lorenzetti, Ambrogio Lorenzetti and others at work elsewhere in the complex.

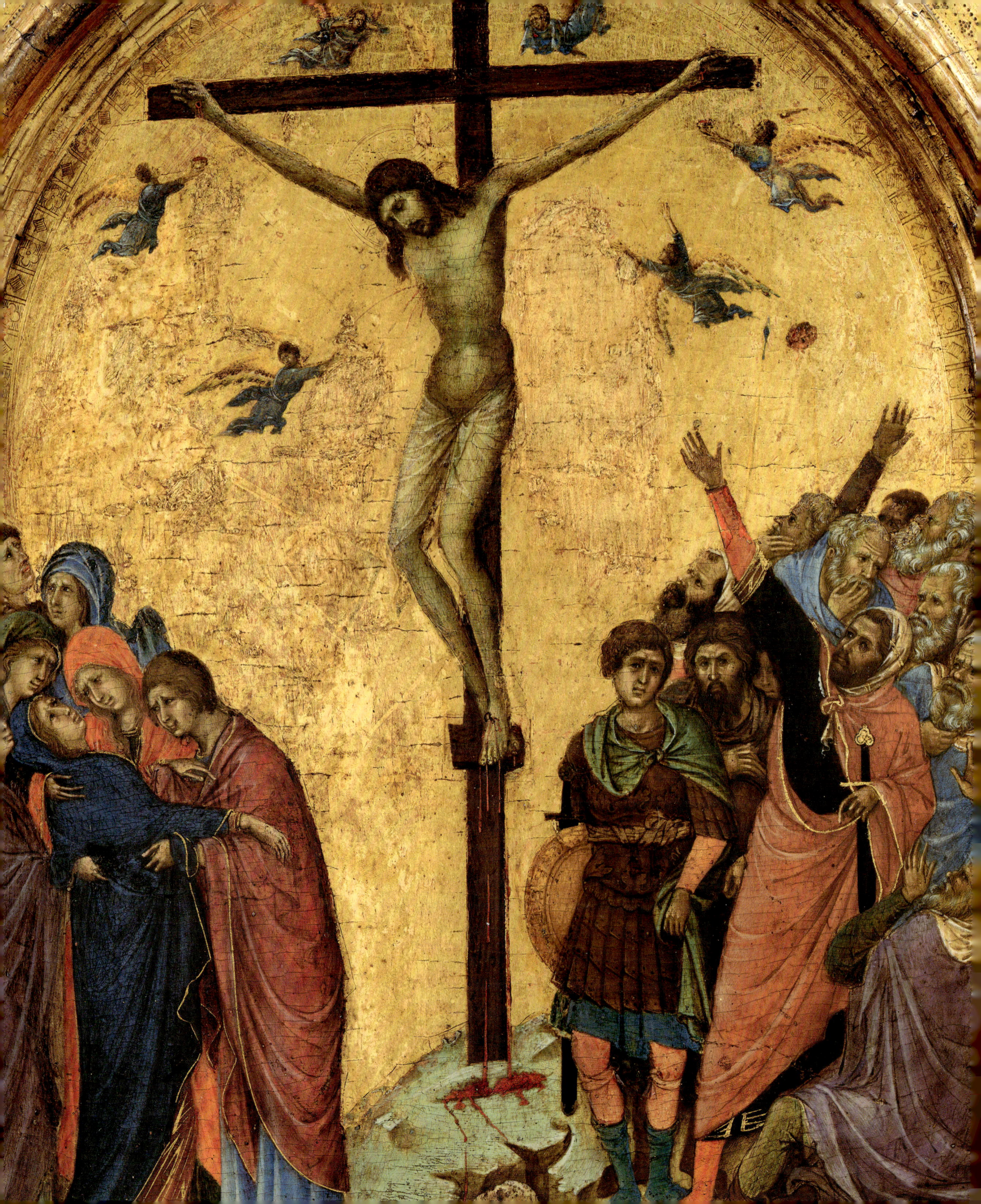

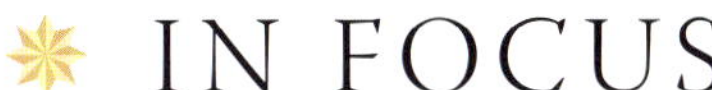

Two Portable Triptychs by Duccio

Joanna Cannon

There is good reason to believe that the Dominican cardinal Niccolò da Prato owned two magnificent portable triptychs painted, in large part, by Duccio, in the years following the installation of the artist's *Maestà* in the Cathedral of Siena.[1] The two works in question are the *Triptych with the Virgin and Child, Saint Dominic, Saint Aurea, Patriarchs and Prophets*, National Gallery, London (fig. 31), and the *Triptych with the Crucifixion, Saint Nicholas, Saint Clement and the Redeemer with Angels*, Museum of Fine Arts, Boston (fig. 32). Exceptionally, the two triptychs have been brought together, probably for the first time in many centuries, in the exhibition that this volume accompanies. Niccolò's will, drawn up in 1321, is one of the first to mention panel paintings among a cardinal's possessions. Included in many very generous benefactions, the Dominican foundation at Prato was to receive three panel paintings that served as altarpieces.[2] The principal link between the two triptychs and Niccolò, who was Cardinal Bishop of Ostia and Velletri, lies in the selection of saints on the triptych wings. Nicholas, the cardinal's name saint, was, admittedly, a popular choice. Clement, less often depicted, was the patron saint of Velletri.[3] Dominic, founder of the order of friars to which Niccolò belonged, seldom appeared in paintings of this time unless the work was directly connected with the Dominicans. Most tellingly of all, Aurea was rarely represented, but as patron saint of Ostia was directly relevant to the cardinal's institutional ties.[4]

Niccolò da Prato's will clearly illustrates the rise of panel paintings as high-status possessions. Unlike the carefully itemised liturgical vessels and vestments used in his private chapel, such as his 'best chalice, cross, thurible and bell of silver', also destined for San Domenico, Prato, the panel paintings were not a liturgical requirement.[5] Their inclusion among the accoutrements of his chapel was a matter of personal taste, and bequeathing them to the cardinal's 'home' convent emphasises their perceived devotional worth set beside the much greater material value of the goldsmith's work that could be recouped if items were traded or melted down.[6]

If we accept that the London and Boston triptychs were two of those three panel paintings,

Detail of FIG. 32

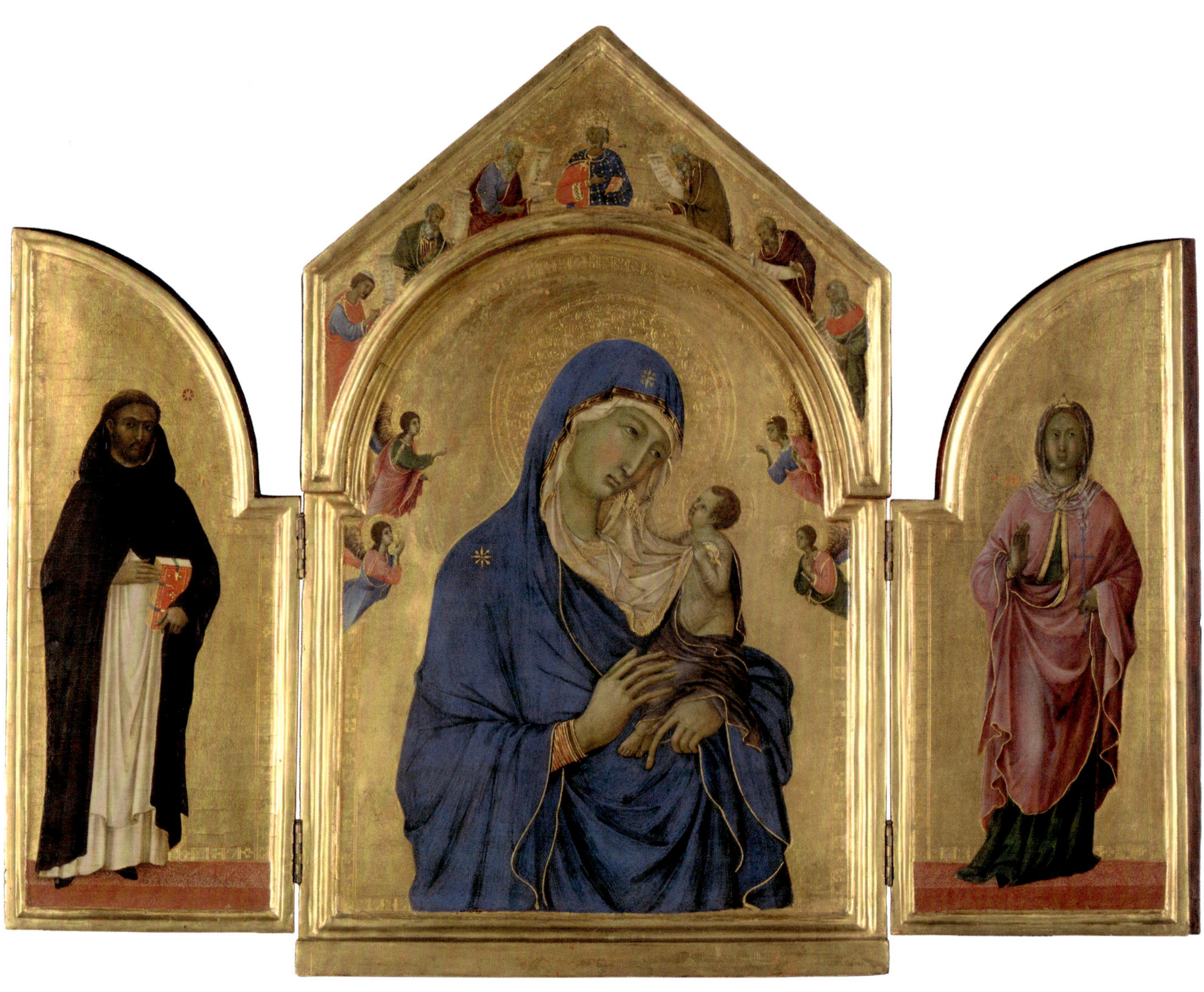

FIG. 31
Duccio (documented 1278; died 1319)
Triptych with the Virgin and Child, Saint Dominic, Saint Aurea, Patriarchs and Prophets, about 1312–15 (?)
Tempera on panel, 61.4 × 39.3 cm (central panel, with engaged frame); 45.2 × 19.3 cm (left wing, with semi-integral frame); 45.2 × 20.6 cm (right wing, with semi-integral frame)
The National Gallery, London. Bought, 1857 (NG566)

FIG. 32
Duccio (documented 1278; died 1319)
Triptych with the Crucifixion, Saint Nicholas, Saint Clement and the Redeemer with Angels, 1311–18
Tempera on panel, 61 × 39.4 cm (central panel, with engaged frame); 45.1 × 19.4 cm (left wing, with engaged frame); 45.1 × 20.2 cm (right wing, with engaged frame)
Museum of Fine Arts, Boston. Grant Walker and Charles Potter Kling Funds (45.880)

how did this wealthy and discerning patron come to choose a Sienese artist, specifically Duccio, to supply these works?[7] As a friar in the Florentine Dominican house of Santa Maria Novella, and subsequently, in 1304, as the Pope's representative based for some months in Florence, Niccolò had ample opportunity to appreciate Duccio's magnificent *Rucellai Madonna* of 1285 (see fig. 6).[8] Following the death of the Dominican Pope Benedict XI in July 1304, the cardinal spent time in Perugia as convenor of the conclave that finally elected his successor, Clement V, in June 1305. The Dominican foundation in Perugia (where Benedict XI was buried) owned a polyptych by Duccio, probably painted around that time, of which only the central panel of the Virgin and Child

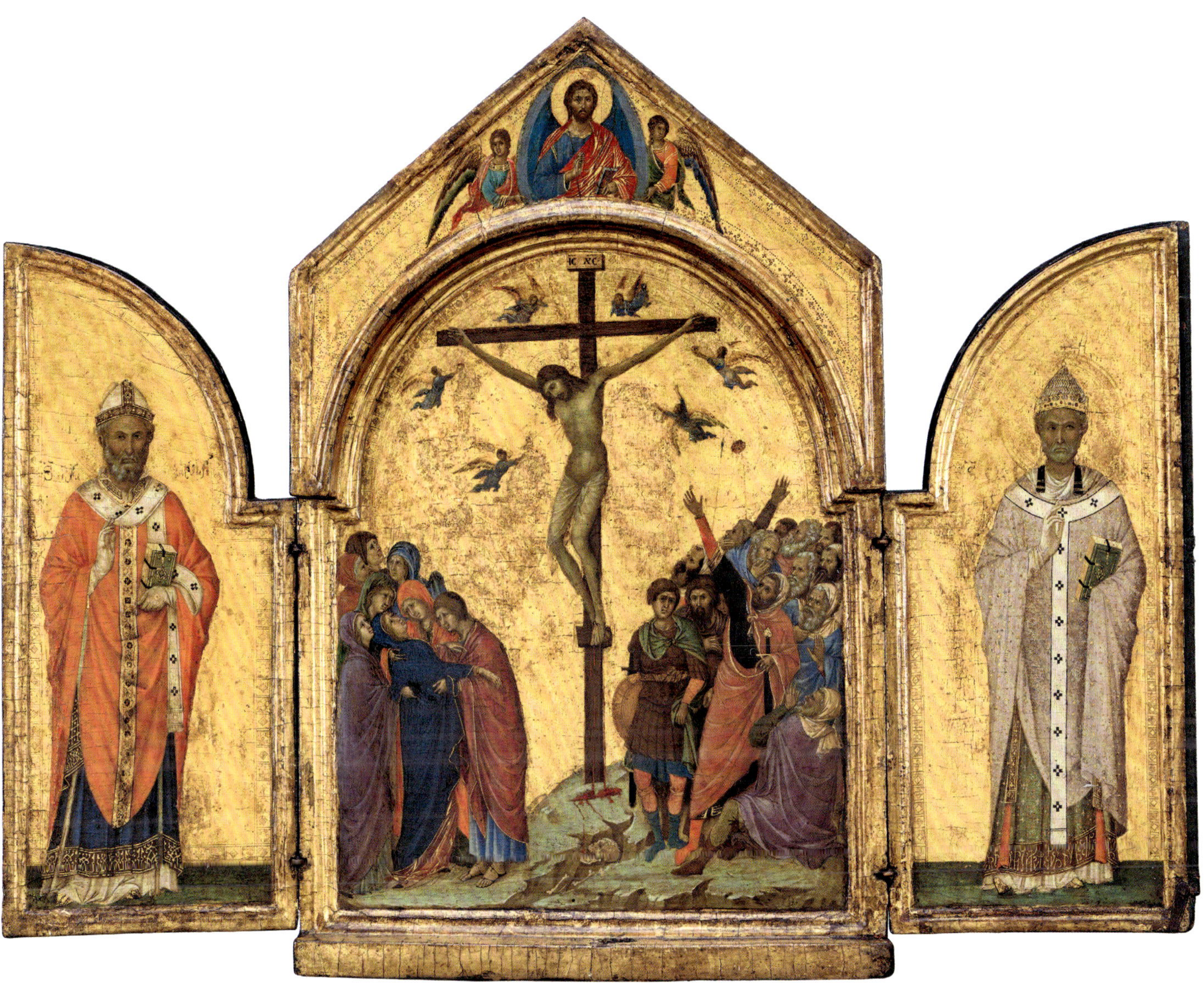

survives.[9] The Virgin and Child of the National Gallery triptych has been convincingly characterised as a reminiscence and elaboration, at reduced scale,[10] of the Perugia composition, likely to have been made at the request of a patron who admired the Perugia painting.[11] Other features of the London triptych, in addition to the choice of the two saints on the wings, also suggest a work tailored to particular requests. Innovatively, six bust-length figures of patriarchs and prophets are assembled in the gable, flanking King David at the apex. Visible even when the triptych wings are closed, all look intently towards the Virgin below, each carrying a scroll with a tiny but legible biblical text, anticipating the virgin birth. Jacob's scroll, '[This is the] house of God and the gate of heaven' (Genesis 28:17), affirms that opening the triptych doors will reveal a celestial vision. The same figures holding, with one exception, the same biblical verses, are found on Duccio's polyptych for Santa Maria della Scala, Siena (now Pinacoteca nazionale, inv. 47), and were perhaps also included in the lost panels of the polyptych for San Domenico, Perugia.[12]

If the National Gallery triptych presents, in concentrated form, aspects of Duccio's polyptychs, the Boston triptych has been considered an abbreviated reminiscence (omitting the two crucified thieves) of the Crucifixion in the Siena Cathedral *Maestà* (installed in 1311).[13] After his stay in Perugia, Niccolò da Prato transferred his main activities to Avignon, where Clement V established the papal

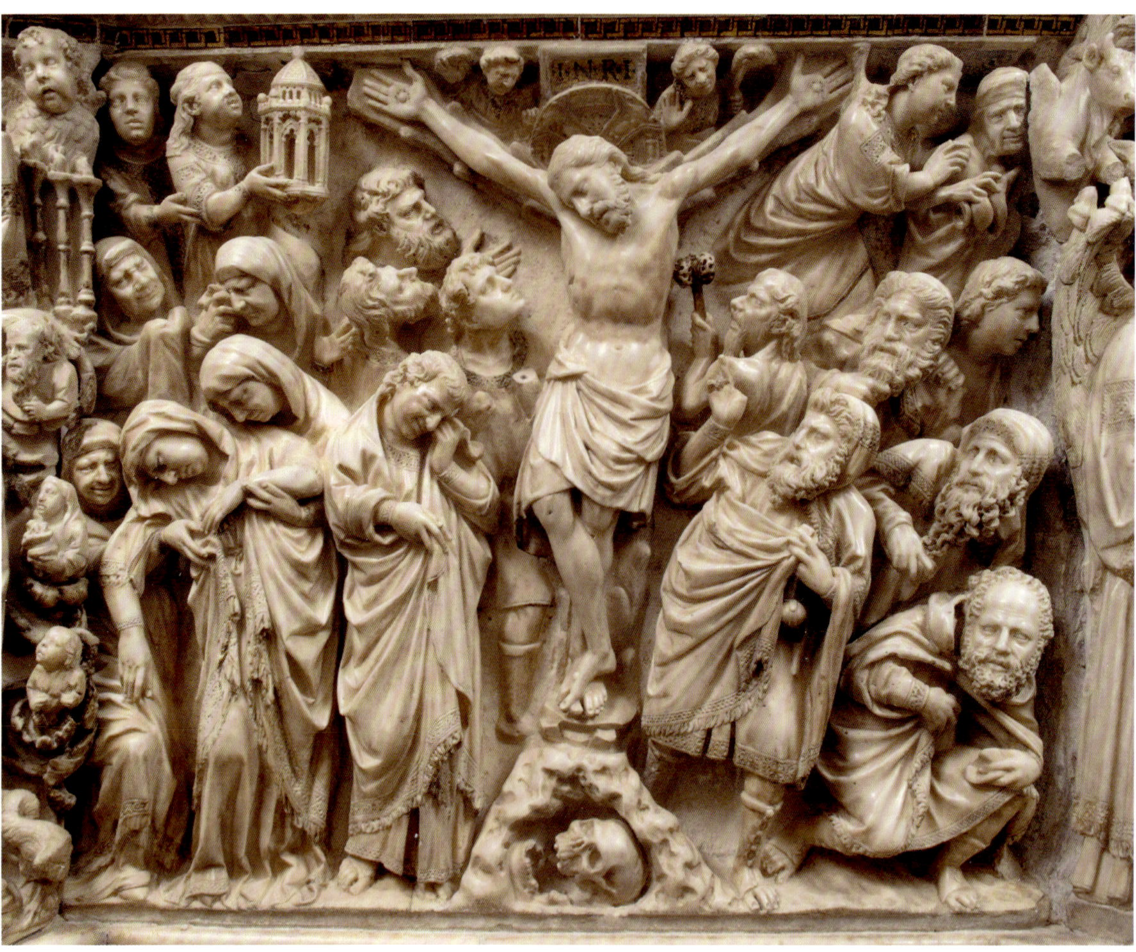

FIG. 33
Nicola Pisano (first mentioned 1258; died between 1278 and 1284)
The Crucifixion, 1265–8
Marble, 84.5 × 94.5 cm
Relief from pulpit in Siena Cathedral

court, but the cardinal returned to central Italy on several occasions, acting as papal representative in 1311–12, just after the completion of Duccio's great work. If, during his journey accompanying Emperor Henry VII to and from his coronation in Rome in 1312, he travelled along the via Francigena, he would have passed through Siena where he is likely to have seen the *Maestà*, and may then have felt the desire and sensed the opportunity to possess a remembrance of this remarkable work, and of the polyptychs that Duccio had previously painted for the Dominicans.[14] Perhaps Niccolò communicated directly with Duccio. Or he may have conveyed his requirements through an agent, possibly aided by drawings supplied by the artist. The almost identical measurements of the two triptychs, and the matching decoration on their exteriors, strongly suggest that they were made as a pair.[15] Once completed the two works would have made their way to the cardinal in Avignon, as his will indicates. Although they were personal possessions they would have been seen by others: his chaplains and possibly also fellow members of the papal court, among them Napoleone Orsini, probable owner of Simone Martini's Orsini Polyptych.[16]

Duccio's triptychs of the Virgin and Child and of the Crucifixion were made at a time of frequent innovation in the treatment of these two very often represented subjects. This involved much fruitful interaction among works of painting, carving and enamelling, and between works produced in Italy and the north.[17] These reciprocal relations can be seen feeding into the design of Duccio's two triptychs. For example, there may be echoes of Parisian works in the National Gallery Virgin and Child not found in those figures in Duccio's large-scale altarpieces: the reduced size of the Christ Child in relation to his mother; his proportions, with small head and elongated body; his intense gaze focused on the Virgin;[18] the censing angels to either side of her head (compare fig. 31 with figs 170 and 172).

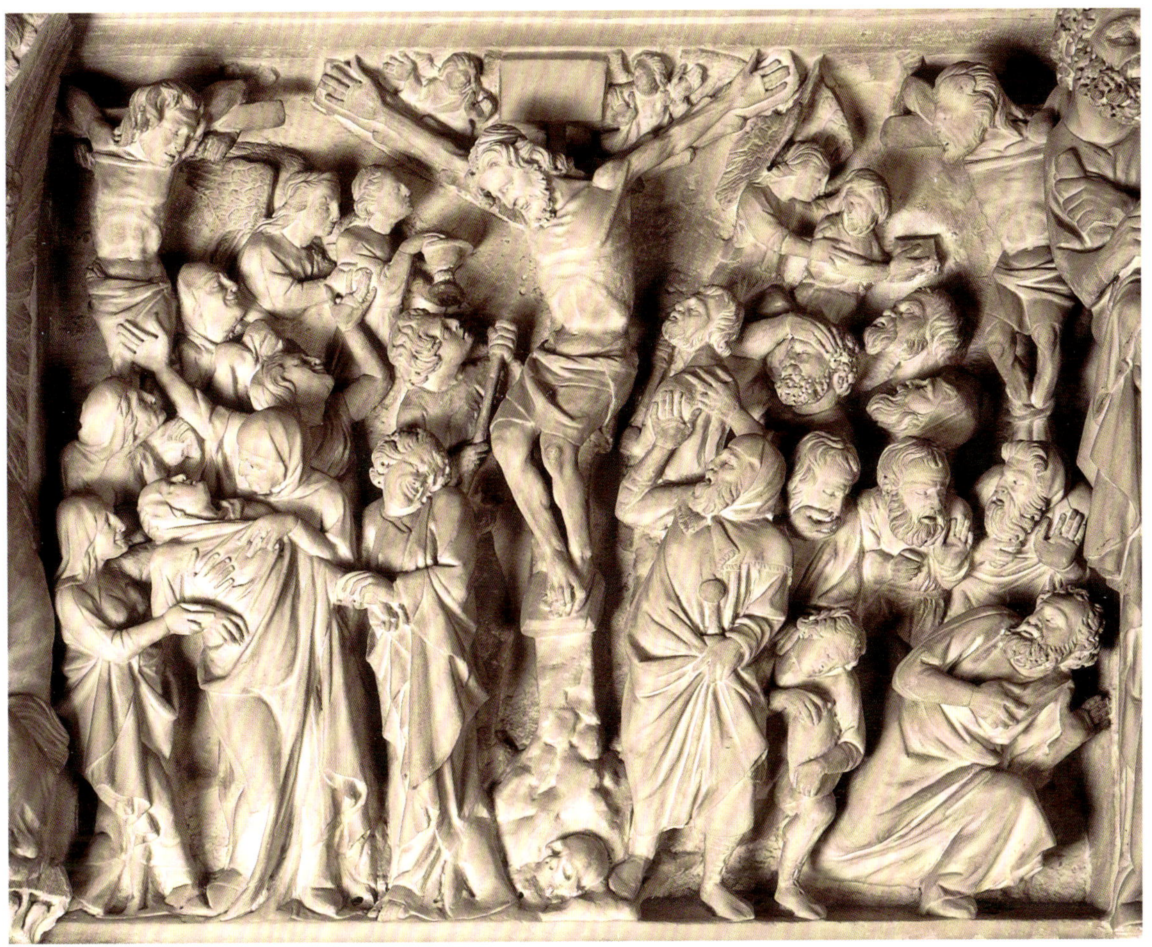

FIG. 34
Giovanni Pisano (born about 1248; died 1319)
The Crucifixion, completed 1301
Marble, 85.5 × 102 cm
Relief from pulpit in Sant'Andrea, Pistoia

A major theme of Sienese Crucifixion scenes, the Virgin swooning in grief and suffering the pains she was spared during childbirth, was initially inspired by Nicola Pisano's relief for the pulpit of Siena Cathedral (fig. 33 and see fig. 15), which itself probably drew on northern manuscript illumination and ivories that were also exploring this motif from around the middle of the thirteenth century onwards (see figs 171 and 172).[19] A rich variety of poses for the Virgin and those supporting her were employed. Duccio's introduction, in the *Maestà* and the Boston triptych, of the backwards collapse of the Virgin, allowing her to look up at her suffering son, may have come from Giovanni Pisano's variation on his father's composition, found in the pulpit for Sant'Andrea, Pistoia, completed in 1301 (figs 34 and 35). Duccio's agitated crowd of gesturing soldiers and priests on the right uses several figures from Cimabue's large-scale Crucifixion in the Upper Church of San Francesco, Assisi, and both painters responded to Nicola Pisano's pulpits.[20] For example, Duccio took the crouching figure at bottom right of the Siena relief and turned him round, so that he mirrors the Virgin's upwards gaze. French ivory diptychs often included the pointing figure to the right of the Cross, and occasionally also the angels flying above, wringing their hands or covering their eyes, perhaps derived at several removes from Duccio's example (see fig. 172).[21] The subsequent rethinking of the *Maestà* Crucifixion within Duccio's circle is exemplified by the Master of Città di Castello (see fig. 206) who added his own variations, as well as returning to some of Duccio's sources, notably the Siena pulpit.[22]

Elements of Duccio's Crucifixion were repeated many times, reaching as far as a small double-sided triptych with translucent enamels, probably made in England in the second quarter of the fourteenth century (see fig. 122).[23] At that distance any connection with Duccio's *Maestà* may well have

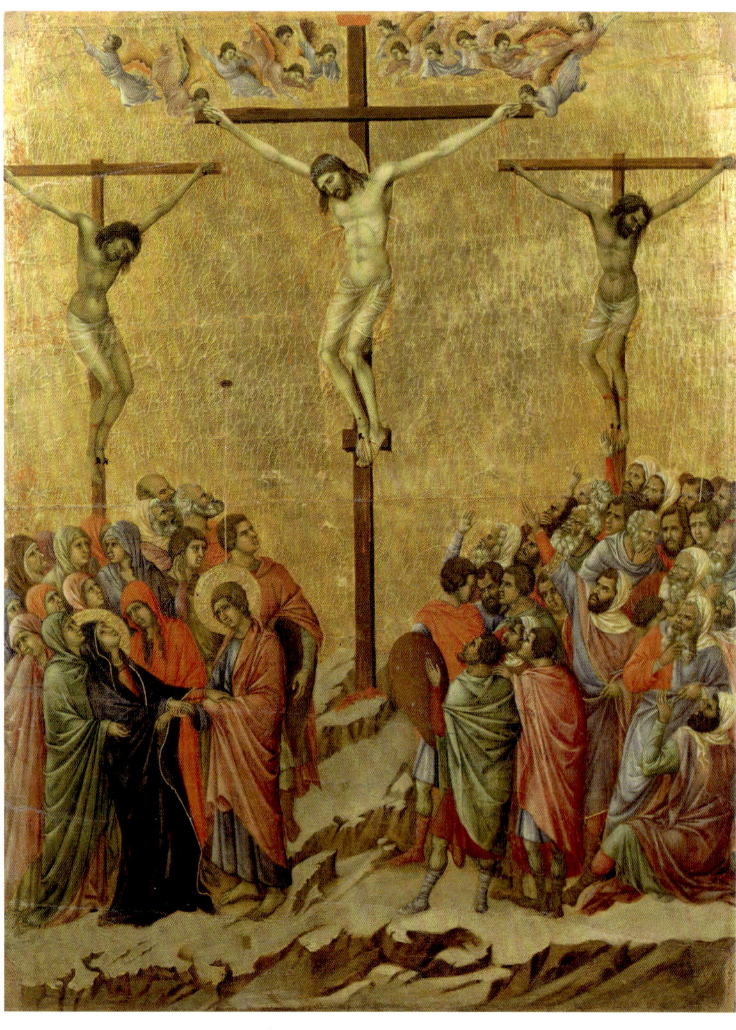

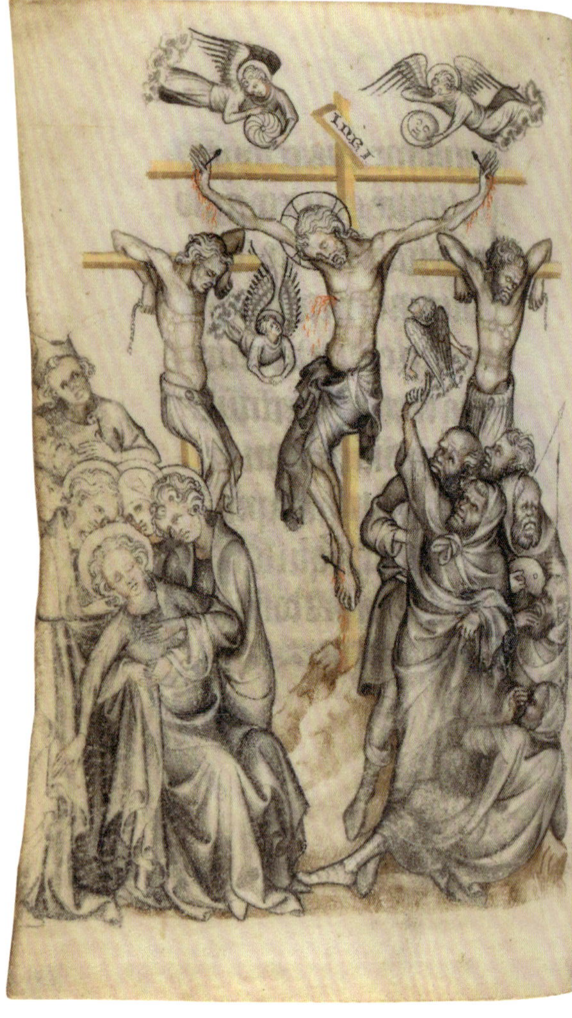

FIG. 35
Detail of the Crucifixion in Duccio's *Maestà* (fig. 9)

FIG. 36
Jean Pucelle
(documented 1319–34)
The Crucifixion,
about 1324–8
The Hours of Jeanne d'Evreux, Queen of France, fol. 68v
Grisaille, tempera and ink on parchment,
9.2 × 6.2 cm (single folio)
The Metropolitan Museum of Art, New York.
The Cloisters Collection, 1954 (54.1.2)

been forgotten, but in some cases the prestige of the original was surely a determining factor in the choice of composition. The exhibition that this book accompanies affords the unparalleled opportunity to see Duccio's recapitulation of his cathedral *Maestà* Crucifixion in the company of another exceptional version of the image found in the tiny book of hours made at the behest of King Charles IV of France for his queen, Jeanne d'Evreux, by Jean Pucelle, the outstanding Parisian illuminator of his time, at some point between about 1324 and 1328 (fig. 36).[24] Choosing to include the two crucified thieves (the bad thief with head turned away from Christ), the rocky Golgotha, the crowded composition to either side and certain details of figure pose and drapery make this, in several respects, a faithful reflection of the original painting. Pucelle engaged very closely and creatively with Duccio's work, rethinking, for example, the gesture of the man crouching at bottom right, whose left hand, shown in an open gesture of amazement in the *Maestà* and in the Boston triptych, is here cupped and turned towards his face to shield his eyes from the sight before him. Whether Pucelle observed the *Maestà* through the medium of a work such as the Boston triptych or, more likely, directly, is a matter of debate.[25] Whatever the mechanism, whether through the movement of people, objects, drawings or memories, new ideas emanating from Siena were taken up with alacrity in different places and art forms. The Boston triptych and Jeanne d'Evreux's book of hours show how Duccio's image of the Crucifixion from his great painting, fixed on the high altar of Siena Cathedral, might be recalled and celebrated: placed by a cardinal on the altar of his private chapel in Avignon or held by the Queen of France in the palm of her hand.

1. For essential discussion of the two triptychs, see Gordon 2011, pp. 188–201; Kanter 1994, pp. 72–6; Ferrante 2018. For the connection with Niccolò da Prato, see also Cannon 1980, pp. 269–70, 315, n. 240; Schmidt 1996; Schmidt 2003a; Schmidt 2003b; Schmidt 2005a, pp. 249–52; Cannon 2013, pp. 207–8; Napione 2013, pp. 292–8. For a fundamental collection of essays on Niccolò da Prato, see Benedetti and Cinelli 2013. The family name Albertini is widely, but incorrectly, applied to Niccolò. See Lorenzini 2013, especially pp. 39–40, 44–6.
2. 'Tres tabulas pictas, quae ponuntur super altare', Paravicini Bagliani 1980, pp. 427–37, p. 430.
3. Previously identified as Gregory. See Schmidt 2005a, p. 252. The inclusion of Saint Clement might also refer to Pope Clement V (reigned 1305–16), whom Niccolò, in his role as cardinal bishop of Ostia, probably consecrated as Pope, and whom he served on several commissions. See Santi 2013, p. 61; Cadili 2013, p. 109.
4. Saints Dominic, Aurea and Nicholas(?) appear on Niccolò's seal. Schmidt 1996, p. 27, p. 29, fig. 12.
5. As pointed out in Gardner 1994.
6. But note the substantial potential cost of the high-quality ultramarine used for the Virgin's garments. Gordon 2011, p. 193.
7. Niccolò's possession of many luxury vestments and hangings, made in a variety of centres including Florence, Rome, Montpellier and England, is demonstrated in the meticulous description of each item in his will. For his apparent preference for northern textiles, notably *Opus Anglicanum* embroideries, see Napione 2013, pp. 296–8, who suggests that Duccio might have been influenced by the cardinal's interests in north European thought and art.
8. For an outline of the cardinal's career, see Redigonda 1960 and, in brief, Lorenzini 2013, pp. 43–4.
9. Galleria Nazionale dell'Umbria, Perugia, inv. 29. Schmidt in Siena 2003–4, cat. 30, pp. 198–9, with further bibliography.
10. Perugia Virgin and Child: 95.5 × 63.8 cm; National Gallery triptych central panel overall dimensions: 61.4 × 39.3 cm. For comparison of the Virgin's veil in the two works, see Hills 2018, pp. 82–4.
11. Suggested by Schmidt 1996, p. 23, and Schmidt 2003b; amplified by Gordon 2011, pp. 198–9; accepted by Napione 2013, p. 294.
12. The exception is Jeremiah. Gordon 2011, p. 199. The San Domenico, Perugia, polyptych is very likely to have included a half-length figure of Saint Dominic, as in Duccio's polyptych thought to have been painted for San Domenico, Siena. For Dominican altarpieces, see Cannon 1982; Cannon 2013, pp. 138–58.
13. Some scholars see the Boston Crucifixion as a precursor of the *Maestà* composition, but Kanter 1994, p. 75, Gordon 2011, pp. 197–9 (with summary of previous opinions), and Ferrante 2018, pp. 7–10, convincingly date the Boston triptych, and its National Gallery companion piece, after the Siena Cathedral *Maestà* of about 1308–11.
14. For the suggestion that Niccolò may have passed through Siena on his way to Henry VII's coronation, see Kanter 1994, p. 75; Schmidt 1996, p. 28; Gordon 2011, p. 198. He certainly visited Siena on other occasions. He spent at least three days there in June 1304. See Cadili 2013, p. 105. In 1307 he supported the appointment as Bishop of Siena of his fellow Dominican, Ruggero da Casole, who may have been closely involved in the planning of Duccio's altarpiece. See Napione 2013, p. 295. For the cardinal's travels in central Italy in 1311 to 1313, see Cadili 2013, pp. 113–23. For the possible circumstances of the commission see also Ferrante 2018, pp. 29–33.
15. Schmidt 2005a, pp. 249–52. For the measurements, see White 1979, pp. 48–52. The matching exteriors are the result of a repainting, probably covering a previous layer of painting and gilding that was also matching. The dating of and reasons for this repainting have yet to be established. Gordon 2011, pp. 194–5, p. 196, figs 12–13.
16. Niccolò worked with Napoleone on various papal commissions. See Cadili 2013, pp. 107–10; Lorenzini 2013, p. 43; Santi 2013, p. 67.
17. For an introduction to Duccio's possible relations with French art, see Deuchler 1984, pp. 176–83. See also Schmidt 2009. For further links between Sienese artists and Avignon, see Gordon, pp. 224–39, in the present volume.
18. For the direction of the Virgin's gaze, see Cannon, p. 39, in the present volume.
19. Neff 1998; Morgan 1988, pp. 57–8, p. 27, fig. 9.
20. Bellosi 1998, pp. 148–9, 183–93; Bellosi 2003–4b, pp. 138–41; Seidel 2012, vol. 1, p. 393; and see Cannon, p. 42, in the present volume.
21. For example, Williamson and Davies 2014, vol. 1, nos 86–7, pp. 266–71; Lowden 2013, no. 8, pp. 68–71. Angels flanking the top of the Cross in French ivories usually carried the emblems of the sun and moon. The identity of the pointing man varies: sometimes shown as a soldier (the centurion who declared 'Truly this man was the Son of God [Matthew 27:54]) and sometimes as one of the Jews.
22. Seidel 2012, vol. 1, p. 392.
23. Campbell in London 1987–8, cat. 583, pp. 459–60.
24. Avril 1978, pp. 13–17, 44–59. The manuscript was later bequeathed to King Charles V of France and subsequently passed to John, Duke of Berry.
25. Those arguing for Pucelle's first-hand knowledge of works in and around Siena include Avril 1978, Ferber 1984 and Pippal 1993–4, all with further bibliography. For arguments against Pucelle's presence in Italy, see Schmidt 1999, pp. 21–8; Schmidt 2005a, pp. 240–2. For possible travels of the de Limbourg brothers in Italy, see Nash, pp. 251–2, in the present volume. For the possible role of drawings in the planning and dissemination of Duccio's compositions, see Ferrante 2018, pp. 40–2.

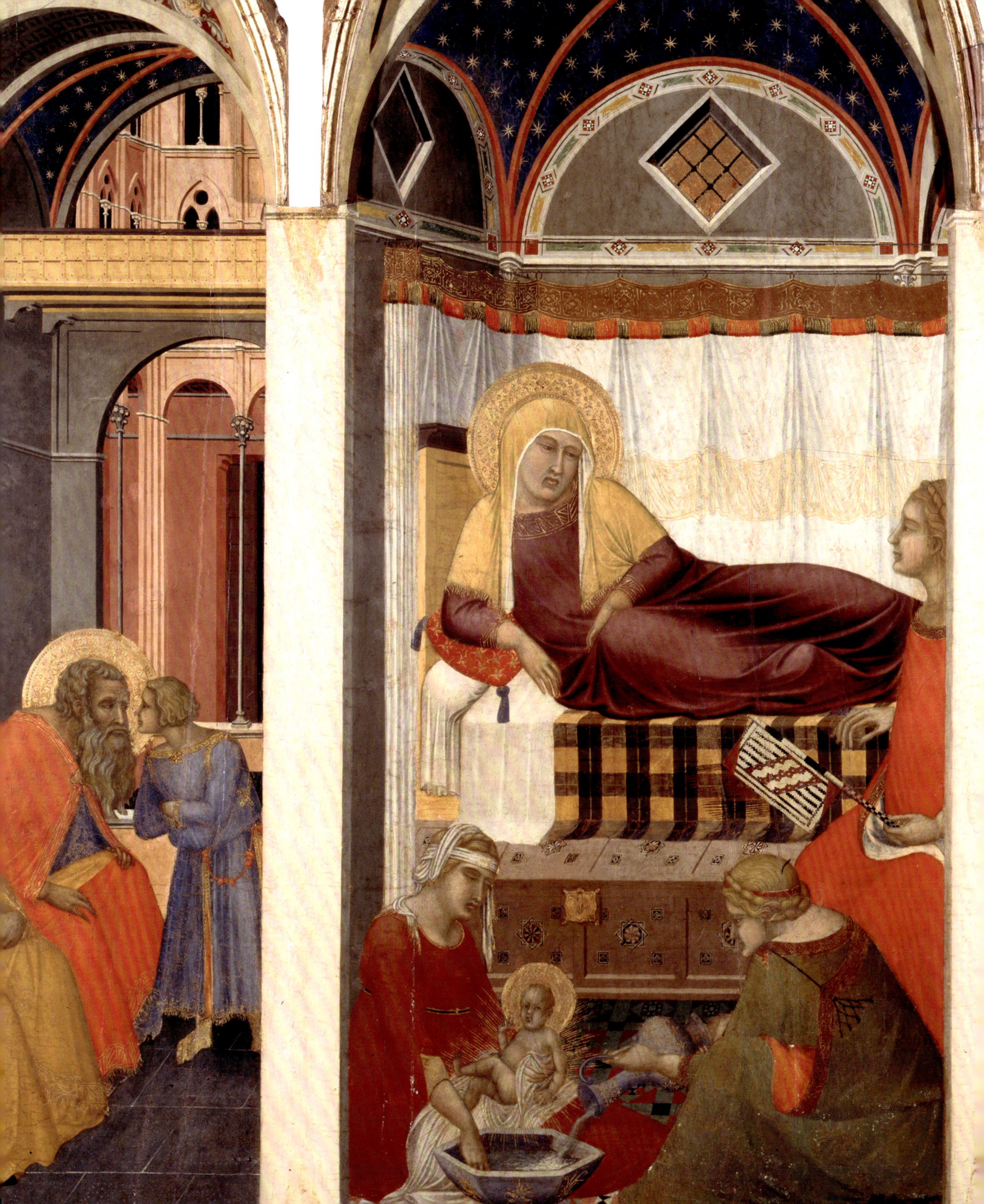

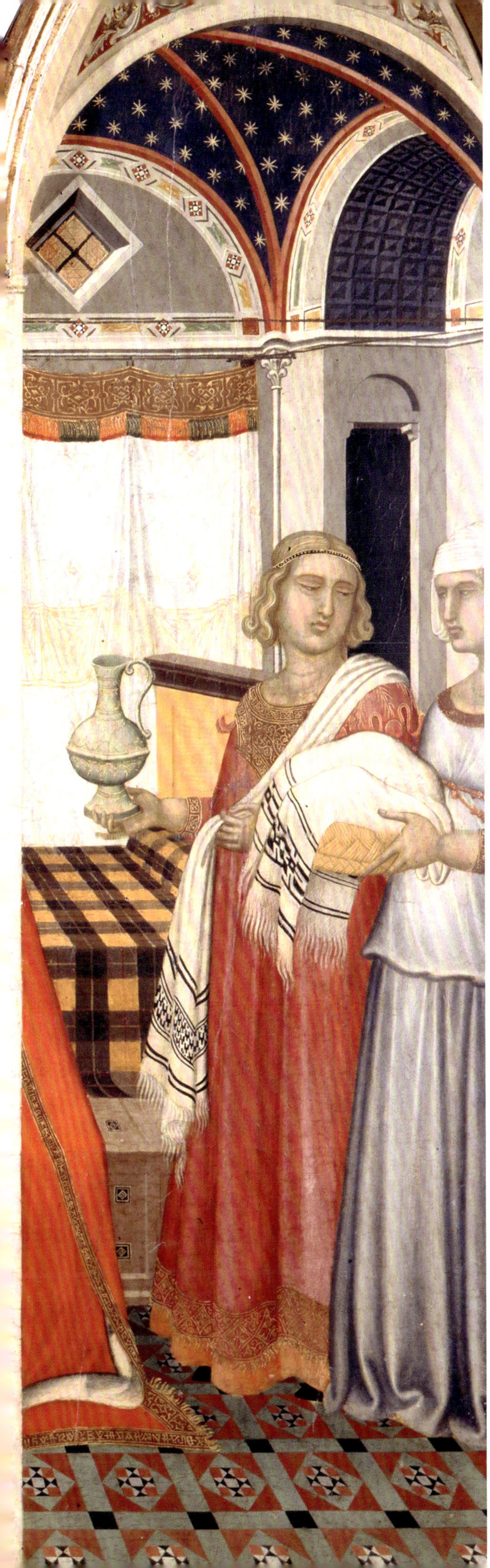

THE HEIRS OF DUCCIO'S *MAESTÀ*

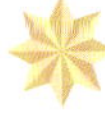

FIG. 37
Pietro Lorenzetti (documented possibly 1306; died probably 1348)
Christ before Pilate, 1340s
Tempera on panel, 37.8 × 27.4 cm
Vatican Museums, Vatican City (inv. 40168)

FIG. 38
Pietro Lorenzetti (documented possibly 1306; died probably 1348)
The Crucifixion, 1340s
Tempera on panel, 41.9 × 31.8 cm (with engaged frame)
The Metropolitan Museum of Art, New York. Purchase, Lila Acheson Wallace Gift and Gwynne Andrews Fund, 2002 (2002.436)

In 1319, after their father's death, Duccio's children renounced their inheritance: anything that remained of his estate would go to their mother.[1] The painter's flesh-and-blood heirs did not receive a financial legacy, but the many artistic heirs of his greatest work, the Siena Cathedral *Maestà*, were richly rewarded. This was a patrimony that was widely shared, but the overall format of the *Maestà* was repeated only once, in the double-sided altarpiece for the Cathedral of Massa Marittima probably made by Duccio and his workshop in about 1316.[2] As Christa Gardner von Teuffel shows (pp. 68–77), the *Maestà*'s legacy for altarpiece design was in the more flexible format of large-scale polyptychs, especially that by Ugolino di Nerio for Santa Croce in Florence, whose predella Passion scenes follow Duccio's cycle in many respects (see figs 48, 50).[3] Portable paintings, notably Simone Martini's Palazzo Pubblico and Orsini polyptychs (discussed here by Laura Llewellyn and Imogen Tedbury, pp. 116–25) and Pietro Lorenzetti's *Christ before Pilate* and the *Crucifixion* (figs 37 and 38), the two surviving pieces of a set of panels (reunited in the exhibition this volume accompanies),

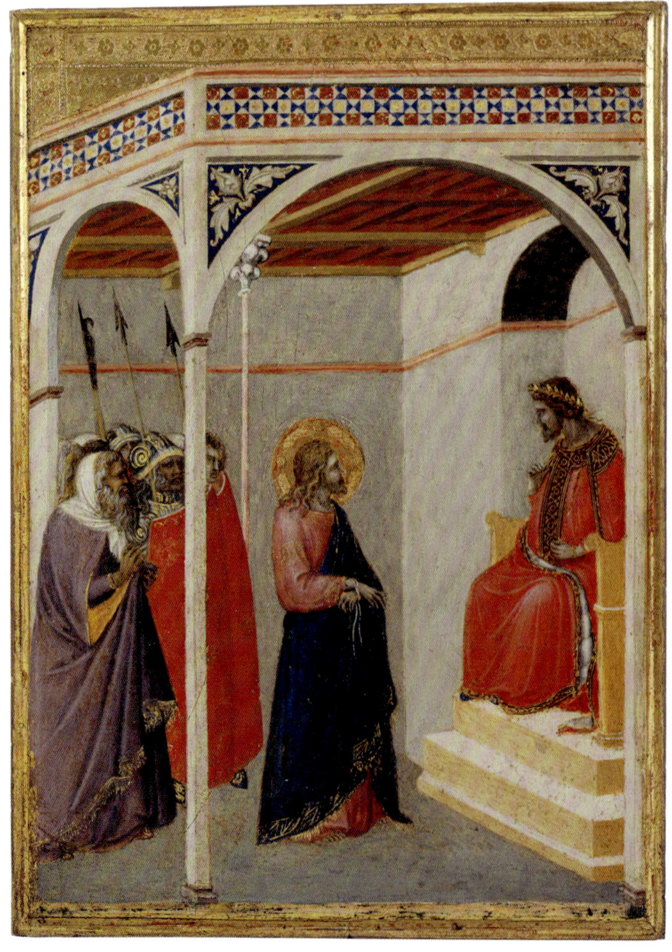

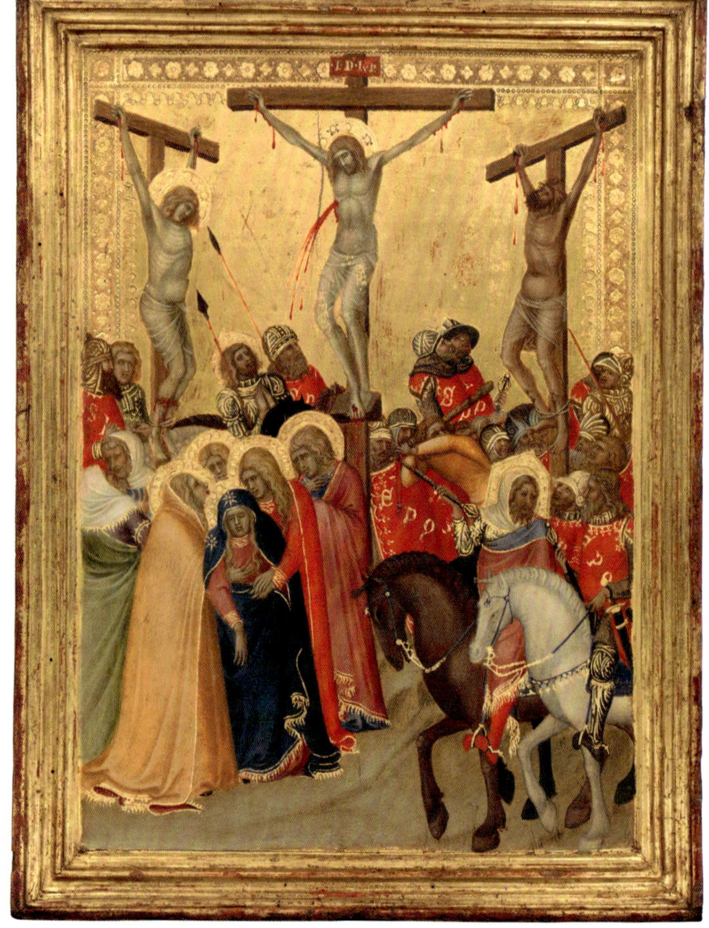

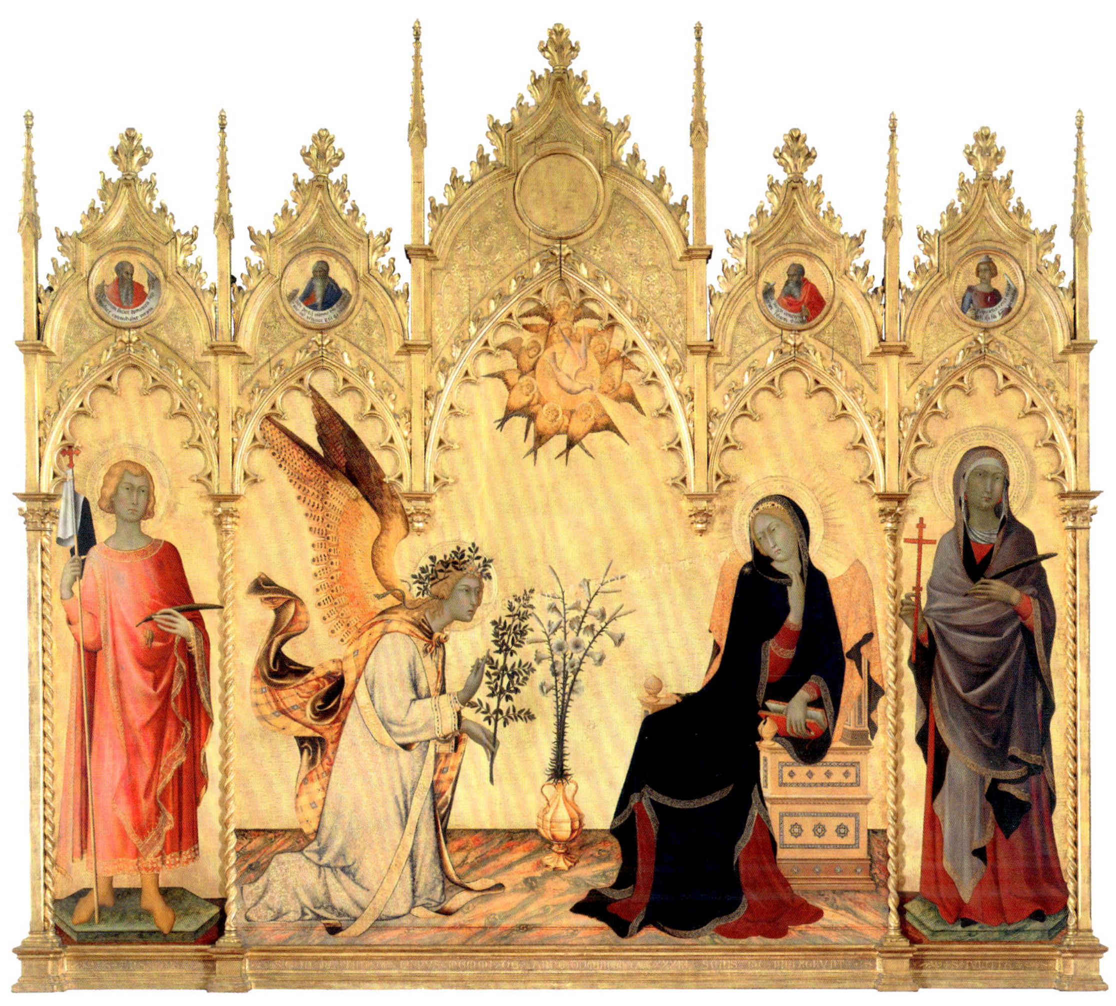

FIG. 39
Simone Martini (about 1284–1344) and **Lippo Memmi** (documented 1317–50)
The Annunciation with Saints Ansanus and Massima, 1333
Tempera on panel, 184 × 210 cm
Gallerie degli Uffizi, Florence
(inv. 1890 nn. 451, 452, 453)

inherited elements of the great work.[4] The influence of the double-sided format of the *Maestà* is also found in the work of sculptors, including Tino di Camaino at Cava dei Tirreni (see fig. 102), and goldsmiths such as Ugolino di Vieri in Orvieto (see figs 47, 126).

Paintings by Duccio's three outstanding successors – Simone Martini, and Pietro and Ambrogio Lorenzetti – once flanked the high altar of Siena Cathedral, on side-altars dedicated to three of the patron saints of Siena: Ansanus, Sabinus and Crescentius.[5] Whether, and if so when, these three artists were members of Duccio's workshop remains a matter of debate, but what is not in doubt is that within his *Maestà* Duccio bequeathed to them invaluable examples of technical refinement, elegant line and, above all, the gift of narrative.[6] The main fields of earlier altarpieces, including Duccio's *Maestà*, presented static images of holy figures, but this trio of pioneering paintings depicts, at large scale, events from the life of the Virgin, each linked to one of her feast days: the *Annunciation* (fig. 39), the *Birth of the Virgin* (fig. 40) and the *Presentation in the Temple* (fig. 41), associated with the feast of the Purification of the Virgin.[7]

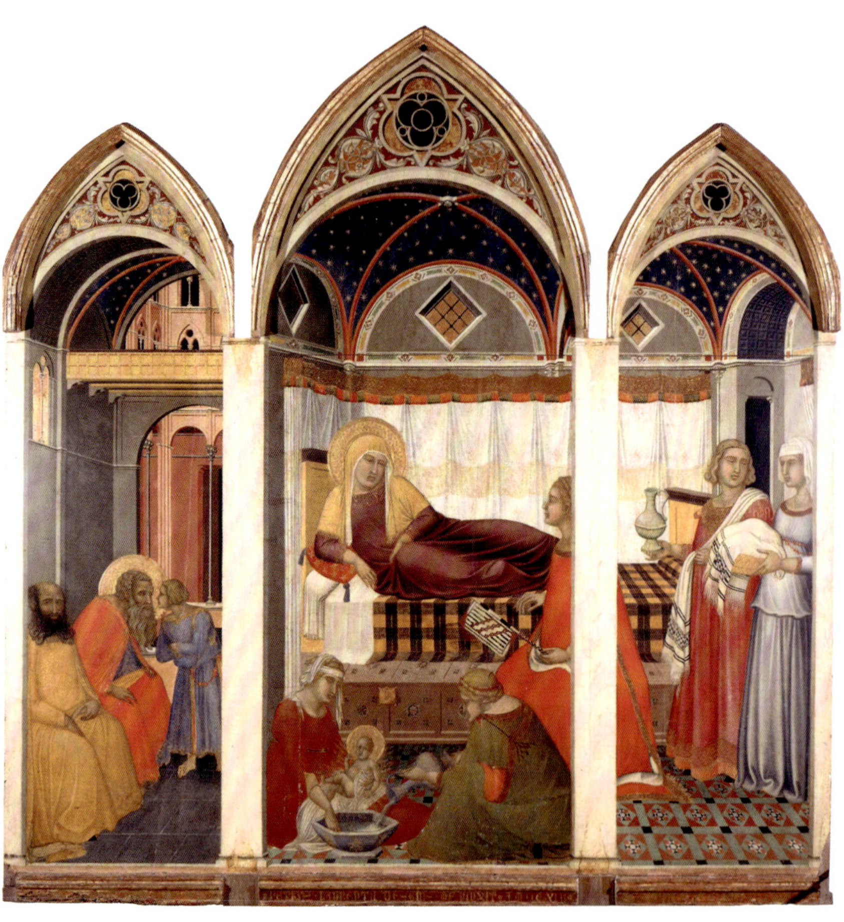

FIG. 40
Pietro Lorenzetti
(documented possibly 1306; died probably 1348)
The Birth of the Virgin, 1335–42
Tempera on panel, 182 × 187 cm
Museo dell'Opera della Metropolitana, Siena

As in the *Maestà*, framing would have played an important part in the appearance of the altarpieces.[8] The frame could act as a transition between the tangible three-dimensional world and that of the painting. Duccio's use of this device, for example in the first Denial of Peter (see figs 9, 11), was developed by Pietro Lorenzetti in the *Birth of the Virgin* (and previously in his *Annunciation* on the Pieve Polyptych, see fig. 61). Framing colonettes (now lost) divided the main panel into unequal thirds, as well as forming the continuation of the four white piers within the painting, so that the figure of the kneeling maidservant in red apparently passed behind, and was partially obscured by, both the actual and the depicted architecture. Pietro also built on Duccio's manipulation of time and space: Anna, the mother of Mary, rests after her labour, while simultaneously, in a different location on the left, the news is brought to Joachim, Mary's father, with a grand, three-storey courtyard glimpsed beyond him, hinting at further depth (compare figs 11 and 26). The oblique view of the rib vaults and of the walls, and the depiction of patterned floor tiles – already explored by Duccio (see fig. 23) – combine here to create spaces in which to set the story.[9] Lessons from Duccio join with those from Giotto's frescoes in Padua, Assisi and Florence. Pietro incised two separate groups of guidelines, one for the checked bedspread, the other for the floor tiles, each leading to independent vanishing points.[10] In a further development, in the *Presentation in the Temple* (fig. 41), Ambrogio employed a system with numerous planning lines, circles and arcs that has been called 'polycentric perspective'. Lines recede towards a single vanishing axis, at the centre of the painting, although not to the single vanishing point found in linear perspective as codified in early fifteenth-century Florence.[11]

Duccio's use of the power of detail is pursued in all three paintings: by Pietro in the water pouring from an elegant jug onto the sparkling surface of the water in a hexagonal bowl in which the newborn is about to be bathed, while a midwife tests the temperature; by Ambrogio in the gilded and enamelled breastplate of the high priest and the pigeons about to be consumed by the flames on the altar of sacrifice before him.[12] Surface texture is treated with great technical skill in the *Annunciation*: the various textiles of Gabriel's garments;[13] the three-dimensional words of the angel's salutation, source of the *Ave Maria*, emerging from the gilded picture surface;[14] the polygonal vase fashioned out of gold leaf: burnished for the mid tones, stippled with three different punches to create highlights, and overlaid with a little translucent brown paint to make the shadows.[15]

The use of narratives on the predella, introduced in the *Maestà*, was probably followed on all three side-altars, with scenes relating to each of the patron saints, although only one panel survives: Pietro Lorenzetti's *Saint Sabinus before the Roman Governor of Tuscany* (fig. 42). The depiction of saints' lives, especially their miracles, was a crucial step in the development of these painters' narrative techniques, as Stephan Wolohojian shows for Ambrogio's Saint Nicholas panels (pp. 136–41), and is true also for Simone's Beato Agostino Novello Triptych (see fig. 90) and Pietro's Beata Umiltà panels.[16]

The three altarpieces grouped around the *Maestà* had actual as well as metaphorical family connections. Pietro and Ambrogio Lorenzetti were brothers, and the *Annunciation* altarpiece was signed by two artists: brothers-in-law Simone Martini and Lippo Memmi.[17] The *Annunciation* was completed first, in 1333, and the two later works, commissioned in 1335 and 1337 respectively, after Simone had left Siena for Avignon, were both installed in 1342.[18] We cannot know whether the prestigious commissions for the cathedral altarpieces passed to the Lorenzetti brothers in the absence of Simone, but it seems certain that the careers of the three artists impinged on one another. In the following contributions Emma Capron outlines Simone Martini's great success in attracting civic commissions, and Donal Cooper and Andrea De Marchi explore how Pietro Lorenzetti 'took to the road' in order to find work away from Simone's dominance. Both Pietro and Ambrogio spent considerable periods of time in Florence.[19] Was there sibling rivalry among these heirs of the *Maestà*? It is hard to imagine three such talents coexisting for several years in the same city without striving to surpass one another. Nevertheless, brotherly love, or, at least, brotherly cooperation, is found at a number of points in the Lorenzetti's careers: working in their own distinctive styles on different parts of the chapter house frescoes of San Francesco, Siena, in the 1320s;[20] jointly signing, explicitly as brothers, two of a series of four frescoes (now lost) on the facade of Santa Maria della Scala in 1335, having completed the project probably left unfinished by Simone in about 1334;[21] and perhaps, intriguingly, contributing the two separate panels of a diptych in about 1345 (see figs 85, 86).[22]

In the Palazzo Pubblico, Siena, two frescoes rival one another in adjacent rooms. Simone Martini's *Maestà* and Ambrogio Lorenzetti's *Good and Bad Government* trace the creative engagement, over a quarter of a century, with the legacy of Duccio's *Maestà*. Simone's painting,

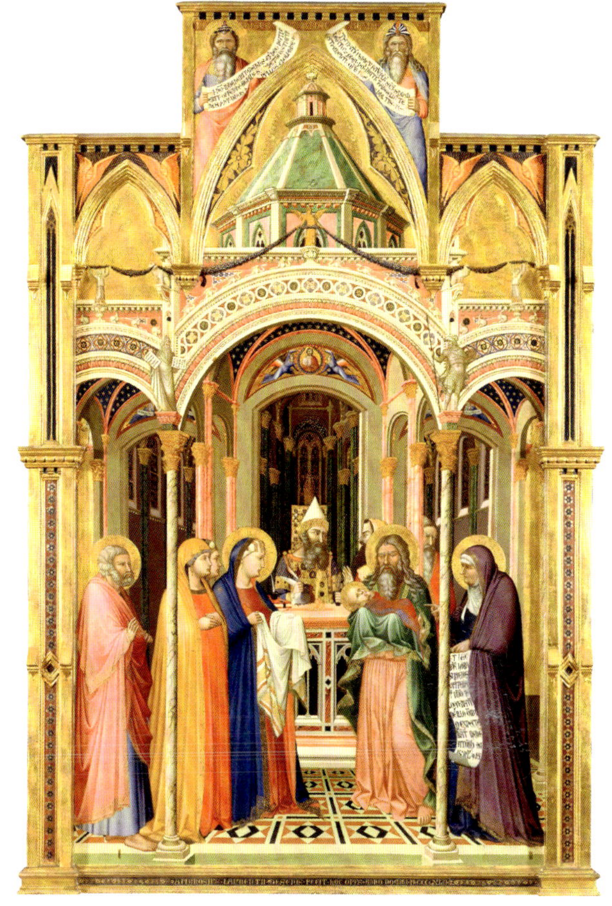

FIG. 41
Ambrogio Lorenzetti
(documented 1319; died 1348/9)
The Presentation in the Temple, 1337–42
Tempera on panel, 257 × 168 cm
Gallerie degli Uffizi, Florence
(inv. 1890 n. 8346)

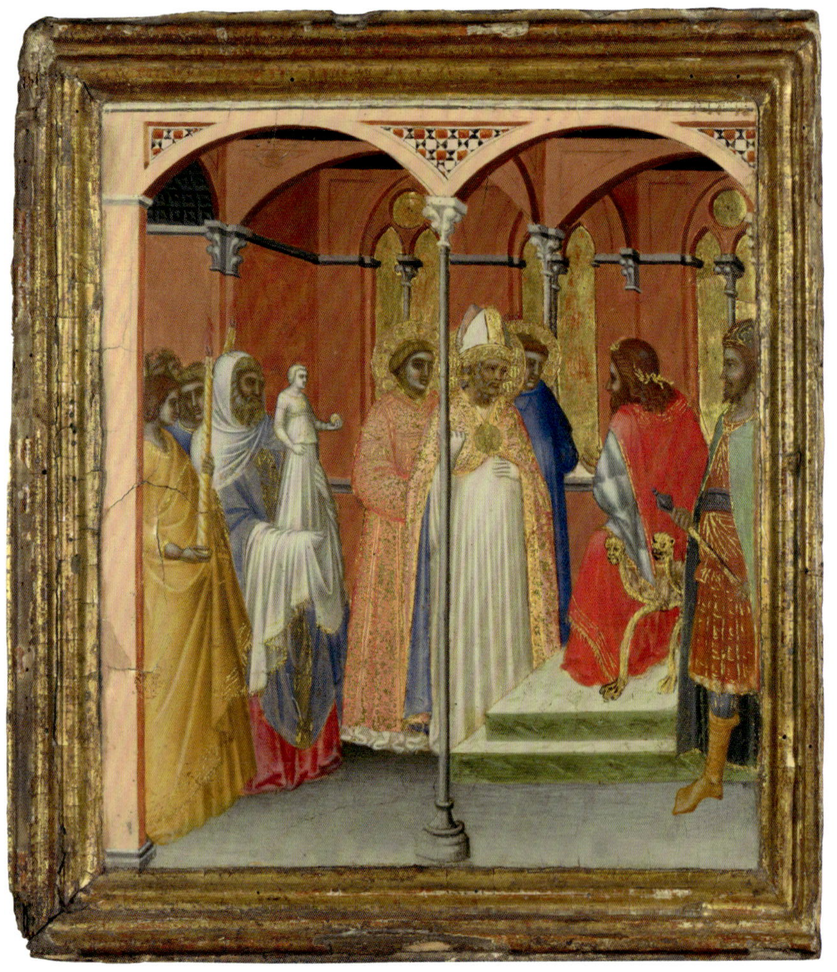

FIG. 42
Pietro Lorenzetti (documented possibly 1306; died probably 1348)
Saint Sabinus before the Roman Governor of Tuscany, 1335–42
Tempera on poplar, 37.7 × 33.2 cm (with engaged frame)
The National Gallery, London. Presented by Charles Fairfax Murray, 1882 (NG1113)

probably begun the year after Duccio's work was completed, is an evident response to the cathedral's high altarpiece, illustrating the government's desire to possess its own *Maestà*. Yet the fresco already offers a reinterpretation, rather than a replica, of the main front panel (compare figs 8 and 65). Duccio's Virgin, as portrayed in the *Maestà* and in his earlier works after about 1300, set a type that was evidently revered in Siena: two major earlier thirteenth-century images of the Virgin and Child enthroned, Coppo di Marcovaldo's *Madonna del Bordone* and Guido da Siena's panel for San Domenico, Siena, both had their faces and veils repainted in Duccio's manner (see fig. 12).[23] These 'refreshed' paintings became, in a sense, heirs of the *Maestà*, even though they belonged to the generation that preceded it. But Simone's Virgin, in her civic setting, acquired a crown and patterned garments, revealed her curling fair hair, and, after a selective repainting for which Simone was paid in 1321, gained a new face (see fig. 152).[24] The Palazzo Pubblico *Maestà* shows that Simone felt free (as Duccio himself had done, around 1300) to paint the Virgin in a new idiom. Ambrogio Lorenzetti's *Good and Bad Government* (1338–9) moves much further on from Duccio's achievements, but the seeds of some aspects of this remarkably innovative fresco programme, notably its portrayal of the well-governed city and countryside (see figs 1 and 140), can be found in the *Maestà*: the crowded cityscape of the *Entry into Jerusalem*, the two street scenes of the rear predella and, most of all, the extraordinary panorama of cities in a mountainous landscape, receding into a darkening distance (see figs 24, 27, 28).

These heirs had, in turn, their own beneficiaries, not only Sienese but also Florentine.[25] Among these was Lorenzo Ghiberti, who devoted half of the second book of his *Commentarii* – the earliest attempt at sketching a history of Tuscan art – to Sienese artists.[26] According to Ghiberti (who was unaware of the existence of Pietro Lorenzetti), 'Master Simone was a very noble and very famous painter. The Sienese painters consider him to be their best, but it seems to me that Ambrogio Lorenzetti was much better, and far more learned than any of the others.'[27] Present-day viewers can continue to debate which of these three outstanding artists they admire the most. *JC*

1. Maginnis 2000, pp. 19–22; Satkowski 2000, pp. 83–8; Siena 2003–4, pp. 513–14; Ragionieri 2003–4, p. 150 (correcting the probable year of Duccio's death to 1319).
2. Bartalini in Siena 2003–4, cat. 36, pp. 244–57; Bartalini in Siena 2017–18, cat. 1, pp. 98–107.
3. For Simone Martini's debts to the *Maestà* in his polyptych design, see De Marchi 2021.
4. Christiansen 2003; Schmidt 2005a, pp. 288–9, 298–301.
5. See Norman 1999b, pp. 66–85; Butzek 2001a; Gordon 2011, pp. 288–98. The altar dedicated to the fourth patron saint, Victor, received an altarpiece by Bartolommeo Bulgarini in about 1350. For Simone Martini's *Annunciation*, see Cecchi 2001a. For Pietro Lorenzetti's *Birth of the Virgin*, see Gordon 2011. For Ambrogio Lorenzetti's *Presentation in the Temple*, see Seidel and Calamai 2022.
6. The hypothesis, in Stubblebine 1979, vol. 1, pp. 39–45, vol. 2, fig. 590, that besides Duccio, eight different artists, including Simone Martini and both Lorenzetti brothers, worked on the *Maestà* has often subsequently been disputed. For Simone's probable training with Duccio, see Spannocchi 2003–4 and Bagnoli in Siena 2003–4, cat. 67, pp. 396–9; for Pietro, see Cooper and De Marchi, p. 80, in the present volume; for the possibility that Ambrogio was involved in the painting of the Massa Marittima *Maestà*, see Bartalini in Siena 2017–18, cat. 12, pp. 104–6.
7. Another candidate for the earliest 'narrative altarpiece', Giotto's *Stigmatisation of Saint Francis*, now in the Musée du Louvre (about 1298, inv. 309), has been shown to have been displayed on the top of a *tramezzo* (screen), rather than on an altar. Cooper 2013.
8. The frame of the *Annunciation* is a nineteenth-century construction. See Cecchi 2001b. Several payments survive for the carpenters, transcribed in Butzek and Cecchi 2001, pp. 129–30. For reconstructions of the frames, see Norman 1999b, p. 77, figs 85 and 86, p. 79, fig. 89; Seidel and Calamai 2022, pp. 88–9.
9. White 1967, pp. 78–83, 93–201.
10. Kemp 1990, pp. 9–11.
11. For Ambrogio's radical arithmetical and geometrical explorations, and his use of 'polycentric perspective', see Seidel and Calamai 2022, pp. 100–67.
12. See Seidel and Calamai 2022 for numerous excellent illustrations.
13. Discussed by Monnas, pp. 208–9, in the present volume. For many fine illustrations, see Cecchi 2001a.
14. AVE GRATIA PLENA DOMINUS TECUM (Luke 1:28); see Van Os 1969, pp. 41–4.
15. Skaug 1994, vol. 1, pp. 67–8, vol. 2, figs 64a and b.
16. Cannon and Vauchez 1999, pp. 65–6, 135–45, with discussion of a lost fresco cycle of Beata Margherita of Cortona, there attributed to the Lorenzetti brothers. For the Beata Umiltà panel, see now Demaria 2021; Bartoli and Parenti 2023.
17. In further family links, Simone's brother Donato, and Lippo's brother Tederigo, are thought to have formed with them collaborative workshops, for which see Israëls 2015b.
18. See Butzek and Cecchi 2001, pp. 129–30, and Capron, pp. 100–15, in the present volume.
19. Ambrogio was enrolled in the Florentine painters' guild at some time between 1328 and 1330. See Siena 2017–18, p. 94. Boskovits 1988, p. 89, suggests that Pietro may have shared a workshop with Ambrogio in Florence for a period between 1332 and 1335. See also Demaria 2021, p. 170.
20. See figs 57, 58, 59, 142, 210.
21. The lost inscription is recorded as 'Hoc opus fecit Petrus Laurentii et Ambrosius eius frater 1335', with the order of names indicating that Pietro was the elder brother. Caffio 2017–18; Norman 2024 (forthcoming), pp. 23–5, nn. 54–64.
22. Boskovits 1988, pp. 91–3. Schmidt 2005a, p. 42, notes that the concave moulding on the Harvard *Crucifixion* suggests that the two panels, although belonging with each other, may not have been hinged together. For a summary of the brothers' joint works in relation to the lost fresco cycle of Margherita of Cortona, and the possibility of a shared workshop, see Cannon and Vauchez 1999, pp. 147–54. For an assessment of the punchwork evidence, see Skaug 1994, vol. 1, pp. 224–5.
23. Hoeniger 1995, pp. 21–42.
24. Here, too, the *Maestà* may have provided a model, if there was a *Coronation of the Virgin*, now lost, on the front face, developed from the crowned Virgin of the Royal Collection triptych (see fig. 150). See Bagnoli 1999 for excellent illustrations and a diagram of the repainting (p. 172).
25. For Sienese responses in subsequent generations, see the foundational study of Van Os 1969 and, in brief, Fattorini 2010; for Florence, see Nethersole 2018, discussing continuing dialogues between Sienese art and Florentine artists into the mid-fifteenth century. Nethersole, p. 123, says, 'From the perspective of the late 1440s, when Ghiberti took up his pen, the history of "modern art" was as much Sienese as it was Florentine'.
26. Ghiberti includes a detailed description of Ambrogio's lost fresco cycle of Peter of Siena in the cloister of San Francesco, Siena. Bartalini 2017–18.
27. 'Maestro Simone fu nobilissimo pictore e molto famoso. Tengono e' pictori sanese fosse el migliore, a me parve molto migliore Ambruogio Lorenzetti et altrimenti dotto che nessuno degli altri.' Ghiberti before 1455 (1998), p. 89.

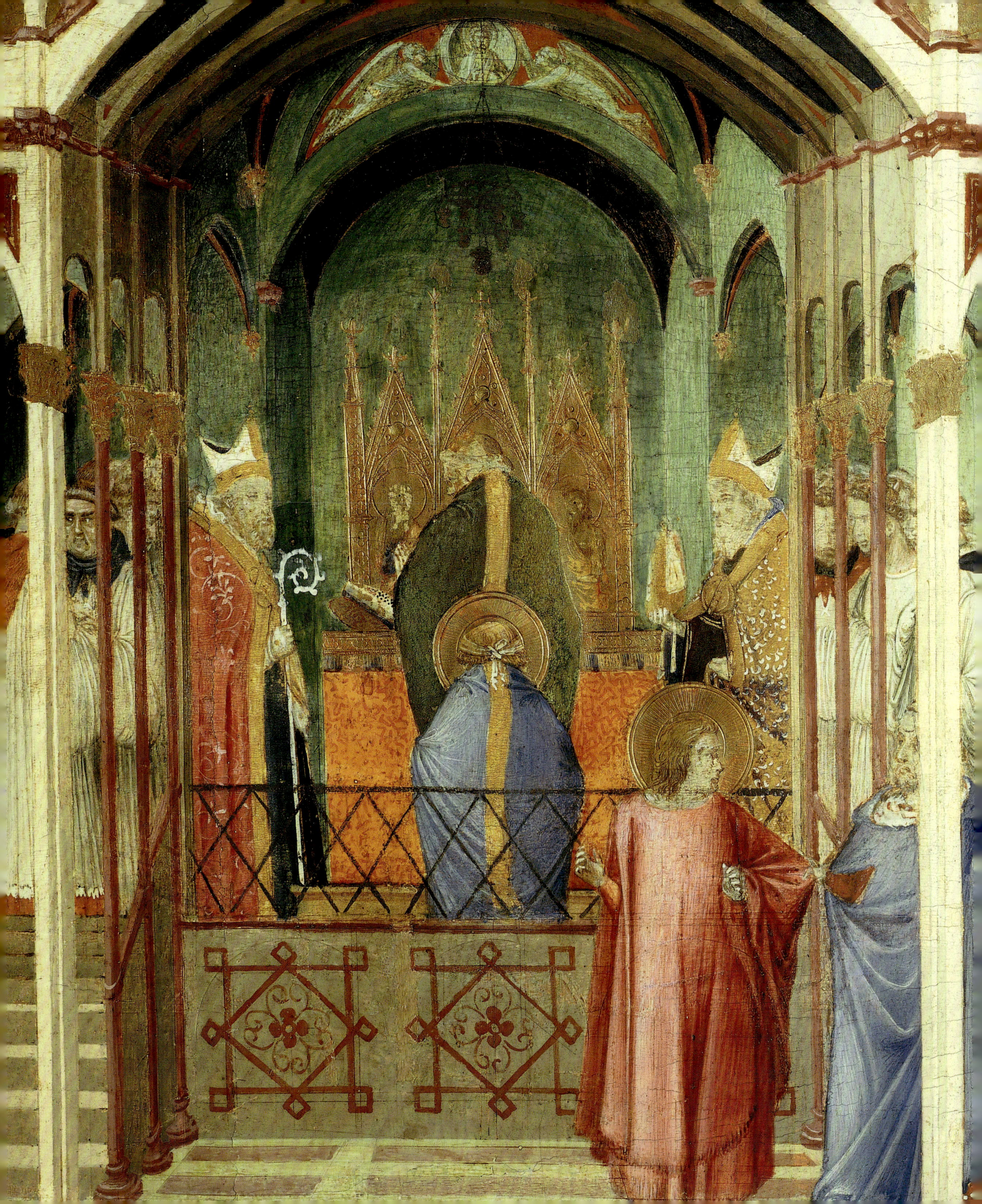

RECONSTRUCTING THE SIENESE ALTARPIECE: PROCEDURES AND PROPOSALS

Christa Gardner von Teuffel

Almost no complete altarpieces from trecento Siena survive. For this reason, the act of envisaging such a thing requires some mental adjustment, and even experts will require some assistance. The guiding principle for art history over the past half century has been reconstruction in its manifold aspects. Therefore, clarity about altarpiece production is fundamental to the whole enterprise. By reconstruction I here mean attempting not only to visualise the original appearance of the painting, but also its setting and its relationship to its patronage and public. Even in central Italy itself, a complete altarpiece in its original setting is extremely rare. An outstanding example is Taddeo di Bartolo's high altarpiece of 1401 in Montepulciano Cathedral, where the setting remains largely authentic.[1] The polyptych that Lippo Vanni frescoed within a niche at the Basilica of San Francesco in Siena in about 1370 constitutes another surviving case (fig. 43).[2] Altarpieces depicted within other paintings can be found, for example, by Ambrogio Lorenzetti in the San Procolo altar panel of Saint Nicholas in Florence (opposite), or a century later in Sassetta's Franciscan high altarpiece for Sansepolcro.[3] However, the evidence provided by such 'fictive' altarpieces is necessarily partial, as painters sought to depict the location of an event near an altar rather than to portray an altarpiece exactly.[4]

All attempts at reconstruction must embrace both construction and deconstruction; the method by which the artefact was initially created and set in place, and the processes by which it was subsequently dismantled and dispersed. It is important to realise that the wooden structure, its subsequent gilding and painting were produced by closely integrated procedures, and that these techniques had an impact on style and vice versa.

A fundamental structural change in altarpiece design and construction occurred towards the end of the thirteenth century, when most wooden structures began to use vertical rather than horizontal planks. This change radically facilitated the development of the monumental, multistoried altarpiece. Picture supports, articulating framework, gilding and painting were planned and executed together within this

p. 68
Ambrogio Lorenzetti
(documented 1319; died 1348/9)
Saint Nicholas consecrated Bishop of Myra, about 1332–4
(detail of fig. 89, p. 138)

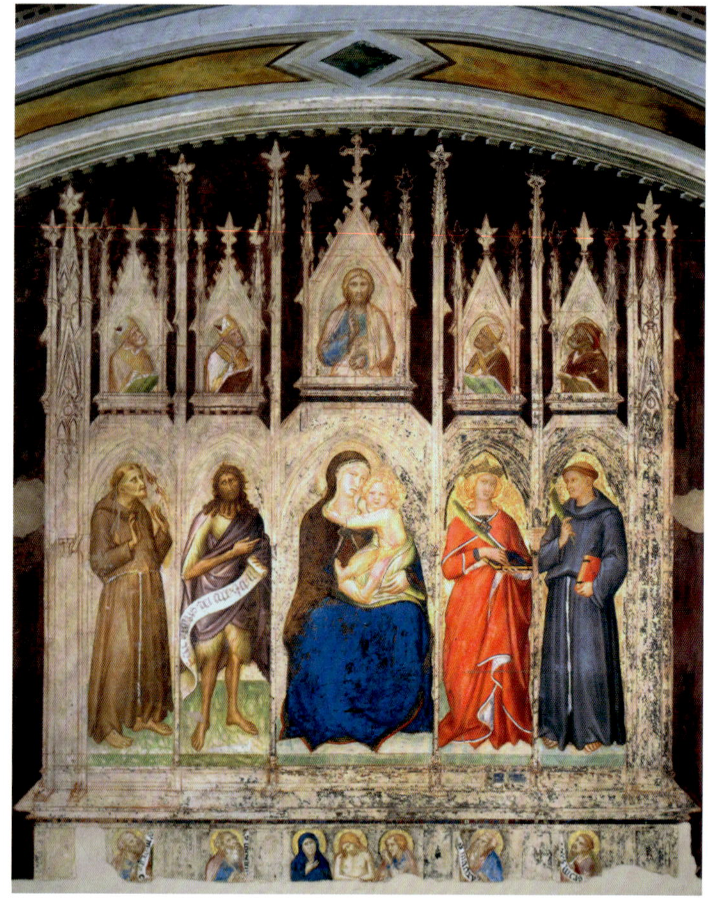

fig. 43
Lippo Vanni (documented 1344–75)
Fictive Altarpiece, about 1370
Fresco
Martinozzi Chapel, Basilica of San Francesco, Siena

new, increasingly vertical design. This production method continued virtually unaltered until the mid-fifteenth century, when a second paradigm shift took place.[5] Thereafter, the painting and its framework, while still planned together, were executed separately and subsequently assembled. Inevitably, this meant that the original frame could be more easily removed and often lost.

Simone Martini's 1319 heptaptych, a seven-part panel from Santa Caterina in Pisa, is a virtually complete altarpiece from the early fourteenth century (fig. 44).[6] Only the original outer buttresses, which supported the heavy wooden structure, and some dividing pilasters and finials are missing. The correct sequence of the main saints can be guaranteed by the presence of wooden pegs or dowels, which once aligned all the main compartments. The original structure is in turn confirmed by the nail pattern of the horizontal battens on the reverse (fig. 45). Simone was the pupil of Siena's most eminent painter, Duccio, and it was he, together with Ugolino di Nerio and the Lorenzetti brothers Pietro and Ambrogio, who was primarily responsible for the successful and widespread dissemination of Duccio's altarpiece concept throughout central Italy.

The Sienese trecento high altarpiece can be characterised as microarchitecture, a result of combining contemporary monumental architecture, best exemplified by the facade of Siena Cathedral itself (see fig. 5),[7] and, on a smaller scale, metalwork such as the famous late thirteenth-century Sienese reliquary of the head of Saint Galganus attributed to Pace di Valentino and his associates (fig. 46).[8] Fashionable Gothic metalwork was either produced locally or imported, and Siena's strategic location on the via Francigena, the ancient route from northern Europe to Rome, facilitated artistic exchanges with northern artisans and patrons.

Familiarity and indeed collaboration between the makers of altarpieces and goldsmiths are strongly suggested by their living and working in the same Sienese neighbourhood of Castelvecchio, as did for example Duccio, the Lorenzetti brothers and the goldsmith Ugolino di Vieri.[9] Significantly, the payments for Ugolino's prestigious and enormously expensive 1338 *Reliquary of the Holy Corporal* for the Orvietan cathedral authorities were handled by the Carmelite prior at Orvieto (fig. 47).[10] Ugolino had probably chosen this prior as his trusted agent because the prior regularly visited San Niccolò dei Carmini, also situated in Castelvecchio.

Woodworkers who carved not only elaborate choir stalls but also provided the wooden cores of silver-clad altar frontals and altarpieces – an outstanding complex survives in San Zeno at Pistoia – were presumably well qualified to create sophisticated architectonic structures to be gessoed, gilded and painted. The Sienese tax system and guild rules sheltered the town's artists and artisans, restricting the intrusion of foreigners. This protectionism, and the custom

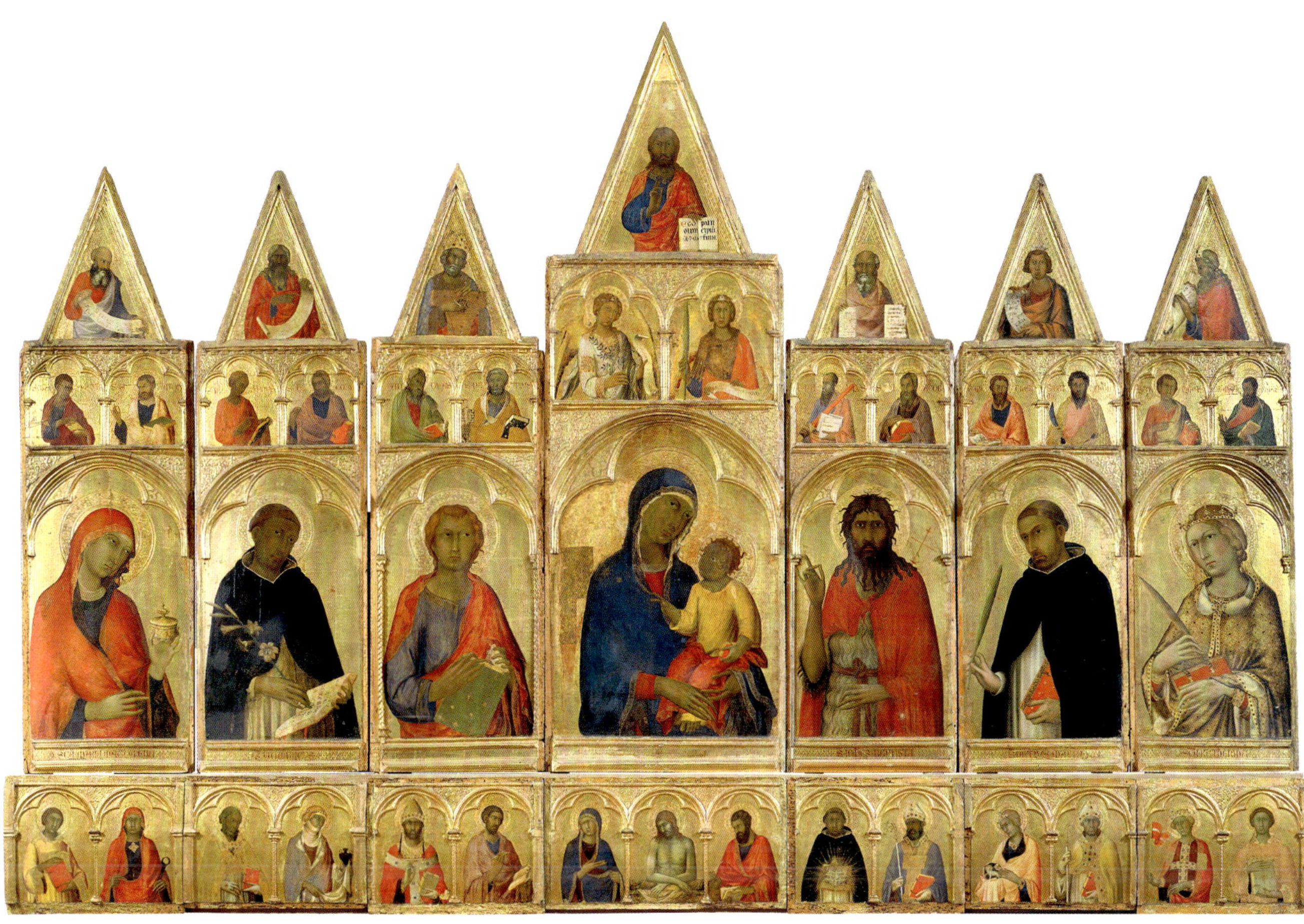

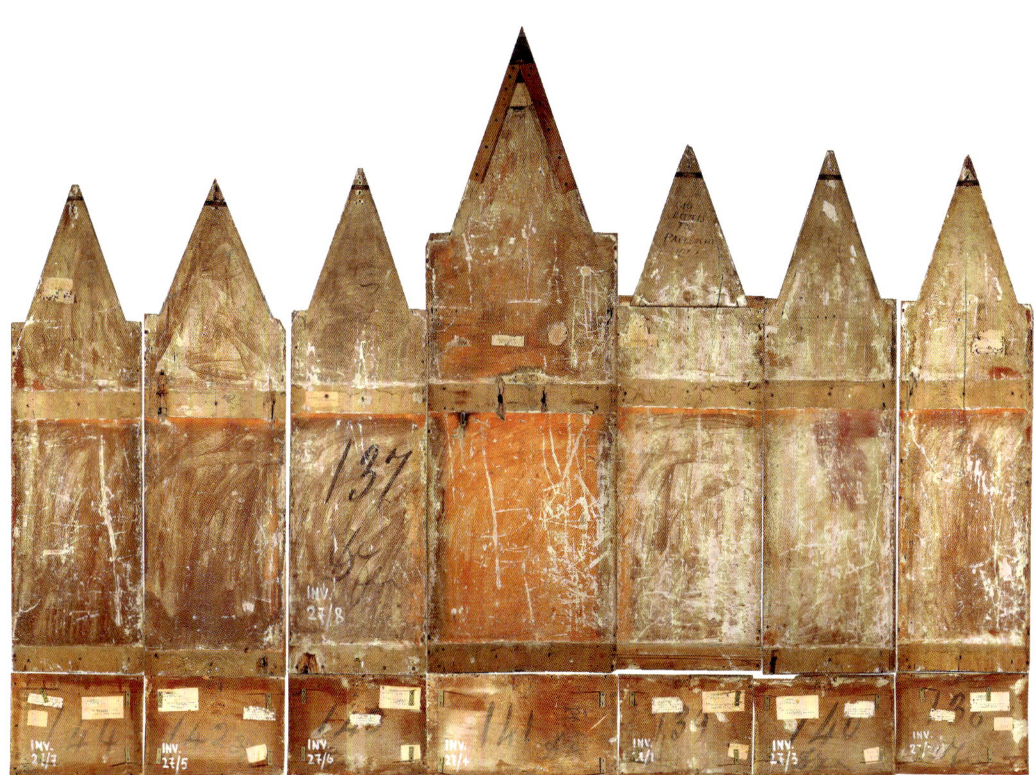

FIG. 44
Simone Martini
(about 1284–1344)
Santa Caterina Polyptych, about 1319
Tempera on poplar, 195 × approx. 340 cm
Museo Nazionale di San Matteo, Pisa

FIG. 45
Reverse of fig. 44

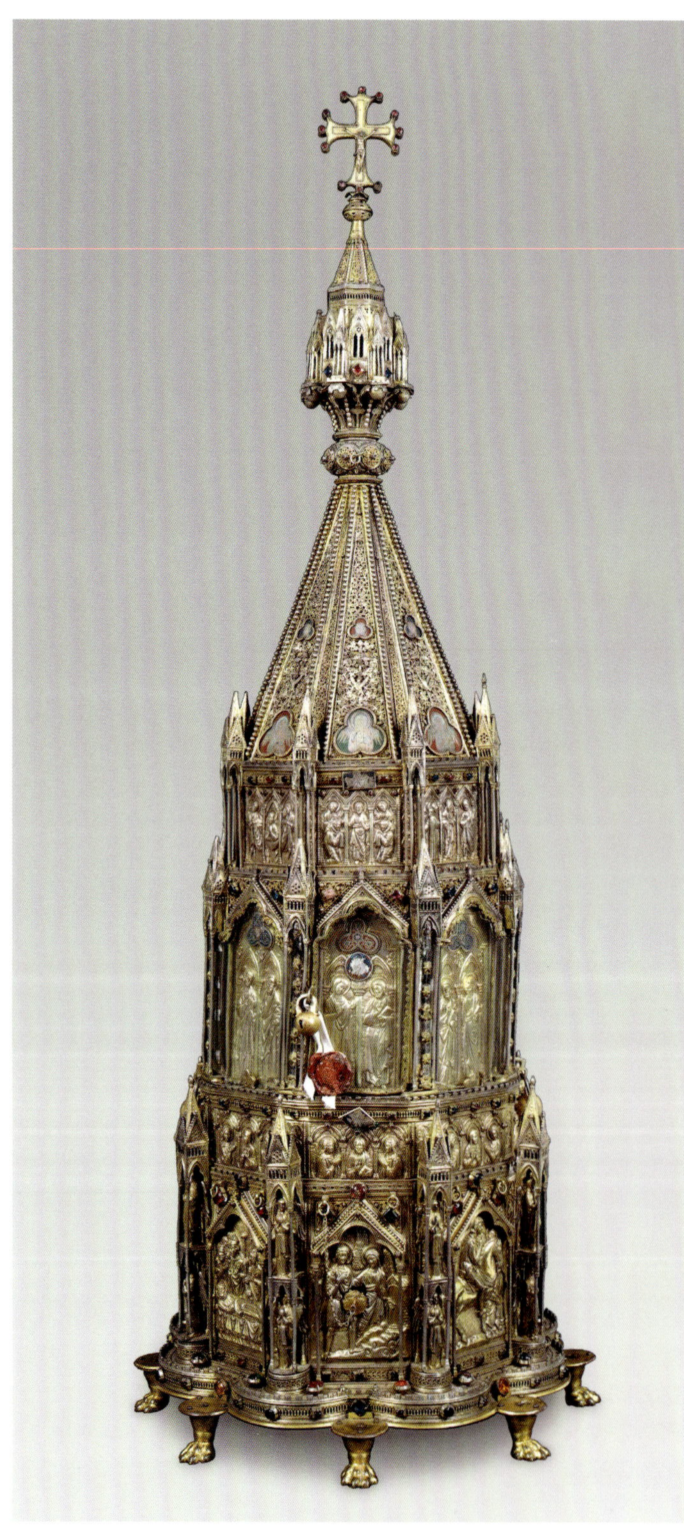

FIG. 46
Attributed to Pace di Valentino (about 1257–1296) **and Associates**
Reliquary of the Head of Saint Galganus, 1338
Gilded copper, bronze and silver with champlevé enamel and precious stones, 99.5 × 36.5 cm
Museo dell'Opera della Metropolitana, Siena

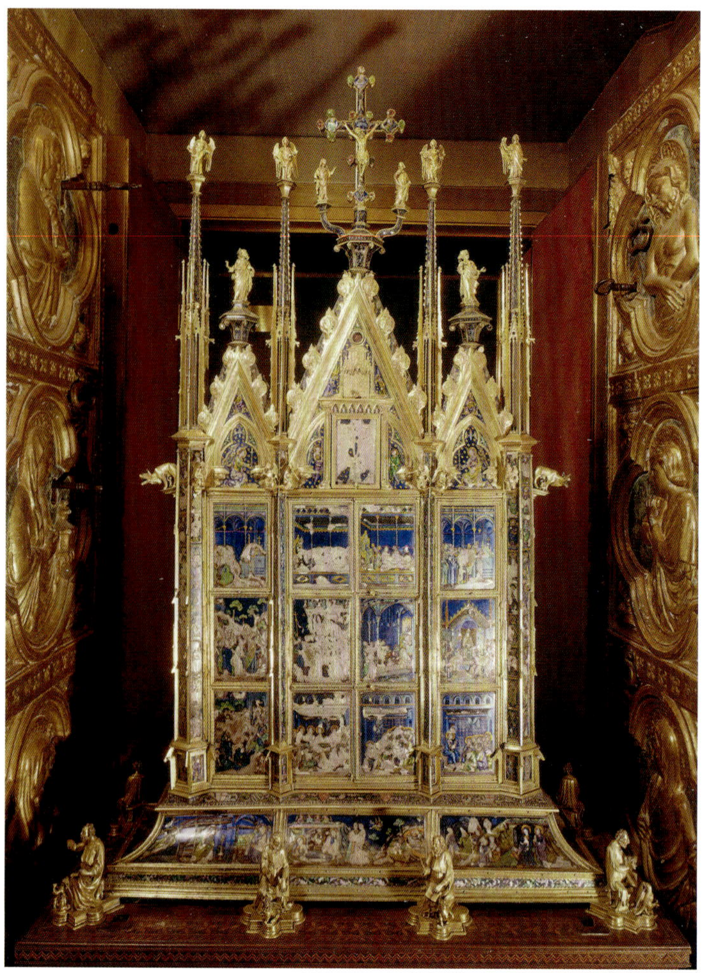

FIG. 47
Ugolino di Vieri (documented 1328–about 1385) **and Associates**
Reliquary of the Holy Corporal, 1338
Silver and gilded silver with translucent enamel, height 139 cm
Museo dell'Opera del Duomo, Orvieto

of awarding communal commissions to local artists, helped forge a Sienese altarpiece style.[11] Sienese artists exported works of art proudly inscribed with their name and provenance, such as Ugolino di Nerio to Florence, Pietro Lorenzetti to Arezzo and Ugolino di Vieri to Orvieto. In contrast, *lignaiuoli* – woodworkers, carpenters and carvers – only very rarely added their signature.

Ugolino di Nerio successfully transferred Sienese altarpiece design concepts to Florence, first to the Dominicans and then to the Franciscans. His first *tabula*, or altar painting, for Santa Maria Novella seems totally lost,[12] and the second for Santa Croce is now dispersed, although major elements of it are preserved in Berlin and London (fig. 48).[13]

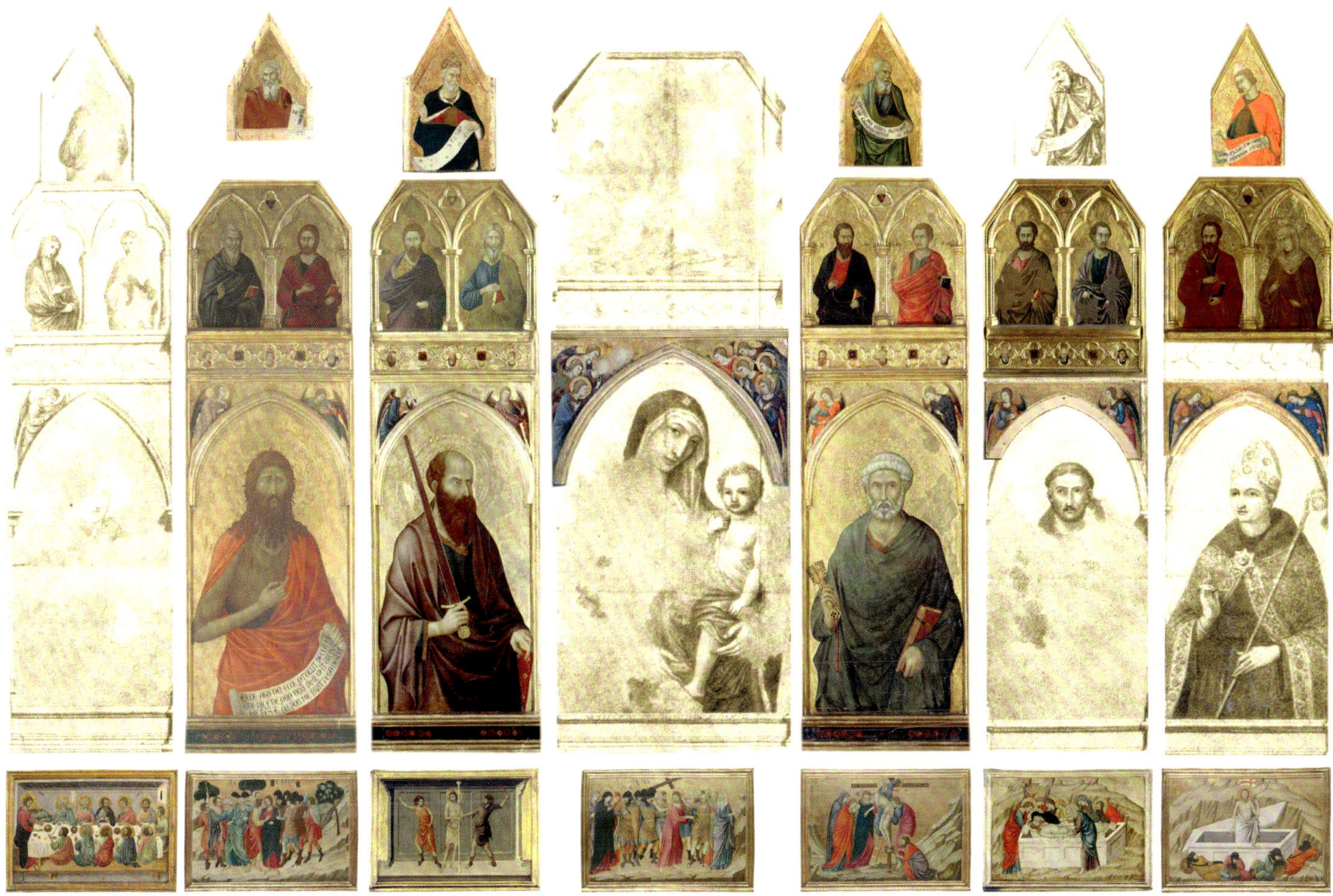

FIG. 48
Photographic montage of the surviving panels of the Santa Croce Altarpiece superimposed on a drawing attributed to Humbert de Superville (1770–1849)

Painted some five years after Simone's Pisan polyptych, it marks a significant development in structure and formal composition, notably in the addition of a narrative predella. Changes in liturgical practice and church interiors account for the dismantling of Ugolino's masterpiece, which was replaced by a large Eucharistic tabernacle in the mid-sixteenth century. Transferred to the convent dormitory, the great altarpiece was radically reduced in size. The Franciscan saints – Francis, Anthony of Padua and Louis of Toulouse – of central importance for the friars' iconographic programme, were lost, but are known from seventeenth-century engravings by Giovanni Antonio Baccanelli. An eighteenth-century drawing attributed to Humbert de Superville appears to show the polyptych in an earlier, but not original, state.[14] Later still, its narrative predella was dismembered and sold as separate scenes to satisfy the growing taste for collecting Italian Primitives (see pp. 255–6). Ugolino di Nerio's heptaptych is a model case for the differing dynamics for destruction and also for the sources of modern reconstruction.

Very few Italian contracts from around 1300 survive, and demonstration drawings, which subsequently became common communication tools, were extremely rare. There are some remarkable exceptions, such as the contract for a surviving polyptych at Arezzo by Pietro Lorenzetti (see pp. 87–8).[15] Another pupil of Duccio, Pietro provided the high altarpiece of the main baptismal church for the local

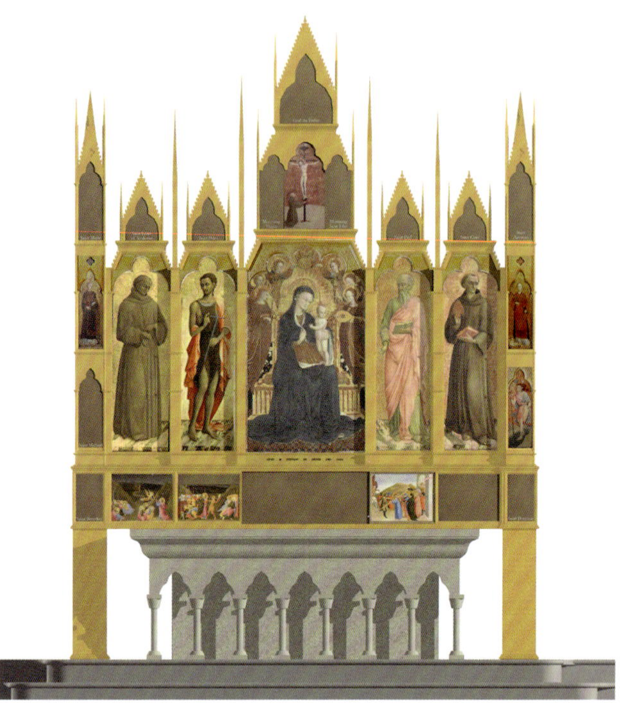

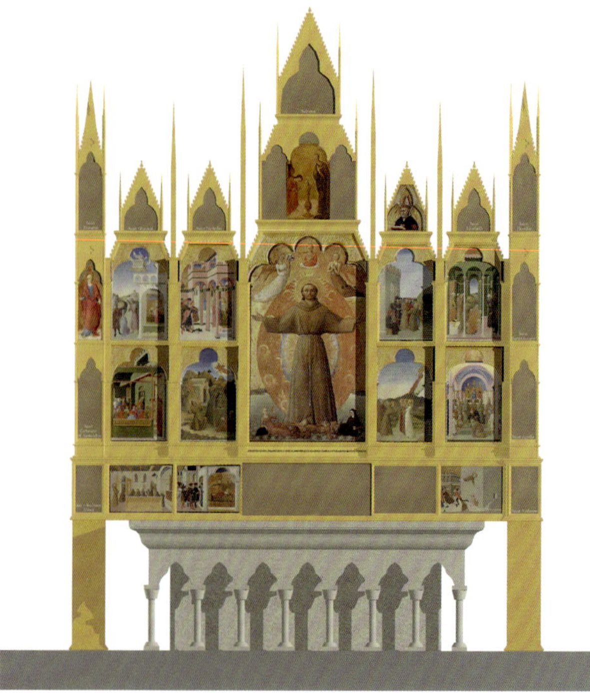

bishop, Guido Tarlati. The 1320 contract specifies the now-lost 'colone da lato', the side buttresses that originally supported the many-storied altarpiece on the free-standing high altar. This constructional device reflected the original structure of Duccio's *Maestà* in Siena Cathedral (see figs 8, 9).[16] Tarlati stipulated a local, somewhat inexperienced woodworker and determined the altarpiece programme for the Pieve, or baptismal church. A central Madonna is flanked by four half-length saints in the main storey. The term *tabula*, indicating a framed panel, is here employed to define the altarpiece type – the now familiar term 'polyptych' is a modern invention.[17]

Further important information about terminology comes from a second early contract, that for Cimabue's lost high altarpiece commission in 1302 (1301 in the modern style) for the hospital church of Santa Chiara in Pisa.[18] This hugely important document provides the first known description of an architecturally conceived altarpiece, strongly suggesting that it was of vertical plank construction. The Latin technical terms *planum*, *tabernaculum*, *predula*, *colonella* and *storia* were extremely flexible in their meanings. In addition, the Pisan altarpiece programme is described following biblical hierarchy and not, as was done later, by the figures' physical location. Only by attempting to understand both contemporary altarpiece structures and iconographic programmes can the modern art historian propose a plausible reconstruction.

Guido Tarlati paid for Pietro's polyptych largely by himself.[19] The mendicant orders routinely used 'crowdfunding' methods for their high altarpieces, amassing small individual donations to cover the high initial cost. At times they also applied to the civic governments of their local communes for financial support, as did the Carmelites at Siena.[20] The patron and the participating craftsmen sometimes communicated by using familiar examples. The predominant term in documents, *modo e forma*, could refer to the altarpiece content, format, frame, material or quality of execution. Following a specific model did not then have any negative charge. Thus, Duccio's *Maestà* provided the model for the cathedral altarpiece at Massa Marittima south of Siena, where an identical wooden structure seems to have been employed.[21] It would appear that religious institutions, and in particular the great international mendicant orders, especially the Franciscans and the Dominicans, used their extensive networks to recommend trusted artisans to their confrères, as the Augustinians at Siena did for their friars at Massa Marittima, or the Dominicans at Pisa for their brothers at Orvieto.[22] However, the details of the construction process, and any preparatory negotiations that

FIG. 49
Reconstruction of Sassetta's Sansepolcro Altarpiece, front and back

may have taken place between the patron and craftsmen, are virtually undocumented. Only at Siena for Duccio's *Maestà*, and at Sansepolcro in the mid-fifteenth century, does one learn something of these essential preliminaries. Delegated friars travelled from Sansepolcro to Siena to agree the detailed programme with Sassetta, which was subsequently confirmed by the convent (fig. 49).[23]

Technical procedures developed and practised in Siena, then almost certainly the leading centre of altarpiece production, were soon widely exported. Lateral pilasters began to be used to buttress multipart polyptychs on free-standing high altars, as the documented polyptychs by Niccolò di Segna (a pupil of Pietro Lorenzetti) and also by Sassetta and Piero della Francesca at Sansepolcro prove.[24] Substantial predellas, with robust box-like structures, soon became a commonly employed mechanism for stabilising and securing monumental altarpieces. Interlocking horizontal cross-battens, which linked the individual vertical compartments at their backs and gave rigidity to the whole structure, were another important innovation (fig. 45).[25] These were presumably introduced by Sienese carpenters to make possible the simultaneous production of different parts of very large altarpieces in the town's small workshops, the separate transport of the main components, and the final assemblage of the altarpieces at their distant destinations. Occasionally, the monumental wooden core was assembled provisionally and erected on an altar to test the stability of the multistoried panel elevation before the woodworker's final payment and the start of the delicate and expensive painting process.[26]

The narrative programme of an altarpiece was fundamentally determined by its patron. The Franciscan friars at Florence and Sansepolcro insisted primarily on the inclusion of their order's saints, while Tarlati concentrated on local saints traditionally venerated in his Aretine diocese. Polyptychs for the mendicant orders, partially surviving or documented, have so far been much better researched than those of the monastic orders like the Benedictines or Cistercians, still mostly known from numerous surviving fragments. Liturgical differences between the religious orders, which demonstrably influenced altarpiece design, have rarely been considered. If the clergy was seated behind the high altar, it becomes obvious that a double-sided altarpiece addressing them as well as the main congregation might be preferred, although it was a notably expensive and uncommon solution.

Saint Bernardino of Siena (1380–1444), preaching in Siena Cathedral, firmly told his congregation to take as their model the devout Virgin Annunciate depicted by Simone Martini in his cathedral altarpiece completed in 1333.[27] Duccio, in his signature on the cathedral *Maestà*, begged the Virgin for peace for Siena and for his own salvation.[28] At other times the patron requested the worshipper to remember his soul or those of his father or family.[29] Or he commended himself to the altar titular (most commonly Mary, to whom the entire city of Siena was dedicated), to his personal name saint or to saints who might intercede on his behalf, as Sebastian was believed to do in times of plague. Other donors were satisfied with their families being memorialised by inscriptions and heraldic shields integrated into their altarpieces, although donor portraits remained exceptional during the trecento. With ever more chapels being built and altar panels erected, patrons also started to compete with one another. In other cases, the resident religious institution determined most of the altar *tituli*, and therefore the overall programme of altars and altarpieces in their church, a practice evident in Siena Cathedral.[30]

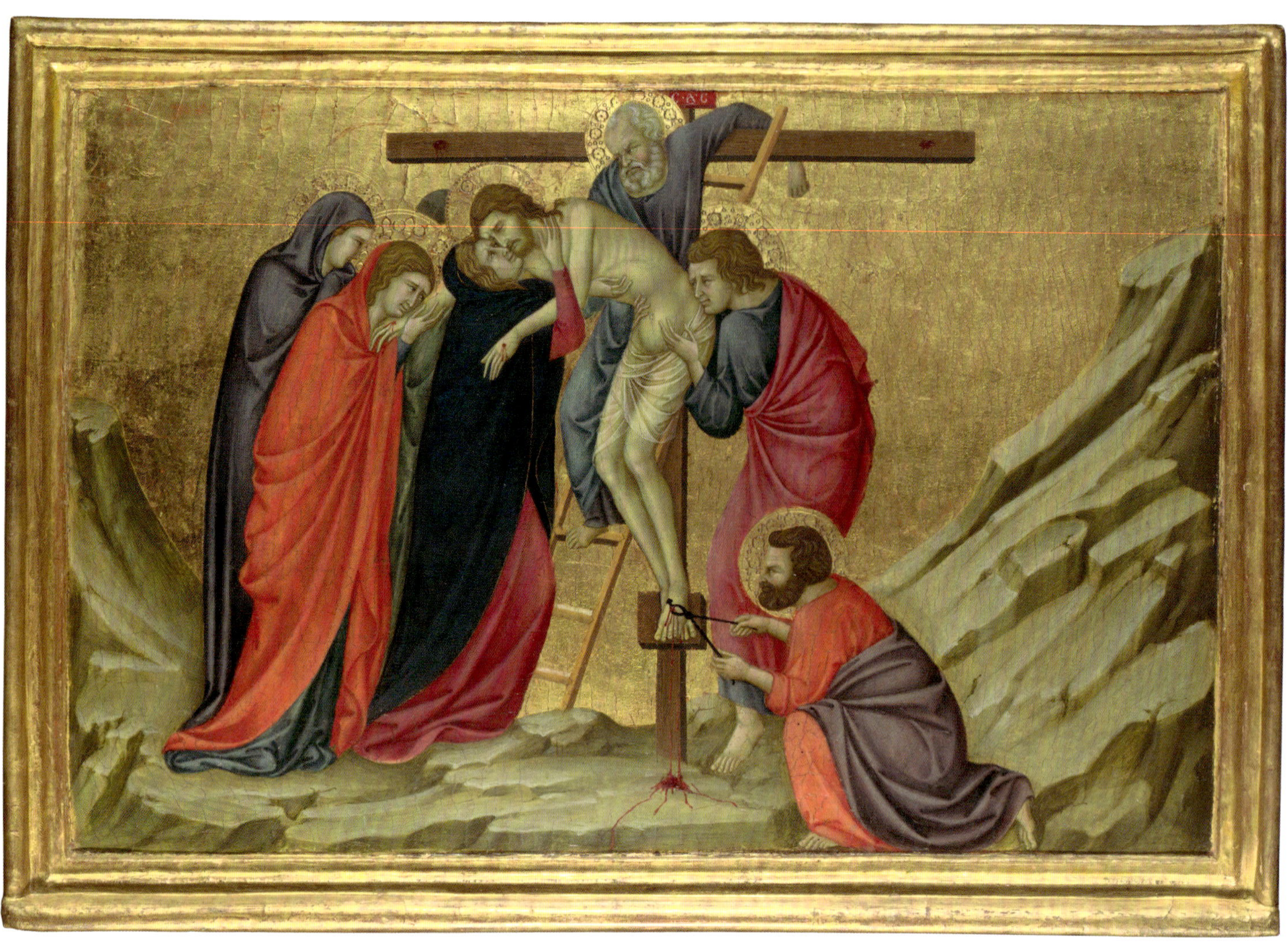

FIG. 50
Ugolino di Nerio (documented 1317–27; died possibly 1329)
The Deposition (from the Santa Croce Altarpiece), about 1325–8
Tempera on panel, 40.7 × 58.6 cm (with engaged frame)
The National Gallery, London. Presented by Henry Wagner, 1918 (NG3375)

Sienese formal compositions were also exported, as demonstrated by Pietro Lorenzetti's *Assumption of the Virgin*, based on the Sienese cathedral oculus, in the crowning pinnacle of his Aretine polyptych (see fig. 61). Panel painters following in the footsteps of Duccio's *Maestà* developed great skills in portraying refined and highly esteemed narratives and observations from daily life and nature. Pietro depicted the Carmelite order's historical development in the predella of their altarpiece in Siena, and Ugolino di Nerio created a Passion Cycle at Florence (fig. 50) that reflected the dedication of Santa Croce, the Franciscan church, to the Holy Cross.[31] Niccolò di Segna, in his *Resurrection flanked by Saints* (mid-fourteenth century; Sansepolcro Cathedral), exported the Sienese cathedral altarpiece scheme of a central scene paired with lateral saints to the Abbey of Sansepolcro.[32] Remarkably, the traditional Sienese colours for Saint Peter, green over blue, reappear in the Santa Croce high altarpiece, and also in Meo da Siena's monastic high altarpiece for Montelabate in Umbria (about 1330; Galleria Nazionale dell'Umbria), rather than the customary Tuscan yellow over blue.[33]

The fact that knowledge of technique extends our understanding of medieval painting was demonstrated by the watershed exhibition of 1989 at the National Gallery, London, *Art in the Making: Italian Painting before 1400*.[34]

The fragment no longer remained an autonomous image ostentatiously reframed or draped in velvet. It became instead a source of vital information about its original design and setting, and one hopes that this splendid precedent will be reiterated in the future. Since that date, restoration reports have become the norm, providing crucial information about wooden structures, painting processes, pigments and the condition of exhibits for the general public.

Unlike the enterprising and inquisitive scholar of earlier centuries, the contemporary art historian now routinely collaborates with scientists and restorers, learning to balance established historical sources with valuable new technical and scientific observations. Traditional-style analysis has become radically insufficient, as knowledge of carpentry and painting techniques has become essential. Information on buttresses, battens, dowels and laminated structures is now as vital as familiarity with gesso, bole and gold leaf, or underdrawing, pentimenti, flesh-painting and pigments, binding media and varnishes.

Modern technology, fortunately, makes it possible to reconstruct a work of art, visually and digitally, before any physical intervention on the painting. Unfortunately, it also facilitates implausible, anachronistic and misleading reconstructions and settings for even the greatest and most familiar altarpieces. Here, too, the thoughtful combination of historical knowledge, technical understanding and common sense remains fundamental. More than ever before, the necessity of understanding and communicating the importance of reconstruction to the concerned viewer has become obvious. With better information available, we can develop a better understanding of how these great altarpieces were created and installed at their original sites.

This is a modified and briefer version of a longer discussion; see Gardner von Teuffel 2021. I owe special thanks to Pierluigi Nieri and Julian Gardner.

1. Solberg 2020, p. 21; Perugia 2020, pp. 180–1.
2. Van Os 1990, pp. 34–7, fig. 5.
3. Amato in Siena 2017–18, cat. 13b, pp. 182–91.
4. Bokody 2015.
5. For a general introduction to panel construction, see London 1989–90; Castelli 2009, pp. 319–33; Castelli 2016.
6. Cannon 2013, pp. 138–48, with full bibliography; Nieri 2022, pp. 74–6, figs 8–9, for the important restoration report; see also Gardner von Teuffel 2021, pp. 8–11.
7. Gardner 2008; see also Guillouët and Vilain 2018.
8. Cioni in Siena 2003–4, cat. 74, pp. 438–45.
9. Maginnis 2001, pp. 49, 54, 193, 228; for Ugolino di Vieri, see Luzi 1866, p. 356: 'nunc priori fratrum capituli et conventi sancta Marie de Monte Carmelo de civitate Urbevetana, procuratori Magistri Ugolini aurificis filii Magistri Veri civis civitatis Senarum de populo Sancti Petri Castri Veteri' ('Current prior of the friars of Santa Maria del Monte Carmelo of the city of Orvieto, procurator of master Ugolino, goldsmith, son of master Vieri, citizen of the neighbourhood of San Pietro in Castelvecchio in Siena').
10. For Ugolino di Vieri's reliquary, see Cioni 1998, pp. 468–621.
11. Maginnis 2001, pp. 85, 196.
12. Cannon 1982, pp. 87–91, remains fundamental. See also Gardner von Teuffel (forthcoming).
13. Weppelmann 2005–6; Weppelmann and Winkler 2005–6, reviewed in Gardner von Teuffel 2006, and Gordon 2011, pp. 430–77.
14. Biblioteca Apostolica Vaticana, Rome, Vat. Lat. 9847, fols 91v–92r. The drawing was published by Loyrette 1978, interpreted by Boskovits 1988, pp. 162–76, Weppelmann 2005–6, Weppelmann and Winkler 2005–6, and reviewed by Gardner von Teuffel 2005, p. 623, Gardner von Teuffel 2006 and Gordon 2011, pp. 430–77. Further, Gardner von Teuffel 2021, pp. 11–14.
15. Becchis 2012, pp. 37–46, 161, reprinted the document, interpreted by Gardner von Teuffel 1979, pp. 33–5, and annotated in Gardner von Teuffel 2005, pp. 125, 623; see also Freni 2000a, although the author's reconstructed Pieve setting does not convince me.
16. Gardner von Teuffel 1979, pp. 35–41, and annotated in Gardner von Teuffel 2005, pp. 622–8; Siena 2003–4, cat. 32, pp. 208–43; Cannon, p. 28, in the present volume.
17. Paris 1990, p. 11.
18. Tanfani Centofani 1897, pp. 119–20, published the contract, interpreted by Hager 1962, pp. 113–14, fig. 164, reinterpreted by Gardner von Teuffel 1979, pp. 42–3, and misunderstood by Flora 2018, pp. 237–41.
19. Guerrini 1988.
20. Lorenzetti's Carmine altarpiece is one prominent example, for which see Becchis 2012, pp. 161–2; Gardner von Teuffel 2015, fig. 17, with full bibliography, pp. 4, 23–7.
21. Bartalini 2003–4.
22. Seidel and Calamai 2017–18a. Gardner von Teuffel 1985 established the provenance of Ambrogio's altarpiece. For Simone Martini at Orvieto, see now Cannon 2013, pp. 143–4; Boston 2022–3.
23. Satkowski 2000, p. 75; Banker published the *scripta* or agreement first in 1991, then in 2009, see Banker 1991; Banker 2009, pp. 571–2; further discussed by Israëls et al. 2009, pp. 166–7; Gardner von Teuffel 2009, pp. 214–17.
24. Gardner von Teuffel 1979, reprinted and annotated in Gardner von Teuffel 2005, pp. 622–8; for Niccolò di Segna, see Gardner von Teuffel 2009, p. 217; for Piero della Francesca, see Banker 2010, p. 21, and Gardner von Teuffel 2010, pp. 74–5.
25. Castelli 2016, pp. 322–5. To the list should now be added Simone Martini's 1319 Pisan altarpiece, see Nieri 2022.
26. This process, documented not in Siena but in Perugia at the end of the fifteenth century, may well reflect long-established practice. See Gardner von Teuffel 2004, p. 147.
27. Banchi 1884, pp. 441–2; Cecchi 2001a.
28. White 1979, p. 100.
29. Bacci 2000, pp. 378–9, 460; Amato in Siena 2017–18, cat. 6, pp. 126–31.
30. Butzek 2001a.
31. Gardner von Teuffel 2015, pp. 23–5; Gordon 2011, pp. 430–77.
32. Gardner von Teuffel 2009, p. 217.
33. Gordon 2011, p. 431; Garibaldi 2015, pp. 186–90.
34. London 1989–90.

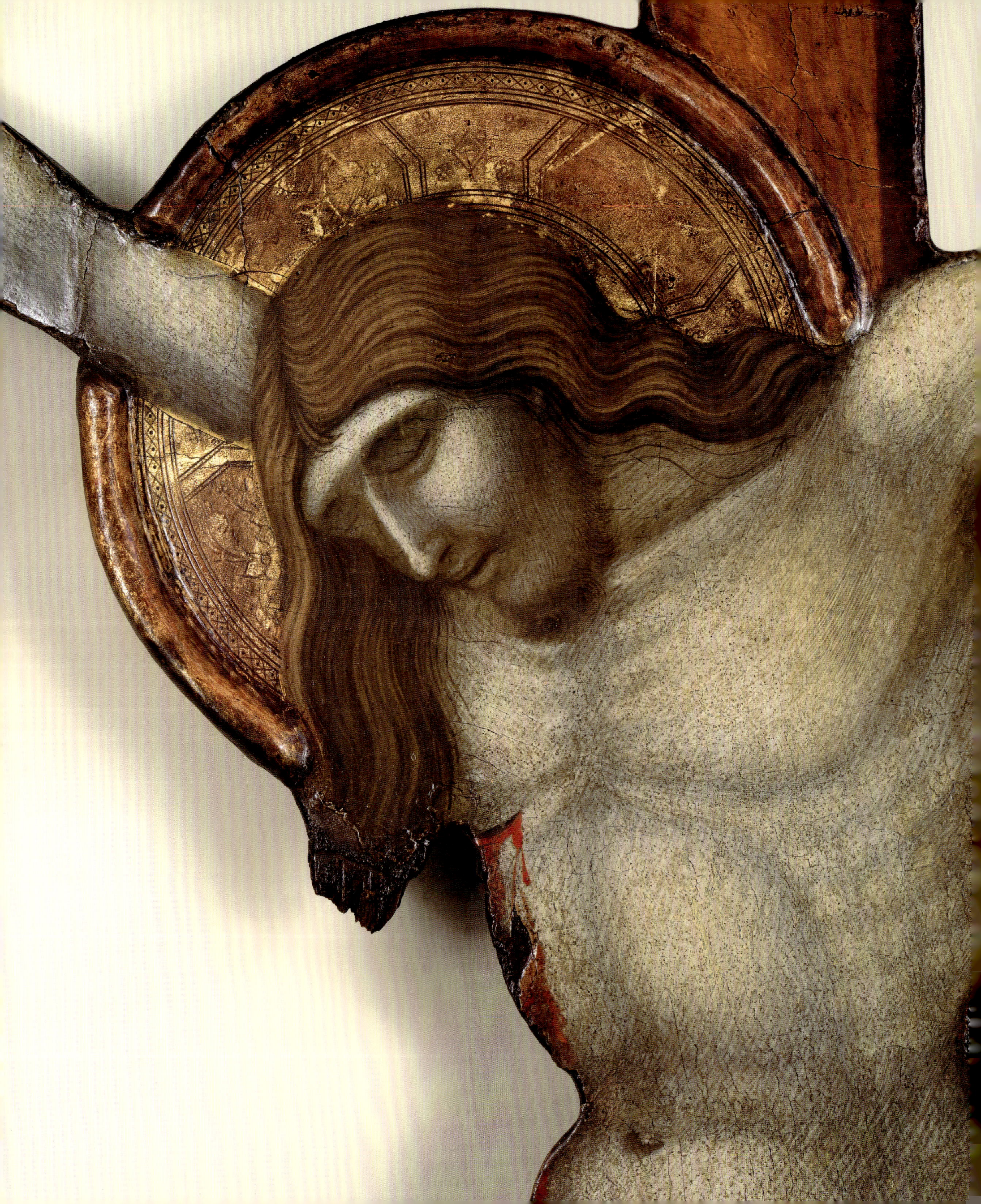

SIENESE ART ON THE ROAD: PIETRO LORENZETTI'S FORMATIVE YEARS AS A PERIPATETIC PAINTER

Donal Cooper and Andrea De Marchi

Composing his *Commentarii* in the early 1450s, Lorenzo Ghiberti lavished praise on the Sienese painter Ambrogio Lorenzetti, 'the most famous and distinctive master [...] the most noble composer [...] learned as no other painter was'.[1] Ghiberti did not even mention Pietro, Ambrogio's older brother and fellow painter. The elder Lorenzetti would only emerge from obscurity a century later in Giorgio Vasari's *Lives of the Artists*, published in 1550 and again, in revised and much expanded form, in 1568.[2] Vasari's brief biography is strewn with inaccuracies, including jumbled claims for Pietro's activity in Pisa's Camposanto and Old Saint Peter's in Rome. Surprisingly, Vasari did not realise that Pietro and Ambrogio were brothers, despite describing in both their lives the same fresco cycle on the facade of the hospital of Santa Maria della Scala in Siena, which was identified by a prominent inscription as a joint work, executed in 1335 or 1337, by Pietro and Ambrogio 'his brother'.[3] Vasari even mistook Pietro's surname as 'Laurati' based on a misreading of the Latin inscription on the painter's altarpiece for San Francesco, Pistoia (now in the Gallerie degli Uffizi, Florence).[4]

Arguably, however, Vasari's confusion is punctuated by shafts of insight. Already in the 1550 edition of the *Lives*, Pietro was said to have worked not only in Siena, but also 'in many other Tuscan cities', while his frescoes at Santa Maria della Scala were said to imitate the manner of Giotto and in technique even to surpass the Florentine master.[5] The 1568 biography is informed by the remodelling of the Pieve church in Arezzo that Vasari – a native of the town – oversaw in the early 1560s. This intervention transformed the Pieve into a mausoleum for Vasari's family and involved the removal from the high altar of Pietro Lorenzetti's polyptych (see fig. 60).[6] Vasari's second life of 'Pietro Laurati' is three times longer than the first, but a lengthy excursus on the author's new high altarpiece for the Pieve accounts for much of the difference. Vasari does, though, include a relatively detailed description of Pietro's polyptych, commissioned in 1320, which he reinstalled on another altar in the church. In the process, Vasari must have looked at these panels closely,

P. 78
Pietro Lorenzetti (documented possibly 1306; died probably 1348)
Cut-out Crucifix, about 1315–20 (detail of fig. 109, p. 159)

FIG. 51
Pietro Lorenzetti (documented possibly 1306; died probably 1348)
The Virgin and Child, about 1312–13
Tempera on poplar, 126 × 83 cm
Museo Diocesano, Cortona

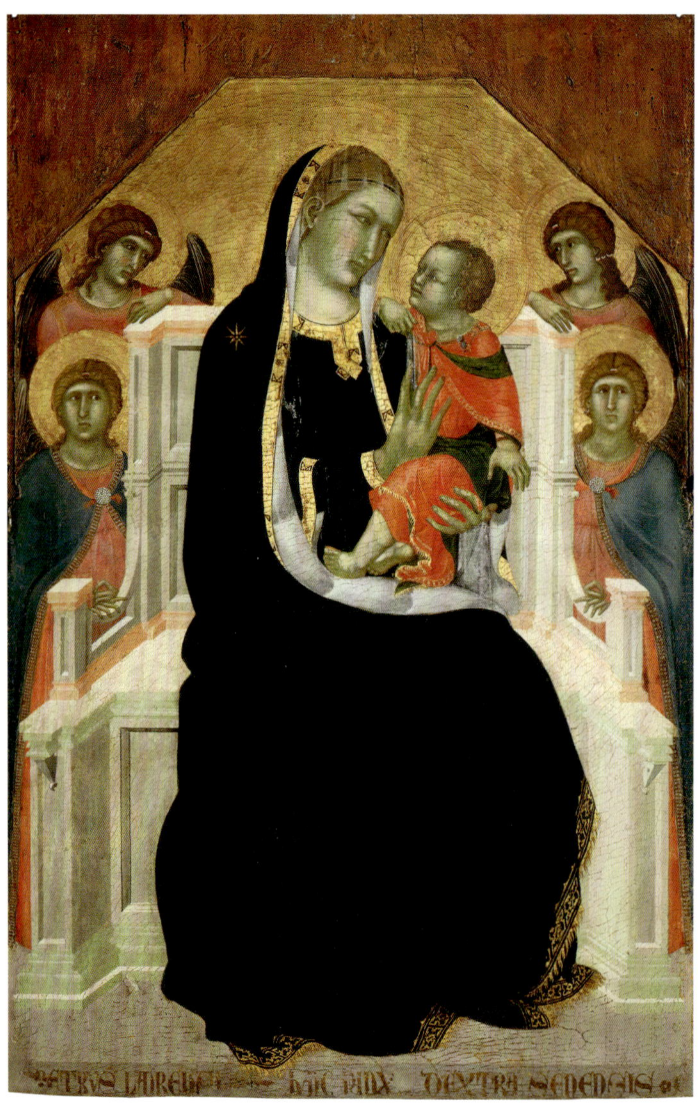

and he praised them as 'truly beautiful and executed in very good manner'.[7] Vasari's estimation may have been spurred by a desire to burnish the artistic prestige and heritage of the Pieve for his own ends, but the 1568 life also suggests a genuine appreciation of Pietro's importance and his qualities as a painter. The claims made in 1550 are now more concrete: Pietro was 'sought after and valued throughout Tuscany'; he not only imitated Giotto's style but also became a greater master than him, or Cimabue, or anyone else. The peripatetic note in Vasari's account is suggestive, and we will argue that Pietro built his career on commissions outside his native Siena, in marked contrast to his principal contemporary and rival among Sienese painters of the generation following Duccio: Simone Martini.

We do not have any information on Pietro's early life: he is often thought to be the 'Petruccio di Lorenzo' paid in February 1306 for additions to the altarpiece painted by Duccio in 1302 for the chapel of the Council of the Nine (or *Nove*), Siena's ruling magistracy, in the Palazzo Pubblico.[8] Recent scholarship does not, however, identify Pietro among Duccio's multiple assistants on the great *Maestà* for Siena Cathedral in the years before 1311. The pattern of Pietro's early commissions suggests that he was dependent on patrons from outside Siena. Works traditionally dated to the mid-1310s include the now disassembled altarpiece for Monticchiello and the *Virgin and Child* at Castiglione d'Orcia, two small settlements to the south-east of Siena.[9] Noting that Pietro would later own property close to nearby Montalcino, Carl Strehlke has proposed that these early commissions may reflect family connections in this area of the Sienese *contado* (countryside).[10] The absence of prominent projects in Siena itself stands in stark contrast to the sensational success of Simone Martini, who during these same years was at work on the enormous frescoed *Maestà* in the Palazzo Pubblico.

The impression of an itinerant artist is reinforced by commissions that drew Pietro further afield, to centres beyond the confines of the Sienese state: Cortona, Florence, Assisi, Arezzo and probably Assisi again. Pietro's earliest surviving work may be the *Virgin and Child* now in Cortona's Museo Diocesano (fig. 51).[11] It confirms his knowledge of the latest developments in both Sienese and Florentine painting and synthesises the two traditions skilfully. The Virgin's splayed marble throne and the angels resting their hands on its upper ledge or gently fingering its sides bear the clear imprint of Duccio's cathedral *Maestà*, completed in 1311, but the sweeping curve of the Virgin's mantle also acknowledges Giotto's earlier *Ognissanti Madonna* (about 1302–3; Gallerie degli Uffizi, Florence).[12] Pietro's panel is unlikely to post-date these masterpieces by long: in the smoky chiaroscuro and rounded faces of the four angels, Pietro is closer to Duccio than he would ever be again. These stylistic affinities suggest that the Cortona panel should be dated before the Monticchiello and Castiglione d'Orcia altarpieces, probably to 1312–13.[13] But while the angels and throne can be characterised as a homage to Duccio, the *Virgin and Child* at Cortona is already distinctively Pietro's own, and the artist's signature speaks of considerable self-confidence: 'PETRUS LAVRENTII HANC PINX[IT] DEXTRA SENENSIS'. The signature is located on the step front of the Virgin's throne, the same location as Duccio's written prayer of authorship on the cathedral *Maestà*.[14] But Pietro's sophisticated formula is far removed from Duccio's pious petition in its professional assurance. The inscription can be roughly translated as 'Pietro di Lorenzo of Siena painted this [work] with his right hand', where – as Christopher Platts has shown – 'dextra' carries additional resonance, signalling Pietro's manual dexterity and invoking the metaphor of the *dextera Dei* (the divine right hand of creation).[15]

The Cortona *Virgin and Child* has lost its original framing elements, but closer inspection of the surviving panel provides some clues as to its original format. Dowel holes on the exposed left and right edges, two on each side at matching heights, establish that the picture was the central element of a larger altarpiece.[16] The pictorial field tapers at the top like Duccio's cathedral *Maestà*, but the panel itself is rectangular, suggesting that the overall shape of the altarpiece followed a more archaic squared format, comparable to the altarpiece painted almost contemporaneously by Memmo di Filippuccio for the Clarissan convent in San Gimignano.[17] While the loss of the lateral panels limits our ability to reconstruct Pietro's Cortona altarpiece, the evidence indicates that here he sought to replicate features of the recently completed *Maestà* within the parameters offered by a carpentry support of much more traditional format, perhaps one that had been supplied by his patrons.

Two other early works firmly attributed to Pietro, both crucifixes, are still in Cortona, suggesting sustained periods of activity in the city, probably around 1312–16. One of these is the monumental crucifix now in the Museo Diocesano but with a provenance from the local Church of San Marco (fig. 52).[18] Measuring 380 × 274 cm, this is the largest surviving crucifix painted to that date by a Sienese artist, although it is still considerably smaller than the late thirteenth-century crosses linked to the Umbrian Maestro di Santa Chiara in nearby Arezzo (San Francesco) and Castiglione Fiorentino (Pinacoteca Comunale), and also

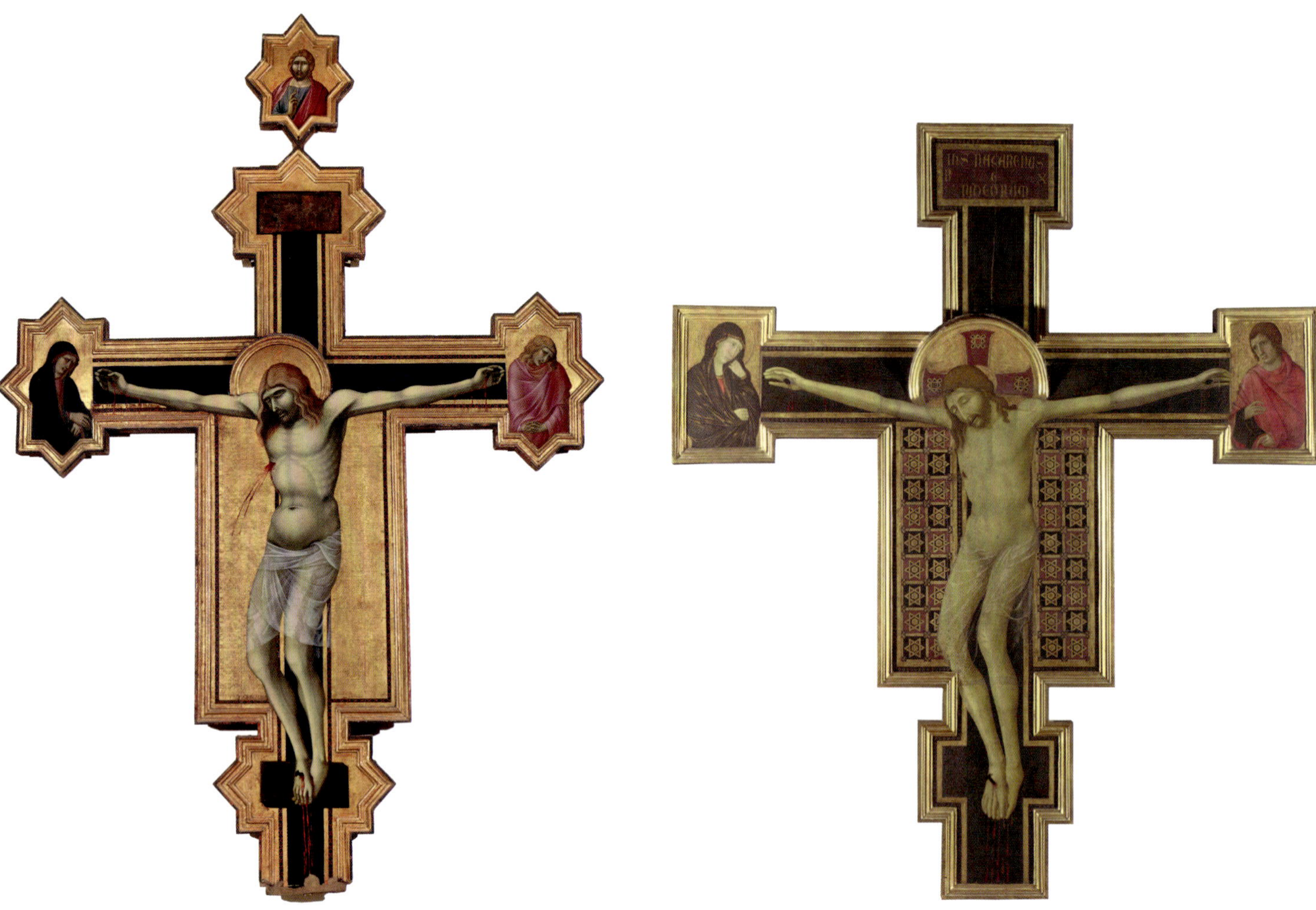

the more recent examples by Giotto and his workshop in Florence (Santa Maria Novella) and Rimini (Tempio Malatestiano).[19] Pietro's Cortona cross can be read as a provocative response to Giotto's latest modifications to the traditional genre of the monumental panel cross. Some details imitate Giotto, for example the blood issuing from the wounds in the hands, running along the wrist and forearms but also dripping down onto the picture border below, reprising the Santa Maria Novella cross. Meanwhile, Christ's reddish hair, falling down to frame his face, seems closer to Giotto's frescoed *Crucifixion* in the Lower Church at Assisi of about 1310–12, which might indicate Pietro's early familiarity with the Basilica of San Francesco. In other respects, however, the large Cortona cross offers distinctive solutions that would become characteristic of Sienese crucifix production as the fourteenth century unfolded. Pietro was surely familiar with the transition that Giotto engineered from plain rectangular to more elaborate cusped quatrefoil terminals, an innovation that seems to have been introduced in the Rimini crucifix of about 1298. In the Cortona cross Pietro formulates his own version of a cusped terminal: a simpler pointed star field, notably elongated, perhaps to allow him to develop more expressive gestures for the Virgin and Saint John. The star device extends to the upper terminal, where the lower point of the *cimasa* (crowning panel) with the Blessing Christ appears to balance delicately on the similarly starred *Titulus Crucis* (the inscription nailed to the top of the cross).

The innovation of the starred terminal would be quickly taken up by other Sienese artists. Segna di Bonaventura deployed it on a larger scale in his monumental cross for the abbey church of Sante Flora e Lucilla in Arezzo, for which

FIG. 52
Pietro Lorenzetti (documented possibly 1306; died probably 1348)
Crucifix, about 1313–16
Tempera on poplar, 380 × 274 cm
Museo Diocesano, Cortona

FIG. 53
Segna di Bonaventura (documented 1298; died 1326/31)
Crucifix, about 1310–15
Tempera on poplar, 213.5 × 184 cm
The National Gallery, London. Bought, 1857 (NG567)

there is good documentary evidence for a date about 1319.[20] Segna's earlier crosses (like the example in the National Gallery, fig. 53) have traditional rectangular terminals, so it seems likely that his adoption of starred terminals for the Arezzo panel depended on the precedent of Pietro's Cortona cross, providing a useful chronological peg to confirm the latter's early date.[21] Simone Martini would soon design his cross at San Casciano in Val di Pesa with starred terminals, and would be followed by Ugolino di Nerio (Santa Maria dei Servi, Siena), Niccolò di Segna (San Niccolò del Carmine, Siena), Pietro's own brother Ambrogio (Montenero d'Orcia) and others.[22] Thus, Pietro's innovation became a leitmotif of Sienese crucifix production during the fourteenth century.

The star motif is also picked up on the apron of the Cortona cross. Here, Pietro eschewed the dominant practice of filling the fields to either side of Christ's body with fictive textile patterns in favour of a plain gold ground. But the gilding is elaborately tooled with a pattern of interlocking stars and crosses, set against a hatched ground and filled with foliate designs.[23] Remarkably, the entire design is executed freehand, a further argument for an early date in the mid-1310s (Pietro seems to have begun using motif punches after the Arezzo Pieve Polyptych commissioned in 1320). The prominent star mouldings and extensive gilding of the framing elements evoke contemporary metalwork, whereas the body of Christ shows an awareness of contemporary sculpture. The striking detail of Christ's grimacing upper teeth was a novelty for a painted cross but was already a distinctive feature of Giovanni Pisano's wooden crucifixes.

Pietro's profound engagement with the sculpture of Giovanni Pisano is confirmed by the other crucifix that he painted for Cortona, the 'cut-out' cross now in the Museo Diocesano with a provenance from the convent of San Girolamo delle Poverelle (fig. 109; see p. 78).[24] Whereas the larger Cortona cross can be set within an evolving tradition of monumental cross design, the smaller cut-out version appears to be unique. For comparable examples we have to wait until the series of cut-out crosses produced by Lorenzo Monaco and his followers in the early 1400s. The only contemporary analogy comes in the form of the cut-out panel of Saint Michael that Giotto included in his fresco of the *Verification of the Stigmata* in the Saint Francis cycle in the Upper Church at Assisi, painted in about 1292. Giotto's fictive panel is remarkably precise and has been taken to indicate both the existence of such cut-out panels and their possible elevated display.[25] The inherent fragility of the format may have limited their survival, but if cut-out panels had been widespread, we would expect more survivals and traces in the sources, and the peculiar features of Pietro's version at Cortona suggest an adventurous and experimental work, in which the artist sought to allude to sculptural qualities in an essentially two-dimensional work.[26]

Several aspects of the panel's construction and design point to this intention. As with many of Giovanni Pisano's crucifixes, Christ's body is forced downwards, opening spaces between the arms and the horizontal bar of the cross. The raised border around the halo is interrupted by the upwards thrust of Christ's right arm, which thus appears to project before the relief moulding. While the straight edges and corners of the cross are carved with rectilinear profiles, the passages where the panel's outline follows Christ's body are more ambiguous. Here, gesso and pigment wrap around the exterior and the reverse, and the panel's edges are chiselled from the rear to accentuate the corporeal form in contrast to the clean geometry of the cross. As Peter Dent observes in the present volume (pp. 150–63), the illusion of

FIG. 54
Pietro Lorenzetti (documented possibly 1306; died probably 1348)
Passion Cycle, about 1317–19 and 1322–3
Fresco
South transept, Lower Church, Basilica of San Francesco, Assisi

sculpture would have been strongest when seen from a range of viewpoints.

The smaller Cortona cross has sometimes been characterised as a processional artwork, and its modest dimensions and cut-out form would have rendered it light enough to be portable. But the inherent fragility of its silhouetted carpentry argues against such a public function, for which genuine sculpted crosses were generally more suitable. An elevated display in the manner of the *Verification* fresco also seems unlikely due to scale and structure. Instead, it probably served as a devotional focus for a religious community, whether over an altar or displayed in an oratory. The panel was found by Ugo Procacci during the Second World War in the convent of San Girolamo delle Poverelle, a Franciscan nunnery that could trace its origins back to groups of religious women established by the local saint Margaret of Cortona in the late thirteenth century.[27] We should probably imagine the cut-out cross as a liturgical and devotional focus for a female religious community, large enough to serve a communal audience, yet sufficiently portable to function in a range of ritual contexts.[28]

The Franciscan link here may be significant in light of the next step in Pietro's career. Nothing in the story thus far prepares us for his move to Assisi around 1317, where he was tasked with completing the fresco scheme of the transept of the Lower Church, begun by Giotto and his workshop. This was one of the most prestigious commissions of the moment, and the choice of the comparatively unknown Sienese painter to fill Giotto's shoes may have surprised contemporaries as much as it still puzzles today's art historians. It is tempting to think that Cortona may have been more of a launching pad for Assisi than traditionally thought. Pietro's large Cortona cross has a provenance from the local Church of San Marco, but there is reason to think that this may not have been the panel's original destination.[29] San Marco had been rebuilt in the thirteenth century, but is difficult to reconstruct today: it was suppressed in 1785 and then dismantled. The building was an important landmark in medieval Cortona, giving its name to one of the city's three districts (or *terzieri*), but it was not one of the larger churches, certainly not large enough to justify a cross on the monumental scale of Lorenzetti's.[30] San Marco, however, was adjacent to Cortona's biggest church, San Francesco, which was under construction in the early years of the fourteenth century with heavy backing from the town's ruling family, the Casali.[31] Pietro's crucifix would have been an appropriate 'crux de medio ecclesiae' for the new Franciscan foundation, dominating the church interior from its location over a rood screen in the centre of the nave.[32] As for the Cortona *Virgin and Child*, first recorded in the Pieve in the nineteenth century, its origins are unclear, but it may well be that Franciscan networks were already shaping Pietro's commissions and movements, even before his call to Assisi.

Other factors were probably at play behind Pietro's arrival in Assisi. Some scholars have sought a connection with Cardinal Napoleone Orsini: Pietro's first work in the Lower Church seems to have been the fictive altarpiece for the cardinal's chapel of Saint John the Baptist at the southern end of the transept, and Orsini was well connected with Cortona, where he had promoted the local cult of Margaret of Cortona, who died in 1297.[33] But by the mid-1310s, the cardinal was a distant figure, based at the papal court in Avignon.[34] A more likely agent on the ground in Assisi was Fra Jacopo del Tondo, the Provincial Minister of the Franciscan order's Umbrian province. Fra Jacopo was from a leading Sienese family but had attracted controversy in Tuscany from more rigorously

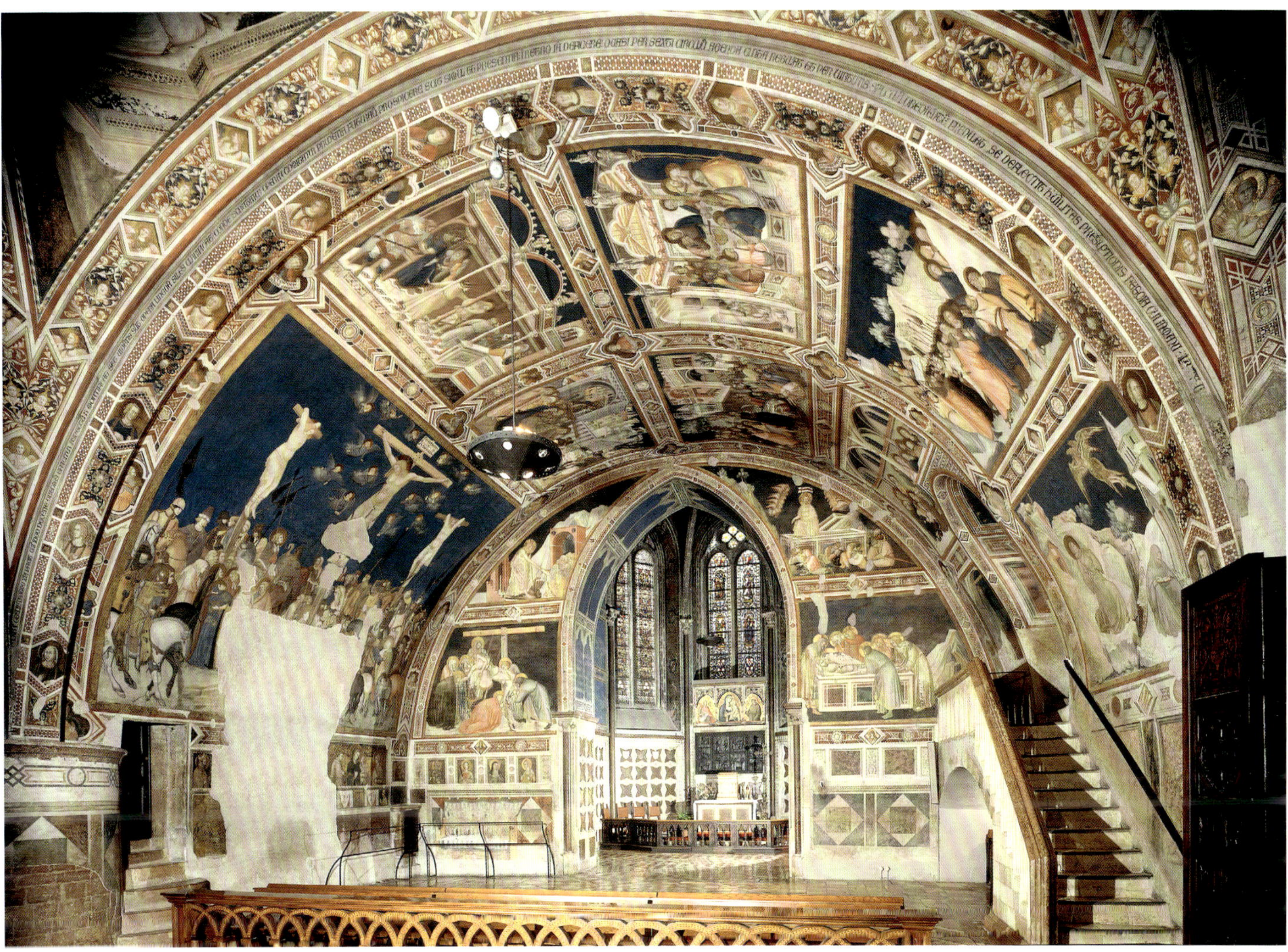

minded friars who thought his interpretation of Franciscan poverty too lax.[35] By the summer of 1311 the Minister General Gonsalvo of Valboa had pragmatically moved Jacopo sideways to Umbria, where he was installed as Provincial Minister with his base at Assisi. In 1313 the order's General Chapter transferred care for the Basilica of San Francesco from the Minister General to the Umbrian Provincial Minister, and so Jacopo would have had direct responsibility for the church from that date. He remained in office until the summer of 1316 when a successor was elected, but maintained active connections with Assisi into the 1320s.

It seems more than a coincidence that Fra Jacopo's term in Umbria occurred at the same time as a decisive turn towards Sienese artists at Assisi, as first Simone Martini and then Pietro Lorenzetti supplanted the hitherto dominant Giotto workshop in the Lower Church. Giotto had already frescoed the northern transept with a cycle of the Infancy of Christ before entrusting his workshop to execute the elaborate allegories of the Franciscan virtues in the 'Vele' vault over the high altar, which must have been completed by around 1313.[36] At that point, whether due to the Giotto workshop being overcommitted elsewhere, or simply due to a desire for change, a decision to engage new painters was made, who may have taken some time to arrive on site.[37] As Provincial Minister with newly confirmed authority over the basilica, Jacopo del Tondo would have been ideally placed to dictate the selection of his Sienese compatriots. Simone's frescoes in the Saint Martin chapel can be dated to about 1315–17, with the fictive retable for the Saint Elizabeth altar following in about 1318–19.[38] Pietro's arrival is often dated to 1317 and his main focus was the south transept where he frescoed a Passion Cycle (fig. 54) to complement

Giotto's Infancy scenes opposite. It is impossible to know but tantalising to speculate whether Pietro and Simone overlapped in the Lower Church, and if so on what terms: as rivals or collaborators. With regard to fresco expertise, Simone could draw on the experience of the monumental Palazzo Pubblico *Maestà*, commissioned in about 1312, but even with this priming the level of technical virtuosity and experimentation displayed in his Assisi frescoes is astonishing.[39] Although for Pietro we have no evidence of prior works in fresco, we should assume from the exceptional quality he achieved at Assisi that these were not his first paintings in the medium.

At Assisi Pietro was required to follow a template that had already been established by Giotto on the other side of the transept. As we have seen, Pietro drew on Giotto even in the Cortona *Maestà* and the early dating that is often given to his panel of Saint Lucy for Santa Lucia dei Magnoli suggests his presence in Florence in the 1310s.[40] Pietro's first fresco at Assisi, the fictive altarpiece for the Baptist's chapel, followed the marble-framed triptych format established by Giotto in the Saint Nicholas chapel at the opposite end of the transept (both chapels being under the patronage of the Orsini family). In the main bay of the south transept Pietro copied exactly the system of fictive marble framing bands that Giotto had used in the north, with bust-length figures set into cusped quatrefoil medallions at the intersections of the grid and midpoints of its vertical bars.[41] The key difference that Pietro introduced was to merge the equivalent of four narrative fields on the eastern wall to create a monumental *Crucifixion*, four times the size of Giotto's equivalent *Crucifixion* in the northern transept, where the need to preserve and incorporate Cimabue's existing *Virgin and Child enthroned with Saint Francis* had prevented a similarly expansive approach. Pietro's *Crucifixion* would later lose its lower central section with the insertion of an altar frame in the seventeenth century, but what survives shows that he probably created the most crowded vision of Calvary realised in Italian painting to that date. Below his vast *Crucifixion* Pietro squeezed a fictive altarpiece for the modest side altar dedicated to Saint John the Evangelist, tucked tightly into the corner of the transept to avoid impeding the flow of pilgrims around the tomb of Saint Francis.[42] Christ's Passion unfolded across the barrel of the transept vault, with the *Stigmatisation of Saint Francis* interpolated almost as a mirror opposite the *Crucifixion*. The four post-Crucifixion scenes of the *Harrowing of Hell*, the *Deposition*, the *Entombment* and the *Resurrection* filled the end walls of the transept, arranged in two registers to either side of the Baptist chapel.

An adequate treatment of Pietro's Passion Cycle and its wealth of narrative invention is not possible within the parameters of this essay. Instead, we focus on the dating of Pietro's Assisi campaign and its patronage, to reassess how the artist's Umbrian sojourn related to his other commissions around 1320, and to his eventual success in Siena later in the decade.[43] Assisi experienced a period of extreme political upheaval in September 1319 with the Ghibelline coup led by Muzio di Francesco, which threw the city into a bitter conflict with neighbouring Perugia backed by the papacy.[44] It is often assumed that Lorenzetti must have completed his cycle before Muzio's revolt, as it is difficult to see how the artist could have continued to work amid the turmoil.[45] In March 1320 Muzio's regime looted the papal treasury secured in the basilica's sacristy, immediately adjacent to the south transept of the Lower Church.

The chronology of the Lorenzetti campaign at Assisi is complicated further by the donor figure and abraded coats of

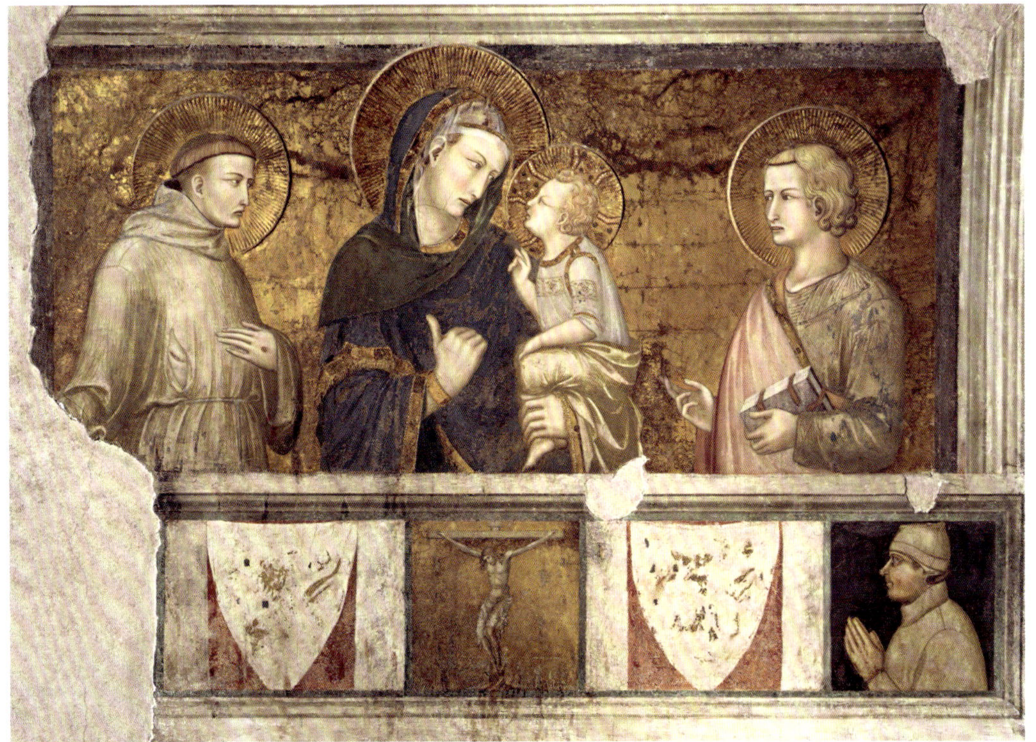

FIG. 55
Pietro Lorenzetti (documented possibly 1306; died probably 1348)
Fictive Retable with the Virgin and Child, Saints Francis and John the Evangelist, the Crucifixion and a Donor in Prayer (Walter VI of Brienne?), about 1322–3
Fresco
South transept, Lower Church, Basilica of San Francesco, Assisi

arms included in the fictive retable above the Saint John altar (fig. 55). The historical identification of the arms as belonging to Walter VI of Brienne, Duke of Athens (and tyrant of Florence in the 1340s), may well be correct, especially given the distinctive detail of the lions' double intertwined tails.[46] The Brienne family had been among the earliest donors at Assisi, but Walter was born in 1304 or 1305 and was still in his minority in 1319, making him an unlikely patron prior to the Ghibelline revolt of that year. The beardless donor figure may be taken as young but is not a child or youth. To consider Walter as a candidate for Lorenzetti's portrait we need to look forward into the 1320s, when he emerged as a significant figure in the Angevin court, marrying King Robert the Wise's niece Beatrice in 1321 and briefly ruling Florence in 1326 as vicar for Count Charles of Calabria.[47]

In fact, there are good stylistic reasons for identifying a break in the fresco scheme of the south transept. Joseph Archer Crowe and Giovanni Battista Cavalcaselle, the first to attribute the cycle to Pietro Lorenzetti in 1885, had already noted the stylistic differences between the lower scenes on the end wall – the *Deposition* and the *Entombment* – and those above.[48] Although Hayden Maginnis believed the cycle to have been completed in a single campaign, the technical evidence that he published in 1976 showed that the lower scenes were executed with fewer *giornate* and had much more extensive *a secco* additions in tempera.[49] The greater monumentality of their figures also suggests a greater assimilation of Giottesque models and contemporary sculpture.[50] While it is difficult to differentiate between the normal succession of *giornata* patches and more significant interruptions, there is a consistent horizontal divide in the *giornate* on the end wall between the two registers, just below the framing band.[51] The second phase of the transept campaign would have encompassed the *Deposition* and *Entombment*, the gallery of saints and illusionistic bench below, and the fictive retable of the Saint John altar around the corner. It can probably be dated to after the fall of Muzio's regime in March 1322, when the besieged city capitulated to the Perugians and a degree of order was restored.

Pietro's appearance in Arezzo to sign the contract for the Pieve Polyptych in April 1320 falls neatly into the gap created by the interruption of the Assisi commission. The Arezzo altarpiece is discussed in detail in the following essay (pp. 95–9), but we note here how the contract foregrounds the role played by Guido Tarlati, Bishop and Lord of Arezzo.

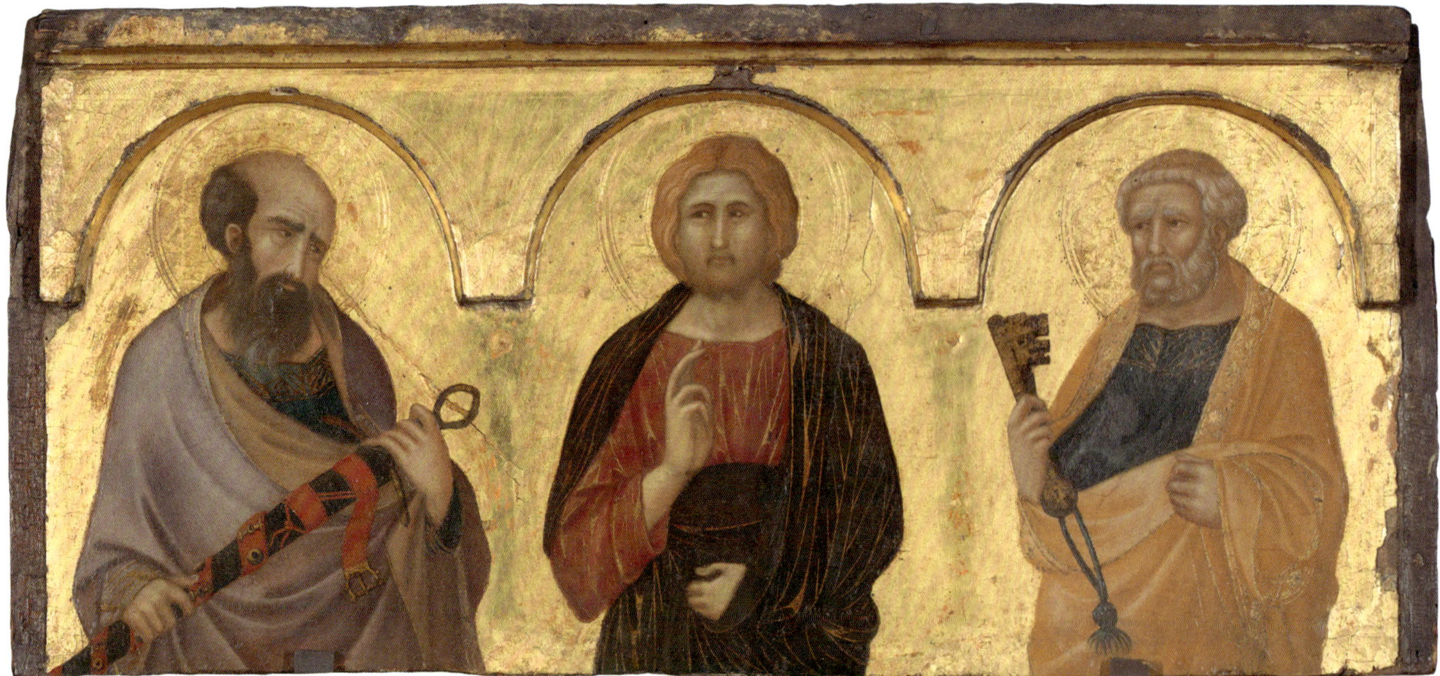

Tarlati was a close ally of Muzio in the wider struggle between rival Ghibelline and Guelph powers across central Italy; indeed, the bishop seems to have received some of the looted objects from the Assisi treasury.[52] Arranging the Pieve commission may have been a diplomatic solution between these Ghibelline allies to the problem of a painter who found himself suddenly out of work. In the 1320 contract Pietro is pointedly referred to as 'formerly of Siena' ('qui fuit de Senis'), which suggests he had not been based there for some time, but there is no indication that he had been residing in Arezzo.[53] More likely, he had moved there from Assisi for the prospect of the Pieve commission.[54]

The first signs of success in Pietro's native Siena may be traceable to the same years. Carl Strehlke has argued that the *Virgin and Child enthroned* (about 1320–3; Philadelphia Museum of Art) should be identified as the central panel from the high altarpiece of Santa Maria dei Servi in Siena, for which the Servite friars sought subsidies from the Sienese government in October 1319 (funds that were duly paid until 1323).[55] The Philadelphia picture has been associated with the recently discovered panel of *Christ between Saints Paul and Peter* (fig. 56).[56]

Pietro's real breakthrough in his hometown, however, was once more thanks to the Franciscans, and may again have arrived via the offices of Fra Jacopo del Tondo.[57] Fra Jacopo had already been guardian of San Francesco, Siena, at the end of the 1290s and by 1322 had re-established himself as one of the convent's senior friars following his term as Provincial Minister in Umbria. He is prominent in the documents that paved the way for the laying of the foundation stone for a vast new Church of San Francesco in 1326, one that would vie with Santa Croce in Florence for pre-eminence in the Tuscan province.[58] The new church was a long-term project and in the short term the Sienese friars focused their artistic patronage on their chapter house. The task of hosting the Tuscan province's annual chapter meetings was dominated by Florence and Siena in the 1320s, and both Franciscan houses decorated their chapter houses with frescoes in these years.[59] In Siena Pietro worked alongside his younger brother Ambrogio to fresco the space. Pietro was responsible for the central wall facing the entrance, and Ambrogio the two end walls. The frescoes were discovered beneath plaster and detached in the 1850s.[60]

Ambrogio's scenes focused on the sainted figures of the order: Francis presenting his friars and the Clarissans with their respective rules (a fragment of which survives, see fig. 210), the profession of Louis of Toulouse, the martyrdom

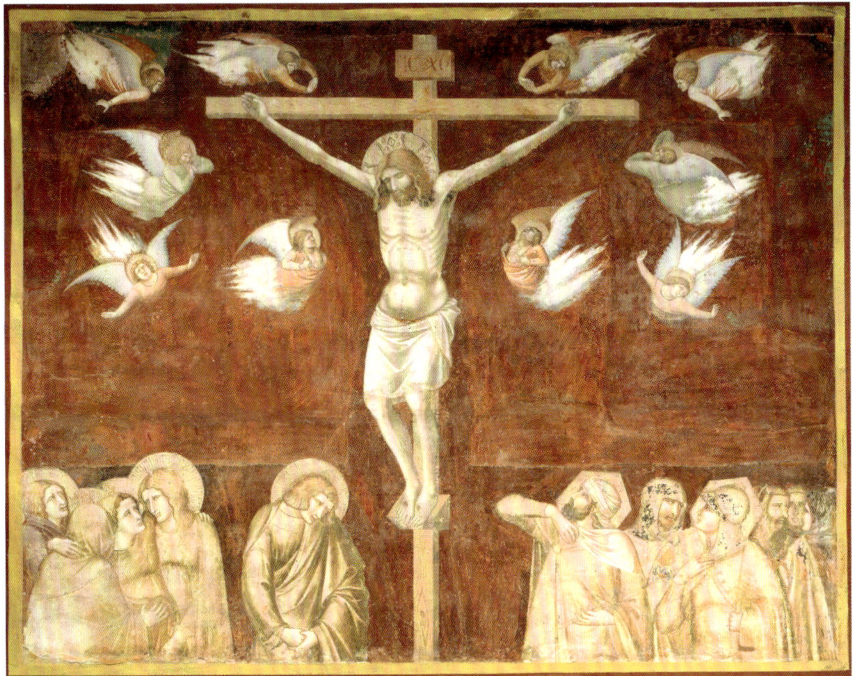

FIG. 56
Pietro Lorenzetti (documented possibly 1306; died probably 1348)
Christ between Saints Paul and Peter, about 1315–20
Tempera on panel, 32.2 × 70.4 cm
Ferens Art Gallery: Hull Museums (2013.125)

FIG. 57
Pietro Lorenzetti (documented possibly 1306; died probably 1348)
The Crucifixion, about 1325
Detached fresco
San Francesco, Siena, formerly chapter house

of the Franciscan missionaries, and a fourth scene that does not survive, probably related to Saint Anthony of Padua.[61] Pietro's subjects were more conventional: a central *Crucifixion* (fig. 57) with a *Resurrection* to the right – the scene to the left does not survive but is likely to have been a *Way to Calvary*. The allocation of the Passion scenes to Pietro may have been informed by the impact of his Assisi cycle on a Franciscan audience. The *Crucifixion* has lost its lower section but retains its emotional force: the crowds present in the Assisi *Crucifixion* are here pared back to the essential protagonists. The tormented angels draw on Giotto, notably the angel tearing its robe in rage. The Virgin seems to collapse between her companions and the consoling hand on her belly indicates that she is experiencing the pains of labour that she had been miraculously spared at Christ's birth.[62] Two figurative medallions survive from the framing bands: a bust of Saint Elizabeth of Hungary set in a hexagonal field (fig. 58) and another of the Virgin (fig. 59), whose hand raised in surprise or alarm identifies her as the Virgin of the Annunciation who would have been paired with another medallion of the Archangel Gabriel.[63] Her frame is a more complex cusped quatrefoil and she was probably set at an intersecting corner in the scheme, perhaps to the top right of the *Crucifixion*.

More work in Siena followed: the high altar for another mendicant order, the Carmelites, in 1327–9, and then – finally – major civic commissions for Santa Maria della Scala and the cathedral in the 1330s.[64] Both Pietro and his brother continued to win commissions in Florence: Sienese penetration of the Florentine artistic arena stands in marked contrast to the total absence of Florentine artists from Siena in this period.[65] But the recognition Pietro received in his later career should not eclipse his earlier years as a largely peripatetic painter, moving with his commissions from town to town during the 1310s. Indeed, the formative experiences of those years – both the exposure to different artistic traditions across central Italy and the networks he forged among his ecclesiastical patrons – in some ways facilitated his later success. Pietro's trajectory suggests the intensity of the Sienese art market in a period when the city was a net exporter in the visual arts. He had to wait until the mid-1320s (and probably aged over 40) before he was firmly established in his hometown, and for many years he could not compete with Simone Martini's grip on civic projects. Simone is sometimes thought to have been left-handed;[66] if so, Pietro's 'dextra' signatures in Cortona and Arezzo may well have carried an additional barb of professional rivalry.[67]

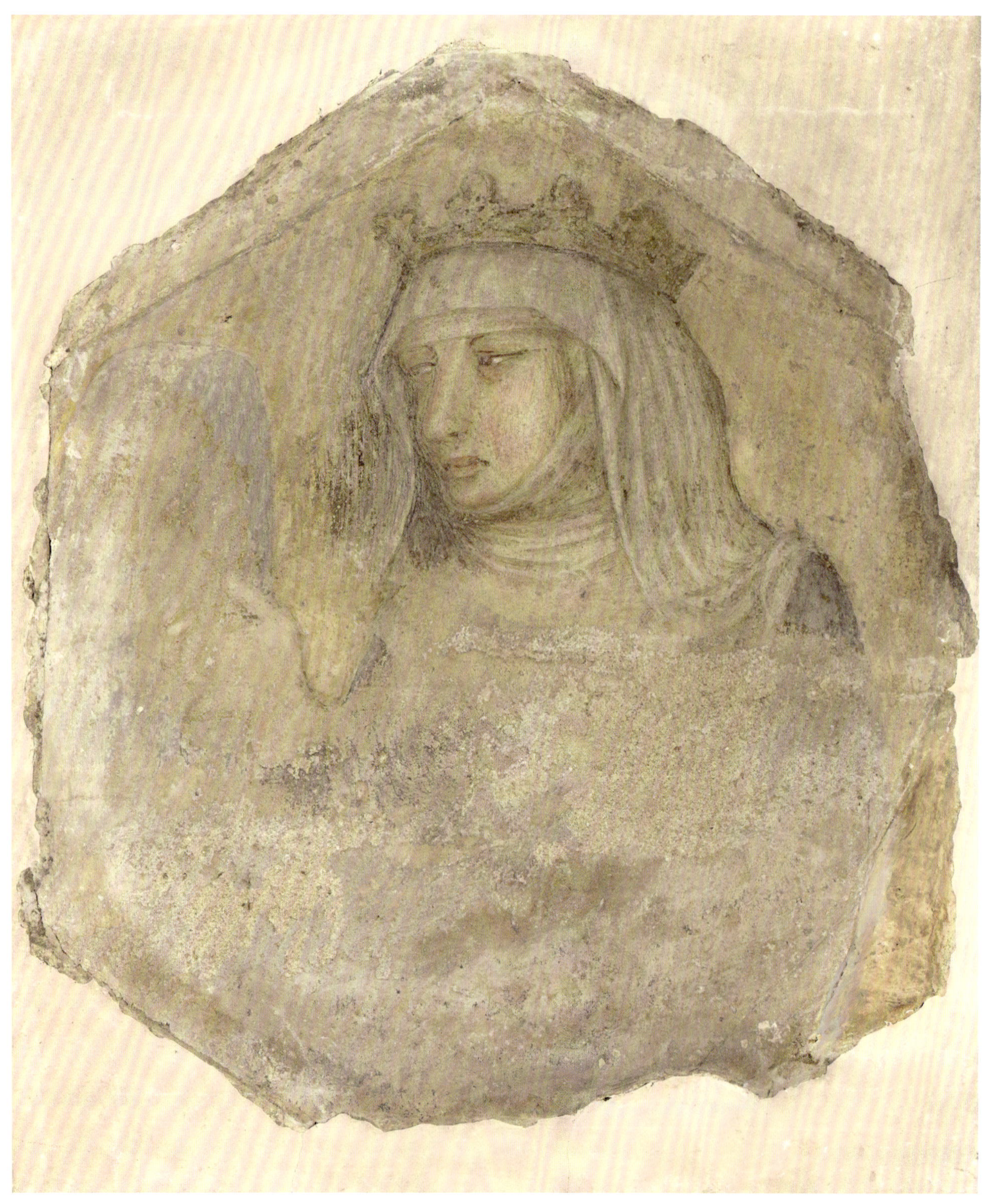

FIG. 58
Pietro Lorenzetti (documented possibly 1306; died probably 1348)
A Crowned Female Figure (Saint Elizabeth of Hungary?),
about 1325
Fresco with areas of secco, 38 × 33 cm
The National Gallery, London. Layard Bequest, 1916 (NG3071)

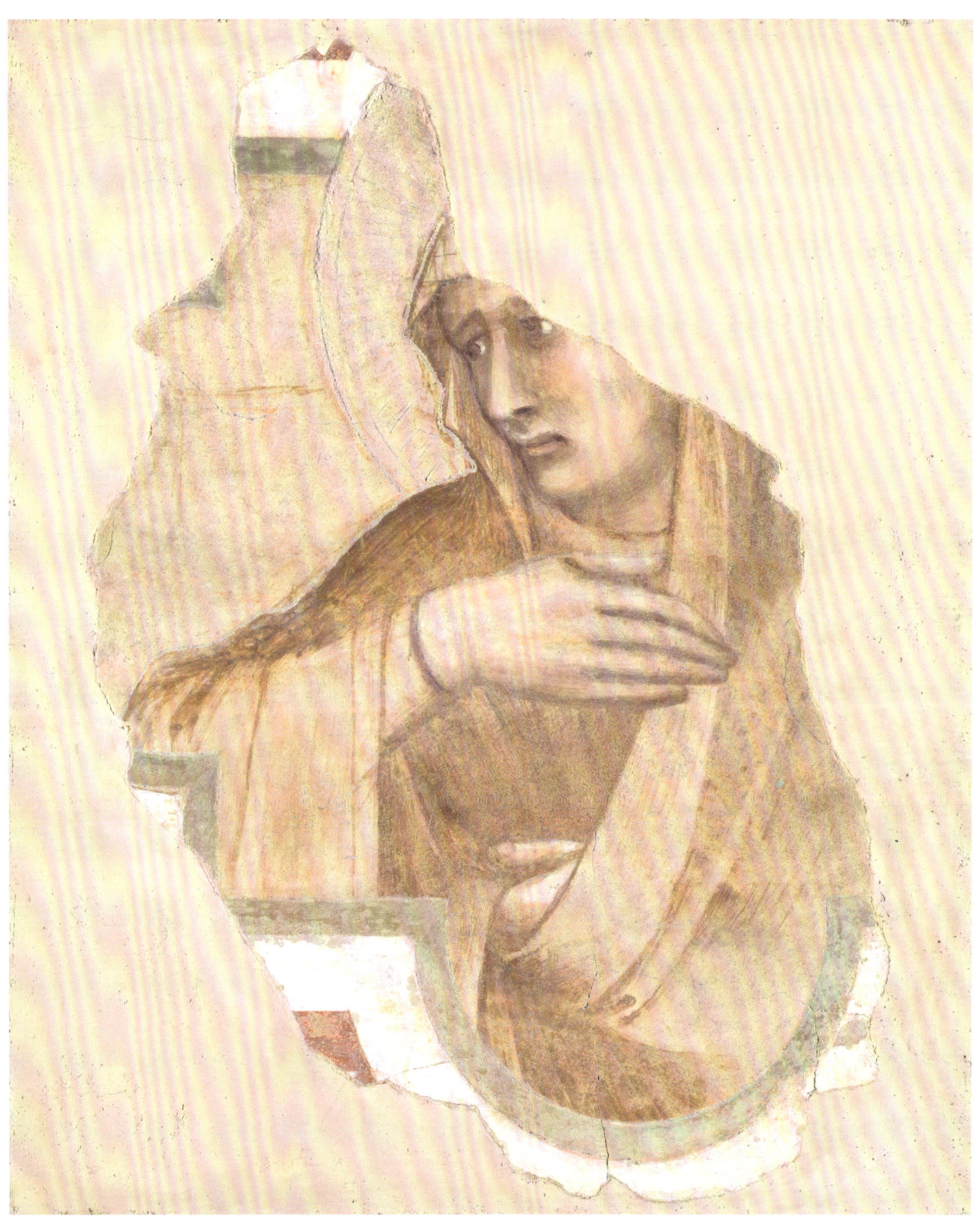

FIG. 59
Pietro Lorenzetti (documented possibly 1306; died probably 1348)
The Annunciate Virgin,
about 1325
Fresco with areas of secco, 39 × 30 cm
The National Gallery, London. Layard Bequest, 1916 (NG3072)

This essay is dedicated to the memory of Janet Robson, who would have relished writing it and whose insight its authors greatly missed. We are grateful to Machtelt Brüggen Israëls, Giovanni Giura, Jeffrey Hamburger, Christopher Platts, Carl Brandon Strehlke and Lucy Wrapson for assistance and advice when preparing this material, and to Joanna Cannon for her close reading of the text. For the sections on Pietro in Arezzo we are much indebted to the scholarship and generosity of Isabella Droandi, who sadly died as this catalogue was being edited for publication.

1. Ghiberti before 1455 (1998), pp. 87–9.
2. Vasari 1550 (1967), pp. 131–4; Vasari 1568 (1996), pp. 131–4.
3. Caffio 2017–18 (the order of the inscription is generally taken as confirmation that Pietro was the elder brother).
4. Inv. 445.
5. Vasari 1550 (1967), p. 143.
6. On Vasari's renovations at the Pieve, see Cornelison 2021.
7. English translation from Vasari 1568 (1996), p. 133.
8. Strehlke 2004, p. 213, argues that under Sienese law Pietro should have been aged at least 25 to receive this payment in 1306, implying a birth date around 1280. The sum of money (1 lire, 10 soldi) was small; for comparisons see Maginnis 2001, pp. 61–73. For recent monographic treatments of Pietro's life and works, see Monciatti 2002; Strehlke 2004, pp. 213–15; Becchis 2012; Laclotte 2015. Among older studies, Seidel 1981 and Volpe 1989 remain valuable.
9. For Pietro's Monticchiello altarpiece, see Israëls 2015a (with a dating to about 1315). For the Castiglione d'Orcia *Virgin and Child*, see Siddi in Siena 2017–18, cat. 3, pp. 110–13 (with a dating to about 1310–15).
10. Strehlke 2004, p. 214, n. 1.
11. Laclotte in Siena 2003–4, cat. 69, pp. 406–7; De Benedictis in Gubbio 2018, cat. 34, pp. 230–1.
12. Inv. 8344.
13. Strehlke 2004, p. 213, suggests a civic dimension to the commission, linked to Cortona's achievement of independence from nearby Arezzo, granted by Emperor Henry VII.
14. On the devotional nature of Duccio's signature on the *Maestà*, see Cannon 2010, pp. 28–31.
15. Platts 2024 (forthcoming). We are grateful to the author for sharing his text prior to publication.
16. For further consideration of its likely format, see De Marchi 2024 (forthcoming).
17. For Memmo's retable for Santa Chiara, San Gimignano, see Cooper 2021, pp. 29–31.
18. For the cross, see Volpe 1989, pp. 119–21; Monciatti 2002, pp. 60–1.
19. For scaled comparisons, see the useful graphic by Utari in Gubbio 2018, pp. 134–5.
20. On Segna's Arezzo cross as a latest possible date for Pietro's Cortona crucifix, see Strehlke 2004, p. 213 (the association with Pietro's Cortona cross having been made by Stubblebine 1979, vol. 1, p. 133). The 1319 document is correctly transcribed by Salmi 1912, p. 34, and Guerrini 1988, p. 11.
21. Gordon 2011, pp. 414–17.
22. For a different reading, considering the starred terminals on Pietro's Cortona crucifix and Segna's Arezzo cross as reflections of Simone Martini's San Casciano crucifix (dating the latter as early as about 1316), see Bagnoli 2022, pp. 16–22; for Ambrogio Lorenzetti's Montenero d'Orcia cross, see Amato in Siena 2017–18, cat. 8, pp. 152–5 (with a dating to about 1320–5).
23. For further discussion of cross and star patterns, see Monnas, p. 201, in the present volume.
24. For the cut-out cross, see Amato in Siena 2017–18, cat. 4, pp. 114–19 (with a dating to about 1315–20).
25. On the fictive images in the *Verification* fresco, see Cooper and Robson 2013, pp. 72–4; Bokody 2015, pp. 82–3, 113–14. It is possible, however, that the cut-out image depicted in Giotto's fresco could have been fashioned from less durable materials. A series of later cut-out angels painted on paper and cloth mounted on card, attributable to a Florentine artist active in the third quarter of the fifteenth century, may indicate a more widespread genre: see Parenti in Boskovits and Fossaluzza 1998, nos 10–11, pp. 84–6.
26. The closest analogy from the period is the rather larger (315 × 173 cm) cut-out crucifix painted on both sides with the donor figure of Cardinal Godin embracing the cross, sometimes attributed to the Master of the San Giorgio Codex and dated to about 1324–34, from the Dominican church in Toulouse and now in the Musée des Augustins, Toulouse (inv. 49 6 15); see Testi Cristiani 1990.
27. For the provenance from San Girolamo, see Amato in Siena 2017–18, cat. 4, p. 114.
28. On crucifixes in nunnery choir spaces (citing examples from Umbria and the Marche), see Zappasodi 2018, pp. 92–4.
29. For the provenance of the cross from San Marco, see De Marchi 2024 (forthcoming).
30. An unpublished testament from the mid-fifteenth century records the presence of a crucifix in San Marco large enough to have a lamp hung in front of it; on 6 November 1448 Archdeacon Benedetto requested burial 'in dicta ecclesia [San Marco] sub figura et lampade Crucifixi'; for this document, see Cooper 2024 (forthcoming). It is possible, however, that the crucifix could already have been removed from its original location by that date. Giotto's crucifix in Santa Maria Novella had been transferred from that church's *tramezzo* screen to the transept by 1421; see De Marchi 2009, p. 607.
31. For the building history of San Francesco, Cortona, see Giura 2018, pp. 80–92, with further discussion in Giura 2024 (forthcoming) and Cooper 2024 (forthcoming). In the 1583 apostolic visitation of Cortona, San Marco was said to be 'almost adjacent' ('fere est contigua') to San Francesco; see Peruzzi 1583 (2012), p. 49.
32. Giura 2018, pp. 83–92, convincingly argues that the late thirteenth-century panel crucifix traditionally associated with San Francesco (now in the Accademia Etrusca, Cortona, attributed to the Maestro delle Croci Loeser-Cortona) is too small to have served as a nave cross for the current church.
33. A proposal noted with some scepticism by Amato in Siena 2017–18, cat. 4, p. 116.
34. Cardinal Napoleone never returned to Italy after relocating to Avignon in about 1310. Schmidt 2005a, p. 260, argues that he nonetheless retained an active interest in artistic projects at Assisi and elsewhere from a distance through correspondence and intermediary agents.
35. On Fra Jacopo del Tondo, see Cooper 2022.
36. Bagnoli 1999, pp. 67–8, 71, established that Simone Martini's Palazzo Pubblico *Maestà*, completed in 1315, shows knowledge of the 'Vele', while Romano 2015 convincingly dates Giotto's campaign in the north transept to 1310–13.
37. Lunghi 2012, p. 188, suggests that the threat of flooding in 1311 may have disrupted the fresco campaign in the Lower Church. It is more likely that the Giotto workshop was called away to Rome for a series of prestigious commissions at St Peter's.
38. Much of the dating debate turns on how firmly one considers the long-expected canonisation of Louis of Toulouse in April 1317 as the earliest possible date for his representation as a saint. Norman 2010b, p. 307, argues that his canonisation had been confidently awaited by the Franciscans for several years before 1317 (although the repainting of the entrance arch indicates that his presence in the Saint Martin chapel was not envisaged at the outset). Emphasising Fra Jacopo's role does not necessarily contradict the hypothesis that Cardinal Gentile da Montefiore, patron of the Saint Martin chapel in the Lower Church, may have encountered Simone when passing through Siena in April 1312; for discussion and bibliography, see Cooper 2022, pp. 107–8. For an alternative timeline for Simone at Assisi, see Bagnoli 1999,

p. 142, with further discussion on pp. 66–72, 120–4.

39. For a detailed account of Lorenzetti's Assisi frescoes, see Volpe 1989, pp. 60–107.
40. On the Saint Lucy panel, see Boskovits 1986, pp. 7–8; Volpe 1989, p. 205. The year 1316 recorded in a later drawing on the elaborate Beata Umiltà Altarpiece for the Florentine nunnery of the Faenza is usually discounted as a transcription error; for the arguments in favour of a dating of about 1330, see Boskovits 1988, pp. 85–91; Demaria 2021.
41. For the overarching conceptual and composition unity of the transept scheme, see Robson 2005.
42. On the flow of pilgrims through the Lower Church, see Cooper 2005.
43. This section develops arguments first presented by De Marchi 2010, pp. 622, 625–6, nn. 30–3.
44. Muzio's seizure of power formed part of a wider struggle across central Italy that pitched Ghibelline (broadly pro-imperial) factions against their Guelph (broadly pro-papal) rivals. On Muzio's brief rule, see Brufani 1989.
45. For a dissenting view, see Strehlke 2004, p. 213.
46. For Fra Ludovico da Pietralunga's late sixteenth-century account, see Pietralunga before 1580 (1982), p. 77.
47. Becchis 2012, pp. 90–1, repeats the case for Brienne's patronage without citing De Marchi (Becchis's book lacks footnotes), but dates the entirety of Pietro's activity at Assisi to the period after 1324, probably to about 1326–7.
48. Crowe and Cavalcaselle 1885, pp. 184–6; De Marchi 2010, pp. 622, 625, n. 30.
49. The term *giornate* describes the separate patches of plaster applied to the wall surface that were then painted while still wet according to the true fresco technique (one *giornata* is sometimes taken to represent a day's painting). Artists could then add extra details once the plaster had dried (*a secco*). Maginnis 1976, p. 204, remarks on 'the large size of the *giornate* and their limited number' in these two scenes, 'possible only because of the limited amount of true fresco used or, in other words, the large amount of [*a secco*] tempera'.
50. On Pietro's debt to Giotto, see Seidel 1981, pp. 144–54.
51. Maginnis 1976, pp. 203–4, figs 9, 10.
52. On Tarlati's backing for the spoliation of the papal treasury, see Guerrini 1988, echoed by Becchis 2012, p. 36.
53. Becchis 2012, p. 36, draws a contrast to Segna di Bonaventura, similarly documented as 'fuit de Senis' in Arezzo in 1319, but with the supplementary 'et nunc moratur Aretii' ('and now resident in Arezzo').
54. Pietro is cited in Arezzo on 21 September 1321 as a witness to a testament alongside two Sienese painters, Mino di Vollia and Mino di Pace, who may have been his assistants, see Droandi 2005, pp. 43–4. The scale of the Assisi campaign would certainly have required a workshop.
55. Strehlke 2004, pp. 219–21, with relevant documents at pp. 467–9. The presence of a Servite friar as donor strengthens the case for the Philadelphia panel, but the artist is not named in the communal sources. For an alternative proposal linking the payments with a *Virgin and Child* by Segna di Bonaventura still in Santa Maria dei Servi, see Padovani 1979, p. 87, n. 8.
56. Further technical examination is required to confirm whether, and if so how, the Ferens and Philadelphia panels formed part of the same altarpiece. Another early commission from nearby Siena must have been the panel of Saint Leonard now in the Abegg Stiftung, Riggisberg, probably painted for the Augustinian hermitage at San Leonardo al Lago: see Seidel 1985, pp. 114–29 (with a date around 1325). Saint Leonard's halo is realised freehand without the benefit of punch-marks, suggesting an earlier date than hitherto thought, perhaps even around 1316.
57. Another Franciscan commission from this phase of Pietro's career is likely to be the *Crucifixion* (about 1318) in the Harvard Art Museums (inv. 1943.119), now the subject of a comprehensive study by Hamburger (forthcoming). This stand-alone devotional panel depicts both saints Clare and Francis kneeling at the foot of the Cross. Hamburger argues that it was painted for a Clarissan audience; for Jacopo del Tondo's interest in the Poor Clares, see Cooper 2022, pp. 95–7. We are very grateful to Jeffrey Hamburger for the chance to read his text prior to publication.
58. Fra Jacopo del Tondo featured prominently in the 1322 testament of Nello de' Pannocchieschi, with responsibility for overseeing (alongside his fellow Franciscan Pietro da Monterio) Nello's substantial bequest for building the main chapel of San Francesco and the decoration of its altar; see Cooper 2022, p. 98.
59. For the early decoration of the sacristy chapter house at Santa Croce, attributed to Jacopo da Casentino, see Zappasodi 2010. The sequence of Tuscan provincial chapters in the 1320s can be reconstructed as follows from the account books of Franciscan inquisitors preserved in the Vatican (Archivio Segreto Vaticano, *Collectoriae* 249 and 250): Florence 1320; Cortona 1321; Montepulciano 1322; Siena 1323; Florence 1327; Siena 1328; Florence 1329 (the registers omit the years 1324 to 1326).
60. For the Siena chapter-house frescoes, see Testa and Interguglielmi 2017–18 (with extensive discussion of the previous literature). For an alternative analysis dating the scheme much later to 1343–4, see Norman 2018, pp. 191–226.
61. For the fragment of Ambrogio Lorenzetti's rule-giving scene (the earliest known example of this iconography), see Gordon 2011, pp. 284–6, and Testa and Interguglielmi 2017–18, pp. 140–2, with reconstruction of the scheme on p. 134, fig. 3. In a sermon given in 1427, San Bernardino described an ecstatic image of Saint Francis in the chapter house, where the saint was portrayed 'lifted outside of himself and transformed by God'; see Norman 2018, p. 201. This has been read as referring to a *Stigmatisation*, but it could also have been an *Apparition of Saint Francis at Arles*, which would have allowed the friars to include Saint Anthony of Padua (who was giving a sermon when the vision occurred) in the scheme. Set in a chapter house, the scene would also have been highly appropriate for the space.
62. For this iconographic tradition, see Neff 1998.
63. Misidentified as a mourning Virgin by Testa and Interguglielmi 2017–18, pp. 132, 135; already recognised as a Virgin Annunciate in Gordon 2011, pp. 299–304.
64. For the Carmelite altarpiece, see Cannon 1987; for the Santa Maria della Scala frescoes, see Caffio 2017–18; for Pietro's *Nativity of the Virgin* for the altar of Saint Sabinus in the Duomo, commissioned in 1335 but only completed in 1342, see De Marchi in Siena 2010, cat. B.1, pp. 148–9; Gordon 2011, pp. 288–98. Both the Lorenzetti brothers in Siena must have benefited from Simone Martini's departure for Avignon in the mid-1330s (in 1335 or even as early as 1334).
65. The Beata Umiltà Altarpiece is datable to about 1330, although see above, n. 40.
66. For technical evidence suggesting Simone was left-handed, see Muller 2012, pp. 167–8, n. 35 (citing communications with Joseph Polzer), to which we may add the sequence of *giornata* patches on the Palazzo Pubblico *Maestà*, mapped in Bagnoli 1999, p. 172, grafico n. 2, as starting at top right, 'contrariamente alla norma' ('contrary to the norm').
67. This deduction was reached in conversation with Joanna Cannon and Lucy Wrapson.

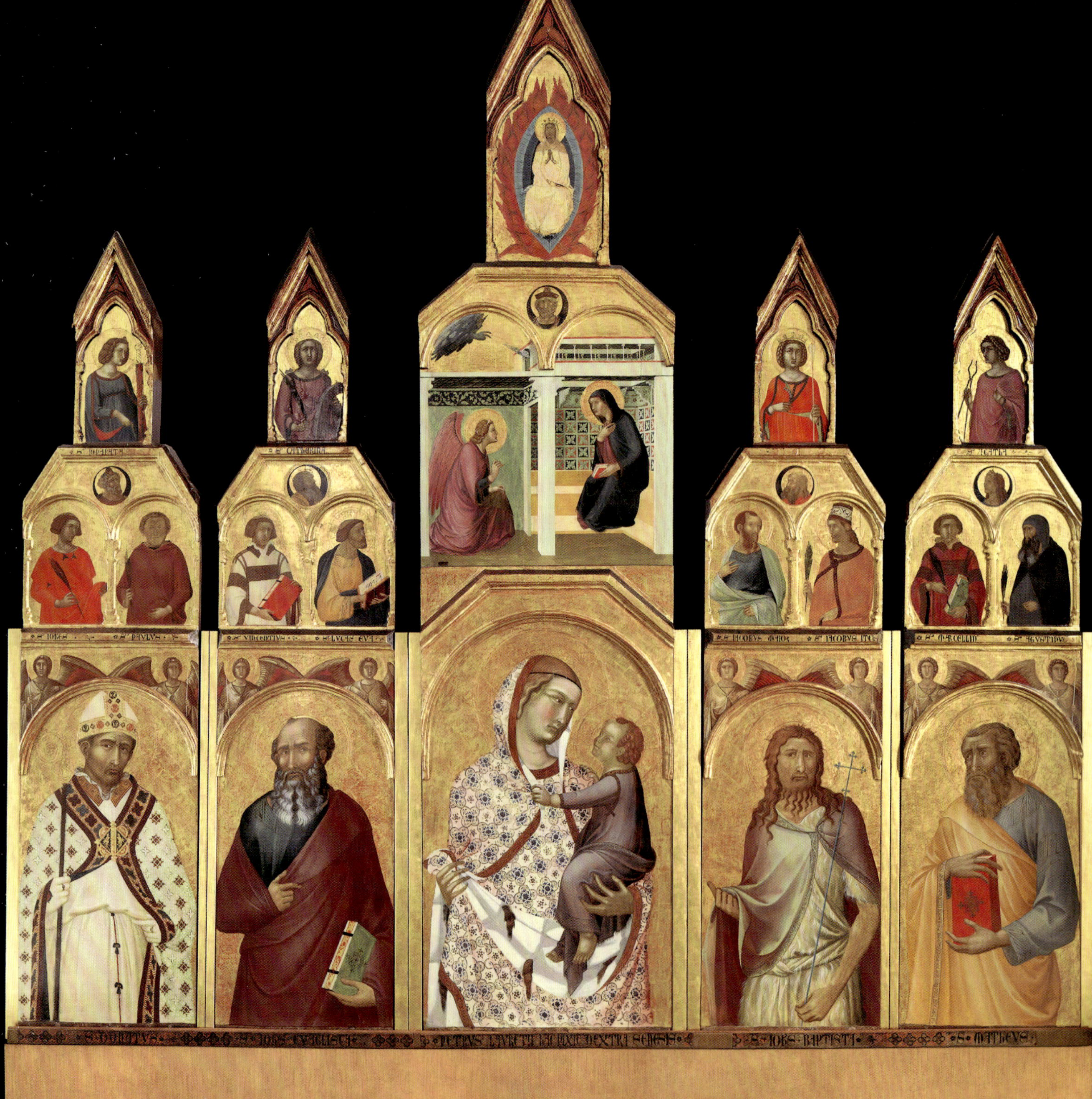

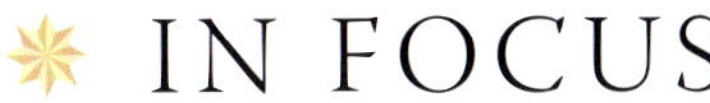

Pietro Lorenzetti's Pieve Polyptych

Donal Cooper and Andrea De Marchi

On 17 April 1320 Pietro Lorenzetti signed a contract with Guido Tarlati, the bishop and de facto ruler of Arezzo, to paint an altarpiece for the Church of Santa Maria in the city, generally known as the 'Pieve'. The commission resulted in the large polyptych still owned by the bishopric of Arezzo and exceptionally loaned to the exhibition this volume accompanies. Pietro's Pieve altarpiece is of central importance for our understanding of Sienese painting in the years following the completion of Duccio's cathedral *Maestà*.[1] As Pietro's first securely dated work, it provides the chronological linchpin for all interpretations of the artist's early career. Alongside Simone Martini's polyptych for Santa Caterina, Pisa (see fig. 44), Pietro's Arezzo commission marks the evolution of the altarpiece format in the wake of the *Maestà* in the hands of the next generation of Sienese artists. The Pieve Polyptych can also be analysed in light of Pietro's 1320 agreement with Bishop Tarlati, one of the earliest surviving contracts for an Italian altarpiece.[2]

According to that document, Pietro promised to paint an altarpiece which was to be 6 *braccia* (about 350 cm) wide and 6 *braccia* high at its central point. The structure would also incorporate two 'columpnae', which – as Christa Gardner von Teuffel demonstrates – were lateral buttresses to stabilise the vertical structure.[3] On the main register Pietro was to paint a Virgin and Child at the centre with two saints on either side, using the best gold, silver and colours, including ultramarine for the blue. In addition, he was to paint figures of prophets and saints in the other fields of the altarpiece and further figures on the 'columpnae'.[4] The figures would be chosen by Bishop Guido, who promised to provide Pietro with the wooden support for the painting. The support was clearly yet to be constructed when the contract was agreed, and the close integration of figures and framing elements in the final work suggests that the artist may have been involved in its design. Once the panel was ready, Pietro committed to working on the altarpiece without interruption and without taking on other commissions until its completion.

The central axis of the altarpiece is dominated by images of the Virgin, reflecting the Marian

FIG. 60
Pietro Lorenzetti
(documented possibly 1306; died probably 1348)
Pieve Polyptych,
about 1320
Tempera on panel,
312 × 295 × 9 cm
Chiesa di Santa Maria della Pieve, Arezzo

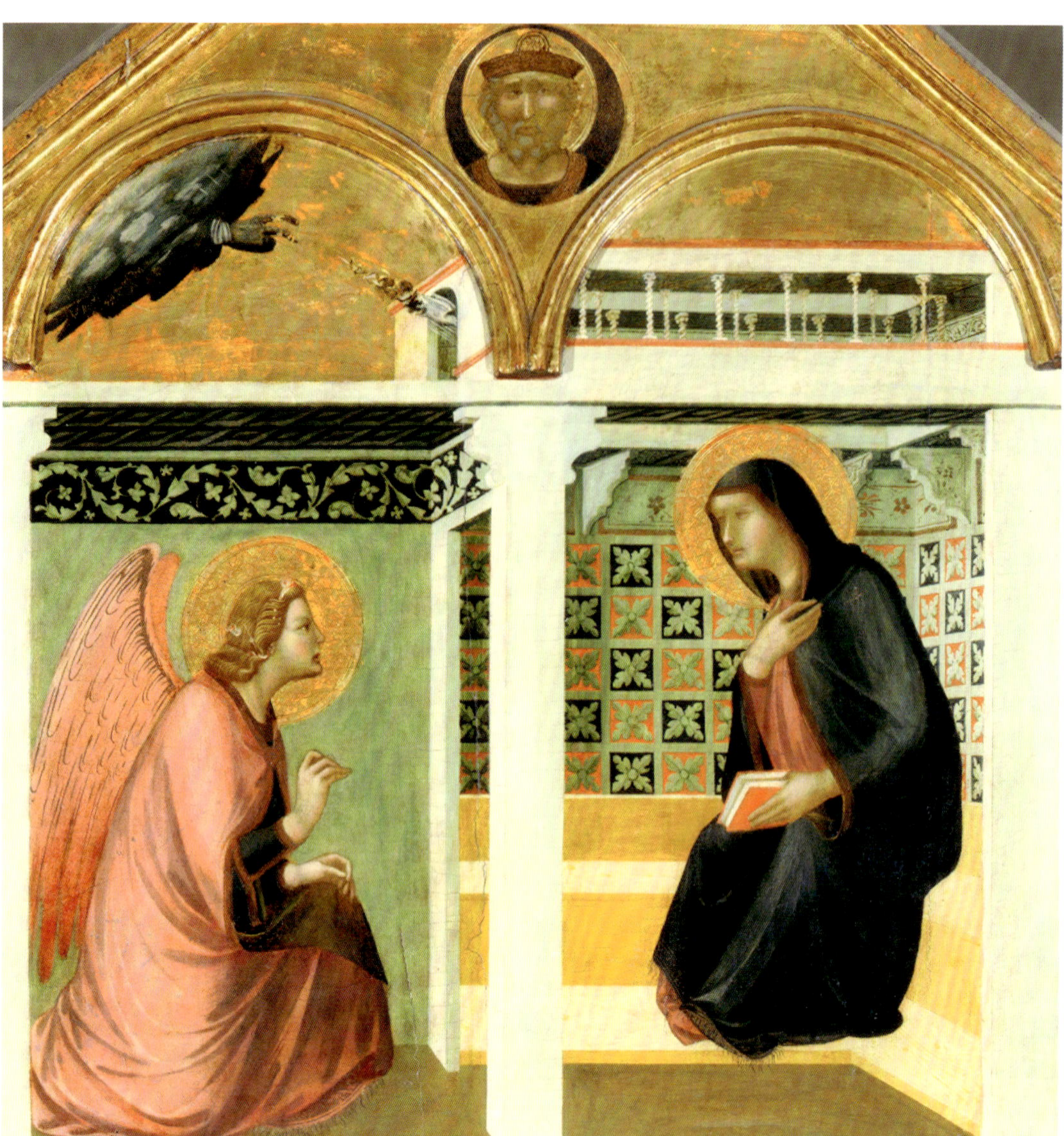

FIG. 61
Detail of the Annunciation

dedication of the Pieve: the Virgin and Child at the centre of the main register are surmounted by the Annunciation in the upper register and the Assumption in the central pinnacle. As Giovanni Freni demonstrates, the choice of saints reflected relics and cults venerated in the Pieve and the Arezzo diocese, and Pietro identified all of them clearly for the viewer with prominent inscriptions.[5] In the main register is Saint Donatus, Arezzo's principal patron saint, whose relics and cult were divided (and in some respects contested) between the Pieve and the city's cathedral. On the upper register is Saint Vincent, patron of nearby Cortona; the rarely depicted Persian martyr James Intercisus was venerated at an altar in the Pieve itself, which boasted an arm relic of the saint; relics of the obscure Tuscan martyrs Augustinus and Marcellinus were held below the Pieve's high altar. The contract specified that the bishop would choose the images for the altarpiece, and he selected a gallery of saints that articulated and underlined the sanctity of the Pieve and of his diocese.

On the central axis Pietro cleverly framed his image of the Annunciation with a double arch to match the paired saints to either side. He used gesture to smooth the transition between the architectural setting of the Annunciation and the adjacent figures. To the right, as Freni observed, Saint James's raised right hand echoes that of the Virgin. To the left, Saint Luke – whose gospel recounts the Annunciation

– gazes up at the scene but also marks his place in his open book, as if the vision has interrupted his reading (again echoing the Virgin, who has closed her book at the arrival of Archangel Gabriel).[6] In the roundels between the saints Pietro included four prophets, whose words were commonly understood as prefigurations of Christ's Incarnation, gazing towards the Annunciation.

In the Annunciation itself, Pietro used a plausibly constructed architectural space to stage the story. The double arch rests on a painted pilaster dividing the Virgin's chamber from the antechamber where Gabriel kneels. The architecture recedes into space, although not to a true vanishing point (a device Pietro would deploy in his later altarpiece of the *Birth of the Virgin* for Siena Cathedral).[7] The recession is slightly offset from the central access, creating an asymmetry that Pietro exploited to show a doorway connecting the two spaces. The Virgin's chamber is enriched with a grid pattern containing alternating blue and red rosettes, while the antechamber has a foliate frieze inspired by ancient reliefs. The building is topped by a clerestory raised on delicately sketched spiral columns and with a strategically placed aperture that allows the dove of the Holy Spirit, descending from the upper left with clouds trailing in its wake, to enter the Virgin's chamber. Compared to Duccio's Annunciation from the *Maestà*, Pietro used architecture in a much more sophisticated fashion to structure the narrative and stress the well-known metaphor of the Virgin as a window in pictorial and spatial terms – an approach he would have seen first-hand in Giotto's frescoes at Assisi.[8] A remarkable detail is the *dextera Dei* – God's blessing right hand, a relatively archaic feature by this date – emerging from the clouds at the upper left and taking their atmospheric form and blue colour. The scene is fittingly overseen by the crowned bust of the royal prophet David in the roundel above.

In the uppermost pinnacles Pietro depicted four female martyrs and a central Assumption of the Virgin, which may reflect the lost Assumption that crowned Duccio's *Maestà*. While the lower tiers are framed with round arches, the pinnacles have pointed arches, following the latest Gothic architectural motifs that Pietro would have known from the new facade of Siena Cathedral (see fig. 5). Simone Martini deployed similarly pointed arches

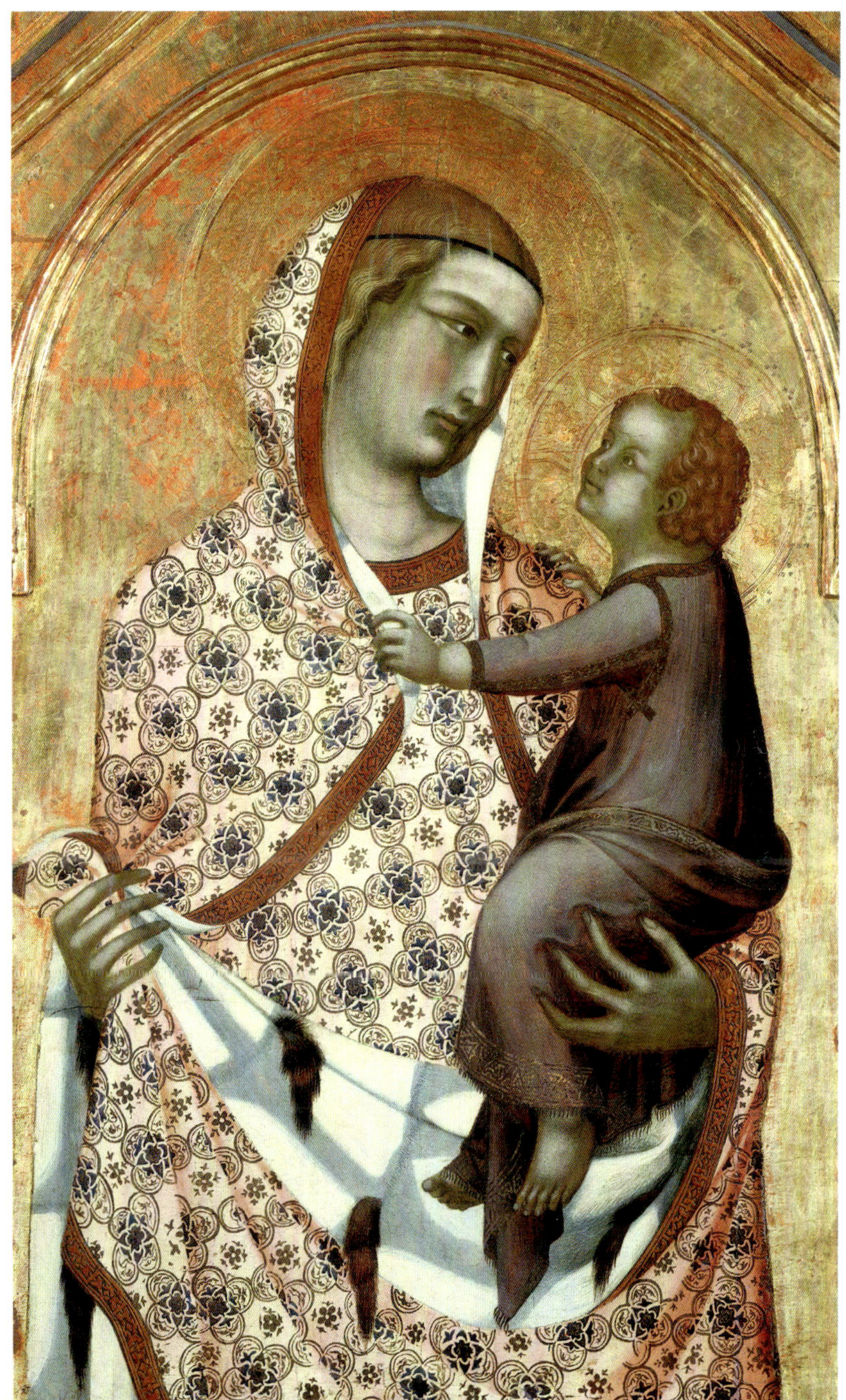

FIG. 62
Detail of the Virgin and Child

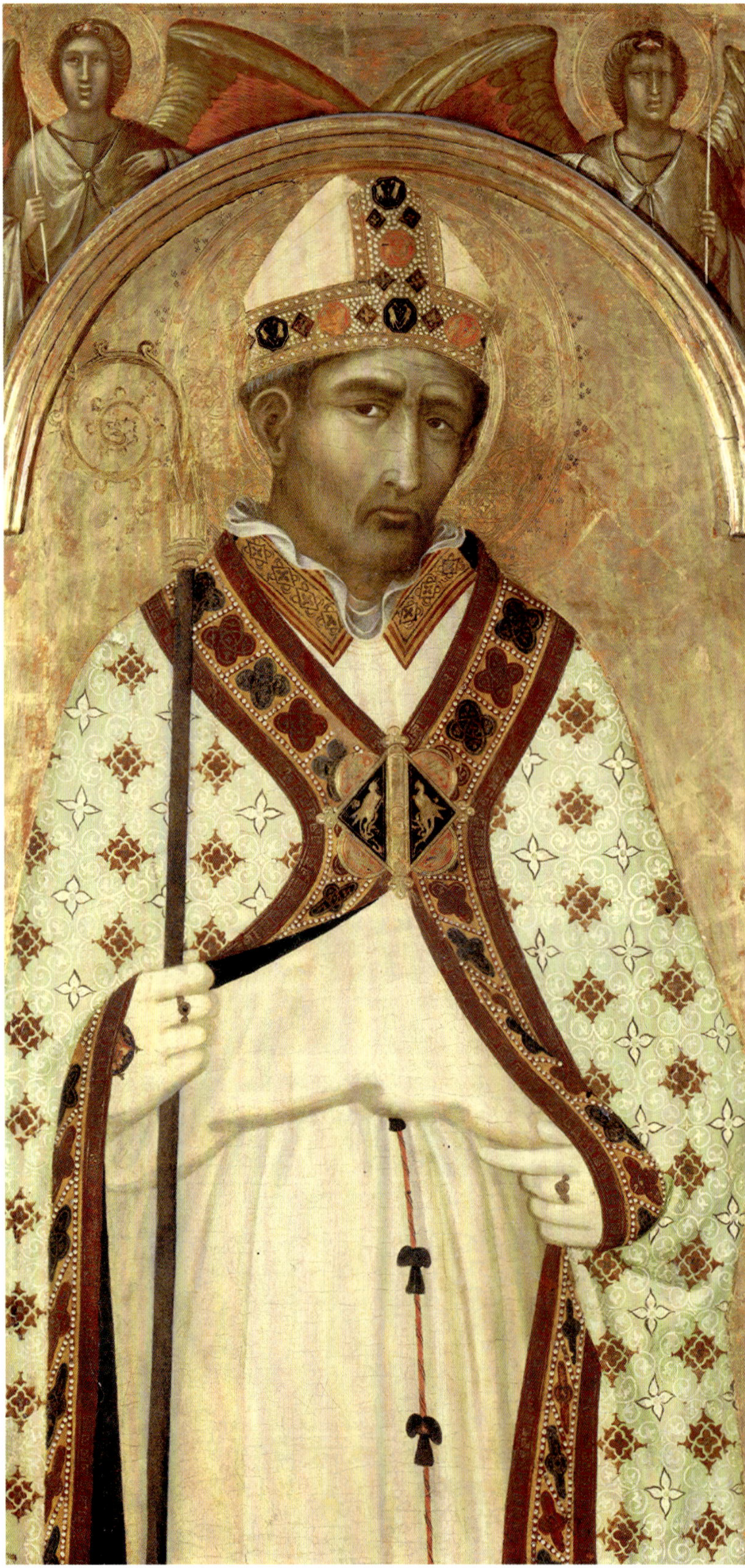

FIG. 63
Detail of Saint Donatus

on his Orvieto altarpieces, and it would become a dominant feature of fourteenth-century Tuscan altarpiece design.[9] Here it allowed Pietro to accentuate the verticality of his altarpiece, which had to compete with the lofty central apse of the Pieve.

According to Giorgio Vasari's first-hand description in the 1568 edition of his *Lives*, the altarpiece originally possessed a predella below the main saints. Vasari's description is vague – he refers only to 'many little figures' – and it is impossible to know for certain whether the predella depicted more saints or a narrative cycle (although the 1320 contract specified saints and prophets rather than narrative scenes).[10] One proposal for the predella is based on two related fragments attributed to Pietro: the *Pietà* now in La Spezia and a *Saint Anthony Abbot* in a private collection.[11] According to this reconstruction, the *Pietà* would have been the predella's central element, reflecting the Eucharistic liturgy of the altar, with the Saint Anthony positioned below one of the left-hand saints. When considering this proposal, it is important to note that the two candidate fragments are painted on vertical supports, rather than the horizontal boards one would expect for a predella box extending across the width of the altarpiece (as was the case with Duccio's *Maestà*). If the pair did form part of the Arezzo predella, their carpentry implies that the main vertical panels of the altarpiece extended downwards to incorporate the predella below.[12]

The central figure of the Virgin reprises the features of Pietro's earlier Madonnas in the Baptist chapel of the Lower Church at Assisi and the Monticchiello Altarpiece, but here her hair is revealed, held back by a thin dark band – details that are visible beneath the transparent veil on Pietro's Cortona Madonna, probably his earliest surviving painting of the Virgin and Child. In Arezzo the interaction between mother and child is more dynamic, with Christ pulling at the Virgin's hem, while she gathers her mantle up in her right hand, revealing its luxurious inner fur lining. The mantle itself is radiant pink with a repeat quatrefoil design, contrasting with the more conventional blue cloak the Virgin wears in the Annunciation above. Like Duccio on the *Maestà*, Pietro signed his name below the Virgin, although in a markedly different way: not as a prayer, but with the artistically self-conscious

Latin formula he had already used on his Cortona *Virgin and Child*: 'PETRUS LAURENTII HANC PINXIT DEXTRA SENENSIS'. This can be translated as 'Pietro Lorenzetti of Siena painted this [work] with his right hand', where 'dextra' carries the additional sense of virtuosity that 'dextrous' can convey in English. As Christopher Platts observes, Pietro's emphasis on his right hand also implied a parallel with the *dextera Dei* in the Annunciation above, aligning his artistic creativity with that of God.[13] Remarkably, Pietro also included a hidden signature elsewhere on his altarpiece, inscribing the silvered sword held by Saint Reparata on the upper left pinnacle with the more straightforward 'PETRUS ME FECIT' ('Pietro made me').

Documented donations towards the altarpiece extended into 1324, but it is unlikely that Pietro laboured over this project for four years.[14] The monumental scale of the altarpiece, even in its distinct components, would have required Pietro's presence in Arezzo and he may have finished the altarpiece significantly earlier.[15] The polyptych was part of a larger renewal of the Pieve in the early 1320s, which encompassed a new choir precinct in the nave before the high altar.[16] Frescoes on the apse walls attributed by Vasari to Pietro were likely to have been executed several decades later,[17] but Tarlati's campaign probably did open a large Gothic window at the centre of the Romanesque apse directly behind the high altar, mirroring and extending the polyptych's Gothic architecture.[18] The interior of the Pieve was remodelled extensively by Vasari in the 1560s and was heavily restored in the nineteenth century: while the altarpiece has returned to the high altar for which it was made, its surroundings have been thoroughly transformed.[19]

1. On the altarpiece, see Guerrini 1988; Volpe 1989, pp. 121–5; Freni 2001; Monciatti 2002, pp. 19–25; Droandi 2005, pp. 41–7; Becchis 2012, pp. 35–46. The polyptych was the subject of conservation campaigns in 1976 and more recently in 2014–20 by RICERCA restauro (which inserted modern copies of the framing elements between the vertical sections of the altarpiece, restoring the polyptych to its original width).
2. The contract has been published several times; for a full transcription and photograph of the original, see Maetzke in Arezzo 1979–80, cat. 5, pp. 33–5.
3. Gardner von Teuffel 1979, pp. 33–4.
4. The contract specified 'duabus columpnis [...] in qualibet esse debeant esse VI figure' ('two columns [...] in which should be six figures'). For a reconstruction incorporating six tiers on each buttress, see Arezzo 1979–80, p. 34, and De Marchi 2004, p. 26, fig. 10; it is more likely, however, that the wording envisaged three figures on each buttress, giving six in total.
5. Freni 2001, pp. 82–90.
6. Ibid., pp. 72–3.
7. Kemp 1990, pp. 10–11, judges Pietro's *Birth of the Virgin* 'a *tour de force* of fourteenth-century perspective', with two vanishing points (or 'converging systems') for the floor tiles and bed covering.
8. For Giotto's fresco of the *Annunciation* in the north transept at Assisi, see Cooper 2018.
9. The date of the three Orvieto polyptychs is debated, see Cannon 2022–3. Israëls 2022 proposes a date of 1330 for the San Domenico Altarpiece at Orvieto, but an earlier date at the very start of the 1320s for the San Francesco Polyptych.
10. Vasari 1568 (1996), p. 133.
11. For this hypothesis, see De Marchi 2004, p. 27, n. 43.
12. Israëls 2022–3, p. 151, suggests a similar predella structure for Simone's altarpiece for San Domenico, Orvieto.
13. For this point and further discussion, see Platts 2024 (forthcoming), and our essay, p. 81, in the present volume.
14. For the financing of the commission, see Freni 2001, pp. 63–8 (with a register of documents at pp. 103–8). Although there is an aspect of 'crowdfunding' here, with a number of pious bequests made by individuals, the guiding role of Tarlati seems clear, particularly in the diversion of fines levied in the local ecclesiastical courts towards the altarpiece.
15. It is likely he had already returned to Assisi to complete his frescoes in the south transept while the final funds for the Arezzo Pieve Polyptych were being collected; see our essay, pp. 87–8, in the present volume for further discussion. The 'Madonna dei Tramonti' at Assisi (see fig. 55) is a further evolution of the central *Virgin and Child* at Arezzo.
16. Freni 2001, pp. 90–3.
17. Vasari 1568 (1996), p. 132, dates these murals to 1355 (by which point Pietro was dead), but Droandi 2005, pp. 44–6, plausibly fixes the fresco campaign to 1340–50/51, the period when the patron mentioned by Vasari (probably on the basis of an inscription), Archpriest Guglielmo, appears in local sources.
18. The large fourteenth-century window is recorded in the eighteenth-century drawing of the apse exterior by Cristofano Conti; see Freni 2001, p. 92, fig. 49. The window was probably plain when Pietro executed his altarpiece, and would only receive stained glass in the early fifteenth century to judge from the agreement of 14 November 1416 between the Chapter of the Pieve and the local merchant Lazzaro di Giovanni Feo, which granted Lazzaro permission to be buried in the choir between the tomb of the canons and the central lectern ('in coro ecclesie dicte plebis inter sepulcrum canonicorum et leggium existentes in dicto coro') and licence to commission a stained-glass window in the apse with images and figures as he saw fit ('faciendi fieri et costrui et apponi ad fenestram maiorem cappelle dicte ecclesie fenestram vitream scultam, figuratam et insignitam illis figuris et ymaginibus de quibus sibi per suam devotionem videbitur'): Florence, Archivio di Stato, Notarile Antecosimiano 9522, at date. Lazzaro honoured the agreement, as Vasari saw the stained glass and attributes the window to Lorenzo Ghiberti: Vasari 1568 (1996), pp. 305–6.
19. For Vasari's later remodelling, see Cornelison 2021.

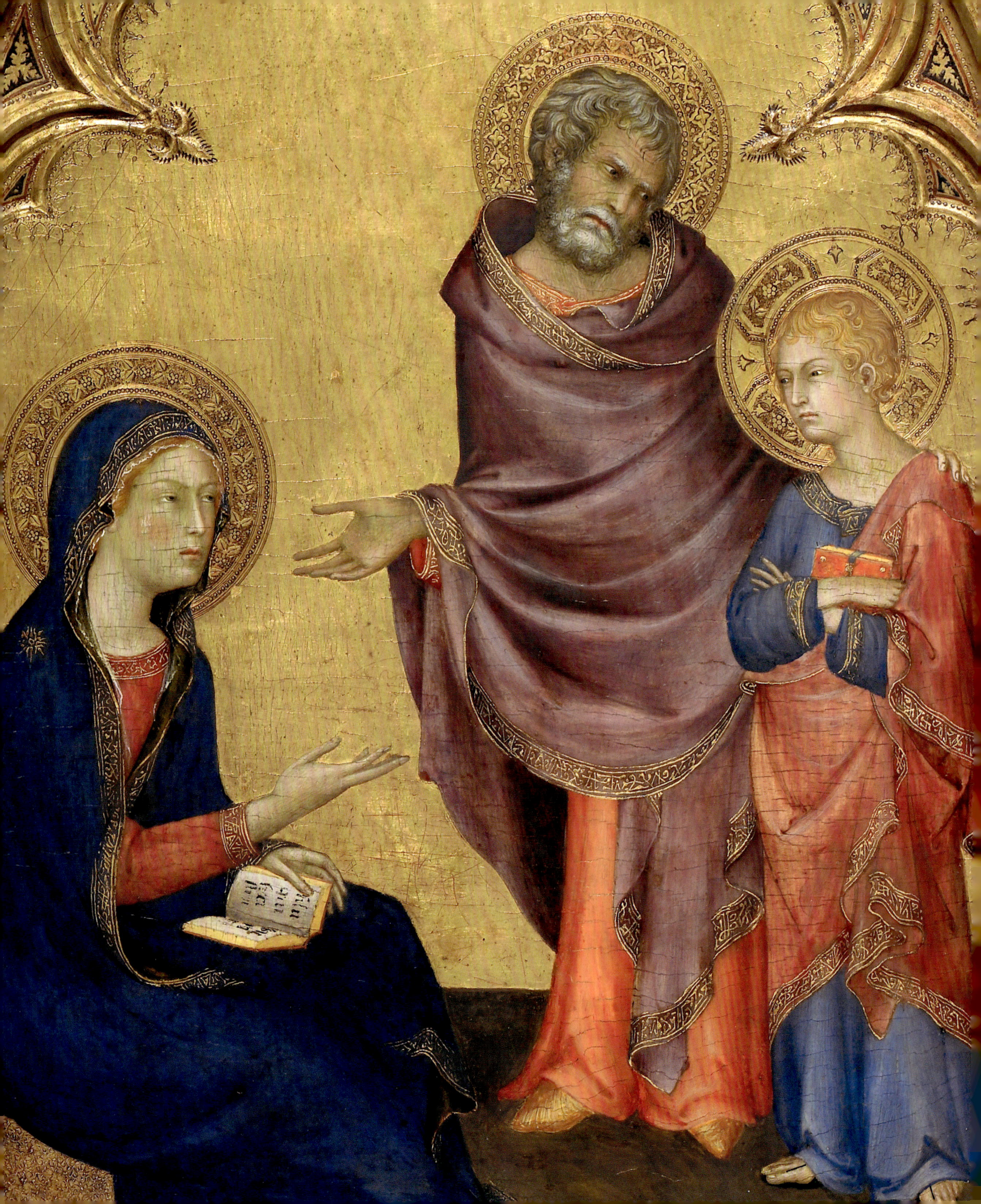

CORTESIA FE': SIMONE MARTINI AND COURT ART

Emma Capron

A Tuscan town during the late Middle Ages. Under the shadow of the communal palace, a richly attired nobleman on horseback looms over a painter dressed in a rumpled frock, standing, brush in hand, outside his modest workshop. His wares are exhibited on the ground beside him. With cheerful confidence, the patron announces to the dismayed artisan: 'I'm bored with triptychs. Paint me a quadriptych.' This cartoon by James Stevenson, published in the *New Yorker* in 1987 (fig. 64), upends the romantic idea of Renaissance artistic genius by showing how curtailed painters' creative licence effectively was by patrons' demands – offering a biting commentary on the timelessness of overbearing clients in the process.

Perhaps equally caricatural, at the other end of the spectrum of late medieval patronage, the court has long been eulogised as a space where artists, freed from the supposedly stifling control of guilds, the financial pressure of securing commissions and the strain of running a workshop, could enter a communion of spirits with an enlightened sovereign.[1] The template for this idealised rapport was established in classical antiquity: in his *Natural History*, Pliny the Elder recounted how the ancient painter Apelles's 'great courtesy of manner' – and legendary talent – endeared him to the otherwise mercurial emperor Alexander the Great.[2] Centuries later, in Avignon, the Italian poet Petrarch wrote a marginal note beside this passage in his own copy of Pliny: 'and in recent times, so was our most delightful Simone, the Sienese.'[3]

This genial Sienese painter so well suited to courtly life was Simone Martini, one of the most accomplished of Duccio's heirs. In a career spanning three decades (about 1312–44), Simone and the workshop he ran with his brother Donato and his brothers-in-law Lippo and Tederigo Memmi brought numerous innovations to the medium of panel painting. This concerned the formats painting could assume, from independent panels to large-scale polyptychs, to smaller, more flexible multi-panelled ensembles. His work was also distinguished by the refinement of its design, its narrative intelligence, deliberate emulation of other materials, and the unsurpassed technical virtuosity

p. 100
Detail of fig. 74

fig. 64
James Stevenson (1929–2017)
'I'm bored with triptychs.
Paint me a quadriptych', 1987
The New Yorker

fig. 65
Simone Martini (about 1284–1344)
Maestà, about 1312–15
Fresco
Palazzo Pubblico, Siena

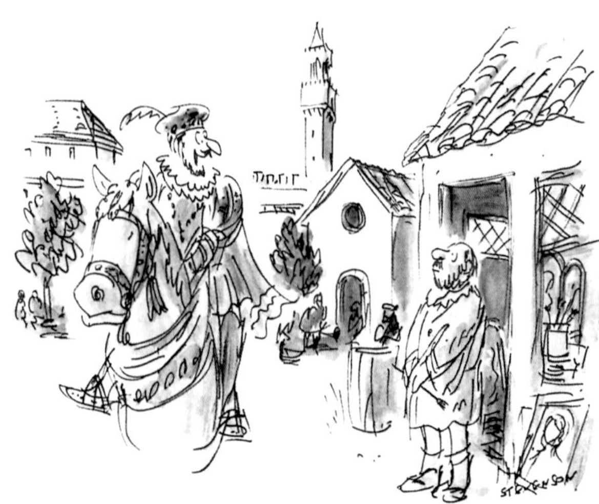

and variety he achieved in the treatment of gold surfaces. Having worked extensively for the Sienese government and furnished altars for mendicant churches across central Italy, Simone spent the final decade of his life in the Provençal city of Avignon, where the papal court was then residing. This is where he befriended the younger Petrarch, who not only reported on his charming demeanour, as mentioned above, but also enshrined him in the canon of vernacular poetry by penning two sonnets in praise of his miraculous brush: of Simone's portrait of the poet's beloved Laura, Petrarch wrote that it appeared as if 'courtliness' itself made it (*Cortesia fe'*).[4] Beyond Petrarch's words, Simone's reputation as a courtly artist was shaped by his stay in Avignon because it made his art available to prelates and princes on visits to the curia from all over Europe: they returned home with recollections – and perhaps, in some cases, with actual samples – of his work that provided a powerful stylistic paradigm for generations of artists working for the courts of Paris, London and Prague well into the fifteenth century.[5]

Simone's exceptional trajectory therefore captures the apparent paradox of a style born and fostered in a communal republic that eventually came to define court art across Europe. However, the lingering problem in addressing Simone's 'courtliness' is that, despite Petrarch's account, no Alexander has been identified to match his Apelles: there is simply no conclusive evidence that Simone was ever officially employed as a court painter, that is, a permanent, salaried member of an individual's household, be it that of a prince of the blood or the Church. Although this might be the result of archival loss, it raises the question of whether the 'fictional Simone'[6] crafted by Petrarch, combined with the preciousness of the artist's style and the afterlife of his work at various courts, consorted to distort our view of his career. Here, the facts of Simone's activity will be confronted with the long shadow of his courtly reputation.

Simone Martini is first documented working on a major public commission for Siena's newly completed Palazzo del Comune, the seat of the city's government: from about 1312 to 1315 he worked on the monumental fresco depicting the Virgin and Child surrounded by the celestial court – the *Maestà* (fig. 65) – elaborating on the theme that Duccio had just treated on the obverse of his high altarpiece for Siena Cathedral.[7] Simone's fresco dominated the Sala del Consiglio, the chamber where the city's councillors met. He altered the work in 1321.[8] From then onwards and until 1333, Simone's name appears almost continuously in Siena's public records working on a string of commissions for the Palazzo del Comune, the majority of which are now lost.[9] In 1321 Simone received payment for what was either a free-standing crucifix or a mural showing the Crucifixion in the chapel of the *Nove*, the city's nine elected governors (lost).[10] For the same chapel, he polychromed two carved angels in 1329 and four years later provided a pedestal for a crucifix and 'other things' (all lost).[11] In 1323 Simone is recorded frescoing a loggia near the Sala della Pace and painting a Saint Christopher for the *Biccherna*, Siena's financial administration, whose office was located on the ground floor of the Palazzo del Comune (both lost).[12] In 1326–7 Simone painted an altarpiece for the Capitano del Popolo, a post that saw a new official appointed every six months.[13] This work is today identified as five panels depicting the Virgin

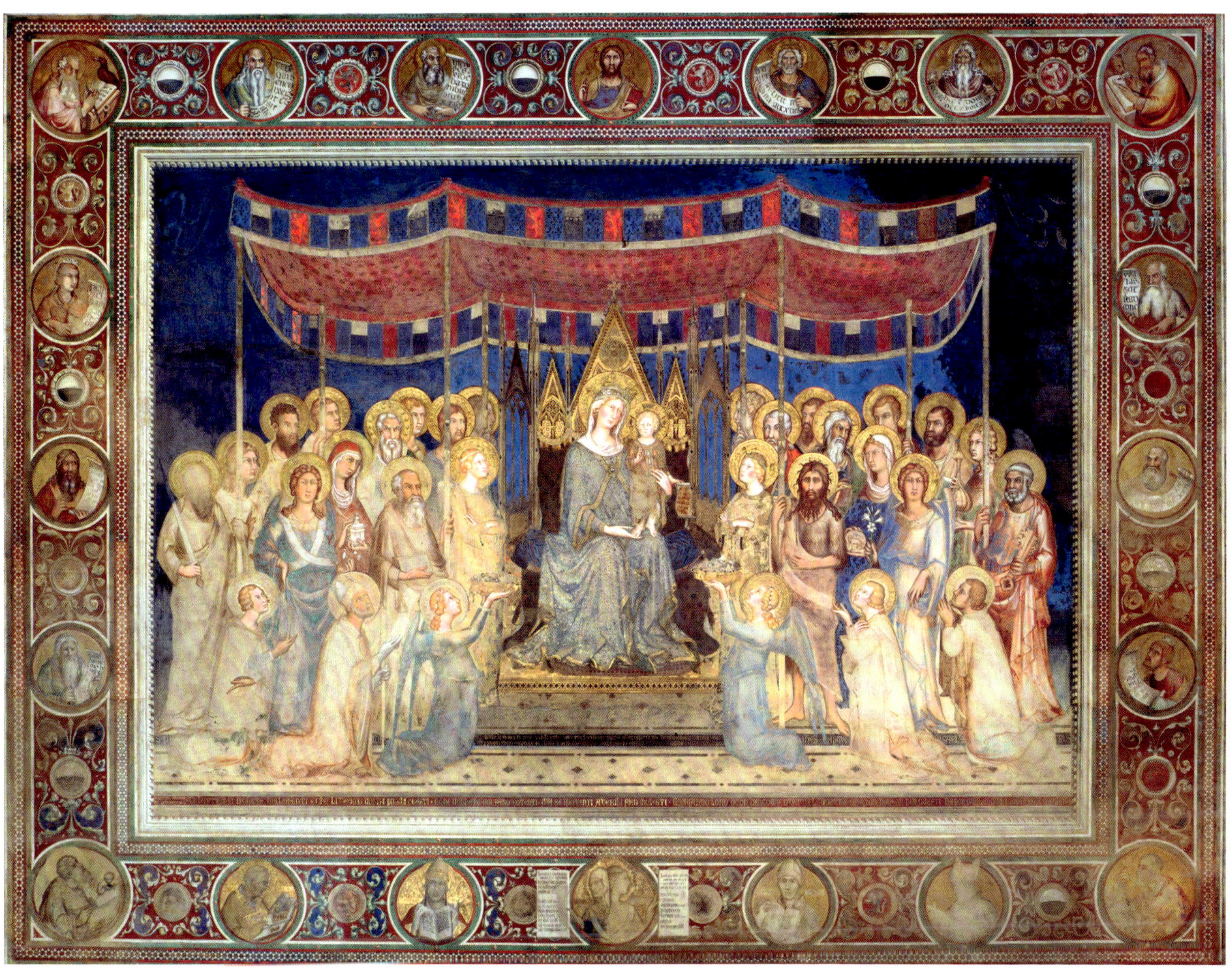

and Child, and saints Andrew, Peter, Luke and Ansanus – one of the city's patron saints – and now split between New York, Madrid and Los Angeles (see pp. 117–19).[14] Their format is deeply unusual for an altarpiece: they all have equal dimensions, are rectangular rather than gabled, have (or had) marbled reverses, and are set in unhinged box frames – characteristics befitting of portable panels rather than fixed altarpieces. These idiosyncrasies seem to reflect Simone's inventive response to the challenge of providing an altarpiece that was not to be set in a permanent location but which instead could be moved and reassembled flexibly each time a new Capitano was appointed.[15] In 1330 Simone returned to the great hall of the Palazzo del Comune where he had painted the *Maestà*. On the opposite wall he was tasked with visualising Siena's military might by portraying fortresses newly secured by the *comune*, territories presented both as tributes to the Virgin painted across the hall and evidence of her support of the city: Montemassi and Sassoforte, and the following year Arcidosso and Castel del Piano.[16] The stern equestrian portrait of the *condottiere* Guidoriccio da Fogliano surveying a barren landscape with the identifiable town of Montemassi is all that remains of this commission.[17] Another secular subject occupying Simone at the Palazzo Pubblico in 1330 was a depiction of the Roman hero Marcus Atilius Regulus – an exemplar of patriotic duty – for the Sala del Concistoro.[18]

Simone's public commissions were not confined to the Palazzo del Comune: around 1329 he frescoed the Porta Romana (the gate to the south-east of the city that pilgrims took on their way down to Rome) with a very large, unfinished Coronation of the Virgin.[19] In the early thirties, he began painting the Antiporto di Camollia (the

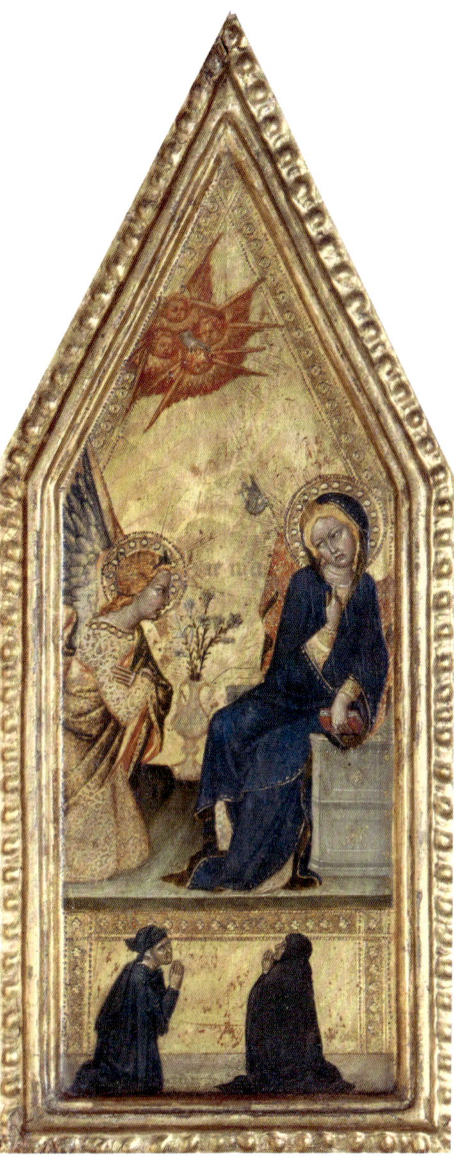
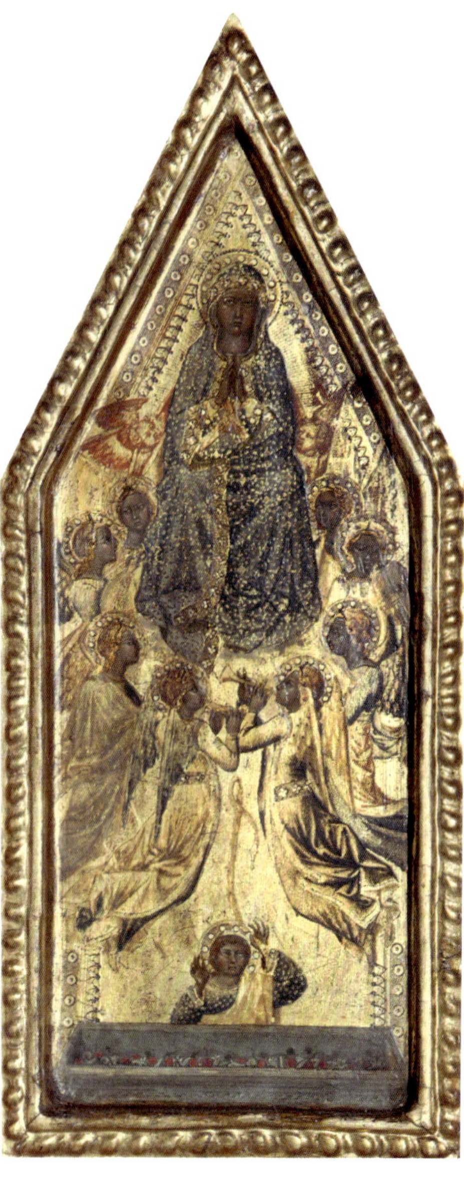

FIG. 66
Francesco di Vannuccio
(documented 1356–89)
Diptych with the Annunciation and the Assumption, about 1380
Tempera on panel, each wing
36 × 15.2 cm (with engaged frame)
The Mistress and Fellows, Girton College, Cambridge (188[a, b])

gate to the north-west) with an Assumption of the Virgin, the daring spatial arrangement of which may be reflected on a diminutive scale in Lippo Memmi's exquisite panel of the same subject (Alte Pinakothek, Munich) and later in a diptych by Francesco di Vannuccio (fig. 66).[20] The *Annunciation* altarpiece that Simone and Lippo Memmi signed in 1333 and placed on the altar of Saint Ansanus – only secondary to the high altar where Duccio's *Maestà* stood – is so much at the heart of Siena's civic identity and devotional life that it also counts as an official commission (see fig. 39).[21] Lorenzo Ghiberti recorded another altarpiece by Simone at the cathedral and, significantly, that he frescoed a Virgin and Child above the doorway of the *Opera del Duomo* – the official body in charge of running the cathedral – and scenes of the life of the Virgin on the facade of another major civic institution, the hospital of Santa Maria della Scala.[22] Although documentation is missing, the role of the *comune* in sponsoring building and decoration projects for the city's major mendicant churches, as well as encouraging local cults, was probably fundamental in the commission of Simone's Beato Agostino Novello Triptych (see fig. 90).[23] Despite the patchiness of the Sienese archives for the first decades of the fourteenth century, and although only a handful of these documented works survive, the picture that emerges from this nearly uninterrupted series of public endeavours is of Simone as the official painter of the *comune* – a 'civic propagandist':[24] the Sienese equivalent of what Giotto was to Florence. Given that Siena's government was anything but monolithic and consisted of a revolving cast of elected officials, the consistency of Simone's employment by the *comune* is all the more remarkable. His role as a public representative of Siena would go on after he had left the city, as testified by a record from 1344 in which he acted on behalf of the hospital of Santa Maria della Scala at the papal court.[25]

Yet the word 'civic' carries a set of visual expectations – sobriety, solidity – that do not conform to what we see at the Palazzo Pubblico. In its vibrantly coloured and prodigiously gilded, silvered, tooled and glass-studded splendour, the *Maestà* emulates the preciosity of enamelled metalwork on a monumental scale, while the sinuous drapery folds, the figures' gentle nods and graceful gestures recall the elegance of French ivory and manuscript illuminations.[26] Simone stages a courtly ceremony of homage before his viewers: the Virgin and Child are shown enthroned under a canopy, surrounded by their heavenly retinue (see also p. 15). Through vernacular inscriptions, Siena's four patron saints petition the Virgin for her protection, while kneeling angels present her with a tribute of roses and lilies gathered in gold dishes. The Virgin replies that she will only grant the city her favour in exchange for good governance, while Christ's scroll further exhorts Siena's councillors to exercise justice. In lieu of her traditional thick blue mantle, the richness of the Virgin's robes of luscious blue silk woven with gold and her blonde tresses, visible underneath the translucent white veil, give her the distinctly secular appearance of an earthly princess (see p. 204).[27]

The courtly accent of the imagery is further enhanced by real-life heraldry: the ceremonial fabric canopy, or baldachin, beneath which the Virgin holds court is emblazoned with the black-and-white *balzana*, the emblem of Siena, the lion symbolising the Sienese people, the French fleur-de-lis and the arms of the Angevins – a cadet branch of the French royal family that had dominion over Anjou, Provence and the Kingdom of Naples.[28] By including their coat of arms, the fresco advertised Siena's close political ties to this influential dynasty and its alignment with the Guelph (pro-papal) interests it promoted across Italy. Such a heraldic baldachin would have called to mind the elaborate processional canopies with which the city welcomed powerful visitors – including several members of the Angevin family – throughout the 1310s and 1320s.[29] The cost of these objects was vertiginous: in addition to the expensive silks themselves, the most Simone is known to have ever been paid by the *comune* was for painting Sienese and French heraldry on two canopies that the city commissioned to celebrate the entry of the Angevin scion Charles of Calabria and his wife Mary of Valois in 1327 – visualising the diplomatic alliance between the city and the dynasty in precisely the same fashion as the *Maestà* did.[30]

Simone's involvement with the Angevins runs like a thread through his career, but the exact terms of his employment by them remain stubbornly out of documentary reach.[31] Angevin-related patronage seems to have drawn Simone to the Franciscan motherhouse at Assisi around the time he was at work on the *Maestà* (from about 1312 to 1315–16), perhaps explaining the apparent interruption in the execution of the fresco, attested by technical evidence,[32] and the hiatus in public commissions carried out by Simone in his hometown between the *Maestà*'s completion in 1315–16 and its repair and modification in 1321.[33] That the *comune* released Simone from his duties halfway through the

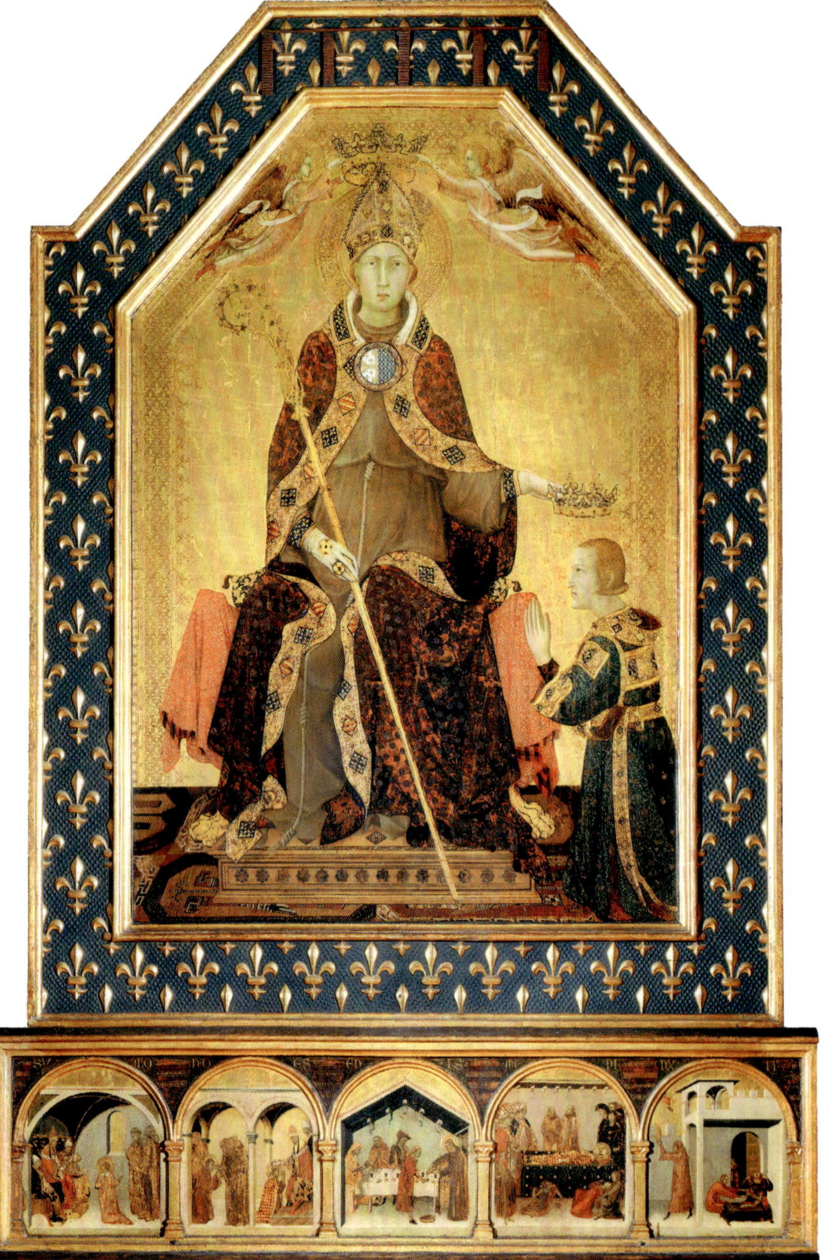

FIG. 67
Simone Martini
(about 1284–1344)
Saint Louis of Toulouse Altarpiece, 1317
Tempera on panel, 200 × 188 cm (without predella)
Museo Nazionale di Capodimonte, Naples

Maestà and dispatched him to Assisi might have constituted a 'diplomatic gift' from Siena to both the Franciscans and the Angevins.[34] In Assisi, Simone painted the chapel of Saint Martin, founded by the leading Angevin ally Cardinal Gentile Partino da Montefiore, who probably visited Siena in the spring of 1312.[35] Gentile was dead by the end of that year and Simone's richly coloured, luminous cycle full of chivalric deeds was probably executed under the guidance of his executors and the friars.[36] The chapel's imagery also hints at a direct involvement – if not an effective takeover of patronage – on the part of the Angevins. The arch that frames the entrance was partially repainted to feature three saints with familial ties to the dynasty: their illustrious ancestor the Valois king Louis IX; King Robert of Naples's brother Saint Louis of Toulouse – both set against heraldic backgrounds of gilded fleurs-de-lis; and Saint Elizabeth of Hungary, a relative of King Robert's mother, the dowager queen of Naples, Mary of Hungary.[37] It is probably for her that Simone frescoed a group of seven saints attending to the Virgin and Child in the north transept: except for Saint Francis, they all

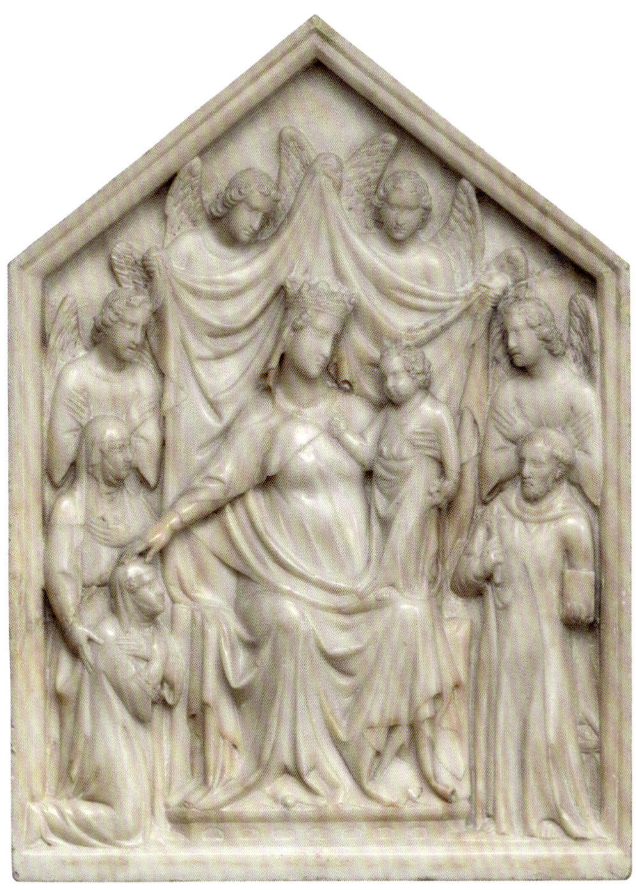

FIG. 68
Tino di Camaino (about 1280–about 1337)
The Virgin and Child with Queen Sancia, Saints and Angels, 1332–3
Marble, 51.4 × 37.8 × 8.5 cm
National Gallery of Art, Washington, Samuel H. Kress Collection (1960.5.1)

hailed from the Hungarian or Angevin royal families.[38] The fact that Mary's son, Saint Louis of Toulouse, appears with a halo throughout the Lower Church suggests that the frescoes were completed after his canonisation in 1317.[39]

The monumental altarpiece that Simone painted to visualise – and legitimise – the Angevin succession to the throne of Naples is believed to date from around that time (fig. 67).[40] It shows the enthroned Saint Louis of Toulouse, who had renounced his royal destiny to embrace a holy life within the Franciscan order, crowning his kneeling younger brother Robert of Anjou, King of Naples. The image at once proclaims the dynasty's political ambitions, affirms its religious sanctity and projects its material splendour. Again, details regarding the painting's commission, execution and destination are missing. The likeliest patron for the work is King Robert himself, but other candidates include his mother, Mary of Hungary, and his brother Philip of Taranto, acting either as individuals or as part of a 'familial enterprise'.[41] Meanwhile, the Angevin-sponsored Franciscan convents of San Lorenzo Maggiore, Santa Chiara and the chapel of Saint Louis of Toulouse in Naples Cathedral have all been proposed as original locations.[42] Whatever the specifics of the commission, Simone does not appear in any of the accounts of the royal household in Naples.[43] In fact, there is no evidence that he ever visited the city, and it is entirely possible that he executed the work from Siena or the temporary workshop he must have established in Assisi during those years.[44] This differs from the extended stays of his compatriots the Sienese goldsmith Lando di Pietro and the sculptor Tino di Camaino in Naples, both of whom resided at court for several years – in the latter's case for over a decade, providing no fewer than 12 royal tombs as well as more intimate works reflecting the Franciscan affinities of the royal family (fig. 68).[45] Simone's patronage by the Angevins also stands in sharp contrast to the situations achieved by the Roman painter Pietro Cavallini and the Florentine Giotto in Naples. Although sources are silent on the nature of his work there, Cavallini was allocated an annual salary and a house during his stay in the city in 1308–9.[46] Giotto is documented at court from 1328 to 1332 – probably over several visits rather than one continuous stay – and established a workshop there.[47] He was originally retained on a monthly emolument until he was granted the status of Robert's *familiaris* in 1330, fuelling Giorgio Vasari's effusive – and Plinian – account of the king's frequent visits to the painter's studio, and the artist's ability to entertain the monarch with his wit as well as his art.[48] Rather than Simone, it is therefore Giotto – albeit remembered nowadays as the quintessentially civic painter – who emerges from the primary sources as the successful court artist.

Meanwhile, following his Angevin commissions, the bulk of Simone's output in the 1320s and early 1330s was destined for religious and public institutions rather than a

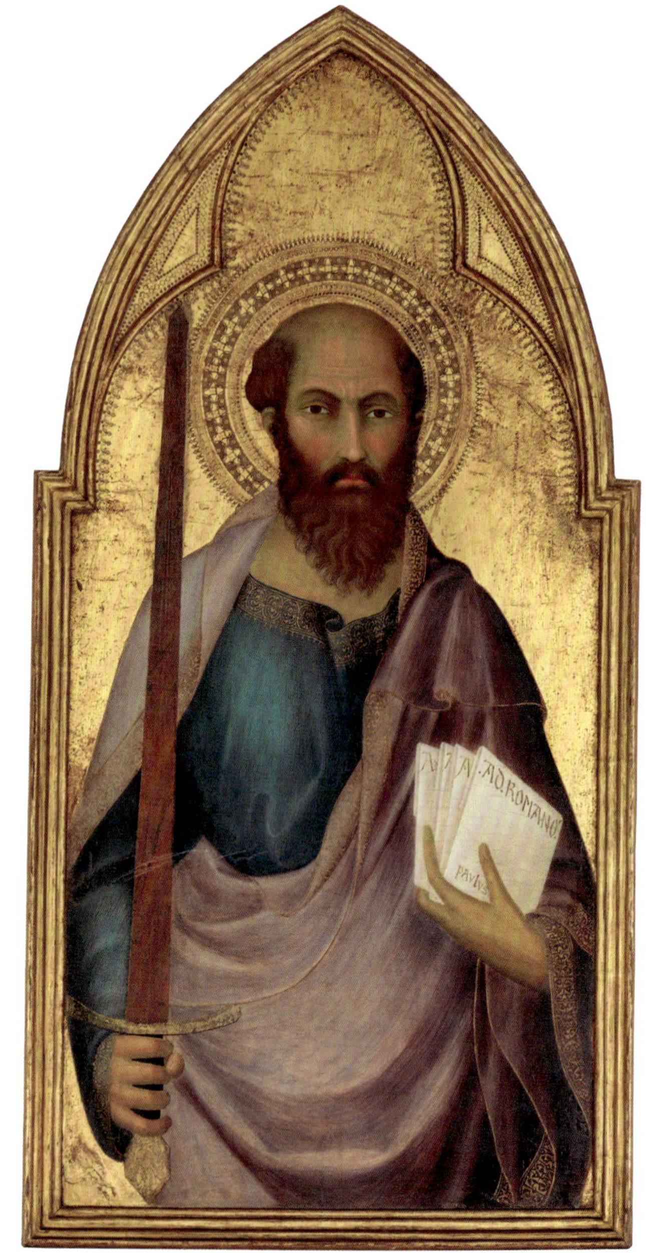

single individual or household. In contrast to the slimmed down operation that may have come with a court position, these works were produced with the assistance of a large workshop that Simone ran together with his brother Donato and the painters Lippo and Tederigo Memmi – a professional venture which became a familial enterprise after Simone married their sister Giovanna Memmi in 1324.[49] So successful were they at crafting a common stylistic idiom modelled on Simone's elegant manner that their hands are sometimes hard to distinguish from one another, leading to many debates over attributions. In addition to the work for the Sienese *comune* already discussed, the Martini-Memmi *compagnia* painted a large number of innovative polyptychs for mendicant convents at San Gimignano (which included Lippo Memmi's *Saint Paul*, fig. 69), Pisa and Orvieto, pushing both formal and iconographic boundaries in altarpiece design.[50] Consistently high in quality and often signed under a single name – usually Simone's – close examination of these works reveals the participation of several craftsmen, capitalising on the possibilities offered by the polyptych to rationalise production by having various assistants work on several panels at once.[51]

Some of the visual strategies deployed in these large-scale endeavours found their way into devotional panels: along with a lost *Virgin* and *Man of Sorrows*, the mourning *Saint John the Evangelist* (fig. 70) – his drapery bristling with grief – formed a portable Passion triptych that distilled on a few square inches the emotional impact of the central predella of Simone's Pisa Polyptych.[52] Similarly drawing from a larger design – this time the *Virgin and Child* from Simone's altarpiece for San Domenico in Orvieto (1320s) – is a small Marian panel (fig. 71). Exquisitely tooled, its reverse splendidly gilded, and replete with vivid and tender details – Christ's toes peering through his mother's fingers – it features along its bottom edge a cast of diminutive saints and a Dominican nun, which suggests it was intended for a member of the convent of San Paolo in Orvieto (the female arm of San Domenico): a miniature, personalised version of an altarpiece, adapted for private contemplation rather than public worship.[53] Lippo Memmi adopted a comparable two-tiered arrangement in the left wing of a diptych now split between New York and Paris, which was certainly destined for a grey friar or nun, given the Franciscan saints depicted

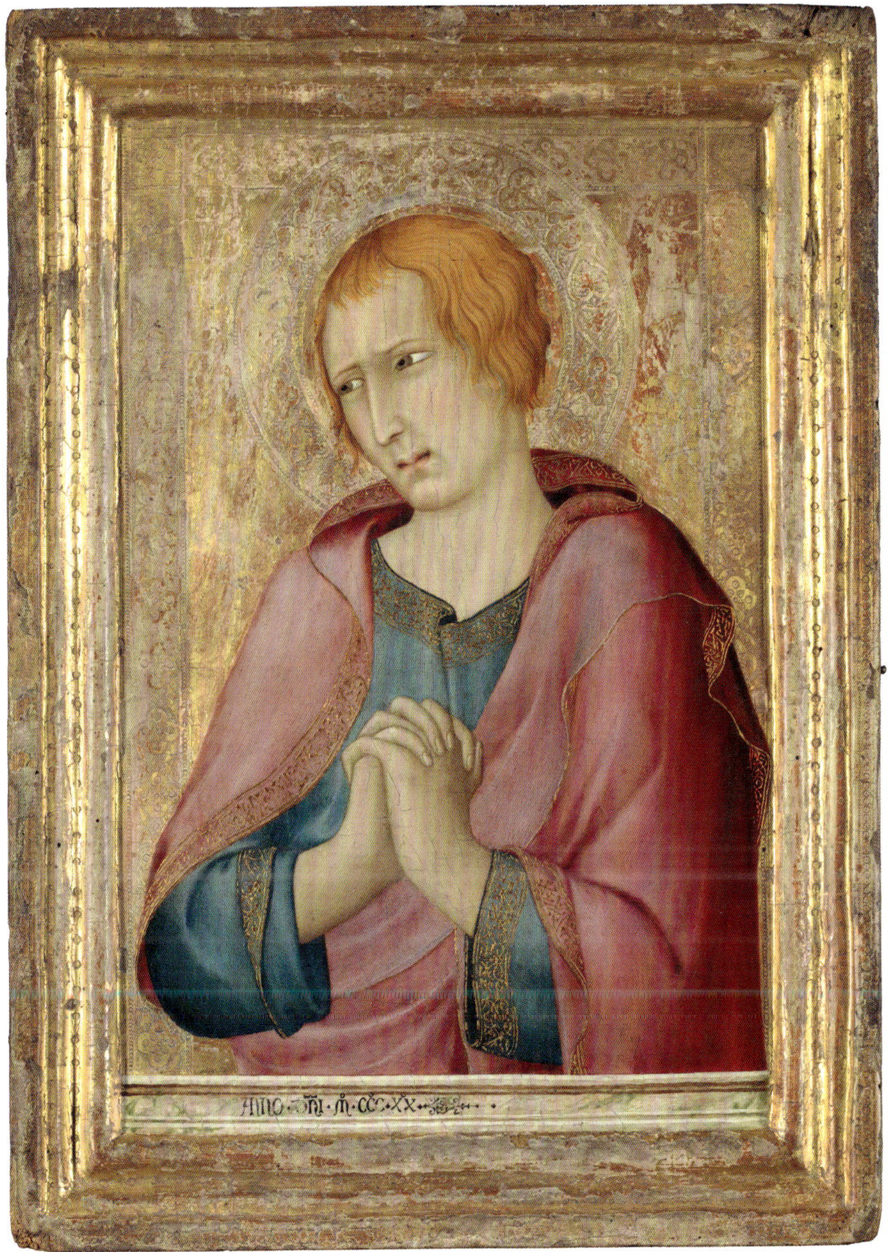

FIG. 69
Lippo Memmi (documented 1317–50)
Saint Paul, about 1330
Tempera on panel, 95.9 × 48.3 cm
(with partially modern engaged frame)
The Metropolitan Museum of Art, New York. Gift of Coudert Brothers, 1888 (88.3.99)

FIG. 70
Simone Martini (about 1284–1344)
Saint John the Evangelist, 1320
Tempera on panel, 41.7 × 30.3 cm
(with engaged frame)
The Henry Barber Trust, the Barber Institute of Fine Arts, University of Birmingham (38.12)

around the Virgin and beneath the lower arches (fig. 72).[54] It includes unusually the nine choirs of angels, their stateliness contrasting with their mourning counterparts on the *Crucifixion* (Musée du Louvre, Paris), which formed the other part of the diptych. By pairing these two panels up, the artist balanced narrative drama with the patron's specific iconic requirements. Although its original function is unknown, Simone's ability to convey monumentality on a small scale is perhaps most evident in the *Christ on the Cross* (see fig. 214) now at Harvard: stripping the scene of all anecdotal details, he confronts viewers with Christ's lone, frail body starkly delineated against the gold background, a field ruptured only by his flowing blood.[55] It was also in Simone's ambit that the highly original *Mystic Marriage of Saint Catherine* (see fig. 213) originated: probably commissioned to commemorate the reconciliation of two warring lords, it is exceptional in its seamless blend of religious imagery and secular concerns.[56] Rather than a homogeneous output, these works demonstrate the endlessly versatile and sophisticated ways with which Simone and

FIG. 71
Simone Martini (about 1284–1344)
The Virgin and Child over Saints Helen, Paul, Dominic, Stephen (?) and a Dominican Nun, about 1325
Tempera on panel, 33.4 × 25.4 cm (with engaged frame)
Isabella Stewart Gardner Museum, Boston (P30w8)

FIG. 72
Lippo Memmi (documented 1317–50)
The Virgin and Child with Saints and Angels, about 1345
Tempera on panel, 66.7 × 33 cm (with partially modern engaged frame)
The Metropolitan Museum of Art, New York. Maitland F. Griggs Collection, Bequest of Maitland F. Griggs, 1943 (43.98.6)

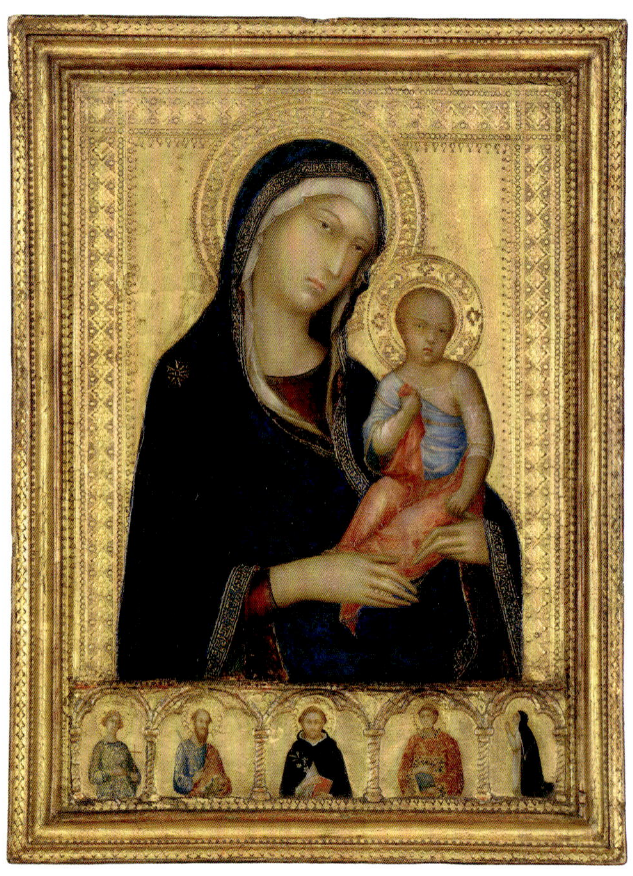

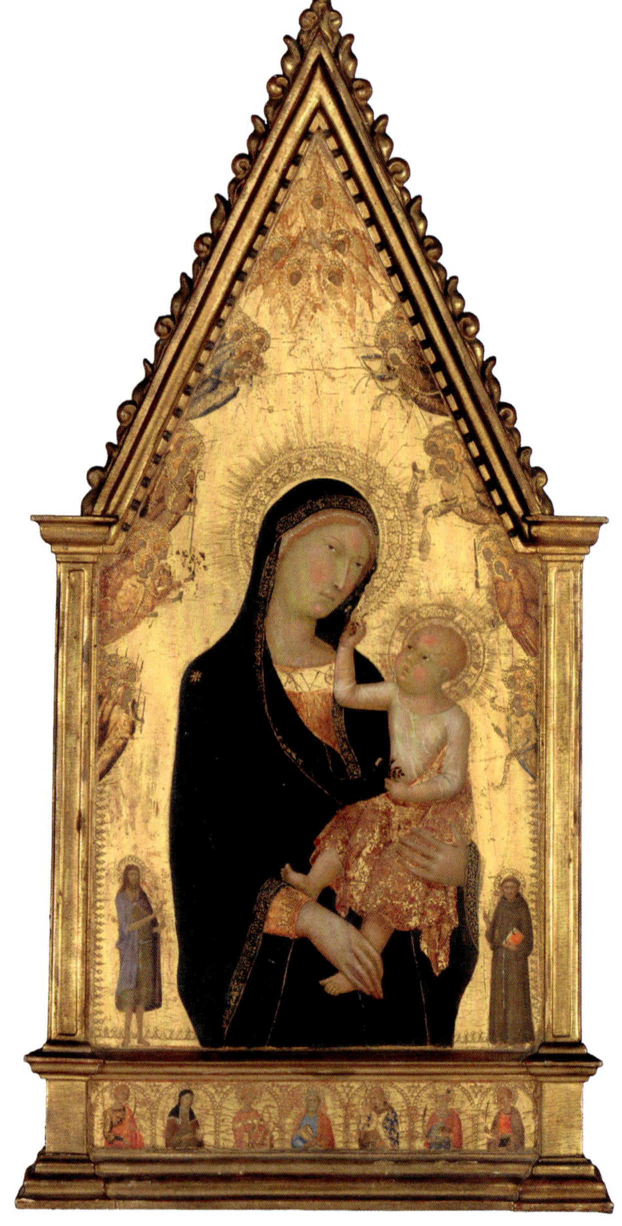

his *compagnia* responded to their many patrons' demands, large and small. Far from rarefied courtly patronage, the impression this corpus conveys is one of effective industry.

What we know of Simone's final years of activity in Avignon seems to conform more closely – at least in part – to what one expects of a court artist. Early Sienese sources claim Simone moved to Avignon at the behest of a cardinal passing through Siena on his way to France.[57] This relocation took place between 1333 and 1336.[58] For Simone to depart from his hometown at a time of great activity for his workshop, no doubt leaving many projects unfinished, suggests indeed a personage of importance and influence.[59] Candidates include Cardinal Jacopo Stefaneschi, for whom Simone painted a fresco cycle on the porch of Avignon's Notre-Dame-des-Doms cathedral,[60] and Stefaneschi's relative, Cardinal Napoleone Orsini, who probably commissioned Simone's eponymous polyptych (about 1326–34; see fig. 80), and whom the artist painted in a lost portrait – a remarkably early instance of the genre.[61] Diana Norman recently made the compelling proposition that Napoleone's first cousin, Giovanni Gaetano Orsini, was the cardinal who poached Simone, as he made a prolonged stay in Siena while en route to Avignon in 1334, coinciding with Simone's transfer to the papal city.[62]

Few paintings survive from Simone's decade in Avignon. Most of them are small and jewel-like, such as the frontispiece of Petrarch's copy of Virgil (fig. 73) and the extraordinary *Christ discovered in the Temple* (fig. 74): both connoisseurs' items that blend exquisite craftsmanship with feats of iconographic invention.[63] Those surviving works give the misleading impression of a drastic drop in both activity and scale, as one would expect from a court painter on a salary, working without a workshop on precious, erudite objects for private use.[64] Yet this reduced corpus seems to result mainly from accidents of survival. Ghiberti, Vasari and, more reliably, the first-hand account of the Florentine merchant Luigi Peruzzi who resided in Avignon in the fifteenth century, tell us that many works by Simone were visible in the papal city.[65] Peruzzi singles out a monumental Marian high altarpiece that Simone signed in 1343 for Avignon's Franciscan church, locally known as the Cordeliers – a prominent and vast convent that was the beating heart of Avignon's Italian community.[66] Although lost, this remains the most important altarpiece – either surviving or merely documented, painted or sculpted – to be recorded during the Avignon papacy. For this sizeable endeavour, Simone would have needed the help of an efficient workshop, and he may have brought or called members of his Sienese *compagnia* to join him.[67]

The specifics of this commission help gain a clearer sense of Simone's circumstances in Avignon. Importantly, he painted this altarpiece not for a cardinal but for a Florentine banker, Lapo di Ruspo, documented in Avignon from 1321 until his death in 1361, and bearing the title of *Cavaliere* from 1352 onwards.[68] Described by economic historians of the Avignon papacy as a peripheral figure, Lapo was nonetheless by the middle of the fourteenth century Florence's second biggest taxpayer, a member of the *gente nuova* who had recently joined the city's political and economic elite.[69] His rise to prominence in the early 1340s coincided with the crash of the major Florentine banking companies in 1343–6 (the Peruzzi, Acciaiuoli and Bardi) and he seems to have benefited from the vacuum left by these key players at the papal court.[70] This broadly coincides with the completion of Simone's altarpiece in 1343, and the commission was probably meant to signal Lapo's rising fortunes. His wife further donated to the Cordeliers a precious silk frontal for the high altar and a chalice bearing her arms.[71] Lapo's name endured in Avignon, where it became synonymous with legendary wealth, as attested by a letter addressed to Francesco Datini in 1401, in which the Prato banker is called a 'modern-day Lapo Ruspi, because of the great fame of [his] wealth'.[72] Simone's altarpiece, a splendid reminder of Lapo's munificence, certainly played a part in ensuring this posthumous fame.

Yet for all his economic success, Lapo di Ruspo jars with the cortège of cardinals and royalty who previously employed Simone. He was not, however, the sole person involved in the commission. The friars undoubtedly kept close control over this image intended for their core liturgical space, and given Simone's history with the order at Assisi and Orvieto, Franciscan networks surely played a fundamental part in securing the artist's services:[73] the Cordeliers chapter included Tuscans who would have been aware of the artist's work,[74] and in 1337 the trial of friar Andrea da Gagliano in Avignon drew to the city several influential Neapolitan friars close to the Angevins and familiar with Simone's Saint Louis of Toulouse Altarpiece (fig. 67).[75] The Angevins themselves

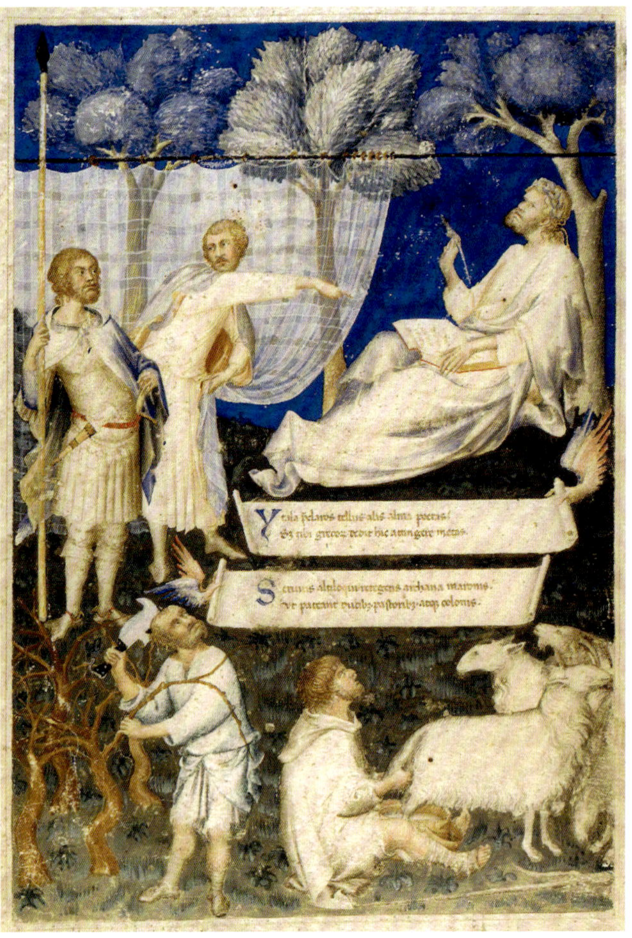

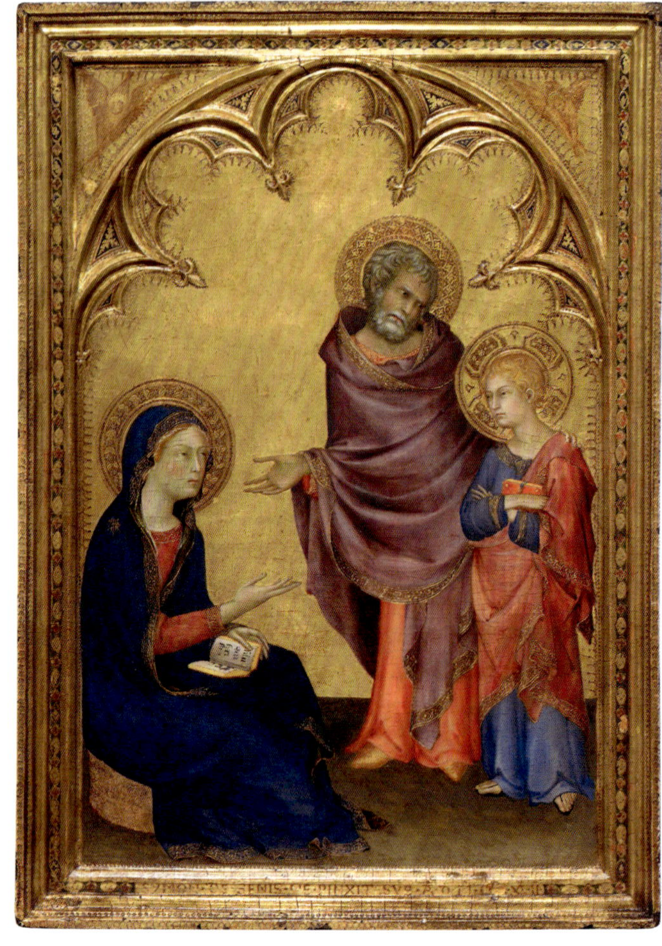

were important Cordeliers benefactors. As lords of the city, their banners proudly hung in the church on feast days,[76] and Queen Sancia of Mallorca had presented the convent with precious liturgical metalwork and three textile antependia (precious cloths that would hang before the altar) specifically for the high altar.[77] If either Queen Sancia or King Robert had any part in brokering the commission of the Cordeliers high altarpiece, this would be yet another instance of their role in the diffusion of Sienese painting in fourteenth-century Europe – and effectively the last such instance considering their respective deaths in 1345 and 1343 (see pp. 195–6).[78] Finally, the Cordeliers were patronised by two of Simone's former curial patrons: Jacopo Stefaneschi and Napoleone Orsini.[79] The latter had a specific interest in the high altar, donating one textile frontal especially for it.[80] He further founded a chapel in the church, which in 1347 received an altarpiece signed by Simone's collaborators Lippo and Tederigo Memmi, possibly the *Maestà* now in the Berenson collection at I Tatti – a commission that may have gone initially to Simone but been executed by his relatives after his death in 1344.[81]

Given that the Cordeliers attracted the benefaction of Simone's most eminent former patrons, the artist's employment there was no coincidence. Any or all of these actors could have served as intermediaries between the local friars and the artist. Rather than Simone seeking the commission, it is likely the friars courted him, harnessing their network to secure his services. Beyond artistic merit, Simone's links to the leading royal and curial dynasties of the day would have made an association with him deeply desirable to the friars, at a time when they probably felt the need to catch up with their rivals in the city, the Dominicans, who had a convent so monumental it had been chosen as a residence by the pope on his arrival in Avignon, and hosted the conclaves and coronations of Benedict XII and Clement VI in 1335 and 1342 respectively.[82] Simone may have acquiesced under the

FIG. 73
Simone Martini (about 1284–1344)
Frontispiece to Petrarch's Virgil, about 1340
Tempera and ink on parchment, 20 × 29.5 cm
Biblioteca Ambrosiana, Milan (S.P. 10.27)

FIG. 74
Simone Martini (about 1284–1344)
Christ discovered in the Temple, 1342
Tempera on panel, 49.5 × 35.1 cm (with engaged frame)
National Museums Liverpool, Walker Art Gallery. Presented by the Liverpool Royal Institution 1948 (2787)

pressure of his former patrons, or as a favour to his putative protector, who may have 'lent' his artist to the Franciscans. Another possibility is that the death of this elusive patron freed the artist from exclusive service: for instance, if Simone did join Giovanni Gaetano Orsini in Avignon, then he would have found himself without patronage almost immediately upon resettling as the cardinal died in August 1335. Following this, Simone might either have worked for a wider client pool or entered another household, such as that of Napoleone Orsini.[83] Napoleone died in March 1342, that is – perhaps not coincidentally – around the time Simone must have accepted the Cordeliers commission. Bearing in mind Peruzzi's testimony that other works by Simone were on public view in Avignon, it appears that whatever his circumstances – court artist or not – Simone took on more than one large-scale project while living in the papal city.

Simone's Cordeliers altarpiece, commissioned by a banker but embedded within a dense courtly network, shows how slippery the definition of 'court artist' can be for the late medieval period. 'Courtly' his style certainly was, but he may never have been a court artist. Simone's career as a whole challenges established categories of court and city, public and private, secular and religious: modern taxonomies reflective of stylistic assumptions as much as hard facts, which fail to account for the enmeshed nature of late medieval patronage. Whatever the label, what Simone's trajectory from Siena to Avignon does capture is the rise in status and international appeal achieved by Sienese painters – and by painting as a medium more generally – by the mid-fourteenth century, a time when, according to Peruzzi, Simone and his compatriots proudly 'held the field'.[84]

1. In a rich yet teleological account, Martin Warnke (1993) saw court as a fundamental step in the rise of the artist from the status of mere urban artisan to respected intellectual during the late medieval and early modern periods. For a response, see Campbell 2004.
2. Pliny (1938), vol. 9, p. 325.
3. Bibliothèque nationale de France, Paris, MS Lat. 6802, fol. 256v: 'Hec fuit et Symoni nostro Sensensi nuper iocundissima'. On this notation, see Baxandall 2006, p. 63; Campbell 2004, especially p. 39; McHam 2013, p. 65. Accounts of Simone's agreeable character also appear in Vasari 1568 (1996), p. 170, and Luigi Peruzzi's manuscript, Biblioteca Medicea Laurenziana, Florence, MS Acquisti e Doni 401, fol. 48v: 'homo honesto e di buona vita'.
4. Petrarca (2001), p. 115, poem 77: 'Per mirar Policleto a prova fiso'. The passage is discussed by Strehlke 2022–3, pp. 68–70. For a demystified account of Petrarch and Simone's relationship, see Anheim 2015, pp. 375–6.
5. See Gordon, pp. 224–39, and Nash, pp. 240–53, in the present volume. It should be acknowledged that the art and architecture of fourteenth-century Avignon provided a model for European courts beyond Simone: in 1344, while on a visit to Pope Clement VI in Avignon, Emperor Charles IV recruited the architect Matthew of Arras to rebuild Prague Cathedral (Recht 2008, p. 172); in 1349, following a stay at the curia, the French king John II commissioned the painter Jean Coste to paint murals inspired by the Papal Palace's Chamber of the Stag at his castle of Vaudreuil, while other murals at the royal residences of Saint Pol and the Louvre also derived from it (Laclotte and Thiébaut 1983, p. 151); in 1406 King Martin I of Aragon sought to procure drawings after Matteo Giovannetti's angels frescoed in the Pope's private chapel of Saint Michael in the Papal Palace, as a template for his own chapel dedicated to the archangel (Castelnuovo 1962, p. 161).
6. Campbell 2004, p. 33.
7. Martindale 1988, no. 35, pp. 204–9; Maginnis 2001, pp. 124–5; Leone de Castris 2003, pp. 228–37, no. 5, pp. 345–6; Bagnoli 1999; Norman 1999b, pp. 48–58; Norman 2018, pp. 51–8.
8. Leone de Castris 2003, pp. 228–36.
9. Martindale 1988, pp. 37–44; Carter Southard 1988.
10. Martindale 1988, no. 29, pp. 203–4; Maginnis 2001, p. 126; Leone de Castris 2003, pp. 237–40.
11. Martindale 1988, nos 30–1, p. 204; Maginnis 2001, p. 127.
12. Martindale 1988, no. 33 (loggia), no. 34 (Saint Christopher), p. 204; Maginnis 2001, p. 126 (loggia), p. 129 (Saint Christopher); Leone de Castris 2003, pp. 366–7.
13. Martindale 1988, no. 27, p. 203; no. 12, p. 217.

14. Boskovits 1974; Christiansen 1994; Leone de Castris 2003, pp. 242–9; no. 26, p. 358; Schmidt 2005a, p. 83.
15. Strehlke 2022–3, pp. 73–4.
16. Martindale 1988, nos 36–7, pp. 209–10; Leone de Castris 2003, pp. 265–74.
17. Martindale 1988, no. 38, p. 210; Leone de Castris 2003, pp. 265–74, no. 30, p. 360. Attribution challenged by Mallory and Moran 1981–2; De Wesselow 2004.
18. Martindale 1988, no. 32, p. 204; Maginnis 2001, p. 129.
19. Ghiberti before 1455 (1998), p. 89; Martindale 1988, no. 40, p. 211; Israëls 2012, pp. 207–8.
20. Leone de Castris 2003, pp. 287–90; Fattorini 2010, pp. 144–5; Fattorini in Siena 2010, cat. B.5, pp. 156–7; Israëls 2012, pp. 201–7. Memmi's panel: inv. WAF 671.
21. Martindale 1988, pp. 41–2; no. 12, pp. 187–90; Leone de Castris 2003, pp. 274–86; no. 32, pp. 361–2; Norman 1999b, pp. 67–85.
22. Ghiberti before 1455 (1998), p. 89; Martindale 1988, no. 24 (cathedral altarpiece), p. 202, no. 25 (facade of the Opera del Duomo), p. 202, no. 26 (hospital), p. 203. On the *Maestà* with the Quattro Santi Coronati painted on the facade of the Opera del Duomo, which probably dates from 1330, see Di Simone 2017. On the frescoes for the facade of the hospital, in which the Lorenzetti brothers were also involved, see Maginnis 1988; Norman 1999b, pp. 87–101; Caffio 2017–18. The lost scheme bore a date of 1335 but Simone may have completed his scenes earlier.
23. Martindale 1988, p. 33, also no. 41, pp. 211–14; Leone de Castris 2003, pp. 256–65, especially 256–7, for the saint's civic relevance. On the *comune*'s active involvement in the cult of new, local mendicant saints, see Vauchez 1977. Israëls 2022–3, pp. 128–9, points out that, similarly, the Orvieto *comune* supported its mendicant churches as 'civic assets'.
24. White 1966, p. 242.
25. Leone de Castris 2003, p. 370.
26. Strehlke 2022–3, pp. 67, 70–1.
27. Monnas 2008, p. 232; Strehlke 2022–3, p. 71.
28. Coat of arms revealed by the restoration of the fresco in 1988–94 and first identified in Bagnoli 1999, pp. 17, 24, 155.
29. Maginnis 2001, pp. 65–6; Norman 2006; Norman 2018, pp. 56–8.
30. Martindale 1988, pp. 37–8; Maginnis 2001, pp. 65–6.
31. The most comprehensive study of the relationship between Simone and the Angevins occurs in Norman 2018, pp. 56–8, 71–2, 133–51, 159–69.
32. Bagnoli 1988, especially p. 109, fig. 1, pp. 113–14; Leone de Castris 2003, pp. 20–4; Norman 2018, pp. 53–4.
33. Simone and his workshop were, however, busy painting polyptychs for important mendicant churches around the same time: in San Gimignano (Sant'Agostino; about 1317), Pisa (Santa Caterina; about 1319–20) and possibly Orvieto (San Francesco and San Domenico; early 1320s).
34. Israëls 2022–3, p. 131: the phrase is used as an attempt to explain how the Angevins obtained Simone's services on the Saint Louis of Toulouse Altarpiece (fig. 67).
35. On the chapel, see Martindale 1988, pp. 19–23; no. 4, pp. 174–81; Leone de Castris 2003, pp. 74–120; no. 8, pp. 347–8; Norman 2010b; Norman 2018, pp. 159–69; Strehlke 2022–3, pp. 74–6.
36. See Norman 2018, p. 169, on the appeal of the chivalric imagery to the Angevins and the Hungarian origins of Saint Martin.
37. Leone de Castris 2003, pp. 122–6; Norman 2010b, pp. 322–3; Norman 2018, pp. 161–2; Strehlke 2022–3, p. 76. A clerical saint became Saint Louis and Saint Ursula was turned into Saint Elizabeth of Hungary. Tintori and Fehm 1983, p. 177: technical evidence indicates that the entrance arch was painted last.
38. Martindale 1988, no. 3, pp. 173–4; Leone de Castris 2003, pp. 131–6, especially p. 134; no. 12, pp. 350–1; Norman 2010b, pp. 324–31; Norman 2018, pp. 164–9.
39. Norman 2018, p. 167.
40. Gardner 1976; Martindale 1988, p. 18; no. 16, pp. 192–4; Hoch 1995; Leone de Castris 2003, pp. 136–54; no. 11, pp. 349–50; Norman 2010a; Aceto 2010; Norman 2014; Norman 2018, pp. 11, 71–2, 133–51; Strehlke 2022–3, pp. 76–81; Israëls 2024 (forthcoming). I am grateful to Machtelt Brüggen Israëls for kindly sharing her unpublished manuscript with me.
41. Angevin involvement is accepted by all scholars except for Francesco Aceto (2010), who sees it as an exclusively Franciscan commission. Israëls 2024 (forthcoming) makes a compelling argument for the patron to be King Robert himself.
42. For an overview of the debate, see Norman 2018, pp. 140–7. Israëls 2024 (forthcoming) makes a new case for San Lorenzo.
43. The presence of a 'Symone Martini milite' at the Angevin court in 1317 has caused much confusion in the past but the record is now dismissed as referring to an Aragonese knight; see Aceto 1992, pp. 53–5.
44. Leone de Castris 2003, p. 143; Schmidt 2005a, pp. 239–40; Strehlke 2022–3, pp. 76–8; Norman 2018, pp. 71–2. Martindale 1988, pp. 6, 216, is tentative and Kozlowski 2015, p. 220, argues that the painting was executed in Naples on account of Robert's precise likeness.
45. On Lando di Pietro in Naples and the attribution of the reliquaries of Saint Louis of Toulouse and Saint Luke (both Musée du Louvre, Paris) to him, see Leone de Castris 1980b; Norman 2018, pp. 72–4. On Tino di Camaino in Naples, see Norman 2018, pp. 97–126, especially pp. 108–9 for the Washington relief. On this object, see also Middeldorf 1976, pp. 5–6.
46. Aceto 1992, p. 62; Fleck 2008, especially pp. 464–7.
47. On Giotto in Naples, see Caglioti 2005, pp. 38–40; Leone de Castris 2006; Fleck 2008, pp. 467–71.
48. About the status of *familiaris*, see Martindale 1972, pp. 36–8; Fleck 2008, pp. 466, 470. Vasari 1568 (1996), pp. 125–6.
49. On the Memmis, see Bennett 1977; Israëls 2015c, pp. 441–5.
50. Cannon 1982; Cannon 1994; Cannon 2022–3.
51. Cannon 2022–3, pp. 109–10.
52. Van Os 1978, pp. 70–2; Martindale 1988, no. 8, pp. 184–5; Hemsoll 1998; Leone de Castris 2003, p. 214; no. 15, p. 353; Schmidt 2005a, p. 145. The authenticity of the signature and the date of 1320 inscribed on the frame has been questioned in the past, but examination undertaken when the picture underwent conservation treatment at the National Gallery in 2020–1 provided no physical evidence to doubt it. I am grateful to Paul Ackroyd for sharing his insights on this matter. About the Pisa Polyptych, see Cannon in Boston 2022–3, cats 1–2, pp. 175–6, 191, n. 45.
53. Martindale 1988, no. 11, pp. 186–7; Leone de Castris 2003, no. 31, p. 361; Israëls in Boston 2022–3, cat. 5, pp. 212–21.
54. Zeri and Gardner 1980, p. 52; Christiansen 2012.
55. Fahy 1978, pp. 382–3; Leone de Castris 2003, no. 35, p. 364.
56. Kanter 1994, no. 91, pp. 91–5; Israëls 2015c, pp. 441, 442, n. 18; Jansen 2018, pp. 188–94. For another work attributed to Simone that might commemorate a truce, see De Wesselow 2022.
57. Sigismondo Tizio, *Historiarum Senensium ab initio urbis Senarum ab annum MDXXVIII*, about 1528, Biblioteca Comunale degli Intronati, Siena, MS B.III, cited in Martindale 1988, pp. 45–6. Uberto Benvoglienti, *Notizie dei Pittori e Statuarij*, cited in Pierini 2000, p. 228, n. 30; Norman 2024 (forthcoming), p. 19, n. 35. I am grateful to Diana Norman for kindly sharing her unpublished manuscript with me.
58. Rowlands 1965 argued on a philological basis that Petrarch wrote the poems in praise of Simone's portrait of Laura before 4 November 1336. Simone is last recorded in Siena in 1333, painting the base of a cross for the Cappella dei Nove (Leone de Castris 2003, p. 369). The *Annunciation* he signed with Lippo Memmi for the cathedral is also dated 1333. The facade of the hospital of Santa Maria della Scala, executed with the Lorenzetti brothers, is dated 1335, but Simone's involvement probably occurred earlier (Caffio 2017–18). The facade of the Opera del Duomo is reported by Della Valle 1785, p. 98, as dated 1335, but more probably dates from 1330 as reported by other early sources and an eighteenth-century drawing (Di Simone 2017). See Norman 2024 (forthcoming), p. 25, n. 63; Anheim 2015, p. 367.

59. Martindale 1990 posits that Simone might have been drawn by a 'Hollywood contract' that would have provided the ageing artist with something akin to a 'retirement'. Anheim 2015, especially pp. 377–8, also interprets Simone's Avignonese period as 'retirement' but not one connected to a court position, rather a winding down of activity afforded by the artist's fame, which would have allowed him to work on projects of his choosing and for the most select patrons.
60. The fresco cycle included the *Virgin of the Humility* and *Salvator Mundi* (both on the east wall), *Saint George and the Dragon* (north wall, destroyed) and *Andrea Corsini healing a Blind Man* (a miracle purported to have taken place on the cathedral porch; south wall, destroyed). For these frescoes, see De Nicola 1906; Enaud 1963; Martindale 1988, pp. 46–8; no. 5, pp. 181–3; Leone de Castris 2003, pp. 310–22, 363–4; Williamson 2007.
61. On the Orsini portrait, see Martindale 1988, pp. 49; no. 7, p. 184; Leone de Castris 2003, pp. 326–7. On the Orsini Polyptych, see Brink 1976; Brink 1983; Martindale 1988, no. 2, pp. 171–4; Leone de Castris 2003, no. 33, pp. 362–3; Schmidt 2005a, pp. 256–60, 281–3. Hueck 1983 argues for the patronage of Giovanni Gaetano Orsini. See also Norman 2024 (forthcoming).
62. Norman 2024 (forthcoming).
63. On the *Virgil*, see Biblioteca Ambrosiana, Milan, MS S.P. 10/27; Martindale 1988, pp. 50–1; no. 15, pp. 191–2; Leone de Castris 2003, pp. 322–5; no. 36, p. 364; Campbell 2004. On *Christ discovered in the Temple*, see Denny 1967; Van Os 1969; Martindale 1988, p. 49; no. 14, pp. 190–1; Leone de Castris 2003, pp. 324–8; no. 37, pp. 364–5; Schmidt 2005a, pp. 193–9.
64. Martindale 1988, pp. 45–6; Martindale 1990, pp. 285–6; Anheim 2015, especially pp. 369–70, 377–9.
65. Vasari 1568 (1996), p. 170; Ghiberti before 1455 (1998), p. 89; Peruzzi's manuscript is in the Biblioteca Medicea Laurenziana, Florence, MS Acquisti e Doni 401, the relevant passage appearing on fols 48v–49v. For a full critical edition of the manuscript, see Ferrante 2016. For the passage on Simone, see Capron 2017; Capron 2019, pp. 40–74.
66. Capron 2017; Capron 2019, pp. 40–74, especially 51–4 for the Cordeliers.
67. Capron 2017, pp. 5, 7. About the size of Franciscan altars, see Gardner 1981; Sirocco 2014.
68. Renouard 1941, pp. 115, 216, 217, 222, 223, 231, 250, 252, 266, 276, 358, 367, 370, 371, 405, 409: Lapo is listed as a changer in Avignon in 1328 when he received a fine for using the wrong weight. The fine was lifted on account of his good relations with the curia. From 1343 to the early 1360s he was among the popes' main bankers. In 1354 he was master of papal coins. See also Arias 1905, especially pp. 311, 328; Sapori 1943, p. 40 (records the first mention of Lapo in Avignon on 27 March 1321); Hayez 2012, pp. 176, 199, n. 72; Ferrante 2016, p. 312, n. 309. Lapo's papers and correspondence are documented by Jérome Hayez (1994, especially p. 81, n. 66) in the archives in the Bibliothèque municipale of Metz, in an uncatalogued volume. The originals are currently missing, but a partial microfilm of them exists at the Archives départementales de Vaucluse, 1MI 301. The poor quality of the reproduction makes this material nearly impossible to exploit. So far Lapo's will has not been found in the Archives départementales de Vaucluse. The Ruspi family arms appear in the Raccolta Ceramelli Papiani, Archivio di Stato, Florence, Ceramelli Papiani, fasc. 4144. Lapo owned a relic of Saint John the Baptist's index, reputedly received from a Byzantine lord and later purchased by the Calimala, Florence's wool merchants guild, for the city's baptistery: see Capron 2019, pp. 46–7; Buoninsegni 1581, p. 724; Minerbeti 1770 (1900), p. 172; Cornelison 1998, pp. 158–61, 168, 172–3, 239, Appendix G, document 1.
69. Arias 1905, pp. 311, 328, describes him as a 'piccolo banchiere fiorentino'; Renouard 1941, p 115, as 'chef d'une petite compagnie'; Hayez 2012, p. 199, n. 72; Brucker 1962, p. 21, n. 84: Lapo is among the *gente nuova* who achieved economic prominence in the 1352 communal tax records.
70. Partner 1965, p. 93: 'the small banking house of Lapo di Ruspo, a rich member of the *gente nuova*, was after 1342 much employed by the papacy; he was also used as a papal moneyer'.
71. Archives départementales de Vaucluse, sacristy inventory of the Cordeliers drawn up in 1369, 24H29, fol. 459v. Inventory published in full in Capron 2019, Appendix 2, pp. 249–52.
72. Nastagio di ser Tommaso a Francesco di Marco Datini, 16 July 1401, Archivio di Stato di Prato, *Datini*, 717, 703467, cited in Hayez 2012, p. 199, n. 72.
73. About the role of mendicant networks in the commissioning of Sienese polyptychs, see Cannon 1982; Cannon 1994; Cannon 2013, pp. 139–60; for Simone in particular, see Cannon 2022–3. For Simone in Orvieto, see Boston 2022–3.
74. Lenoble 2013, p. 381. The frequent use of vernacular Italian in the Cordeliers documents confirms that there was a sizeable Italian contingent among the Avignon friars in the second half of the fourteenth century.
75. Lenoble 2013, pp. 76–7: Francesco, guardian of the Neapolitan house of San Lorenzo Maggiore, and Pietro da Cadeneto, chaplain to Queen Sancia of Mallorca, came to Avignon to testify. Raymond de Stranillis, then guardian of the Cordeliers, had previously been the vicar of the monastery of Santa Chiara in Naples. About the trial, see Pasztor 1955, pp. 3–48; Schmitt 1959, pp. 181–7.
76. Archives départementales de Vaucluse, 24H29, fol. 458.
77. Archives départementales de Vaucluse, 24H29, fol. 459v.
78. On this topic, see Norman 2018.
79. Archives départementales de Vaucluse 24H29, fols 458–457v; also discussed by Lenoble 2013, pp. 55–6.
80. Archives départementales de Vaucluse, 24H29, fol. 458v. Napoleone had been created cardinal by the Franciscan Pope Nicholas IV and was generally very close to the order, including some of its spiritual members such as Ubertino da Casale, who had been his chaplain. During his tenure as papal legate in Umbria, Napoleone had founded not one but two chapels in the transept of the Lower Church of San Francesco at Assisi, both completed before 1306. About Napoleone's ties to the Franciscans, see Graham 2013.
81. Our knowledge of the Orsini Chapel and the Memmi altarpiece derives exclusively from the account of the antiquarian Joseph Marie de Suarès, *De rebus Avenionensibus*, Biblioteca Apostolica Vaticana, Rome, MS Barberini Lat. 3055, fol. 212, first cited in De Nicola 1906, p. 340, n. 6. For identification of the altarpiece to the Berenson *Maestà*, see Israëls in Strehlke and Israëls 2015, no. 69, pp. 452–8, pl. 69. Israëls 2015c, pp. 442–3: the Memmi brothers are not documented in Siena from 1343 to 1347 and it is probable that they spent those years at Avignon, either assisting Simone on Lapo di Ruspo's high altarpiece or settling his estate after his death.
82. About Avignon's Dominican convent, see Capron 2019, pp. 34–5, 61–2; Labande and Requin 1910; Guillemain 1979, pp. 225–6; Rollo-Koster 2015, p. 219; Schimmelpfennig 1990, pp. 179–96, especially p. 186.
83. Norman 2024 (forthcoming) traces the trajectory of Simone's compatriot, the cleric Vanni Paparoni, who seemed to have left Siena for Avignon in Giovanni Gaetano Orsini's retinue before transferring to Napoleone's service upon the former's death. As discussed, Napoleone is the likeliest patron of the Orsini Polyptych. He had his portrait painted by Simone in Avignon, and has been proposed as the man behind the commission of *Christ discovered in the Temple* (fig. 74). See Cameron 2022.
84. Biblioteca Medicea Laurenziana, Florence, MS Acquisti e Doni 401, fol. 48v. This is a backhanded compliment on Peruzzi's part, since it draws on a passage from Dante's *Purgatorio* 11:94–7 on the fading of earthly fame.

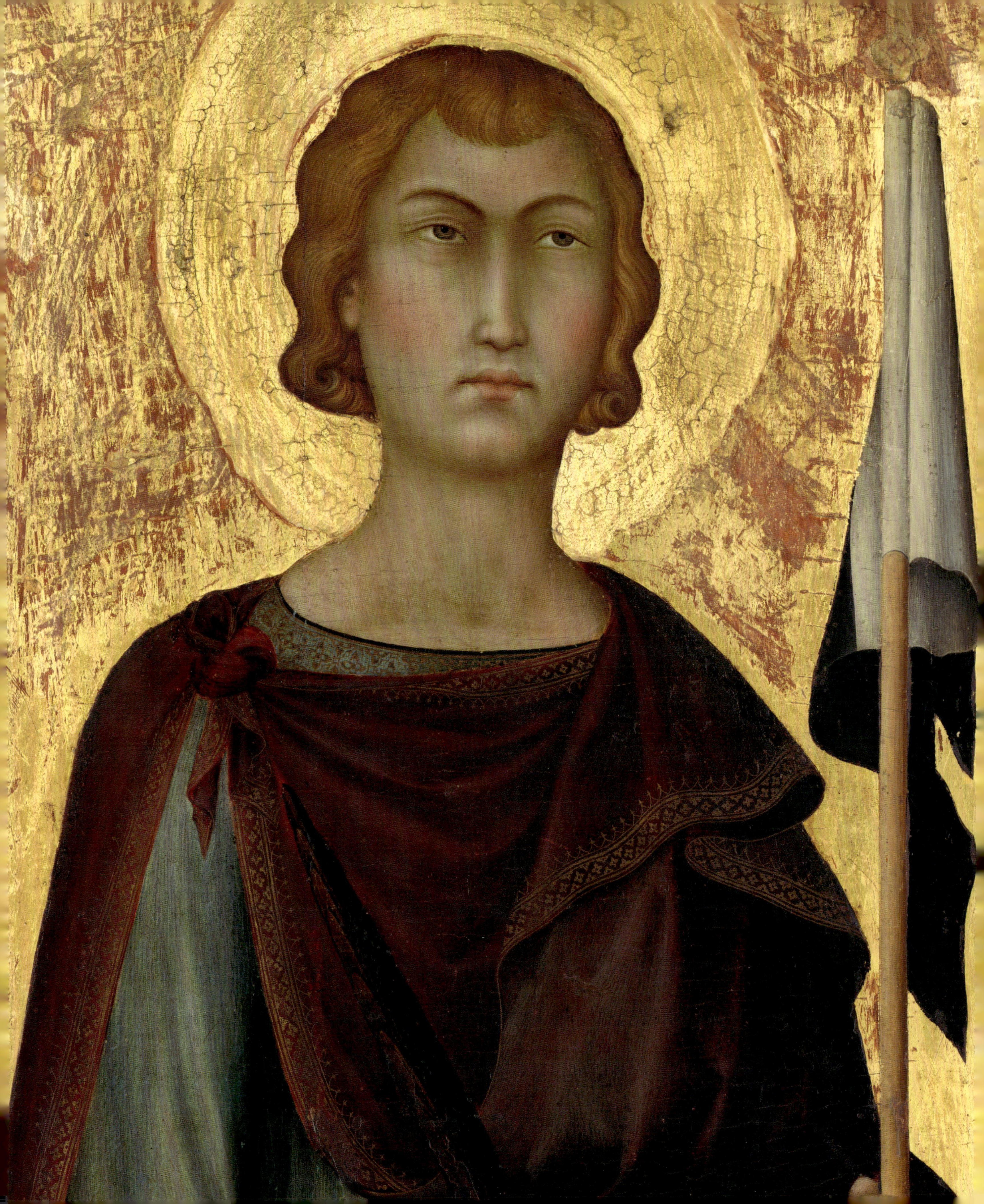

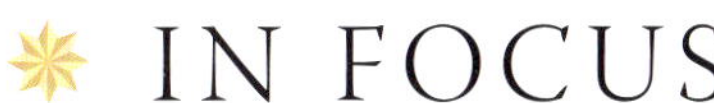

IN FOCUS

Two Portable Altarpieces by Simone Martini

Laura Llewellyn and Imogen Tedbury

Simone Martini's extraordinary inventiveness is encapsulated in a pair of remarkable multi-panelled works. Two very different commissions, one public and one private, these works develop Simone's experimentation with ensembles created from multiple rectangular panels, a format explored in the earlier assembly from which *Saint John the Evangelist* (see fig. 70) originated.[1] Both works, in their way, are also heirs to Duccio's *Maestà* (see figs 8, 9). One represents a uniquely flexible take on the iconic heavenly court of the front, while the other, itself a double-sided object, develops the narrative innovations of the reverse. These ensembles are brought together for the first time in centuries in the exhibition this publication accompanies, an occasion that may prompt new directions for further investigation.

THE PALAZZO PUBBLICO ALTARPIECE PANELS

For much of the twentieth century, when the contours of Simone's surviving corpus were still blurred, the paintings now divided between New York, Madrid and Los Angeles had orphan status. Nothing was known about where they originated or for whom they were painted.[2] Nor was there any consensus on their date, their relationship to each other or their attribution, which swung from Simone to Lippo Vanni to an unknown artist working in Simone's circle.[3] Although their imagery – a Virgin and Child with attendant saints – points towards their original function as an altarpiece, their physical structure is at odds with a traditional Sienese polyptych of the period (fig. 75–9).[4] The panels are not gabled and their rectangular box frames are of a type associated with smaller, portable works. Equally unusually, the panels are all the same size (rather than the central panel with the Virgin being larger). Finally, there is no physical evidence to suggest that the panels were originally hinged or nailed together, or indeed assembled into a bigger polyptych structure.

Technical study has revealed the engaged frames to be original, so corroborating their relationship as a group.[5] The date at which they were separated is not known, although it might have been as early as the seventeenth century.[6] Certainly, their differing

Detail of FIG. 75

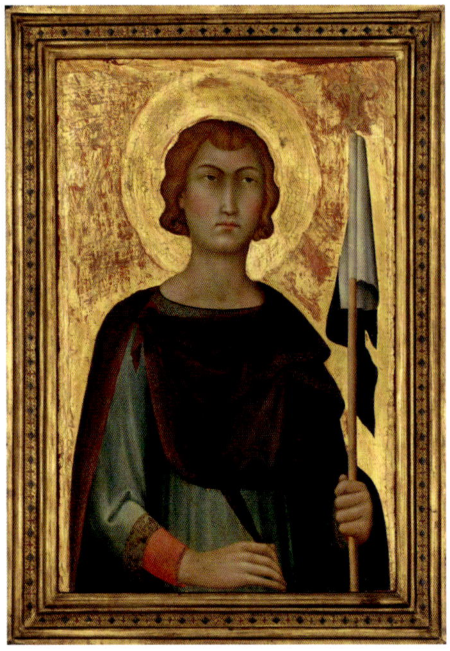

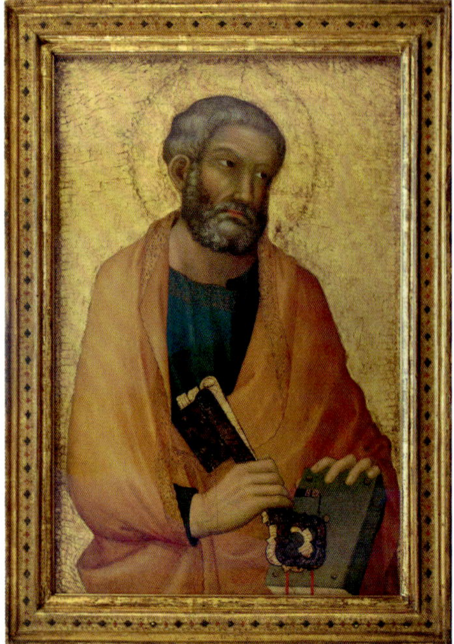

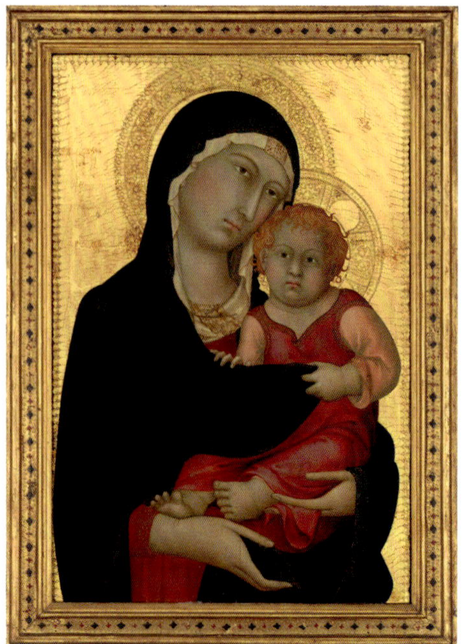

FIGS 75–9
Simone Martini
(about 1284–1344)
The Palazzo Pubblico Altarpiece

FIG. 75
Saint Ansanus, about 1326–30
Tempera on panel, 57.5 × 38.1 cm (with original frame)
The Metropolitan Museum of Art, New York. Robert Lehman Collection, 1975 (1975.1.13)

FIG. 76
Saint Peter, about 1326–7
Tempera on panel, 58 × 38.5 cm (with original frame)
Colección Carmen Thyssen (CTB.1997.20)

FIG. 77
The Virgin and Child, about 1326–7
Tempera on panel, 58.7 × 39.4 cm (with original frame)
The Metropolitan Museum of Art, New York. Robert Lehman Collection, 1975 (1975.1.12)

states of conservation indicate divergent afterlives. All the New York panels – *Saint Andrew* (fig. 78), *Saint Ansanus* (fig. 75) and the *Virgin and Child* (fig. 77) – and Madrid's *Saint Peter* (fig. 76) have been thinned and cradled. Their engaged frames have been removed and then reattached upside down. The Getty's *Saint Luke* is the best preserved (fig. 79), and therefore particularly important for reconstructing the original appearance and function of the group. Its wooden panel support is painted on the reverse and sides with imitation porphyry, a strong indication that it has not been trimmed, and that it was conceived as a portable object. It also bears an identifying inscription on the gold backdrop at either side of the saint's head ('S LUC[AS] S EV[ANGE] LSTA'); the *Saint Andrew* retains traces of a similar inscription. We can assume this feature was once shared by all the panels.

When the paintings' earliest attribution to Simone Martini was re-established, it was tentatively suggested that these panels could be identified with a work 'to keep in the Palazzo del Capitano' ('per tenere nel Palazzo del Capitano') for which Simone took payment of 30 lire in 1326.[7] The words 'per tenere' are revealing, seemingly indicating that the palace of the Capitano was a temporary or sometime repository rather than a permanent home. Archival research has confirmed that the five panels should indeed be associated with Simone's 1326 commission, and so belong to his mid-career period during which time Simone was running a prolific workshop in his native city, together with his brother-in-law Lippo Memmi.

For this work, many of the key records in fact date to the following century, when the panels had been moved to the newly established Cappella dei Signori in the Palazzo Pubblico.[8] In the mid-fifteenth century the five panels were set into a new surrounding frame and given a predella depicting the episodes from the life of the Virgin, painted by Sano di Pietro.[9] Here, they were probably seen by the Florentine sculptor and goldsmith Lorenzo Ghiberti, who wrote of his admiration for Simone Martini in his *Commentarii*, where he remarked that the people of Siena considered Simone to be their greatest artist.[10] Such recycling or refurbishment of earlier panels in later centuries is relatively rare, although not exceptional, and often points to the singular reputation of the painter in question.[11] Certainly Siena retained a particular pride in the achievements of earlier artists, Simone foremost among them. The figurative and literal reframing of Simone's panels speaks to the reverence in which he was posthumously held in his native city.

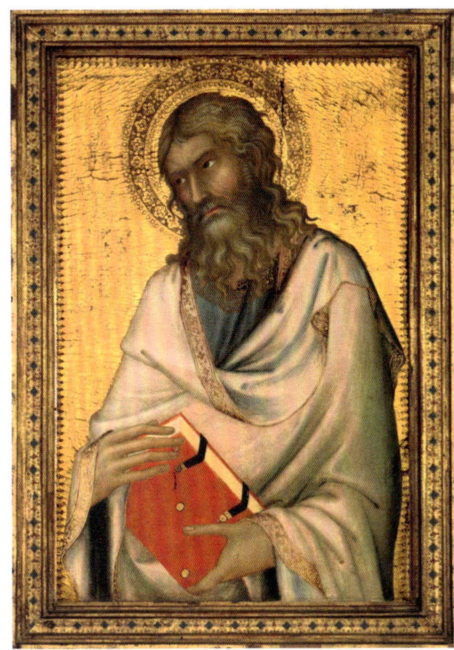

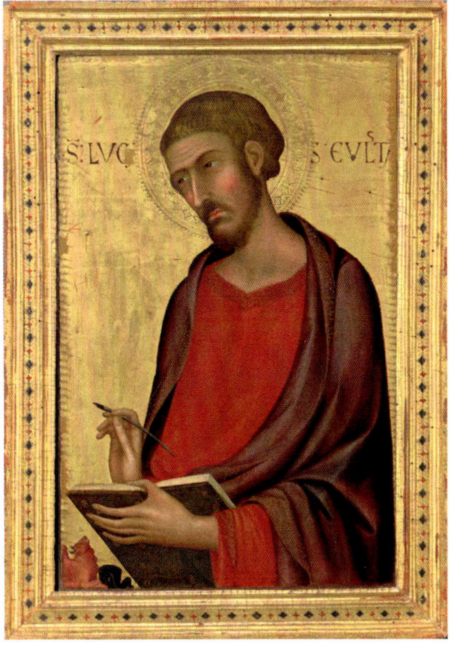

It is the trecento documents, however, that are of particular interest for understanding how the panels were first used, and for understanding how they were conceived at the point of production. In February 1327, six months after Simone had taken payment, what seems to be the same work was lent by the *comune* to the residence of the Podestà and later returned to the Palazzo Pubblico.[12] The 'per tenere' (to keep) of the 1326 payment and the 1327 document noting the loan of the panel to the Podestà show that, from the outset, Simone's panels were on the move between different buildings associated with the Council of the Nine (*Nove*): transported from the residence of the Capitano, to the house of the Podestà and to the town hall. There are also much later documents that appear to suggest the panels were transferred from one room to another within the Palazzo Pubblico.[13] This flexible and movable solution acquires particular logic when we consider that change was the mainstay of Sienese political life, with new members of the *Nove* elected every two months.[14] Simone had apparently produced the panels specifically so that they could be rearranged, transplanted and even borrowed externally.

The work itself was also scalable. The 1327 record describes the paintings in question as only three panels: the *Virgin and Child*, *Saint Peter* and *Saint Andrew*. *Saint Ansanus* and *Saint Luke* are not mentioned. Perhaps these outermost panels were not required and left behind. However, it has also been hypothesised that they were not part of the original commission but added to the set at a later date.[15] The idea is intriguing and may explain some of the slight differences in the punchwork. *Saint Peter* and *Saint Ansanus* have both sustained significant damage to their gilded background. Of the three panels that survive with their punched decoration intact, the Virgin's and Andrew's haloes share outer borders of incised lines, while Luke's halo is rather different in conception, bordered by a fringe of punchwork. This technique was introduced by the Martini-Memmi workshop in the 1320s, initially to distinguish the Virgin and Child in the San Domenico Polyptych, Orvieto.[16] Further technical analysis may cast light on this question. What seems clear is that flexibility was a key component of Simone's design brief: easily portable and with no hinging hardware to enable use as a partial or complete set. In this respect, the Palazzo Pubblico Altarpiece, ostensibly conventional on first encounter, is in fact a daring experiment with form and structure, and encapsulates Simone's singular ability to fuse tradition with innovation. *LL*

FIG. 78
Saint Andrew, about 1326–7
Tempera on panel, 57.2 × 37.8 cm (with original frame)
The Metropolitan Museum of Art, New York. Gift of George Blumenthal, 1941 (41.100.23)

FIG. 79
Saint Luke, about 1326–30
Tempera on panel, 67.5 × 48.3 cm (with engaged frame)
J. Paul Getty Museum, Los Angeles (82.PB.72)

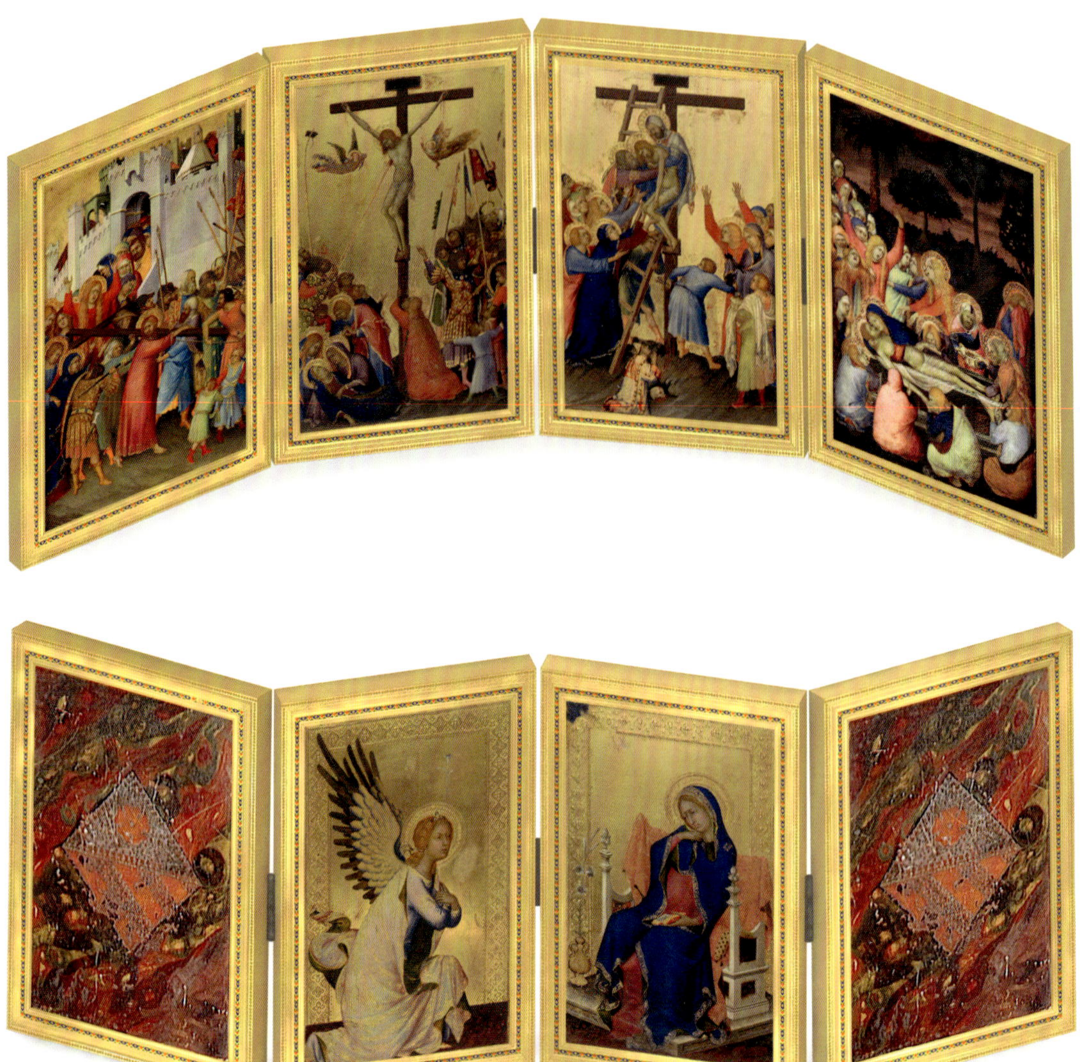

FIG. 80
Reconstruction of the inner and outer faces of the Orsini Polyptych, courtesy of Matilde Grimaldi

THE ORSINI POLYPTYCH

Tradition and innovation are fused again in the conception and construction of the ensemble known as the Orsini Polyptych. Today divided between Antwerp, Paris and Berlin, the work was originally constructed from four rectangular panels, each painted on both sides (fig. 80).[17] Physical evidence of attachments survives on the right of the *Way to Calvary* panel (see fig. 189), suggesting that the panels were almost certainly joined together with hinges that would have permitted the work to fold as a 'concertina', a mechanism used by goldsmiths and ivory carvers (for example, see fig. 173).[18] The original order of the panels is confirmed by the inscription that once ran across the four consecutive narrative scenes from the Passion: 'HOC OPUS' (recorded on the frame of the *Way to Calvary*), 'SYMON' (still present on the *Crucifixion*'s frame), 'PINXIT' (on the *Deposition*'s frame) and, very likely, a lost inscription on the *Entombment* panel too, either the date or 'DE SENIS'.[19] The *Entombment*'s frame was removed at an unknown date, perhaps during the same campaign that the panel's gold background was painted over with a nighttime landscape. Close examination of the Antwerp panels confirms that the *Angel Gabriel* and *Annunciate Virgin* (fig. 81) once formed the back of the *Deposition* and *Crucifixion* (see figs 192, 197) panels before being sawn apart at an unknown date.[20] The reverse of the *Way to*

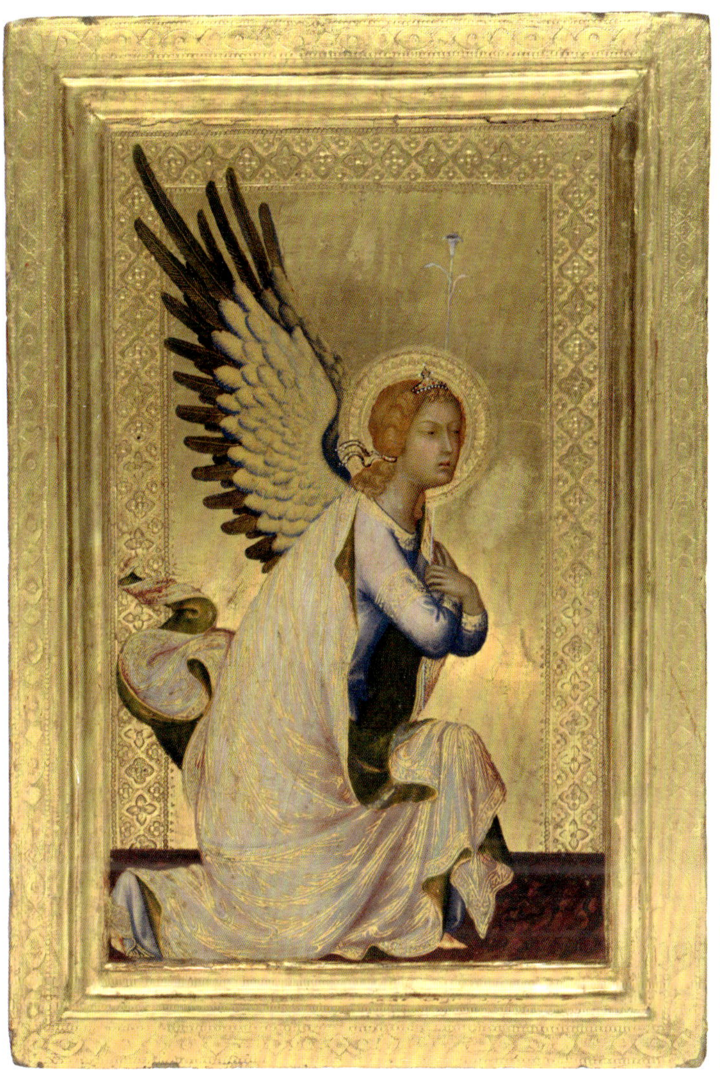

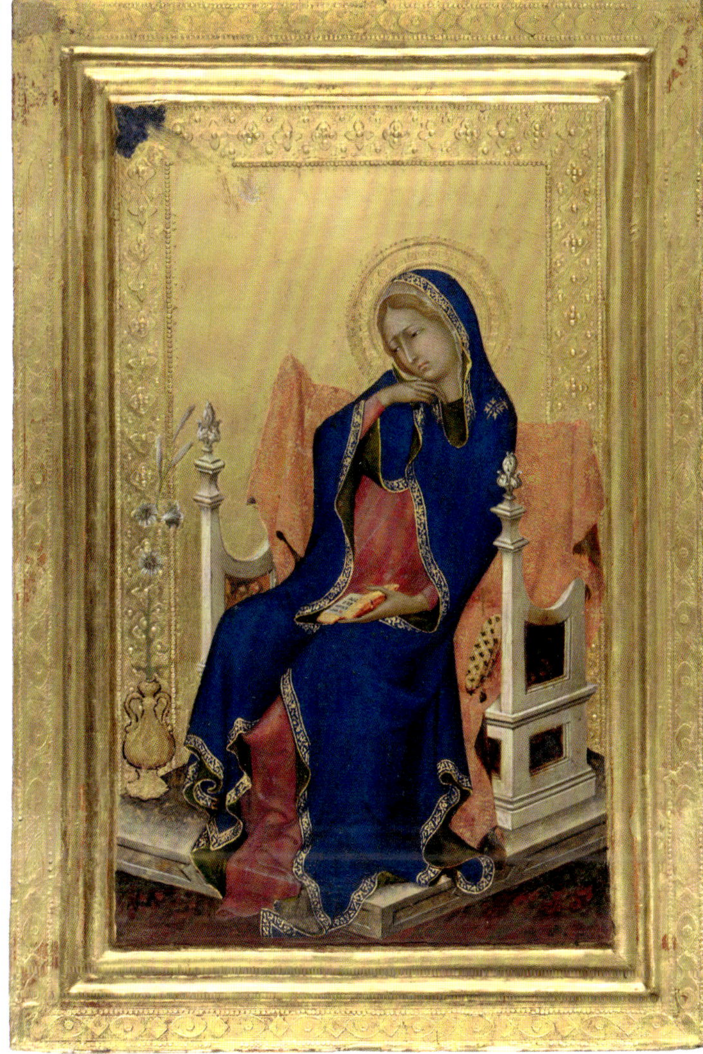

Calvary bears the Orsini family arms on fictive marble protected by a gold frame; the *Entombment* panel has been thinned and cut down but probably carried similar decoration on its reverse.[21] Closed for transportation, this small block of gold and painted marble would have been the size of a large book – personalised, portable and highly prestigious – but opened, it would have functioned as a free-standing, miniature, double-sided altarpiece, with the silent, stately Annunciation on one side and the four scenes from Christ's Passion, wild, crowded and chaotic, on the other.[22]

While Simone's authorship has never been questioned, there is little agreement about when – and where – the work was created. All possible options have been put forward, ranging from the earliest 'Ducciesque' phase in Simone's career[23] and the years around 1320,[24] to the mid-1320s,[25] a period around 1335–6 immediately preceding the painter's departure for Avignon,[26] and the last years of his life in the papal city.[27] Close study of the techniques employed in the panels' decoration can provide some clues, however. Their punchwork may associate them with paintings produced by Simone and Lippo from the mid-1320s onwards in Siena, and although Simone used a textured *sgraffito* on the hanging draped over the Virgin's throne, this surface is lacking the granulation introduced in Gabriel's tunic in the *Annunciation* of 1333.[28] The polyptych's impact on contemporary artists can also help to date – and

FIG. 81
Simone Martini
(about 1284–1344)
The Angel Gabriel and
The Annunciate Virgin,
about 1326–34
Tempera on poplar,
29.7 × 20.5 cm (each,
with engaged frames)
Collection KMSKA -
Flemish Community
(public domain) (257, 258)

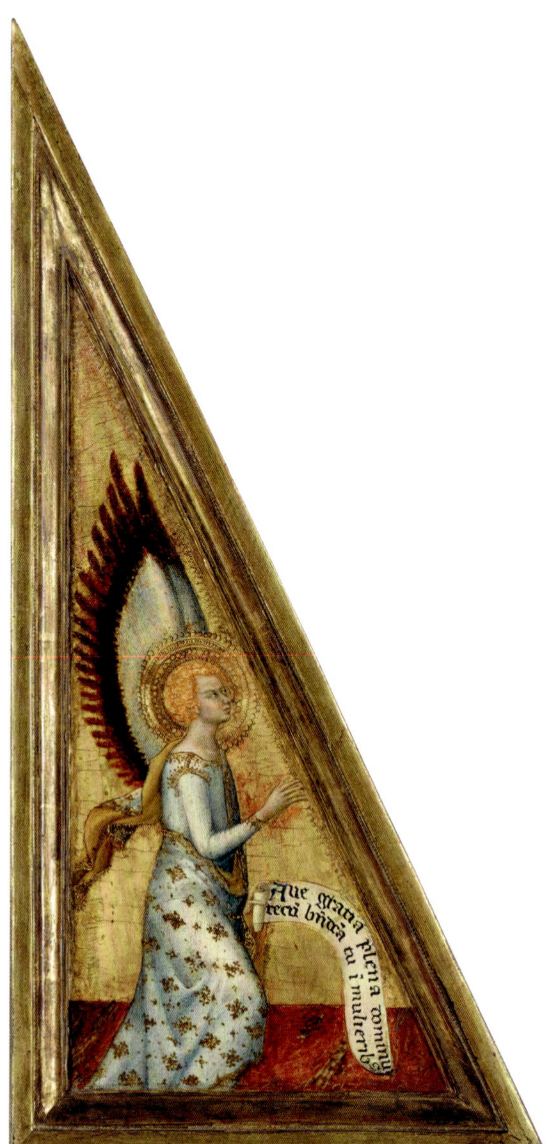

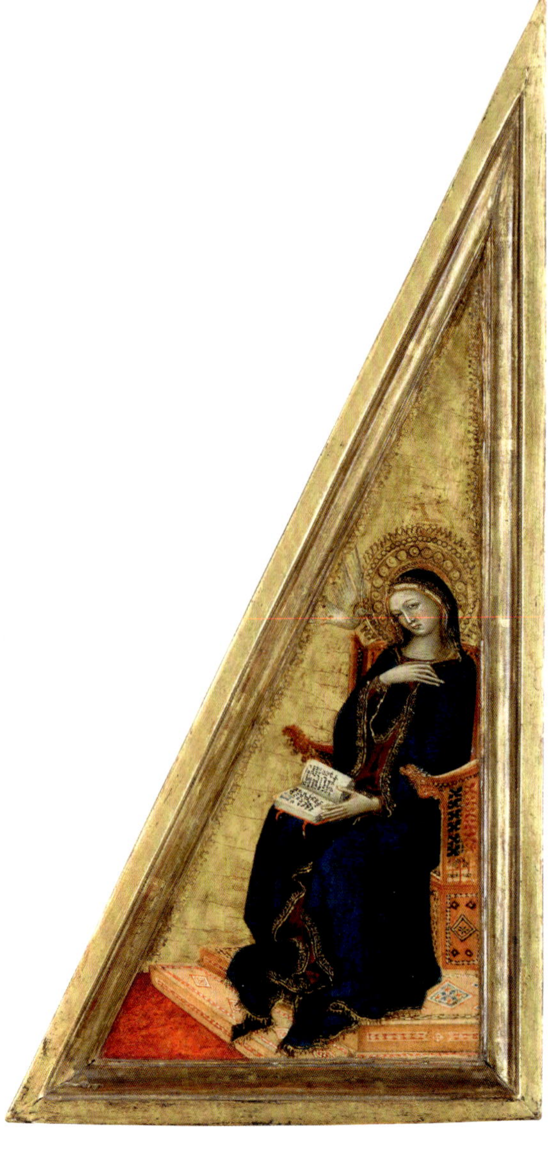

FIG. 82
Matteo Giovannetti
(about 1300–1369)
The Angel of the Annunciation and *The Virgin of the Annunciation*, about 1345
Tempera on canvas, transferred from panel, 41 × 22 cm each
Musée du Louvre, Paris
(RF 1996 4, RF 1996 3)

locate – its production. Echoes of the Passion Cycle's innovative iconography have been observed in works associated with the Martini-Memmi workshop dated or datable between 1335 and 1340, such as the frescoes in the Collegiata, San Gimignano, suggesting that Simone's inventions were known in his circle by that date.[29] The polyptych also seems to have been known by artists in Avignon, such as Giovannetti (fig. 82). Both connections invite interrogation: how – and when – might a small painting destined for private use become familiar to other artists? If the polyptych had been painted in Siena before Simone's departure, artists in Simone's circle might have been present during its production or perhaps been aware of workshop drawings. Matteo Giovannetti, on the other hand, may have seen the polyptych after it had passed into the possession of its new owner, who is depicted in the panel of the *Deposition*, an elderly mitred prelate, participating in what has been called 'a pious game of virtual reality'.[30]

This owner was almost certainly one of three powerful Orsini cardinals who ended their careers at the papal court in Avignon.[31] Matteo Orsini, a Dominican, bequeathed his 'large panel with pictures made in the city of Siena' to the Dominicans of Avignon, although it is hard to imagine Simone's exquisite polyptych ever being described as 'tabulam meam magnam' ('my large panel').[32]

Another candidate is Giovanni Gaetano Orsini, Cardinal of San Teodoro from 1316, who died in Avignon in 1335.[33] Giovanni Gaetano is documented visiting Siena on two separate occasions, in 1327 and for several months in 1334, and would have had ample opportunity to become acquainted with Simone's work. It is generally agreed that the most likely contender is Giovanni Gaetano's first cousin, Cardinal Napoleone Orsini, a known patron of artistic commissions, including from Simone himself, who, according to Petrarch, painted a lost posthumous portrait of Napoleone.[34] The extraordinary expressiveness of Simone's Passion scenes has been persuasively connected to a text written by Napoleone's chaplain, Ubertino da Casale, who encouraged meditation on the instruments of the Passion.[35] Napoleone himself even owned a relic of one of the holy nails, which might explain why the supplicant is included in the *Deposition* (not the *Crucifixion*, which is more usual), gazing intently at the bloody nails held out by the holy woman in mauve.[36] It has recently been suggested that the polyptych might have been made for Napoleone, but with the involvement of Giovanni Gaetano.[37] Napoleone moved to Avignon around 1310 and never returned to Italy, but remained politically active in life on the peninsula through letters, agents and messengers, one of whom could well have been Giovanni Gaetano, who began his career as a retainer in Napoleone's household.[38] Whether Giovanni Gaetano acted as an agent in the commission on Napoleone's behalf or commissioned the painting as a gift for his powerful cousin, Simone may have based the supplicant image on a frescoed portrait of Napoleone, identified by inscription, painted by associates of Giotto between 1295 and 1300 in the Saint Nicholas Chapel of the Lower Church of Assisi.

The commission of the Orsini Polyptych exemplifies a broader, possibly competitive, interest in portable, precious, personal paintings among the papal curia in Avignon, several of whom owned panel paintings by Sienese artists (see pp. 224–39). Napoleone Orsini worked with Niccolò da Prato on various papal commissions and may well have known the pair of triptychs by Duccio that he is thought to have owned.[39] James Stevenson's cartoon of a demanding patron – 'I'm bored with triptychs. Paint me a quadriptych' (see fig. 64) – invites consideration of the one-upmanship that might have had an impact on the production of these structurally advanced objects.[40] Although inspired by the hinging technologies used in French ivory or metalwork quadriptychs, the Orsini Polyptych is, uniquely, two works in one, both Annunciation diptych and Passion Cycle quadriptych together. Its rectangular panels are also proportioned according to true measure, an aspect ratio familiar to our eyes but innovative at the time.[41] Smaller, sleeker, more compact, and the latest in structural and narrative innovations, this technologically advanced and iconographically varied object might have outperformed even a pair of triptychs. *IT*

***

It has been observed before that Simone Martini's altarpiece for the Palazzo Pubblico is a significant precedent for the Orsini Polyptych in its experimentation with form.[42] If the Orsini Polyptych was made in the second half of the 1320s – Giovanni Gaetano Orsini was in Siena briefly in 1327 – Simone may have begun work on it almost immediately after his panels for the town hall, or even worked on the two commissions contemporaneously, if a later date for the *Saint Luke* and *Saint Ansanus* panels is entertained. Nonetheless, both ensembles push the formal possibilities of works assembled from multiple rectangular panels in very different directions. The Palazzo Pubblico panels constitute a series of iconic images scaled for group viewing, their inherent flexibility resulting from the absence of connecting hardware. By contrast, hinging hardware is key to the Orsini Polyptych's presentation of two intricate narrative sequences, which are packed full of significance for the private appreciation of their intended owner. These consummately sensitive and unique responses to their patrons' requirements foreshadow Simone's extraordinary *Christ discovered in the Temple* (see fig. 74), apparently a stand-alone panel, which presents emotional family drama as a subject for personal devotion.[43]

1. For this work, see Capron, p. 108, in the present volume.
2. Three of the panels were first known in Paris: *Saint Ansanus* was supposedly bought in a bookshop there before 1915; *Saint Peter* and *Saint Luke* appeared with Parisian dealer E. Bonesi. The *Virgin and Child* was first known in the collection of Bishop Alessandro Toti, Colle di Val d'Elsa, in 1900. Robert Langton Douglas acquired *Saint Andrew* from the Earl of Northesk or Earl of Southesk in 1915. For the panels' full provenance, see Leone de Castris 2003, p. 358.
3. For the panels' earlier critical history, see Pope-Hennessy and Kanter 1987, pp. 18–22; Martindale 1988, pp. 38–40, 194–5.
4. See Gardner von Teuffel, pp. 68–77, in the present volume; Cannon 2022–3, pp. 104–23.
5. For the frames, see Newbery and Kanter in New York 1990, cat. 1, p. 33; Newbery 2007, pp. 6–9. Macro-X-ray fluorescence gold maps for the *Saint Luke* panel show that the original sheets of gold leaf extend from the panel over the frame. See MacLennan et al. 2019, fig. 2d.
6. In 1686 the altarpiece in the chapel where they are thought to have stood was dismantled and replaced by Sodoma's *Holy Family with Saint Leonard* (1533; Palazzo Pubblico, Siena). See Christiansen 1994, pp. 149–50.
7. Boskovits 1974, p. 376, whose rejection of the historic attribution to Lippo Vanni in favour of Simone is now widely accepted, was the first to suggest this group of paintings might be associated with the documented work of 1326, although his proposal was not universally accepted initially. Eisenberg 1981, p. 147, n. 50, considers 30 lire too little for an altarpiece. See Christiansen 1994, Appendix, document I, p. 159. Cited in Romagnoli 1976, vol. 1, pp. 587–8, and transcribed in Bacci 1944, pp. 148–9.
8. Keith Christiansen's meticulous archival research, illuminating the panels' fifteenth-century history, seems to confirm the association made by Boskovits in 1974 (Christiansen 1994). Leone de Castris 2003, no. 26, p. 358, and Schmidt 2005a, p. 283, accept the identification. Others maintain the panels are earlier works: Bagnoli 1994, pp. 124–42; Pierini 2000, p. 122.
9. Sano di Pietro's predella took as its inspiration the frescoes by Simone Martini and the Lorenzetti brothers on the exterior of Santa Maria della Scala, now lost. The panels (dating from 1448 to 1452) are: *Birth of the Virgin* (University of Michigan Museum of Art, Ann Arbor), *The Presentation in the Temple* (Pinacoteca Vaticana, Rome), *The Assumption of the Virgin* and *The Virgin returning to the House of her Parents* (Staatliches Lindenau-Museum, Altenburg) and *The Marriage of the Virgin* (The Metropolitan Museum of Art, New York). Sano's predella replaced an earlier, additional predella, commissioned in 1401–2, for which, see Christiansen 1994, p. 151, and Appendix, documents III and IV, pp. 159–60.
10. Ghiberti before 1455 (1998), p. 89.
11. Later generations of Sienese painters remained indebted to Simone Martini and the Lorenzetti (see Fattorini 2010). The renovation of earlier artworks was undertaken across Tuscany, as adaptations of Giotto's Baroncelli Altarpiece and Fra Angelico's San Domenico Altarpiece demonstrate, but the practice was particularly prevalent in Siena, where works were repainted as well as reframed. For example, Lippo Memmi's *Madonna del Popolo* (about 1325–30; Museo Diocesano, Siena) was given an *all'antica* frame (Hoeniger 1995, pp. 112–13, p. 115, fig. 79), and Butzek 2001b argues, convincingly, that the thirteenth-century paintings in the cathedral, the *Madonna dell'Opera* and the *Madonna del Voto*, were given new frames by Francesco and Andrea Vanni in about 1380 and about 1400 respectively.
12. The 1327 document refers to a 'tavola' valued at 30 lire. Christiansen 1994, pp. 155–6, and Appendix, document II, p. 159.
13. Christiansen 1994, pp. 149–50, summarises what is known of the panels' movements after their replacement by Sodoma's altarpiece.
14. See Campbell, p. 13, in the present volume.
15. Christiansen 1994, pp. 156–8, and Leone de Castris 2003, p. 249, mention the possibility that *Saint Ansanus* and *Saint Luke* may have been painted slightly later than the other three panels. Andrea De Marchi makes this argument in Siena 2010, no. B.10, p. 172.
16. Leone de Castris 2003, p. 249, p. 194, n. 48, discusses this feature of the punchwork.
17. As Susie Nash notes in the present volume, pp. 240–53, the panels were almost certainly at the Burgundian court by around 1400, and may have remained in Dijon until the nineteenth century. The four Antwerp panels were bequeathed to the Museum voor Schone Kunsten van Antwerpen in 1840 by Legs Van Ertborn, who had purchased them in Dijon in 1826. The *Way to Calvary* was recorded at the Chartreuse of Dijon in 1791 and purchased by the Musée du Louvre from L'Saint-Denis in 1834. See Monget 1898–1905, vol. 3, p. 75.
18. Schmidt 2005a, pp. 281–306, suggests this formation and discusses the Orsini Polyptych within a broader corpus of multi-panelled paintings, as well as the relationship of these works to folding ivories and metalwork objects. See also Schmidt 2002b.
19. The *Way to Calvary* had the inscription 'HOC OPUS' on its frame in 1791 (see above, n. 13), but this text was probably lost when the panel's frame was regilded. For the *Entombment* inscription, Leone de Castris 1989, p. 113, considers 'DE SENIS' most likely.
20. Brink 1976, p. 11, observes that the saw marks and worm furrows visible on the backs of the Antwerp panels confirm the reconstruction proposed by Van Os and Rinkleff-Reinders 1972. The Louvre panel was added to the complex with the Antwerp panels by Crowe and Cavalcaselle 1885, p. 114, and the Berlin panel by Gosche 1899, p. 87, n. 1.
21. Reinach 1927 was the first to recognise the arms of the Orsini family on the Louvre panel. Both sides of each panel would have had an engaged frame, projecting 5.5 mm from the Passion scenes and 2 mm from the Annunciation and fictive marble surfaces.
22. Martindale 1988, p. 172, discusses the extraordinary contrast in mood on the polyptych's two sides.
23. Peter 1939, p. 164, considers the polyptych pre-Assisi; Caleca 1977 suggests a Ducciesque phase.
24. Pope-Hennessy 1939; Paccagnini 1955, pp. 110–21; Brandl 1985. Pierini 2000, p. 227, also prefers a window of 1317–25.
25. Polzer 2010; Norman 2024 (forthcoming).
26. Gosche 1899; Gnudi 1956; Gozzoli 1970; De Benedictis 1976; De Benedictis 1979; Leone de Castris 1989, no. 26, pp. 11–21; Leone de Castris 2003, p. 300.
27. Oertel 1968, p. 213; White 1966, p. 241; Martindale 1988, pp. 51–3, p. 172.
28. Polzer 2010 observes the affinity with punches used in the mid-1320s onwards. In addition to the Orsini Polyptych *Annunciate Virgin* and the 1333 *Annunciation*, Simone uses *sgraffito* in only one other panel: the 1342 *Christ discovered in the Temple* at Liverpool (fig. 74). See Monnas 2008, pp. 73–6; Monnas, pp. 198–215, in the present volume.
29. Also, *Christ bearing the Cross* (fig. 211) and Ugolino di Vieri's *Reliquary of the Holy Corporal* (figs 47, 97, 126).
30. Schmidt 2005a, p. 259.
31. The identification of the Orsini arms has ruled out other proposed patrons, like Giacomo Colonna and Jacopo Stefaneschi.
32. 'tabulam meam magnam cum ymaginibus pictam in civitate senarum' (Cannon 2013, p. 222, n. 86, citing Forte 1967, p. 242). D'Urso 1991 argues that the Orsini Polyptych is Matteo's 'tabulam magnam', for which see Cannon 2013, pp. 219–23.
33. Hueck 2001 makes this suggestion, drawing attention to the prominence given to Saint John the Evangelist: Giovanni Gaetano's name saint.

34. For this portrait, see Martindale 1988, pp. 49, 184; Brink 1976, pp. 17–18. For Petrarch's relationship with Simone, see Capron, pp. 101–2, in the present volume.
35. Brink has made this argument on several occasions. Brink 1976, pp. 17–23; Brink 1977a; Brink 1983.
36. Brink 1977a, pp. 7–8; Polzer 2010, pp. 321–2; Schmidt 2005a, pp. 258–60. Brink also identifies one of the figures at the *Entombment* as an image of Clare of Montefalco, to whom Napoleone was also dedicated. See Brink 1983.
37. Norman 2024 (forthcoming). With huge thanks to Diana Norman for kindly sharing her article with us in advance of its publication.
38. Giovanni was in Napoleone's household by 1316. Norman 2024 (forthcoming), citing Beattie 2007, p. 43.
39. See Cannon, p. 53, in the present volume.
40. Cardinal Gozio Battagli's eight-panelled ensemble, probably commissioned in Avignon from a Sienese artist, should also be considered in this context. See Gordon, p. 226, in the present volume.
41. Brink 1976, p. 7, n. 1, notes Simone's use of these true measure rectangles in the 1342 *Christ discovered in the Temple* (fig. 74) and his frontispiece for Petrarch's *Virgil* (fig. 73). True measure rectangles have an aspect ratio of the square root of two (particularly familiar to users of A4 paper).
42. Schmidt 2005a, pp. 281–3.
43. For this painting, see Schmidt 2005a, pp. 193–9; and Capron, p. 111, in the present volume.

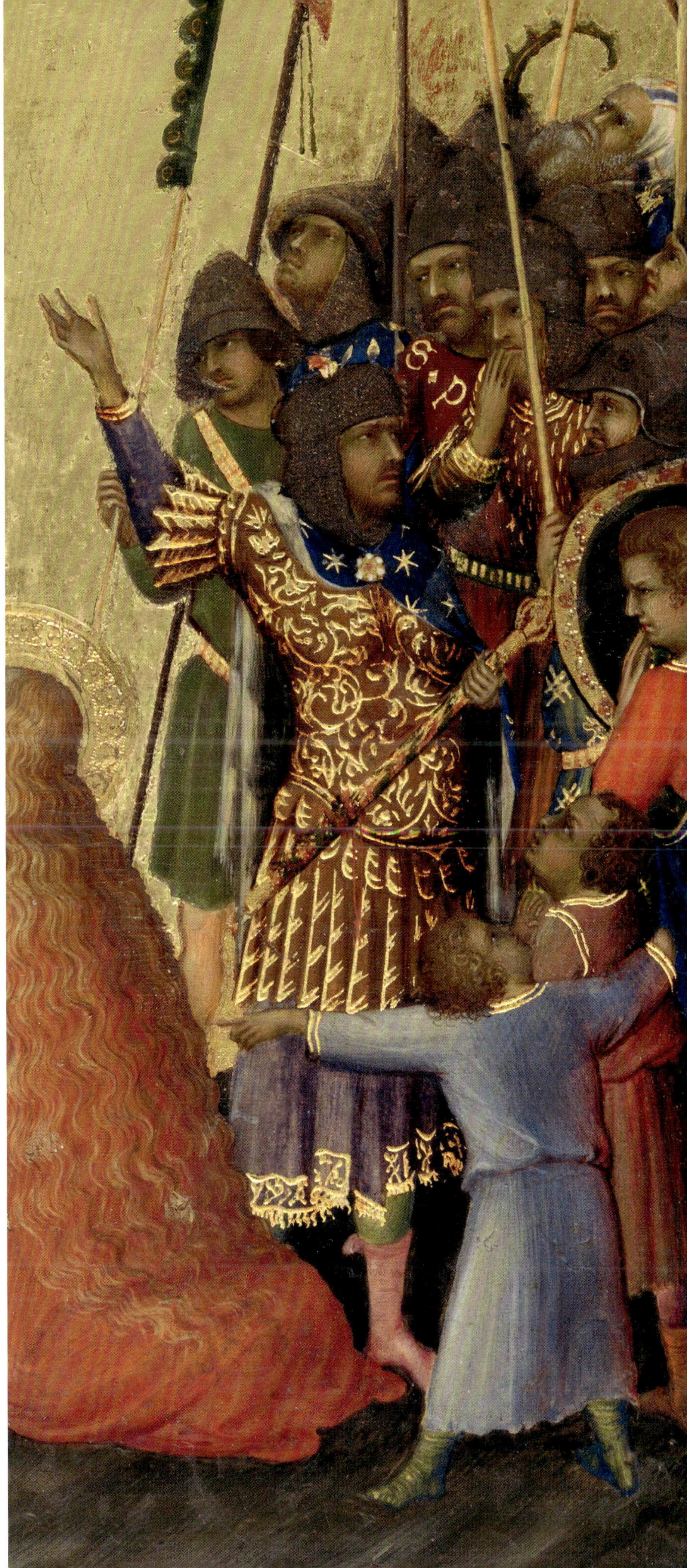

Detail of Simone Martini's *Crucifixion* from the Orsini Polyptych (fig. 80; see also fig. 197)

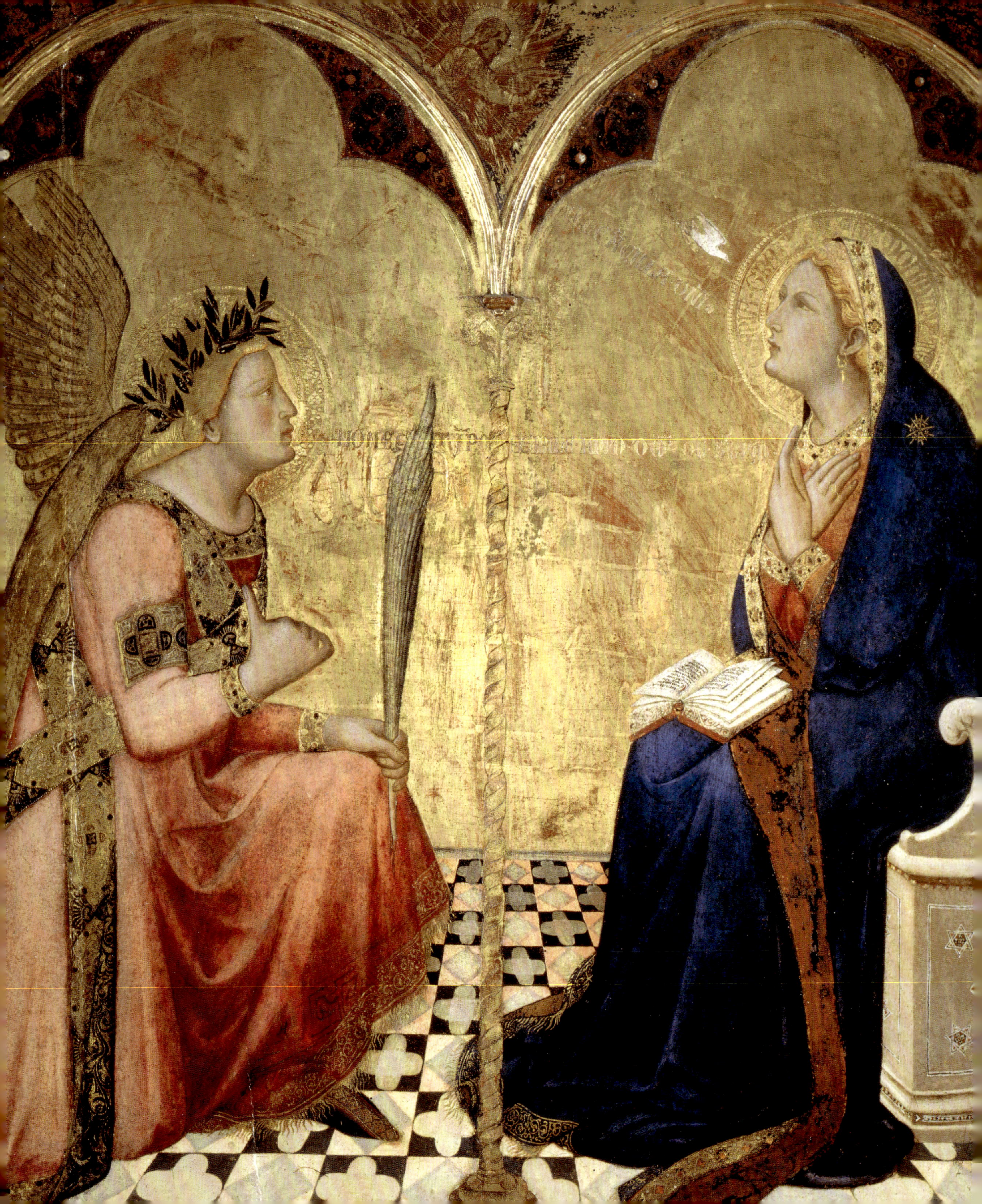

'A MOST FAMOUS AND OUTSTANDING PAINTER': AMBROGIO LORENZETTI

Stephan Wolohojian

Written in Florence, around 1447, Lorenzo Ghiberti's seminal treatise on art theory, history and practice, *I commentarii*, presents an especially favourable assessment of Ambrogio Lorenzetti. In the work's second volume, an exploration of the art that immediately preceded his own, Ghiberti expresses a particular admiration for Sienese painters of the fourteenth century. Throughout the meditation he frames as 'arte moderna', he privileges Ambrogio Lorenzetti as one of only two artists – the only painter – to receive his highest praise. Ghiberti singles out Ambrogio as *famosissimo e singolarissimo* (most famous and outstanding), a 'man of great genius and a most noble designer, very skilful in the theory of painting'. He returns to words such as *docto* (scholarly/learned) and *perito* (highly skilled/knowledgeable) to describe his talent, summing him up as a man of great genius (*di grande ingegno*) and *arte*.[1] A century after this, Giorgio Vasari based his own account of Ambrogio on Ghiberti's text, further praising the artist's intellectual interests, his powers of composition and his ability to portray complex figural compositions. At the end of his biographical assessment, this forerunner of modern art history admired Ambrogio above all for his associations with men of letters and for his engagement with the Sienese republic, concluding that he was as much, if not more, a learned gentleman and a philosopher as he was an artist.[2] By concluding in such a laudatory way, Vasari, like Ghiberti, singled out this fourteenth-century Sienese artist as making a higher claim for their profession, elevating it both socially and intellectually, and propelling the art of painting away from the mechanical work of the craftsman, into the realm of a learned practitioner.

In the context of a twenty-first-century exhibition, it is difficult to present the full intellectual and artistic reach of this extraordinary artist. The very paintings that excited Ghiberti and Vasari, a series of frescoes in the cloister of a Franciscan friary depicting a martyrdom occurring during a dramatic storm (a bravura feat they clearly recognised), were destroyed in the eighteenth century.[3] Likewise, only

P.126
Detail of FIG. 87

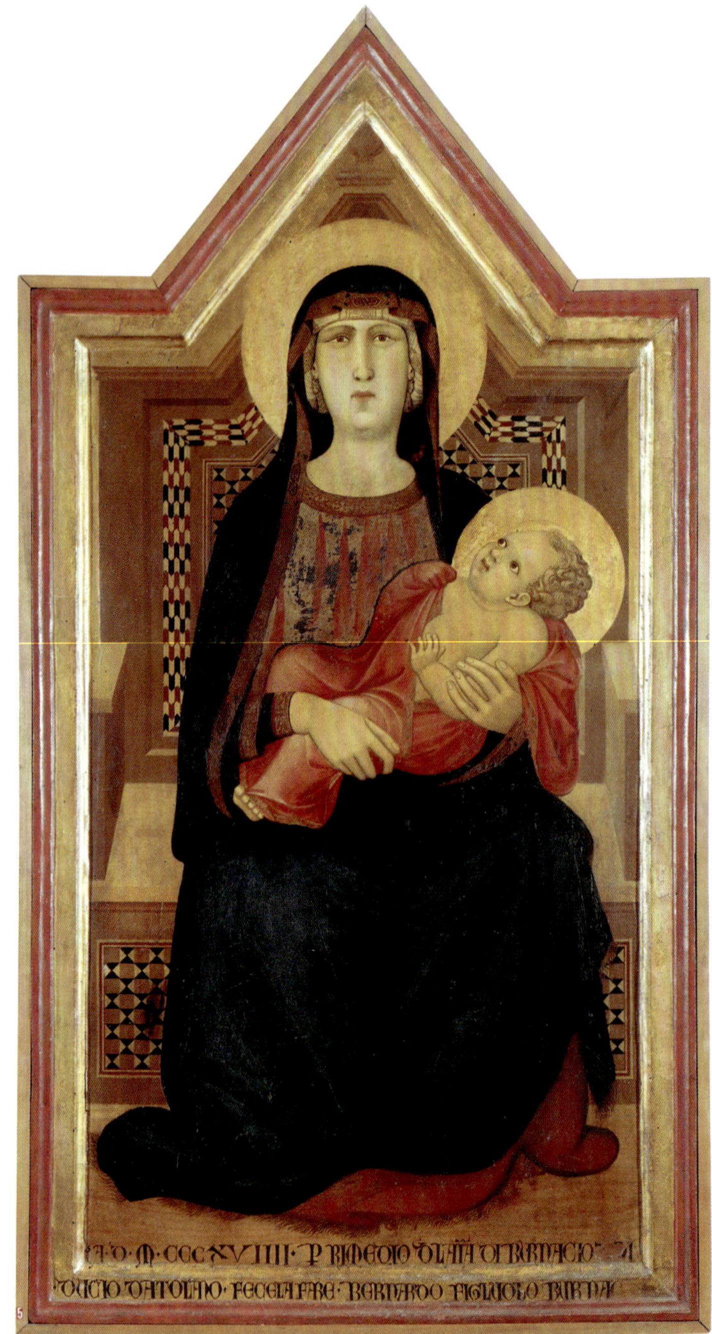

FIG. 83
Ambrogio Lorenzetti
(documented 1319; died 1348/9)
Madonna di Vico l'Abate, 1319
Tempera on panel, 148.5 × 78 cm
Museo di Arte Sacra, San Casciano Val di Pesa

a few track marks forming concentric rings on the walls of the great council hall in the Palazzo Pubblico – the city's town hall – record the site of a large rotating world map that Ambrogio painted there in 1345.[4] Although the map is long gone, the meeting hall still bears the name, the Sala del Mappamondo, a residual presence of Ambrogio's project that placed Siena at the global centre of a cartographic wheel. In the wall paintings that survive in the adjoining council room, frescoes of the so-called *Good and Bad Government*, Ambrogio tested the possibilities of pictorial allegory. In this panoramic mural, he portrays the effects of government in two parallel depictions of the city: one vibrant and in harmony with its well-governed territory, the other, a vision of urban ruin, ruled by tyrants. The two scenes, meant to guide the government leaders who assembled beneath them, laid out an ambitious political theory that is still marvelled at today.[5] Such works obviously cannot be included in an exhibition, nor can Ambrogio's massive altarpieces, for example the *Maestà* from Massa Marittima, the artist's stunning reformulation of Duccio's and then Simone Martini's large-scale images that came before it.[6] This brief overview of Ambrogio's work focuses instead on the portable works in the exhibition this accompanies, to serve as an introduction to the remarkable painter so admired by these early writers.

To lead us into these works, it is instructive to look at Ambrogio's *Madonna di Vico l'Abate*, named after the Tuscan town in which it was found (fig. 83).[7] Its inscription, dated 1319, makes it the artist's first securely dated painting.[8] It is a curious work for a young artist because it looks as much back in time as it sets a course forward. For an artist who most likely worked and trained under Duccio, and witnessed his progressive strategies towards naturalism, the backward-looking and archaic qualities of this panel must be understood as a considered artistic decision providing insight into Ambrogio's analytic approach to painting. The task the artist seems to have set about was to represent the history of the image, while making it new and instilling it with his own vision. At first glance, the enthroned Virgin's rigid posture and frontal gaze are surprising in their archaicism. Her head and halo push out of the rectangular confines of the picture into a gable that contains them within

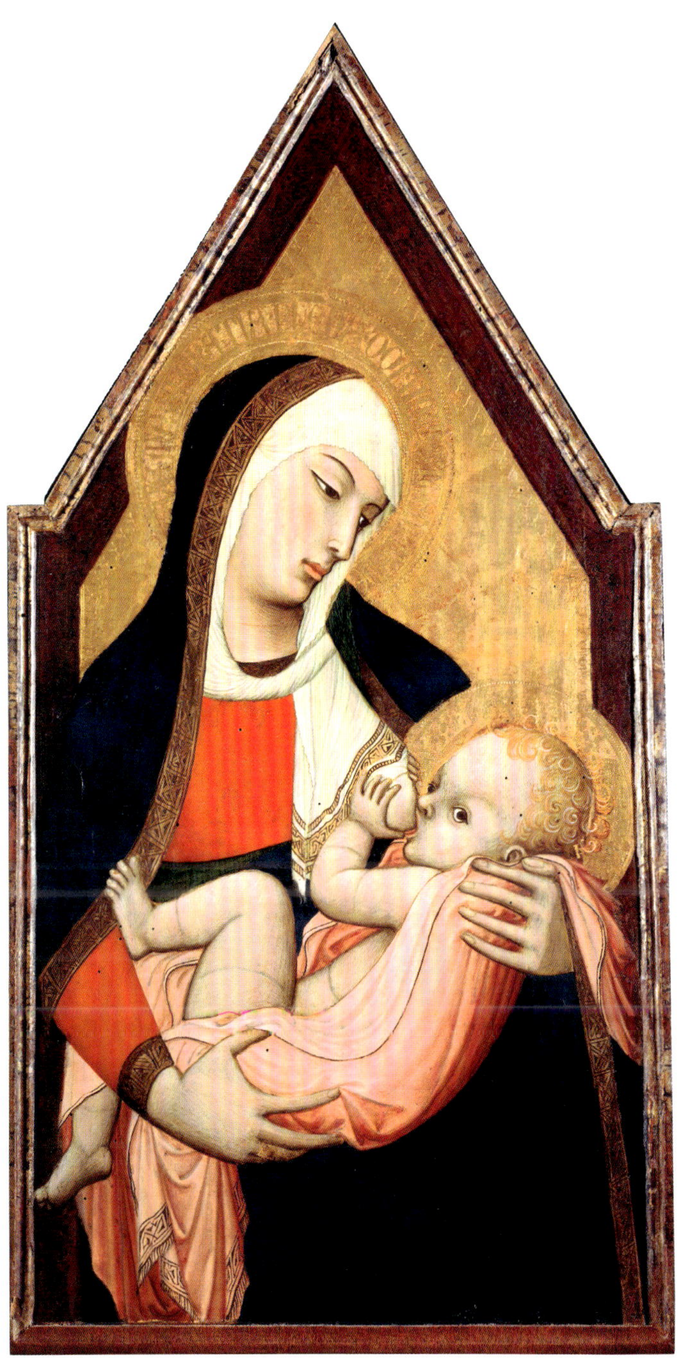

FIG. 84
Ambrogio Lorenzetti
(documented 1319; died 1348/9)
Madonna del Latte, about 1325
Tempera on panel, 96 × 49.1 cm
Arcidiocesi di Siena - Colle di
Val d'Elsa - Montalcino,
Museo Diocesano, Siena

the picture field. It is difficult to reconcile such an image with others from approximately the same period, such as Pietro Lorenzetti's Pieve Polyptych, commissioned for Santa Maria della Pieve in Arezzo a year later (see pp. 94–9). To make sense of it, we need to look at an important image of a century prior, the so-called *Madonna of the Large Eyes*, by the Master of Tressa, one of the earliest paintings made for Siena's cathedral, and a launching point for any understanding of the cult image in that city (see fig. 2).[9] This early thirteenth-century painting, presenting the cult image in low relief within the raised pattern of the frame, complicates the relationship between the dimensionality of sculpture and the flat picture plane. Details like the earrings commonly found on such cult statues contrast with the tight and regular folds of the close-fitting coif covering the Virgin's hair, while the rigid *maphorion* on top of it looks back to Byzantine prototypes (see also figs 13, 14).[10] Pressing against the confines of its frame, Ambrogio's large, enthroned figure reformulates the experience of looking at early cult images, in this case, the starting point of painted images of the Virgin in Siena, expressing an awareness of time by pictorialising it through a different stylistic mode.[11] The Virgin, no longer a dimensional polychromed sculpture, becomes a painted image.

Writing about this work, Bruce Cole observed that Ambrogio drew stylistic inspiration, but not style, from the thirteenth century; moreover, that he obtained the psychological content of these earlier images without a detailed imitation of their formal devices.[12] Although Cole concludes that Ambrogio 'gave his patron a very modern work of art, full of the spirit of a dead past', I would argue that the originality of this work is actually rooted in its retrospective glance. Ambrogio provides a cradle for the animated Christ Child, whose playfulness and humanity herald a new dimension of felt likeness in Italian painting. Using the flat field of the painted surface to explore the complex interplay between the old and the new, he offers an aperture into an understanding of an analytic approach to image-making, even at this early step in his career.

The tender and vivacious depiction of the Christ Child in Ambrogio's painting of 1319 makes it possible to give a date

FIG. 85
Pietro Lorenzetti
(documented possibly 1306;
died probably 1348)
The Virgin and Child enthroned,
about 1345
Tempera on panel, 34.8 × 30.8 cm
(with remains of original
framing elements)
Staatliche Museen zu Berlin,
Gemäldegalerie (Kat. Nr. 1384)

FIG. 86
Ambrogio Lorenzetti
(documented 1319; died 1348/9)
The Crucifixion, about 1345
Tempera on panel, 71.5 × 35.5 cm
(with engaged frame)
Harvard Art Museums/Fogg
Museum, Gift of Paul J. Sachs
in honor of Edward W. Forbes's
thirtieth year as Director of the
Fogg Museum (1939.113)

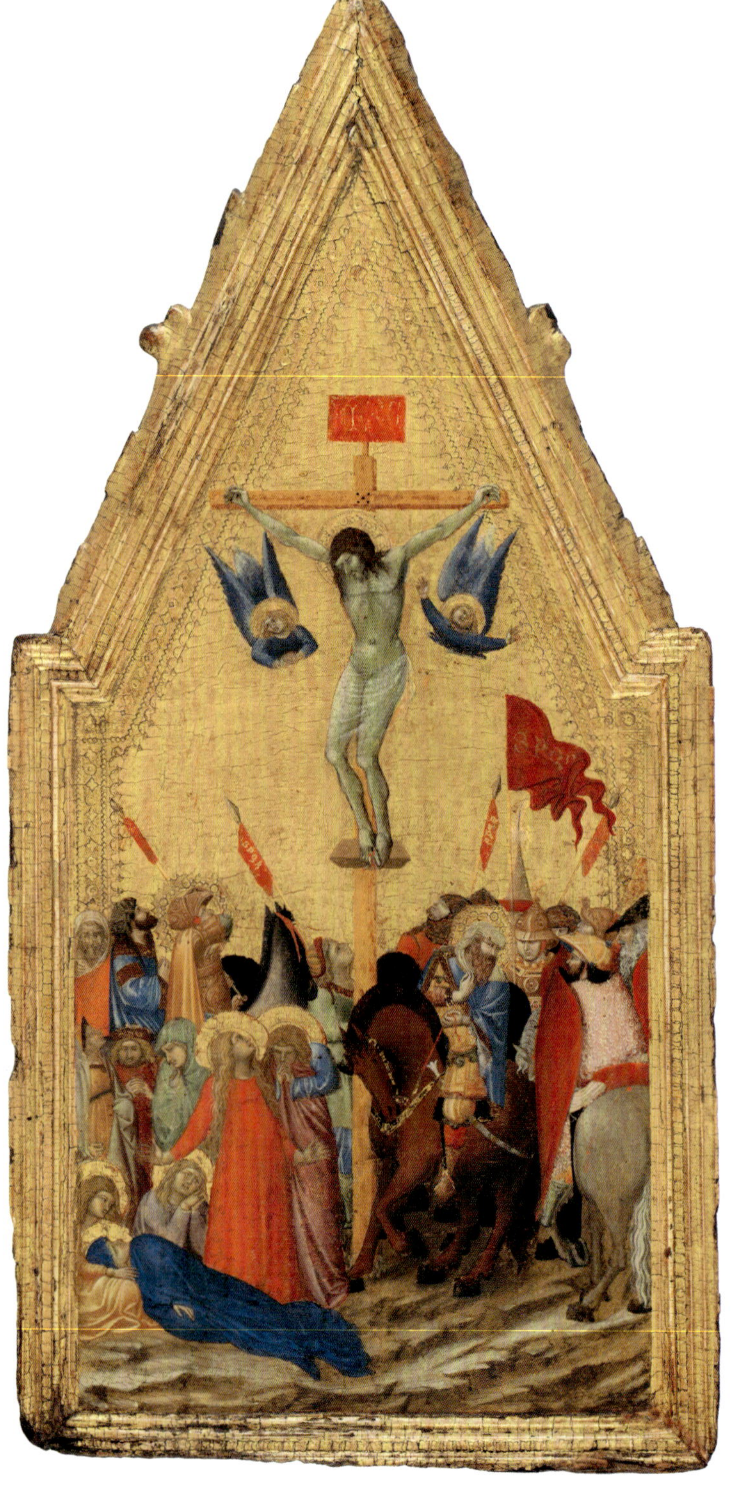

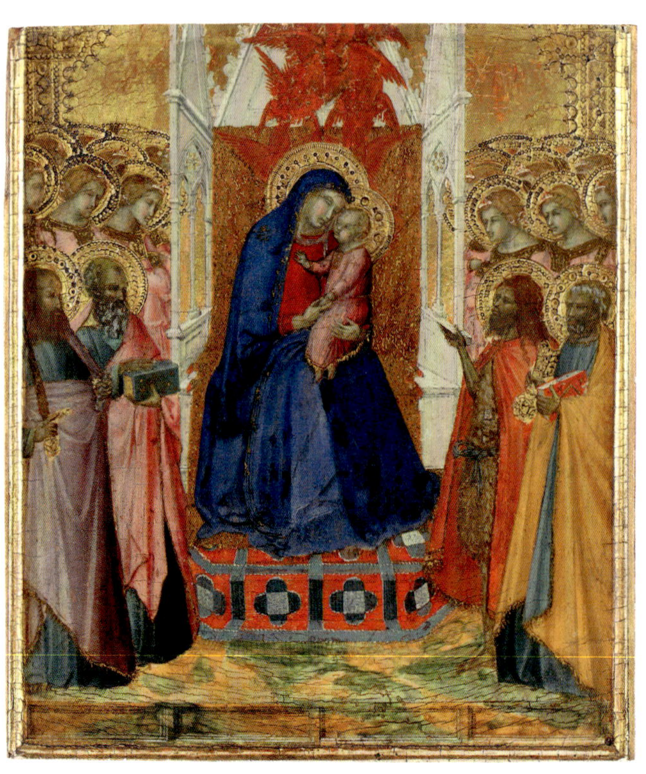

of around 1325 to one of his most innovative and admired images, the *Madonna del Latte*, or *Nursing Madonna*, where the baby with a blaze of golden locks takes this one step further (fig. 84).[13] Particularly beloved by nineteenth-century British artists and aesthetes, this painting has held a privileged place in Ambrogio's oeuvre.[14] Measuring nearly a metre high, the panel seems outsized for personal devotion, and yet, like Ambrogio's earlier *Madonna* at Vico l'Abate, there is no indication that it was part of a larger altarpiece ensemble. This singular image was probably conceived to stand on its own.[15] It replaces the rigid axiality of the artist's earlier image with the dynamic interplay of the Virgin, whose haloed face dominates the upper-left of the picture field, with her nursing child as a counterweight to it at the right. Ambrogio has subordinated the symbolic elements of the religious image to display human action and emotion. The Virgin, looking tenderly at her child, has been described as the embodiment of motherhood, allowing the human and the divine to intersect. Likewise, the adorably engaging Christ Child asserts the human aspect of his dual nature.[16] This essential duality is spelt out in the halo of the Virgin, among the very first in Italian painting. The halo delicately interweaves the letters of the words spoken in the Annunciation by the Archangel Gabriel into the tooled decoration.[17] This interplay of word and image would become central to the work of Ambrogio and his fellow Sienese painters.[18] The inscription here provides a resonant foil both to Mary's corporeality, as she nurses her naked baby, and to her knowing glance, as she cradles him in a manner that almost suggests a *pietà*.

If the physicality of the Virgin is also a focal point in Ambrogio's dramatic *Crucifixion*, painted in the final decade of his career, its distinction here is the artist's unforgettable presentation of a figure with a total absence of weight and being (fig. 86). Ambrogio again visualises an idea: a grief so raw that it consumes the body. The anguished mother lies seemingly bodiless, a wrinkled mass of blue drapery, closest to the viewer within the picture plane. Few realisations of this central Christian scene, by any artist, are as complex and considered as this. The entire panel bristles with emotion and dramatic energy, from the ragged rocks on which the scene is staged, to the gilded flames carved on the upper edges of its frame. Having swooned from witnessing her son crucified, the Virgin anchors the group of holy figures at the left side of the Cross. Saint John the Evangelist, Mary Magdalene and the two other Marys are brought together in a web of emotion, both introspective and directed to engage with the painting's beholder. Ambrogio again lays out a composition through the interplay of oppositions. The Virgin's lifeless body is set against the strength of the erect Magdalen, whose red robe and cascading golden tresses draw an axis from the Virgin to her crucified son above. The Magdalen's upward gaze and open arms are contrasted with the Evangelist's clasped hands and pious downward look, just as the ascending thrust of one of the bewailing angels at the side of the Cross is contrasted with its plunging counterpart. The artist harnesses every element to animate the moment, down even to the considered placement of the horses – the sloping curve of one mane redirected by the other to lead the gaze both upward and downward. This is a painting conceived by one of art's great storytellers. Ambrogio's carefully crafted composition dispenses drama and contemplation in equal measure, never allowing one mode to overtake the other.

Few Crucifixions from this period balance narrative, clarity of composition and devotional focus in such a unified

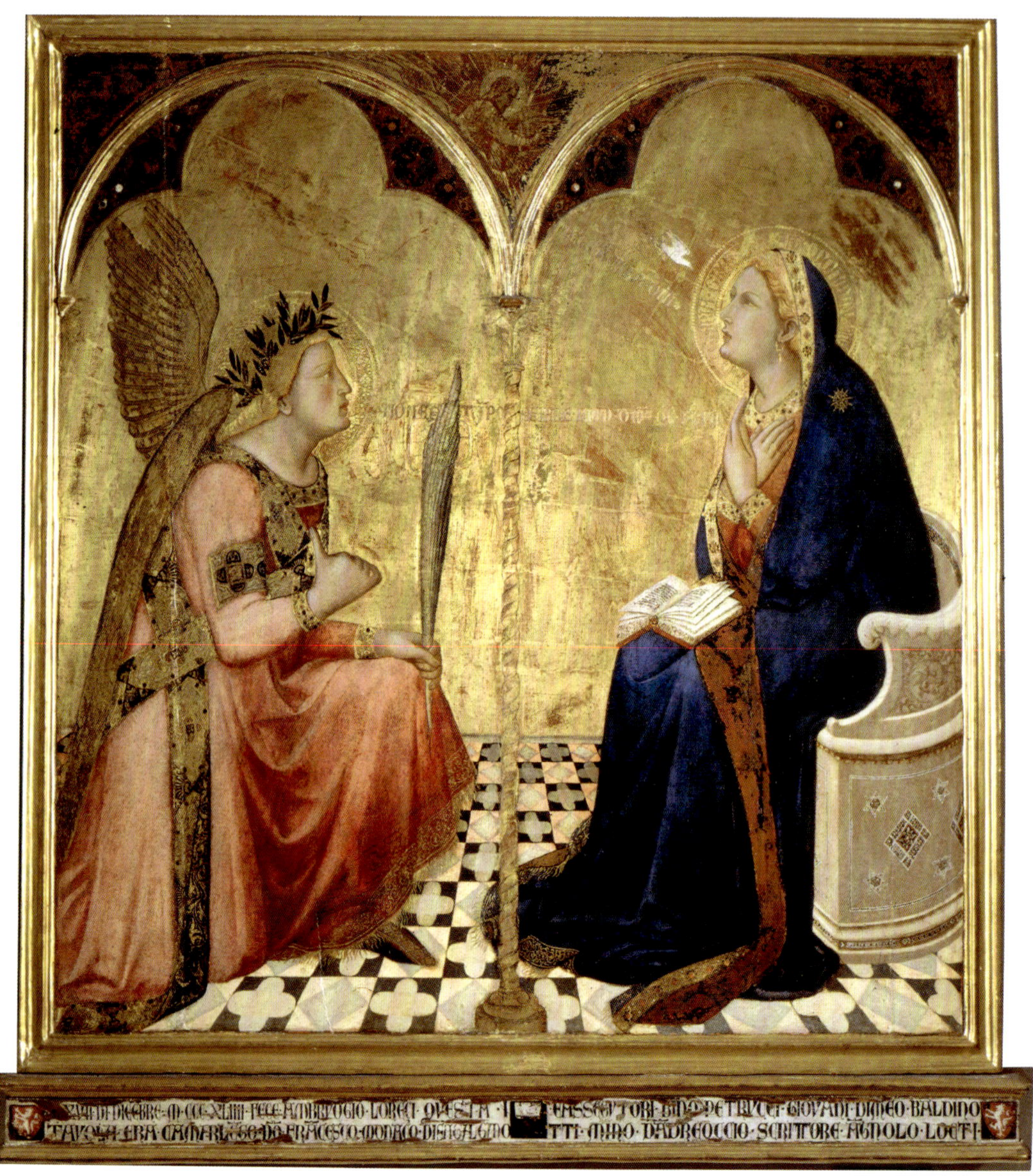

FIG. 87
Ambrogio Lorenzetti
(documented 1319; died 1348/9)
The Annunciation, 1344
Tempera on panel, 130 × 152 cm
(with original frame)
Pinacoteca nazionale di Siena,
musei nazionali di Siena (88)

and resolved way. However, unlike the *Madonna di Vico l'Abate* and the *Madonna del Latte*, it is difficult to imagine that this small painting stood independently, as it does now at the Harvard Art Museums. It most likely formed part of a diptych or portable polyptych, but the concave edges on its two sides and the unusual absence of any traces of hinging make it difficult to understand how it would have been attached.[19] In 1971 two scholars independently associated this work with an enthroned Virgin and Child, a *Maestà*, in the Gemäldegalerie in Berlin (fig. 85).[20] The pairing of an enthroned Virgin with a Crucifixion was common in the fourteenth century, but what prompted the union of these panels was that the elaborately worked pattern of the gold in each of them is identical, made from the same tools and punches. Although the Berlin panel is compromised, with its gable having been cut down at some early point and the edges of its remaining frame trimmed, the dimension of its picture field is identical with that of the *Crucifixion*.[21]

If the connection between the two works is clear, their association raises many questions. For one, the painting in Berlin has always been attributed to Ambrogio's brother, Pietro Lorenzetti, and never to him.[22] Although a document of 1335 confirms that the brothers worked on a large fresco programme for the facade of Siena's hospital of Santa

Maria della Scala, uniting these panels assumes that they worked on more modest projects together as well.[23] Such a collaboration suggests a fluid relationship between their workshops despite their different styles and approaches to painting. Their collaboration may have been on the most basic level a matter of ordering panels from the same carpenter, or one brother may have had a larger supply of these small panels than he needed and shared them with the other. We know that Sienese painters often borrowed expensive punch tools from other workshops, but what complicates things further here is that the patterns found on these two panels, frequently produced in Ambrogio's shop, are absent in any paintings that survive of his brother's.[24] We could also assume that someone in Ambrogio's workshop might have prepared panels for Pietro to paint later and that these two panels were never together in the fourteenth century. However, if we do imagine that they were intended as a pair, they point to the important possibility that these great painters, who dominated the city's artistic scene after Simone's departure to France, kept a joint practice at the height of their careers.

Ambrogio's last signed and dated painting to come down to us, his *Annunciation* of 1344, is often considered his artistic *summa* (fig. 87).[25] Despite its subject and size, it is not an altarpiece but rather a civic commission, painted for the Magistrati di Gabella, the office of Siena's tax magistrates, housed in Siena's Palazzo Pubblico.[26] The novel square format, taken up by Florentine painters in the following century, is divided equally by two semicircular arches of a simple raised moulding. Situated beneath them are the Archangel Gabriel and the Annunciate Virgin, whose size and monumentality within the aperture of the picture field have no precedence in Italian panel painting. Ambrogio had painted this narrative episode on a grand scale in fresco a decade earlier in the chapel connected to the sanctuary church of San Galgano in Montesiepi, where Gabriel and Mary are separated by a window, integrated by Ambrogio into the fictive architecture to use the source of light to convey the divine illumination that accompanies the angel's word (fig. 88).[27] The Montesiepi *Annunciation*, remarkable in ways far too numerous to elaborate here, presents the scene in a box-like room with an ample floor and barrel-vaulted ceiling. In an entirely unprecedented move, in the Pinacoteca *Annunciation* Ambrogio dispenses with the built architecture of the Virgin's chamber – the walls and ceiling – grounding the entire composition of this later work on a chequered ground within a frame.

Three elements define Ambrogio's last *Annunciation*: the frame, the figures and the word. The artist designed the raised arcs of the frame to structure the spatial organisation of the picture plane and to anchor the figures within it. He juxtaposes the touched and the seen by painting detailed cusps below the arcs and decorating the spandrels at either side above – ornament that must have been sumptuous before the silver and other materials that were used to make it tarnished or disappeared with time. Most astonishing, however, is the spiralling gold column at the centre of the picture field that bridges the vast expanse of gold ground with the fictive space of the pictorial stage of the figures. It is tooled – not painted – traced and stippled directly into the gold such that it becomes both tactile and reflective. This column seems to operate both within and outside the picture plane: it is in the painting when it meets the lower edge of the picture, and outside of it when it meets the springing of the framed arches above.[28] As the vertical axis of the painted field, it generates energy by

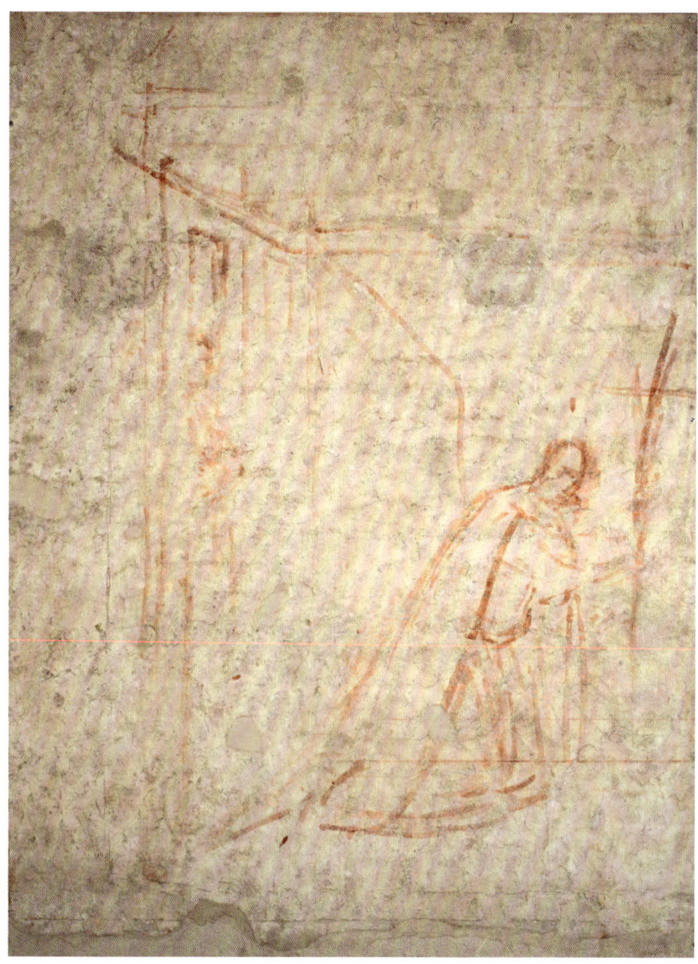

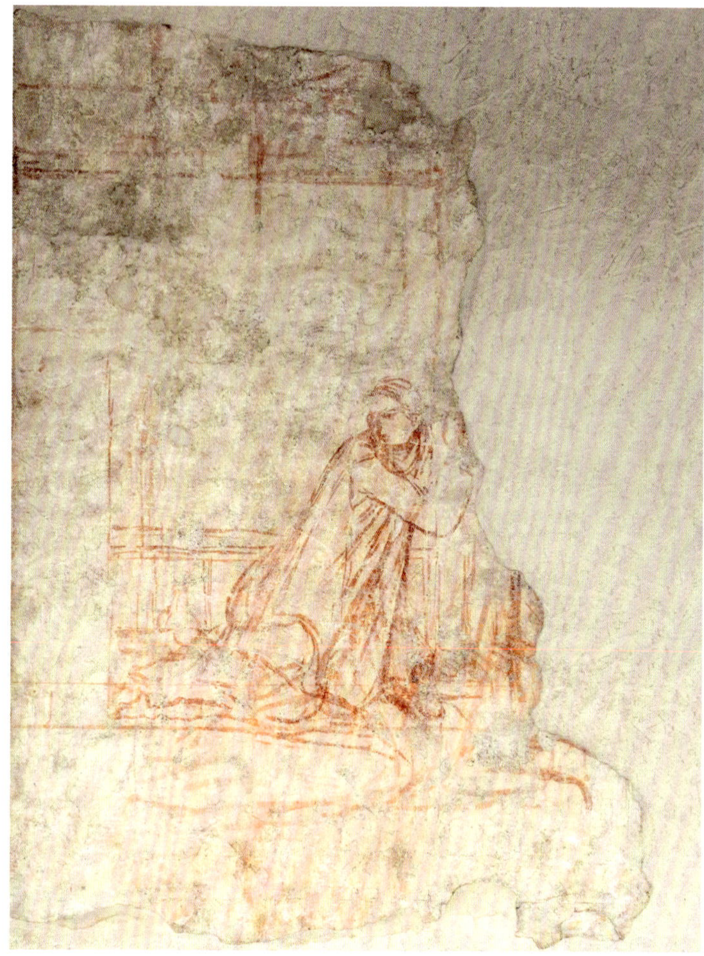

dividing the tip of the Virgin's blue robe from the rest of the garment, just as the actual frame at its edges clips the ends of the angel's wings and breaks the energetic sweep of the Virgin's throne as it dips behind it. Furthermore, the column gives dimension to Gabriel's annunciation, written across the panel, which after being spoken, first passes in front of the palm frond and then behind the column to meet the clasped hands of the Virgin.[29] Within this rectilinear frame, Ambrogio sets out important first steps towards linear perspective, even if not fully achieving it. He fixes the viewer at the centre of the composition, at the site of the spiralling column, by tracing orthogonal lines that converge towards a vanishing point hidden behind it.

Less than three decades after Duccio died in 1319, Ambrogio Lorenzetti signed his will. It was 9 June 1348 and Siena was gripped by a catastrophic plague, which eventually took his life and that of his daughters, along with half of the population of his native city.[30] His brother Pietro may also have died in the calamity.[31] Simone Martini, having left for Avignon a decade earlier, had died in 1344. The arc of Sienese painting, which starting with Duccio had reached so high to these great artists, came to a crushing end.

FIG. 88
Ambrogio Lorenzetti
(documented 1319; died 1348/9)
The Angel Gabriel and the Annunciate Virgin, about 1334–6
Sinopia on plaster, 241 × 173.4 and 242.4 × 172.8 cm
Arcidiocesi di Siena - Colle di Val d'Elsa - Montalcino, Eremo di San Galgano a Montesiepi, Chiusdino

1. Ghiberti before 1455 (1998), pp. 87–9. For Ghiberti's focus on Sienese painting from the previous century, see Ercoli 1980.
2. Vasari 1568 (1996) pp. 157–9. See Norman 1999a.
3. A few fragments of sky uncovered in the cloister of San Francesco in the late 1970s show darkened skies with hailstones that bear witness to these accounts. See Bartalini in Siena 2017–18, cats 19a, 19b, pp. 268–77, for a full account of the project.
4. Kupfer 1996; De Wesselow 2000.
5. The literature on this chamber, the Sala dei Nove, is vast. See, most recently, Piccinni 2022.
6. For the altarpiece, see Norman 1995b; Seidel and Calamai in Siena 2017–18, cat. 17, pp. 232–61.
7. The attribution was first proposed by Giacomo De Nicola, in 1922, and has been universally accepted. For a full discussion of this painting, including questions of its date and attribution, see Amato in Siena 2017–18, cat. 6, pp. 126–31.
8. The inscription, surely not written by the artist, may have been added by the patron to commemorate the commission.
9. The history of Madonna images in the cathedral is long and complicated. See Campbell, pp. 11–12, in the present volume. For the relationship of this painting to the early cathedral images, see Butzek 2001b, pp. 97–109, fig. 1.
10. The relationship of historic images to current practice is explored, in part, in Nagel and Wood 2010, especially pp. 108–22, although my understanding of Ambrogio's interest here is his focus on a history of the Madonna image in Tuscany, and Siena more specifically, through its origin in the cathedral image, rather than in the origin image of the Virgin and Child itself.
11. Maginnis 1997, p. 116, aligns this with the development of mechanised time and the rapid spread of the mechanical clock at the end of the thirteenth century.
12. Cole 1973, p. 241.
13. See Mallory 1969; and Visa Guerrero in Siena 2017–18, cat. 9, pp. 156–61, for the full discussion.
14. On the positive reception of Ambrogio's painting in the Victorian era, see Tedbury, pp. 254–69, in the present volume, as well as Robinson 1975; Matar 2019, pp. 117–19, offers a more fraught and personal reading of the painting.
15. The work is first mentioned in 1439, at the Augustinian hermitage of Lecceto, near Siena, but was moved, in its seventeenth-century frame, to a seminary chapel in San Francesco, Siena, in 1866, where it remained until 1966.
16. Mallory 1969, p. 41.
17. 'AVE . MARIA . GRATIA . PLENA . DOMINUS . TECUM . BENE(dicta)'. Another early example of this practice is found in Simone Martini's polyptych for the Dominicans of Orvieto, for which see Cannon 2013, p. 151. For an overview of the depiction and veneration of Mary and an overview of the Annunciation, see Pelikan 1996, pp. 12–15. For the theology around the Hail Mary and the immaculate conception by Thomas Aquinas and other theologians around 1300, see Lamy 2000, especially chapters 4 and 5.
18. The most well-known work that plays against this dynamic is Simone Martini's *Annunciation* (fig. 39). See Cecchi 2001a; De Marchi 2006..
19. Schmidt 2005a, p. 42, for this question.
20. Frinta 1971, pp. 307–9; Zeri 1971, pp. 20–4, pls 13–14. Thought to be by Ambrogio when it belonged to William Young Ottley in the late eighteenth and early nineteenth century, the *Crucifixion* was associated with the Roman painter Pietro Cavallini when it belonged to Cyril B. Harcourt, London, by 1829 and then to Charles Fairfax Murray, London, who thought it was by Ambrogio's brother, Pietro Lorenzetti. The panel in Berlin was acquired by the Berlin museum in 1821 from Edward Sully, an Englishman living in Berlin.
21. Although trimmed, the Berlin panel still preserves the original fictive marble painted on its reverse. See Boskovits 1988, no. 35, pp. 91–3.
22. Ibid., p. 92, for the history of its attribution.
23. Maginnis 1988.
24. For the detailed study of punch tools in workshop practice, see Skaug 1994.
25. Seidel and Calamai 2022, p. 333. For a brief overview, see Caffio in Siena 2017–18, cat. 29, pp. 346–51.
26. Muller 1977. For the long-standing practice of Sienese artists working for treasury officials of Siena, see, in brief, Cannon, p. 37, in the present volume.
27. See Norman 1993; Seidel and Calamai in Siena 2017–18, cat. 15, pp. 198–227.
28. The introductory pages of David Kim's recent book provide a provocative framework in which to consider the relationship of the picture field and the various layers of 'ground'. See Kim 2022, pp. 1–10.
29. For a discussion of the restoration of this area of the inscription, see Muller 1977, p. 3, figs 4–5.
30. Ambrogio's will designated his three daughters as his primary beneficiaries who must have also perished in the plague since his estate ultimately benefited a Sienese religious confraternity, the Company of the Virgin Mary, which may also have had an altarpiece by him. See Wainwright 1975.
31. The last document associated with Pietro Lorenzetti is dated 1345.

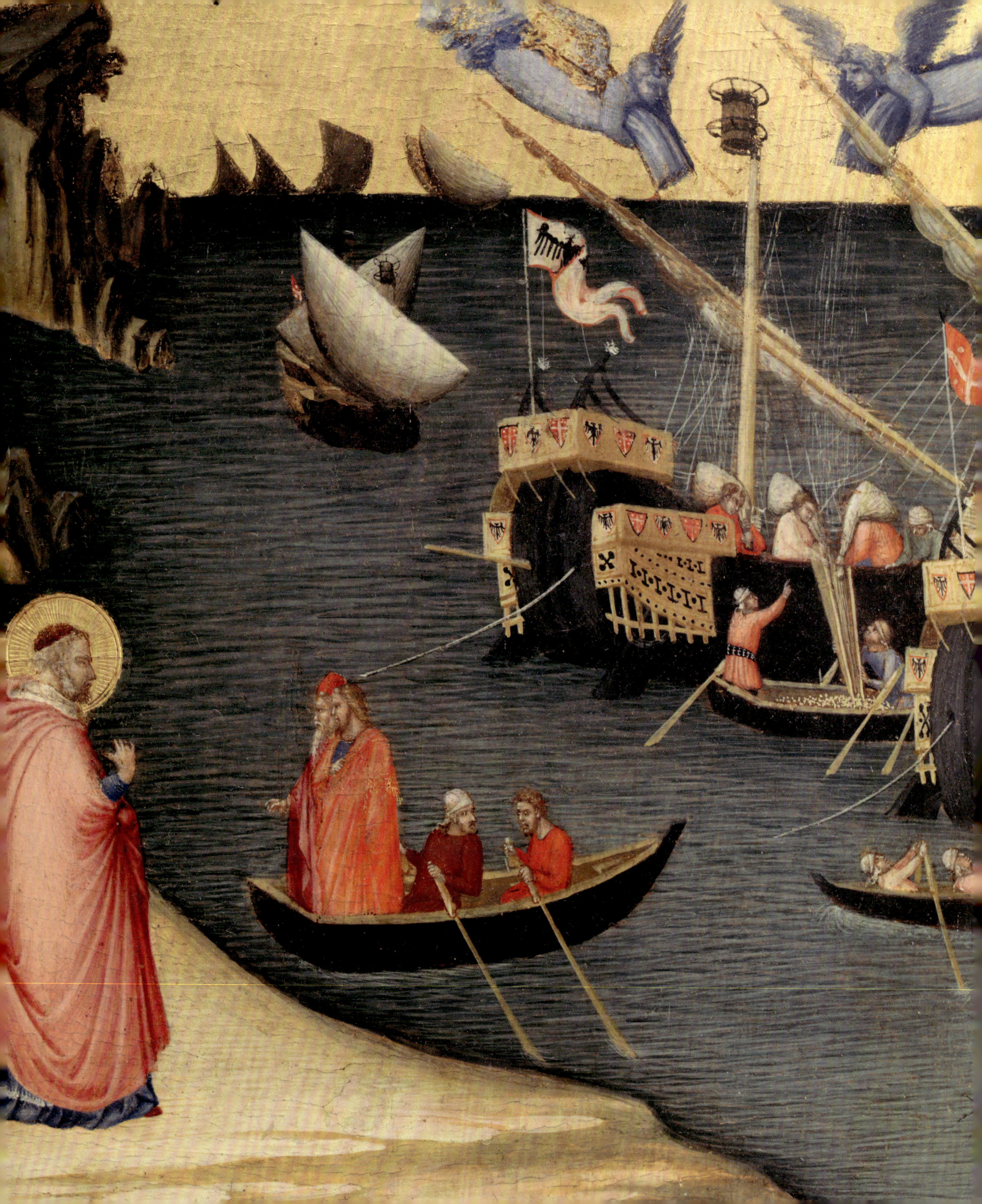

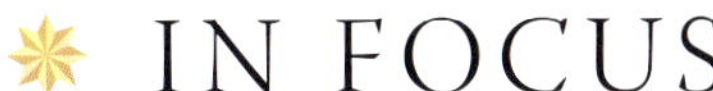

IN FOCUS

The Stories of Saint Nicholas

Stephan Wolohojian

Ambrogio Lorenzetti was one of the great storytellers of the fourteenth century, exploring storyline, setting and plot. In ways even more complex, he arrived at the sophistication of allegory, a mode not easily adaptable to visual representation, in his grand fresco scheme in the chamber of the city councillors, in the Palazzo Pubblico, Siena's town hall. There is every reason to believe that Ambrogio collaborated with Duccio and his team of assistants on the cathedral's *Maestà*, and that, as one of the youngest of the group, he most likely worked on the complex narratives of Christ's life that unfold across the back of the renowned altarpiece. No training ground could have better prepared an artist interested in the potential of narrative.

Dating from the early 1330s, the *Stories from the Life of Saint Nicholas* (fig. 89) explore complex modes of narrative and visual representation: four multifaceted meditations on word and image that map the miraculous life of this early Christian from the ancient city of Myra. They offer an exceptional opportunity to examine this aspect of Ambrogio's work. The narratives are painted on two large vertical panels of poplar wood and most likely flanked a central image of Nicholas himself, in keeping with other cult images, such as Simone Martini's Beato Agostino Novello Triptych, of about a decade earlier, where the cult figure stands with a bank of scenes from his life at each side (fig. 90).[1] Lorenzo Ghiberti, a great admirer of Ambrogio, was the first to record the panels, noting that the paintings were in a 'cappella' in the Benedictine parish church of San Procolo, Florence.[2] Later, Giorgio Vasari, presumably an eyewitness as well, added that this chapel contained 'the stories of S. Nicholas with little figures'.[3] As with Simone's panel, the Nicholas stories were probably not elements of an altarpiece in the strict sense, adorning the site of liturgical celebration, nor were they part of a built chapel, but were instead components of a devotional image centred on the veneration of this bishop saint.[4] If we can be relatively sure about what kind of object these remarkable images were from, less clear is their place in the chronology of the artist's work. Like many Sienese painters, and so few Florentine painters in reverse, Ambrogio established himself in Florence in 1327, registering in the guild to which painters belonged,

Detail of FIG. 89

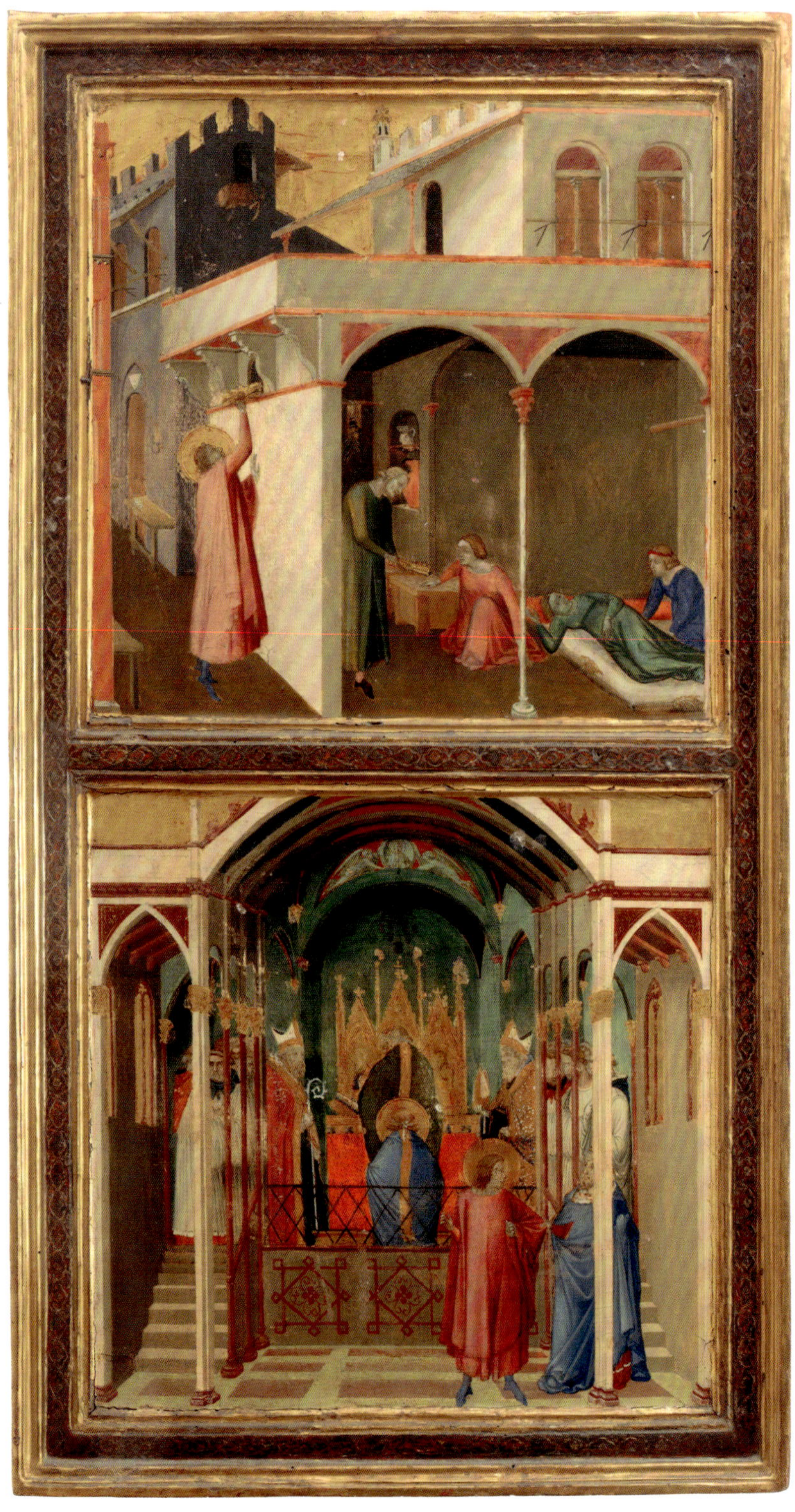

FIG. 89
Ambrogio Lorenzetti (documented 1319; died 1348/9)
Stories from the Life of Saint Nicholas, about 1332–4
Tempera on panel, 96.2 × 52.3 cm and 95.8 × 52.3 cm
(with partially original frames)
Gallerie degli Uffizi, Florence (inv. 1890 nn. 8348, 8349)

the Arte dei Medici e Speziali.[5] His arrival there in the 1320s has prompted some to precipitously date the Saint Nicholas project to this early moment, but Janet Robson has convincingly argued that the paintings were commissioned by the Florentine Taldo Valori, and that they most likely refer to the grain shortages in Florence in the years around 1332.[6]

Drawn mainly from episodes in the *Life of Saint Nicholas* in Jacobus de Voragine's *Golden Legend*, a hagiographic compilation written in the previous century (about 1260–98), Ambrogio engages his beholder in four astonishingly rich and complex biographical tableaux.[7] In some instances, he follows his source with such accuracy that it is difficult not to read his images as an attempt at a strict translation of the written word into image. In others, Ambrogio seizes upon the image's ability to express psychology and human response in ways that the Latin text from which it was drawn could not.

The four square fields are set apart by an engaged frame, embellished by a decorative pattern that has been associated with elements used to secure enamel reliquary plaques.[8] The stories unfold from the top left and proceed anticlockwise. The artist has made a clear division between the two narratives on the left, which depict scenes from the saint's youth, and those on the right, which show miracles, the final scene taking place after his death.

Ambrogio uses architecture – urban, domestic and ecclesiastical – to anchor his narratives. The first is a scene of Christian charity, *Saint Nicholas gives Dowries to Three Maidens*. In it, we see Nicholas, born to rich parents, sharing his wealth by placing gold wrapped in a piece of cloth through the window of his neighbours' house after hearing that the father, whose financial fortune had been lost, was considering forcing his three daughters into prostitution to attain their dowries. This is the most direct of the four scenes, and Ambrogio engages us with the figure of the young saint, springing on tiptoes to reach into the window to distribute his life-altering gift.

The Choice and Consecration of Saint Nicholas as Bishop of Myra that follows unfolds on two levels. In the foreground, the saint, clad in the same garment as in the scene before, is pulled aside by the bishop to hear the unexpected news of his consecration. The viewer is drawn into the narrative through the 'little figures' Vasari described, who move through the complexities of the church space. The presentation of the episcopal insignia, the crosier and mitre, that Nicholas will receive as Bishop of Myra flank him at either side. The act takes place before an altarpiece, a carefully rendered painting within a painting, not unlike Ambrogio's three-panelled altarpiece for San Procolo, which would have been seen nearby (fig. 91).[9]

One of the most memorable scenes, *Saint Nicholas and the Grain Ships*, takes place during a period of famine, which may have resonated with the contemporary Florentine audience at a time of food insecurity. Nicholas learnt that boats transporting grain from Alexandria to Rome had docked at Myra. Asking if some of their cargo could be shared to help feed Myra's citizens, the saint was told that the shipments had been carefully measured when they left port in Alexandria and had to be delivered to Rome intact. Nicholas assured the sailors that they would arrive at their destination as planned, with no shortage of grain, if they shared their precious cargo. Ambrogio includes several sequential moments from the narrative within this astonishing maritime setting. The aged Nicholas, grey-haired and bearded, addresses the merchant-seamen standing in the boat, but the viewer has already concluded that they have ceded their valuable goods to him by the fact that the oarsmen are beginning to row back towards the imperial fleet, where we find sailors pouring grain from sacks that then cascades down a chute into waiting boats. The materiality of the grain, shown by the speed by which it passes through the channel, is reinforced by the weight it then gives to the vessels it fills. Ambrogio conveys the drag of the low-riding boat with two men leaning back as they heave on the oars to bring their heavy load ashore. Two blue angels direct grain from the heavens, which streams down from celestial sacks to replenish the vessels.

Ambrogio's depiction of the energetic transfer of grain, laboured and miraculous, the different states of the ships, docked and in full sail, and the golden cliffs of the ragged landscape illuminated by Nicholas's beatific act is nothing short of mesmerising, as is the startling post-mortem scene, *Saint Nicholas resuscitates a Boy strangled by the Devil*. Ambrogio's rendering of this story, which does not feature in Italian painting until the fourteenth century, closely follows the account in the *Golden Legend* and tells

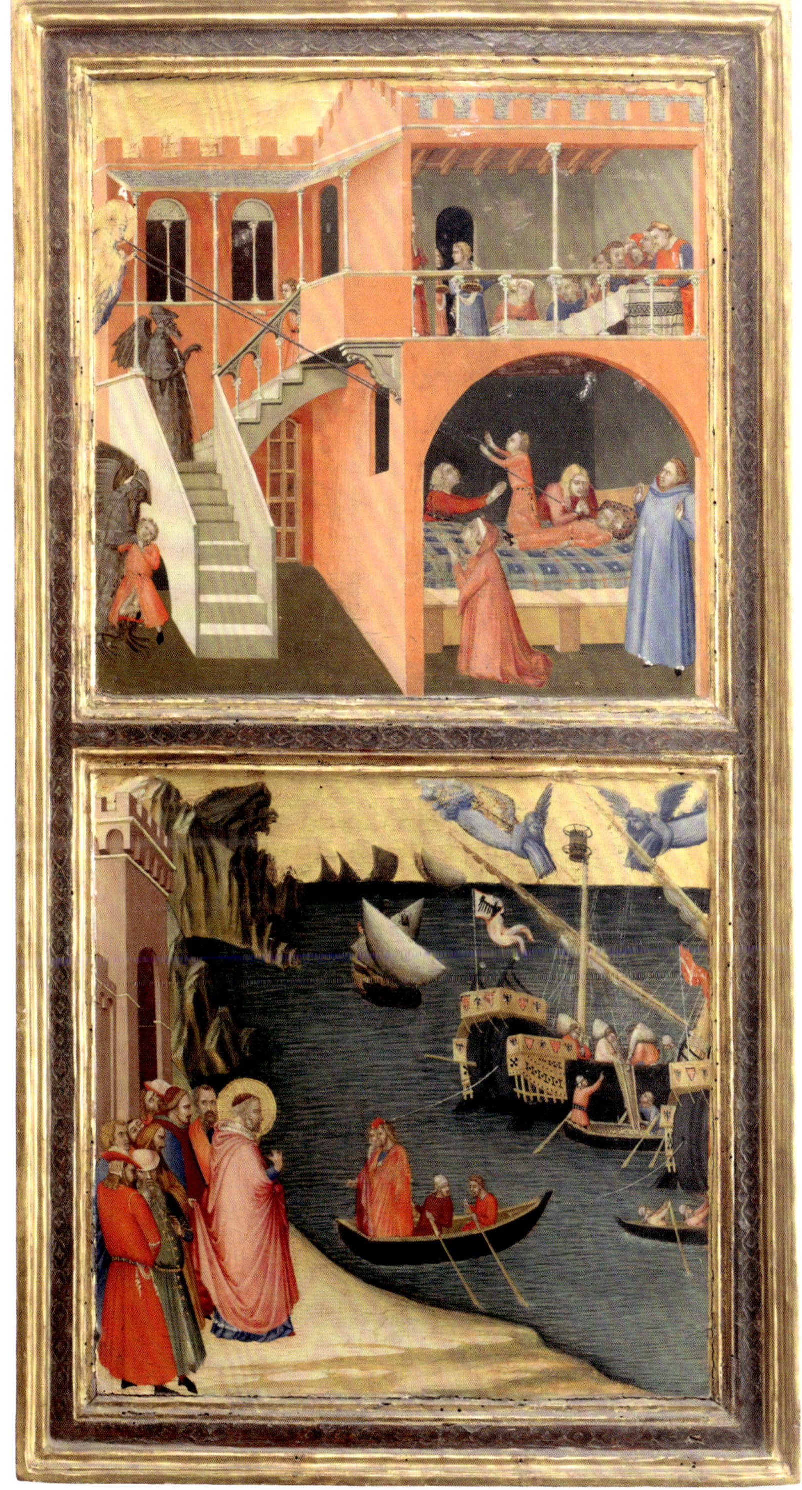

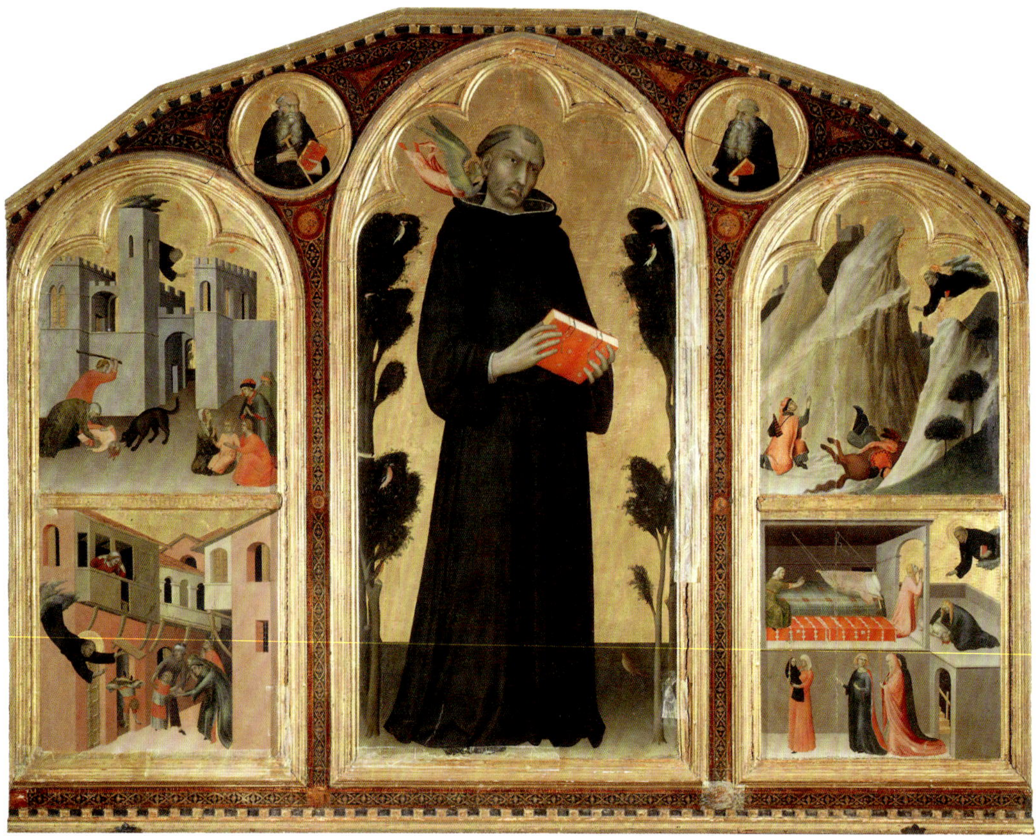

FIG. 90
Simone Martini
(about 1284–1344)
Beato Agostino Novello Triptych, 1324–8
Tempera on panel, 198 × 257 cm
Pinacoteca nazionale di Siena, musei nazionali di Siena

the chilling tale of a murdered child. The instructive function of the scene is especially interesting because it is no longer the saint who is the exemplar, but rather his lay devotees. The first vignette in this story is the banquet of a wealthy man celebrating Saint Nicholas's feast day, which is a pious use of his wealth. While clerics and other guests dine, the devil, disguised as a pilgrim, knocks at the door begging. The beggar has fled by the time the man's young son goes to offer alms, another act of lay piety. Seeing no one at the door, the boy pursues him, but when he finally catches up, the devil-pilgrim, now with clawed feet, grabs the child and strangles him. Returning home with his son's body, the grief-stricken father appeals to Saint Nicholas, who appears in his resurrected state at the upper-left side of the frame and sends beaming rays towards the dead child, who upon receiving them opens his eyes and sits up. Ambrogio nimbly juxtaposes the luminous radiance of the weightlessly floating Nicholas, with his assured gaze and healing hand, with the conniving tilt of the bearded and menacing devil's head and the clawed hand that killed the boy.

Ambrogio constructs a complex, multi-episodic narrative, winding through the interior spaces of a house, its exterior staircase and the street beyond. He explores modes of depicting time, arriving at the ingenious invention of conveying a resurrection miracle by setting a supine and a revitalised figure beside each other. Joanna Cannon notes that this motif, which later became common in the portrayal of such miracles in Tuscan painting, appears here for the first time in Sienese art.[10]

The series stands out not just in Ambrogio's work but in fourteenth-century European painting at large for the way in which the architectural and spatial volumes respond so dynamically with the figural elements of the story. Space and figure achieve a unity and balance that the artist would master in his mature paintings, such as the fresco cycle of the *Good and Bad Government* that he undertook in Siena's Palazzo Pubblico later in the 1330s (see figs 1 and 140). It would take Florentine artists until the start of the next century to accomplish such cohesion within the frame of a picture.

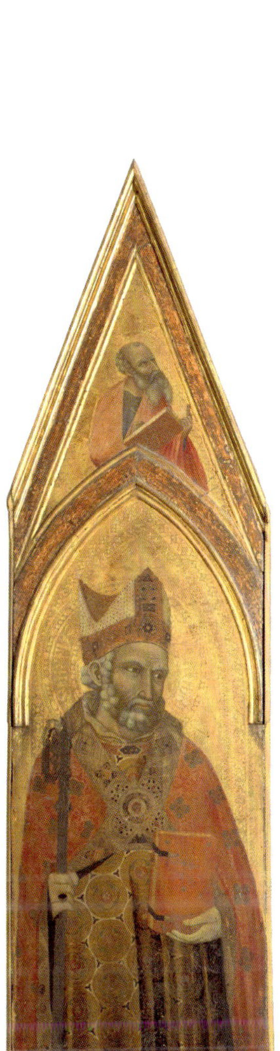
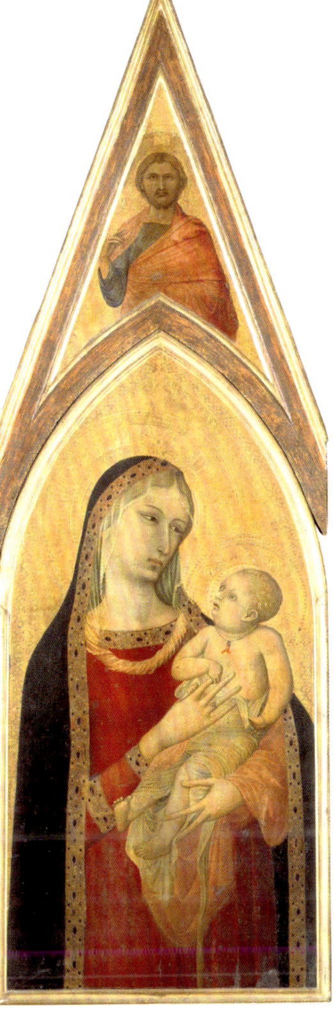
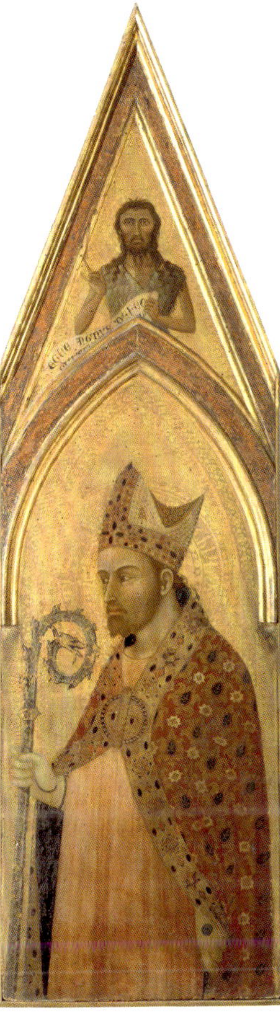

FIG. 91
Ambrogio Lorenzetti
(documented 1319; died 1348/9)
San Procolo Altarpiece, 1332
Tempera on panel, 167 × 56 cm (central panel), 145 × 43 cm (each side panel)
Gallerie degli Uffizi, Florence
(inv. 1890 n. 9411)

1. On Simone's painting and the cult, see Seidel 1985. On the Sant'Agostino shrine and the panel, see Seidel 1988.
2. Ghiberti before 1455 (1998), p. 89. This was a strange use of the word as the church had no built chapel spaces.
3. Vasari 1568 (1996), p. 158: 'After these works, proceeding to Florence, he made a panel in S. Procolo, and in a chapel he painted the stories of S. Nicholas with little figures, in order to satisfy certain of his friends, who desired to see his method of working; and, being much practiced, he executed this work in so short a time that there accrued to him fame and infinite repute.'
4. See Cannon 2013, pp. 251–9, for the fluidity of terms such as *cappella* in Dominican churches.
5. Giorgi and Moscadelli 2017–18, document 4, p. 475.
6. The basis for a dating to the 1330s coincides with a polyptych by Ambrogio for the same church that is signed and dated 1332. See Amato in Siena 2017–18, cat. 12, pp. 174–80. Robson 2022 has recently clarified that both the Nicholas dossal and that altarpiece were most likely exhibited in proximity to each other in a chapel area devoted to the saint and commissioned by a member of the Valori family. The original disposition of Ambrogio's altarpiece in that church must have resembled the three-panel format of the altarpiece in Ambrogio's consecration scene in this narrative series.
7. De Voragine 2012, pp. 21–7.
8. Amato in Siena 2017–18, cat. 13, p. 182. It should be noted that only the outer frame of each panel is original; those at the top and bottom and inner side are later.
9. Said to have been signed 'Ambrogio Lorenzetti of Siena, 1332'. Amato in Siena 2017–18, cat. 12, pp. 174–80.
10. Cannon and Vauchez 1999, pp. 137–8.

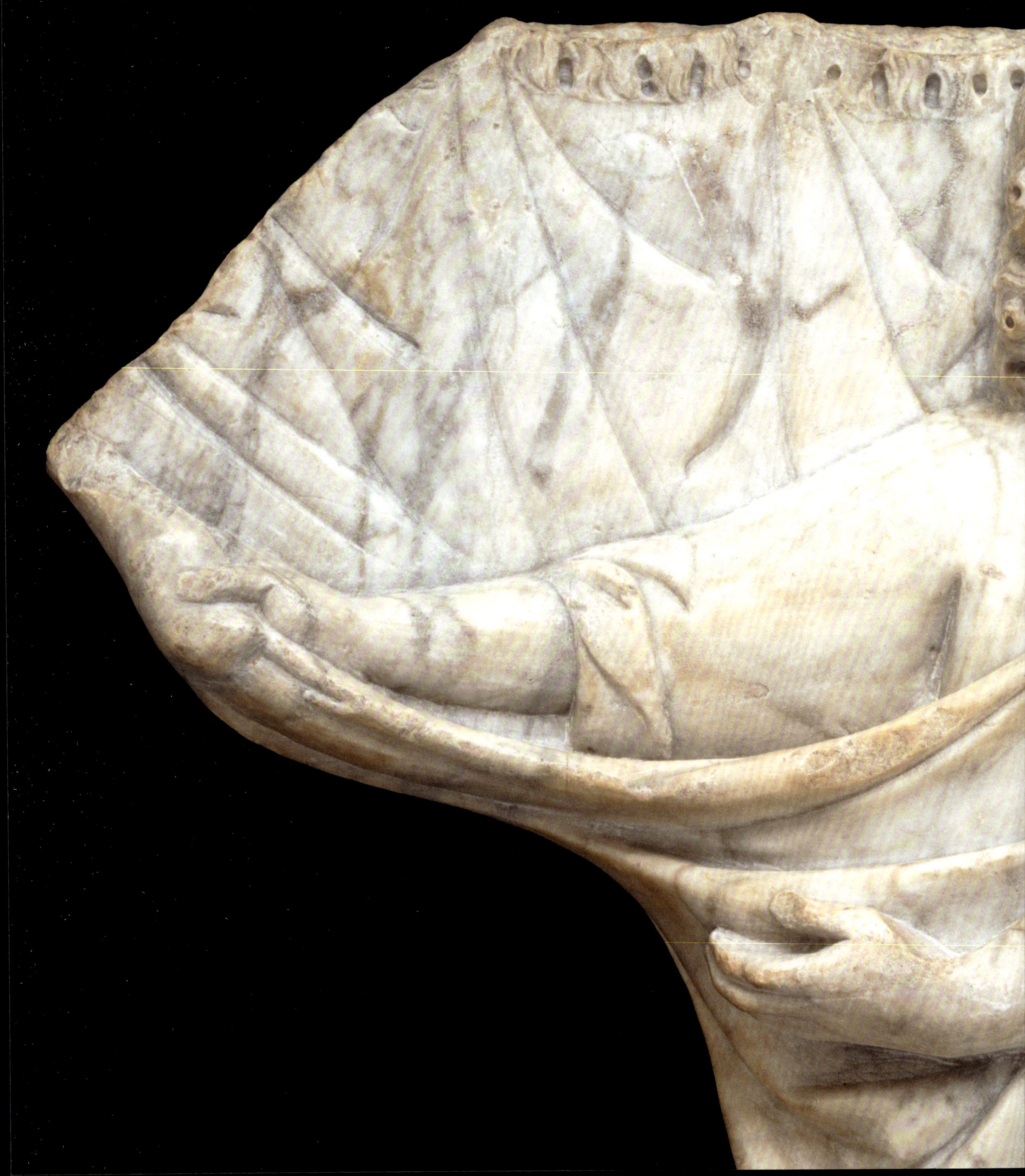

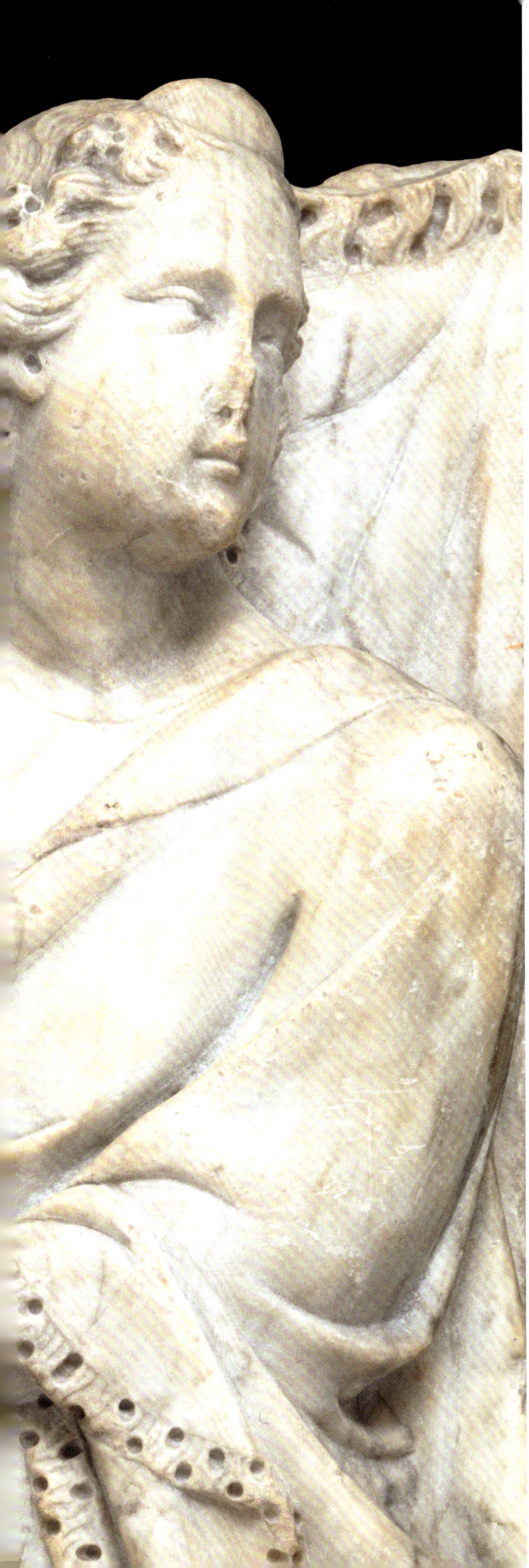

SIENESE CONTEMPORARIES

In the same years as Duccio was painting the *Rucellai Madonna* for Santa Maria Novella in Florence (see fig. 6), the Sienese goldsmith Guccio di Mannaia was signing a chalice made for Pope Nicholas IV, presented to San Francesco at Assisi, embellished with the earliest known examples of translucent enamelwork (see fig. 121), and the Pisan sculptor Giovanni Pisano, granted Sienese citizenship in 1285, was involved for more than a decade on the design of the Gothic facade of Siena Cathedral, executing the sculptures of prophets, patriarchs and philosophers that adorned its lower register (see fig. 5).[1]

These three contemporaries, each one technically and conceptually innovative in his own field, illustrate the talents that could coexist in Siena. This is a story of both convergence and divergence. Artists working in different media learnt from one another, enriching their visual vocabularies. But the specific materials, and the varying traditions and functions within which their creations existed, also dictated significant contrasts. For example, the bold, deep, looping folds of Gothic sculpture were emulated, in three dimensions, by Sienese sculptors such as Gano di Fazio (fig. 92), sometimes accented by touches of colour and gilding reminiscent of Parisian ivory carvings (see figs 170, 173, 174, 175), and in two dimensions by masters including Duccio, Pietro Lorenzetti and Simone Martini (see figs 31, 60, 74). When depicting unpatterned drapery, the painters used tonal variation, often employing three shades: the original hue, and two lighter values, produced by adding different amounts of white (see fig. 21).[2] A goldsmith working in champlevé enamel

FIG. 92
Gano di Fazio (documented 1302; died before 1318)
Old Saint, Saint John the Baptist, Saint Peter and *Young Saint with a Book*, about 1315–18
Marble with traces of polychromy, heights 73.7, 73.3, 78.6 and 75.1 cm
Museo di San Pietro all'Orto, from the Cattedrale di San Cerbone in Massa Marittima (sala II inv. 8–11)

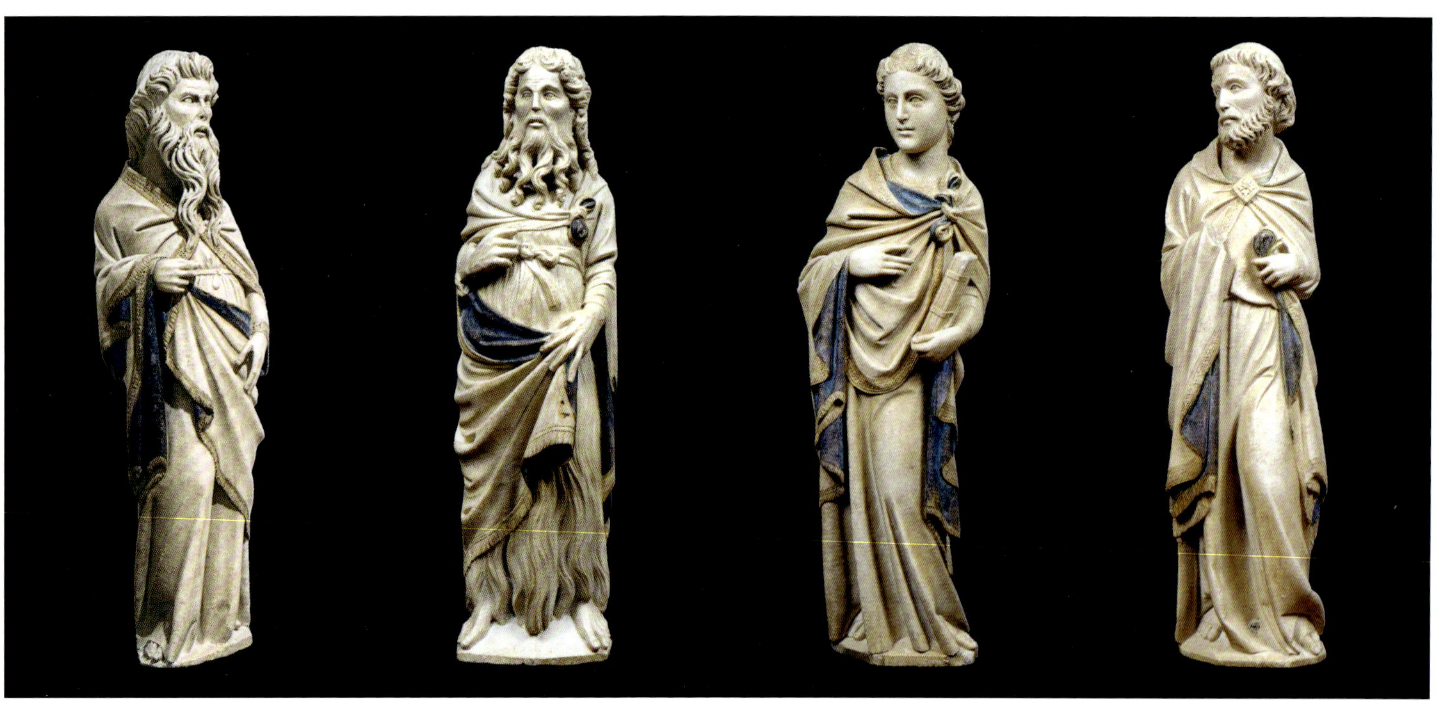

was generally restricted to two or three colours: the gilded copper or silver into which the design was engraved, and the enamel that filled the excavated channels (fig. 93).[3] In this technique, line rather than tone played the key role in describing form. Images made from gilded glass, as discussed by Beth Williamson (pp. 184–9), also depended on line and a limited choice of colours. The removal of thin lines of gold leaf, set against a backing layer painted in a single hue, resembled the fine strokes of a drawing (but with the lines created by the absence rather than the presence of ink or pigment), while the remaining gold formed shimmering highlights (see fig. 137). Most subtle of all was basse-taille enamel, in which the design was punched and engraved in very low relief into a silver ground, which was then flooded with translucent enamel, available in a range of strong colours (but opaque rather than translucent reds, which had yet to be developed). The drapery folds were enhanced by the varying tones of the enamel through which they were visible: the deeper the excavation, the darker the tone, marrying colour modelling and drawing (see figs 118, 126). Regrettably, this subtle yet powerful effect is now often lost, because of damage to the fragile glass surface, but the refinement of the engraving can still be admired, for instance in the plaque showing Saint Galganus kneeling in prayer before his sword, plunged into the rock of Montesiepi to form an improvised cross, as his elegant horse paws the ground beside him (fig. 94). As these examples suggest, there were fundamental contrasts between the basic characteristics of different media. These could spark experimentation, and lead to more complex explorations of what was possible given the particular qualities and textures of various materials, as Peter Dent's contribution (pp. 154–63) so evocatively explores.

The four painters at the heart of this volume all benefited from studying the sculpture and metalwork of their Sienese contemporaries.[4] They excelled in finding methods through which to represent goldsmiths' work, creating on the actual picture surface, with the use of tooled gold leaf, gesso and paint, textures that helped to suggest the depicted surface textures of precious objects: the crosier and jewelled mitre of Duccio's Saint Sabinus (see p. 24), the crosier, mitre and morse of Pietro Lorenzetti's Saint Donatus (see fig. 63), or the vases in Simone Martini's Orsini Polyptych *Annunciation* (see fig. 81), and Ambrogio Lorenzetti's *Piccola Maestà* (see fig. 145). Conversely, a sculptor – Tino di Camaino – seems to have been influenced by two-dimensional methods of representation. Two angels, fragments from an unidentified tomb, draw curtains ornamented with meandering borders that blend with their own garments, carved largely in low relief (fig. 95).[5] A sculptural relief might echo elements of the design of a single-panel painting, as in the marble panel attributed to Giovanni di Agostino (fig. 96), in which the composition of the figures, with background daringly cut away, is set

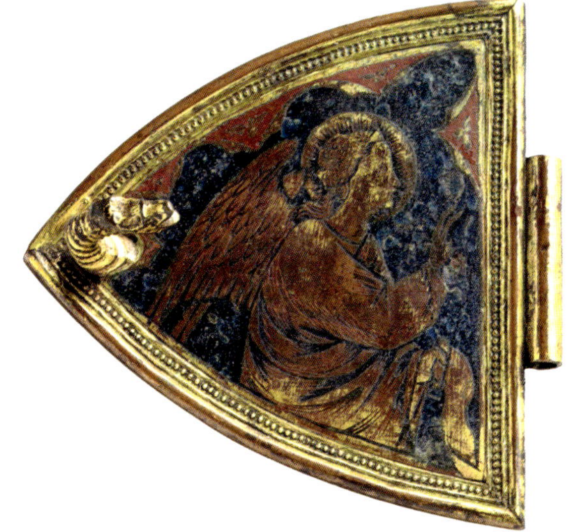

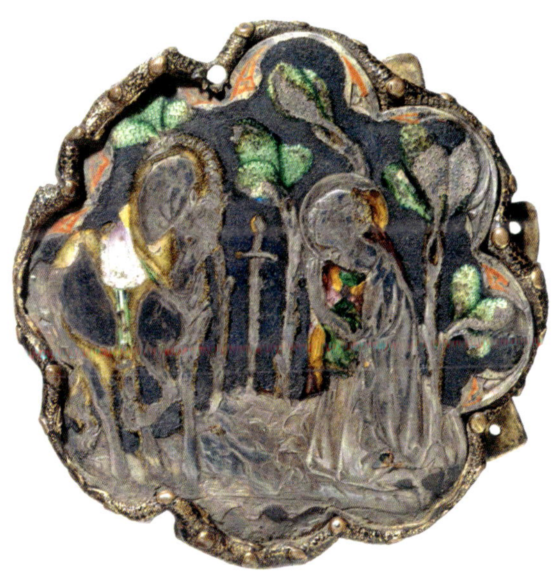

FIG. 93
Sienese artist
Angel from the Lid of an Incense Boat, about 1325–50
Gilded copper with champlevé enamel, 9.1 × 9 × 2.6 cm
The Metropolitan Museum of Art, New York. Gift of Brimo de Laroussilhe, 2006 (2006.316)

FIG. 94
Sienese goldsmith
Medallion with Saint Galganus in Prayer, about 1320–30
Silver and gilded copper with translucent enamel, 7.7 × 7.7 cm
Musée Cluny, Paris (Cl. 21557)

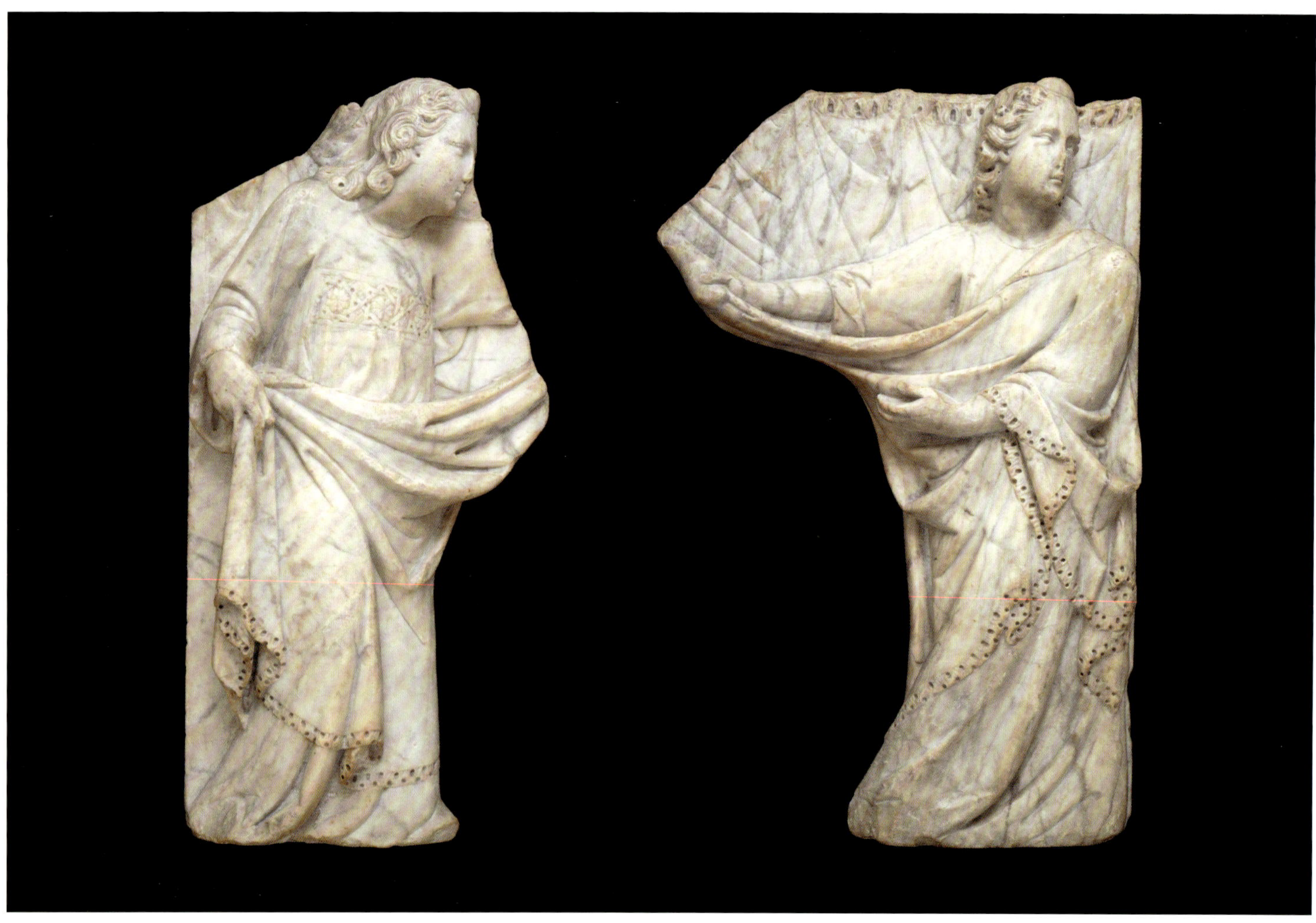

FIG. 95
Tino di Camaino (about 1280–about 1337)
Two Angels holding Curtains, 1319–21
Marble, 63 × 32 × 12 cm and 64 × 43 × 12.5 cm
Victoria and Albert Museum
(7567–1861, 7566–1861)

FIG. 96
Giovanni di Agostino (about 1310–1370)
The Virgin and Child with Saints Catherine and John the Baptist, about 1340–50
Marble with traces of polychromy and gilding, 70.5 × 52.5 × 5.9 cm
The Cleveland Museum of Art, In memory of Henry G. Dalton by his nephews, George S. Kendrick and Harry D. Kendrick (1942.1162)

FIG. 97
Scene showing the Bishop of Orvieto taking possession of the Holy Corporal in the Church of Santa Cristina, from Ugolino di Vieri's *Reliquary of the Holy Corporal* (fig. 47)

within a rectangular frame, beneath a Gothic gabled canopy reminiscent of carpentered frames, local goldsmiths' work and imported ivories (see figs 43, 47, 172, 174).[6] The *Reliquary of the Holy Corporal* in Orvieto, an extraordinary masterpiece created by Ugolino di Vieri and his associates, responded to an entire altarpiece, following at smaller scale the design of the back of Duccio's *Maestà* (see fig. 47). The goldsmiths recreated, in basse-taille enamel, the innovative methods of storytelling used by Duccio, Simone Martini and Pietro and Ambrogio Lorenzetti, arranging figures in action within credible architectural settings.[7] Like the *Maestà*, the Orvieto reliquary was fully worked on both sides, but quite unlike the *Maestà* (apart from its initial triumphant installation in Siena) the reliquary was designed to be carried through the town annually on the feast of Corpus Christi.[8] Similarly, as Williamson shows, the Cleveland and Fitzwilliam Reliquary was intended both for standing upon an altar and for processional display. 'Front' and 'back' were terms that could be applied interchangeably, depending on what feast was being celebrated, or the position of an onlooker witnessing a procession.

Although the creations of painters, goldsmiths and sculptors coexisted in religious settings, their functions diverged. As Glyn Davies discusses (pp. 170–83), goldsmiths produced items essential to the celebration of Mass and other religious rituals, such as the altar cross, candlesticks, hanging lamp and crosier depicted in the scene of the Bishop of Orvieto taking possession of the Holy Corporal in the Church of Santa Cristina on the Orvieto *Reliquary of the Holy Corporal* (fig. 97). Sculptors worked on tombs and shrines that provided a focus for commemorative or supplicatory prayer. Paintings gradually became an expected part of the furnishing of an altar but they were not a liturgical requirement. Sienese painters could, however, be involved in creating a new type of reliquary, as Williamson shows, or in the ornamentation of a liturgical necessity: the choir books containing the sung parts of church services. Lippo Vanni, who produced frescoes (see fig. 43) and panel paintings such as the elegant vision of *Saint Peter as Pope* (fig. 99), was also, together with members of his workshop, a prolific illuminator of antiphonaries (books for the hours – regular communal prayer) and graduals (for Mass).[9] The lavishly decorated leaf now in the Victoria and Albert Museum, probably from a house of Camaldolese nuns in Siena, bears the opening words of Psalm 24, 'Ad te levavi animam meam. Deus meus in te confi[do]' (To thee, O Lord, have I lifted up my soul. In thee, O my God, I put my trust), chanted by the nuns' choir at the start of Mass on the first Sunday of Advent (fig. 100). At the foot of the page, a group of nuns gaze in adoration towards the image of King David, set in the lower portion of the large letter A, himself raising up his small, prayerful, soul towards the blessing Christ, descending, among seraphim, in the upper part of the initial. Like many of his Sienese contemporaries, Vanni also executed important Florentine commissions, including an initial A framing a beautiful if disturbing image of the martyr Saint Agatha, one of five surviving cuttings from a lost antiphonary thought to have been made for Florence Cathedral (fig. 98).[10]

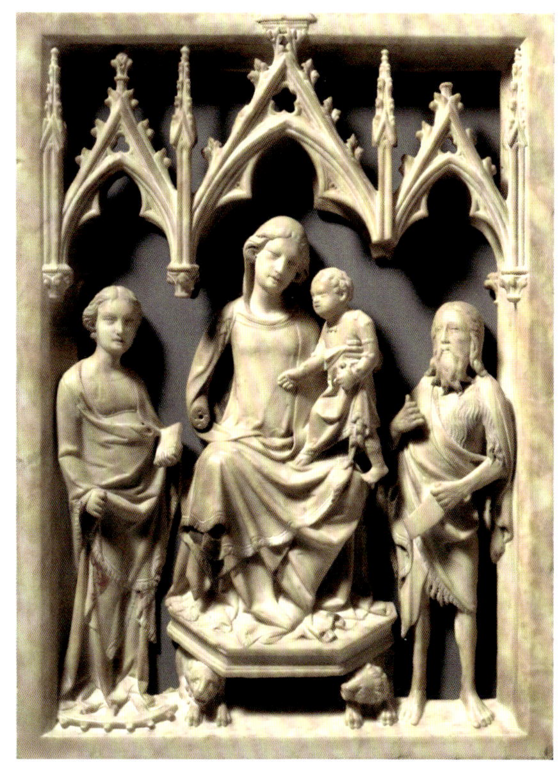

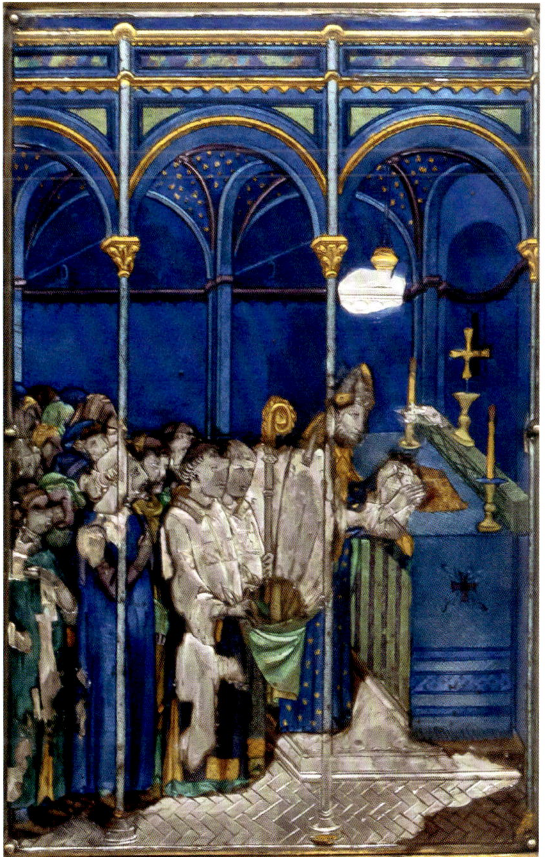

Besides working to the requirements of the formal liturgy, what did Sienese painters and their contemporaries think about the religious functions of their art? This complex question is very difficult to address, but one fascinating piece of evidence was revealed as a result of the lamentable destruction, during the Second World War, of a large wooden crucifix carved and painted by the goldsmith, engineer, architect and sculptor Lando di Pietro (see fig. 130).[11] Two pieces of parchment were rescued from the surviving fragments, one from within the head (fig. 101), the other from the knee. Within the head Lando had written, at the start of a lengthy prayer for mercy for himself, his family and all mankind, that this cross was carved by him, at God's urging, 'to recall for people Christ's Passion'.[12] In the right margin of the parchment strip Lando added that in January 1337 (1338 modern style) 'this figure was completed in the likeness

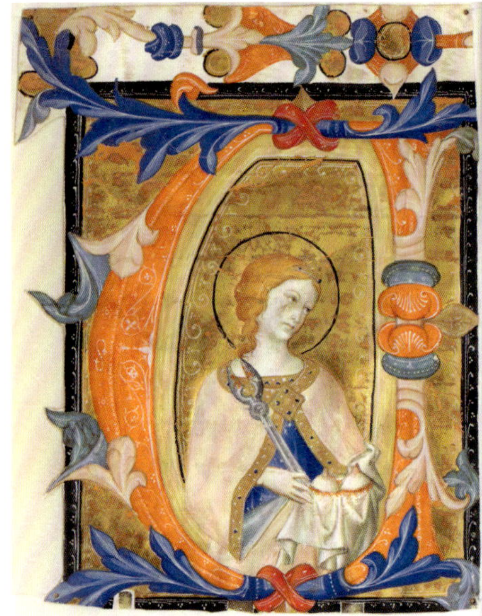

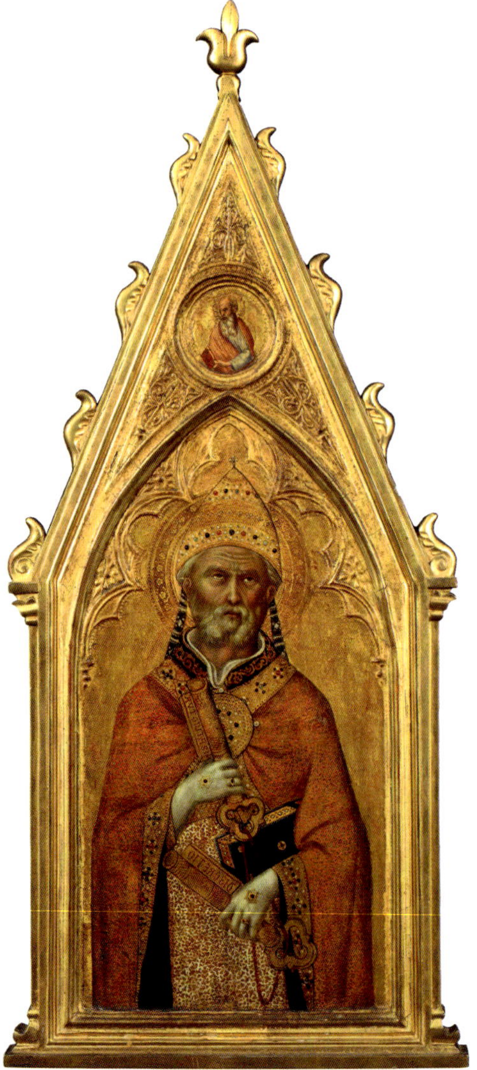

(*similitudine*) of Jesus Christ Crucified, true and living son of God. And one should venerate him and not this wood'.[13] These statements capture two of the fundamental theological attitudes to the function of Christian art in the period. A beautiful three-dimensional painted likeness of the crucified Christ had an important role to play in reminding people of Christ's suffering, and in recommending Lando's soul to God, but at the same time idolatry must be avoided: worship was due to Christ and not to an inanimate piece of wood.[14]

Both Lando di Pietro and Tino di Camaino had illustrious careers, working in the orbit of Emperor Henry VII in the 1310s, and subsequently, in common with Simone Martini, for the Angevins.[15] In Naples Tino produced an unprecedented series of tombs, Lando is credited with exquisite reliquaries (see fig. 131) and Simone contributed the remarkable painting of Saint Louis of Toulouse (see fig. 67). At this elite level – 'inimitable' works to echo Davies (pp. 175–7) – the oeuvres of these three artists illustrate the high reputation of goldsmiths, sculptors and painters from Siena. At a more modest level – the level of the 'imitable' – the Sienese practice of signing goldsmiths' work and, also, paintings, with the artist's city of origin contributed to wider recognition.[16] We can ask whether, during the first half of the fourteenth century, the prestige of one form of art – painting – was rising particularly rapidly. How did the careers of painters from Siena, and the status of the works that they produced, compare with those of Sienese sculptors and goldsmiths? There is, of course, no single simple answer to this question, but the contributions to this section provide opportunities to explore crucial aspects of divergence and convergence among artistic contemporaries in Siena. *JC*

FIG. 98
Lippo Vanni (documented 1344–75)
Cutting from a Choir Book with Saint Agatha, about 1366–70
Tempera and ink on parchment, 22 × 17.2 cm
Private collection

FIG. 99
Lippo Vanni (documented 1344–75)
Saint Peter as Pope, about 1365
Tempera on panel, 74.1 × 32.9 cm (with modern engaged frame)
The Courtauld, London (Samuel Courtauld Trust) (P.1966.GP.469)

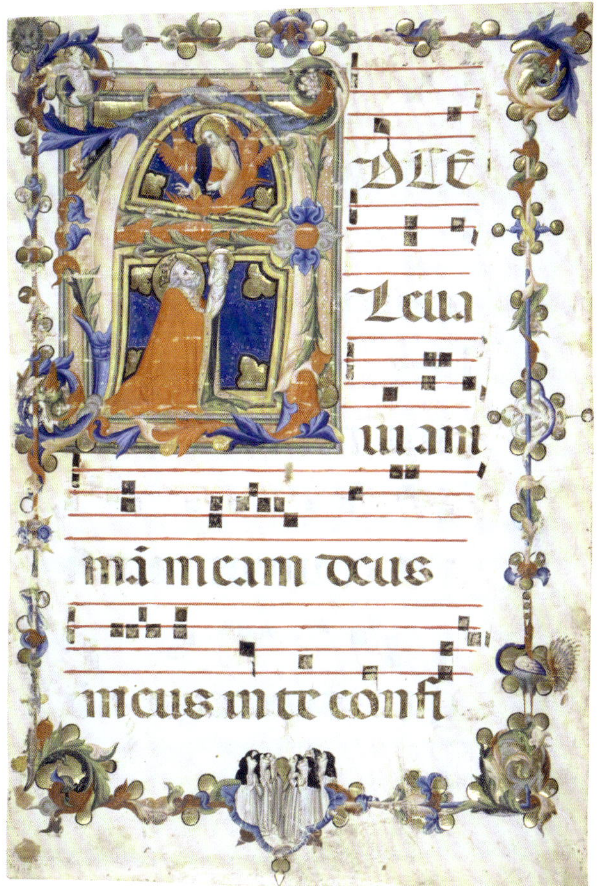

FIG. 100
Lippo Vanni (documented 1344–75)
Leaf from a Gradual with King David raising his Soul to Christ, about 1350
Tempera and ink on parchment, 57 × 38.5 cm
Victoria and Albert Museum (4149)

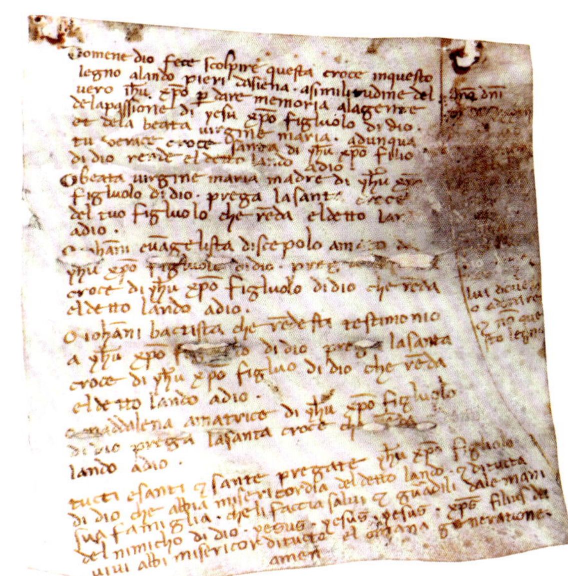

FIG. 101
Lando di Pietro (about 1280–1340)
Ex-voto, 1338
Ink on parchment, 10.3 × 9.9 cm
Basilica di San Bernardino all'Osservanza, Siena. Museo Castelli

1. The *Rucellai Madonna* was commissioned in 1285; Nicholas IV's chalice was made during his papacy (1288–92); Giovanni Pisano was associated with work on the facade of Siena Cathedral from 1287, when he was appointed Master of Works, until his departure from Siena in 1296 or 1297. See Butzek 2006, pp. 24, 26, 28–9; see also Bartalini 2023. Giovanni's Sienese successor was Camaino di Crescentino, father of Tino di Camaino.
2. See Cannon, p. 43, in the present volume.
3. See Davies, pp. 170–83, in the present volume.
4. For goldsmiths, sculptors and Gothic art in Siena, see Bartalini and Cioni 2003–4, and the exhibition catalogues Siena 1982 and Avignon 1983, which remain fundamental resources. For Simone Martini and goldsmiths' work, see Bellosi 1988b; Bagnoli 1999, pp. 40–5; Leone De Castris 2003, pp. 41–50. For Pietro Lorenzetti, see Cioni 1998, especially pp. 417–18. For Ambrogio Lorenzetti, see Seidel and Calamai 2022, pp. 265–85. For Simone Martini and reciprocal relations with contemporary sculpture, see Middeldorf Kosegarten 1988; Kreytenberg 1988. For Pietro Lorenzetti and Tino di Camaino, see Dent, pp. 150–63, in the present volume.
5. For the placement of such angels, drawing the curtains of the mortuary chamber, see Marzullo, fig. 111, in the present volume.
6. Bartalini 2011b, pp. 337, 350–1, 363.
7. Several scenes from the Passion Cycle follow Duccio's *Maestà* or resemble the work of Pietro Lorenzetti or Simone Martini, specifically his Orsini Polyptych, see figs 126 and 194. See Cioni 1998, pp. 553–602. For the suggestion of a direct collaboration with Ambrogio Lorenzetti in the Holy Corporal cycle scenes, see Seidel and Calamai 2022, pp. 279–85. For the Holy Corporal cycle, see also Freni 2000b, pp. 121–30.
8. Freni 2000b, pp. 130–4, 152–3.
9. For Lippo Vanni in the context of Sienese manuscript illumination, see Labriola, De Benedictis and Freuler 2002, pp. 105–45, especially pp. 129–40, 319. For the leaf in the Victoria and Albert Museum, see Wainwright 1988, pp. 27–9, 31–3.
10. Labriola, De Benedictis and Freuler 2002, pp. 138–9, 319.
11. See Davies, pp. 150–63, in the present volume.
12. 'Domene dio fece scolpire questa croce in questo legno alando pieri da Siena asimilitudine del vero ihu xpo per dare memoria ala gente de la passione di yesu xpo figluolo di Dio.' See Bagnoli in Siena 1987, cat. 12, pp. 65–8. For the translations used here and important analysis of the inscriptions, see Cooper 2006.
13. 'Anno Domini MCCCXXXVII di gennaio fu compiuta questa figura a similitudine di yhu xpo crocifisso figluolo di dio vivo et vero. Et lui dovendo adorare et non questo legno.' See Bagnoli in Siena 1987, cat. 12, p. 68; Cooper 2006, p. 48.
14. For an introduction to these views in a Dominican context, and further bibliography, see Cannon 2013, pp. 51–6, 342–3.
15. Lando made the crown for Henry VII's coronation as King of Italy, in Milan, in 1311, and Tino sculpted Henry's tomb, in Pisa, in around 1315. See Dent, pp. 150–63, Davies, pp. 170–83, and the biographical notes by Marzullo, pp. 270–1, in the present volume. For the artists' employment in Naples, see Norman 2018, pp. 71–126.
16. Davies, pp. 172–3, in the present volume; Donato 2003; Donato 2011–12, especially pp. 5–15. For an unfavourable fifteenth-century reaction to the Sienese fondness for signing works, see Capron 2017, p. 4.

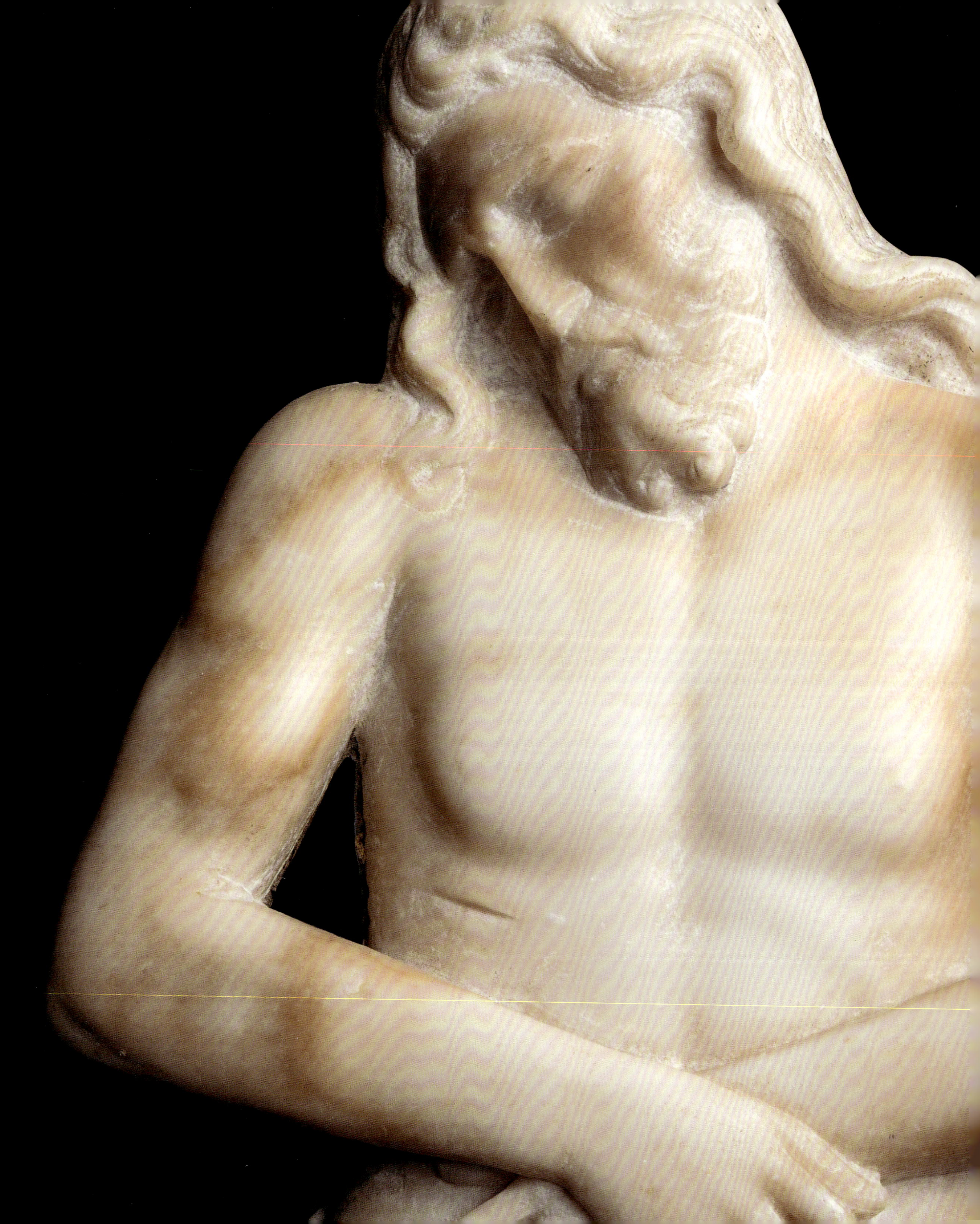

TINO DI CAMAINO, PIETRO LORENZETTI AND THE BODY OF CHRIST

Peter Dent

Towards the end of his life, in the early 1330s, the Sienese sculptor Tino di Camaino was commissioned by Abbot Philip de Haya of the Benedictine community Santissima Trinità at Cava dei Tirreni to sculpt a marble altarpiece for the high altar of the abbey's church. A lost inscription transcribed in 1780 recorded his patronage: 'Brother Philip de Haya abbot of this monastery of Cava had this panel made in order to honour God.'[1]

Only fragments survive of what must have been an extraordinary marble altarpiece, executed in low relief. These fragments include two large panels, one depicting Mary, John the Evangelist and their companions, all in attitudes of grief (fig. 102), and the other a group of soldiers.[2] These panels were clearly once part of a larger composition with a Crucifixion at the centre. Further sculptures at the abbey, in particular a small, framed narrative relief of the Massacre of the Innocents, suggest that the altarpiece incorporated a predella.[3] Even more intriguingly, two fragments of a monumental Virgin and Child have given rise to the suggestion that the altarpiece may once have been double-sided. The scene of the Crucifixion would have overlooked the monks' choir, while the Virgin and Child, accompanied no doubt by saints, probably addressed the congregation in the nave.

The altarpiece embodies much of what makes Tino perhaps the most significant and innovative sculptor of his generation. The commission itself, for an extremely powerful Benedictine foundation in the south of the peninsula, demonstrates the incredible level of penetration that Sienese artists had achieved at the Neapolitan court by about 1330.[4] It confirms the high esteem in which Tino and his workshop were held by patrons with connections to that court.[5] Philip de Haya's brother Giovanni was rector of the Corte della Vicaria, the court of justice. He was described in his funeral eulogy in 1337 as the most important official of the kingdom.[6] Among his services to King Robert (reigned 1309–43) and his son Charles, Duke of Calabria, he administered various

P. 150
Detail of FIG. 105

FIG. 102
Tino di Camaino (about 1280–about 1337)
Mary, Saint John the Evangelist and Companions at the Foot of the Cross, about 1329–31
Marble, 98 × 75 cm
Abbazia della Santissima Trinità, Cava dei Tirreni

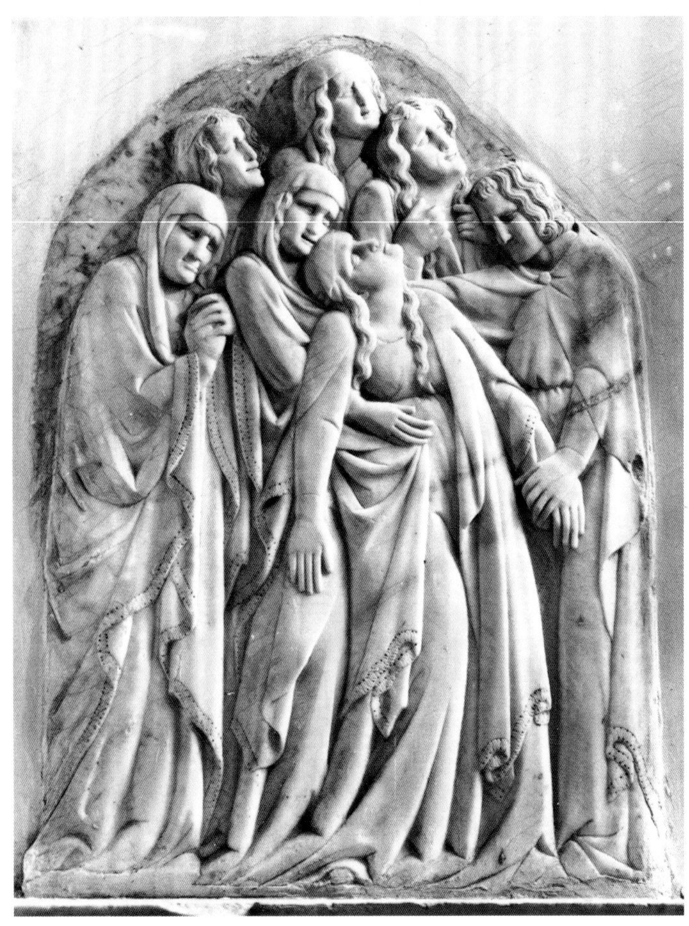

royal construction projects. A document of 9 March 1329 issued by Giovanni de Haya, relating to construction of the castle of Belforte, also names Tino da Siena.[7] It is probably through this connection that Tino won the commission at Cava dei Tirreni.[8] Tino had arrived in Naples early in 1324 and was soon employed on funerary monuments for members of the royal family and other nobles.[9] Indeed, he also appears to have sculpted a tomb for Philip de Haya at the abbey, including low-relief images of an enthroned Virgin and Child, a Saint Benedict and Philip himself presented to the Virgin by the founder of the community, Saint Alferio.[10]

The prospect of a double-sided altarpiece immediately calls to mind Duccio's *Maestà* (see figs 8, 9). The iconography, with a Crucifixion on one side and an enthroned Virgin on the other, along with a predella incorporating narrative scenes, corresponds with that celebrated Sienese model, with which Tino would have been closely acquainted.[11] The format declares the sculptor's interest in emulating the art of painting.[12] We know that Tino certainly produced one double-sided marble altarpiece on a smaller scale. This survives as two separate triptychs executed in relief and clearly designed to imitate a panel painting. One panel carries bust-length images of the Virgin and Child, John the Baptist and Catherine of Alexandria (fig. 103); the other, Christ as the Man of Sorrows flanked by the Virgin and John the Evangelist (fig. 104).[13] When first brought together for comparison, these were found not only to possess identical proportions but also corresponding damage to the backs, indicating that they once formed an integral block that was subsequently sawn apart.[14] At this scale, the object was presumably designed for the more intimate context of private devotion, although the rather unique two-sided format suggests either a setting with particular requirements or perhaps even a patron wishing to own a personalised version of a public work like Duccio's.[15] This too emulates the basic iconography of the *Maestà* on a smaller scale, with the bust-length Man of Sorrows replacing Christ Crucified in this abbreviated format.

It is perhaps possible that the images of mourners and soldiers at the foot of the Cross in the Cava dei Tirreni fragment were designed to frame a pre-existing crucifix by another sculptor, now lost. Whether or not the lost

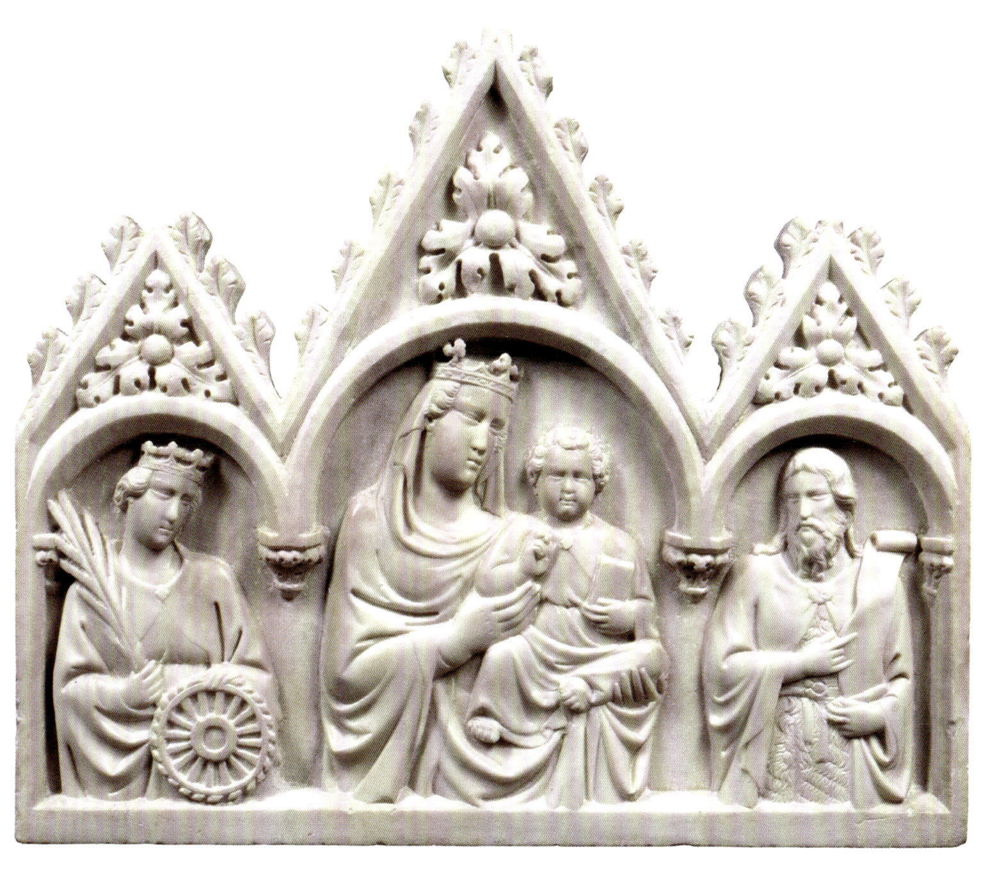

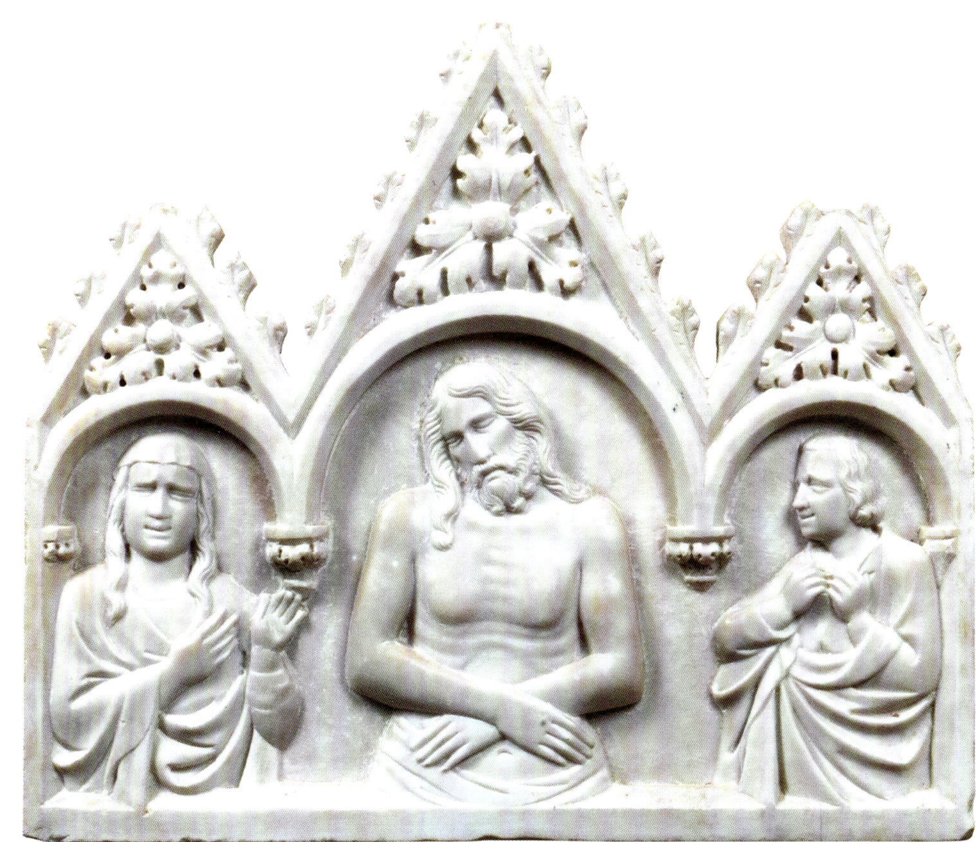

FIG. 103
Tino di Camaino (about 1280–about 1337)
The Virgin and Child with Saint Catherine and Saint John the Baptist, about 1329–32
Marble, 55 × 65 cm
Monte dei Paschi, Siena

FIG. 104
Tino di Camaino (about 1280–about 1337)
The Man of Sorrows with the Virgin and Saint John the Evangelist, about 1329–32
Marble, 55 × 65 cm
Salini Collection, Castello di Gallico

image of Christ Crucified was indeed a work in low relief by Tino, it draws attention to a significant lacuna in his career. Although a relatively large number of works in both stone and wood can be attributed to Tino on the basis of signature inscriptions, documentary evidence and stylistic arguments, none of this material includes an image of Christ on the Cross.[16] There are depictions of Christ's baptismal body, his dead body and his resurrected body, and multiple examples of his infant body. Apart from the reliefs at Cava, however, the only other evidence that Tino had previously attempted the image of Christ on the Cross – perhaps the most common iconography of this period alongside the Virgin and Child – is an incomplete panel of the Crucifixion now in the Museo dell'Opera di Santa Chiara in Naples.[17] This too probably formed part of a large, sculpted altarpiece. Not only is this fragmented, so that the figure of Christ is missing from the hips upward, but also the carving was left unfinished, as though the project was aborted.[18]

The limited evidence for Tino's engagement with the image of Christ Crucified may just be an accident of survival. But it is a problematic one in terms of understanding his development as a sculptor. His early career was spent in close proximity to Giovanni Pisano who, apart from Arnolfo di Cambio, was perhaps the most significant central Italian sculptor of the previous generation.[19] Giovanni had a direct impact at Siena where he was employed as master of works on the cathedral facade.[20] After Giovanni's departure from this role in 1297, Tino followed him to Pisa, where he remained until 1315.[21] Of all Giovanni's followers, Tino is distinguished for his ability to carve out an independent career within the older sculptor's orbit. At Pisa, he was responsible for significant commissions in his own right, such as the tomb-altar for San Ranieri and the monument for Emperor Henry VII.[22] Despite his proximity to Giovanni, or possibly precisely because of it, Tino seems to have actively developed an artistic language in partial opposition to Giovanni's example. Where, for instance, Giovanni pursued three-dimensional form to its fullest extent, Tino appears more interested in pictorial effects. Already in the San Ranieri tomb-altar he seems to have taken Giotto's *Saint Francis of Assisi receiving the Stigmata* (about 1300; Musée du Louvre) as his model.[23] Although problematic as evidence of character, the early signature inscriptions also seem to strike an oppositional tone. The long inscription on Giovanni's Pisa pulpit is notable for its many variations on the word 'sculpture'.[24] In contrast, Tino's lost baptismal font that faced it in the south transept associated him instead with an 'art of colours'.[25] Later, the inscription on the tomb for the Florentine bishop Antonio degli Orsi places Tino's skill second to that of his father Crescentino, in stark contrast to Giovanni's declaration on the Pistoia pulpit that he was Nicola's son but 'blessed with greater skill'.[26]

The works that most epitomise Giovanni's sculptural language are his wooden crucifixes, one of the earliest of which survives in Siena.[27] These depict Christ in increasingly complex three-dimensional poses, twisted, coiled and compressed as he hangs against the Cross. These tortured forms are supplemented with a detailed sculptural definition of the ribs, tendons, muscles and ligaments, each rendered as though seen at the very pitch of stress and strain.[28] The same conception also appears in the Crucifixion panels of his pulpits. It is against this image of the suffering Christ, expressed emphatically in sculptural terms rather than relying on the effects of surface polychromy, that the absence of anything comparable in Tino's work is notable.[29] The incomplete relief of the Crucifixion from Naples suggests,

FIG. 105
Tino di Camaino (about 1280–about 1337)
Man of Sorrows, about 1329–32
Marble, 25.5 × 20 × 4 cm
Private collection

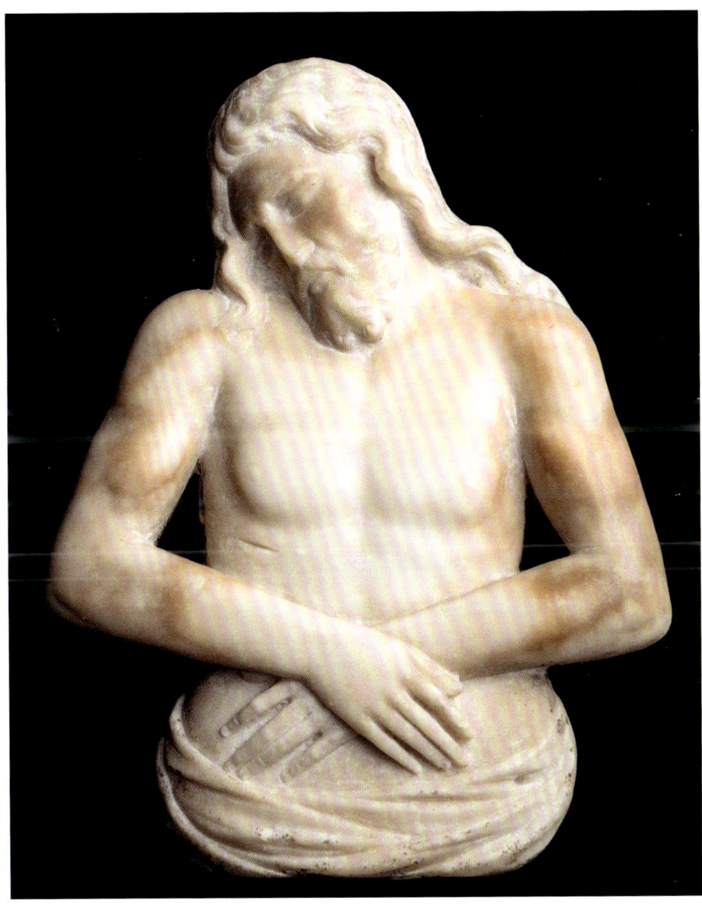

instead, an interest in pictorial models, and we can probably speculate that the same was true of the lost crucifix at Cava. Indeed, the evidence suggests in both cases that Tino was pursuing a carving technique much closer to two-dimensional representation than the kind of deep excavation that Giovanni practised when working in relief, for example, on the aforementioned Crucifixion panels at Pistoia and Pisa.[30]

The closest version to Christ's Passion body that we can substitute for this absence is the Man of Sorrows. There are three surviving cases where Tino attempted a version of this figure, all attributable to the Neapolitan phase of his career: in the double-sided triptych already mentioned; within a roundel on the tomb monument for Catherine of Austria in San Lorenzo Maggiore in Naples; and in a small isolated relief, without further context.[31] In the first two cases, the flanking figures of Mary and John in mourning situate the Man of Sorrows as a substitute for Christ on the Cross. Giovanni Pisano was responsible for two versions of the same figure, probably intended for Epistle lecterns on his pulpits.[32] Even allowing for the radically divergent functions, the differences in execution reinforce the impression that Tino was responding to pictorial sources for his versions rather than to the sculptural language developed by Giovanni. On the Pisa and Pistoia lecterns, for example, the body of Christ has been deeply excavated from the marble ground. By contrast, Tino's versions all present the same body in much lower relief, almost entirely integrated into the planar surface of the ground with negligible undercutting of the contour.

To a certain extent, the articulation of the body differs as well. Although more subdued than his Crucifixions, Giovanni's versions are nevertheless rooted in those images of suffering. The difference in Tino's approach is clearest in the most highly finished of his figures: the small, isolated relief (fig. 105).[33] Almost all trace of the Passion has been eliminated from the depiction of the body. Christ's head is inclined gently as though in untroubled sleep, rather than bowed after the agonies of death. His hair trails softly over his shoulders. His arms are held without strain across his abdomen and his fingers are poised delicately above the textile around his waist. The execution tends towards a simplicity, a flatness – almost a blankness – that differentiates it from the three-dimensional elaboration of

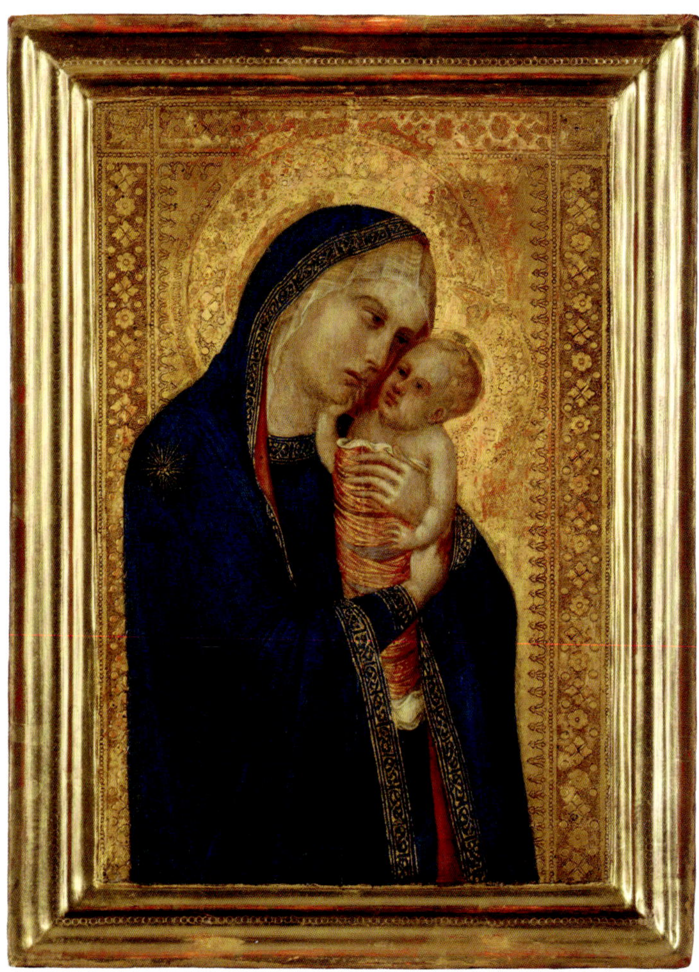

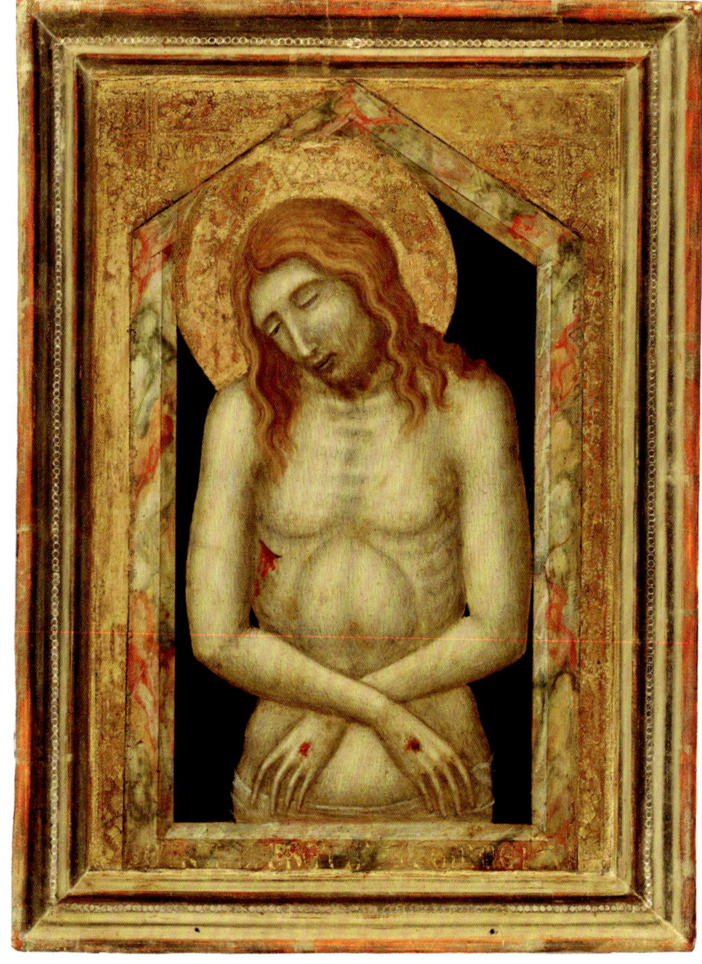

Giovanni's figures. There is a reduction and softening not only of anatomical detail, but also of surface articulation of any sort except in the fine detailing of the face and the fingertips. As a statement of Tino's conception of the Passion body of Christ, it diverges fundamentally from Giovanni Pisano's model.

This small Man of Sorrows relief is in many respects an enigmatic object, although the black marble inserts by the crook of each arm offer some suggestive evidence for its original appearance. The application of black as a backdrop to a Man of Sorrows corresponds closely to another image, also by a Sienese artist of the same generation, Pietro Lorenzetti. In a panel at Altenburg, Lorenzetti has depicted Christ framed against the black interior of a gabled tomb that bears his signature along the lower edge (fig. 106).[34] This panel forms the right valve of a compact devotional diptych. In the other valve, Mary clutches her child tight in his swaddling clothes as she gazes across at the image of his future death. The black marble inserts on Tino's version rather suggest that his Man of Sorrows would have been surrounded by a similar gabled tomb. Indeed, without further framing, this would produce an object identical in structure to a remarkable series of Virgin and Child panels attributed to Tino.[35] These clearly imitate the format and scale of devotional panels and suggest that Tino's workshop was engaged in a limited form of serial production, comparable to similar practices already established for devotional panels by Duccio. These 'chiselled images' were perhaps intended for an elite group of patrons connected with the Neapolitan court.[36]

Can we imagine the Man of Sorrows paired with one of these? The scale of the figure suggests not. While it is comparable in height to Lorenzetti's painted figure of the Man of Sorrows, it is more than 5 cm shorter than

FIG. 106
Pietro Lorenzetti (documented possibly 1306; died probably 1348)
Diptych with the Virgin and Child and the Man of Sorrows, about 1340–5
Tempera on panel, 35 × 25.9 and 35.1 × 25.9 cm (with engaged frames)
Lindenau-Museum Altenburg, Germany (Inv. 47, 48)

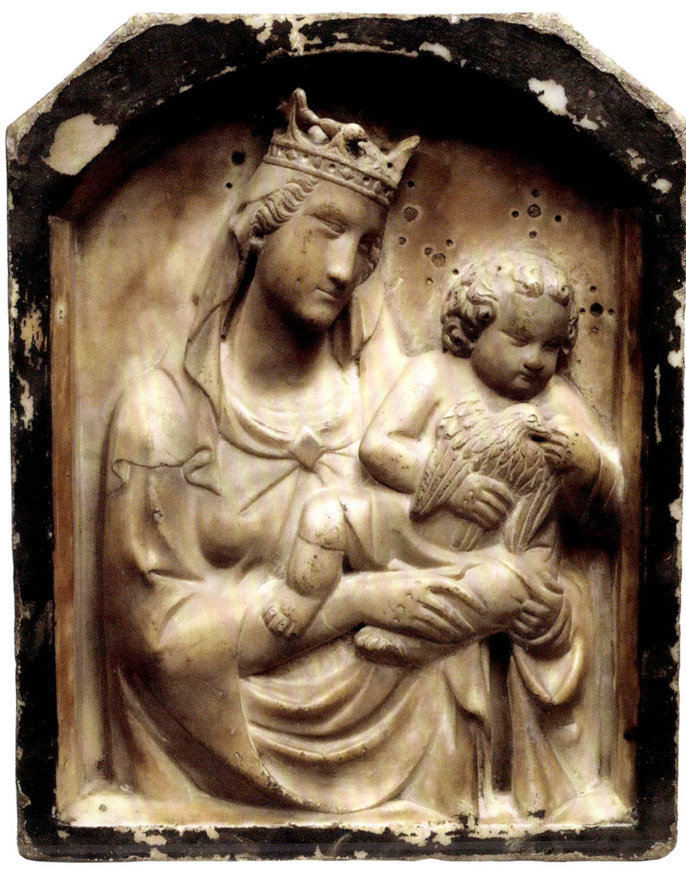

FIG. 107
Tino di Camaino (about 1280–about 1337)
The Virgin and Child, about 1335
Marble, 31 × 26 cm
State Hermitage Museum, St Petersburg (H.ck-1056)

the equivalent bust-length images of the Virgin in this sculpted group. However, a slightly different version of the composition now in the State Hermitage Museum in St Petersburg, Russia (fig. 107), is on a smaller scale, and the Virgin does share the same dimensions, give or take a centimetre.[37] One interesting divergence from the iconography of the other Virgin and Child panels in this case is the strong turn of the Christ Child to look along the same sight line as his mother, as though focused on something lying outside the image to his left (our right). In a painted panel, we might take this as evidence that the image was once part of a diptych or a triptych. A paired panel of this sort executed in marble would be unique in Tino's career but not entirely unknown elsewhere, and sculpted diptychs were obviously a common category in ivory. The Hermitage panel has an arched rather than a gabled frame but it helps us to imagine, in terms of scale and execution, what such a diptych might have looked like if the Man of Sorrows were combined with a Virgin and Child as a sculptural equivalent to the kind of devotional diptychs fashioned by Sienese painters.

In all of these small reliefs, at the very least the clothing, the Virgin's crown, the goldfinch, the pomegranate, the hair and the eyes would no doubt once have been polychromed.[38] The background might also have been gilded or otherwise decorated, and both figures supplied with halos. In the Hermitage Virgin and Child, some polychromy remains on the frame, although this may not be original. There are also drill holes for inserting material around the halos. It is much harder to imagine that surface polychromy played such an extensive role on the marble Man of Sorrows. This is suggested in part by the use of a black marble ground. If the sculptor anticipated extensive polychromy, this would have been an unnecessary inclusion. Some colour applied as paint must nevertheless have played a role. Although the side wound is defined in the marble, the wound on the front hand is not and this was presumably painted onto the surface. Perhaps Christ's hair, the details of his facial features and the cloth around his waist were once also given further definition through the application of colour, along with blood for the visible wounds.[39] It seems unlikely, however, that the flesh of the body would have been treated in this way. The marble has been given a noticeably finer level of polish wherever Christ's skin is visible, and this draws out some of the warmer variegated tonal interest of the material itself.

The conceit of marble as flesh developed in sophisticated ways during the fifteenth century, but it is hard to say at what date sculptors first began to exploit the approach in serious terms.[40] Although we expect much medieval sculpture to be painted, selective polychromy of stone was probably always practised to some extent. However, its potential is emphatically demonstrated in the decade following Tino's death, in Andrea Pisano's *Madonna del Latte* (about 1343–7; Museo Nazionale di San Matteo, Pisa), where the exquisite

FIG. 108
Sienese artist (**Guccio di Mannaia** [documented 1295–1318]?)
The Crucifixion, about 1310–20
Marble and coloured wax, 44.8 × 28 × 3.2 cm
Arcidiocesi di Siena - Colle di Val d'Elsa - Montalcino, Siena, Palazzo Arcivescovile
(from Chiesa di San Pellegrino alla Sapienza)

FIG. 109
Pietro Lorenzetti (documented possibly 1306; died probably 1348)
Cut-out Crucifix, about 1315–20
Tempera on panel, 145 × 90 cm
Museo Diocesano, Cortona

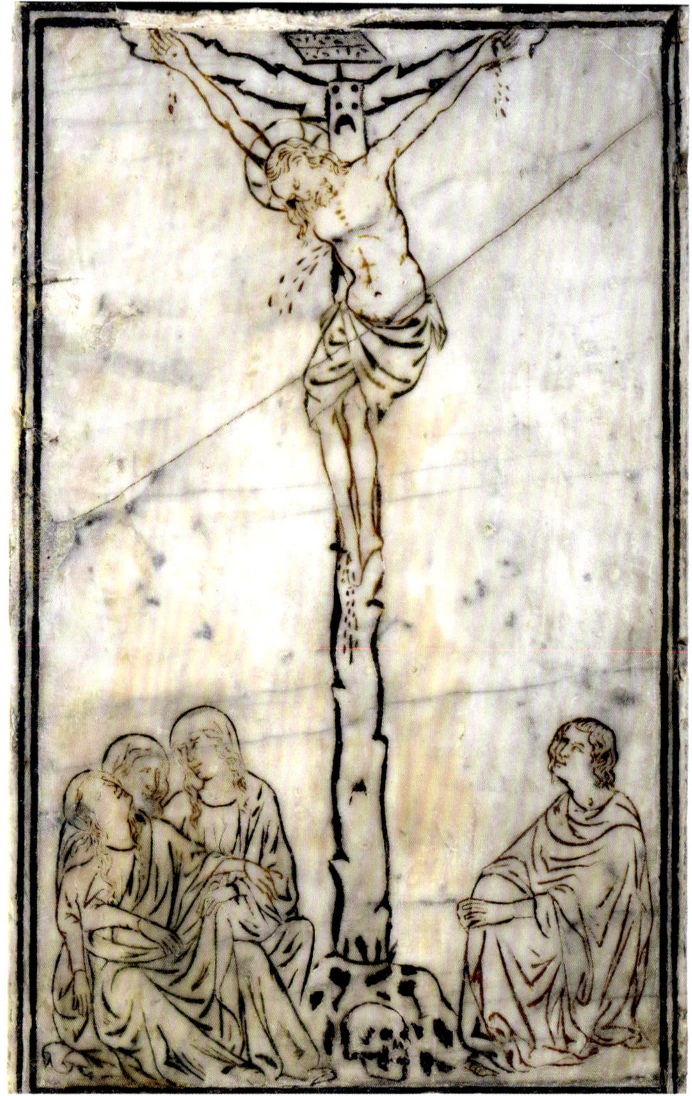

quality of the surviving gilding against the high polish of the exposed marble surface, especially where it serves as the milky flesh of the Virgin's breast and of Christ's face as he suckles, indicates a clear appreciation of the subtle aesthetic qualities that could be drawn out of the material itself.[41] Tino's Man of Sorrows may be a pioneering experiment in this direction, but it may also be reductive to interpret this quality of his work entirely through the lens of a fifteenth-century conceit.

It is more fruitful, perhaps, to situate it within the general turn to pictorial models in his work, itself part of a distinctive trend in Sienese sculpture that developed in spite of, or in reaction to, Giovanni's earlier presence in the city.[42] The simplified conception of Christ's body, spare in its detail, that draws the material ground into its representational language finds some interesting resonances in this turn. Within the Sienese context, another devotional image associated with Lorenzetti experiments with a similar kind of simplicity in which marble takes on a subtle representational value. This object, an image of Christ on the Cross flanked by seated figures of John, Mary and her companions, sits right on the boundary between two-dimensional and three-dimensional imagery (fig. 108).[43] It clearly expresses the special kind of dialogue between media that developed in this period in the Sienese context. The design has been lightly engraved, possibly with the fine edge of a chisel, into a block of marble that could have easily accommodated deeper carving. Coloured wax of different hues pressed into these lines gives the design greater body against the pale stone and articulates, to a certain extent, the boundaries of different materials, such as wood or flesh. But there is no indication of any further surface detail or colour. The bodies are elegantly conjured out of the simple linear contours. With these in place, the lightly mottled surface of the marble not only functions as the ground for the 'drawing', dissolving into open space behind the figures, but also gently evokes Christ's pale flesh stretched on the Cross.

Although the sensitive handling of the incised lines suggests the intervention of somebody skilled in working marble, the design has been attributed to Pietro Lorenzetti himself or somebody influenced by his manner. Another work attributed to Lorenzetti indicates an interest, comparable to Tino's, in experimenting at the boundary between flatness and three-dimensionality. This is the cut-out crucifix from Cortona, the earliest surviving example of its type (fig. 109).[44] It is not only the liberation of the form

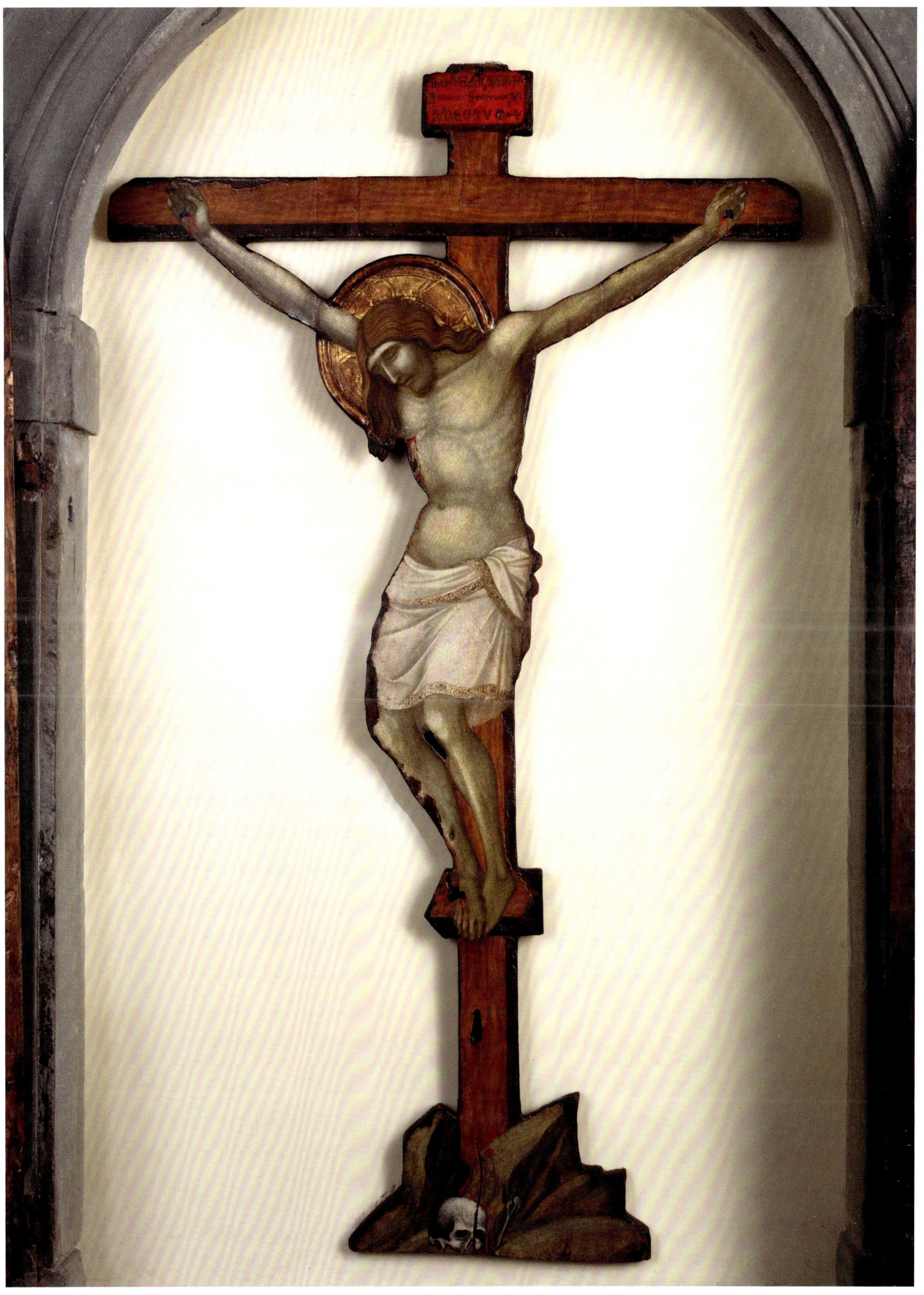

of Christ on the Cross from the context of a larger panel that gives this object something of a sculptural quality; the finishing also gestures towards relief. Traces of pigment and linen support that extend beyond the front face, and the partial sculptural definition of Christ's body on the reverse, indicate that the work was designed to entertain views from other directions.[45] In its original state, the crucifix must have presented a deeply ambiguous mixture of illusionistic and real volumes. Indeed, the cut-out gap between the knees produces a similar effect to the black marble insert of Tino's Man of Sorrows. As such, it represents a distinct phase in the long dialogue between painted and sculpted images of Christ Crucified in particular.[46] In its own fashion, the execution of the incised marble Crucifixion seems designed to capture something of this ambiguity. In ways that evoke the sculptural line normally associated with Florentine artists of the following century, the incisions vary in thickness along their length, as though turning around a three-dimensional contour before being lost to the eye.

Once again, the scale and subject matter of this incised panel of the Crucifixion suggest an image designed for personal devotional purposes. The scene is framed by a double border and this detail, in combination with the linear design and the sheet-like quality of the marble, evokes the effect of an ink drawing on parchment. Indeed, a celebrated late thirteenth-century Italian manuscript, the *Supplicationes variae*, has a cycle of full-page drawings framed with double borders.[47] Towards the conclusion of this cycle, a Man of Sorrows is included as a devotional focus after the narrative sequence of Christ's Life, Death and Resurrection (fig. 110).[48] This drawing in particular, linear and spare in execution, shares some of the character of the engraved Crucifixion panel and Tino's Man of Sorrows. In other images, the artist has introduced coloured wash but here the application of colour is much reduced, and the depiction perhaps draws on a widespread association of the material of the page with the flesh of Christ. This unique manuscript was designed to function as a sophisticated meditational path, leading the reader-viewer towards contemplation of the divine, a path in which the image cycle is the final stage. We might imagine the marble 'drawing' of the Crucifixion and Tino's Man of Sorrows as comparable and rather unique attempts to develop images in different media that could function in a similar way. All three may bear witness to the increasingly refined appetite in late medieval culture for devotional images. Where Giovanni Pisano might supply a surfeit of detail to populate the viewer's mind, these images literally leave space for the devotee to exercise their own imagination.

In dwelling in this way on Tino's Man of Sorrows, a contemporary viewer might treat it as a narrative image of Christ's body entombed in the hiatus between death and resurrection.[49] This could entail mentally inscribing the blank canvas of the body with the marks of the Passion narrative itself. The image of Christ Crucified is certainly described in these terms in contemporary texts, as a book on which scriptural events are written as wounds.[50] The body literally carries the narrative. In this context, the blemishes in the marble across the arms might evoke the memory of Passion violence still clinging to Christ's flesh.[51] Equally, the polished quality of the marble might serve to articulate the attention paid to Christ's dead body as it was kissed and caressed and anointed in preparation for the tomb. However, the iconography of Christ upright in the tomb, as if in suspended animation, is itself a kind of anti-narrative image. While Christ's body awaits resurrection, the narrative flow

– the Harrowing of Hell – unfolds elsewhere. With the body rendered almost void of detail in this way, it becomes the symbol of this narrative hiatus, the image of the pause, as the body sleeps, now beyond reach of the Passion, until called forth from the tomb to rejoin the world. With its delicate accents on the face and fingers, Tino infuses Christ with an uncanny sense of potential that anticipates this imminent return to life.

On the other hand, the Man of Sorrows is not only a narrative image. It was also understood in this period as a visualisation of Christ's body within the consecrated bread and wine.[52] The desire to see the consecrated host, not just at the elevation but also outside this liturgical context, was just taking hold in central Italy in the first decades of the fourteenth century.[53] As a visible point of attraction, however, the plain white disc of bread was also frustratingly dissimilar in its appearance to the underlying reality of Christ's body. There is evidence from elsewhere in Europe at this date that hosts might be stamped with the image of the Man of Sorrows.[54] Such impressed images were probably relatively simple. Considering Tino's relief, with the Eucharist in mind, a devotee might also connect the whiteness, flatness and relative blankness – perhaps even opacity – of Christ's body with these qualities of the consecrated host.[55]

In other words, for all its simplicity in comparison to the detailed visual rhetoric – the legibility – of Giovanni Pisano's version of Christ's body, Tino's Man of Sorrows offers itself to the active devotional gaze like a subtly nuanced screen onto which a variety of thoughts can be projected. Certainly, these thoughts could range across both interpretations of the iconography. Indeed, if the Man of Sorrows was once surrounded by a gabled tomb like that in Pietro Lorenzetti's painted panel, the evocation of a tabernacle would help draw

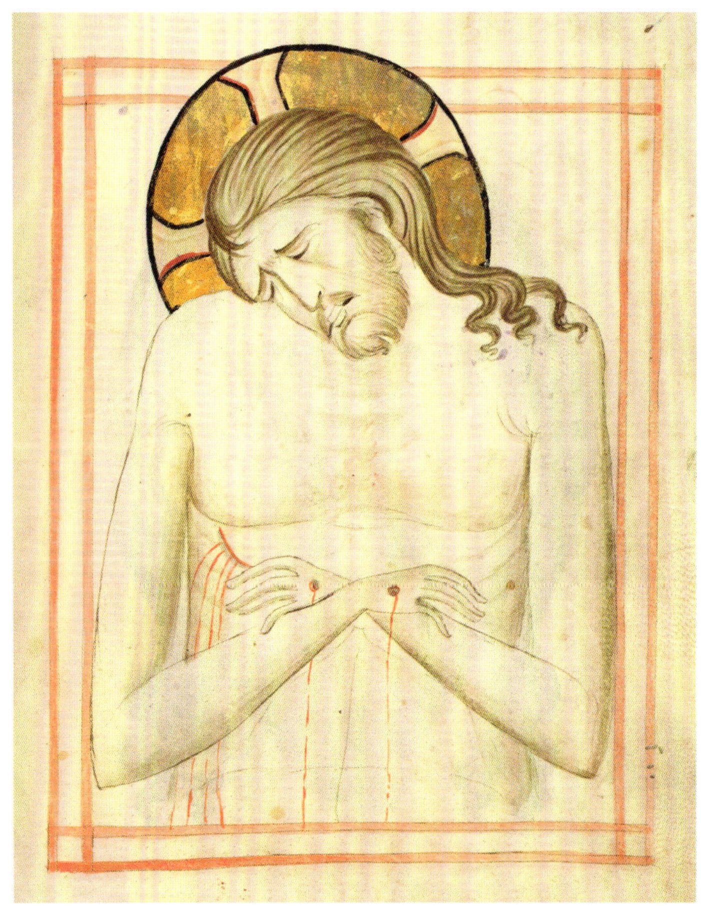

FIG. 110
Artist from the Veneto
The Man of Sorrows, 1293
Ink and wash on parchment, 27 × 19.5 cm
Supplicationes variae, MS Plut. 25.3, fol. 387r
Biblioteca Medicea Laurenziana, Florence

out the Eucharistic implications for the viewer. Returning now to that image, the diptych from Altenburg, in the light of Tino's Man of Sorrows, is instructive.

On the reverse of the panel the painter conjures up a complex illusion, perhaps intended to recall a portable altar: the elaborate pattern punched into the silver ground that runs in a thick band around the edges evokes a precious metal frame designed to encase the fictive marble slab depicted at the centre.[56] This exterior decoration interacts in interesting ways with the imagery within, particularly in so far as it engages both the narrative and Eucharistic significance of the Man of Sorrows. On the one hand, the interior pairing of the Virgin and Child with the image of Christ in the tomb encapsulates the narrative arc of Christ's life, setting birth and death together across the two wings in such a way that the Virgin's gaze spans these two moments and she experiences future sorrow in the midst of present joy. On the other hand, the relationship between the two sides of the Man of Sorrows panel draws out the Eucharistic connotation of that body. The visual conceit here involves a portable altar, encouraging us to imagine the presence of the consecrated host. But this altar can also be opened to reveal the actual body of Christ within. In other words, these two orientations cohere, as they must, in the Man of Sorrows.

This intertwining of the Eucharistic and narrative aspects is reinforced by the framing of Christ's body. On the exterior of the panel, the punched gilding encloses the fictive marble. Both elements also appear on the interior face, but here the marble has retreated to become a second frame around the corpse. With this move, the framing activates the liturgical symbolism of the altar as Christ's tomb.[57] In opening the diptych it is as though we have lifted the fictive marble slab – or rolled away the stone – to find Christ there, waiting in suspended animation. And here Lorenzetti appears to have carried these ideas a step further in his handling of Christ himself. The figure's slightly mottled skin tone with its subtle greens and browns, along with the stronger accents of the whiter highlights and the red blood of the wounds, are all picked up in the stony palette of the variegated marble tomb with its veins of green, brown, white and red. It is as though Christ's body has taken on the rich but implacable character of the stone, reinforcing the thought that his flesh endures the narrative closure of death, which is now held in suspension rather than completed. This is not a body petrified and lifeless, but rather the 'living stone rejected by men' that triumphs over mortality and offers that triumph, through this body, to humankind.[58]

This dialogue of skin and stone, this play with the connotations of different materials, speaks to the intimate dialogue between Sienese sculptors and painters in this period. Surviving documents indicate that in the early 1340s, a few years after Tino's death, Pietro Lorenzetti acted on behalf of Tino's sons in several Sienese property transactions, hinting at a long-standing connection between painter and sculptor.[59] Whether an artistic dialogue occurred directly between the two men is impossible to say, but the visual evidence is suggestive. The works considered in this essay testify to a deeply productive back-and-forth between Sienese artists, working at the limits of their media as they negotiated the evolving devotional needs of their patrons.

1. 'FRATER PHILIPPUS DE HAYA ABBAS HUIUS MONASTERII CAVENSIS AD HONOREM DEI FIERI FECIT TABULAM ISTAM'. Bartalini 2011a, p. 199.
2. Ibid., no. 6, p. 199 (98 × 75 cm and 86 × 75 cm respectively).
3. Ibid., nos 7–10, pp. 199–200.
4. Norman 2018.
5. For his activities in Naples, see Aceto 2011; Norman 2018, pp. 74–88, 97–126.
6. On Giovanni de Haya, see Boyer 2016.
7. Bartalini 2011a, p. 194.
8. Aceto 2011, p. 189.
9. Norman 2018, pp. 97–126.
10. Bartalini 2011a, no. 22, p. 203 (see also no. 23).
11. Tino was based in Pisa when Duccio's altarpiece was installed in 1311, but he fled the city in 1315 and returned to Siena, where he was documented as working for the cathedral in 1318 and named lead sculptor there in 1320. While in Siena, he executed the funerary monument of Cardinal Riccardo Petroni, who died on 26 February 1314, for the chapel of Saint Catherine in the cathedral. Bardelloni 2011.
12. Seidel 1989.
13. Bartalini 2011a, no. 17, p. 201 (both 55 × 65 cm).
14. Kreytenberg 2001.
15. On this phenomenon, see Schmidt 2005a, pp. 169–204. It is also possible that the work was located in a small chapel.
16. For the most recent monographic study, see Baldelli 2007; Bartalini 2011a, pp. 119–231.
17. Bartalini 2011a, no. 14, p. 201 (79 × 64 × 9 cm).
18. Remarkably, this is one of several unfinished works by Tino that reveal aspects of his sculptural practice. See also Bartalini 2011a, nos 17, 19, p. 140.
19. Moskowitz 2001, pp. 44–93.
20. Tigler 2007.
21. Bardelloni 2011.
22. Bartalini 2011a, nos 1, 3–11, pp. 134–9.
23. INV 309; MR 253. Kreytenberg 1995, especially pp. 29–31.
24. In the upper inscription: 'SCVLPSERE [...] SCVLPTVRE [...] SCVLPENS [...] SCVLPERE [...] SCVLPTORES [...] SCVLPTVRAS'.
25. Bartalini 2011a, no. 2, pp. 134–5: 'TINI SCULPTORIS DE SENIS ARTE COLORIS'. See also Dietl 2009, pp. 37–9.
26. Pistoia pulpit: 'SCVLPSIT JOH[ANN]ES QVI RES NO[N] EGIT INANES / NICOLI NAT[VS] SENSIA MELIORE BEATVS'. Tomb of Bishop Antonio degli Orsi (Bartalini 2011a, no. 44, pp. 146–7): 'OPERU[M] DE SENIS NATUS EX MAG[IST]RO CAMAINO IN / HOC SITU FLORENTINO TINUS SCULPSIT O[MN]E LAT[US] / HU[N]C P[RO] PATRE GENETIVO DECET INCLINARI / UT MAGISTER ILLO VIVO NOLIT APPELLARI'.
27. On the Siena crucifix, see Spannocchi (with earlier bibliography) in Casole d'Elsa 2010, cat. 2, pp. 156–8.
28. Seidel 1976; Seidel 2000.
29. For Giovanni's attitude to polychromy, see Seidel 1991, p. 70.
30. On Giovanni, see Bullard 1977, pp. 76–124. On Tino's orientation towards pictorial form, see Seidel 1989; Baldelli 2007, pp. 349–92.
31. For the tomb, see Bartalini 2011a, no. 1, p. 196.
32. Dent 2008; Dent 2011.
33. Bartalini 2011a, no. 18, p. 202 (25.5 cm × 20 cm × 4 cm); Seidel 1989; Kreytenberg in New York 2002–3, Tino di Camaino, *Imago Pietatis*, pp. 14–17.
34. 35 × 25.8 cm including frame (other valve 35 × 26 cm including frame). See Eclercy in Hamburg 2011–12, cat. 5, p. 132; Paris 2009, pp. 51–5; Labriola in Siena 2008, cat. 4, pp. 44–9; Volpe 1989, no. 173, pp. 193–4.
35. Kreytenberg 2013; De Giorgio 2021.
36. The phrase is from Seidel 1989.
37. Bartalini 2011a, no. 38, p. 207 (31 × 26 cm).
38. On the polychromy of stone sculpture for this period in Tuscany, see Andreuccetti 2008; Ames-Lewis 1997, pp. 31–8.
39. For the close interaction between sculpture and polychromy in Tino's work, see Barbavara di Gravellona, Samarelli and Lalli 1998, pp. 182–4, and more generally Andreuccetti 2008, p. 102.
40. Fehrenbach 2020a.
41. Ames-Lewis 1997, pp. 36–7.
42. Bartalini 2005, pp. 271–89; Middeldorf Kosegarten 1966; Moskowitz 2001, pp. 96–102.
43. 44.8 × 28 × 3.2 cm. Cioni in Siena 2003–4, cat. 84, pp. 482–5.
44. 125 cm, about 1315–20. Amato in Siena 2017–18, cat. 4, pp. 114–18.
45. Maginnis 1980.
46. Whittington 2022.
47. For this manuscript, see above all Neff 2019.
48. 27 × 19.5 cm. Neff 2019, pp. 164–7 in particular.
49. For the complex meaning of the iconography, see Belting 1981. For a discussion of the iconography in the context of Tuscan sculpture of this period, see Dent 2005.
50. Dent 2017.
51. It is not impossible that the marble was selected with this possibility in mind.
52. This meaning is apparent from the location of the Man of Sorrows lectern in the programme for Giovanni Pisano's pulpits, for example. See Dent 2011; Dent 2008.
53. Dumoutet 1926.
54. See, for example, the representation of the elevation of the host from an early fourteenth-century Anglo-French manuscript, *Manière d'entendre la messe*, Bibliothèque nationale de France, Département des manuscrits, Paris, Français 13342, fols 46v–47, where the elevated host contains a miniature image of the Man of Sorrows.
55. Indeed, the material at Christ's waist might not only evoke the loincloth or shroud, but also a corporal, the white linen cloth on which the vessels containing the consecrated bread and wine are placed during the liturgy.
56. See Eclercy in Hamburg 2011–12, cat. 5, p. 132; Schmidt 2005a, p. 45. The following interpretation builds on their observations.
57. Although the marble exterior might also suggest the Stone of Unction on which Christ's body was anointed before burial.
58. 1 Peter 2:4.
59. Carmi and Felicetti 2007, pp. 451–2, docs 95–7.

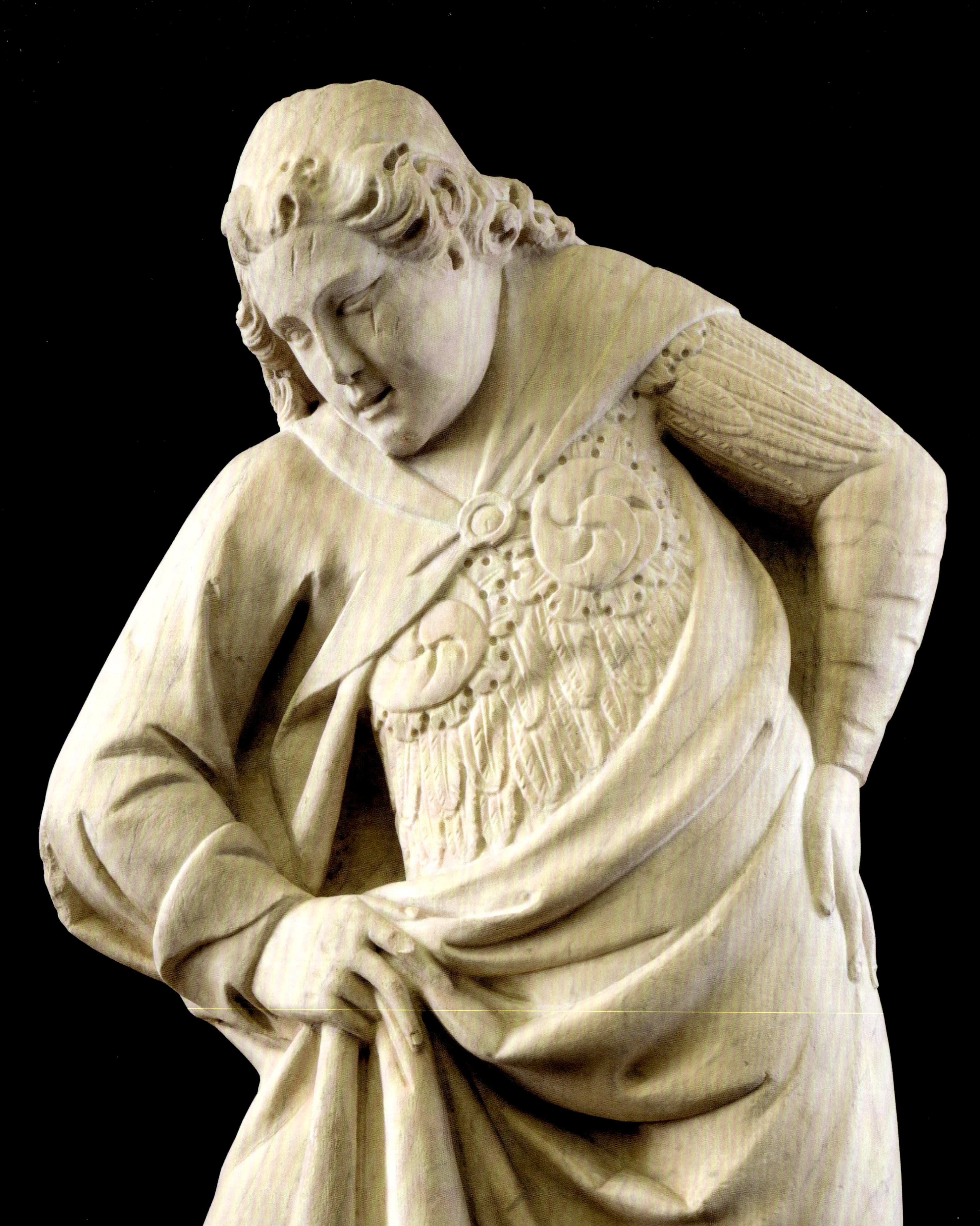

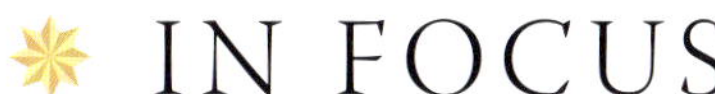

The Tomb of Gastone della Torre by Tino di Camaino

Francesca Marzullo

It was by chance that Gastone della Torre, a high-ranking cleric of Milanese origin, perished in Florence on 20 August 1318. Having recently been elected Patriarch of Aquileia, the former Archbishop of Milan was journeying from Naples to Friuli to assume his new seat when he fell from his horse near the Tuscan city and died there of his injuries. His body was interred in the Franciscan Church of Santa Croce, where a lavish marble tomb was erected in his honour. Originally suspended on the right wall of the nave in a privileged position near the transept, the monument fell victim to Giorgio Vasari's renovations of 1566, which resulted in its transfer to the first cloister, beside the Pazzi Chapel.[1] A consequence of this move was the ensemble's partial dismemberment and the scattering of some of its parts. After the disastrous flood of the Arno in 1966, the work was relocated yet again, this time to the Museo dell'Opera di Santa Croce, where its central elements remain (fig. 111). The other surviving components are six figural sculptures and possibly a fragment of an aedicule, now dispersed between collections in Florence and Frankfurt.[2]

Although Florence was the place where Gastone drew his last breath, why it should have become his eternal resting ground is not immediately apparent. He had no ties to the Florentine clergy and it is somewhat surprising that his remains were not taken to Friuli, where his great-uncle Raimondo della Torre, who had himself served as Patriarch of Aquileia from 1273 to 1299, had built a burial chapel in which he and other prominent members of the della Torre family were entombed. Following his accident, Gastone expired in the home of the Barucci family of Florence and it has commonly been said that it was the Barucci who commissioned his sepulchre in Santa Croce. The insufficient documentary evidence to this effect, however, leaves room for other hypotheses, and it has been argued more recently that the tomb's patronage should be understood in the context of the pro-Guelph, pro-Angevin political climate in Florence at the time.[3] Tuscan authorities with an interest in celebrating the Guelph cause may have seen Gastone's passing as an opportunity to publicly memorialise an illustrious ecclesiastic who had suffered at the hands of the

Detail of FIG. 116

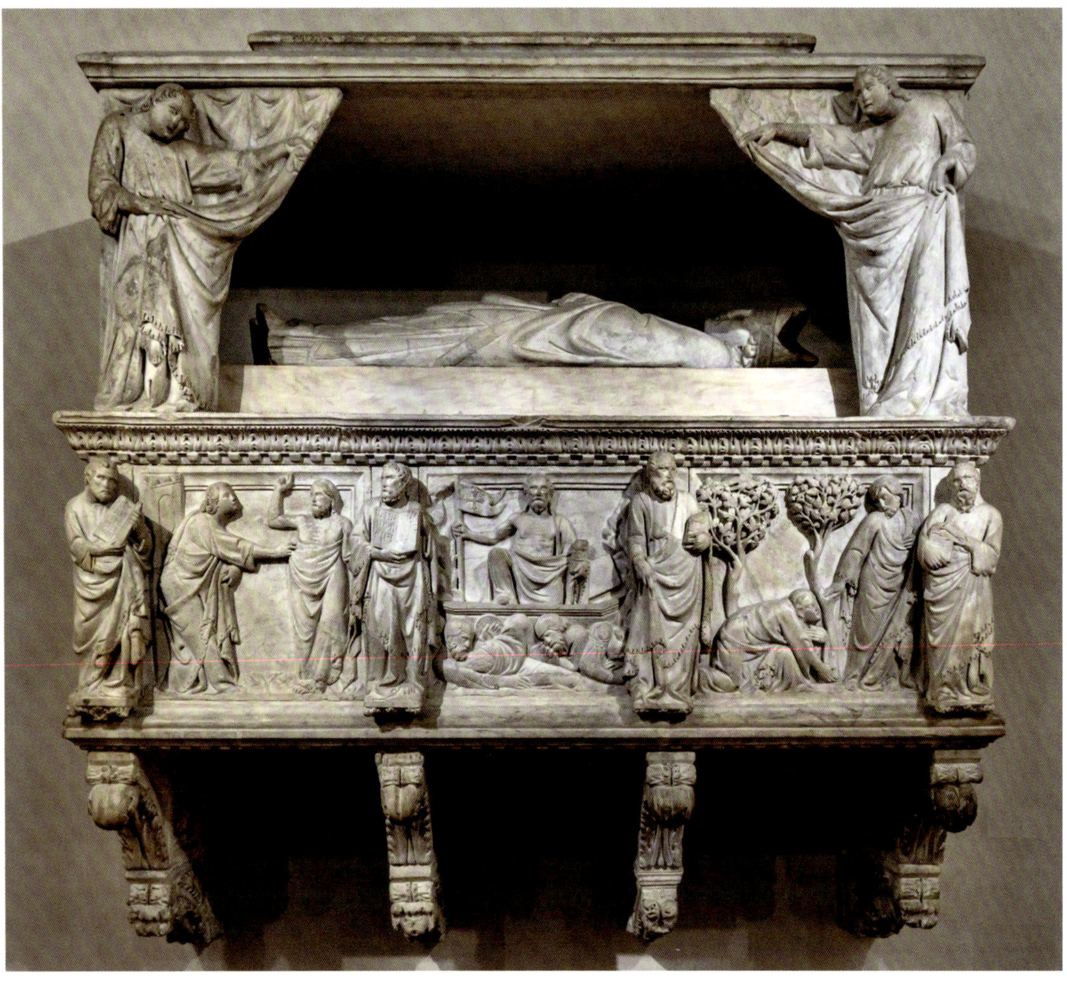

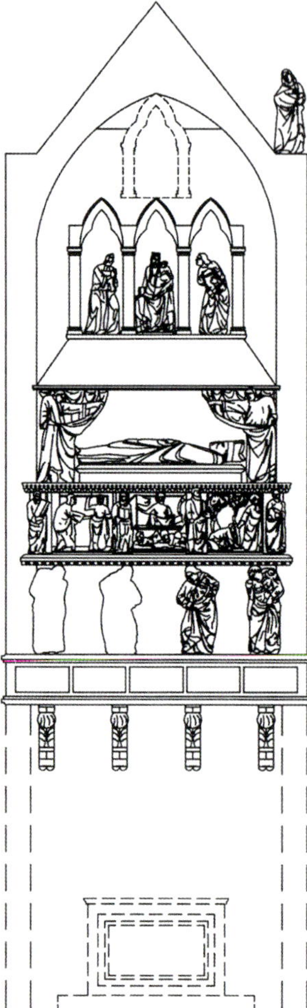

FIG. 111
Tino di Camaino
(about 1280–1337)
Tomb of Gastone della Torre: Sarcophagus with Gisant, Consoles and Angels, about 1318–19
Marble, 84 × 252 cm (sarcophagus), 94 cm (height of angels)
Museo dell'Opera di Santa Croce, Florence

FIG. 112
Reconstruction by Francesca Baldelli, 2007

Ghibelline Visconti – the rivals of the Guelph della Torre in Gastone's homeland of Milan – before ascending to the title of Patriarch of Aquileia by favour of King Robert of Anjou.

Whether it was the Barucci or local officials who were responsible for Gastone's tomb, the patron of this important undertaking chose an artist who was also a foreigner to the city: the Sienese sculptor Tino di Camaino, who had until this point worked in Siena and in Pisa, where he had received the extremely prestigious commission of the sepulchre of Emperor Henry VII (now disassembled). Most likely called to Florence expressly for the della Torre project, Tino executed the sculptures in around 1318–19, taking as his principal model the funerary monument of Cardinal Riccardo Petroni in the Cathedral of Siena, which he had completed a few years earlier (fig. 113).[4] The two wall tombs share key characteristics and probably followed a similar compositional scheme prior to the latter's dismantling, although the differences between them are meaningful as well. In both, a pair of angels draws back the curtains of the mortuary chamber to reveal the *gisant* – the recumbent figure of the deceased – who lies on a slab or bed atop his sarcophagus. The same sequence of narrative scenes representing Christ's reappearances after death, albeit in reverse order, is carved in relief on the tomb chest, with the Resurrection at centre.[5]

The pieces of the della Torre monument that have been identified in modern times allow us to have a reasonable idea of what it looked like in its original state. Gert Kreytenberg's 1979 reconstruction is still largely accepted, with slight revisions proposed in 2007 by Francesca Baldelli, who raised the possibility that the tomb was initially situated above an altar (fig. 112).[6] For both authors, though, the overall arrangement of the extant figures is the same. Positioned directly beneath the sarcophagus, the caryatids (figures used in place of columns as architectural supports) would have appeared to hold up the sepulchre above (figs 115, 116, 117, now in the Museo Nazionale del Bargello, Florence, and the Liebieghaus Skulpturensammlung, Frankfurt). Unlike the Petroni tomb bearers, who carry their burden with little visible effort, Gastone's caryatids bend under the weight of the chest. Tino balances the strain conveyed by their bowed heads and hunched shoulders with the graceful curve of their bodies. The caryatids, of which there were presumably two more, would have stood on a shelf supported by the four consoles, or brackets, that are currently installed just below the sarcophagus. Up above, the seated Virgin and Child (fig. 114, now also in the Bargello) most likely surmounted the pitched roof of the funerary chamber, flanked on one side by a praying angel (now in the Palazzo Vecchio, Florence), and on the other by the kneeling Gastone and his angelic companion (fig. 115, now in the Liebieghaus). The separation of the Virgin and Child from Gastone and the angel who presents him deprives today's viewers of what is perhaps the work's most poignant moment. To see them together again is to witness in vivid terms the longing for salvation that animated the lives, and indeed the deaths, of the Christian faithful. As Gastone gazes ardently upwards, his hands crossed over his chest in reverence before the divine, the Christ Child responds by raising his right fingers in a gesture of blessing, appearing to climb onto his mother's knee as if to draw nearer to his pious follower. The upward sweep of Christ's drapery is met by the falling folds of the archbishop's cope, forming an arc that eloquently connects the two figures across the space between them.

It is notable that in its intended form the della Torre tomb featured not one but two images of Gastone, who is pictured both in death, as the supine *gisant* resting on his sarcophagus, and in life, as the fervent devotee who commends his soul to Christ and the Virgin.[7] The practice of adorning sepulchres with sculpted effigies of the deceased rose to popularity in northern Europe in the late eleventh and twelfth centuries. Italian artists looked to these Romanesque models, and by Tino's time, effigial wall tombs were not uncommon in Florence but remained highly exclusive, reserved for powerful ecclesiastics and others of special religious eminence.[8] In its doubling of the effigy, Tino's monument for Gastone departs from the Petroni tomb and finds precedent instead in Arnolfo di Cambio's tomb of Cardinal Guillaume de Braye, of about 1282, in the Church of San Domenico in Orvieto, which similarly juxtaposes the figure of the corpse with that of the living cardinal who kneels before the Virgin and Child.[9] The de Braye and della Torre sepulchres stage a complex discourse between past, present and future. As an evocation of the expired body that has been laid to rest, the *gisant* stands in for the earthly cadaver of the defunct, whose actual state of decay is hidden from view. Above this, the portrayal of the worshipful Gastone with a youthful countenance serves as a recollection of the subject's past life while simultaneously conjuring the immortal life of the soul, or *anima*,

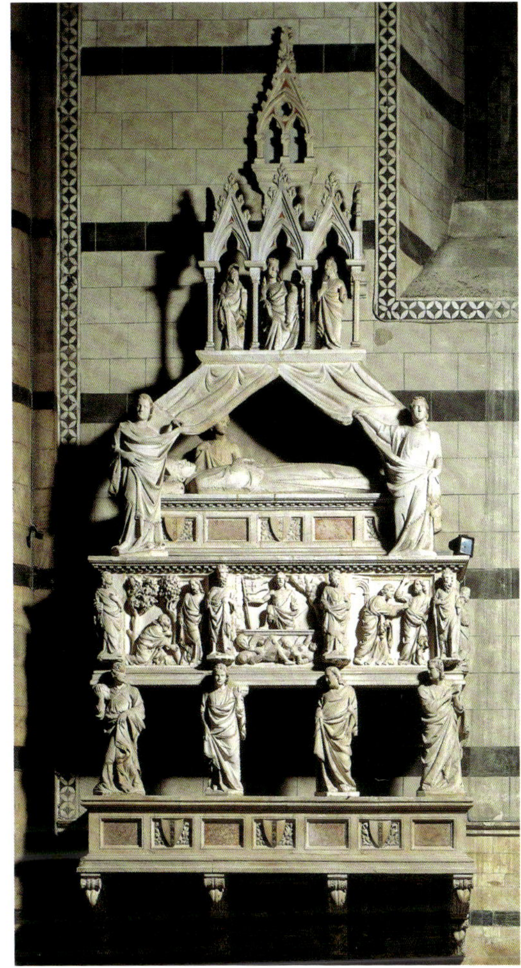

FIG. 113
Tino di Camaino
(about 1280–1337)
Tomb of Cardinal Riccardo Petroni, about 1315
Marble, 771 × 285 cm
Siena Cathedral

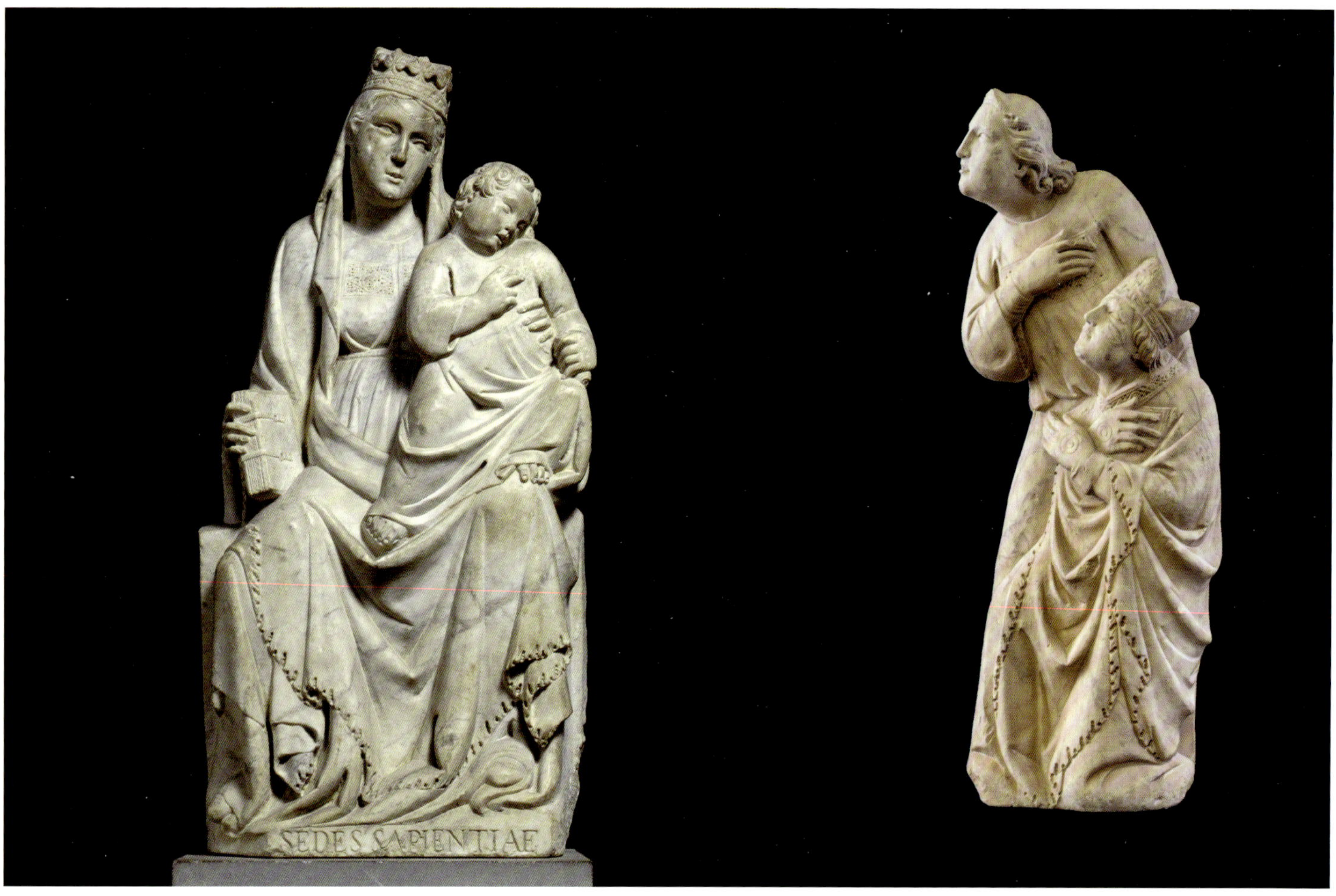

FIG. 114
Tino di Camaino
(about 1280–about 1337)
The Virgin and Child,
1318–21
Marble, 78 × 39 cm
Museo Nazionale del Bargello, Florence (434)

FIG. 115
Tino di Camaino
(about 1280–about 1337)
Angel presenting a Bishop,
1318–21
Marble, 81.5 × 32 × 14 cm
Liebieghaus Skulpturensammlung, Frankfurt am Main (955)

which will one day be reunited with the flesh in the moment of bodily resurrection. This last point, fundamental to Christian eschatology, is underscored by the reliefs of the sarcophagus, which depict Christ as having risen triumphantly from his tomb.

The sarcophagal reliefs bring us to a recurrent theme in the literature on Tino – one that Peter Dent illuminates in the present volume (pp. 150–63) – which is the sculptor's intimate and generative engagement with the art of painting. It was observed by Kreytenberg that when compared to the corresponding reliefs on the Petroni monument, those of the della Torre tomb exhibit a shift away from the three-dimensionality of the medium and towards the creation of an illusionistic space inspired by painting, and especially by the work of Simone Martini.[10] Max Seidel and Peter Dent have further explored the conscious pursuit of pictorial effects that would continue to shape Tino's visual language and set him apart from Giovanni Pisano, under whose influence he received his early training.[11] Indeed, Tino's pictorial sensibility is seen not only in the reliefs of Gastone's tomb, but also in the free-standing figures. The *Virgin and Child*, for example, are broad and planar in construction, articulated by shallow modelling that is legible from a frontal view rather than by deep incision into the marble block. It might also be considered that painters, in turn, may well have looked to Tino's accomplishments in the della Torre monument for their own compositions. An echo of the *Virgin and Child*, for instance, can be found in Pietro Lorenzetti's altarpiece of about 1327–9 for the Church of San Niccolò al Carmine in Siena, pointing to a relationship of mutual exchange between Sienese painters and sculptors.

That the della Torre tomb, a major commission of both spiritual significance and civic pride, was

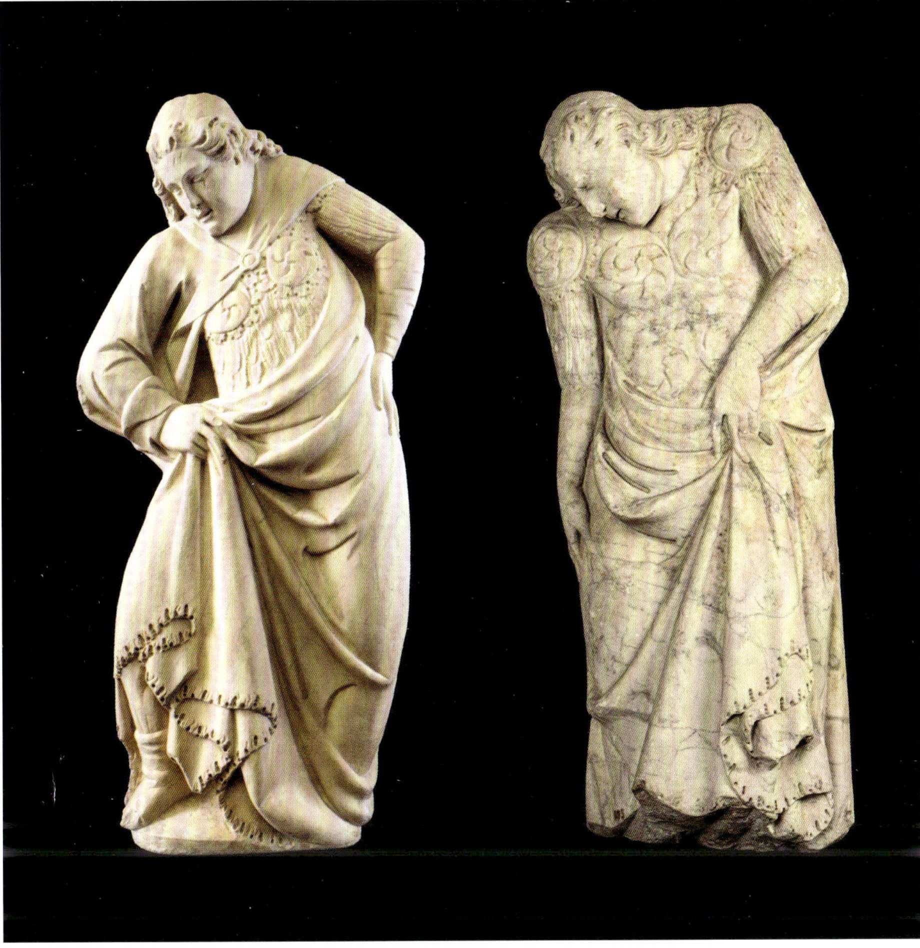

awarded to an artist with no prior presence in Florence attests to the fame Tino had achieved beyond his native Siena by this point in his career. He would go on to complete the sepulchral monument of Bishop Antonio d'Orso in Florence Cathedral, as well as sculptures for the baptistery, before his vaunted reputation took him yet further away to Naples, where he soon went to work for patrons of the highest order, fashioning the tombs of Angevin royals and other elites. Although his output was by no means limited to funerary sculpture, the ingenuity and versatility of his contributions in this field, from his early tomb of Emperor Henry VII to his later Neapolitan projects, made him a crucial figure during a formative period in the development of the Italian wall tomb.

FIG. 116
Tino di Camaino
(about 1280–about 1337)
Caryatid, 1318–21
Marble, 87 × 42 × 15 cm
Liebieghaus Skulpturensammlung, Frankfurt am Main (881)

FIG. 117
Tino di Camaino
(about 1280–about 1337)
Caryatid, 1318–21
Marble, height 80 cm
Museo Nazionale del Bargello, Florence (495)

1. On the tomb's original location and subsequent fate, see Novelli 2011, p. 132; Bardelloni 2011, p. 143; Baldelli 2007, p. 405.
2. For entries on the tomb's central elements and the dispersed figural sculptures, with bibliographies of the relevant literature, see Bardelloni 2011, pp. 143–5; Baldelli 2007, pp. 405–6. In addition to the works illustrated in the present volume, there are the *Annunciate Virgin* (Museo dell'Opera di Santa Croce, Florence) and the *Adoring Angel* (Palazzo Vecchio, Florence). On the fragment of an aedicule (Lapidario di Santa Croce, Florence), see Tigler 2004, pp. 52–4; Baldelli 2007, pp. 185–7; Novelli 2011, p. 132, fig. 3.
3. Novelli 2011.
4. The date of about 1318–19 is based on stylistic and circumstantial grounds. On Tino's authorship, see Baldelli 2007, p. 170; Barbavara di Gravellona 2001, p. 266, n. 4. Kreytenberg 1979, p. 50, and Baldelli 2007, p. 187, n. 26, speculate that della Torre may have seen the Petroni monument shortly before his death.
5. From left to right, the reliefs on the della Torre sarcophagus depict Christ on the Road to Emmaus, the Incredulity of Saint Thomas, the Resurrection, the Noli me Tangere, and the Three Maries at the Tomb. Tigler 2004, p. 54, suggests that the scenes were meant to be viewed from right to left.
6. For the various reconstructions, see Valentiner 1935; Valentiner 1954; Kreytenberg 1979; Baldelli 2007. On the hypothetical altar, see Baldelli 2007, p. 187. On the existence and function of Sienese tomb-altars, and possible earlier examples by Tino, including the Petroni tomb, see Cannon 2000b.
7. On effigial doubling in the della Torre tomb and other monuments, see Fehrenbach 2020b, pp. 69–77.
8. On Romanesque tomb effigies, see Fozi 2021; on Florentine tomb typologies, see Butterfield 1994.
9. Fehrenbach 2020b, p. 75.
10. Kreytenberg 1986, pp. 32–3; Kreytenberg 1988 elaborates on the relationship between Tino and Simone.
11. Seidel 2005c; Dent 2007.

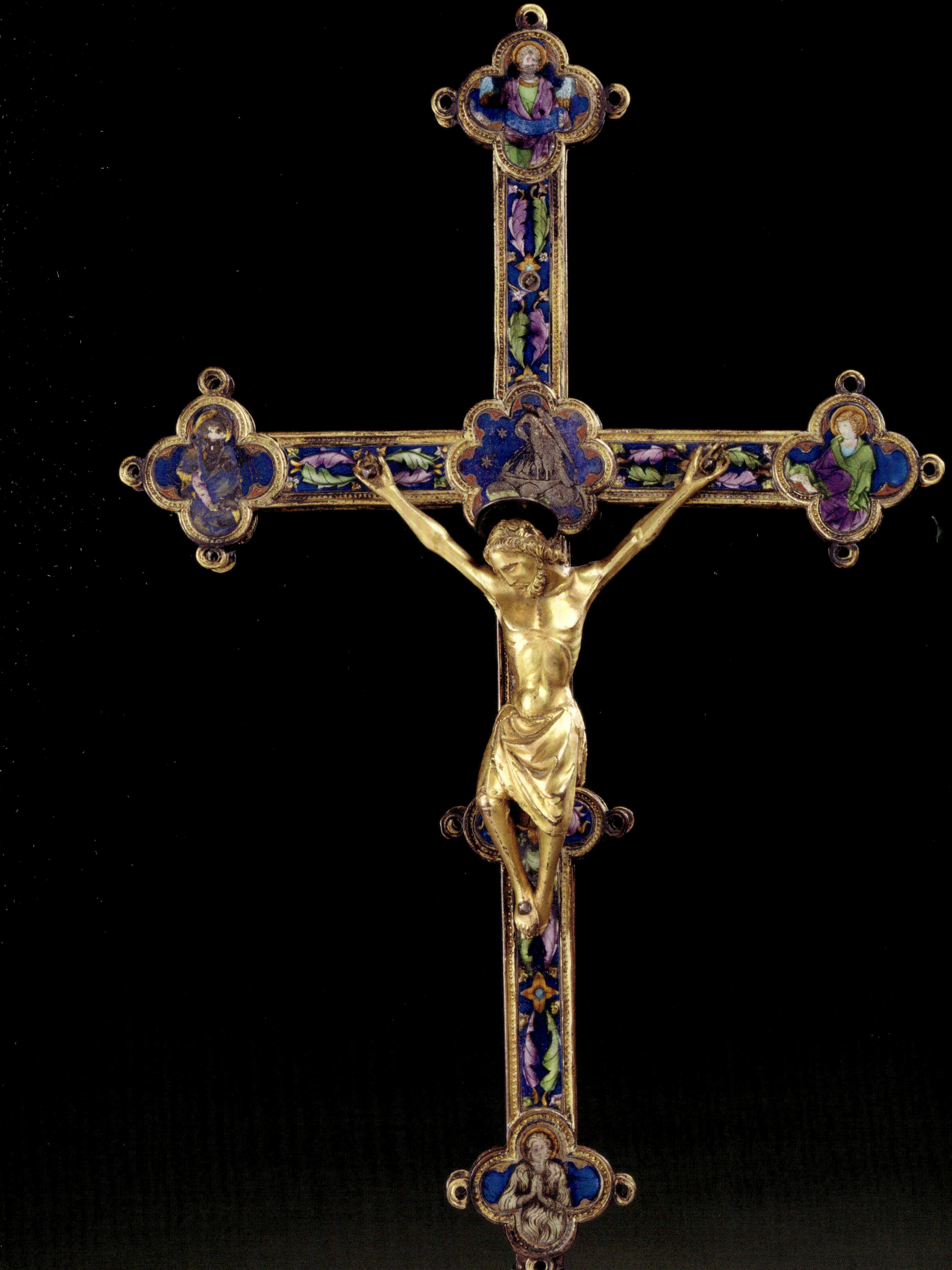

SIENESE GOLDSMITHS IN SIENA AND BEYOND

Glyn Davies

From at least the 1260s, the goldsmiths of Siena began to enjoy a reputation outside their own city that is remarkable both for how sustained it was, and for how far its tendrils spread. This reputation went hand in hand with the influence of Siena's painters outside the city walls, and was often disseminated in the same regions. Goldsmiths held a relatively high status among artists and artisans because of the intrinsic value of the raw materials with which they worked. They were entrusted with precious metals, jewels and the manufacture of items such as official seals, which would be used by individuals and institutions to authenticate documents. Over the course of a successful career, a Sienese goldsmith might expect to fulfil commissions for churches and mendicant convents, secular authorities such as the Council of the Nine (the *Nove*), as well as potentially lucrative commissions from foreign rulers and church dignitaries. Many of them also created works in other media, notably items in base metals such as copper, the founding of large works in bronze, and the production of marble and wood sculpture, as well as engineering and architectural projects. A number of Sienese goldsmiths held public office in the city. While no Sienese goldsmith ever earned the friendship and praise of a figure like Petrarch, in the way that the painter Simone Martini did, the goldsmith Lando di Pietro was still described by the General Council of Siena as 'a most knowledgeable man, not only in his own area, but in many others; a man of the greatest ingenuity and invention, both with regard to the building of churches and the erection of palaces and private houses; a talented engineer for roads, bridges and fountains.'[1]

The geographical boundaries of the Sienese goldsmiths' popularity are quite markedly defined. There were three main areas. The first was the central Italian zone comprising Tuscany, Umbria, Lazio and parts of the Marche. This is perhaps surprising, since there were excellent goldsmithing centres in a number of other cities throughout this territory: Florence, Lucca, Pistoia, Pisa and Bologna all possessed communities of goldsmiths of real talent in the trecento and the quattrocento. The second area was the papal court, or Curia. Sienese goldsmiths obtained a foothold as members

FIG. 118 (P. 170)
Attributed to Tondino di Guerrino
(documented 1322–42)
Crucifix, about 1325–30
Gilded silver with translucent enamel, 42.6 × 22.5 cm
Musée du Louvre, Département des Objets d'art, Paris (OA 10656)

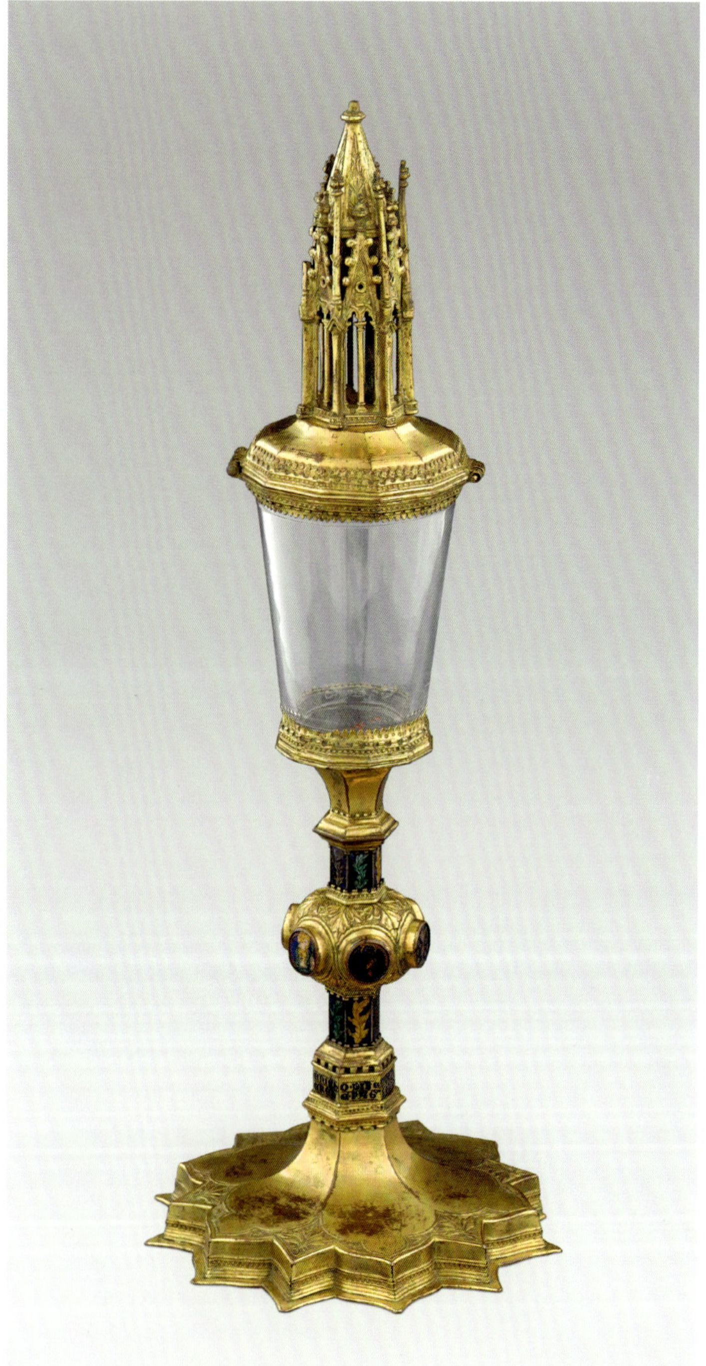

FIG. 119
Sienese goldsmith
Reliquary-monstrance, 1331
Glass and gilded copper with translucent enamel, 45.5 × 17.7 cm
Musée Cluny, Paris (Cl. 9190)

of the papal *familia* ('household') from the later thirteenth century, and this continued into the period of the so-called 'Babylonian Captivity', when the papacy dwelt in Avignon. Related to this southern French activity, there was a limited penetration into Spain. This papal context was different in character from the goldsmiths' influence in central Italy, since it involved them spending extensive spells of time away from their native city. The nature of art patronage within the Curia was heterogeneous in its taste, combining artists and styles from various regions to create a hybrid visual context. Nevertheless, Sienese goldsmiths were employed at Avignon throughout the time that the papacy lived there. The final area of notable enthusiasm for the work of Sienese goldsmiths was in territories controlled by the Angevin dynasty in Naples, Sicily and Hungary. This phenomenon was probably linked to the goldsmiths' association with the papal household to which the Angevins were intimately connected, and to Siena's role as a Guelph city state from the 1270s to the 1350s, which enjoyed good diplomatic relations with Naples.[2] The pattern of documents and surviving works in the Angevin sphere suggests that Sienese goldsmiths' work was almost wholly associated with the ruling dynasty itself and its close allies.[3]

There is little trace today of the work of Sienese goldsmiths making its way to northern France, Germany or England, although this may be down to the matter of survival rather than actuality. Nevertheless, it contrasts with the rather greater impact that Sienese painting had in these regions (see pp. 224–39). Sienese goldsmiths were certainly aware of artistic trends in the north, particularly in Paris. It seems likely that it was the import of French manuscripts, goldsmiths' work and ivories into Italy that was the conduit for this, rather than journeys made by Sienese goldsmiths into the north.[4]

We are able to reconstruct the lives and careers of many Sienese goldsmiths because of the relatively copious documentation that survives regarding them, and because of the frequent practice in Siena of applying inscriptions naming the maker to many of the objects that they produced, particularly chalices and reliquaries. Goldsmiths such as Guccio di Mannaia and Duccio di Donato did this from an

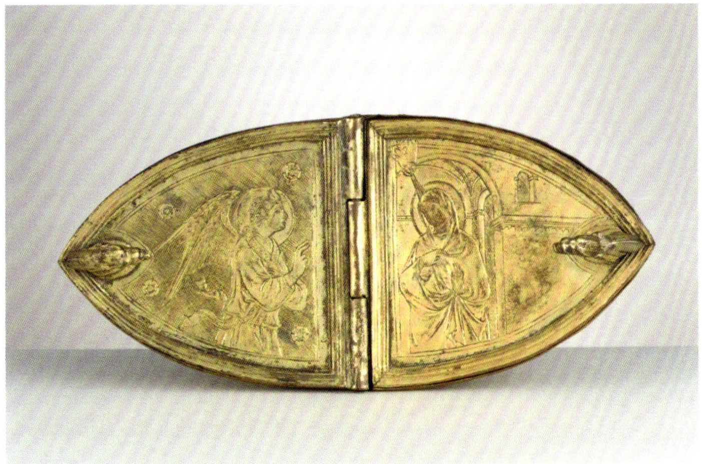

FIG. 120
Sienese goldsmith
Incense Boat with the Annunciation, about 1350–75
Gilded copper, 10.2 × 9 × 21.5 cm
Musée Cluny, Paris (Cl. 11157)

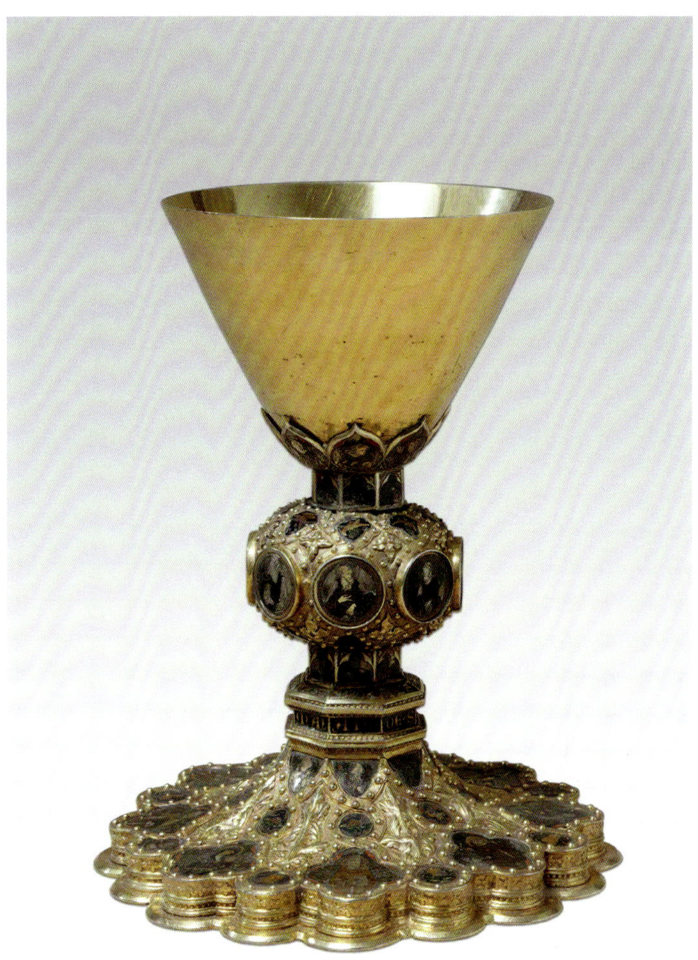

FIG. 121
Guccio di Mannaia
(documented 1291–1322)
Chalice, about 1290
Gilded silver with translucent enamel, height 22 cm
Museo del Tesoro, Basilica of San Francesco, Assisi

early date. This practice parallels similar examples in Sienese painting during the same period, and both groups may have been inspired by Tuscan sculptors like Nicola and Giovanni Pisano. Although the placing of goldsmiths' names on their products also occurred in other centres, including Florence, Pistoia, Lucca and the Abruzzo, it was an especially common strategy in Siena.[5] Reliquaries very often bear the names of their commissioners, either in addition to the goldsmith's name, or instead of it (fig. 119). It should be emphasised that although ecclesiastical commissions such as chalices, crosses (fig. 118), navettes for holding incense (fig. 120), morses (clasps for liturgical vestments) and reliquaries had a far greater chance of surviving to the present day – and are therefore the subject of much of the discussion in this chapter – a large proportion of the goldsmiths' time would have been taken up with secular productions. Inventories provide information on these sorts of objects, with both jewellery and items for dining – knives, cups, basins, mugs and flasks – being produced regularly.[6]

The emergence of Sienese goldsmiths onto the international scene was rapid: they arrived as acknowledged masters, fully formed, in the upper echelons of art patronage. Probably the earliest example is Pace di Valentino, who was active from the 1250s until his death around 1300. In 1265 he was summoned to Pistoia to examine a gold chalice, and produce a companion equal to it for use on the altar of San Zeno.[7] A chalice still surviving in Pistoia has been attributed to Pace as a separate commission.[8] A goldsmith called 'Magister Pax' (in Italian, Maestro Pace) worked for a number of popes from 1278 until his retirement in 1296 – that is, Nicholas III, Martin IV, Honorius IV and Boniface VIII – and it seems likely that this was the same man.[9] One Pope is conspicuously absent from the list – Nicholas IV (reigned 1288–92) – but for him, the Sienese goldsmith Guccio di Mannaia produced perhaps the most significant of the early surviving pieces: the chalice at the convent of San Francesco, Assisi (fig. 121).[10]

The chalice bears two inscriptions. The first names Guccio as the chalice's maker, while the second names the patron, Nicholas IV. Unlike the gifts of liturgical apparatus

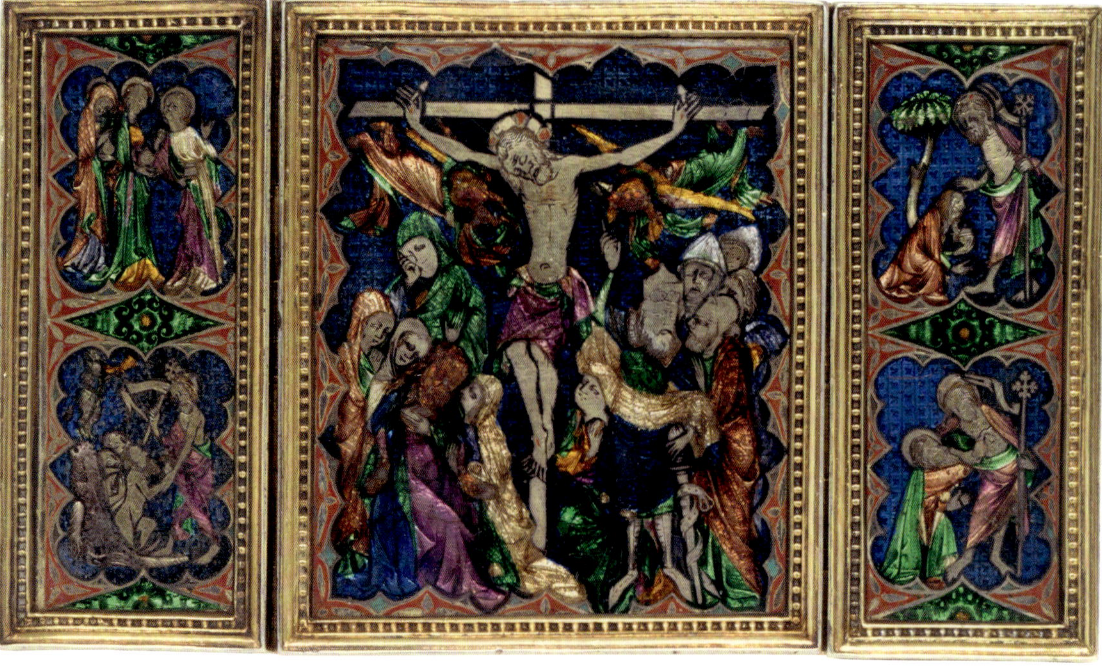

FIG. 122
English goldsmith
Triptych with Scenes from the Life of Christ, about 1325–50
Gilded silver with translucent enamel, 6.6 × 11.3 × 0.6 cm
Victoria and Albert Museum. Salting Bequest. (M.545–1910)

given by Nicholas to the basilica at Assisi immediately after his coronation as Pope, which seem to have been objects already in existence, the specifically Franciscan character of the chalice's iconography as well as the inclusion of an image of Nicholas himself as Pope strongly suggest that it was a commission specifically undertaken for presentation to San Francesco.[11] Guccio is otherwise only documented producing high-status seals within Siena. This style of chalice, with its lavish use of figurative translucent enamels, which allowed for a sophisticated iconographic programme, would become synonymous with Sienese goldsmithing.

TECHNIQUES AND WORKSHOPS

The sudden popularity of Siena's precious metalwork has sometimes been almost solely attributed to the development in the late thirteenth century of basse-taille enamel: the use of translucent coloured glass (or enamel) over a very low-relief silver figurative base.[12] Siena was the earliest site to develop an easy mastery over this technique, as Guccio's chalice in Assisi demonstrates. However, it is true to say that by at least the 1320s other centres were also producing similar high-quality enamels, in Italy, Paris and elsewhere (fig. 122). The reputation of Sienese goldsmithing can be dated to before the invention of translucent enamel, and it continued much later than their possession of a unique technique.

Sienese goldsmiths also made virtuoso use of two other enamelling techniques. The first of these was traditional champlevé enamel, where opaque enamel is laid into channels in a metal base and different colours are separated. The second method was one that seems to have been associated primarily with the goldsmiths of Paris: enamel 'de plique', in which wirework separates the cells of enamel (or 'cloisons') and opaque and translucent enamels are mixed to create patterns. Examples of French work of this type must have been known to Sienese goldsmiths, as they sometimes emulated the effects of this sort of enamel, without quite duplicating the technique. Centres like the papal court or the Angevin court in Naples may have been the venues for such exchange.[13] Certainly, French goldsmiths were active at the court in Naples in the early part of the fourteenth century, as, for example, in 1304 when Etienne Godefroy, Milet d'Auxerre and Guillaume de Verdelay produced a reliquary of Saint Gennaro for the cathedral.[14] Enamels 'de plique' are strikingly depicted in a Sienese panel representing Saint Lucy now in the Berenson Collection at Villa I Tatti.[15] The transmission of technical ideas between Siena and Paris, whether basse-taille or enamels 'de plique', seems to have gone both ways, and although the mechanisms for this transmission are not fully

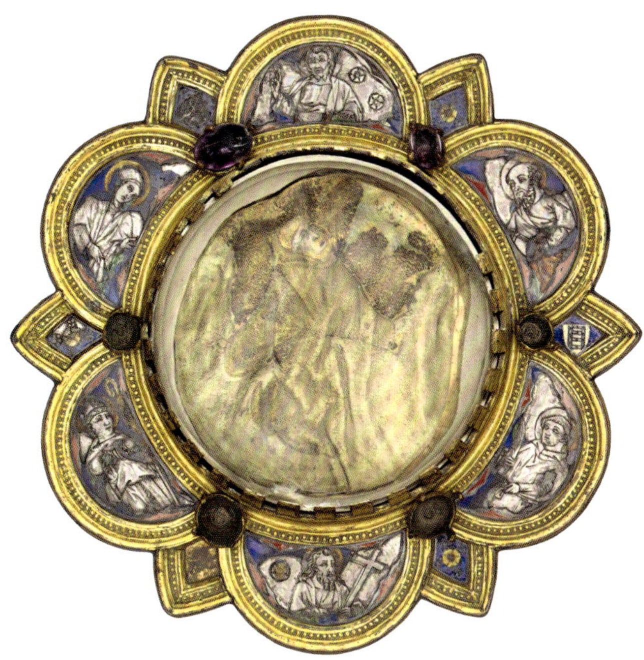

FIG. 123
Sienese artist
Morse with Saint Francis receiving the Stigmata, mid-fourteenth century
Gilded copper, silver, translucent enamel, parchment and glass gems, 12.9 × 12.9 × 4 cm; rock-crystal centre: 6.9 × 1 cm
The Metropolitan Museum of Art, New York. Gift of J. Pierpont Morgan, 1917 (17.190.767)

understood, there was a fertile period of exchange in the early years of the fourteenth century.

In addition to enamel, goldsmiths employed a variety of other techniques to create their works. Vessels were produced through 'raising' a sheet into a form using a planishing tool, hammering it on a relatively soft support such as pitch. Figures, ornaments and architectural details were made by stamping, modelling, manufacturing moulds and lost wax casting. Surface decoration could be fashioned through engraving, punching and chasing. Precious and imitation jewels could be applied into settings (fig. 123). Silver and copper could be enriched with gilding.

As with the city's painters, there were a variety of tasks, some more specialist than others, and it is impossible to be certain about the ways in which such work was divided in any given workshop. Most *maestri* ('masters') would have employed one or more adult workers, among them goldsmiths, wire-workers and gilders, as well as several apprentices, as copious references to *lavorenti* ('workers'), *gignori* ('young apprentices' or more experienced workers) and *discipuli* ('pupils') in the Sienese guild regulations make clear.[16] Associations between masters, and between different workshops, were also common. Such relationships could take the form of one-off subcontracts, but could be formalised into associations (*soci*) or companies (*compagnie*) for which legal instruments were sometimes drawn up.[17] Within the close-knit world of the Sienese goldsmith, family dynasties also developed. For example, Guccio di Mannaia may have had a goldsmithing brother, Giovanni di Mannaia, and certainly had three sons who became goldsmiths, Giacomo, Montigiano and Mannaia (also known as 'Mannaino' or 'little Mannaia'), who were active in the 1320s.[18]

IMITABILITY AND INIMITABILITY

Another ingredient in the success and influence of Sienese goldsmithing in the late thirteenth and fourteenth centuries is the way in which although the most impressive pieces were inimitable displays of skill and design, the opportunity to codify the basic 'look' of Sienese designs, and offer them at lower prices, meant that a wide market could be supplied with up-to-the-minute designs. Guccio di Mannaia's chalice for Assisi took a remarkable new form, incorporating abundant Gothic ornament, increased verticality and lavish use of figurative enamels depicting Christ and the saints. Guccio's precocious embrace of a northern Gothic vocabulary may be attributed in part to the presence at Assisi of frescoes produced most likely in the 1270s by the so-called 'Northern Master' and his team. There has been much debate over whether the Northern Master was French, German or English, but the team worked in the north transept of the Upper Church, and either they or other northern artists were also involved in the related stained-glass programme.[19]

Given the prestige of the Assisi chalice commission from the Pope, it may be that Guccio's chalice was the very first of its kind to be produced; certainly, it is the earliest survival.[20] Very quickly, however, this chalice form was codified, simplified and imitated. The fact that the Franciscan mother

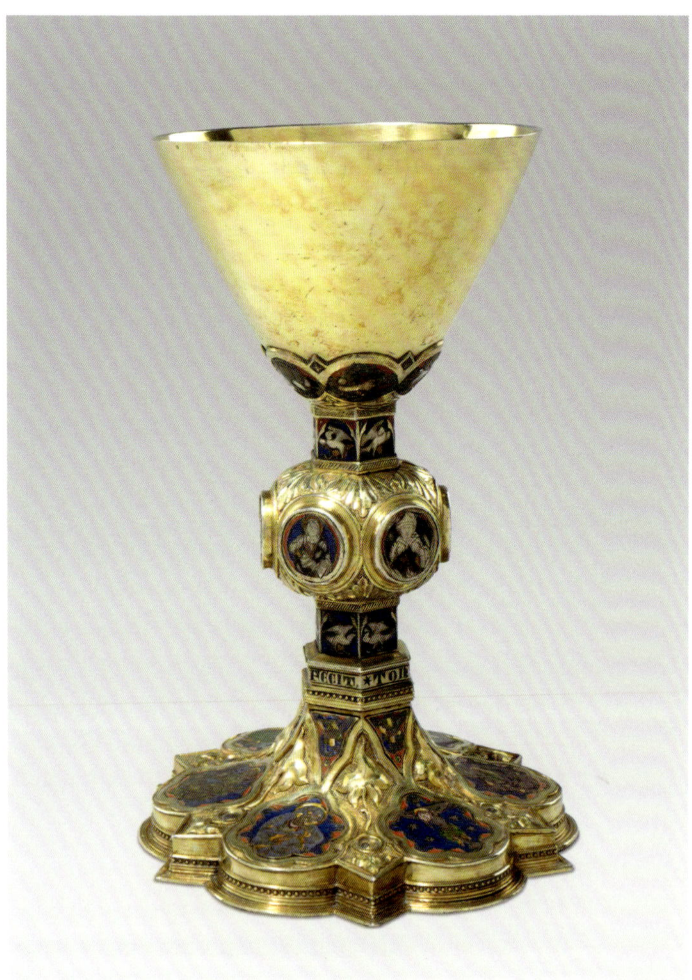

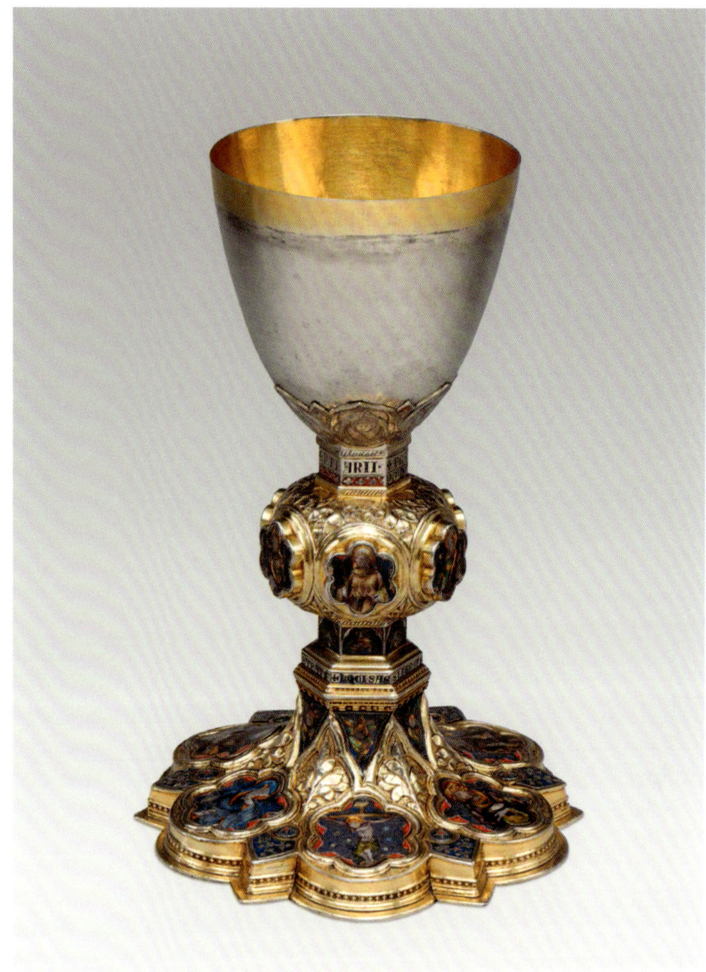

house possessed the example of Guccio's chalice seems to have inspired a range of other Franciscan houses to acquire chalices of this type in the first half of the trecento.[21] The chalice by Tondino di Guerrino and Andrea Riguardi now at the British Museum, manufactured most likely between about 1317 and the early 1320s, must have been one such, since the iconography depicts not only Saint Francis, but also the other Franciscan saints, Louis of Toulouse and Elizabeth of Hungary (fig. 124). Another example, also plausibly made by Tondino di Guerrino, is the somewhat later chalice given by the papal penitentiary Peter of Sassoferrato to the Franciscans of that town in about 1341–2 (fig. 125).

Initially, the new chalices were made of silver, but soon cheaper options were created in gilded copper, with only the chalice bowl itself in silver. Variations of this form were manufactured in Siena for another hundred years. The type acquired a wider currency in central Italy, with examples being produced in centres such as Florence, Lucca and Pisa. This diffusion of the style was facilitated through commissions and sales outside of the city. For example, in 1325 a legal dispute took place in Florence between the Florentine goldsmith Gellino di Geri and the makers of the British Museum chalice, Tondino di Guerrino and Andrea Riguardi. Gellino had purchased a chalice from them, apparently intending to sell it on in Florence.[22] Gellino had only paid part of the money towards this, and still owed the pair the sum of 4 libre, 4 soldi and 2 denarii in Florentine currency.

This chalice type was clearly associated with Siena, as several documents make clear. A Florentine guild statute of 1408 is especially revealing: it establishes that no one could sell or import silver objects not in accordance with the Florentine standard of silver purity and the other rules of the guild 'except for chalices and other ecclesiastical works, which are not worked here, and are partly of silver and partly of copper

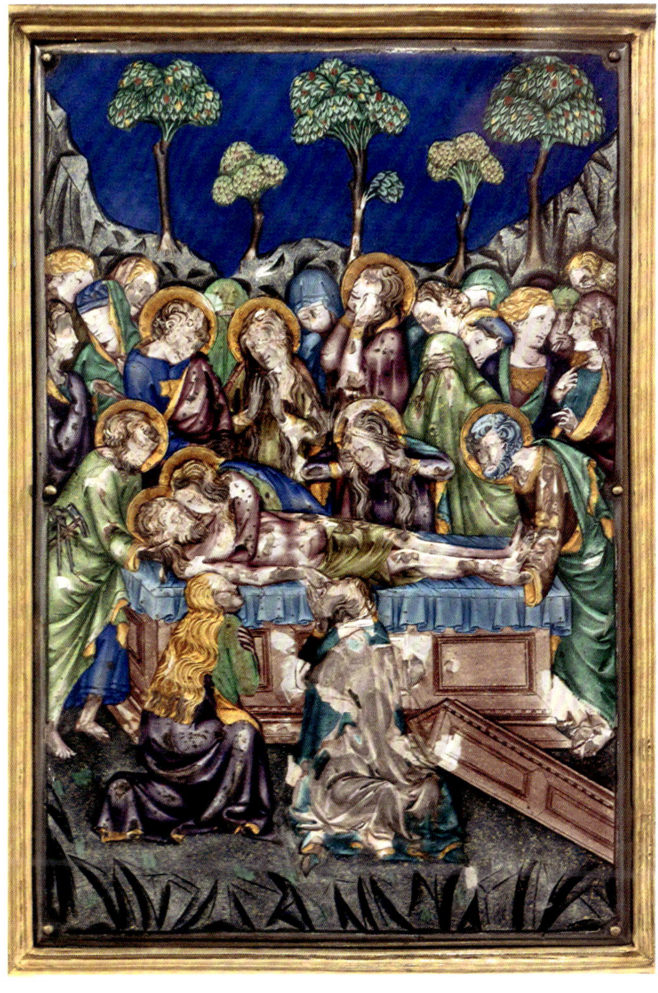

FIG. 124
Tondino di Guerrino (documented 1322–42) and **Andrea Riguardi** (documented 1325)
Chalice, about 1320
Gilded silver with translucent and champlevé enamel, 21 × 13.8 cm
Trustees of the British Museum, London. Purchased with a contribution from the Art Fund (as NACF) (1960,1203.1)

FIG. 125
Attributed to Tondino di Guerrino (documented 1322–42)
Chalice of Peter of Sassoferrato, 1341–2
Gilded silver with translucent enamel, 21.7 × 14.9 cm
The Metropolitan Museum of Art, New York. The Cloisters Collection, 1988 (1988.67)

FIG. 126
Ugolino di Vieri (documented 1328–about 1385) **and Associates**
The Entombment (detail from the *Reliquary of the Holy Corporal*), 1338
Silver and gilded silver with translucent enamel, height 139 cm
Museo dell'Opera del Duomo, Orvieto

such as those which are made in Siena or elsewhere: these one can legally cause to be brought in, stocked and sold.'[23] The significance of this statute is quite wide-ranging: Sienese chalices made of copper with silver cups were a recognisable commodity associated with the town, and were exported to Florence and sold there by Florentine goldsmiths.

If a significant portion of the business of Sienese goldsmiths was taken up in producing relatively straightforward commissions in a recognisably 'Sienese' style, there were nevertheless throughout the fourteenth and fifteenth centuries regular opportunities to create something outstanding. Reliquaries to hold significant relics became some of the most spectacular works made by Sienese goldsmiths. One of the most remarkable to survive today is undoubtedly the *Reliquary of the Holy Corporal* produced in 1338 for the Duomo in Orvieto (fig. 47). The Corporal is a relic of a miracle that occurred at Bolsena in northern Lazio in 1263, when a consecrated wafer began to bleed real blood onto the cloth placed beneath the chalice and Host during Mass. The Orvieto reliquary bears an inscription confirming that it was manufactured by 'Master Ugolino and associates, goldsmiths of Siena.'[24]

Ugolino di Vieri was a goldsmith who enjoyed a long and varied career, working for clients in Perugia and Pistoia, and living into the 1380s.[25] The identity of the associated *maestri* who collaborated on the production of the reliquary is unknown, although throughout his career Ugolino regularly worked in association with Viva di Lando. He also had two goldsmith brothers, Luca and Domenico di Maestro Vieri, who are likely to have been collaborators (for Luca as the potential author of the Cleveland reliquary tabernacle, see pp. 184–9).

The Holy Corporal Reliquary is decorated with daringly large translucent enamel images illustrating the story of the relic in addition to a cycle of the Infancy, Ministry and Passion of Christ. The narrative of the Bolsena miracle is the earliest surviving depiction of the story. The enamels demonstrate the mastery of the Sienese goldsmiths over this difficult technique, and its ability to draw on and to provide an equivalent to narrative painting (albeit on a much smaller scale). The reliquary also features expressive sculptural elements. These sorts of showpieces were essentially inimitable, and survivals like this give the best idea of the attractiveness of Sienese goldsmiths' work to powerful commissioners across central Italy.

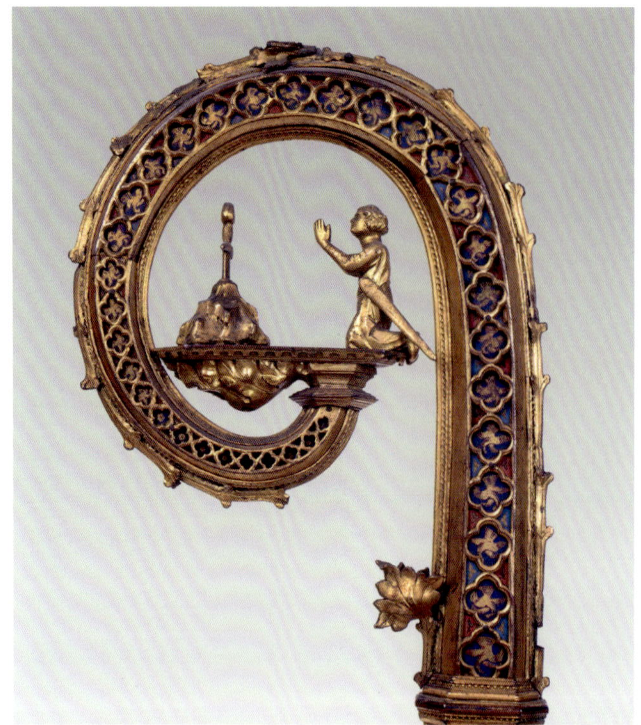

FIG. 127
Master of the San Galgano Crosier
Crosier, about 1315–20
Gilded copper with enamel,
193 × 14 cm
Museo dell'Opera della Metropolitana, Siena

FIG. 128
Possibly by Goro di Gregorio
(documented 1311–24)
Crosier (detail of Virgin and Child), about 1324
Silver gilt with translucent enamel
(dimensions not available)
Museo Diocesano, Città di Castello

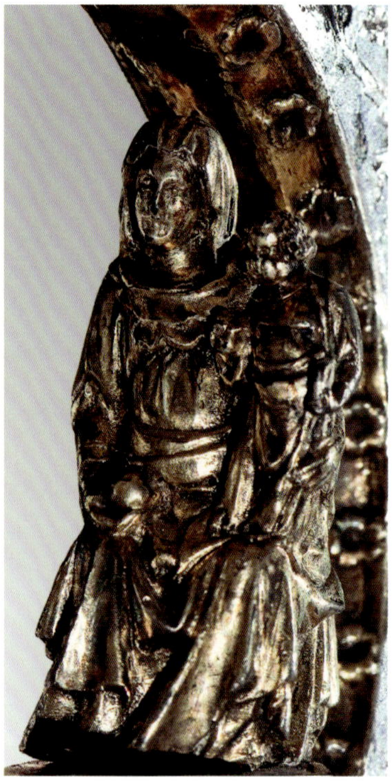

GOLDSMITHS AND THE OTHER ARTS

Goldsmiths – expert in metal, in casting and in working stones – also had associations with artists in other media. They sometimes worked closely with Sienese painters, as, for instance, when Biagio di Goro Ghezzi (a painter with links to the Lorenzetti) provided the goldsmith Michele di Ser Memmo with tin, gold and mordant in 1370.[26] Sienese goldsmiths also created works in other media. For example, the fifteenth-century goldsmith Francesco d'Antonio produced a gilded wooden tabernacle in 1448 for use during the Corpus Christi festivities at Siena Cathedral. He followed up two years later with a version in silver.[27]

Perhaps of greater significance, and another indicator of the high status enjoyed by goldsmiths in the city, is the number of architectural and engineering projects that they undertook. Michele di Ser Memmo, whom we saw working alongside the painter Biagio di Goro, also acted during his career as *capomaestro* ('master of works') for the Palazzo del Comune in Pistoia, as the *capomaestro* for the Cappella di Piazza project on the facade of the Palazzo Pubblico in Siena, as well as repairing clocks and bells for the city.[28] Earlier in the fourteenth century, the multitalented Lando di Pietro made the gilt-iron crown for the coronation of Emperor Henry VII, was active casting bells in Florence and Siena, worked as an architect in Paganico and Siena, and produced wooden sculpture.[29]

The most significant aspect of Sienese goldsmiths' work in other fields was undoubtedly sculpture. This is unsurprising, as even their usual productions frequently included sculptural elements. The reliquary of Saint Sabinus by Ugolino di Vieri and Viva di Lando (Museo dell'Opera del Duomo, Orvieto) incorporates a beautiful figure of the Virgin and Child. It has been suggested that sculptors sometimes created models for goldsmiths working on such elements. This might explain a crosier from Città di Castello featuring cast silver figures, an angel and a bishop praying to the Virgin and Child, which bear striking similarities to the work of the sculptor Goro di Gregorio (figs 128, 129). In 1414 a large-scale silver figure of Saint Sabinus for the Duomo in Siena was designed by the sculptor Francesco di Domenico (called Valdambrino) and executed by the goldsmith Turino di Sano, with enamels by his son Giovanni di Turino.[30]

However, goldsmiths were entirely capable of producing sculpture on their own. In some cases, this simply meant sizing up the sorts of figures that they created for reliquary busts, as when in 1301 the Sienese goldsmith Manno di

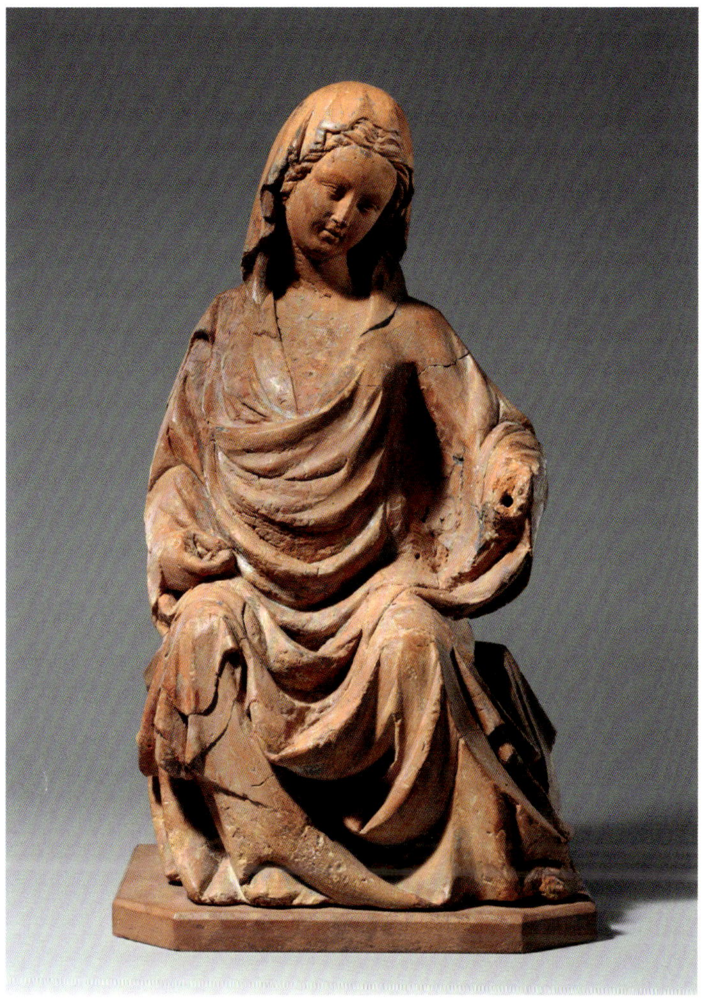

FIG. 129
Goro di Gregorio (documented 1311–24)
Enthroned Virgin, first half of the fourteenth century
Terracotta, 44.8 × 25.4 × 24.1 cm
The Metropolitan Museum of Art, New York. The Cloisters Collection and Rogers Fund, 1998 (1998.214)

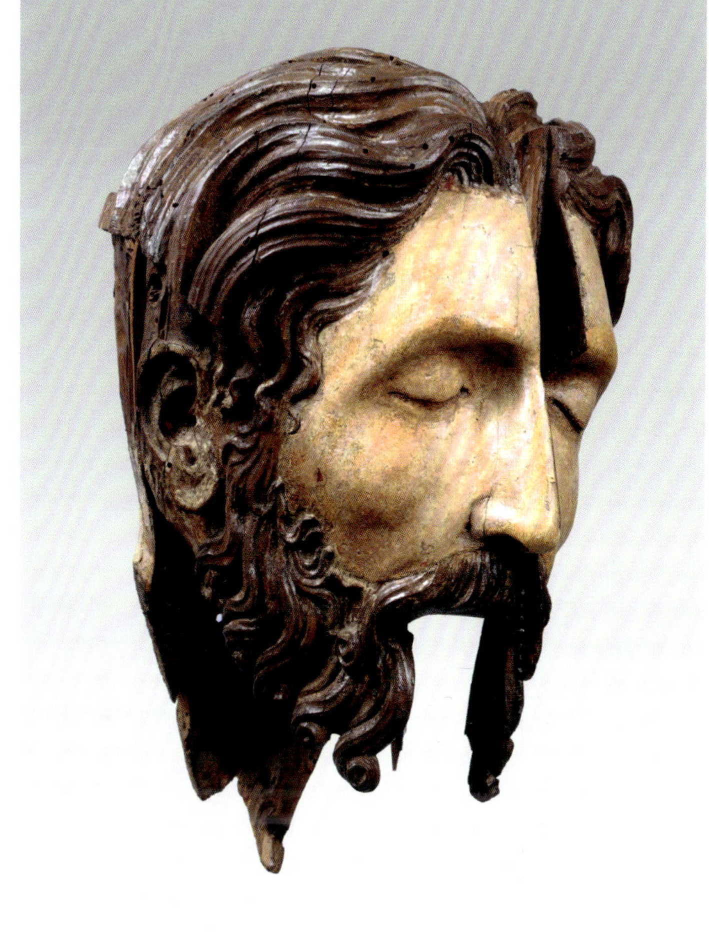

FIG. 130
Lando di Pietro (about 1280–1340)
Head of Christ (fragment of crucifix), 1338
Tempera on walnut, 31 × 22 × 18 cm
Basilica di San Bernardino all'Osservanza, Siena. Museo Castelli

Bandino, who lived and worked in Bologna, fashioned an enormous statue of Pope Boniface VIII in gilded copper for the facade of the Palazzo Comunale in that city.[31] But goldsmiths' statuary need not always be scaled-up reliquaries. Nor need they always be made of metal. In 1338 Lando di Pietro produced a wooden crucifix. Sadly, this was partially destroyed by a bomb in 1944. Only fragments now remain in the Basilica of the Osservanza in Siena (fig. 130), but due to the damage, a remarkable find was made within the figure. Wedged inside were two little parchment sheets, one in the head, the other in the knee. They contained a passionate prayer in Italian naming Lando as the maker, dramatically confirming his authorship.[32] In the 1370s and 1380s a number of Sienese goldsmiths executed marble figures of saints for the Cappella di Piazza project.[33] One of them, Mariano d'Agnolo Romanelli, also produced an Archangel Michael for the hospital of Santa Maria della Scala, which was painted by Bartolo di Fredi.[34] Comparison with Mariano's marble sculptures has allowed a convincing attribution to him of the reliquary bust dated 1381 depicting the saint Pope Mark at the abbey of San Salvatore near Siena.[35]

The involvement of Sienese goldsmiths in the production of large-scale statuary noticeably increased during the second half of the fourteenth century, paralleling a

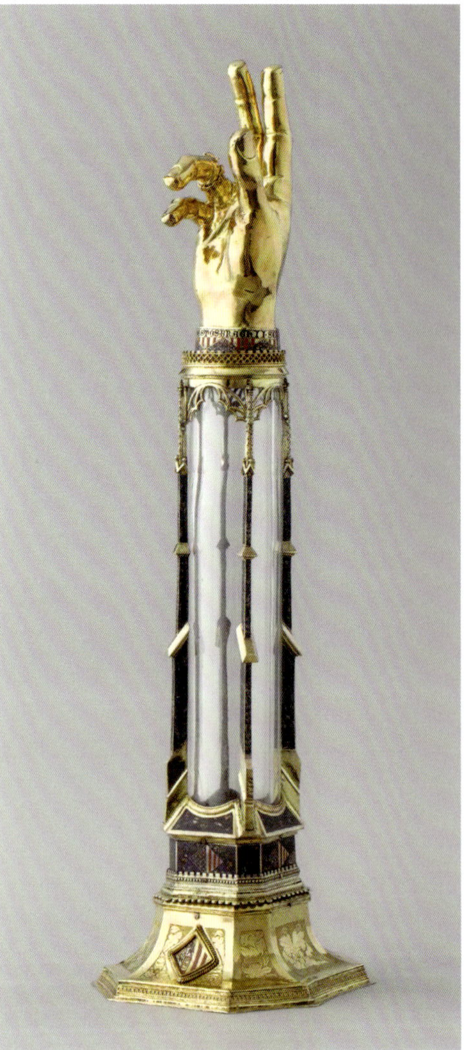

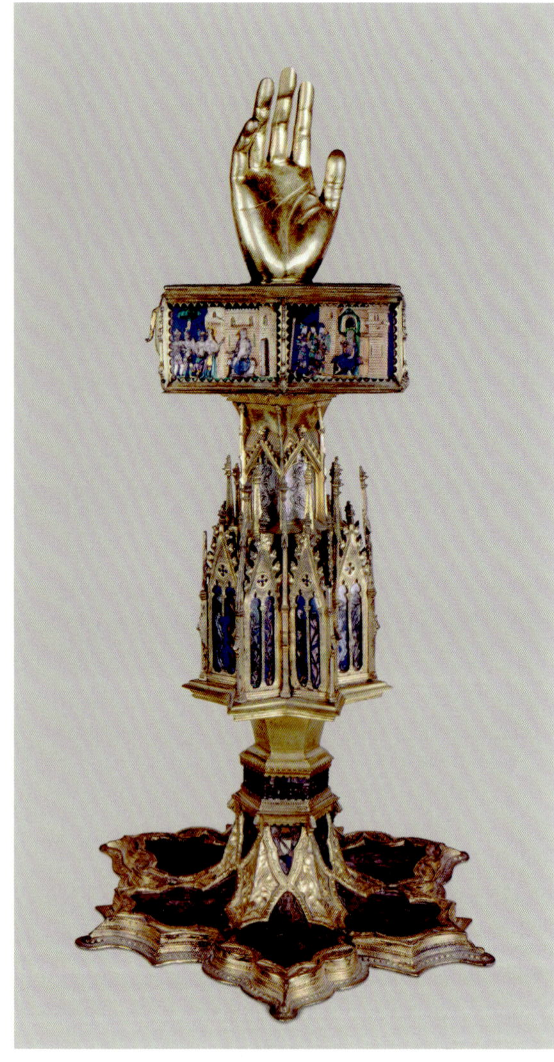

FIG. 131
Possibly by Lando di Pietro (about 1280–1340)
Arm Reliquary of Saint Louis of Toulouse, about 1336–8
Gilded silver with translucent enamel and rock crystal, 62.5 × 17.5 × 17.5 cm
Musée du Louvre, Paris (OA 3254)

FIG. 132
Giacomo di Tondo (documented 1343–76) and Andrea di Petruccio (documented 1363–73)
Hand Reliquary of Saint Lucy, about 1350–60
Gilded silver with translucent enamel, 65.5 × 36.5 × 36.5 cm
Catedral Primada Museum, Toledo

contemporaneous phenomenon in Florence. In that city, artists who would become known as sculptors – including Filippo Brunelleschi, Lorenzo Ghiberti and Donatello – all trained as or worked as goldsmiths when young in the latter part of the trecento. Donatello, indeed, was often described as *orafo* ('goldsmith') in documents during the early part of his career, and when he came to Siena in the 1420s to work on the baptistery font, he was employed alongside Sienese goldsmith-sculptors such as Giovanni di Turino, Goro di Ser Neroccio and Jacopo della Quercia, who was the son of the goldsmith Piero d'Angelo.[36] Goldsmiths and sculptors shared many techniques, and a solid grounding in goldsmithing and *disegno* ('design') was the best foundation for a career as a sculptor, especially one who worked with bronze.

SIENESE GOLDSMITHS ABROAD

Some Sienese goldsmiths were regularly active outside their home city. Lando di Pietro worked in both Florence and Naples. It was from Naples that he was called back at the end of his life to take over as *capomaestro* of the Siena Duomo.[37] The arm reliquary of Louis of Toulouse, now in the Musée du Louvre, Paris, has been proposed as one of his works, possibly made while on his Neapolitan sojourn (fig. 131).[38] Lando was one of a number of prominent Sienese artists lured into producing work for the Angevins during the period from about 1317 into the 1330s, including Simone Martini and Tino da Camaino.[39] Sienese goldsmiths such as Manno di Bandino in Bologna, Andrea di Naddo di Guidarello in Pisa, Michele di Ser Memmo in Pistoia and

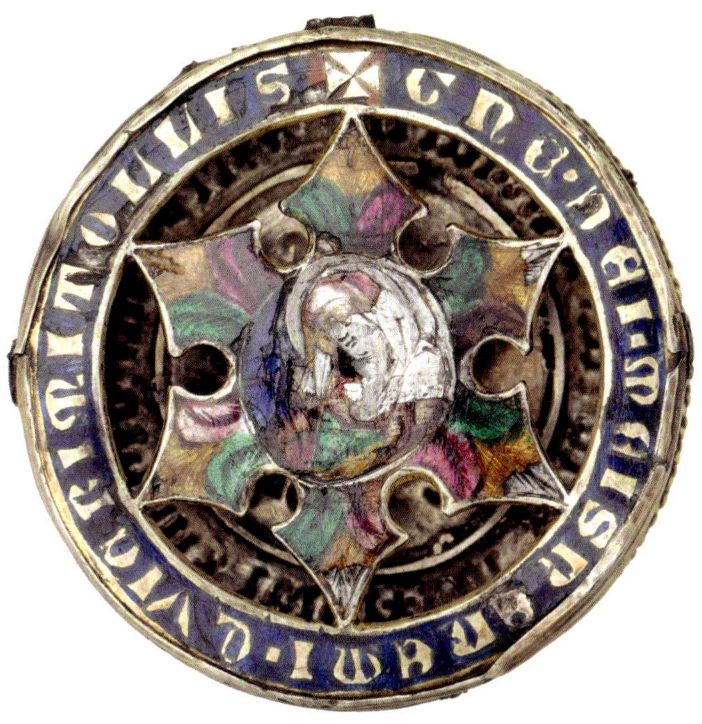

FIG. 133
Sienese goldsmith (upper part)
Container for an Agnus Dei, about 1320–30
(lower face a fifteenth-century replacement)
Silver with translucent and champlevé
enamel, 4.2 × 4.2 cm
Musée Cluny, Paris (Cl. 11460)

Niccolino di Paolo in Lucca spent much or even all of their working careers based in other Italian cities.[40]

The established trend for the employment of Sienese goldsmiths at the papal court continued with the transfer of the papacy to Avignon. The Italian orientation of the papacy with regard to precious metals is perhaps most clearly illustrated by the fact that the Avignon Curia retained the lower silver standard used in Italian centres rather than adopting the local, purer, silver standard of southern France.[41]

The Avignon Curia was the source of a number of surviving Sienese works now in Spain. The earliest is the crosier in the Museo Arqueológico in Madrid, which although it is unsigned, bears close similarities to Sienese examples.[42] Rather more problematic, in that it has a somewhat hybrid character, is the cross 'dels lleonets' formerly in the treasury of Tortosa Cathedral (current whereabouts unknown). If a Sienese goldsmith was involved in the creation of this object, then they must have been operating in a foreign workshop and collaborating with locals trained in a different tradition.[43] This is entirely possible, since we know of at least one Sienese goldsmith, a man referred to as 'Tuxto', who was active in Barcelona in the second and third decades of the trecento.[44] The most impressive of this group of survivals is the hand reliquary of Saint Lucy, probably dating to the 1350s, inscribed by the goldsmiths Giacomo di Tondo and Andrea di Petruccio, which was once owned by Cardinal Albornoz, and is now in Toledo Cathedral (fig. 132).[45] Other objects apparently by Sienese goldsmiths working in Avignon are unsigned, such as the upper part of an *Agnus Dei* (container for wax) now at the Musée Cluny in Paris (fig. 133).

Two of the most prominent Sienese goldsmiths working in Avignon were Minucchio da Siena and Giovanni di Bartolo. Minucchio was active at the papal court between 1327 and 1347 and, among a large number of other commissions, produced 18 gold roses for the Pope, which were ceremonially presented as gifts on Laetare Sunday, the fourth Sunday of Lent. Only one of these survives, giving us an idea of the spectacular artifice possible when working for the wealthiest patrons (fig. 134).

Giovanni di Bartolo worked for the popes in both Avignon and Rome from the 1360s to the 1380s. Most significantly, in 1369 he produced the important reliquary busts of saints Peter and Paul that were once in the Church of Saint John Lateran in Rome, now sadly lost. Fortunately, another reliquary bust by Giovanni does survive: that of Saint Agatha conserved in the cathedral treasury of Catania.[46] This was commissioned by Martial, Bishop of Catania, and was

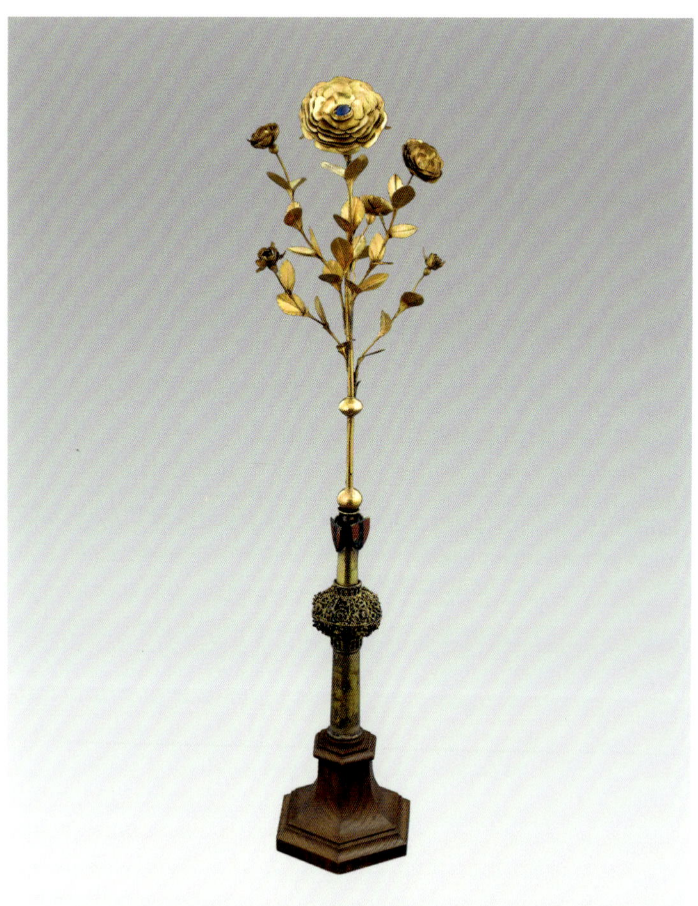

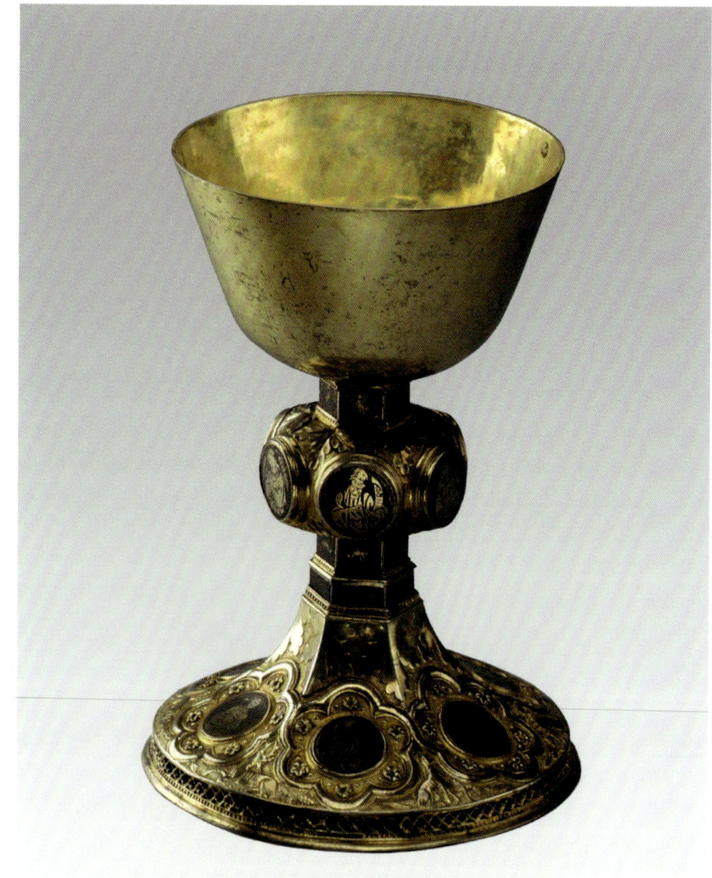

completed under his successor Elia in 1376. The bust has been much added to, and today is usually covered in a garment made from jewellery and ex-votos (gifts donated to honour promises made during prayer). Despite the later accretions, some of the novel elements introduced by Giovanni to his reliquary busts are immediately apparent: the use of a three-quarter figure that allowed for the inclusion of hands holding attributes, and the painting of the figure's face. This feature can also be seen in the fragmentary bust of Saint Juliana now in The Metropolitan Museum of Art, New York, possibly a work by the same artist.[47]

Sienese goldsmiths were also active in Hungary – Pietro and Niccolo Gallicus are certainly documented as working there.[48] A striking chalice featuring the Anjou arms comes from the Hungarian church of Vizakna (now in Estonia), an important silver-mining centre.[49] It differs from the standard Sienese silver chalice in several details: for example, the foot is engraved rather than embossed. Similar discrepancies from the standard Sienese form can be found on another survival from central Europe, the chalice from the parish church of Saint Vitus in Lipnic (Moldova), today in the Prague Museum of Decorative Arts (fig. 135).[50] As with the chalice from Vizakna, despite this object's evidently Sienese character, several elements of the decoration are unusual in the context of surviving Sienese examples, notably the flat, engraved foliage decoration on the foot, the somewhat muted mouldings separating the various elements, and the fact that the enamels of both foot and knop are of equal size, and repeat iconographies (there are two plaques depicting the Crucifixion). It is unclear whether these chalices were produced by Sienese goldsmiths, or like the cross in Tortosa were created under the influence of Sienese craftsmanship, or by a Sienese artist working in an unfamiliar workshop context. Nevertheless, both chalices serve to underline the international dimension of Sienese goldsmiths' work during the trecento, a story that both parallels and complements the reputation of Sienese painting.

FIG. 134
Minucchio da Siena
(documented 1327–1347)
Ceremonial Rose, 1330
Gold with champlevé enamel and semi-precious stone, height 60 cm
Musée Cluny, Paris (Cl. 2351)

FIG. 135
Unknown goldsmith, probably Sienese
Chalice, about 1320–50
Gilded silver with translucent enamel, height 20 cm
Museum of Decorative Arts, Prague (7090)

1. 'est homo legalissimus, et non solum in arte sua predicta, sed in multis aliis, preter dictam suam artem, est homo magne subtilitatis et adinventionis, tam his que spectant ad edificationes palatiorum et domorum comunis et viarum, et pontium, et fontium'. See Milanesi 1854, vol. 1, doc. 50, p. 228.
2. Norman 2018.
3. Leone de Castris 1988.
4. Cioni 1998, pp. 33–57; see also Guérin, pp. 216–23, in the present volume.
5. Donato 2011–12; Davies 2014, pp. 210–44.
6. For a discussion of the inventory of Mary of Hungary in this context, see Leone de Castris 1988, pp. 119–22.
7. Beani 1906, pp. 7–8.
8. Hueck 1982; Cioni 1998, pp. 20–3; Hueck 2007, pp. 53–4.
9. For his career, see Cioni 2005 and further documents published in Le Pogam 2004, p. 169.
10. Inscribed 'NICHOLAUS PAPA QUARTUS / GUCCIUS MANAIE DE SENIS FECIT', 'Pope Nicholas IV / Guccio di Mannaia of Siena made this'. See Callori di Vignale and Santamaria 2014, which lists much of the extensive earlier bibliography on this object.
11. The gifts given in 1288 included a number of silver liturgical vessels. See Cooper and Robson 2013, p. 36.
12. Leone de Castris 1991.
13. Gaborit-Chopin 1996; Taburet-Delahaye 1994; Gaborit-Chopin 1999; Distefano 2021; Guérin (forthcoming).
14. Leone de Castris 1988, p. 128.
15. Strehlke and Israëls 2015, pp. 444–51, pl. 68b.
16. Davies 2009; Davies 2014, pp. 106–27.
17. Davies 2014, pp. 245–312.
18. For Guccio's sons, see Machetti 1929, p. 39; Cioni 1998, p. 627, n. 12; Cioni 2005, p. 341; Ermini 2016, pp. 108–10.
19. Bellosi 1988b; Binski 2002; Cooper and Robson 2013, p. 82.
20. For this argument, see Collareta 1983, pp. 3, 6.
21. Davies 2022.
22. Cioni 1998, pp. 360–2; Davies 2014, pp. 140–1.
23. 'excetto i calici e altri lavori eclesiastichi, i quali non fossono lavorati qui et fossono parte d'ariento e parte di rame chome quegli che ssi fanno in Siena o altrove: questi sieno leciti potere fare venire, tenere et vendere'. See Dorini 1942, p. 400. For a discussion, see Davies 2009, pp. 37–40.
24. 'PER MAGISTRUM UGOLINUM ET SOTIOS AUREFICIES DE SENIS FACTUM FUIT'. For the reliquary, see Cioni 1998, pp. 469–618; Freni 2000b; Donato 2011–12, no. 5.S.3.1, pp. 80–6.
25. Documents in Milanesi 1854, vol. 1, pp. 210–13; Machetti 1929, pp. 21–2; Ermini 2016, pp. 106–8. Elisabetta Cioni has proposed that Guidino di Guido was responsible for much of the enamelling on the reliquary; see Cioni 1998, p. 553.
26. Freuler 1981, p. 38.
27. Israëls 2006, p. 198. For Francesco d'Antonio's career, see Cioni and Fattorini 2021.
28. Machetti 1929, p. 36; Lisini 1904, p. 652; Pichi 2003, pp. 56–7.
29. Moretti 2004.
30. For this commission, see Cioni 2018, p. 14. For a biography of Giovanni di Turino, see Siena 2010, p. 619.
31. Pini 2006.
32. Siena 1987, pp. 65–8.
33. Borgherini 2001, pp. 110–24; Giorgi and Moscadelli 2005, pp. 264–71; Siena 2010, p. 425; Cioni 2018, p. 20.
34. Freuler 1994, p. 283. For a biography of Mariano, see Siena 2010, p. 622.
35. Bagnoli 2018; Cioni in Siena 2010, cat. F.5, pp. 440–1.
36. For Donatello and goldsmithing, see Bloch 2023.
37. Moretti 2004.
38. Leone de Castris 1988, pp. 130–2.
39. Norman 2018, pp. 71–96.
40. Moretti 2007; Capitanio in Lucca 1990, vol. 2, cat. 81, p. 418; Concioni, Ghilarducci and Ferri 1991, pp. 12, 34.
41. Taburet-Delahaye 1995.
42. Inv. 52160.
43. Cioni 1998, pp. 178–87.
44. De Dalmases 1992, vol. 2, pp. 145, 193–6.
45. Cioni 1998, pp. 673–84; Cioni 2010, pp. 156–8; Cros Gutiérrez 2008, vol. 1, pp. 273–5.
46. For this work, and for Giovanni's career, see Cioni 2010.
47. Inv. 61.266. Boehm in New York 2006–7, cat. 73, pp. 180–2; Cioni in Siena 2010, cat. F.4, pp. 436–7.
48. Mihalik 1926–7.
49. The chalice is now in the Hungarian National Museum, Budapest. See Budapest and Luxembourg 2006, p. 104.
50. Stehlikova 1994, pp. 650–3; Cioni 1998, pp. 22–5.

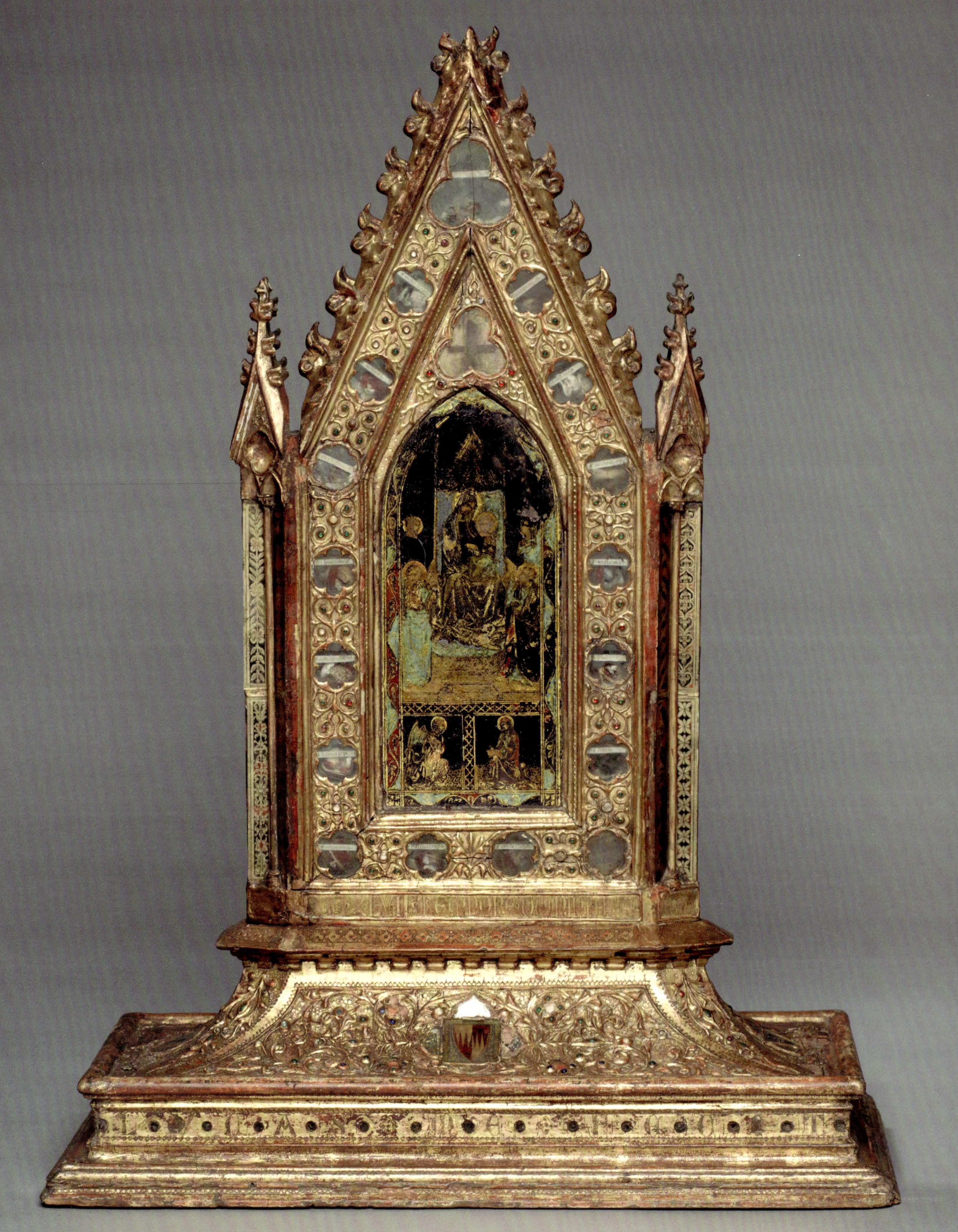

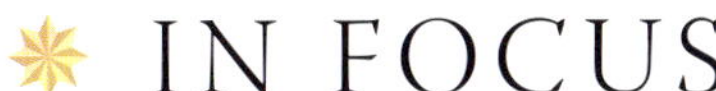

IN FOCUS

The Fitzwilliam Gilded Glass and the Cleveland Reliquary Frame

Beth Williamson

A reliquary frame in the Cleveland Museum of Art consists of a gilded wooden core structure, embellished with modelled gesso, inset 'gems' of polished glass, and gilded glass (fig. 136). Displaying saints' relics, the frame has 17 glass-covered apertures: 16 six-lobed rosettes and a trefoil at the apex. As the structure is double-sided, it affords viewing from both sides. The gabled rectangular frame housing the relics was designed to be detachable from the base, so that it could be mounted on a pole and carried in procession. It has been clear for many years that the gilded glass panel, now in the Fitzwilliam Museum in Cambridge (fig. 137), once sat at the centre of the Cleveland frame.[1] The exhibition this volume accompanies brings these two objects back together for the first time since they became known to scholars, offering a unique opportunity to reimagine the composite object once formed by these two pieces, a key example of a Sienese reliquary tabernacle.

There are at least eleven surviving published examples of this type of object.[2] They follow a common form: a wooden panel with a pointed apex, supported on a wooden base, containing at its centre an image (usually painted), which is surrounded by apertures housing relics of saints and holy places. Sometimes the central gabled section is a single panel, as in the Cleveland frame, and sometimes it has wings that can fold over the central panel (as in the Wyvern Collection triptych, see fig. 171, which has, exceptionally, a fourteenth-century French ivory diptych embedded in the central panel). The relic apertures in these tabernacles were originally covered with glass, but now in most instances the glass and relics have been lost and the apertures are empty. The Cleveland frame, however, retains relics, wrapped in cloth and labelled, in each of the compartments disposed around the edges of the wooden panel.[3] A few other tabernacles, including that attributed to Naddo Ceccarelli in Baltimore (fig. 138), and that by Francesco di Vannuccio in Siena,[4] still contain relics, but the condition of the relic apertures' coverings in both cases may indicate significant repairs and alterations.[5]

The frame at the Cleveland Museum of Art was acquired in 1978.[6] By analogy with other examples of this reliquary tabernacle type, it was clear it would

Photographic montage of the complete reliquary (reverse), reuniting figs 136 and 137

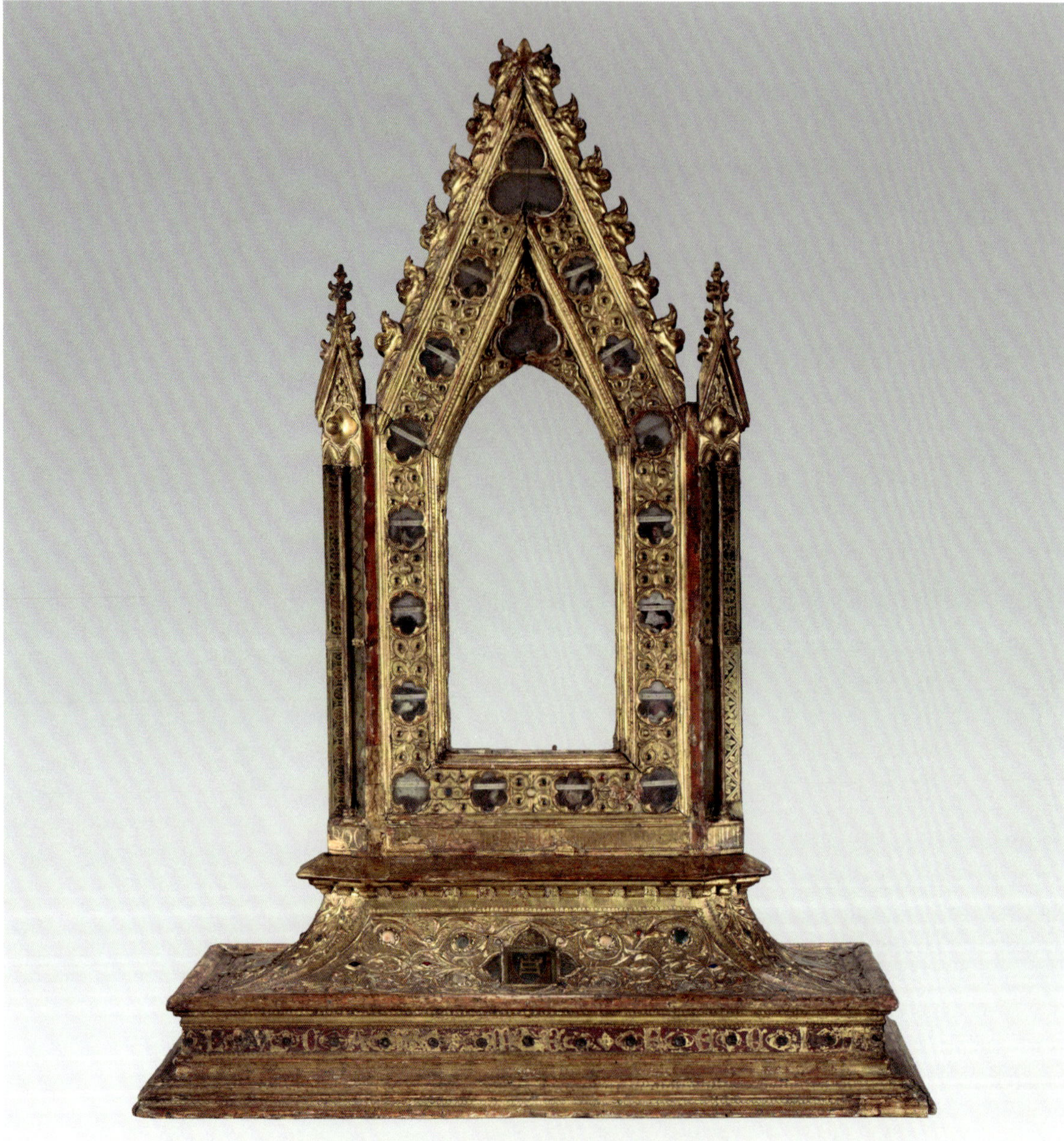

FIG. 136
Sienese artist (?)
Frame for a portable reliquary icon (obverse), 1347
Gilded wood, modelled gesso, gilded glass, glass cabochons and relics, 66.7 × 51.3 × 25.3 cm
The Cleveland Museum of Art, Gift of Ruth Blumka in memory of Leopold Blumka (1978.26)

FIG. 137
Sienese artist (?)
The Virgin and Child with Saints and the Annunciation, 1347
Gilded glass, 25.1 × 10.5 cm
The Syndics of the Fitzwilliam Museum, University of Cambridge (M.56 & A-1904)

have framed some kind of image, but it was not then known precisely what that might be. William Wixom suggested the frame had once contained a painted panel on one side and a gilded glass panel on the other, one of them representing the Virgin and Child, like the double-sided processional image signed by the Sienese painter Francesco di Vannuccio and dated 1380, now in the Gemäldegalerie in Berlin.[7] The Fitzwilliam glass depicts a Virgin and Child enthroned, accompanied by Saint James Major, an evangelist (?) and two angels, with an Annunciation below. It was bequeathed to the museum in 1904 and published in 1912.[8] Although it was evident the panel must once have been part of something larger, it was not known what. The glass is currently displayed in a later, possibly fifteenth-century, gessoed and gilded wooden frame. After the acquisition and publication of the Cleveland frame, Dillian Gordon recognised that the dimensions of the Fitzwilliam glass – 25.1 cm high and 10.5 cm wide – matched exactly those of the central aperture in the Cleveland frame; in addition, there are several correspondences between decorative features in the frame and in the glass.[9] She linked the Cleveland frame with a 'tabernacolo' mentioned in 1791 by Girolamo Macchi, the archivist of the hospital of Santa Maria della Scala, in Siena.[10] Macchi's description showed that Wixom had been right in part about the iconographical subjects at the centre of the Cleveland frame (although not the inclusion of a painted panel). Macchi confirms that there was an image of the Crucified Christ on one side, and 'the Most Holy Virgin' on the other, both made of gilded glass.

Aspects of the frame itself also provide links with the hospital. Two coats of arms each appear twice on the frame's base. One, showing a golden ladder on a black background, is that of the hospital of Santa Maria della Scala.[11] On the reverse, and the right-hand short side, are gold and red diagonally quartered and indented coats of arms, which are those of the Cinughi family, a Sienese patrician dynasty.[12] The inscription on the frame gives a date of 1347, and names a certain 'MINI/CINI'.[13] This was surely Mino di Cino Cinughi, rector of the hospital from 1340 until his death in 1351.[14] The coats of arms, the inscription and Macchi's eighteenth-century description confirm that we are justified in considering this object as 'Sienese'. The gabled reliquary tabernacle appears to have developed in Siena, in the early fourteenth century, in the circles of Sienese artists such as Pietro Lorenzetti and Naddo Ceccarelli.[15] The Fitzwilliam glass must have been made by someone familiar with the visual culture of Siena: its images relate both compositionally and stylistically to Sienese works of the early fourteenth century, especially, but not exclusively, to the circle of Simone Martini and his workshop.[16]

While style, composition, patronage and object type point to Siena, localising the technique of the Fitzwilliam glass is more complex. Given that the majority of surviving examples of medieval Italian gilded glass come from Umbria rather than Tuscany, can we confidently describe this element of the tabernacle as 'Sienese'? The technique used by the artist of the Fitzwilliam glass largely conforms to that described by Cennino Cennini in his late fourteenth-century *Craftsman's Handbook*. Cennino instructs the artist to lay gold leaf on a sheet of glass, and lightly draw a design onto the gold with a thin stylus or needle. When the design is established, the areas of gold beyond the outlines of the drawn figures are to be rubbed away, and paint of different

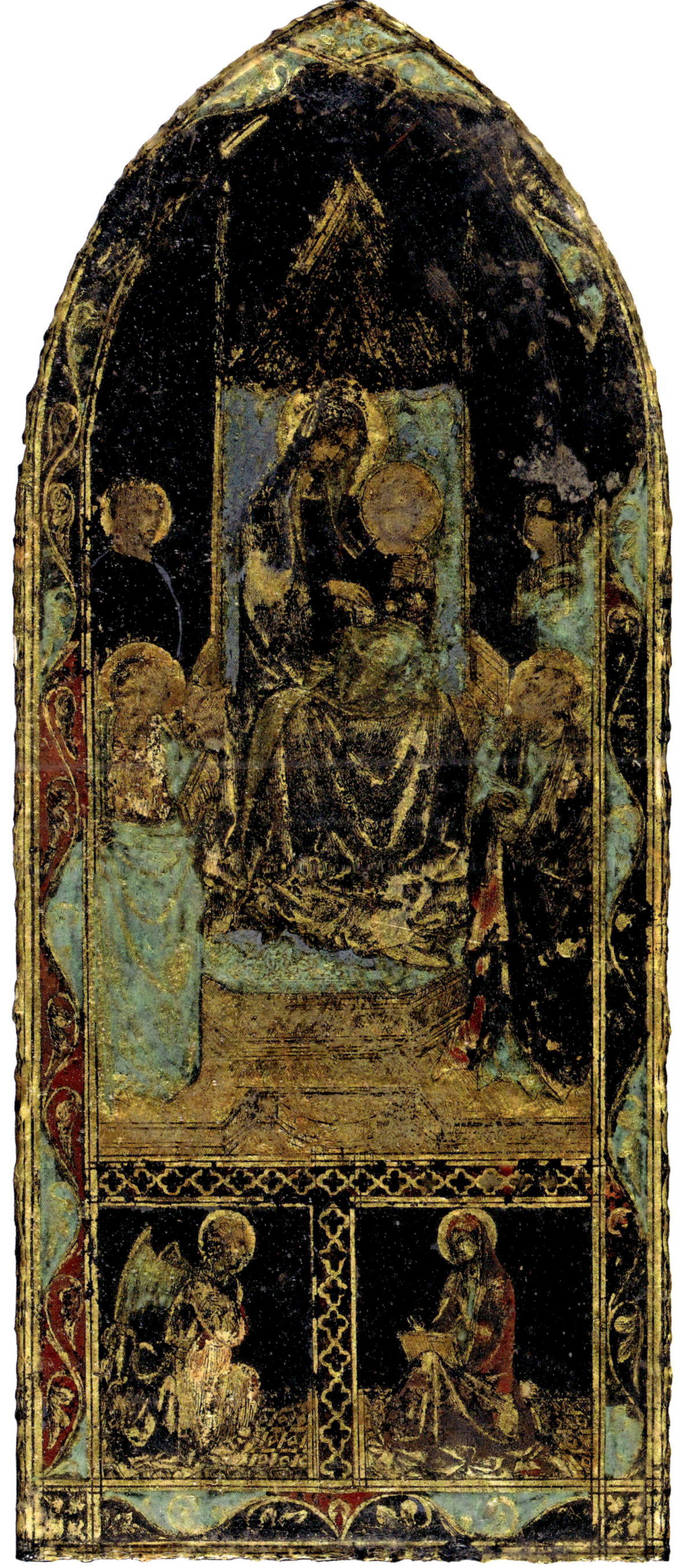

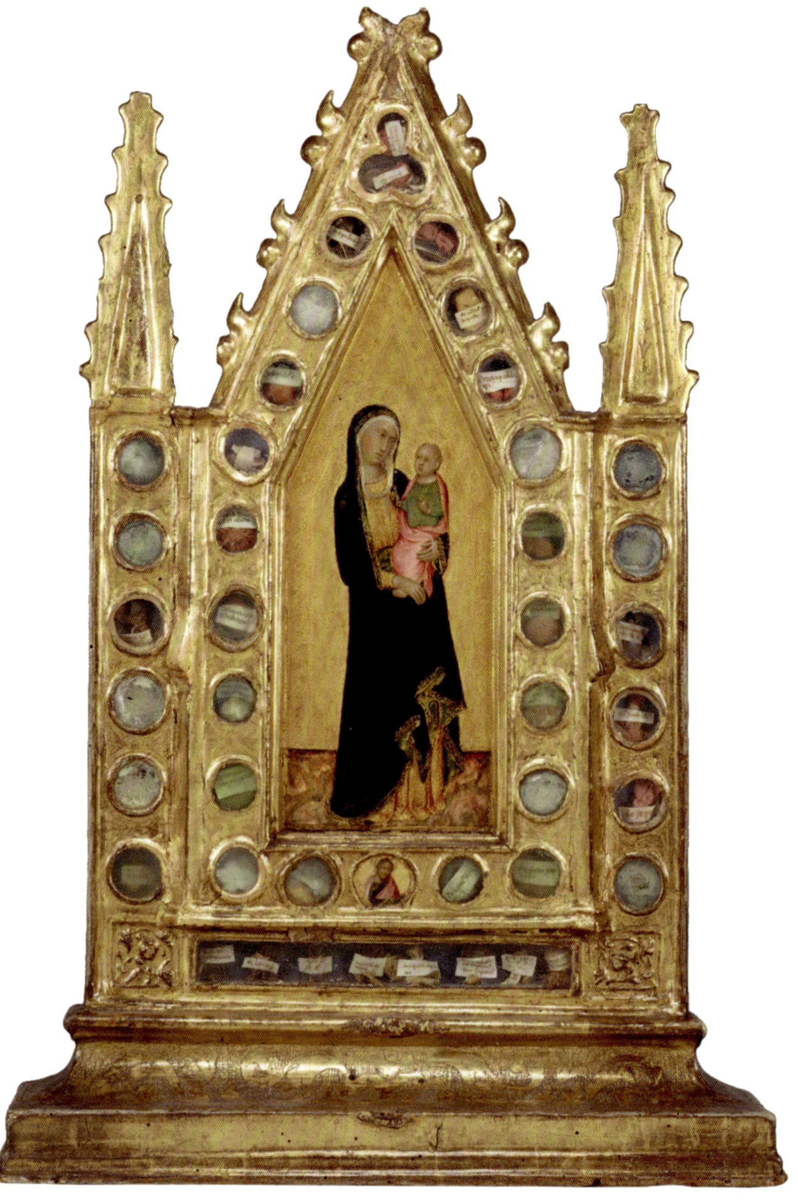

FIG. 138
Naddo Ceccarelli
(documented about 1330–60)
Tabernacle with Standing Virgin, about 1350
Tempera on panel with glass, paper and relics, 62 × 43 × 9.4 cm
Walters Art Museum, Baltimore. Acquired by Henry Walters, 1920 (37.1159)

FIG. 139
Detail of fig. 137

colours applied to the glass.[17] Creating an image in gilded glass was an exceptionally demanding process. Everything must be drawn in reverse, and once the gold has been removed, a mistake cannot be rectified.[18] Many fourteenth-century artists do not appear to have been as exacting as Cennino might have wished. As Gordon pointed out, in the majority of fourteenth-century gilded glasses the gold is cut away rather crudely, with the resulting spaces blocked in with colour.[19] But the technique in the Fitzwilliam glass is exceptionally fine. The artist has used very delicate modelling and hatching, following Cennino's advice to create strong shadows by going with the tip of the needle all the way through the gold to the glass; medium shadows are created by not passing all the way through the gold (fig. 139).[20] Much of the original colour has been lost from the Fitzwilliam glass. The Virgin's robe was presumably once backed in blue. The robes of Saint James are a pale green, and the brocade cloth on the throne varies in different areas from a blue-green to a pale green. The lining of the outer robes of the right-hand figure is backed in red, and his undergarment is pale green. The Annunciate Virgin and Gabriel both appear to have worn red robes, though much of the colour is now lost. Red, blue and pale green all feature in the foliate border. Despite the colour losses, it can be seen what a rich and vibrant object this must once have been.

Who might have produced this unusual object, which fits squarely within a Sienese patronage context, and which shows knowledge of Sienese painting? An inscription on the tabernacle's plinth declares that 'LUCAS ME FECIT' (Lucas made me). Various possibilities for the identity of 'Lucas' have been suggested, but there is no documented Sienese painter of that name whose style seems consistent with the object. However, there was a Sienese goldsmith named Luca, documented between 1348 and 1363.[21] He came from a family of goldsmiths, his brother being Ugolino di Vieri, who made the gold and enamelled *Reliquary of the Holy Corporal* in Orvieto, completed in 1338 (see fig. 47). It is possible this Luca might have been aware of – or even worked on – the Orvietan reliquary that bears his brother's name. It can certainly be suggested that an artist trained in goldsmiths' work, and charged with creating an example of a relatively new type of object, might have turned to gilded glass to execute its central imagery. In doing so, he produced a bold multimedia work that made an especially rich and varied contribution to the development of this form of reliquary, in painted and embellished wood, rather than the metalwork traditionally used.[22] If the 'Lucas' of the tabernacle's inscription is indeed the Sienese goldsmith Luca di Vieri, then every aspect of this object – patronage, design, production, devotional context – can be linked with Siena of the fourteenth century, making clear, as do so many contemporary Sienese works, the extraordinary power and innovation of Sienese art in this period.

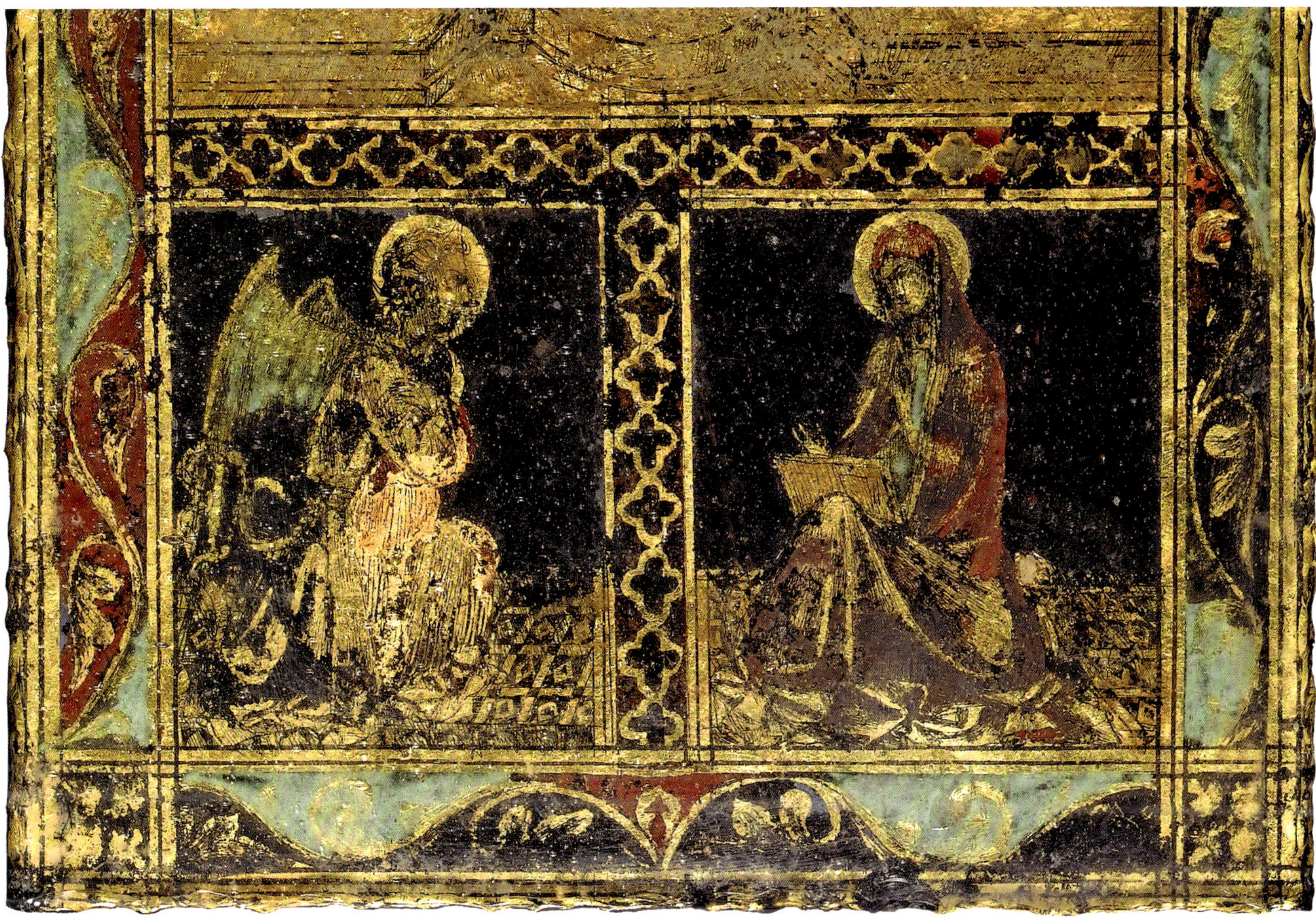

1. Gordon 1981.
2. Williamson 2020, Appendix, pp. 180–1.
3. For a list of the relics, see Williamson 2020, p. 30, n. 7.
4. Fondazione dei Monte dei Paschi, Siena (inv. 101551 [2642]). See Williamson 2020, colour plate XI.
5. Williamson 2020, pp. 56–7.
6. Wixom 1979, pp. 128–32.
7. Inv. 1062B. Wixom 1979, pp. 131–2. For the Vannuccio processional image, see Brilliant 2014, p. 86, figs 9 and 10.
8. Dalton 1912, pp. 116–17.
9. Gordon 1981, p. 153.
10. Ibid., p. 153, n. 36.
11. Ibid., p. 150.
12. Wixom 1979, p. 131.
13. On what is normally termed the 'obverse' of the object, an inscription runs from the outer edge of the left pinnacle to the outer edge of the right pinnacle, over two short fields and a central long field: 'HOC/OPUS. FACTUM. FUIT. SUB. ANNO/DOMINI.' The forward slash here indicates the boundary between the short fields and the long one. On the 'reverse' is inscribed: '[small loss – presumed to be 'M']/CCC.XLVII. TEMPORE DOMINI. MINI/CINI.'
14. Brilliant 2014, p. 72.
15. Williamson 2020, chapter 2, 'The Earliest Examples.'
16. The enthroned Virgin and Child has been compared with Simone Martini's *Maestà* (see fig. 65), and the Annunciation has been compared with several of the Annunciation scenes produced by Simone and his workshop: see Gordon 1981, pp. 149–50. Gordon also suggests comparisons with the work of Ugolino di Vieri and of Ambrogio Lorenzetti (Gordon 1981, p. 150). Several details can be compared with the *Maestà* by Simone's older contemporary, Duccio: see Williamson 2020, p. 36.
17. Cennini 2015, pp. 227–9.
18. 'Make sure that the first drawing does not show very much because you can never rub it out.' Cennini 2015, p. 228. Cennino even goes so far as to recommend that the hand should be rested the day before beginning work.
19. Gordon 1981, p. 149.
20. Cennini 2015, p. 228.
21. Gordon 1981, p. 153.
22. These early Sienese reliquary tabernacles bear a close resemblance in shape with the Saint Galganus reliquary, which might well have been a key object in the development towards these reliquary tabernacles with painted images at the centre. See Williamson 2020, pp. 61–3, where the Saint Galganus reliquary is described as of unknown whereabouts, following its theft in 1989. Since the publication of that book in 2020, the Saint Galganus reliquary has been recovered and returned to the Archdiocese of Siena.

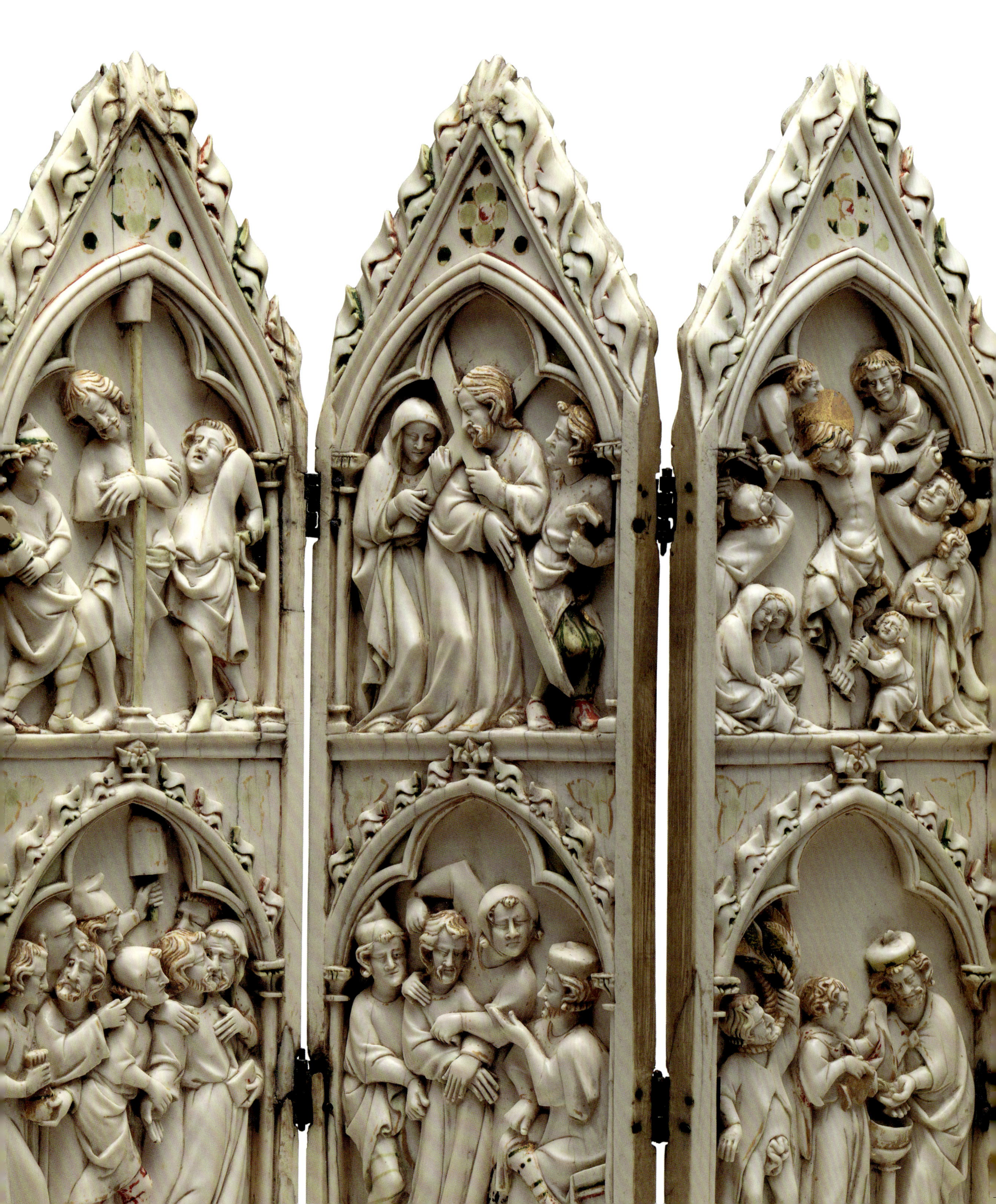

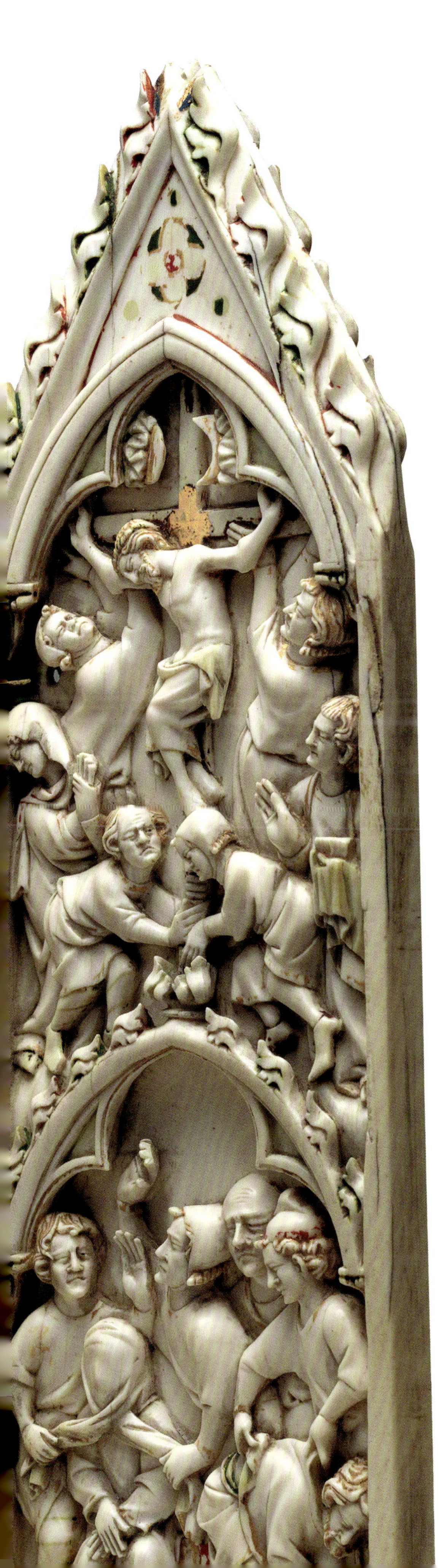

SIENA AND THE WIDER WORLD

As Ambrogio Lorenzetti's fresco of *Good Government in the City and Countryside* famously shows, the walls of Siena express the entity of the city and the security of its inhabitants, with the city gates allowing the controlled passage of those entering, leaving or perhaps passing through, en route between the north and south of Europe on the via Francigena (fig. 140).[1] A journey might be made for many reasons and by various means: for employment, trade, pilgrimage, diplomacy or war; walking, riding or by cart or carriage.[2] Many of the travels mentioned earlier in this volume did not go far from Siena: to Florence, Arezzo, Cortona, Perugia and Assisi, or further afield to Naples and Avignon. Siena was also connected to a wider world. In the distance of Ambrogio's fresco we see the port of Talamone, which allowed Siena precious access to the sea and to one of the routes for links to global trade in the first half of the fourteenth century.[3]

The path from city gate to wider world is powerfully expressed in Ambrogio's depiction of the Miracle of the Grain Ships in one of his Saint Nicholas panels (fig. 141). The gate at Myra, in present-day Turkey, gives on to a port where shipments of grain (miraculously replenished at a time of famine) are unloaded from two large vessels and ferried to shore. Beyond the harbour, on an expanse of sea, sails filled with wind convey

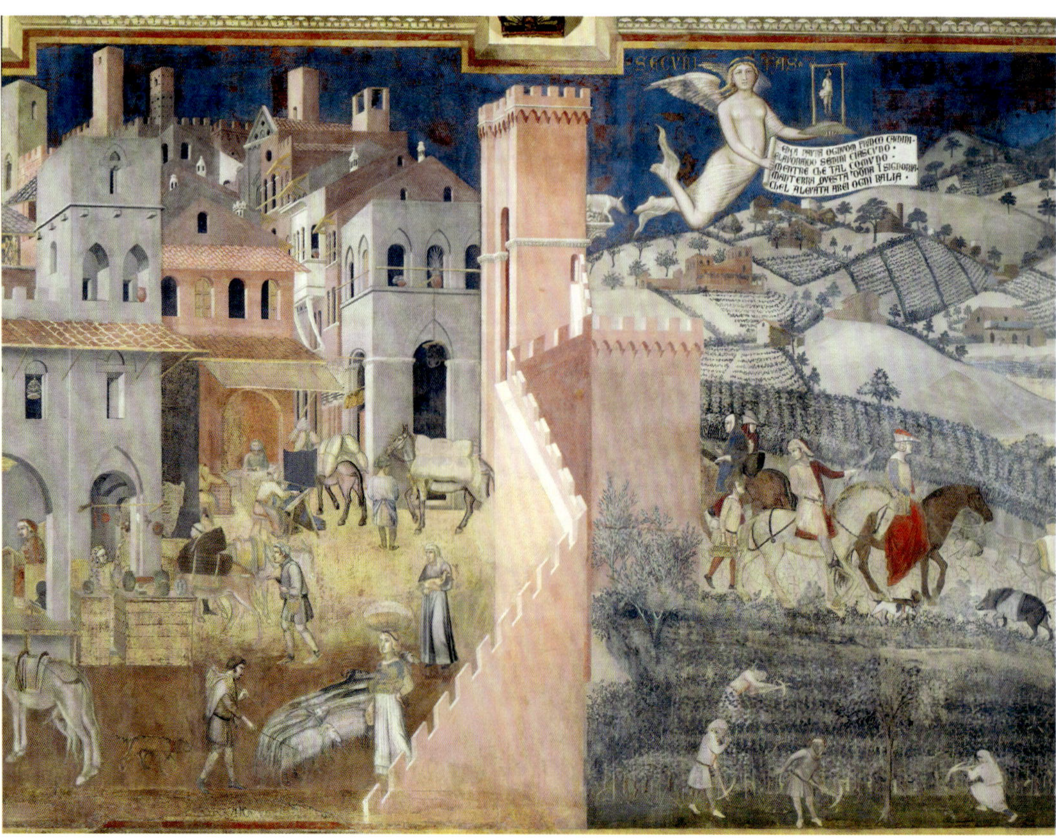

FIG. 140
Ambrogio Lorenzetti
(documented 1319; died 1348/9)
Good Government in the City and Countryside
(detail), 1338
Fresco
Palazzo Pubblico, Siena

the speed with which ships might reach, and seem to sink below, the darkening horizon, on their journeys to and from distant destinations.[4] Sienese merchants participated in a trading network that reached across Europe to the Baltic (including Paris, London and Bruges), around the Mediterranean, as far south as sub-Saharan Africa, and eastwards from Tabriz, across central Asia.[5] Ambrogio's painted seascape depended, for some of its materials, on contacts with the wider world: gold from West Africa for the shining sky;[6] lapis lazuli from Badakhshan (in present-day Afghanistan) for the ultramarine angels delivering miraculous grain;[7] lac (*lacca*) from India, other parts of southern Asia and southern China, or kermes from the Mediterranean or the near east for the crimson-coloured lake pigments of the cloak of Saint Nicholas.[8] Some pigments could be sourced, in small quantities, closer to home. Cinnabar, the naturally occurring form of vermilion, came from Spain, but could also be found in Tuscany on Monte Amiata.[9] Azurite might come from Germany, Hungary or the Tyrol, but some was also found around Siena.[10] Siena was itself a major source of ochre and red earth pigments.[11]

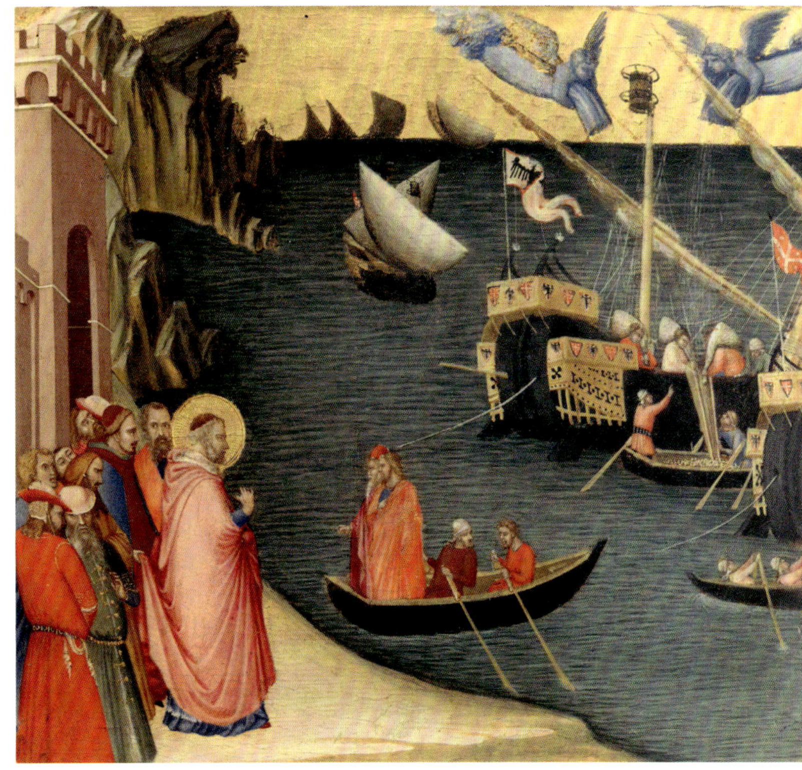

FIG. 141
Detail of the Miracle of the Grain Ships in Ambrogio Lorenzetti's *Stories from the Life of Saint Nicholas* (fig. 89)

Long-distance trade was generally conducted in numerous short stages, but during the period of Mongol domination – the 'Pax Mongolica' (Mongol peace), from the mid-thirteenth to mid-fourteenth centuries – it was possible (if rare) for Italian merchants to journey across Asia to China.[12] Some Italians took up residence in Mongol lands.[13] For example, a Sienese, Tommaso Ugi, served at the Mongol Ilkhanid court in Tabriz and led an embassy westwards, to Pope Clement V, Philip IV of France and to Edward I and his successor Edward II of England in 1307–8.[14] Bartolomeo Abagliati, a Dominican from Siena, was appointed bishop of Tabriz in 1318, serving until 1329. Franciscan and Dominican missionaries travelled east on a variety of routes. Among them was the Franciscan Peter of Siena, who set out for China with three companion friars and journeyed as far as Tana (present-day Thane, now part of Mumbai) where their mission ended in martyrdom in 1321. Peter's story was represented in a fresco cycle painted by Ambrogio Lorenzetti in the cloister of the convent of San Francesco, Siena, in 1336. The frescoes were later singled out for the highest praise by Lorenzo Ghiberti, but regrettably only a few fragments have survived.[15]

Ambrogio also painted a scene of Franciscan martyrdom in the chapter house at San Francesco (fig. 142). There is disagreement over what event is represented: the martyrdom at Ceuta (on the north coast of

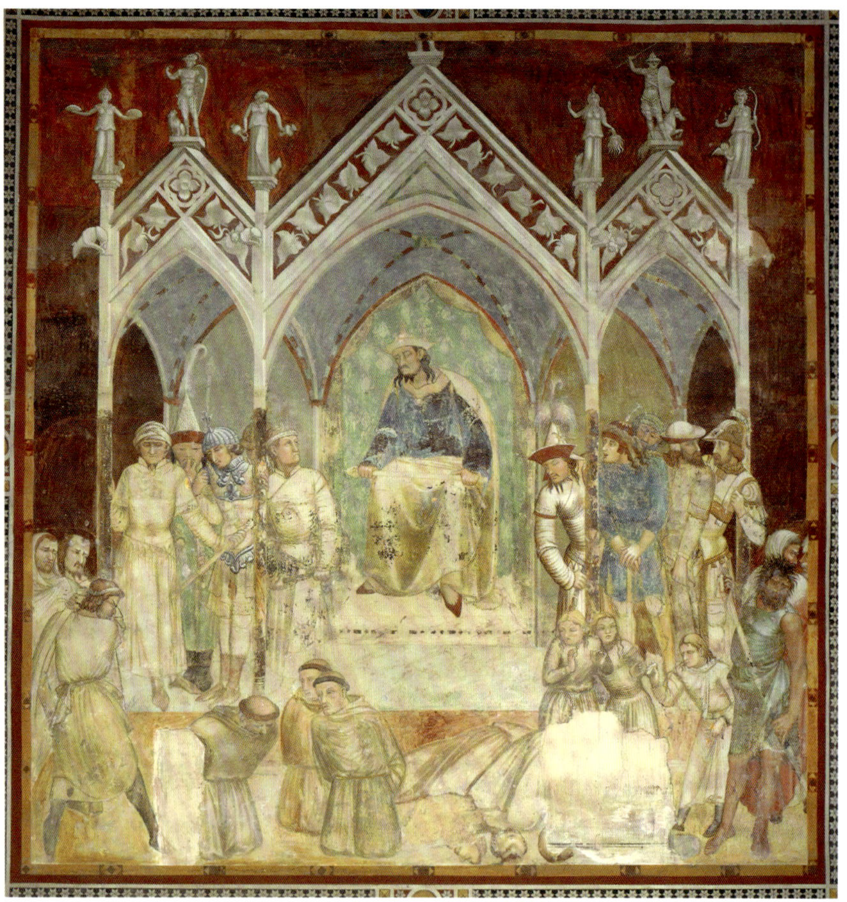

Africa) in 1227; or at Almalyq in central Asia (in present-day China near the Kazakhstan border) in 1339; or, more likely, a composite scene, painted in the mid-1320s, before the Peter of Siena cycle, intended to refer, more broadly, to the variety of distant lands and peoples that Franciscan missionaries might reach and to commemorate all Franciscan martyrs.[16] Ambrogio's depiction of onlookers, witnessing the martyrdom, draws on a range of contacts with foreign cultures. Some figures are undoubtedly shown as Mongols, with distinctive features and dress. Some details – such as the conical hat with a plume, worn by a figure on the right – could have been relayed to Ambrogio by word of mouth, by a traveller, or someone who witnessed one of the Mongol embassies to the papal court, but the precision with which his tunic is described suggests first-hand experience of such a Mongol garment.[17] On the other hand, the ruler is seated in a Western manner, with Western footwear. Other figures have a variety of physiognomies, and a parade of exotic headwear: turbans, helmets and headbands, perhaps intended to evoke the multi-ethnic composition of the Mongol court.[18] It seems probable that Lorenzetti readily mixed a range of specific information with the fruits of his imagination.[19]

FIG. 142
Ambrogio Lorenzetti
(documented 1319; died 1348/9)
Martyrdom of the Franciscan Missionaries, about 1325
Fresco
Basilica of San Francesco, Siena, formerly chapter house

FIG. 143
Avignon or Naples
The Adoration of the Magi, about 1340–4
Tempera on panel, 66.4 × 46.7 cm (with engaged frame)
The Metropolitan Museum of Art, New York. Robert Lehman Collection, 1975 (1975.1.9)

The lives of the later-medieval elites – royalty, aristocracy, civic leaders and princes of the Church – frequently involved travel. This encouraged the production of artworks for personal use that could be handled and then stored for safe transport. Northern European artists made small-scale luxury works, in precious metals, enamel and ivory, in two, three or four pieces, that could be folded and kept in protective pouches, generally made of leather (see figs 122, 173).[20] As discussed in earlier chapters, Sienese painters devised multi-panel works on a rather larger scale, the reverses often silvered or painted in imitation of marble, that could also be folded, secured and transported (see figs 37, 38, 70, 80).[21] The high status of Sienese portable panel types, techniques and ideas is exemplified by a painting that itself illustrates a royal journey: the *Adoration of the Magi* (fig. 143), which, together with panels of the *Annunciation* and *Nativity*, now in the Musée Granet, Aix-en-Provence, probably formed part of a four-part work, possibly folding in accordion style, which may have been given by Robert of Anjou (King of Naples, reigned 1309–43) and his

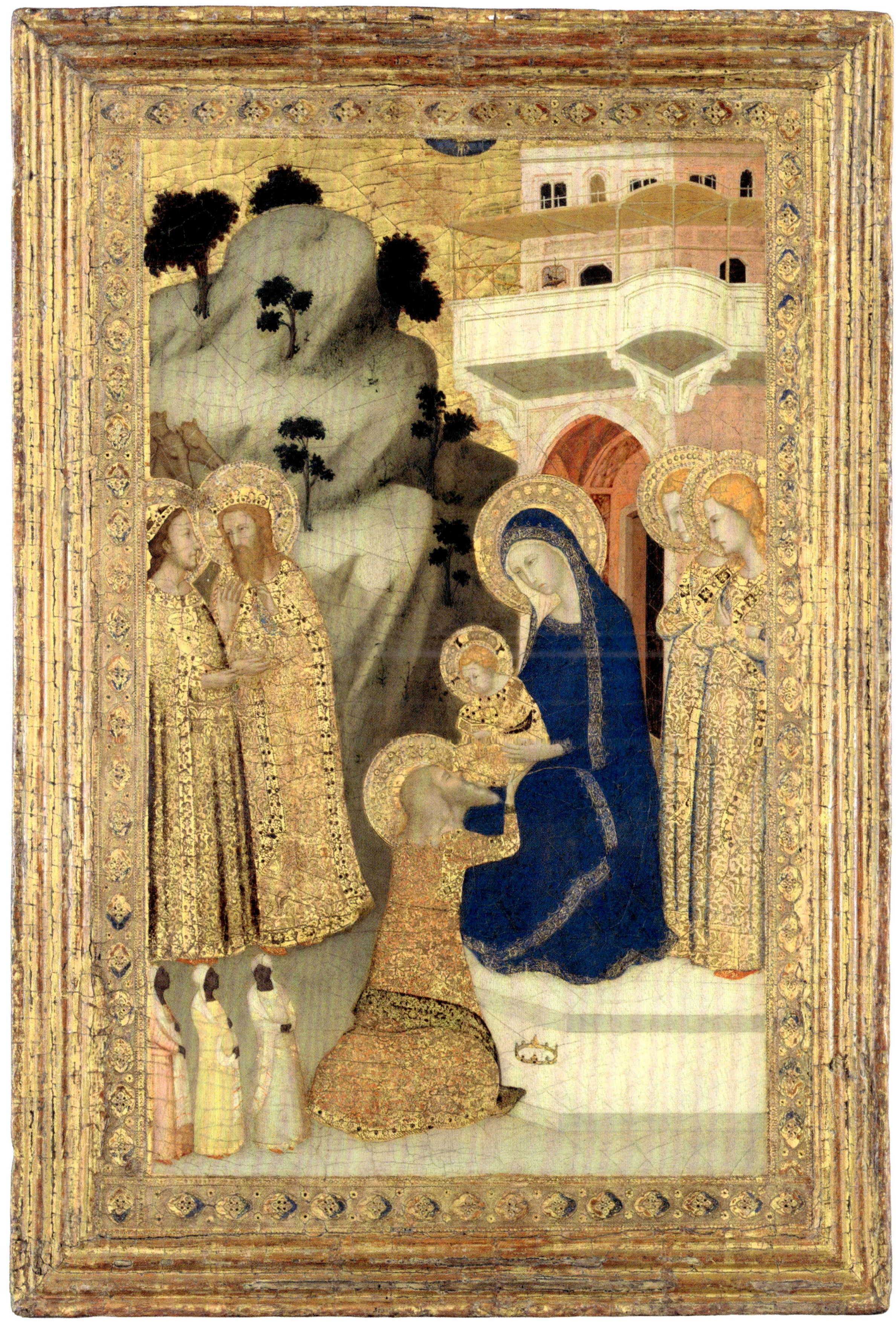

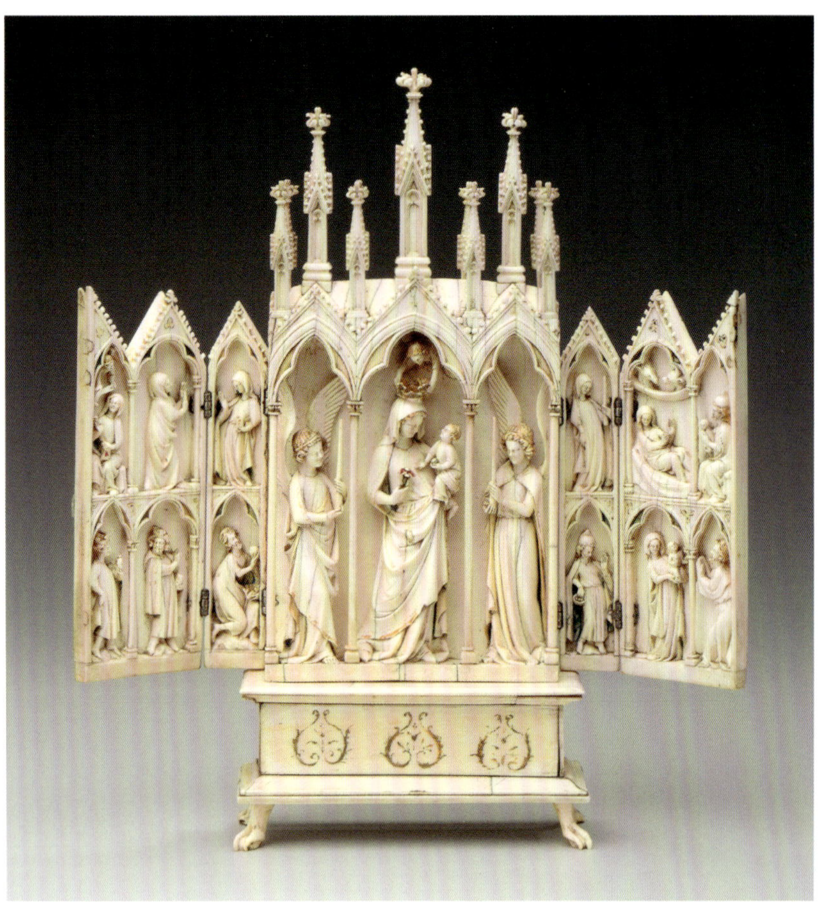

FIG. 144
Paris, France
Polyptych with the Virgin and Child and Scenes from the Infancy of Christ, 1280s
Ivory with traces of polychromy and gilding with metal hinges, 29.4 × 26.7 cm (open); 29.4 × 11.2 cm (closed)
Toledo Museum of Art, OH. Purchased with funds from the Libbey Endowment, Gift of Edward Drummond Libbey (1950.304)

queen, Sancia of Mallorca, to the Clarissan nuns of Aix-en-Provence whose house the queen founded in the late 1330s.[22] The refined painting technique, exquisite handling of punchwork, and use of *sgraffito* work and tooled gold to evoke figured silks (see pp. 207–9) point to a Sienese artist, but the ensemble has also been attributed to a painter working in Naples and Avignon, possibly a Neapolitan follower of Giotto. In either case, the decorative vocabulary is undoubtedly Sienese and the environment courtly. The intriguing inclusion in the Magi's train of three richly attired Africans may be a contemporary reference to the Nubian Christians known to tend shrines in the holy land, and shows, as in Ambrogio Lorenzetti's works, an engagement with a specific facet of the wider world.[23]

The five contributions in this section address different aspects of the interactions between the works of Sienese painters and the world beyond the city walls.[24] Lisa Monnas shows how a Sienese painter might encounter and seek to emulate figured silks. The surviving fragments of oriental and Iberian silks displayed in the exhibition this volume accompanies, some known to have been in central Italy by 1300, and the examples of Lucchese silks that imitated them, are precious traces of the luxury products imported from afar and remind us of the uses such fabrics were put to in enhancing the appeal and status of paintings created by Sienese artists.

The ivories discussed by Sarah M. Guérin made two long-distance journeys: the first, as elephant tusks, from the interior of south-east Africa, over land and sea to northern Europe; and the second, as worked material fashioned into desirable objects, from Paris to other parts of Europe, including central Italy, by a variety of means (fig. 144).[25] Guérin presents specific evidence for examples of their presence in Italy as one likely conduit for an awareness of Gothic forms among Sienese painters.

Dillian Gordon demonstrates that the recognisably Sienese manner of painting that reached Avignon through the movement of objects and, subsequently, artists stimulated a taste for the private ownership of such works among the royalty and aristocracy of central and northern Europe: Bohemia, Flanders, France, Burgundy and England. Susie Nash focuses on a single example of the work of a Sienese artist – Simone Martini's Orsini Polyptych – being studied closely by painters from a different environment, working in a different art form, some eighty years after the polyptych had been produced. The de Limbourg brothers were granted privileged access to the interior of a prized private possession, and reacted with great creativity. Through travel to Assisi, Nash argues, the de Limbourgs probably also had the opportunity to experience at large scale, and draw selectively on, a more public Sienese work: Pietro Lorenzetti's Passion Cycle.

The Orsini Polyptych was cherished as it moved from its original owner into the possession of the dukes of Burgundy, but at some unknown moment the panels, like so many other Sienese multi-panel works, both portable and fixed, were separated and dispersed. In her contribution Imogen Tedbury explores the story of such dispersals, and of the renewed appreciation, in the last two centuries, of Sienese painting of the fourteenth century among English-speaking artists, dealers, connoisseurs, collectors, curators and exhibition visitors. *JC*

1. The most popular route between Rome and northern Europe, also known as the via Romea. See Spufford 2002, pp. 181–7, 208–15. For an introduction to Siena, see Campbell, pp. 10–17, in the present volume. For an evocation of the tight-packed life of artists within the city, see Strehlke 2022–3, pp. 64–5, and, in more detail, Maginnis 2001, pp. 48–53. For the present-day experience of passing through the city gates, see Matar 2019, pp. 50–5.
2. Florence 2015; Spufford 2002, especially the 'road revolution' of the later thirteenth century, pp. 181–7.
3. Norman 1997, pp. 331–2. For the applicability of the term 'global' to the thirteenth and fourteenth centuries, see Walker 2012, with further bibliography.
4. Effects of space and light are discussed in detail in Seidel and Calamai 2022, pp. 306–21. For a Florentine merchant's connection to the painting, see Robson 2022, pp. 146–8.
5. Spufford 2002, especially pp. 112–13, 136. For land and sea routes to and from central Italy, see ibid., pp. 168–73; and, in summary, Spufford 2010. For Sienese merchants in the Levant, see Derbes 1989, pp. 195–7.
6. Wright 2022–3, pp. 41–4; Strehlke 2022–3, p. 64; Guérin 2019, especially pp. 182–4, all with further bibliography.
7. Spufford 2010, p. 12; Kirby, Nash and Cannon 2010, p. 259. For shipping of pigments to Italy in general, see DeLancey 2010.
8. DeLancey 2010, pp. 79–80, p. 81, fig. 4; Kirby, Nash and Cannon 2010, p. 453.
9. According to Cennino Cennini, writing around 1400. See Broecke 2015, p. 64.
10. Ibid., p. 86.
11. Hence 'burnt Sienna'. Ibid., pp. 70–1. During the thirteenth century, silver was mined near Siena. Spufford 2002, p. 356; Spufford 2010, p. 16.
12. Spufford 2010, pp. 13–14. For a valuable summary sketching out the changing relations between the Mongol Empire and the Latin West, and further bibliography, see Shea 2020, pp. 124–6, 129–31.
13. Liberati 2023.
14. Bandlien 2014, pp. 60–1.
15. Bartalini 2017–18. For Bartolomeo Abagliati, see Loenertz 1937, pp. 155–6.
16. For arguments for Almalyq, see Burke 2002, accepted, among others, by Norman 2018, pp. 202–6, 222, with further bibliography. Prazniak 2010, pp. 202–3, 209–10, proposes that the scene 'is and is not Almalyq'. See also Prazniak 2019, pp. 96–8. Ceuta and Almalyq are both rejected in Testa and Interguglielmi 2017–18, pp. 140, 150, n. 36. Shea 2020, pp. 122, 131–2, expresses uncertainty about what event is depicted and notes the mixture of Mongol and non-Mongol dress.
17. My thanks to Lisa Monnas for advice on this issue. For Mongol court dress, see Shea 2020. For the proposal that works of art, including Mongol manuscripts, were a source of information, see Prazniak 2010, pp. 204–8; Shea 2020, pp. 131–6. For the possibility that Ambrogio might have studied the physiognomy of 'Tartar' slaves in Tuscany, see Origo 1955, p. 325; Prazniak 2010, p. 206; Shea 2020, pp. 136–8.
18. Prazniak 2019, pp. 79–80, considers that several figures are not to be read as Mongols: 'Others in the group on the right have clothing styles, hats, and features that identify them as Mediterranean – altogether a very cosmopolitan setting, an artistic fusion of Lorenzetti's own political imaginary.' She suggests that the helmet with bulging segments, on the left, might be 'Persian or central Eurasian'. Shea 2020, pp. 122, 131, says that while some figures are convincingly Mongol, other figures wear 'elaborate armour – helmets and breastplates – evocative of some ambiguous past, perhaps Rome or Persia'.
19. Exercising what Guérin, p. 217, in the present volume, so aptly calls 'the voracious visual imagination of fourteenth-century artists'.
20. Schmidt 2005a, pp. 281–320. See also Gordon, pp. 224–39, in the present volume.
21. Works with as many as eight panels have been recorded. See Gordon, p. 226, in the present volume.
22. Dated to about 1340–3. Musée Granet, Aix-en-Provence, inv. 820.I.II and 820.I.II bis. See Thiébaut in Paris 2013, cats 27–9, pp. 200–7. See also Kozlowski 2022, pp. 26, 160–8; and Gordon, p. 226, in the present volume.
23. I thank Imogen Tedbury, who is preparing a detailed study of this ensemble, and the significance of the three Africans, for her advice.
24. The continuing interactions with Byzantium, touched on by Cannon, pp. 34–42, in the present volume, but not explored in this section, are demonstrated by the remarkable purchase of a collection of Byzantine relics and reliquaries by the hospital of Santa Maria della Scala, Siena, in 1359. See Gerevini 2022.
25. 'trade routes that carried elephant tusks 16,000 km over land and sea … from the interior of south-east Africa, through the Indian Ocean, via the Red Sea, into the Mediterranean and finally to northern Europe', Guérin 2010, *passim*; here pp. 156–8.

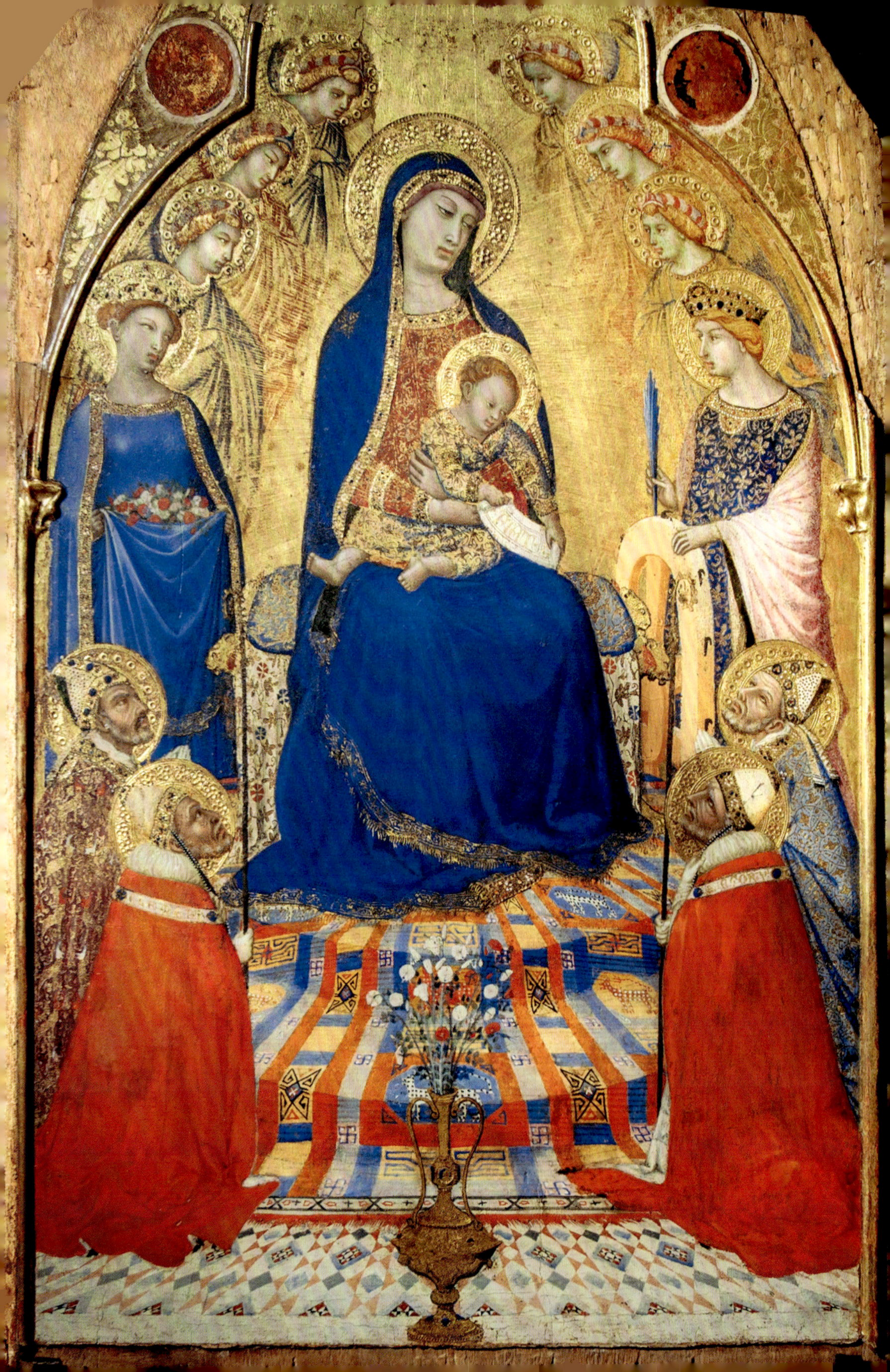

IMITATION AND IMAGINATION: FIGURED SILKS IN THE PAINTINGS OF DUCCIO, SIMONE MARTINI AND PIETRO AND AMBROGIO LORENZETTI

Lisa Monnas

In the *Piccola Maestà*, Ambrogio Lorenzetti depicted several of the holy figures wearing clothing made of silk interwoven with precious gold thread (fig. 145). In reality, the fabrics that inspired this vision were prohibitively expensive. In his lifetime, only the higher clergy, rulers and their wealthiest subjects wore cloth of gold, or even silk, an exclusivity that was enshrined in Sienese sumptuary laws.[1] Although artists did not wear such fabrics, or keep samples as props, there were plentiful opportunities to see them, particularly in church. Liturgical vestments were exempt from sumptuary legislation and the clergy celebrated Mass vested in silk at richly dressed altars, while on feast days churches were decorated with silk hangings in the choir. Most of this was purposely made, but pious offerings of secular garments were also converted into vestments, curtains or clothing for figures of the Virgin or Christ, as well as costumes for liturgical dramas.[2] The formal reception of foreign dignitaries into the city of Siena, the bridal processions of wealthy Sienese families or civic festivities accompanying major religious feasts were all occasions for display.[3] Painters were not just bystanders at these events: there are records of payment for their involvement in the preparations, including painting baldachins and banners for royal entries to Siena.[4]

Siena did not have its own silk-weaving industry, but goods taxed by the *comune* in 1332 included linen, wool, furs, 'Saracen' carpets, cloth of gold and silks.[5] During the thirteenth century, silks were obtained from nearby Lucca, and linen and wool from the fairs of Champagne and from elsewhere in France.[6] Later in the century, Sienese merchants operated in Tabriz, in Greater Iran.[7] Oriental and Levantine textiles, which mainly reached the Italian peninsula via Genoa and Venice, came to Siena through the port of Pisa.[8] In 1338 a shipment of silk fabrics, cloths of gold and accessories was purchased by Benuccio Salimbeni from a Syrian merchant in Porto Ercole for 130,000 florins, an astonishing sum that far exceeded the annual taxation revenue for the *comune* of Siena.[9] The cargo was first viewed at the Salimbeni house in Siena, then 20 brokers acting for the Salimbeni set up warehouses and sales outlets on the via

FIG. 145
Ambrogio Lorenzetti
(documented 1319; died 1348/9)
Piccola Maestà, about 1342–4
Tempera on panel, 50.4 × 33.9 cm
Pinacoteca nazionale di Siena, musei nazionali di Siena (65)

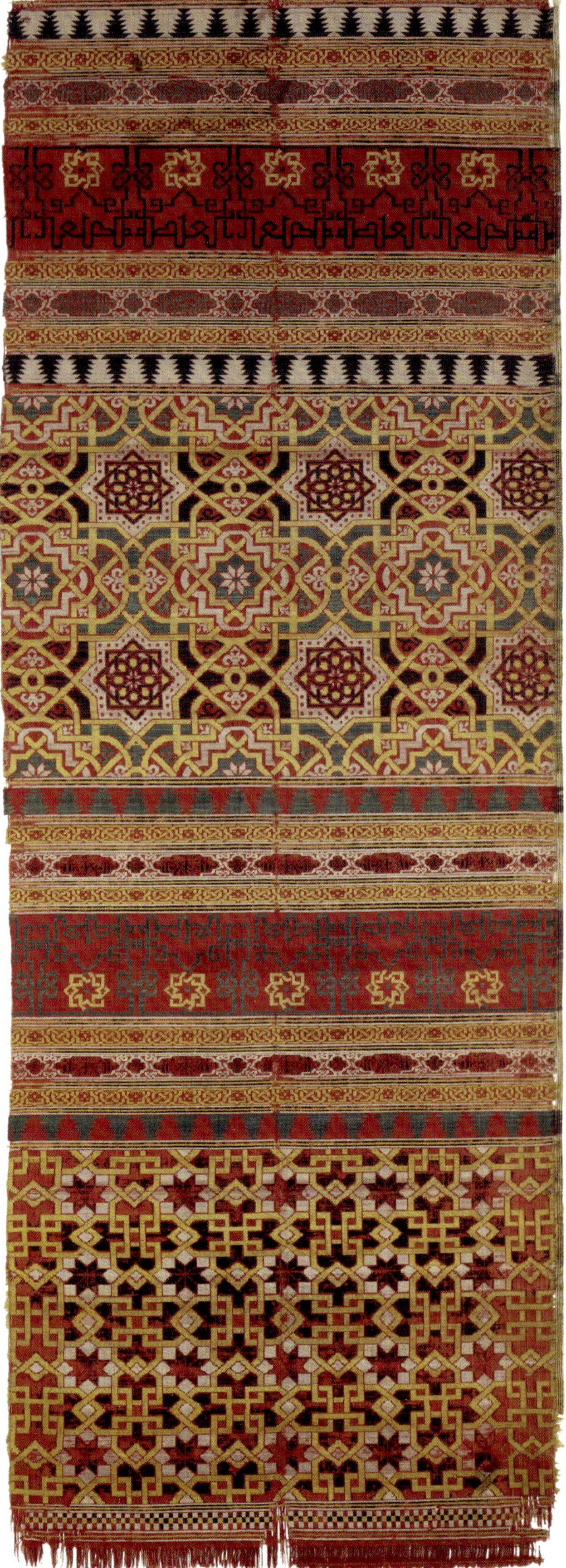

FIG. 146
Nasrid workshop, Iberia
Textile fragment with a geometric design, featuring naskhi and kufic inscriptions, fourteenth century
Silk; twill-tabby lampas weave, 102 × 36.3 cm
The Metropolitan Museum of Art, New York. Fletcher Fund, 1929 (29.22)

Rinaldini. Such was the demand for these luxuries that they almost sold out within a year.[10]

Like other trecento painters, Sienese artists would have worked from drawings and model books, but they also responded directly to the world about them, including details of contemporary dress and furnishings in their paintings. In this respect, their work has been compared to the *dolce stil nuovo* ('new sweet style') in the poetry of Dante and Guido Cavalcanti.[11] Their approach was also consistent with contemporary religious texts, such as the *Golden Legend* and the *Meditations on the Life of Christ*, that encouraged the devout to imagine in vivid detail the lives of the holy family and saints.[12] In depicting textiles, this entailed the gradual abandonment by painters of chrysography – gold lines on garments, which, in Byzantine art, signified a divine spiritual radiance – and the adoption of new styles of figured silks, with attention given to conveying their weight and texture.[13] The representation of textiles in paintings was a creative, selective process that incorporated realistic effects into carefully chosen or invented designs.

GEOMETRIC TEXTILES IN MONUMENTAL PANEL PAINTINGS AND FRESCOES

In the thirteenth century, the rise of the mendicant orders led to the erection of churches with large naves to accommodate congregations attracted by the preaching friars, in which monumental painted crucifixes and images of the Virgin provided focuses of worship. In these images, the Virgin's blue and red clothing retained its traditional, Byzantine appearance, while furnishings were less constrained by convention. Colourful geometric interlace designs, possibly imitating silks from al-Andalus (Iberia),

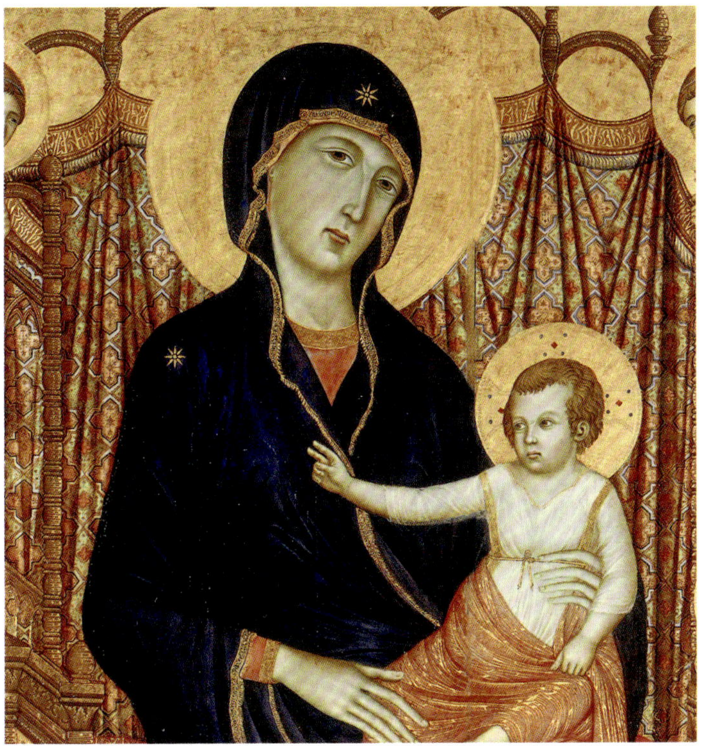

FIG. 147
Detail of the Virgin and Child in Duccio's *Rucellai Madonna* (fig. 6)

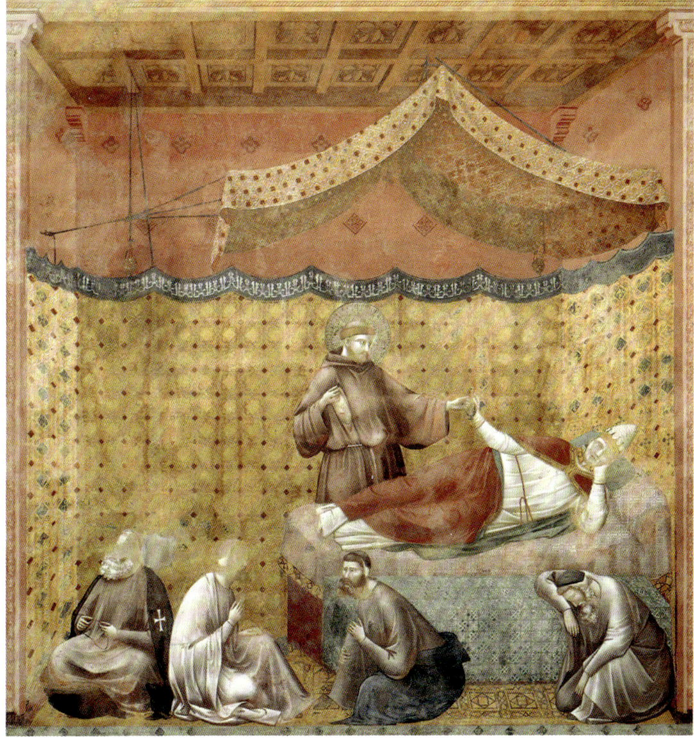

FIG. 148
Giotto (about 1267/76–1337)
Dream of Pope Gregory IX, about 1290–6
Fresco
Upper Church, Basilica of San Francesco, Assisi

were introduced as throne coverings (fig. 146).[14] Similar designs decorated the crucifixes' lateral panels, giving the impression of silks hanging behind the Cross.[15] These may have been inspired by real textiles suspended behind smaller crucifixes displayed upon altars.[16]

Duccio's *Rucellai Madonna* (fig. 147, see fig. 6), formerly in Santa Maria Novella, Florence, has a fictive silk throne-hanging 'woven' with interlocking stars and crosses.[17] A monumental crucifix subsequently painted by Giotto for the same church, about 1312, has a complementary design on its lateral panels.[18] 'Star and cross' designs were popular throughout the Islamic world, found in tile as well as textile decoration.[19] With potential allusions to the Star of Bethlehem and to the Crucifixion, they were also adopted by Christian artists.[20] Geometric designs persisted on large Tuscan crucifixes for decades, despite a burgeoning taste for wearing silks with plant and animal designs.[21] This may suggest a formulaic approach, but perhaps abstract designs, particularly with cruciform motifs, were actively considered more appropriate for the Crucifixion.

In the nave of the Upper Church of the Basilica of San Francesco at Assisi, illusionistic hangings with geometric interlace designs painted on the lower part of the walls resonate with similar fabrics represented in the narrative frescoes above.[22] In the narrative scenes, the textile designs are exploited for their space-defining properties. In the *Approval of the Rule*, the *Dream of Pope Gregory IX* (fig. 148) and the *Dream of Pope Innocent III*, the rooms have bedcovers, canopies and wall hangings whose foreshortened geometric patterns define the pictorial space and whose coordinated designs and repeated epigraphic headings unify the picture plane.[23] This sophisticated orchestration of space and surface pattern through textiles was quite new in Italian painting. Its obvious impact can be seen in Simone Martini's *Dream of Saint Martin* (about 1313–17) at Assisi and, more subtly expressed, in Duccio's and Simone's *Maestàs*.[24]

FIG. 149
Nasrid workshop, Iberia
Textile fragment with a geometric interlace design, featuring a mirrored kufic inscription (from the tomb of Don Felipe, Infante of Castile and Leon [died 1274]), 1250–75
Silk, with pattern wefts of silk and of wrapped gold thread; weft-faced compound tabby (taqueté) weave, 21 × 13 cm
The Metropolitan Museum of Art, New York. Fletcher Fund, 1946 (46.156.8)

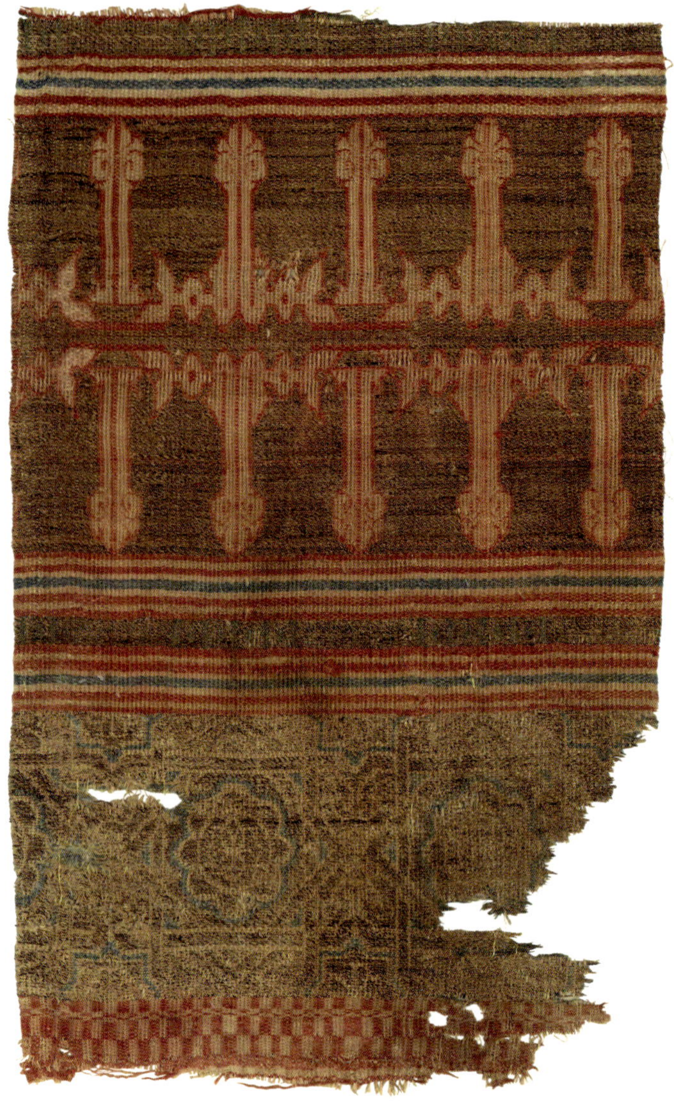

TEXTILES WITH ARABIC OR PSEUDO-ARABIC SCRIPT

Textiles with Arabic inscriptions are generally called 'tiraz' (from the Persian *tarazidan*, 'to embroider'), a term that came to be applied to textiles woven with inscriptions, to the inscribed bands themselves and, by extension, to the workshops in which such fabrics were produced. The custom of adding auspicious inscriptions to textiles originated in Sassanian Persia, and was adopted by Muslim caliphs, spreading throughout the Islamic world (fig. 149).[25] With felicitous phrases often glorifying the giver, tiraz fabrics became a staple component of robes of honour.[26] It has been argued that not all of the Arabic inscriptions in trecento paintings should be prefaced 'pseudo', since some consist of debased but legible Arabic script, often repeating *al-mulk*, truncated from *al-mulk* [*li-lah*]: 'the power belongs to God'.[27] In the *Rucellai Madonna* the silk draping the Virgin's throne has a separate, fringed heading of gold epigraphy (fig. 6).[28] Bands of glittering gold script adorn her cushion, the angels' tunics and the sparkling border of her blue *maphorion* (the long mantle covering the Virgin's head).[29] The mantle's border, with its fluttering fringe, is depicted with infinite care and precision, drawing the spectator's gaze up the tall panel to the faces of the holy figures.[30] It remains uncertain whether Duccio and his contemporaries, even when copying decipherable letters, understood their precise meanings.[31] Although they were imitating a style of writing unknown in Christ's lifetime, the lettering was probably intended to evoke the land of his birth, as well as representing something exotic and precious.[32]

A VISION OF HEAVEN: THE *MAESTÀ* IN SIENA

Doubly revered in Siena as Queen of Heaven and protector of the city, the Virgin enthroned in majesty became an important subject in Sienese art. Duccio's small triptych with a central Crucifixion in the Royal Collection (see fig. 17) presents contrasting images of the enthroned Virgin. In the left wing she holds the infant Christ on her lap, and in the opposite wing she is enthroned as Queen of Heaven beside Christ (fig. 150). The textiles are harmoniously disposed. In the wings, the lavish chrysography on Mary's *maphorion* and the adult Christ's clothing links them to Mary and John in the Crucifixion. In the right wing, the Virgin is presented as a contemporary queen, crowned, with a short white veil and a

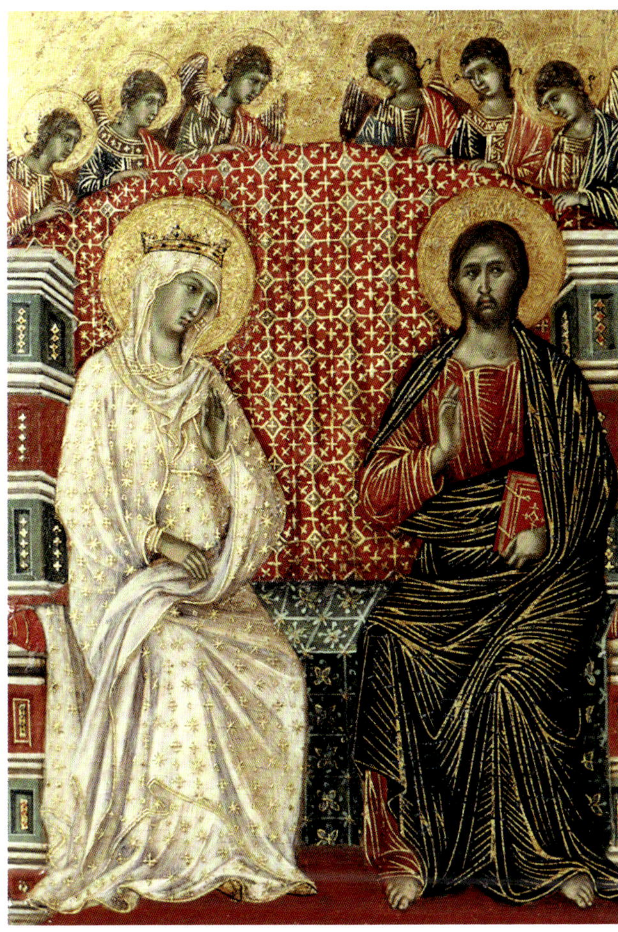

FIG. 150
Detail of the Virgin and Christ enthroned in Duccio's *Triptych with the Crucifixion and Other Scenes* (fig. 17)

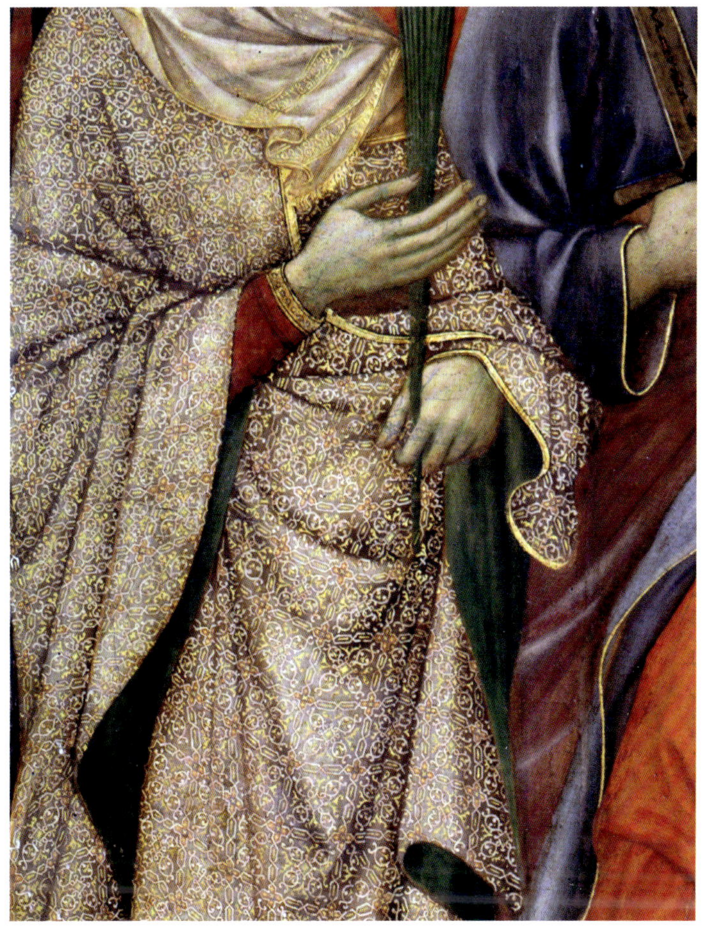

FIG. 151
Detail of Saint Catherine in Duccio's *Maestà* (fig. 8)

white silk dress and mantle 'embroidered' with gold stars and crosses.[33] This is picked up in gold crosses covering the Virgin's two thrones, linking them thematically with the Crucifixion.

In Duccio's altarpiece of the *Maestà* (see fig. 8), painted for Siena Cathedral in 1308–11, in the main scene of the Virgin enthroned, discreet details of chrysography are visible on her clothing.[34] 'Real' figured cloths of gold with intricate geometric designs cover her throne, and are worn by saints Catherine, Agnes and Sabinus. Their shimmering silks create a point and counterpoint across the picture, reminiscent of the interplay of pattern at Assisi, and in the triptych discussed above.[35] The treatment of drapery in the *Maestà* is, however, more sophisticated than anything previously seen in Duccio's work.[36] Instead of painting dark shading over a flat pattern, as in the *Rucellai Madonna*, the patterns in the *Maestà* are carefully distorted and discontinued to suggest draped fabric (fig. 151). The *Maestà* is such an astonishing work that it is easy to overlook Duccio's achievement in representing 'folded' patterns with precision. Duccio may have seen the skilfully foreshortened pattern on Saint Nicholas's chasuble in Giotto's Badia Polyptych (about 1300; Gallerie degli Uffizi, Florence), which, it has been suggested, may have been drawn from life.[37] Duccio's figured draperies in the *Maestà* look even more convincing. Comparison of the throne-hanging in the *Maestà* with an Iberian silk in Berlin suggests that Duccio probably based his design upon a real textile, and observed the distortions that occur in drapery folds.[38] His designs are too intricate to have been sketched from a passing

FIG. 152
Detail of the Virgin and Child enthroned in Simone Martini's *Maestà* (fig. 65)

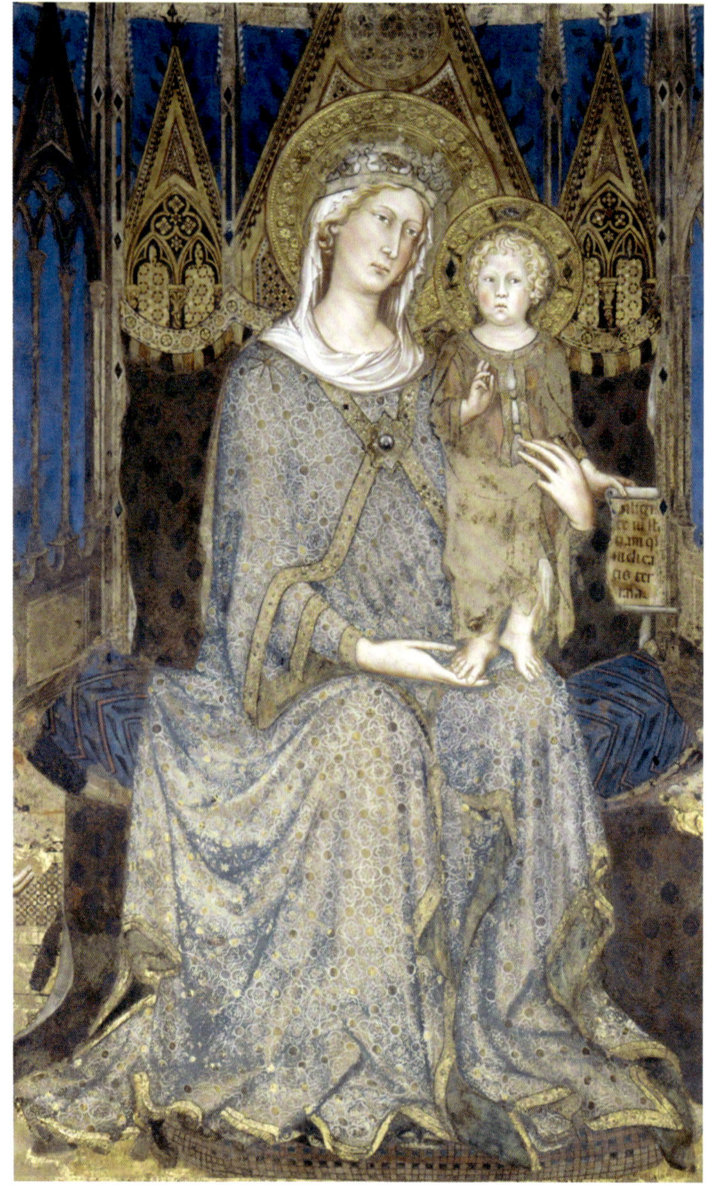

procession or glimpsed during Mass. It seems possible that, while fulfilling this commission, Duccio could have been given the opportunity by the cathedral authorities to study their vestments. This does not mean that he habitually worked from life. Duccio's recycled textile designs from the *Maestà* in the fragmentary *Coronation of the Virgin* (about 1310–15; Museum of Fine Arts, Budapest) point to the existence of pattern drawings.[39]

In 1312–15 Simone Martini reinterpreted the theme of Duccio's *Maestà* in his fresco in the Sala del Consiglio in the Palazzo Pubblico (see fig. 65). The scene unfolds beneath an enormous processional canopy, as if the Virgin had just arrived to preside over the great council chamber.[40] The canopy's space-defining properties are enhanced by the foreshortened geometric interlace pattern of its lining. In this imposing, secular setting, the Virgin's authority is underlined by her regal appearance (fig. 152). She is crowned, with a softly draped white veil, and clothed in Iberian cloth of gold whose geometric pattern, though slightly simpler than Duccio's designs in his *Maestà*, is equally carefully articulated.[41] The Virgin's layered, matching outfit of cloth of gold represents contemporary formal royal dress.[42] The pinnacled Gothic throne is similarly dressed in correct courtly fashion, not only with silk covering its back, but also with seat- and foot-cushions.[43]

'TARTAR SILKS' AND SIMONE MARTINI

In the thirteenth and fourteenth centuries, silks from Mongol territories, collectively called *panni tartarici* ('tartar cloths'), reached Italy.[44] Following the death of Genghis Khan in 1227, safe passage was established overland across Greater Iran and Central Asia to China itself, as vividly described by the Florentine merchant Francesco Balducci Pegolotti.[45] Contact with the Mongols was established not only by merchants and Christian missionaries, but also through diplomatic exchanges with the rulers of Western Europe, including the Pope.[46] In 1300 an embassy of 100 men bearing gifts was sent to Rome for Pope Boniface VIII's jubilee by the Ilkhanid ruler of Iran, Ghazan. This must have been a splendid sight, as must the subsequent Ilkhanid embassies in 1302, 1303 and 1304.[47]

The arrival in Italy of exotic *panni tartarici* introduced new weaves, including satin and velvet, and heralded a profound change in textile design.[48] Previously, designs with roundels enclosing paired birds or animals, or purely

FIG. 153
Central Asia or Greater Iran
Textile fragment with small flowers and leaves (from the cope of Pope Benedict XI), late thirteenth–early fourteenth century
Silk, with pattern weft of flat gold thread; tabby-tabby lampas weave, 12.1 × 18.2 cm
The Metropolitan Museum of Art, New York. Rogers Fund, 1919 (19.191.3)

FIG. 154
Central Asia
Textile fragment, faded red silk with large palmette design, late thirteenth–mid-fourteenth century
Silk, with pattern weft of wrapped gold thread; weft-patterned tabby weave, 85.5 × 35 cm
The Cleveland Museum of Art, John L. Severance Fund (1993.253)

geometric forms, had predominated. Many of the new designs were asymmetrical and others were crowded with tiny motifs (fig. 153).[49] They included swooping birds, leaping animals, meandering plant forms, and palmettes (fig. 154).[50] *Panni tartarici* were received with enthusiasm in the West. They have been found in church treasuries and elite tombs throughout Europe, notably, in Italy, that of Cangrande della Scala, ruler of Verona, who died in 1329.[51] Numerous examples are listed in the papal inventory of Boniface VIII (1295) and further examples (doubtless gifts from Mongol embassies) in that of Clement V (1311).[52] During the fourteenth century, the Basilica of San Francesco at Assisi acquired many tartar silk vestments, including several given or bequeathed by Simone's patrons, the Neapolitan Angevin family and Cardinal Gentile Partino da Montefiore dell'Aso, who died in 1312.[53] The success of *panni tartarici* had important consequences for the silk industry in Italy, where the weavers of Lucca and Venice responded by producing their own versions.[54]

Sienese artists were among the first to represent 'tartar-style' silks. An early example can be seen on Saint Augustine's cope in Duccio's polyptych no. 28 (about 1305; Pinacoteca nazionale di Siena), with swirling leaf-tendrils and small flowers.[55] This design was not replicated elsewhere.[56] A different style of tartar silk, with tiny plant motifs, was more widely adopted by Sienese artists. Simone depicted examples

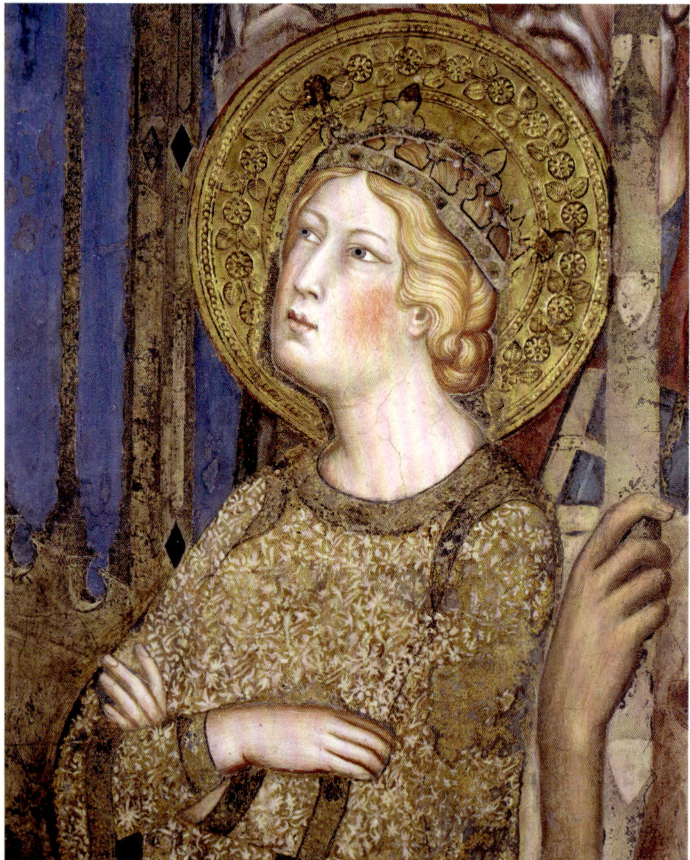

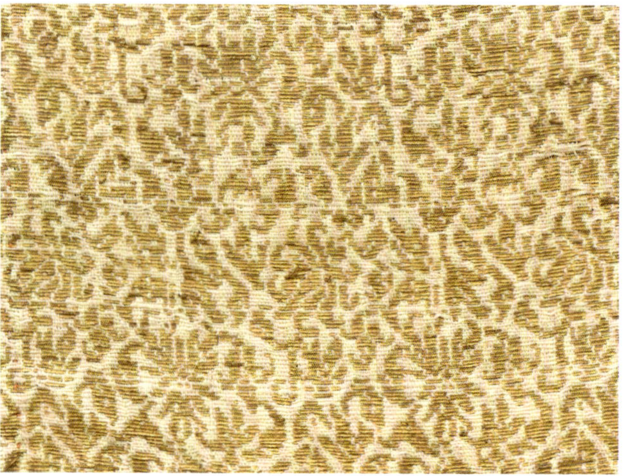

FIG. 155
Detail of Saint Catherine in Simone Martini's *Maestà* (fig. 65)

FIG. 156
Central Asia or Greater Iran
Textile with small flowers and leaves, late thirteenth or early fourteenth century (detail of the dalmatic of Pope Benedict XI)
Silk, with flat gold pattern weft; weft-patterned tabby weave, pattern repeat: 9.9 × 4.4 cm
Museo Beato Benedetto XI, Perugia

in his *Maestà*, worn by Saint Catherine and Saint Ursula (?) (fig. 155). Kneeling on either side of the Virgin's throne, they wear coordinated designs, recalling the 'point and counterpoint' of Duccio's *Maestà* and the frescoes at Assisi. Saint Catherine's textile resembles a specific tartar silk with small gold flowers and leaves on a dalmatic reputedly of Pope Benedict XI (reigned 1303–4) (fig. 156).[57] It is so similar that Simone may have seen this vestment or another example of this textile.[58] There are some adjustments. The pattern, which on the dalmatic measures just 9.9 × 4.4 cm, has been inflated in scale, doubtless for legibility. Whereas in comparable fabrics the pattern is normally gold, Saint Catherine's pattern is white on gold. This reversal was probably dictated by the demands of executing an intricate design on the large surface area of this frescoed figure, since it would have been easier and quicker to paint in white over gold.

In the Saint Louis of Toulouse Altarpiece, Simone depicted royal figures who could have owned the costly tartar silks with rich, heraldic embroidery in which they were portrayed (fig. 157, see fig. 67). Robert of Anjou, King of Naples, is shown kneeling before his enthroned, newly canonised brother, Louis, Bishop of Toulouse.[59] Louis confers the crown of Naples upon his younger brother, while receiving the heavenly crown (of sainthood) himself. The silk of Robert's dalmatic has meandering leaves in light greenish-blue, with gold palmettes on a darker ground.[60] It was perhaps similar to a green tartar silk with gold 'pine-cones' that he gave to the Basilica of San Francesco at Assisi.[61] It is also comparable to an extant silk, on a mitre in the Museo Diocesano Albani, Urbino (fig. 158).[62] A 1334 inventory of King Robert's treasury confirms that he owned coronation vestments of tartar silk with bejewelled embroidery, reminiscent of (but not identical to) the outfit painted by Simone.[63] Saint Louis, who is mitred and carrying a gold crosier, wears a cope of magnificent crimson velvet with a design of gold octagonal discs over a Franciscan habit (other matching vestments are shown in the predella). The velvet is comparable to a group of velvets attributed to late thirteenth- or early fourteenth-century Tabriz (fig. 159).[64] A red velvet with gold discs was listed in 1295 among the

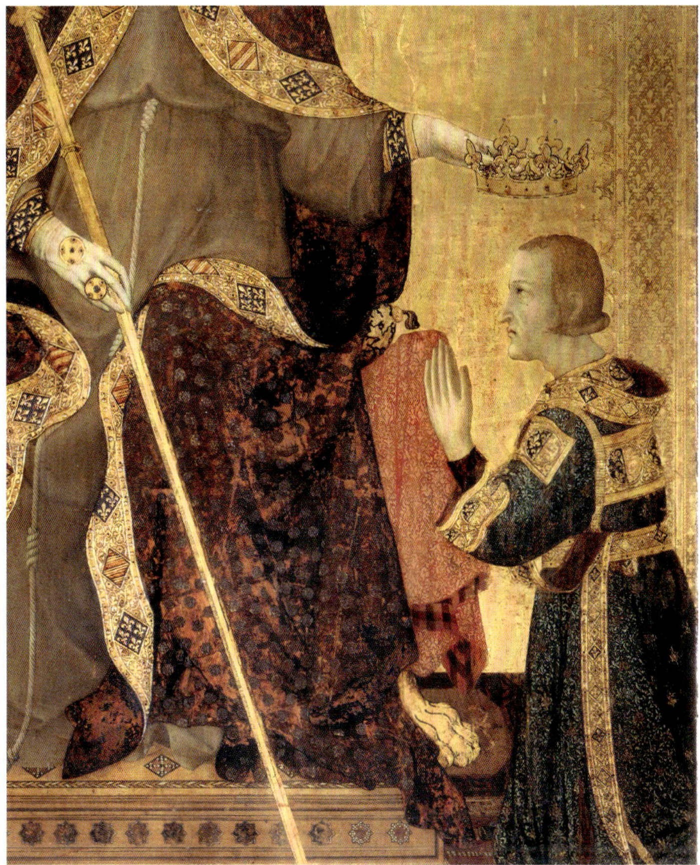

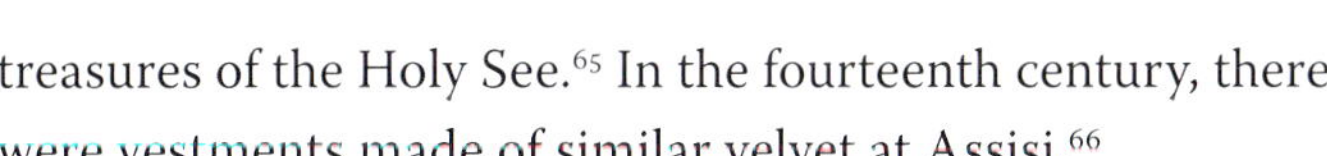

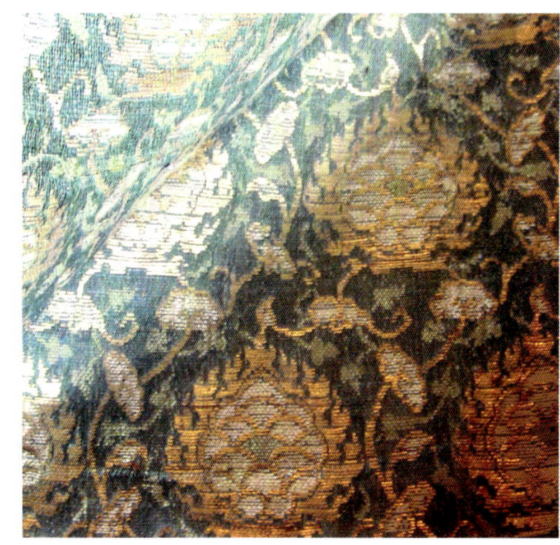

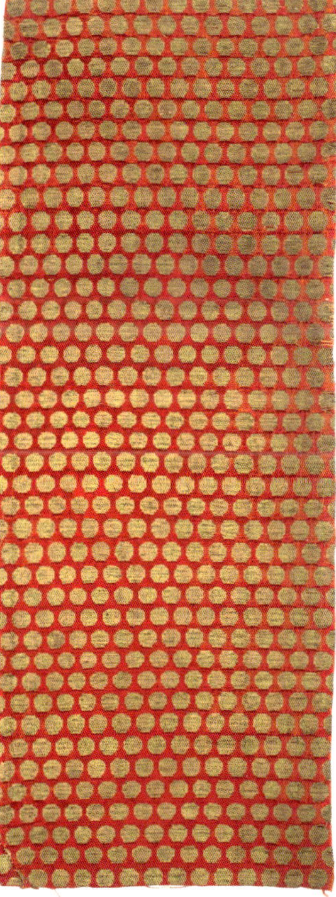

FIG. 157
Detail of the crowning of King Robert in Simone Martini's *Saint Louis of Toulouse Altarpiece* (fig. 67)

FIG. 158
Central Asia or Greater Iran
Textile with flaming jewel clusters amid fungi and leaves (detail of the lining of a mitre associated with Oddone Colonna), first quarter of the fourteenth century
Silk, with silk and flat gold pattern wefts; lampas weave, pattern repeat: about 13 × about 7.5 cm
Museo Diocesano Albani, Urbino

FIG. 159
Greater Iran, probably Tabriz
Textile fragment, crimson velvet with gold octagonal discs, late thirteenth or early fourteenth century
Silk, with pattern weft of wrapped gold thread; velvet, 58.4 × 22.9 cm
The Metropolitan Museum of Art, New York. Fletcher Fund, 1946 (46.156.72)

treasures of the Holy See.[65] In the fourteenth century, there were vestments made of similar velvet at Assisi.[66]

Velvet cloth of gold was the rarest, most expensive fabric available at the time. Simone employed a complex technique of raised, gilded and textured gesso (*pastiglia*) for the discs, with crimson glazes over silver leaf for the pile.[67] He also used *pastiglia* to suggest pearls and couched gold thread in the 'embroidered' heraldic decoration of the garments and of King Robert's stole.[68] In the predella, Saint Louis is shown receiving a cope directly over his habit.[69] At his consecration in 1296, Louis reportedly wore a habit beneath his vestments.[70] On that occasion, however, before receiving the cope he would have been solemnly dressed in vestments worn for celebrating Mass, a tunicle, dalmatic and chasuble, placed one on top of the other, obscuring the habit (see fig. 89, left). Simone's portrayal of the saint in just a cope and habit became a blueprint for representing Saint Louis of Toulouse, but in later examples the cope often has a conventional heraldic design of gold Angevin lilies, unlike Simone's depiction of a specific velvet.[71]

In the predella of the Saint Louis of Toulouse Altarpiece, Simone depicted the saint's velvet vestments by painstakingly outlining the disc design in a red glaze over gold leaf, reserving tiny gold dots.[72] Subsequently, for more challenging 'tartar-style' plant designs he exploited the technique of *sgraffito* and the use of stencils.[73] In *sgraffito*, a layer of gold or silver leaf was first laid, then covered with a layer of paint.

FIG. 160
Detail of Simone Martini and Lippo Memmi's *Annunciation* (fig. 39)

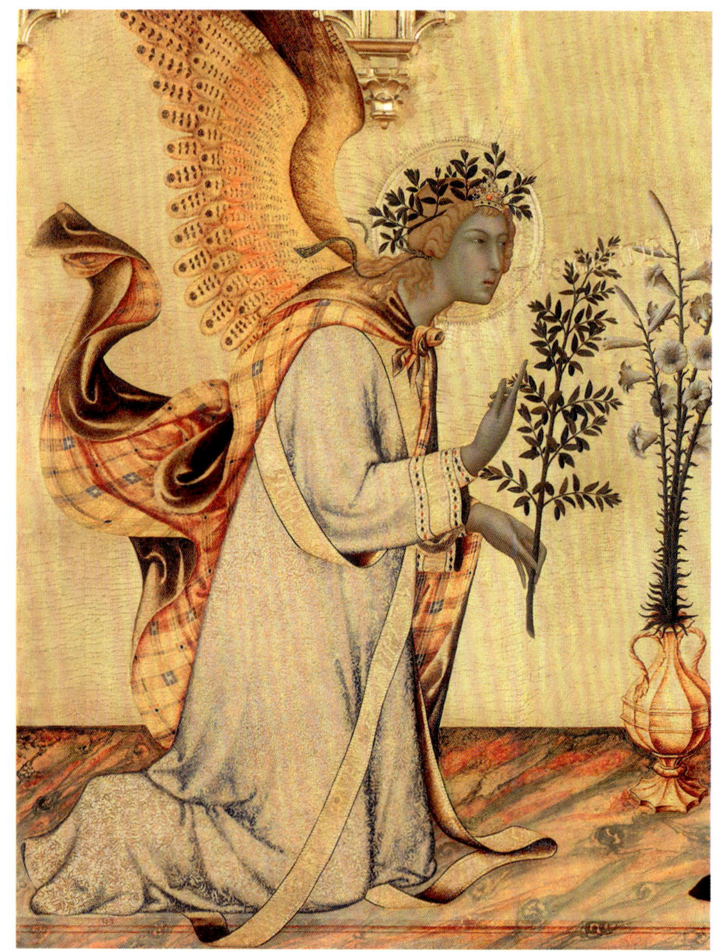

A design was drawn onto the surface, then the designated areas of paint were scraped away to create a gold (or silver) pattern. When the exposed metal surface is smooth it can be described as 'untooled' (as opposed to 'tooled', which indicates a surface textured with a pointed stylus or an ornamental punch or 'rosette'). Simple, untooled *sgraffito*, often executed over silver, already existed in thirteenth-century Tuscan painting.[74] In the Orsini Polyptych (about 1320–30), Simone employed *sgraffito* more elaborately to depict an intricate 'tartar-style' plant design on the red cloth of gold covering the Annunciate Virgin's throne, leaving the smooth, exposed gold to form the pattern (see fig. 81).[75]

In that polyptych, Archangel Gabriel wears a traditional tunic and a fluttering, rectangular mantle (or pallium) adorned with chrysography, ultimately derived from Byzantine imagery.[76] In a new departure, in the *Annunciation* signed by Simone Martini and Lippo Memmi in 1333, Gabriel wears a version of a contemporary priestly dalmatic and stole, although still paired with a pallium (fig. 160).[77] The dalmatic's cuff bears Gabriel's name, and the stole, legible to the celebrant at the altar, carries texts from Saint Luke, referring to the interconnected themes of the Annunciation and Incarnation of Christ.[78] The foreshortened pattern of the Archangel's chequered mantle, swirling beneath its soaring wings, is key to the illusion that it has just alighted: an immediacy underscored by letters spelling its message moulded in gilded gesso seemingly emanating from its lips, and by the Virgin's fearful response.[79] The dalmatic is made of up-to-date 'tartar' cloth of gold in white, and a red version of the same textile covers the Virgin's throne.[80] In 1333 viewers would have recognised that Gabriel was wearing a desirable 'tartar' fabric. Even the mantle's lining would have seemed familiar, since chequered silk linings were expressly permitted in a Sienese law of 1330.[81] Unlike those simple silks, the mantle's lining is painted as a cloth of gold. Instead of chrysography on clothing, rays of divine light incised in the gold ground radiate from the figures' haloes. The substitution of 'real' cloths of gold for chrysography in the *Annunciation* was a logical extension of Duccio and Simone's previous treatment of the Virgin's and saints' clothing in their *Maestàs*.

Unlike Saint Catherine's textile in Simone's *Maestà*, with a design crowded with small motifs (fig. 155), the dalmatic and throne covering in the *Annunciation* have larger, repeating palmettes, possibly plotted with a stencil. In a new refinement, the exposed gold was tooled to replicate the texture of gold thread, with folds painted over the pattern.[82] The result, which is slightly three-dimensional, conveys the texture and weight of heavy material. Gabriel's mantle was depicted in two related but contrasting techniques. There are effects of translucent glazes over gold previously textured

FIG. 161
Central Asia or Greater Iran
Textile fragment with small leaves,
late thirteenth–mid-fourteenth century
Silk, with pattern weft of flat gold thread;
weft-patterned tabby weave, 14.5 × 15.5 cm
The Cleveland Museum of Art,
Dudley P. Allen Fund (1985.33)

with a rosette for the heavier face of the mantle, and glazes over untooled gold with some incised details for its lighter, smooth lining. The juxtaposition of elaborate effects on Gabriel's clothing may have been inspired by goldsmiths' work, including translucent enamelling, for which Siena was renowned (see p. 174).

The laborious, expensive technique of tooled *sgraffito* was employed sparingly by Simone's contemporaries, but it became widely disseminated in the second half of the fourteenth century. In some ways, this represented a backward step, because *sgraffito* patterns, especially when stencils were involved, were necessarily unforeshortened and overpainted with folds, just as they had been in the *Rucellai Madonna*. Instead of creating increasingly realistic folded draperies with foreshortened patterns, painters explored a different aesthetic, experimenting with textures created with styluses or rosettes, and exploiting the contrasting refractive qualities of tooled and untooled gold. Simone's work at Assisi (a destination of international pilgrimage), at the Angevin court in Naples and at the papal court in Avignon extended knowledge of his art well beyond the Italian peninsula. Whether through direct exposure or through intermediary works, during the second half of the fourteenth century tooled *sgraffito* spread to northern Europe. An exceptionally refined example can be seen in the Wilton Diptych (see pp. 233–6).[83]

AMBROGIO AND PIETRO LORENZETTI: SELECTION AND INVENTION

Ambrogio Lorenzetti was an artist of great subtlety and ingenuity, and the impression made upon him by Simone and Lippo's 1333 *Annunciation* is evident in the *Piccola Maestà* (fig. 145) in the use of tooled *sgraffito* for cloth of gold, and his sophisticated treatment of the divine radiance emanating from the Virgin and Child.[84] Ambrogio looked carefully at textiles, sometimes extrapolating motifs from larger designs and creating his own variations. A particular leaf that he favoured recurs in so many surviving silks that it is hard to pinpoint a particular source (figs 163, 165, 166). Like Simone, both Ambrogio and his brother Pietro depicted small-patterned tartar silks, but they opted for simpler versions, often just repeating a single abstract shape (see fig. 42).[85] This was not an unthinking simplification because real textiles like this existed (fig. 161).[86] The Lorenzettian 'small patterns' enjoyed wider currency than Simone's more intricate designs, and continued to appear in fifteenth-century Sienese paintings long after the real textiles had ceased to be fashionable.[87] They never enjoyed comparable popularity with Florentine artists.

Camacas silks with scrolling grapevine designs, of the 1320s onwards, were among the first Italian silks to incorporate Mongol design principles in a Western idiom (fig. 163).[88] Woven in Lucca and possibly also in Florence, they appear in Sienese and Florentine paintings.[89] Lucchese camacas were figured silks, sometimes brocaded with small areas of gold thread.[90] Their popularity among Florentine women is attested in a list of prohibited clothing of 1343–5, which records many camacas garments with grapevines.[91] Through their association with the Eucharist, grapevine silks

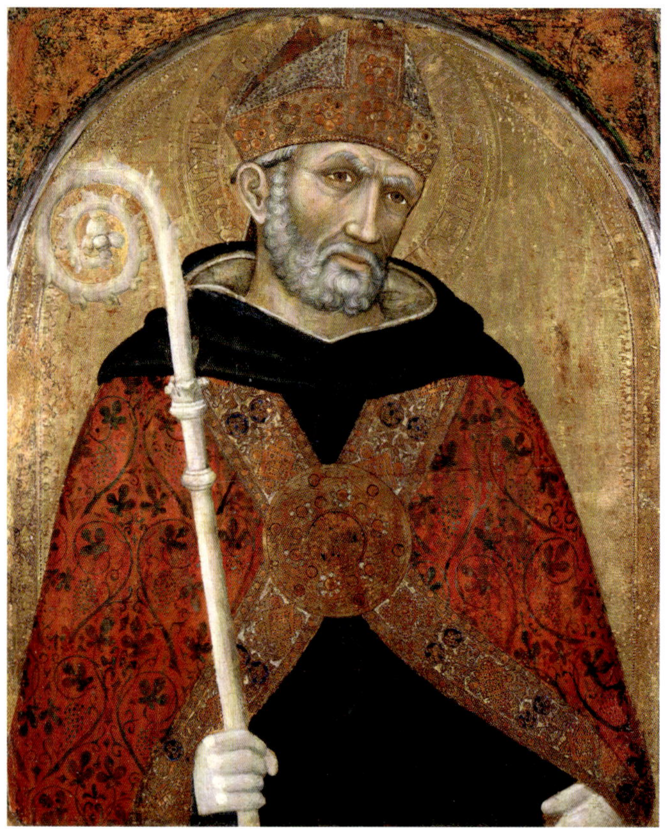

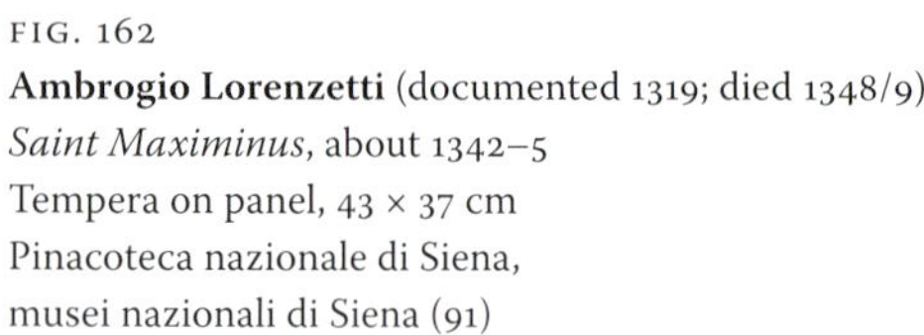

FIG. 162
Ambrogio Lorenzetti (documented 1319; died 1348/9)
Saint Maximinus, about 1342–5
Tempera on panel, 43 × 37 cm
Pinacoteca nazionale di Siena,
musei nazionali di Siena (91)

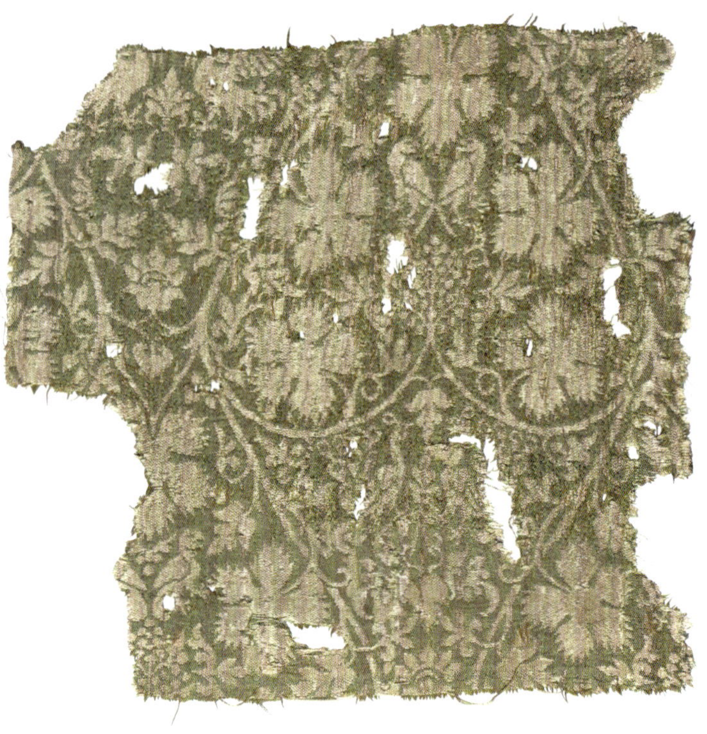

FIG. 163
Lucca, Italy
Textile fragment with grapevines and birds,
second quarter of the fourteenth century
Silk; tabby-tabby lampas weave, 24.1 × 25.4 cm
The Cleveland Museum of Art, Florence and Charles
Abel Oriental Rug Collection by exchange (1971.75)

were also ideal for liturgical vestments. A good example can be seen in Ambrogio Lorenzetti's depiction of Saint Maximinus of Aix, the first-century Bishop of Provence (fig. 162).[92] The colouring of the saint's cope recalls a red example with green vines recorded in Siena Cathedral in 1389, and the design resembles existing silks.[93] Maximinus's cope was not drawn from life. Copes are semicircular vestments, normally constructed from complete loom widths, aligned vertically so that the pattern is seen the right way up on the back, falling over the shoulders at an oblique angle on the front.[94] Here, Ambrogio's chief concern seems to have been the legible depiction of a recognisable, meaningful design.

The *Piccola Maestà* has an unusually rich concentration of patterned textiles (figs 145, 164). The composition is beautifully orchestrated. 'Real' flowers in the vase, or held by Saint Dorothy (?) or in the angels' garlands, resonate with flowers 'woven' into the Virgin's throne covering, while the animals on Saint Nicholas's cope are echoed in the carpet. None of the designs can be traced to a specific source.[95] The animals on the cope faintly recall the quadrupeds on Italian diasper silks, figured silks that were normally monochrome or two-colour, with details brocaded in gold.[96] Ambrogio has represented something more precious, similar to a fragment of silk in The Metropolitan Museum of Art that has a predominantly gold design with (originally) red details (fig. 165).[97] The Virgin's red dress, with gold stripes and butterflies, is reminiscent of an extant group of Italian lampas silks that mimic cloths of gold from Central Asia, with multicoloured stripes containing exotic beasts and birds.[98] The Italian imitations feature animals drawn from Western iconography, and exist both in cloth of gold and all-silk versions, as seen in fig. 166.[99] Ambrogio's 'cloth of gold'

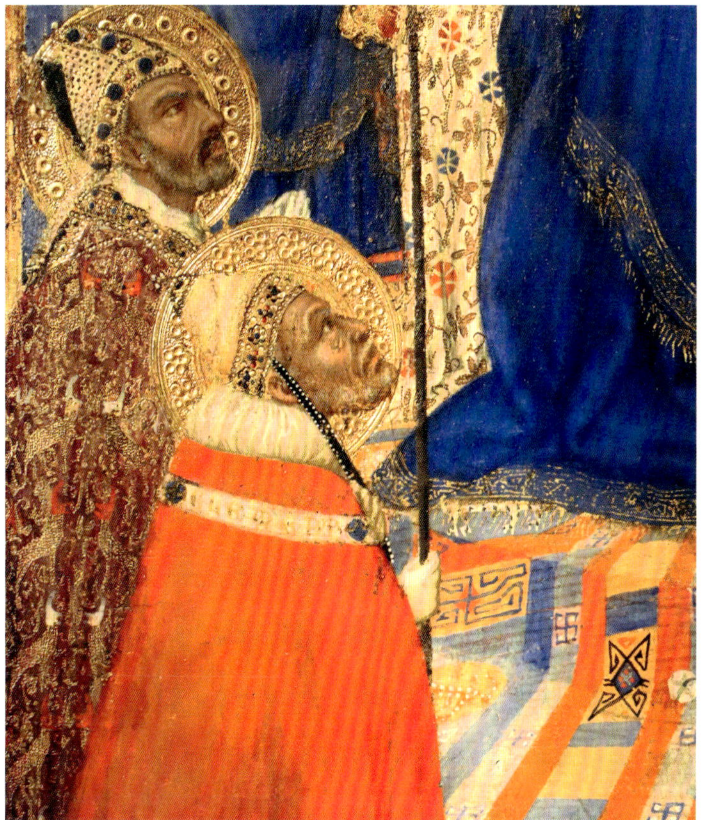

FIG. 164
Detail of Saint Nicholas and Pope Clement I in Ambrogio Lorenzetti's *Piccola Maestà* (fig. 145)

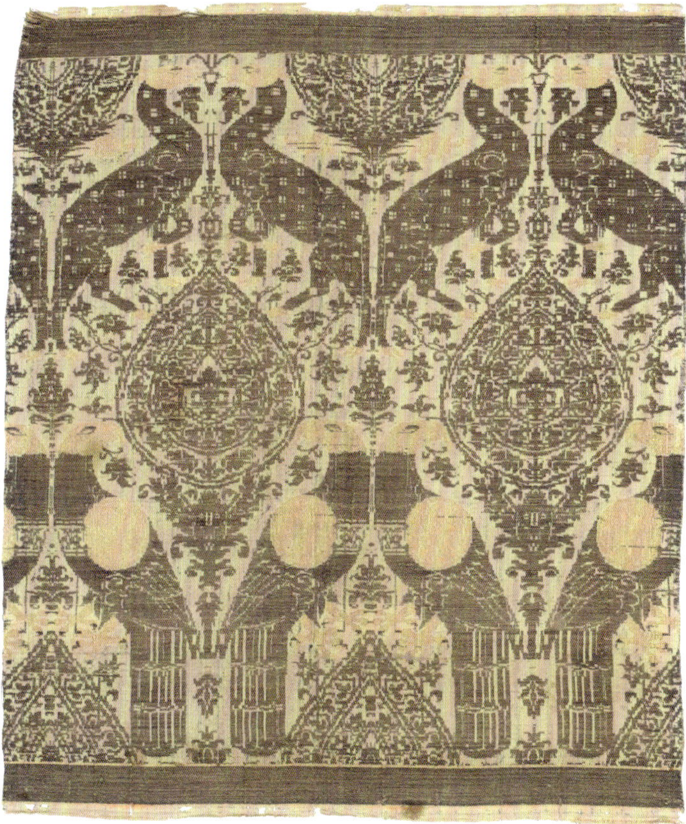

FIG. 165
Lucca, Italy
Textile fragment with quadrupeds and birds,
late thirteenth–early fourteenth century
Silk, with brocading weft of silk and pattern weft of wrapped gold thread; tabby-tabby lampas weave, 47.2 × 40.7 cm
The Metropolitan Museum of Art, New York. Rogers Fund, 1931 (31.69)

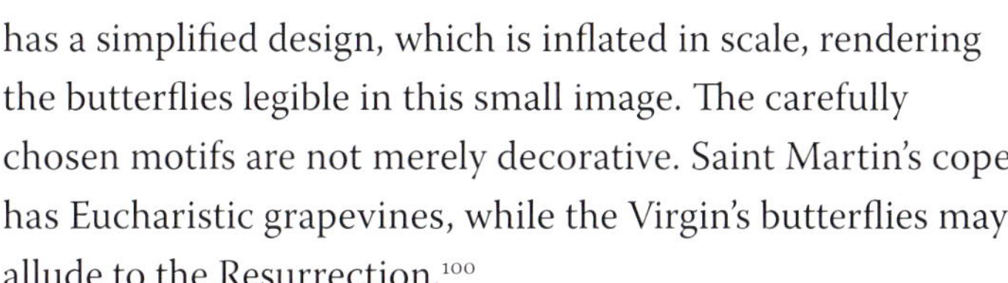

has a simplified design, which is inflated in scale, rendering the butterflies legible in this small image. The carefully chosen motifs are not merely decorative. Saint Martin's cope has Eucharistic grapevines, while the Virgin's butterflies may allude to the Resurrection.[100]

It is striking that in the second half of the fourteenth century Florentine artists, notably the Cione brothers and their circle, often depicted silks displaying plants and animals, whereas Sienese artists favoured more abstract ornament. In 1322–5 making or wearing clothing decorated with animal and plant designs actually became the target of sumptuary legislation in Florence, whereby men, women and children of any station were forbidden such clothing without exemption.[101] In practice, Florentines subsequently paid standard fines in order to continue to wear their finery, as detailed in the *Prammatica sulle vesti delle donne* (1343–5).[102]

In 1330 a Sienese law (reiterated in 1343) forbade wearing any clothing (including headgear) painted, stitched, drawn, woven or applied with 'trees, fruit, flowers, fronds [or] animals or [fantastical] animals.'[103] Unlike the comprehensive Florentine prohibition, in Siena prostitutes (*meretrici*) and entertainers (*giocolieri*) were expressly exempted and allowed to wear such decoration.[104] The Sienese law has previously been discussed in connection with the dancers in Ambrogio Lorenzetti's *Good and Bad Government* (see fig. 1), whose flamboyantly decorated clothing seems to align perfectly with the statutes, but could it also have affected the choice of textiles in religious paintings? Perhaps a lingering stigma stemming from the legislation influenced the continuing preference for abstract textile designs in Sienese religious art, exemplified in the work of Niccolò di Buonaccorso (fig. 167).[105]

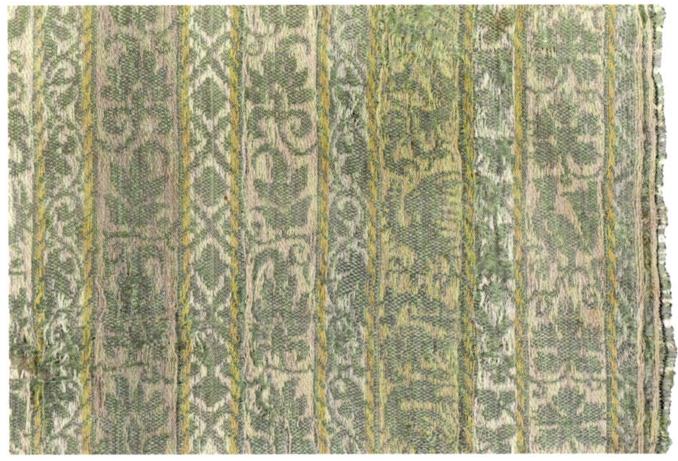

FIG. 166
Lucca, Italy
Textile fragment with stripes containing small leaves, animals and birds (from the shroud of Saint Florent), second quarter of the fourteenth century
Silk; twill-tabby lampas weave, 29.5 × 25.6 cm
Musée Cluny, Paris (Cl. 3363)

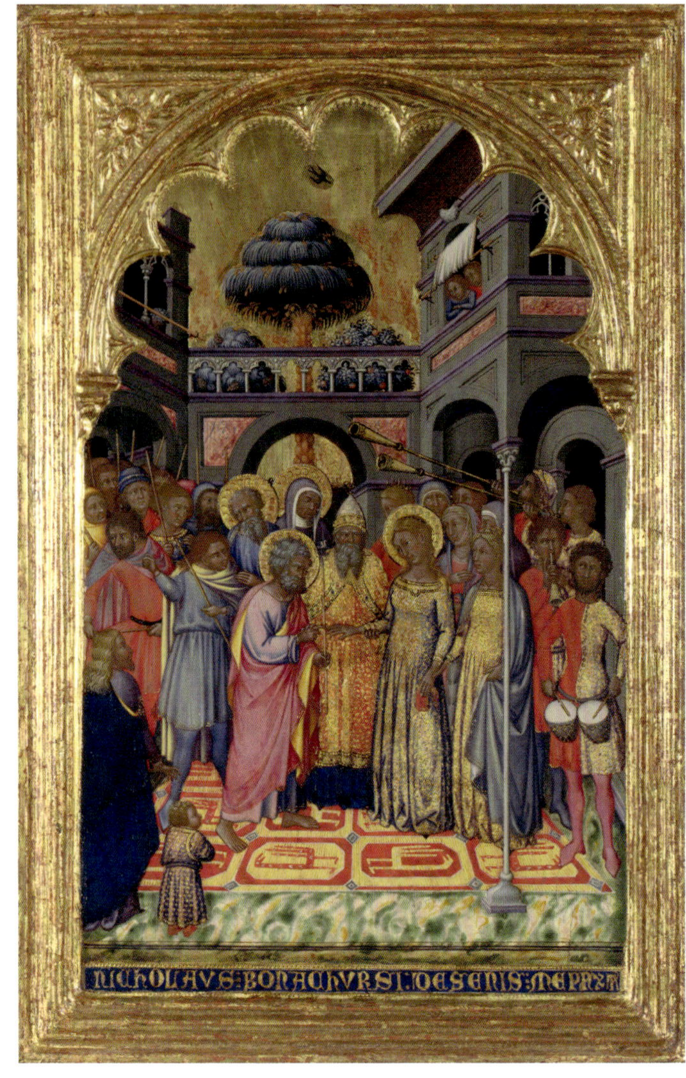

FIG. 167
Niccolò di Buonaccorso (documented 1372; died 1388)
The Marriage of the Virgin, about 1380
Tempera on poplar, 50.9 × 33 cm
The National Gallery, London. Bought, 1881 (NG1109)

CARPETS IN SIENESE PAINTINGS

In the later Middle Ages, carpets were used indoors and outdoors as ceremonial furnishings. In processions marking liturgical feasts or royal entries, canopies were held over the principals, with carpets sometimes laid underfoot.[106] Like throne coverings, expensive carpets were integral to royal interiors and, by extension, to the iconography of royalty. In the Saint Louis of Toulouse Altarpiece (see fig. 67), the saint's throne rests upon an impressive carpet featuring birds of prey. Simone has painstakingly painted rows of tufts, suggesting knotted pile, and its subdued colouring is replicated in later, surviving Anatolian carpets. It seems possible that this, like other textiles in this painting, was based on a real example, perhaps one owned by King Robert.[107] Carpets depicted beneath the Virgin's throne honoured her by emulating those placed beneath royal thrones.[108]

In the *Piccola Maestà* (fig. 145), the Virgin is enthroned upon a carpet with spotted animals and abstract ornament, whose bold stripes position the viewer centrally, drawing the eye towards the enthroned figures. In a Sienese context, the carpet seems rather elaborate. Sienese artists generally favoured simpler designs featuring large birds and animals, as seen in Niccolò di Buonaccorso's *Marriage of the Virgin* (fig. 167).[109] Marco Spallanzani has observed that carpets with similar zoomorphic decoration continued to be represented in Sienese paintings for 150 years.[110] He partly attributes their longevity to the existence of a local production of modestly priced, possibly flat-woven carpets.[111] A few inventories record the ownership of costly imported knotted-pile carpets in Siena.[112] In 1423 Gregorio di Cecco di Luca depicted an example with animal motifs in his *Marriage of the Virgin* (fig. 168).[113] A rare fourteenth-century Anatolian carpet in The Metropolitan Museum of Art, New York, exemplifies the type of carpet that inspired him (fig. 169).[114]

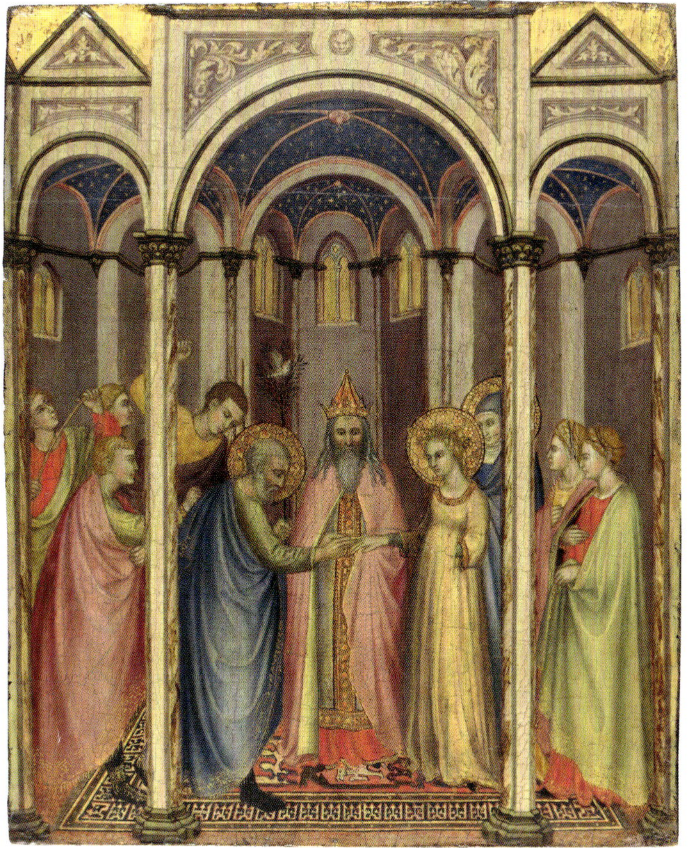

FIG. 168
Gregorio di Cecco di Luca (documented 1389; died 1428?)
The Marriage of the Virgin, about 1423
Tempera on panel, 41 × 33.2 cm
The National Gallery, London. Bought, 1890 (NG1317)

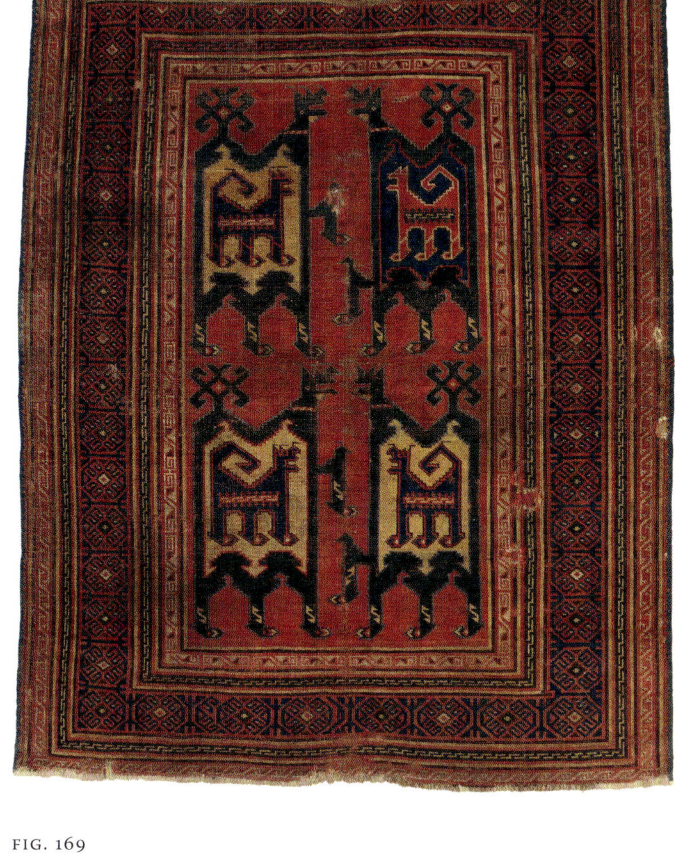

FIG. 169
Turkey (attributed)
Rug with confronted animals, fourteenth century
Wool (warp, weft and pile); symmetrically knotted pile, 165.1 × 138.4 cm
The Metropolitan Museum of Art, New York. Purchase, Harris Brisbane Dick Fund, Joseph Pulitzer Bequest, Louis V. Bell Fund and Fletcher, Pfeiffer and Rogers Funds, 1990 (1990.61)

***

In the first half of the fourteenth century, the close attention that Sienese artists paid to the material world placed them at the forefront of artistic innovation. Their work reveals a new concern for showing different textures and realistically draped, figured textiles. This was combined with an awareness of international courtly culture, expressed in specific details of clothing and furnishings. It is futile, however, to try to impose a straightforward pattern of development on the representation of figured textiles, because this was a process of individual creativity. Artists exhibited a flexible approach in the use of chrysography, and sometimes favoured legibility over verisimilitude. Not all painters' aesthetic decisions were simple matters of personal inclination: the choice and treatment of textile designs was affected by iconographic and practical considerations, and by patrons' individual tastes. There were other, external factors. The adoption of stencils was, for example, encouraged by the advent of 'tartar-style' designs, while the range of designs in Sienese religious art may have been inhibited by local attitudes manifested in Sienese sumptuary provisions. Simone Martini's pioneering development of tooled *sgraffito* influenced depictions of cloth of gold in Siena and beyond for generations. After 1350, the widespread adoption of this technique, fuelled by the popularity of complex figurative textile designs, temporarily sidelined the early achievements of Duccio, Giotto and Simone in painting drapery with elaborate, foreshortened, geometric patterns, which remained unsurpassed until the next century.

1. Lisini 1930, p. 57; Ceppari Ridolfi and Turrini 1993, pp. 146–7, 150–1, 178–9.
2. For example, in Pisa Cathedral (1367), Barsotti 1959, pp. 62–3, 64, 66–7; at Padua, Jacobus 2019, *passim*.
3. Outdoor festivities: Campbell 2001, p. 243.
4. Maginnis 2001, p. 66.
5. Ceppari Ridolfi and Turrini 1993, pp. 212–19.
6. Tangheroni 1987, p. 27; Bonito Fanelli 1994, p. 50.
7. Ashtor 1983, pp. 58–9; Prazniak 2010, pp. 179, 184.
8. Prazniak 2010, p. 178.
9. In Siena, in 1338, one gold florin = 62s. 11d. to 63s. 6d., Spufford 1986, p. 53; tax revenue in 1338, £267,889 14s. (about 85,000 florins), Bowsky 1970, p. 298.
10. Tura del Grasso 1933, p. 521; Jacoby 2016, pp. 111, 119.
11. Belting 1994, p. 371.
12. For the *Golden Legend*, see De Voragine 2012, *passim*; for *Meditations on the Life of Christ*, see Ragusa and Green 1961, *passim*; see Thode 1885, *passim*; Derbes 1996, pp. 16–24.
13. Folda 2015, *passim*.
14. The band of kufic inscription reads 'Felicity'; the naskhi inscriptions within the cartouches read 'Good luck and prosperity'. Partearrogo in Granada and New York 1992, cat. 97, p. 335.
15. For patterned lateral panels ('aprons') on crucifixes, see Derbes 1996, p. 5.
16. In 1385–8 a 'dorsor' was ordered for the crucifix in King Richard II's chapel, TNA E101/401/16, mem. 4; on 'crucifix' textiles and altar frontals, see Cooper 2006, pp. 53–4.
17. For the *Rucellai Madonna*, see Klesse 1967, p. 39; p. 53, fig. 34; no. 23, p. 176; for Duccio's design and fictive textiles on the wall of Saint Gregory's chapel, see Stubblebine 1973, p. 19; Hills 1987, p. 100; Bellosi 2002, p. 156.
18. Ciatti 2002, pp. 49–50.
19. New York and Los Angeles 2002–3, p. 174, fig. 204.
20. For the Westminster Retable (about 1269–72), see Michael 2009; for the English embroidered Vatican cope (about 1280–1300), see Browne and Zöschg in London 2016, cat. 23, pp. 146–50.
21. Klesse 1967, no. 19a, p. 174; no. 37, p. 185; no. 70, p. 206; no. 79, pp. 209–10; nos 84–6, pp. 209–10; nos 93–4, pp. 215–16; no. 95a, p. 216.
22. Ibid., p. 44; no. 50, p. 190; Cooper and Robson 2013, text p. 86; pp. 140–1, figs 126–7; p. 149, fig. 134; p. 167, fig. 148; p. 212, fig. 185.
23. Klesse 1967, text pp. 29, 35, 45; p. 29, figs 6, 7; p. 45, fig. 22; nos 16, 17, p. 173; no. 83, p. 208.
24. For the *Dream of Saint Martin*, see Leone de Castris 2003, p. 117.
25. The mirrored kufic inscription repeats 'Felicity'. Baker 1995, pp. 53–62; Mack 2002, pp. 54–5; Snyder 2014.
26. Mack 2002, pp. 51–71.
27. Napolitano 2016, p. 338, and *passim*.
28. For Mongol and Arabic script in the *Rucellai Madonna*, see Prazniak 2010, pp. 190–1; for doubts about Mongol script in Italian paintings, see Shea 2020, p. 128.
29. The Byzantine *maphorion* was a protective mantle, worn outdoors, see Monnas 2024 (forthcoming b).
30. Stubblebine 1979, vol. 1, p. 19.
31. Fontana 2002, *passim*.
32. Mack 2002, pp. 56; Folda 2015, p. 219; Snyder 2014, pp. 8, 12.
33. For Cimabue's *Coronation of the Virgin* at Assisi as a precedent for Duccio's Virgin and Christ enthroned in the triptych, see Cannon and Pemberton-Pigott 2002, p. 11; for the Virgin's veil and Duccio, see Hills 2018, pp. 82–4; Monnas 2024 (forthcoming b).
34. Folda 2015, pp. 236–44.
35. Klesse 1967, no. 27, p. 178; nos 388, 389, p. 403; Monnas 2008, p. 69; Frattaroli 2009–10, pp. 37–8.
36. Hills 1987, pp. 97, 100.
37. Scarpelli 2012, p. 123; p. 125, fig. 20.
38. Klesse 1967, text pp. 34, 35, figs 25, 26; no. 21, p. 175; for the Iberian lampas silk, see Wilckens 1992, no. 118, pp. 67–8; see also Hills 1987, pp. 100–1, fig. 57; Hoeniger 1995, pp. 155–6.
39. Klesse 1967, pp. 183–4, figs 181–3; nos 27, 27a, p. 178; nos 388, 388a, p. 403.
40. On canopies for royal entries, see Maginnis 2001, pp. 65–6; Norman 2006, *passim*; Monnas 2008, p. 258.
41. Klesse 1967, no. 54, p. 193; Monnas 2019, p. 109.
42. On 'suits' for Philippa of Hainault, see Newton 1981, pp. 342–4.
43. Monnas 2001, pp. 15–16; Monnas 2008, pp. 31–2.
44. Jacoby 2016, *passim*.
45. Balducci Pegolotti 1936, pp. 21–3.
46. Shea 2020, pp. 122–6.
47. Verona 1983, p. 234.
48. Del Punta and Rosati 2017, pp. 22–33.
49. See Cleveland and New York 1997–8, cat. 46, pp. 160–1.
50. Ibid., cat. 37, pp. 146–7.
51. Verona 1983, *passim*; Verona 2004–5, *passim*; Rosati 2020, *passim*.
52. Wardwell 1988–9, pp. 134–44.
53. For gifts by Robert of Anjou, see Norman 2018, p. 165; for Cardinal Gentile's vestments, see Kleinschmidt 1928, nos 174, 188, p. 34; for redating the '1338' Assisi inventory, see Cenci 1985, *passim*; for Simone and Cardinal Gentile, see Frattaroli 2009–10, pp. 39–41.
54. Monnas 2010, *passim*.
55. Klesse 1967, text p. 103; p. 106, fig. 130; no. 382, p. 399.
56. 'Variants' in Klesse 1967, no. 382 a) and b), p. 400, do not resemble Duccio's design.
57. Verona 1983, pp. 164–9; Monnas 2008, p. 73; Rosati 2016.
58. Frattaroli 2009–10, pp. 39–41.
59. On the Saint Louis of Toulouse Altarpiece, see Gardner 1976, *passim*; Hoeniger 1991, pp. 159–60; Monnas 1993b, *passim*; Monnas 2008, pp. 63, 232–3; Norman 2018, pp. 133–47.
60. Klesse 1967, p. 131; no. 134, p. 243.
61. Kleinschmidt 1928, no. 130, p. 5.
62. The mitre is reputedly of Oddone Colonna (Bishop of Urbino 1380–1408; Pope Martin V, 1417–31), but the tartar silk is earlier, see Rosati 2016, pp. 181–2.
63. Barone 1886, p. 579; Klesse 1967, no. 134, p. 56; Monnas 2008, p. 234; Monnas 2019, pp. 101–2.
64. Wardwell 1988–9, p. 111; Monnas 1993b, p. 170; Sonday 1999–2000, *passim*; Monnas 2019, p. 100, fig. 2; Florence 2017, pp. 246–7.
65. Wardwell 1988–9, no. 51, p. 139.
66. Kleinschmidt 1928, no. 204, p. 34; the inventory does not connect these vestments with the Neapolitan Angevins.
67. See Naples 1960, pp. 32–8; Hoeniger 1991, pp. 159–60.
68. Monnas 1993b, p. 173, n. 24.
69. Norman 2018, p. 14.
70. Toynbee 1929, p. 113; Monnas 1993b, p. 169.
71. For example, Lippo Memmi, *Saint Louis of Toulouse*, about 1330, Pinacoteca nazionale di Siena (inv. 48), see Torriti 1980, p. 89.
72. Monnas 1993b, p. 170; Leone de Castris 2003, pp. 147–9.
73. On Archangel Gabriel's dalmatic, see Verona 1983, pp. 27, 188–9; Verona 2004–5, p. 151; Frattaroli 2009–10, p. 38, fig. 9; Hoeniger 1991, pp. 158–9; Monnas 2008, p. 73.
74. Muller 1988, p. 147; Hoeniger 1991, p. 156.
75. With many thanks to Gwen Borms for her technical advice; on the Orsini Polyptych's date, see Schmidt 2005a, pp. 256–9, especially p. 257.
76. Folda 2015, p. 298, and *passim*.
77. See Hoeniger 1991, pp.156–8; Hills 1987, p. 113.
78. On the lettering on the cuff and texts on the stole (Luke 1:30 and Luke 1:35), see Martindale 1988, p. 188.
79. Discussed in ibid., p. 42; on the text, 'AVE MARIA GRATIA PLENA DOMINVS TECVM' (Luke 1:28), see ibid., p. 188.
80. Klesse catalogues the designs of Gabriel's dalmatic and the Virgin's throne covering as identical, see Klesse 1967, no. 136, p. 244.
81. Lisini 1930, no. VII, p. 57; on chequered linings in Florence 1343–5, see Gérard-Marchant 2013, no. 6, p. 4; no. 817, p. 200; no. 1305, p. 203; no. 1320, p. 205 etc.; discussed in Orsi Landini 2019, pp. 70–1; on other chequered linings by Simone, see Monnas 1993b, pp. 171–2.
82. On tooled *sgraffito*, see London 1989–90, pp. 130–5, pls 116–18; on Gabriel's dalmatic, see Hoeniger 1991, pp. 156–7.
83. Plesters and Roy 1986, p. 29.

84. Hills 1987, p. 113; Seidel and Calamai 2017–18b, especially pp. 44–5.
85. Klesse 1967, no. 149, pp. 256–7; no. 151, pp. 258–9; no. 152, pp. 260–1.
86. Cleveland and New York 1997–8, cat. 38, p. 148.
87. For example, Giovanni di Paolo, *Adoration of the Magi*, about 1460, The Metropolitan Museum of Art, New York (inv. 1982.60.4).
88. Wardwell 1976–7, p. 182; Monnas 2024 (forthcoming a).
89. On Florentine camacas, see Monnas 1993a, p. 742, n. 8; on examples painted by Bernardo Daddi, see Monnas 2008, pp. 77–83.
90. On camacas and its weave structure, see King and King 1988, pp. 68–70, figs 3, 4; Monnas 1993a, *passim*.
91. Gérard-Marchant 2013, index pp. 560–2. Discussed in Monnas 2024 (forthcoming b).
92. On Saint Maximinus, see Mascolo in Siena 2017–18, cat. 26g, pp. 322–33.
93. On the inventory, see Kleinschmidt 1928, no. 126, p. 26; on comparable silks, see Wilckens 1992, no. 249, p. 122; no. 250, p. 123.
94. On medieval cope constructions, see Borkopp-Restle 2019, *passim*.
95. Klesse compares the throne covering to a polychrome velvet (Kunstgewerbemuseum, Cologne), see Klesse 1967, text p. 103; figs 136–7, p. 109; no. 404, p. 413; Markowsky 1976, no. 352, p. 244, dates the velvet '2nd quarter 17th century', but it may be early fifteenth century.
96. On diasper silks, see King 1960, *passim*; King and King 1988, pp. 68–9; there is a diasper chasuble in the Museo dell'Opera della Metropolitana, Siena (Inv. Gen. no. 1), see Fineschi in Siena 1994, cat. 1, p. 101.
97. For technical details of another example of the same silk in the Deutsches Textilmuseum, Krefeld, see Tietzel 1984, no. 43, pp. 43–4.
98. Wardwell 1988–9, pp. 98–101, figs 13–14, 25, 41–2, 45; Von Fircks and Schorta 2016, *passim*.
99. On fig. 166, see Desrosiers et al. 2004, p. 190; for an example of polychrome, striped lampas cloth of gold with animals, Abegg-Stiftung inv. no. 219, see Otavský and Wardwell 2011, no. 81, pp. 219–21.
100. On butterflies, see Ferguson 1954 (1961), p. 13.
101. Orsi Landini 2019, p. 20.
102. Gérard-Marchant 2013, *passim*.
103. Lisini 1930, p. 56; Ceppari Ridolfi and Turrini 1993, pp. 180–1; identical restrictions were later imposed in Città di Castello and Gubbio, without exemption for prostitutes or players, see Nico Ottaviani 2005, pp. 312, 581.
104. Campbell 2001, pp. 241–8.
105. Gordon 2011, pp. 380–93.
106. Maginnis 2001, p. 88; Norman 2006.
107. Monnas 1993b, p. 168.
108. Monnas 2008, pp. 242–4.
109. Mills 1975 (1983), pp. 4–5.
110. Spallanzani 2014, p. 38.
111. Ibid., pp. 2–3, 6.
112. Ibid., pp. 3, 28, 31.
113. Gordon 2003, pp. 118–21.
114. Denny 2014, p. 57, fig. 43; Spallanzani 2014, pp. 38, 43, pls 12, 13.

GLOSSARY

Animal substrate: a narrow strip of leather or, in Italy, often ox-gut membrane, which is gilded for metal thread

Baldachin: a ceremonial canopy

Brocaded: with a pattern formed by a brocading weft

Camacas: historic term for a type of tabby-tabby lampas silk, with details sometimes brocaded in gold

Chasuble: a sleeveless vestment, worn by the priest celebrating Mass

Cloth of gold: any textile woven with gold thread

Cope: a processional vestment; a long, semicircular cloak worn by the clergy and the choir

Dalmatic: a sleeved tunic: either a Mass vestment, worn by the deacon, or an ankle-length coronation vestment

Diasper: historic term for a type of tabby-tabby lampas silk, usually with details brocaded in gold

Figured: a textile with a complex pattern woven on a loom with a figure harness

Flat gold thread: in the examples in this essay, a slender strip of gilded animal substrate

Lampas (weave): a figured weave, presenting contrasting textures of a warp-faced ground and weft-faced pattern. In the ground, the main warp binds the ground weft; the pattern is formed by one or more pattern wefts (with optional brocading) bound by a binding warp

Maphorion (from Byzantine Greek μαφόριον): the long blue mantle of the Virgin, covering her head

Pallium: a rectangle of cloth, various meanings; in this essay, a rectangular mantle

Pattern weft (USA, **supplementary weft**): a supplementary weft shot across the entire loom width of a textile, from selvedge to selvedge

Tabby (weave) synonymous with **Plain weave**: a simple weave, in which the first warp thread passes over one and under one weft thread, and the second warp thread under one and over one, repeating

Tabby-tabby lampas (weave): lampas with a tabby ground and tabby pattern

Tunicle: a Mass vestment, a sleeved tunic worn by the subdeacon

Twill (weave): Warp-faced twill: the warp passes over two (or three) wefts, and under one, creating short warp floats. Weft-faced twill: the warp passes under two (or three) wefts and over one, creating short weft floats.

Twill-tabby lampas (weave): lampas with a twill ground and tabby pattern

Warp: threads attached to the loom, which run the length of a textile

Warp-faced: where warp threads predominate on the face of the textile

Weft: threads passed horizontally across the loom by the weaver

Weft-faced: where weft threads predominate on the face of the textile

Weft-faced compound tabby (taqueté) (weave): a figured weave presenting a uniform surface of weft floats bound in tabby. It is composed of a main warp, a binding warp and two or more series of weft threads.

Weft-patterned tabby: a textile with a tabby ground, whose pattern is formed by a supplementary pattern weft, bound in tabby by selected main warp threads

Wrapped gold thread (filé): in this essay, slender strips of gilded animal substrate spun around a core of silk (figs 154 and 159) or of linen (fig. 165)

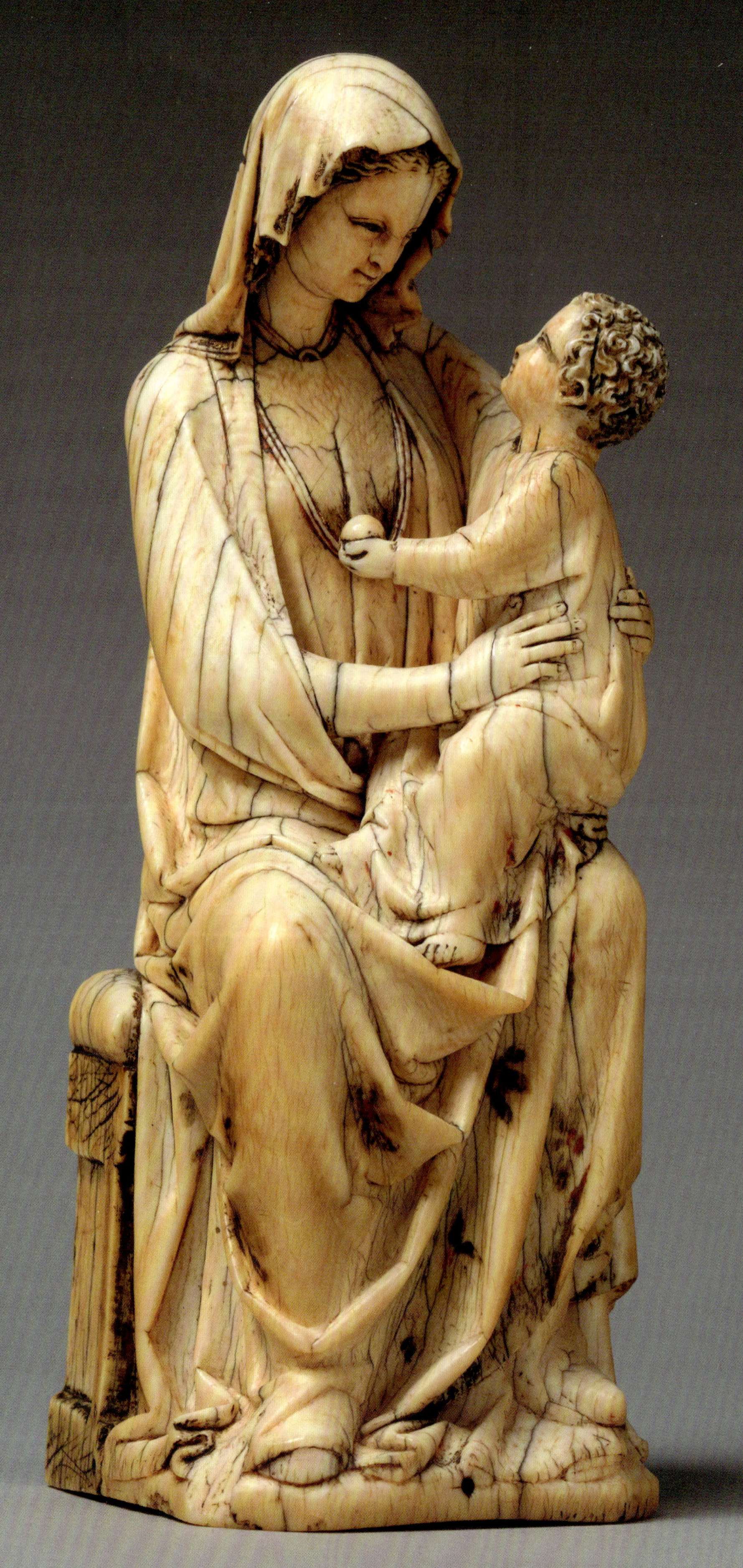

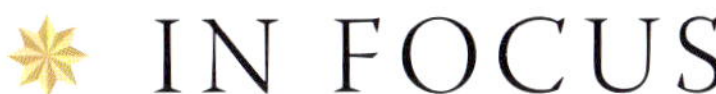

IN FOCUS

Gothic Ivories in Italy: Reviewing the Evidence

Sarah M. Guérin

The impact of French Gothic on Siena's artistic development around 1300 is a recurring theme in the scholarship. Experts have long proposed the travelling artist as the primary mode for the transfer of artistic ideas: Duccio supposedly working in the Ile-de-France as formative for his elegant and polished style, or Jean Pucelle perhaps travelling to Tuscany to drink in the innovations of the trecento.[1] Little evidence, however, outside of formal similarities, supports such hypotheses.[2] Other vectors surely played a role in transmitting foreign visual concepts – portable works of art like drawings, manuscripts or metalwork mediated between monuments and the voracious visual imagination of fourteenth-century artists.

One strand in the manifold relations between Sienese art and the north that deserves closer study is the role Gothic ivories played in the transmission of ideas, object types, style and iconography. Max Seidel underscored the importance of ivories carved in the French kingdom as models of transalpine Gothic available to Tuscan artists.[3] Imported small-scale ivory Virgin and Child statuettes had a monumental impact on the work of the receptive sculptor Giovanni Pisano, but a similar transfer of ideas has also been argued for Duccio.[4] The Metropolitan Museum of Art's *Stoclet Madonna* (see fig. 18) could be placed beside the seated ivory Virgin now at the Cloisters (fig. 170), a work of the highest Parisian artistic pedigree.[5] In particular, the tender gesture of the infant Jesus reaching up to tug at his mother's veil, and the absorbed gaze shared by mother and child, bring the *Stoclet Madonna* closer to the Parisian ivory than to other devotional predecessors, including the famous Byzantine *Eleousa* type, or Virgin of Tenderness.[6] Both ivory and painted panel are small works that speak to the intimacy of private devotion via handheld scale and tender sentiments. Sculpture, however, did not have to be miniature to migrate: for example, a large (70 cm) pear wood sculpture from northern France travelled across the Alps and is today in the Museo dell'Opera del Duomo in Orvieto, the favoured residence of the French thirteenth-century popes.[7] Large-scale sculpture might offer scholars more grounded points of stylistic comparison than ivories,

FIG. 170
Paris, France
Enthroned Virgin and Child, about 1260–80
Ivory with traces of polychromy, 18.4 × 7.6 × 7.3 cm
The Metropolitan Museum of Art, New York. Purchase, The Cloisters Collection and Michel David-Weill Gift, 1999 (1999.208)

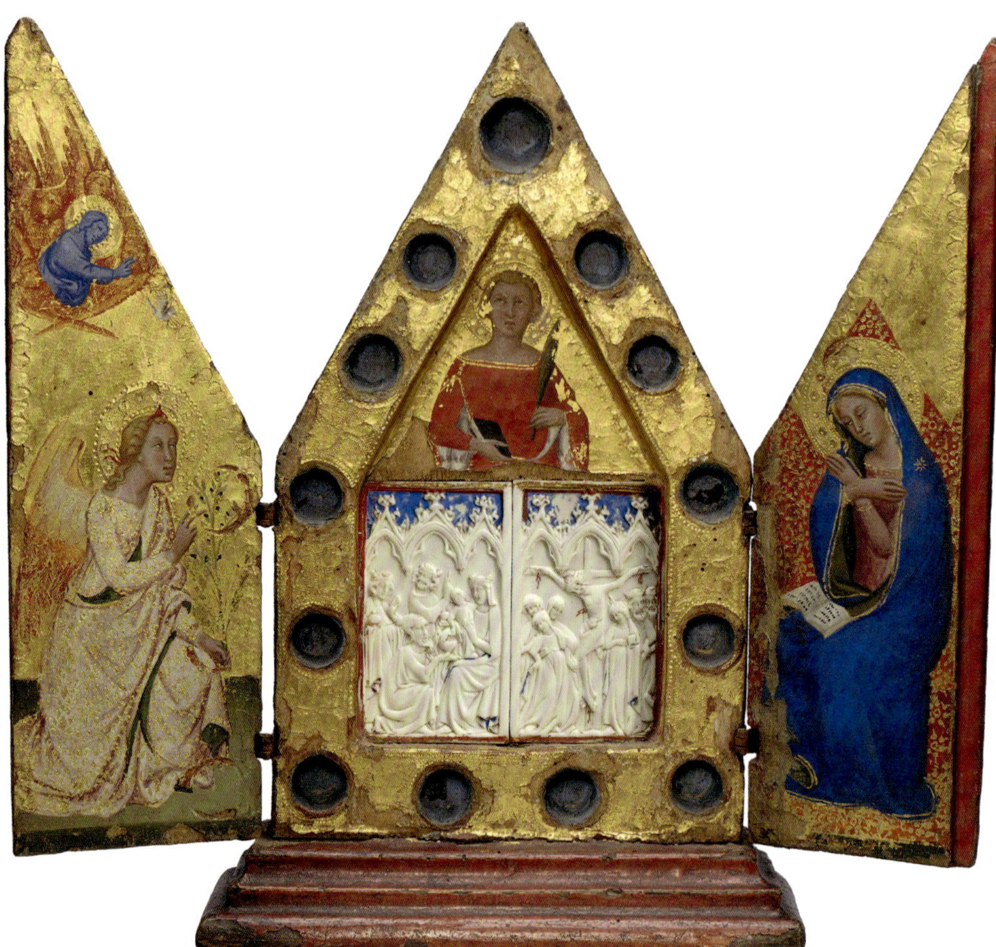

FIG. 171
Bartolo di Fredi (documented 1353–1410) (triptych) and **French artist** (ivory plaques)
Reliquary Triptych with the Annunciation, Saint Ansanus, the Adoration of the Magi and the Crucifixion, about 1370 (triptych); about 1350–70 (ivory plaques)
Tempera on panel with gilded and polychromed ivory, 35.5 × 38.5 cm (open)
The Wyvern Collection, UK (0442)

which all too frequently lack provenance before the nineteenth century.

One exceptional object that proves the presence of French ivories in Siena in the trecento is a pair of ivory writing tablets from about 1350–70 depicting the Adoration of the Magi and the Crucifixion, inserted as the centrepiece of a painted wooden reliquary triptych attributed to the Sienese painter Bartolo di Fredi, in about 1370 (fig. 171).[8] This triptych now in the Wyvern Collection not only confirms the existence of Gothic ivories in a Sienese milieu, but also the sophistication with which contemporary artists and patrons responded to the medium. The inclusion of the ivory reliefs, themselves supports for the written word on wax, between the two figures of the Annunciation – the moment when the word became flesh – demonstrates that whoever conceived of this unusual admixture of painted panel, relics and French Gothic ivories did so as a knowing and reflective consumer.[9]

In the decades leading up to 1300, documents show that Gothic ivories, some of exceptional quality, were owned, used, gifted and even sold in Rome, across the Papal States, in the Angevin territories and their capital in Naples.[10] Evidence from ecclesiastical circles allows us to imagine the types of objects that might have served Duccio, and other fertile artistic minds of his generation, as inspiration in the forging of new synthetic forms.

The archives of the wealthy and cosmopolitan members of the papal Curia offer ample evidence.[11] Eudes de Châteauroux, French cardinal and papal legate, who died at the papal court in Orvieto in 1273, left to the abbey of Sainte-Geneviève in Paris an ivory Virgin and Child statuette on a silver base.[12] The donations made in 1289 by Cardinal Bentivenga dei Bentivegni, the year before his death, to the convent of San Fortunato in Todi included 'a small icon of the blessed Virgin with her son in arms of ivory.'[13] The 1287 inventory of Cardinal Goffredo da Alatri's possessions

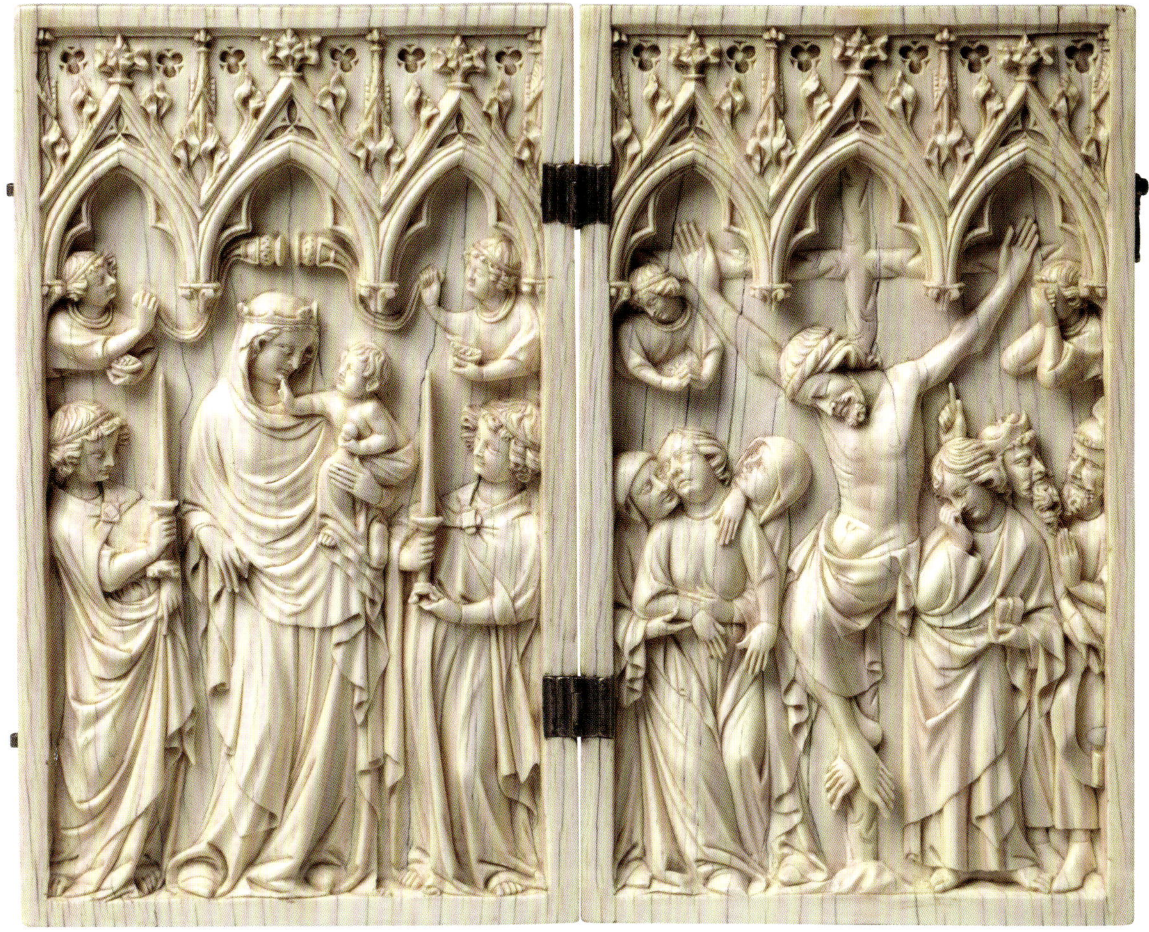

FIG. 172
Paris, France
Diptych with the Glorification of the Virgin and the Crucifixion, about 1325–50
Ivory with later silver hinges and ebony backing, 18.1 × 22.2 × 0.8 cm (open)
The Courtauld, London (Samuel Courtauld Trust) (O.1966.GP.10)

on his death in Rome listed 'a certain image of the Blessed Mary of ivory' worth one gold florin.[14] Upon his death in 1280, Pope Nicholas III (Giovanni Gaetano Orsini) left Santa Maria in Trastevere two images, one of silver and the other of ivory.[15] Although none of these works have yet been identified, and there is no mention of their provenance, it is almost certain that all of these ivory statuettes were carved in Paris, the centre of production in the decades leading up to the year 1300.[16]

The papal collections offer even stronger evidence. Two inventories attest to the treasures of the apostolic see, made soon before the move to Avignon: the first in 1295, when Boniface VIII sent the papal treasure from Naples to his hometown of Anagni, and the second in 1311, when Clement V was moving the papacy to Avignon and needed a list of the treasure that had been in Perugia since the death of Benedict XI in 1304.[17] The 1295 inventory recorded 1,657 items, categorised according to material.[18] The section 'Icones de ebore', or icons of ivory, comprises 20 objects, including some of novel manufacture not easily grouped elsewhere.[19] Ten items are explicitly of ivory or of mixed media; for another three the medium is not specified, but we may safely assume they are of ivory. For example, 'an icon with two tablets in one of which is the Crucifixion and in the other an image of the Virgin with her Son',[20] corresponds to the most popular pairing on Gothic ivory diptychs, the Crucifixion with the Glorification of the Virgin, or the crowned Virgin and Child flanked by venerating angels. Like the Courtauld diptych (fig. 172), such items in the 1295 inventory were surely of ivory.[21]

The succinct descriptions of the 1295 inventory are fleshed out by the 1311 inventory, where the redactors meticulously recorded iconographies, object types and materials in a manner that rivals modern cataloguing.[22] For example, while the Virgin and Child statuette on a base was described simply

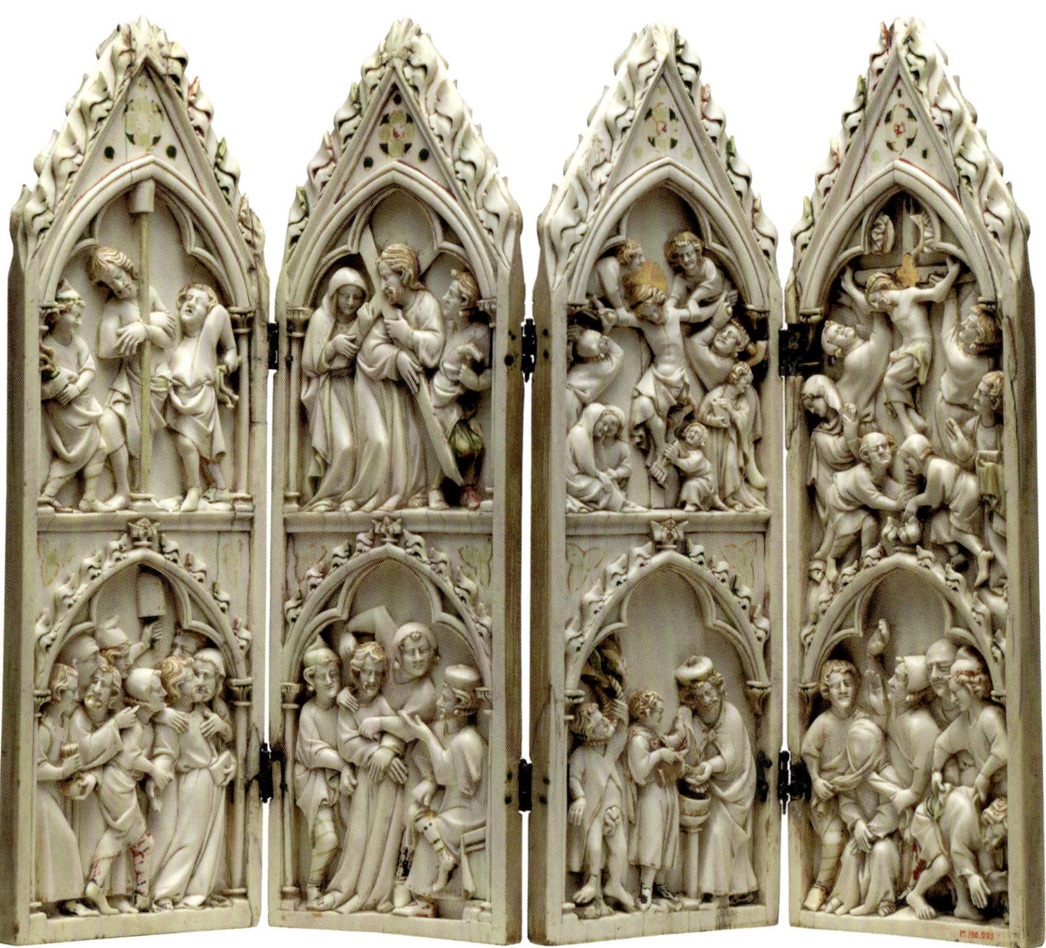

FIG. 173
Paris, France or Cologne, Germany
Quadriptych with Scenes from Christ's Passion, about 1300
Ivory with traces of polychromy (with some original hinges), 23.9 × 32.1 × 1 cm (open)
The Metropolitan Museum of Art, New York. Gift of J. Pierpont Morgan, 1917 (17.190.205)

in 1295 as 'Item, an icon of ivory with the image of the blessed Virgin holding her son in arms and sitting in a certain podium or tabernacle',[23] in 1311 we are provided with other details: 'A large image of the blessed Virgin with her son, of ivory, which image has a crown and is elevated on four feet of the same ivory, and the son does not have an arm and a hand, because they are broken.'[24]

This statuette and a good portion of the other ivories are described as broken in both the 1295 and 1311 inventories. By 1311, a Virgin and Child and a mixed-media triptych were in such bad condition that they were wrapped up together in a linen cloth with fragments that had fallen off these and other pieces.[25] This is surprising given that a number of the ivories had their own carrying cases: a small triptych 'all of ivory, beautiful, and complete' was wrapped in linen and placed in its own leather case, probably of boiled leather (*cuir boulli*).[26] Such a compact work could be folded up for safekeeping and tucked away in its travelling case, protecting the fragile surface during transit from one pontifical residence to the next.[27] Victor Schmidt argues that innovative multi-panelled forms in ivory, that is, diptychs, triptychs and even quadriptychs like the exceptional example at The Metropolitan Museum of Art (fig. 173), inspired Sienese painters to create devotional objects such as the Orsini Polyptych (see fig. 80).[28] The folding forms in dentine offered compelling models in terms of format, iconography and, most importantly, portability for peripatetic ecclesiastical clients including cardinals and papal legates.

'A beautiful tabernacle made of three ivory tablets' was added to the papal collection between the two inventories, probably under the auspices of Boniface VIII.[29] It can be identified with the exceptional and masterful triptych from the parish Church of Saint-Sulpice-sur-Tarn, now in the Musée Cluny (fig. 174).[30] The precision of the 1311 inventory allowed Danielle Gaborit-Chopin to

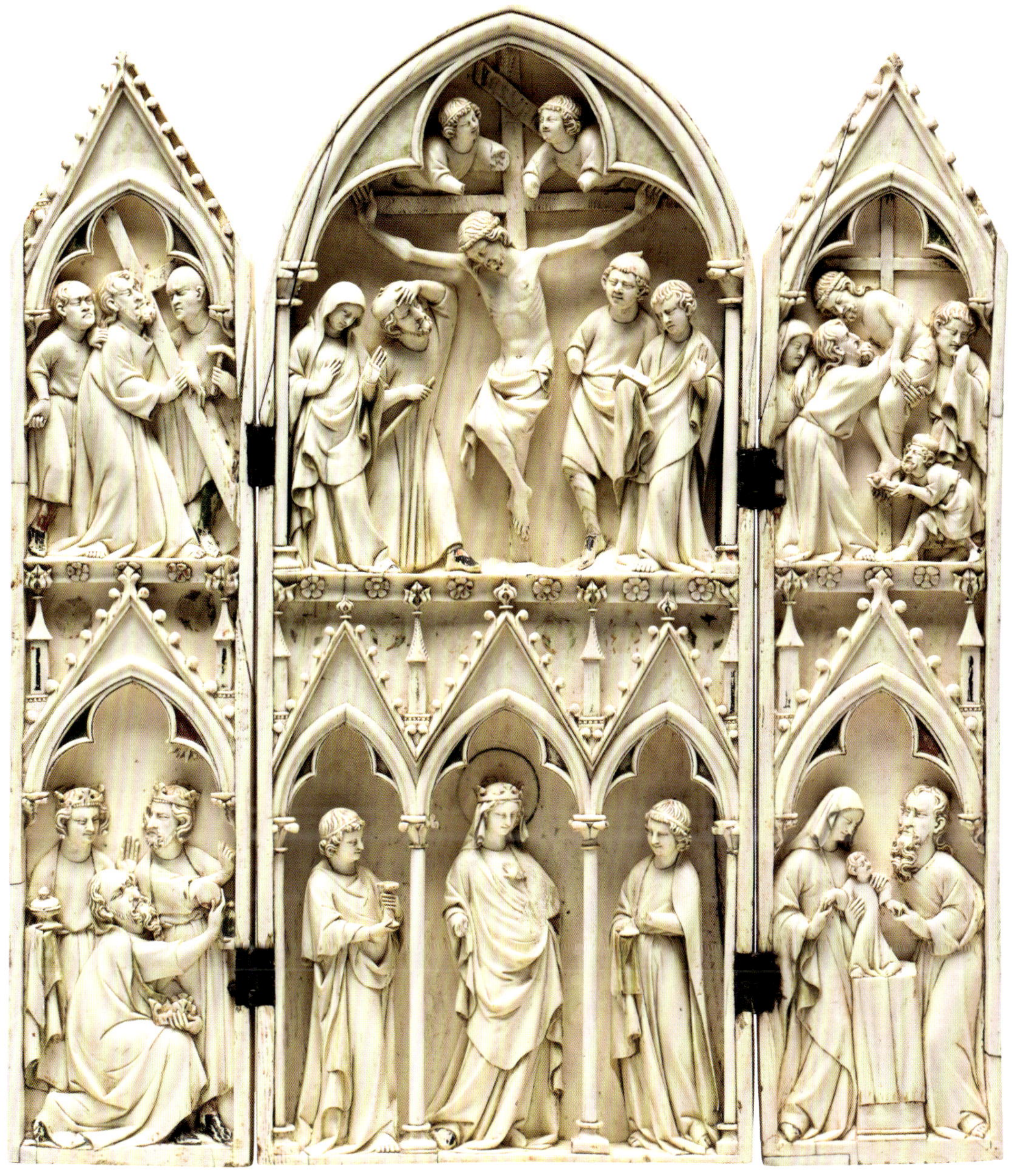

FIG. 174
Paris, France
Saint-Sulpice Triptych, 1296–1303
Ivory with traces of polychromy (with modern hinges), 32 × 28.4 cm (open)
Musée Cluny, Paris (Cl. 13101)

match the triptych with the description, which are identical except for an unusual Last Judgement scene appended to the top, representing Christ in Majesty with an angel carrying the wood of the Cross, and a third figure already missing. Very unusually, this scene seems to have been composed from separately carved figures pinned atop the upper edge of the triptych.[31] The ambitious carver of the Saint-Sulpice Triptych was not limited by the natural parameters of an elephant tusk, even one of extraordinary size (over 14 cm wide): using additive techniques he strove to surpass his materials and to impress elite patrons, like the Pope, with larger-than-life works of sumptuous ivory. The marriage of material splendour and technical virtuosity appealed to patrons of the highest order.

Without knowing its provenance in the papal collections, scholars had already noted that the sensitive execution of the Crucified Christ on the Saint-Sulpice Triptych might have served as a model for Duccio's softening of the Crucified Christ in the Passion scenes on the *Maestà* (see fig. 35).[32] Florens Deuchler mentions the acutely bent knees, the drape of the loincloth and the strong diagonal sweep of the

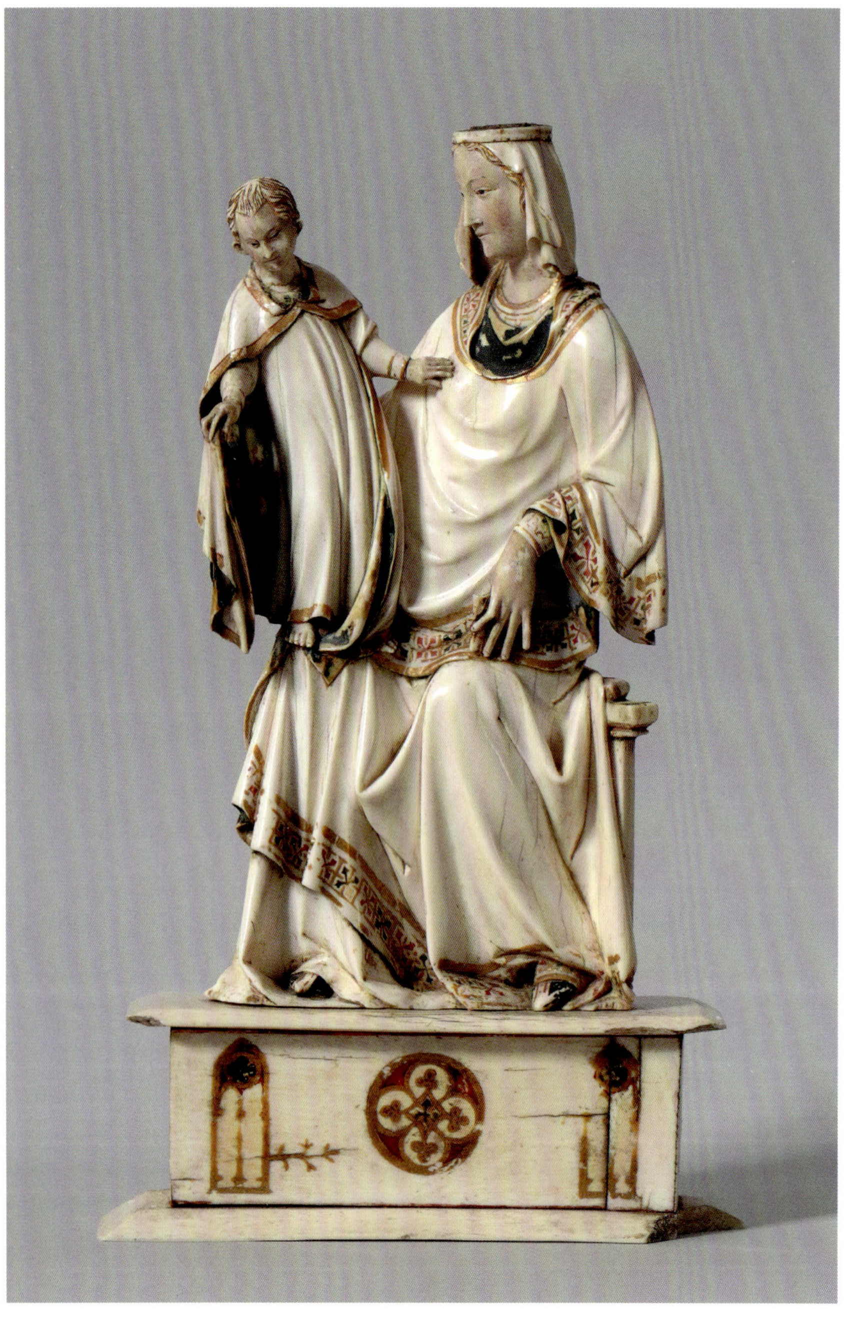

FIG. 175
Paris, France
The Virgin and Child,
1290–1300
Ivory with polychromy,
25.3 × 15.5 × 6 cm
(with original base)
Museo del Tesoro della Basilica di San Francesco, Assisi (88)

outstretched arms.[33] We might add the similarities in the rendering of the abdomen and thoracic cage, with the linea alba and the tendinous intersections of the abdominals depicted softly through modelling, rather than rigidly through line.[34] Today, we are not only able to locate the ivory on the Italian peninsula during the very period of the gestation of the *Maestà*, but we can also place Duccio and the papal treasury in the same place at the same time: soon after 1304, Duccio painted a polyptych for the Dominicans of Perugia, the foundation where Pope Benedict XI was buried and where the treasury was possibly kept.[35] Could the Perugian commission have afforded an opportunity for Duccio to study the extraordinary papal treasury?

The Virgin and Child statuette in the treasury of the Basilica of San Francesco, Assisi, is one of the highest-quality ivories with provenance in Italy in the trecento (fig. 175). As it happens, it was fashioned by the same artist as the Saint-Sulpice Triptych – the most prominent Parisian ivory carver of around 1300 – and it can be dated to the same decade.[36] A 1370 inventory of the Assisi sacristy described the statuette as 'Item, another image of the Blessed Virgin with her son in arms of ivory: beautiful enough [*satis pulchra*]'.[37] The statuette, however, was not listed in the 1360–1 copy of the 1338 sacristy inventory, a text that integrated works added to the treasury after 1338 without signalling their more recent provenance. Understanding this textual evidence allows the arrival of the ivory in the treasury to be pinpointed between 1361 and 1370, although it might have been kept elsewhere at the convent before that date.[38]

Like the Saint-Sulpice Triptych, the Assisi statuette makes masterful use of awkwardly shaped material. Its gently rounded back is covered with abundant cementum (the more calciferous outer layer of the tusk) and the front face of the Assisi Virgin is slightly convex, not flat, which suggests that this piece of ivory was taken from around the tusk's nerve cavity. The carver thus used a section of the tusk unsuitable for panel-making to create a daring sculpture, devising a unique Marian iconography: a toddler Christ stands on his mother's knee, wearing a long mantle that he holds out delicately as he leans away from her. The thinness of this garment is remarkable, and is echoed by Mary's mantle, tossed over her left shoulder, similarly tapering to an exceptional thinness. The artisan specifically chose this unusual composition to suit perfectly the piece of dentine before him, and that he produced such an exquisite work from what others would consider an undesirable part of the tusk is all the more noteworthy. Such artistic economy and bravura surely impressed the artists of the early trecento, making these small-scale ivory masterpieces worthy ambassadors of the Gothic style.

1. For Duccio, see Stubblebine 1979, vol. 1, pp. 6, 26, and *passim*; Bellosi 2003, especially p. 106. For Jean Pucelle, see Meiss 1967, vol. 1, p. 19; Avril in Paris 1981–2, cat. 239, pp. 292–3; Ferber 1984.
2. The *Duche de Siene* in the 1297 and 1298 Parisian tax rolls deserves to be better studied. Stubblebine 1979, vol. 1, p. 4.
3. Seidel 2005b. Hohenfeld 2014, pp. 127–32, claims there is no concrete evidence that French ivories circulated in Italy in the late thirteenth century – which is patently incorrect – and posits that Giovanni Pisano also travelled to the Ile-de-France.
4. See, for example, Deuchler 1984, pp. 181–3.
5. Guérin 2012.
6. In the *Crevole Madonna* (about 1283–4; Museo dell'Opera della Metropolitana, Siena, inv. 37), as with Byzantine examples, the Virgin's gaze is outward.
7. Urban IV in the 1260s and Martin IV from 1281 to 1285. Formerly in the Chiesa di Santa Lucia, which was rebuilt after extensive earthquake damage in 1874. Orvieto 2006–7, cat. 15, p. 62. See also a standing Virgin and Child in the Pinacoteca Nazionale in Pisa (about 1300), which until 1970 was installed within a niche on the facade of the Palazzo Orsini Baroni in via Santa Maria in Pisa. Burresi 2001, pp. 51–2.
8. Williamson 2019, no. 105, pp. 212–13; Williamson 2018.
9. For resonances of ivory and wax, see Guérin 2022, pp. 46–9.
10. The Angevin material is exceptionally rich, but beyond the scope of this essay. For ivories on sale at the Roman Curia around the Jubilee of 1300, see Opitz 2017; Guérin 2022, pp. 252–3.
11. Gardner 1990b, especially p. 87.
12. Guérin 2022, pp. 129–32.
13. Tenneroni 1888, p. 262: 'Item una yconia parva beata virginis de ebore retientis filium in brachiis'.
14. Prou 1885, p. 401: 'inv. 271. Item, quedam ymago Beate Marie de ebore, flor. I'.
15. Egidi 1908, vol. 1, p. 97: 'Ob. d. Nicolaus papa III de domo Ursinorum qui rel. fll. L. et duas imagines, unam de ebhore et aliam de argento ad figuras, que nunc sunt in sacristia nostra' ('Obit Pope Nicholas III, of the house of the Orsini, who left 50 florins and two images, one of ivory and the other of silver with figures, which are now in our sacristy').
16. Guérin 2022, pp. 49–60, and *passim*.
17. See Gardner 2001–2; Burkart 2006 (discussing a number of other inventories); and Gauthier 1983, who instead suggests (p. 531) that the inventory was drawn up in preparation for the papal treasure being shipped from Naples to Rome on 15 February 1295.
18. Molinier 1888.
19. Ibid., chapter 38, pp. 76–7. Objects such as what seems to be a micromosaic (*de opera mosayco*) and Venetian (*opere Venetico/ Veneticorum*) composite icons of hardstones and rock crystal are also included. Molinier 1888, p. 77, inv. 715 and 722.
20. Molinier 1888, p. 77, inv. 720: 'una iconam cum duabus tabulis in una quarum est Crucifixus et in alia imago Virginis cum Filio'.
21. Lowden 2013, no. 8, pp. 68–71.
22. Inventarium 1892.
23. Molinier 1888, p. 76, inv. 706: 'Item, unam yconam de ebore cum imagine beate Virginis tenentis Filium in brachio et sedentis in quodam podio sive tabernaculo'.
24. Inventarium 1892, p. 447: 'Unam magnam ymaginem beate Virginis cum filio suo, de ebore, que ymago habet coronam et est elevate in quatuor pedibus de eodem ebore, et filius non habet unum brachium nec manum, quia fuit fractum'. Relatively few ivories have their original socles, but the Assisi Virgin discussed here is a rare exception.
25. Ibid.: 'Cum quibusdam aliis fragmentis minutis de ebore et de osse et de ligno, que fuerunt in ornamentis predictarum vel aliarum ymaginum et tabernaculorum … et est ligata cum proximis dictis tribus tabulis et involuta cum ipsis, et aliis fragmentis in panno lineo' ('with certain other small fragments of ivory and bone and wood, which ornamented the aforementioned or other images and tabernacles … and it is secured with the previously described three tablets and wrapped up with them and other fragments in a linen textile').
26. Ibid.: 'Item aliam yconam sive ymaginem, *totam de ebore, pulcram, integram*, factam de tribus tabulis … et est involute in panno lineo. Et habet tecam de corio' ('Item another icon or image all of ivory, beautiful, whole, made of three tablets … it is wrapped in a linen fabric and it has a case of leather'). The same as Molinier 1888, p. 76, inv. 711. The rare iconography of Synagoga and Ecclesia identify the triptych as by a master carver active in northern France in the mid-thirteenth century (1240–60). It is very close to a triptych at the Victoria and Albert Museum (inv. 175–1866), which twice depicts a contemporary bishop, indicating that it too was made for an ecclesiastic. A diptych in the Vatican Museums (inv. MV.62444.0.0; old inv. A.82) is from the same atelier, but has no provenance. Guérin 2022, pp. 106–10.
27. For Boniface VIII moving the treasure throughout his reign, see Schmidt 1984, no. 2202, p. 288; no. 2204, p. 289; no. 2654, p. 340; no. 2669, p. 342; no. 2675, p. 343. Gardner 2001–2, p. 72, n. 13.
28. Schmidt 2005a, pp. 281–328, especially pp. 303–4, 314.
29. Gardner 2001–2, p. 72; Guérin 2022, pp. 247–55. The 1311 inventory includes ivories obviously *not* of French origin, such as Siculo-Arabic caskets (p. 446), and several Sicilian crosiers (p. 450).
30. Inventarium 1892, p. 447: 'Item aliud taberncului pulcrum de tribus tabulis de ebore factum…'; Gaborit-Chopin 2013–14, p. 124; Guérin 2022, pp. 212–55, especially pp. 247–55.
31. Two symmetrical dowel holes in the 4 cm-thick upper frame of the Saint-Sulpice Triptych might be the physical evidence to substantiate the identification. See Guérin 2022, p. 249.
32. Carli 1961, p. 30, suggests French ivory corpora in general; Deuchler 1984, p. 183, names the Saint-Sulpice Triptych in particular.
33. Deuchler 1984 proposes the robes of Saint Catherine and Saint Agnese on the *Maestà*, depicted as gold on a cream-coloured ground, as having been inspired by gilded ivory. Rather, Mongolian cloth of gold, or its imitations, is the referent. Hoeniger 1991, p. 156; Monnas 2008, pp. 14, 70; and Monnas, p. 208, in the present volume. I thank Brooke Wrubel for exploring this material with me.
34. Compare with Cimabue's San Domenico Crucifix, Arezzo, where the linearity is particularly marked. One could also productively contrast Giotto's corpulent Santa Maria Novella Crucifix, where the abdominals are hidden under a sagging paunch.
35. Cannon 1982, especially pp. 80–2; see also White 1979, pp. 62–3; Bagnoli et al. 2003, p. 196. I thank Joanna Cannon for pointing out this happy coincidence. For the movement of the treasure in spring 1312, see Gardner 2001–2, p. 72; Ehrle 1885, pp. 231–5. For the Dominican Benedict XI's burial arrangements at San Domenico in Perugia, see Grandjean 1905, col. 615, no. 1018. When he arrived in Perugia on 6 May 1304, Benedict was in residence at the Canonica of San Lorenzo, the episcopal seat. Fabretti 1850, p. 60. This is where he passed away two months later. Among the Pope's dying wishes was the safety of the papal treasure. Ehrle 1889, pp. 585–6. No document attests, however, as to whether the treasure stayed at the Canonica or was transferred with the Pope's other belongings to San Domenico.
36. Guérin 2022, pp. 239–47.
37. See Alessandri 1920, p. 46. In the seventeenth century it was placed on the altar of the Virgin's veil, a relic donated in 1604, in the transept of the Lower Church.
38. Cenci 1985, especially p. 487; Guérin 2022, p. 242.

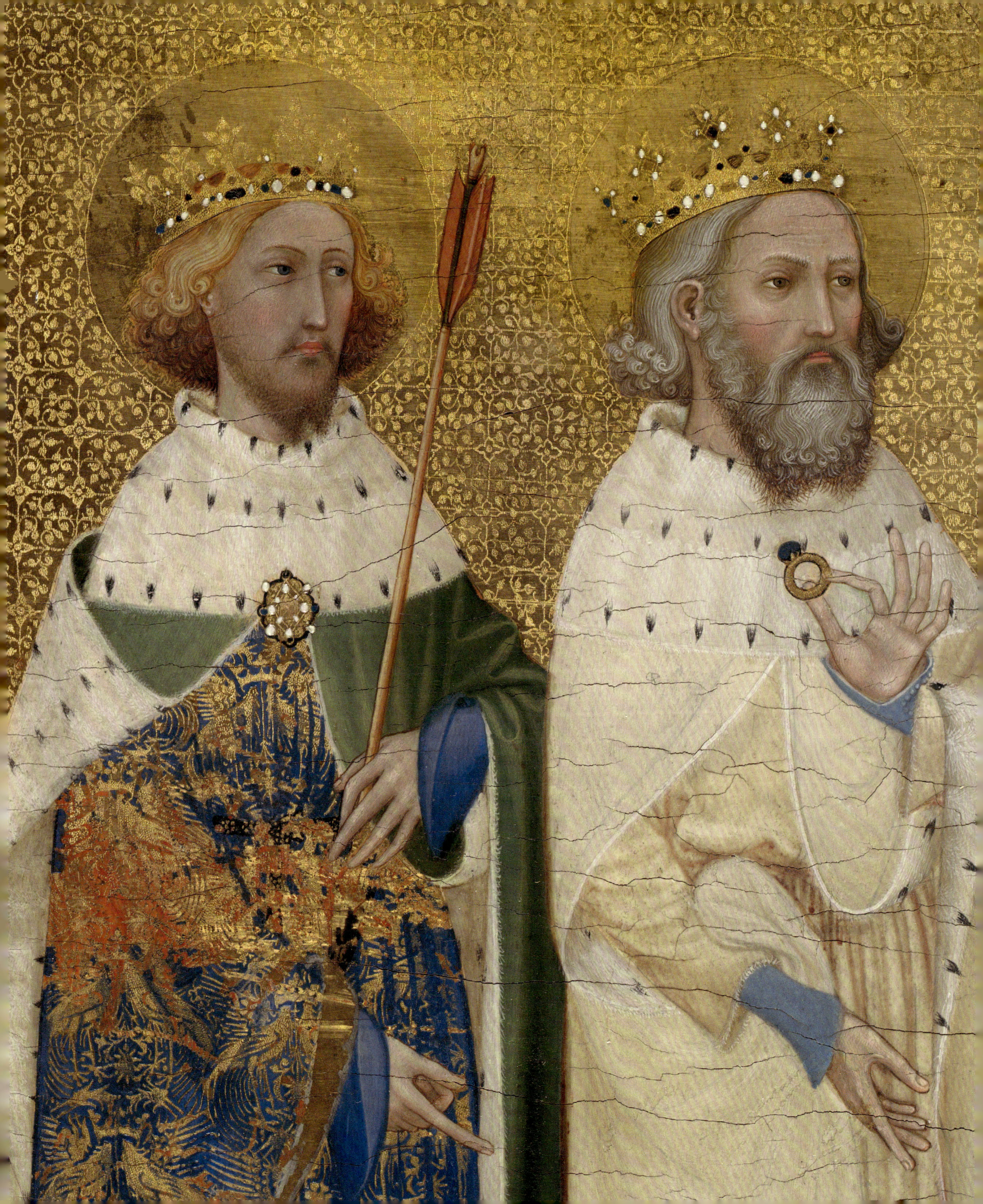

COURTLY RESPONSES TO SIENESE PAINTING: FROM SIENA TO NORTHERN EUROPE VIA AVIGNON

Dillian Gordon

The taste among members of the courts of northern Europe for exquisitely refined, jewel-like objects fostered a deep admiration for works produced by French and Sienese artists. The courts were intricately interconnected, either through marriage or diplomacy, with the result that exchanges of gifts and the movements of peripatetic painters encouraged the diffusion of the so-called International Gothic style. A key component of this was the Sienese style of painting and decoration, emanating largely from Avignon, the seat of the papal Curia (court) from 1309 to 1362, and again from 1378 during the Great Schism, when there was a Pope in Rome and an antipope in Avignon.[1]

Three panel paintings that exemplify the influence of Sienese painting in northern Europe during the fourteenth century are the Bohemian *Virgin and Child enthroned* in New York (fig. 176), the *Annunciation* in the Cleveland Museum of Art (fig. 181), and the Wilton Diptych in the National Gallery in London (fig. 184).

AVIGNON

One of the greatest clusters of Sienese paintings outside Tuscany in the fourteenth century was to be found in Avignon. When Simone Martini moved there in the late 1330s, a number of other Sienese painters followed in his wake. Many of their works are now lost. Not only was there once a painting signed by Simone for the Franciscan church in Avignon dated 1343,[2] but there are also records of lost works signed by other Sienese painters, including Lippo and Tederigo Memmi,[3] Pietro Ceccarelli (which suggests that Naddo Ceccarelli, possibly his brother, also went),[4] Giovanni di Duccio da Siena and Paolo da Siena. One substantial Sienese work in Avignon was the large altarpiece (now lost) that the Dominican cardinal Matteo Orsini, who died in 1340, had commissioned in Siena, which was always displayed on his altar in Avignon, bequeathed to the Dominicans of Avignon if he died there.[5]

The desire among members of the papal Curia to possess a Sienese painting may have been inspired by the Dominican

P. 224
Detail of FIG. 184

FIG. 176
Bohemian painter, here attributed to the **Master of the Vyšší Brod Altarpiece** (active about 1345–50?)
The Virgin and Child enthroned, about 1346 (?)
Oil (?) on panel, 25.8 × 20.2 cm
The Metropolitan Museum of Art, New York. Purchase, George T. Delacorte Jr. Gift, by exchange; Michel David-Weill Gift; The Lesley and Emma Sheafer Collection, Bequest of Emma A. Sheafer and Gift of Mr and Mrs Malcom P. Ripley, by exchange; The Rendl Fund; Lila Acheson Wallace Gift; and funds from various donors, by exchange, 2020 (2020.209)

cardinal Niccolò da Prato, the presumed patron of two triptychs by Duccio (see figs 31, 32), one of them perhaps in collaboration with Simone.[6] Niccolò da Prato, who almost certainly commissioned them in Siena (and possibly a third), may well have taken them with him to Avignon, where he died in 1321. Many Sienese paintings can be linked with Avignon. It has been suggested that the *Fall of the Rebel Angels* (about 1340; Musée du Louvre, Paris) with Saint Martin on the reverse (see also below), by an unidentified Sienese painter, was made in Avignon for Aymery de Chatelus, cardinal priest of San Martino ai Monti in Rome, who died in Avignon in 1349.[7] Victor Schmidt has identified a diptych depicting the *Adoration of the Magi* (Musée des Beaux Arts, Tours), attributed to Naddo Ceccarelli and painted in the 1340s, as that inventoried as part of the papal treasure in Avignon in 1353.[8] Close in style, although not by the same hand, are the *Annunciation* and *Nativity* (both Musée Granet, Aix-en-Provence), and the *Adoration of the Magi* (see fig. 143). These are almost certainly Sienese, with their connections to Neapolitan painting explicable by the fact that the painter/painters may have been part of Simone Martini's workshop in Naples (see p. 107); missing is probably a fourth scene from the childhood of Christ.[9] The reverse of the *Annunciation* is silvered, with the remains of the arms of Aragon and Anjou (see fig. 182). This, along with the evidence of hinges, suggests that these panels originally formed a folding quadriptych, like the Orsini Polyptych (see fig. 80; see also below). Certainly commissioned in Avignon, and probably Sienese, was a folding eight-panelled work bequeathed to Sant'Agnese, Rimini, by Cardinal Gozio Battagli, who died in 1348, as well as a very similar eight-panelled work bequeathed to his burial chapel in San Francesco, Rimini (both works are now lost).[10]

BOHEMIA

Avignon was a focal point not only for high-ranking members of the clergy but also for visiting aristocracy. Among them was Charles IV (1316–1378), who acceded to the throne of Bohemia in 1346 (crowned in 1347). The Bohemian *Virgin and Child enthroned* (fig. 176), possibly painted around 1346 and now in The Metropolitan Museum of Art in New York, may have been commissioned by him.[11]

This small devotional panel was almost certainly the centre of a triptych, as indicated by the composition of the architecture around the centrally placed figures of the Virgin and Child, probably flanked on either side by half-width wings with standing saints and/or narrative scenes, their picture surfaces divided into two compartments.[12] The arms of the patron could have been on the exterior of the wings. The painting of the reverse with imitation jasper, and the representation of the embrasures and arcade of the architecture as inlaid with semi-precious stones and coloured marble, reflect Charles's predilection for these materials. Subsequently, the king was unusual in employing lapidary polishers,[13] and the walls of his chapels in Karlštejn were decorated with actual semi-precious stones, including green jasper.[14]

The painting is rich in symbolism. Keith Christiansen suggested that the contrasting sides of the architecture may represent Solomon's Porch of Judgement (I Kings 7:7), the open arches on the Virgin's right alluding to the righteous, and the barred rectangular openings on her left to the ungodly.[15] Shown as the Queen of Heaven, the Virgin has a halo of gradated blue and a veil edged with white dots, probably symbolising pearls. The fleurons of her crown are unusual in representing vine leaves referring to the

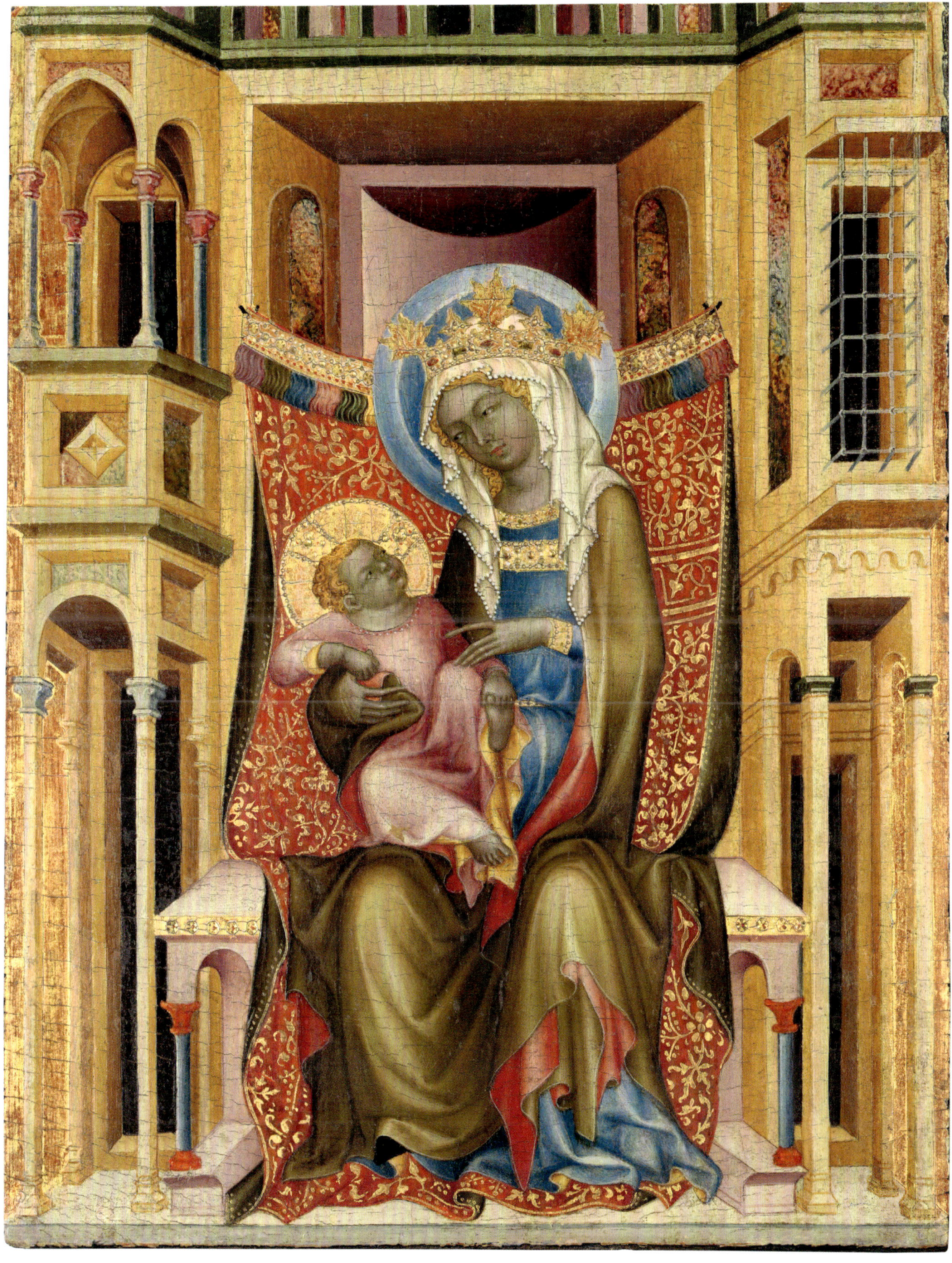

FIG. 177
Master of the Vyšší Brod Altarpiece
(active about 1345–50?)
The Virgin and Child, about 1347 (?)
Tempera (?) on beech, 21.5 × 16.5 cm
National Gallery, Prague (O 1439)

FIG. 178
Master of the Vyšší Brod Altarpiece
(active about 1345–50?)
Diptych with the Virgin and Child and the Man of Sorrows, about 1347–50 (?)
Oil (?) on panel, 25 × 18.5 cm (each panel)
Kunsthalle, Karlsruhe (2431a-b)

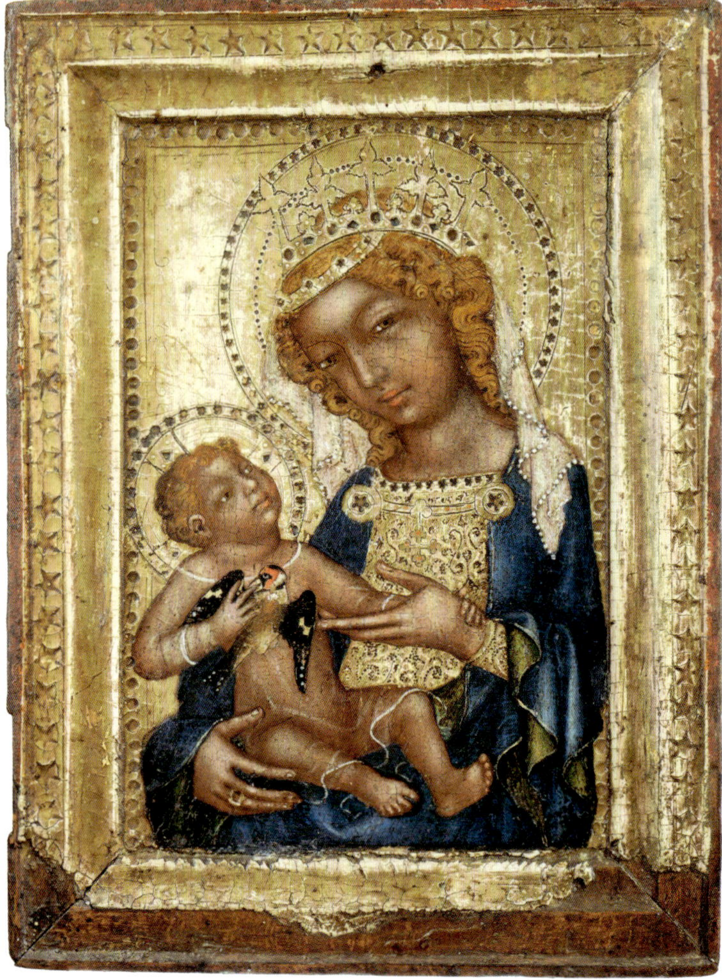

Eucharist, as does the vine leaf and grape pattern in the fringed red and gold Cloth of Honour suspended from two small hooks, which may also represent an altar cloth (see also pp. 209–10, fig. 162).

The Christ Child grasps his toes in the way babies naturally play with their feet. However, playing with his toes while holding his foot in order to display the sole also has symbolic significance and was already found in northern Europe in the context of sculpture, for example in the *Virgin and Child* dating from the end of the thirteenth/beginning of the fourteenth century in the nave of St Lorenz, Nuremberg,[16] and in later northern French works and in later Italian painting.[17] It is widely accepted that the display of the sole of the Child's foot (seen also in the Wilton Diptych, fig. 184) symbolises the Passion, since it will be pierced by a nail at the Crucifixion (possibly depicted in one of the hypothetical wings of the New York panel).[18]

The display of the sole of the foot features in two paintings that Jan Klípa has associated with the New York panel and which share a number of other features with it.[19] Probably by the same hand is a *Virgin and Child* now in Prague, formerly Rome (fig. 177), which was once part of a diptych, perhaps with a Man of Sorrows.[20] It is closely related iconographically, in the Virgin's double crown and the Child holding a goldfinch while showing the sole of his foot, to the larger *Madonna of Zbraslav* (on loan to the National Gallery, Prague) by an anonymous Bohemian painter in the immediate circle of the Master of Vyšši Brod, datable to around 1345–50.[21] Also likely to be by the same hand as the New York panel is a diptych showing the *Virgin and Child* with the *Man of Sorrows* now in Karlsruhe (fig. 178), in which the backward arching Child stems from Italo-Byzantine paintings.[22] All three small-scale devotional works are attributable to the master of the workshop responsible for the Vyšší Brod (Hohenfurth)

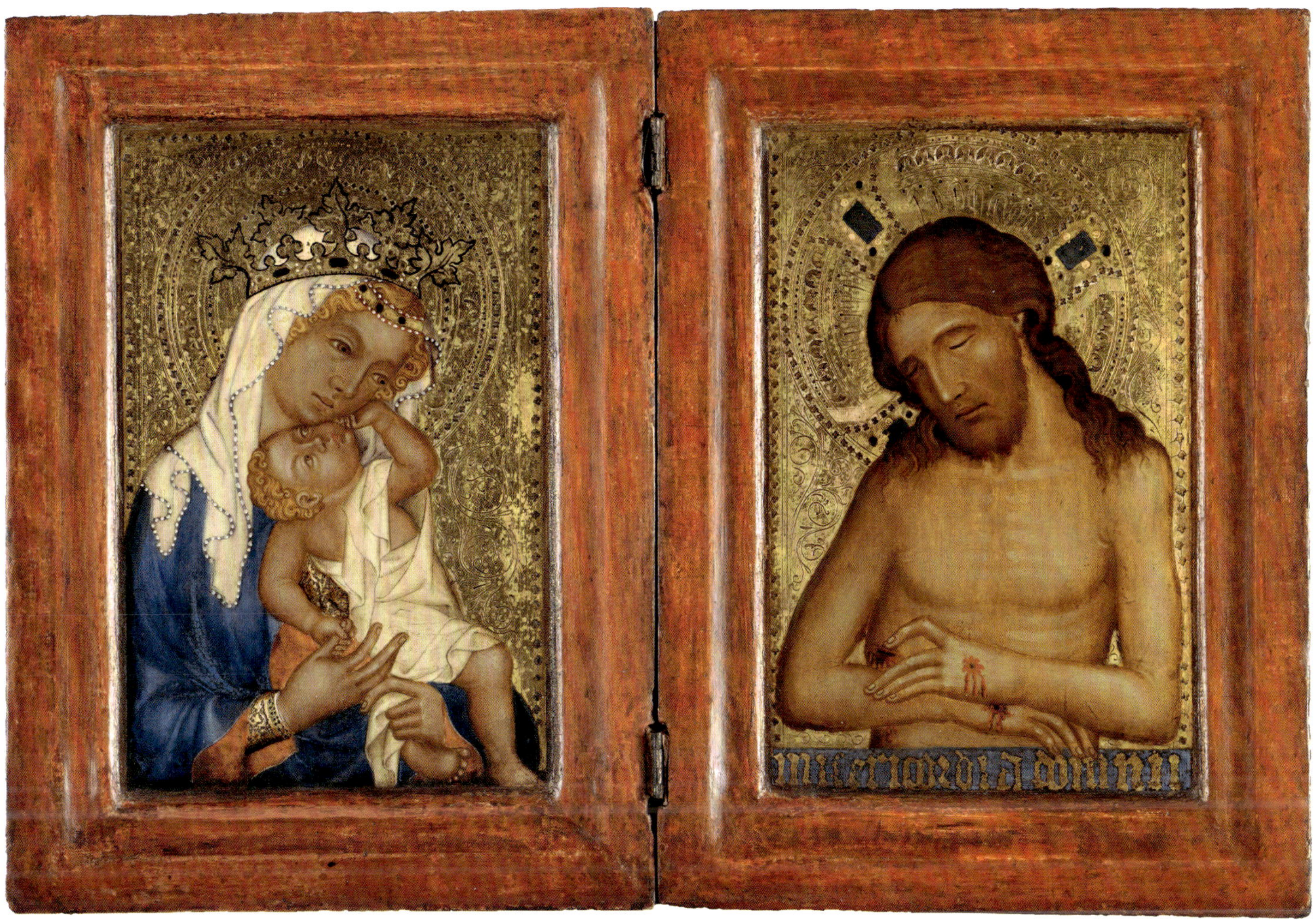

Altarpiece (National Gallery, Prague) whose patron, Peter I of Rožmberk (Rosenberg), is depicted in the (bottom) central panel of the altarpiece showing the *Nativity* beneath the *Crucifixion*.[23] Probably commissioned by Peter and funded by his son after his death in 1347, the altarpiece is thought to have been completed by 1350.[24] Klípa, who (tentatively) attributed the New York panel to the master himself,[25] noted that the punchwork along the top of the hanging and edge of the throne has been done with (probably) the same tool as that used in the Vyšší Brod Altarpiece.[26]

The technique of the *Virgin and Child enthroned* reflects Italian practice in the painting of the flesh tones, which were built up with thin layers of pink paint made from lead white, vermilion and ochre, modelled over what appears to be *terra verde* underpaint.[27] *Terra verde* was commonly used for the underpainting of flesh in Italian panel paintings,[28] and although the Master of the Vyšší Brod Altarpiece was painting with oil (as opposed to egg),[29] he was clearly familiar with Italian techniques. In the scenes in the Vyšší Brod Altarpiece attributed to the master, namely the *Annunciation*, *Nativity*, *Adoration of the Magi* (fig. 179) and *Christ on the Mount of Olives* (that is, the first four scenes chronologically in the Life of Christ), the painter used the same range of pigments as in the New York panel, including *terra verde* underpainting for the flesh, but with an intermediary layer of dark red,[30] with the result that the final appearance of the flesh painting in the New York panel compared with the Vyšší Brod Altarpiece seems somewhat different. A comparison of, for example, the physiognomy of the Child in the New York painting, the ex-Rome and Karlsruhe panels and the *Adoration of the Magi* (fig. 180) in the Vyšší Brod Altarpiece suggests that the Vyšší Brod Master became less Italianate and more Bohemian as he moved away from the likely Italian model (see below). Moreover, the New York painting is considerably

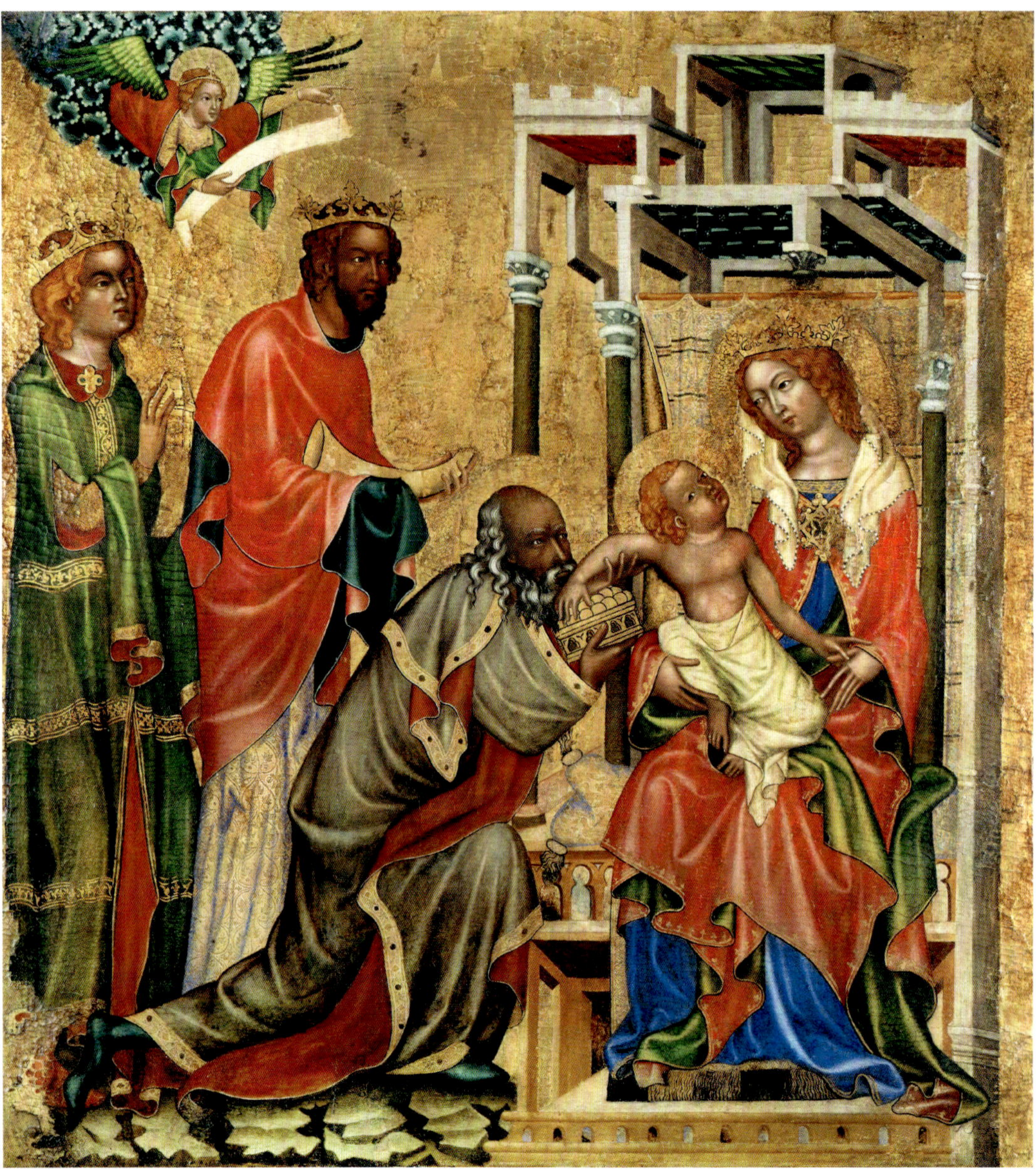

FIG. 179
Master of the Vyšší Brod Altarpiece
(active about 1345–50?)
The Adoration of the Magi (one of nine scenes from the Vyšší Brod Altarpiece), about 1347–50
Oil on maple, 99.5 × 92.5 cm
National Gallery, Prague (CO Vyšší Brod, VO 13506, formerly O 6788)

smaller in scale than the *Adoration of the Magi* (at least one third smaller) and therefore more refined, and designed for closer devotional contemplation rather than to be viewed at a distance like the Vyšší Brod Altarpiece.

The New York painting seems to have been modelled on a Sienese painting. The chubby-cheeked Child with a button nose and rosebud mouth resembles the Child in Duccio's National Gallery triptych (see fig. 31), as does the way in which mother and child look into each other's eyes. The difference in tone and softer modelling in the face of the Child in the New York panel as compared with, for example, the Vyšší Brod Altarpiece suggests the painter was closely observing or indeed mimicking something like the work by Duccio. The curling tendril motif delicately incised in the Child's halo in the *Virgin and Child enthroned*, which occurs again in the background of the Karlsruhe diptych, is typically found in early Sienese painting, and was widespread in works by Duccio and his circle (see figs 15 and 31).[31] The sinuous drapery folds and the imitation (untooled) *sgraffito* of the red and gold Cloth of Honour in the New York panel also suggest the influence of Sienese painters, particularly something like the Cloth of Honour in the *Annunciation* which formed part of the Orsini Polyptych (see fig. 81), while the small-scale pattern of the (tooled) *sgraffito* of the

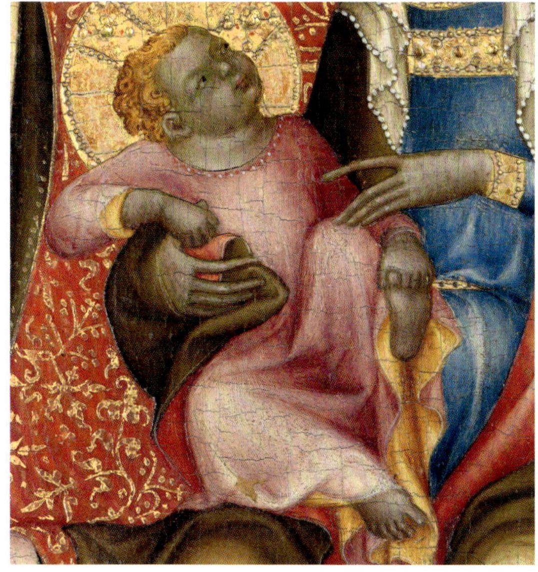
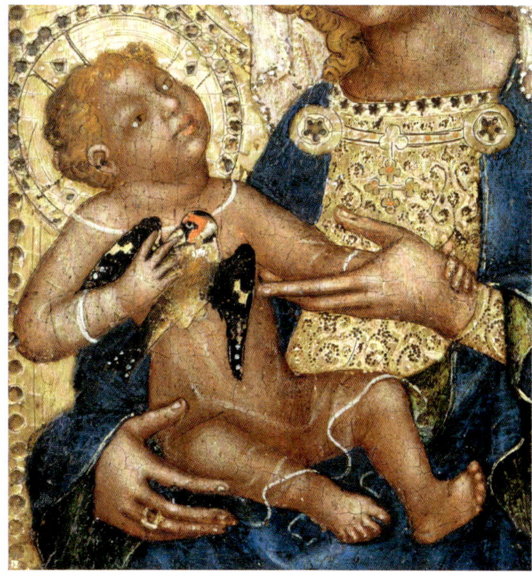
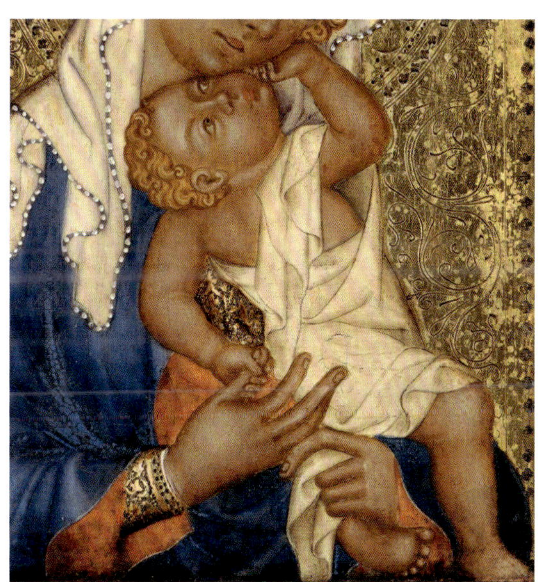
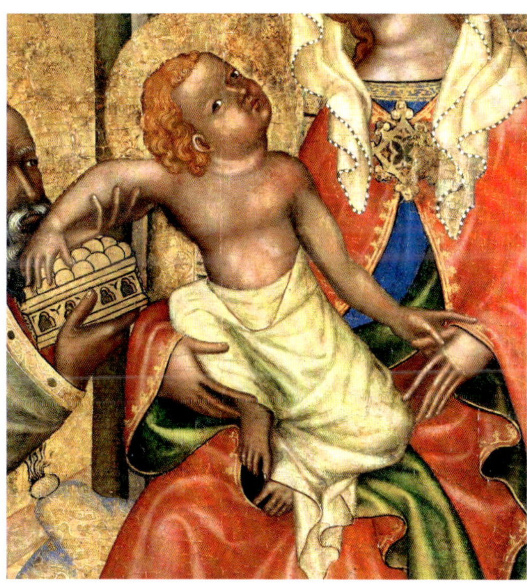

FIG. 180
Details of the Christ Child from figs 176–9

Virgin's cream-coloured dress in the ex-Rome and Karlsruhe panels is typically Sienese (see p. 201). The imitation gems on the gold border along the neckline of the Virgin's robe and crown are often found in works by Simone Martini.[32]

Charles IV clearly admired Sienese painting, an admiration that may have originated in one of his many trips to Avignon (for example, in 1334, 1340, 1344 and 1346, among others).[33] Luigi Coletti and Robert Gibbs considered the wall painting showing Charles and his wife on either side of the *Virgin and Child enthroned* above the altar in the Chapel of Saint Catherine (consecrated in 1357) in Karlštejn to be Sienese,[34] and Gibbs describes the diptych commissioned by Charles from Tomaso da Modena in the 1350s as a 'virtual pastiche' of works by Simone Martini, presumably at Charles's instigation.[35]

The *Virgin and Child enthroned* may have been commissioned with a similar prescription. It is possible that the patron of the New York panel, here presumed to be Charles, requested a 'virtual pastiche' of a Sienese work, perhaps one seen in Avignon. At the very least the painter of the New York panel, here presumed to be the Master of the Vyšší Brod Altarpiece himself, was influenced by Sienese painting. However, the general question of where he would have seen Sienese paintings – in Avignon, Siena or elsewhere – remains open.[36]

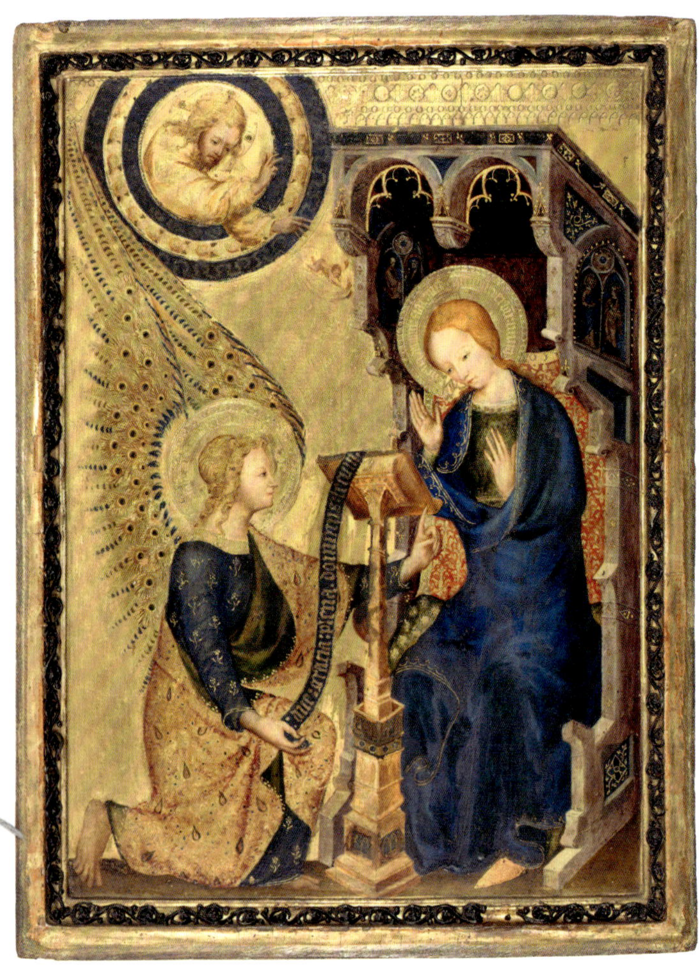

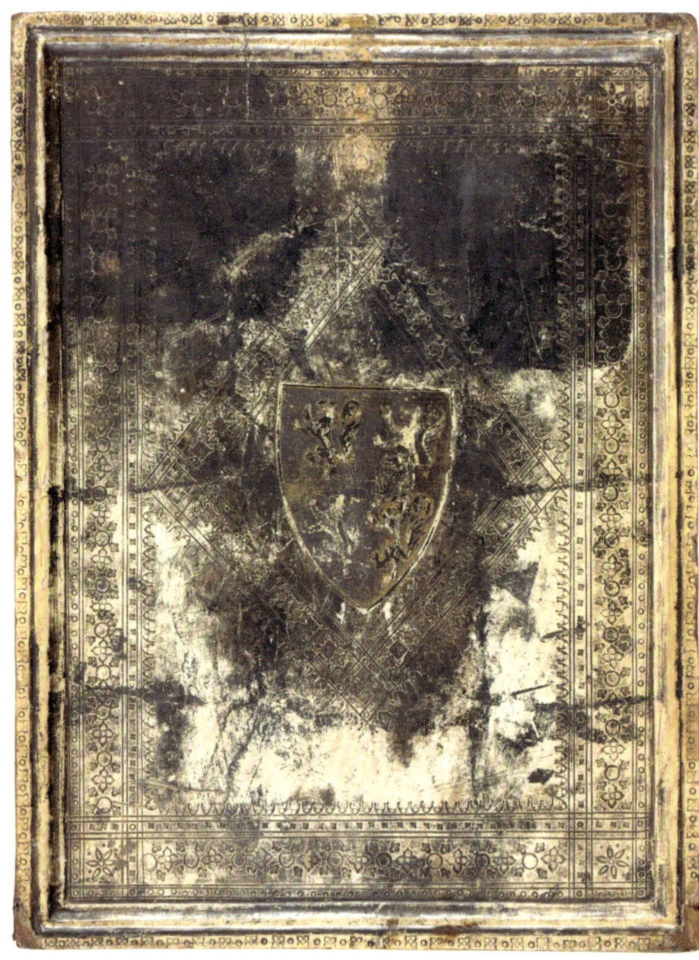

HAINAUT (?)

The impact of Sienese painting on the courts of northern Europe is further exemplified by the *Annunciation* now in the Cleveland Museum of Art, the 'Sachs *Annunciation*' by an unidentified French/Franco-Flemish (?) artist (fig. 181).[37] This was once part of a diptych or possibly a folding polyptych. The arms on the reverse are those of Hainaut-Holland (fig. 182),[38] but its date and who exactly commissioned the work have been disputed.

Due to the arms on the reverse, the Cleveland *Annunciation* has previously been linked by Diane Scillia, followed by Albert Châtelet, with the double wedding of siblings that took place in Cambrai in 1385, when John of Nevers (John the Fearless), son of Philip the Bold, Duke of Burgundy, married Margaret of Bavaria, daughter of Albert of Bavaria, Regent of Hainaut-Holland, and at the same time Albert's son, William, Count of Ostrevant, married Philip's daughter, Margaret.[39] However, any connection with either of the marriages (or William's betrothal to a French princess)[40] is ruled out by the fact that the Hainaut-Holland arms of both Margaret of Bavaria and William of Bavaria were quartered with those of Bavaria.[41] Moreover, the Cleveland *Annunciation* has convincingly been dated around 1350 by Gerhard Schmidt and Victor Schmidt,[42] and around 1350/60 by Stephan Kemperdick.[43]

It is most likely that the Cleveland *Annunciation* was made for Margaret of Avesnes (died 1356), second wife of Ludwig IV of Bavaria, Holy Roman Emperor (died 1347). On 15 January 1346 in Nuremberg, following the death of Margaret's brother William, Count of Hainaut, in 1345, Ludwig made her Countess of Hainaut-Holland in her own right.[44] The reverse, with the shield containing the Hainaut-Holland arms within a lozenge, indicates it was made for a woman.[45] Moreover, the unusual pattern of what appear to be marguerite daisies on the angel's robe refers to her name,[46] and daisies also seem to be in the cast metal frame

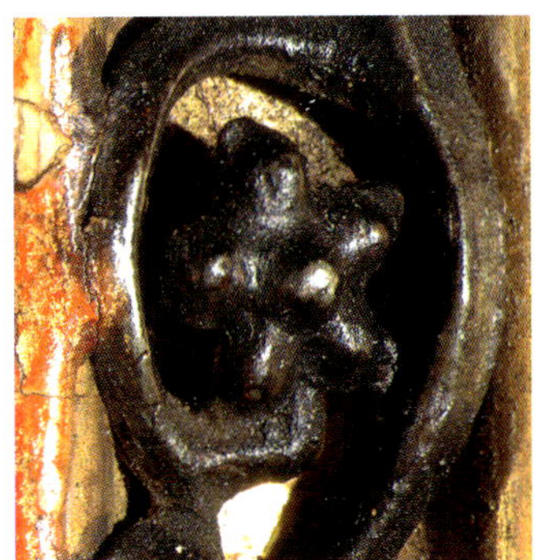

FIG. 181
French/Franco-Flemish (?) artist
The Annunciation, probably 1346–56
Tempera (?) and oil on panel,
35.2 × 26.7 cm (with engaged frame)
Cleveland Museum of Art,
Mr. and Mrs. William H. Marlatt Fund (1954.393)

FIG. 182
Reverse of fig. 181; with the arms of Hainaut-Holland

FIG. 183
Detail of a daisy in the frame of fig. 181

(fig. 183) – now difficult to read – which at the very least presumably reflects the original frame,[47] since, as Helen Howard has observed, it echoes the pattern along the top of the Virgin's throne.[48] Margaret was at the heart of European nobility. Not only was her husband Holy Roman Emperor, but also her uncle, Philip VI, was King of France, and one of her sisters, Philippa, was married to the King of England, Edward III. Margaret was a woman of independent means (and debts), and probably commissioned the *Annunciation* herself, although, given her peripatetic life, where she might have done so is difficult to determine. She spent a considerable amount of time in the county of Hainaut, and she was in Paris in May 1353, which is also a possibility.[49]

The kneeling angel with peacock wings would have resonated with Margaret, since the house of Hainaut-Holland was one of the families whose crest was a 'panache' of peacock feathers.[50] Peacock wings for the Archangel Gabriel may have their origins in Sienese painting. Seen in the *Annunciation* signed by Simone Martini and Lippo Memmi and dated 1333 (see fig. 39), this motif may have circulated in small-scale versions. The patterns of the punchwork in the Cleveland *Annunciation*, particularly the trefoil arches, are typical of Memmi, presumably copied from one of his works, while the tooling of the borders – along the upper edge of the front and around all four edges of the reverse – is similar to that found in Sienese panels, such as the Orsini Polyptych and Memmi's *Virgin lactans* (about 1340; Gemäldegalerie, Berlin).[51] Victor Schmidt noted that the silvered reverse of the Cleveland *Annunciation* is almost identical in design to the reverse of Memmi's *Virgin lactans*.[52] The angel's cloak is imitation *sgraffito* (see below), as is the red Cloth of Honour that hangs behind the Virgin's throne, much as in the New York Bohemian panel.[53]

ENGLAND

The impact of Sienese and also French art is manifest in the Wilton Diptych (fig. 184). It was almost certainly commissioned by the King of England, Richard II, for his personal use, probably around 1397/8, after his marriage in 1396 to Isabelle, eldest surviving daughter of Charles VI of France, and before his deposition on 29 September 1399.[54] It shows Richard presented by saints Edmund, Edward the Confessor and John the Baptist to the Virgin and Child with angels. The exterior bears the royal arms of England impaled with the mythical arms of Edward the Confessor and Richard's emblem of a white hart (fig. 185). The diptych has long been described as having drawn in various ways on Paris and Siena for its style and iconography.[55]

The composition of the left wing seems to derive from a French prototype. There are numerous French examples of a saint presenting a supplicant by touching their back or shoulder just as the Baptist touches Richard's shoulder.[56] The pose of the Virgin and the drapery folds across her front have affinities with fourteenth-century French sculpture.[57] The unruly hair of the angels occurs in French art, for example in *The Angel with a Book* in the Angers Apocalypse tapestries of 1377–80 designed by Jean Bondol, court painter to Charles V (reigned 1364–80).[58] This motif may have been circulating in pattern books, as seen in two possibly Bohemian drawings of the head of the Angel of the Annunciation (Harvard University Art Museums, Cambridge) and Kunsthistorisches Museum (Kunstkammer, Vienna) of around the same date.[59]

The fact that the Wilton Diptych was painted on oak with a chalk (rather than gesso) ground indicates that it was

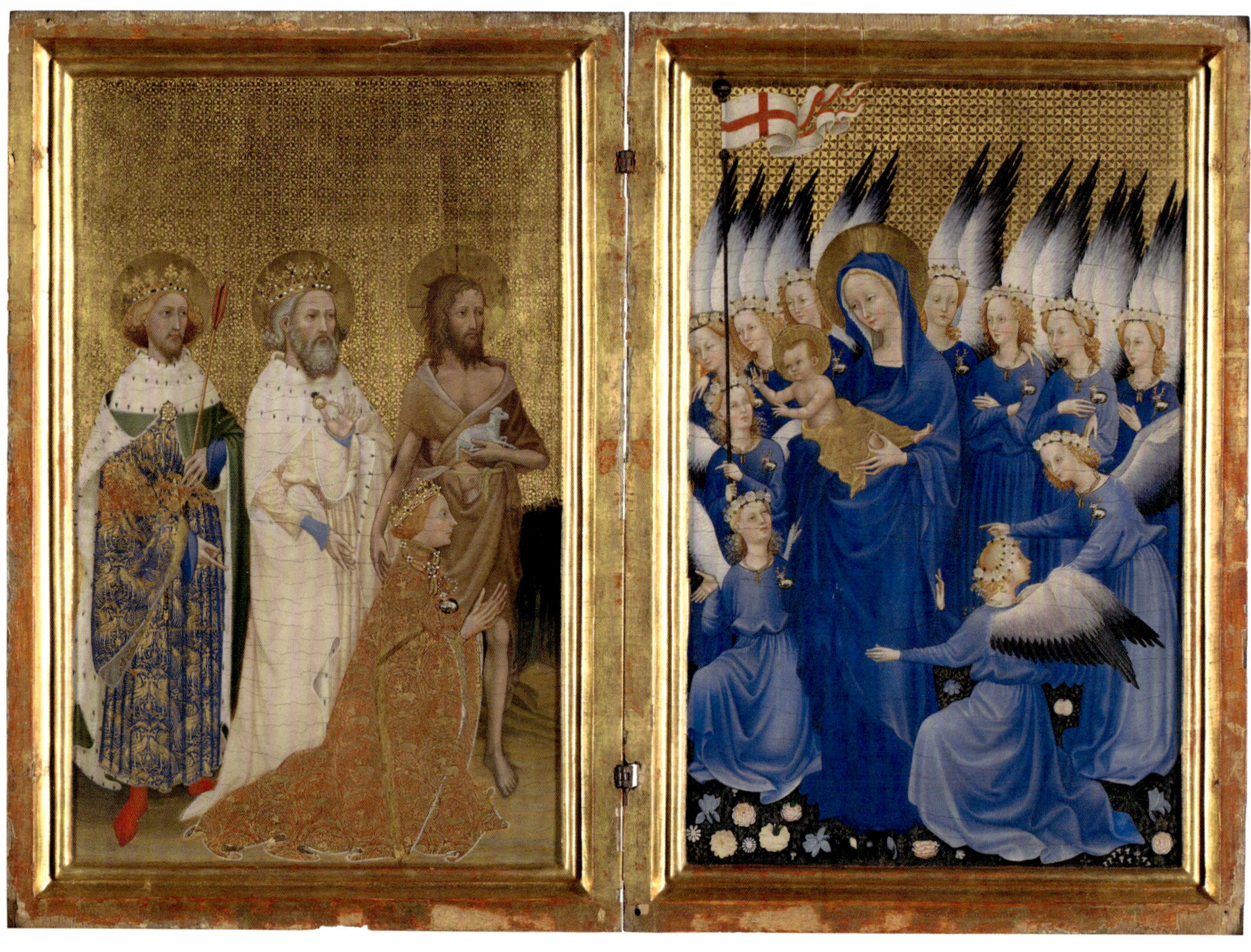

FIG. 184
English or French artist (?)
The Wilton Diptych, about 1396–9
Richard II presented by Saints John the Baptist, Edward the Confessor and Edmund; *The Virgin and Child with Angels*
Tempera on oak, 53 × 37 cm (each wing, with integral frame)
The National Gallery, London. Bought with a special grant and contributions from Samuel Courtauld, Viscount Rothermere, C.T. Stoop and the Art Fund, 1929 (NG4451)

FIG. 185
The reverse of fig. 184: *The royal arms of England and France ancient impaled with the arms of Edward the Confessor, with a helmet, cap of maintenance and a crowned lion passant guardant*; *The white hart lying on a bank of foliage and flowers*

painted in northern Europe. However, no northern painting dating from the end of the fourteenth century precisely mirrors the technique of the diptych, which is largely Italian. The medium is egg and the flesh is underpainted with *terra verde* mixed with lead white, both typical of thirteenth- and fourteenth-century Italian painting:[60] by this date the use of oil as a medium was well established throughout northern Europe.[61] Widely practised in Italy to convey the patterns and textures of textiles was *sgraffito*, here used for the robes of Richard and Saint Edmund. True *sgraffito*, which involved applying pigment over gold leaf, scraping the pigment away to expose the gold parts of the design and then stippling to define the shapes within the pattern, was rarely encountered in northern panel paintings, in which imitation *sgraffito*, the result of artists' observation of true *sgraffito*, is more usual.[62] David Peggie has commented that *sgraffito* could be best

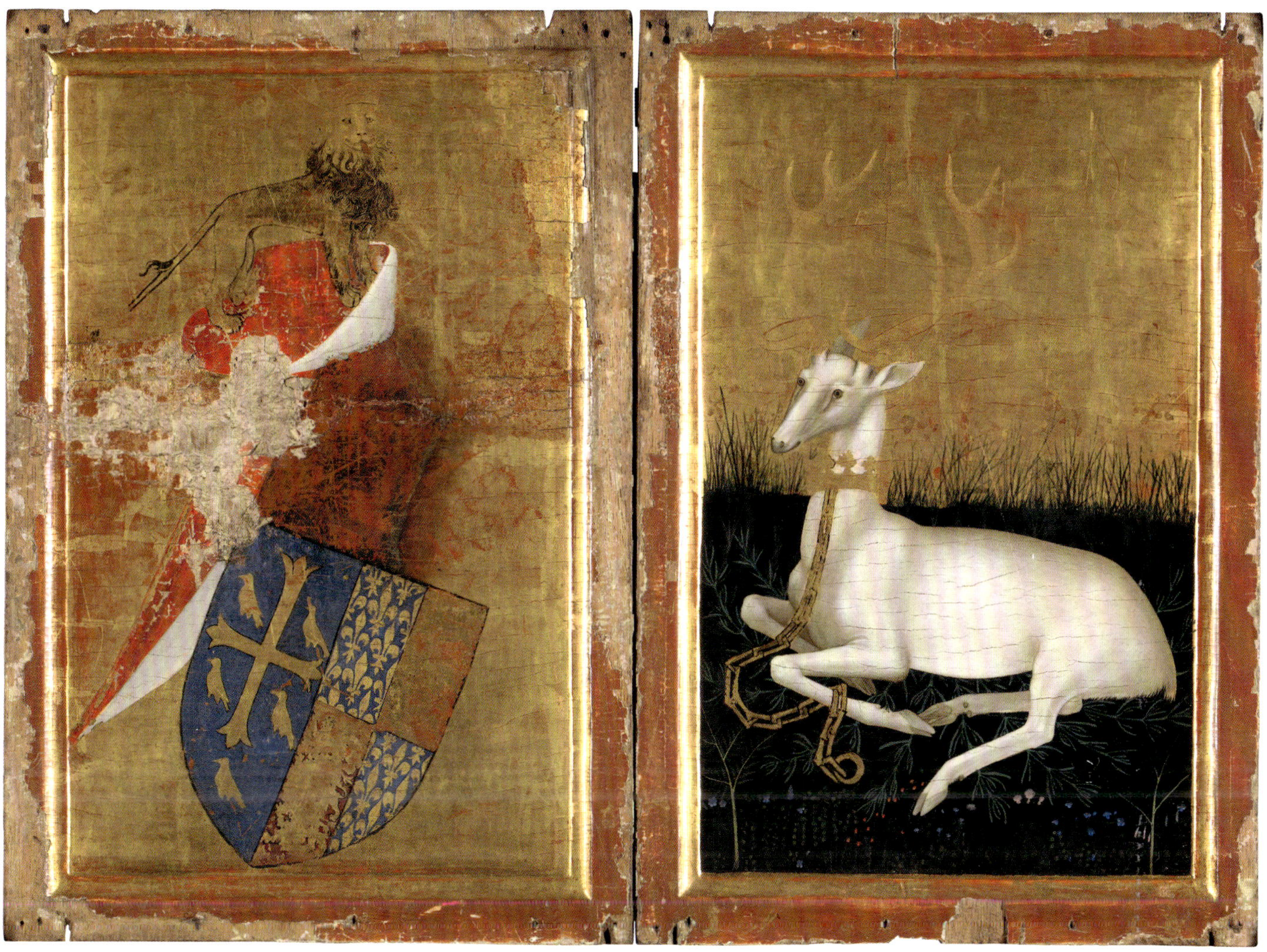

achieved with pigments tempered with egg, and that egg enables the painter to exploit the full purity and intrinsic colour of certain pigments, in this case natural ultramarine.[63] A painter of the calibre of the Wilton Diptych must have been aware of the use of oil but, partly perhaps due to the importance of the textiles of Edmund and Richard with their heraldic references,[64] deliberately chose egg as the medium.[65] Moreover, he was almost certainly attempting to mimic an Italian (presumably Sienese) panel painting – it so happens that an example of the Virgin and Child with angels all entirely in blue is Sienese: the *Virgin and Child enthroned* dated 1344 by Pietro Lorenzetti in the Uffizi, Florence.

The naturalistic depiction of the hart in the Wilton Diptych has been said to have originated under the influence of Lombard painting.[66] However, the artist chose not to render the antlers in paint, but to convey their three-dimensionality in stippling that catches the light. This type of decoration was perfected in Parisian goldsmiths' work of around 1400,[67] but is also seen in Sienese paintings, for example the vase in the Orsini Polyptych (see fig. 81). The refined elegance and some compositional details of the Wilton Diptych seem partly to have their roots in the work of Simone Martini and his workshop and followers, who were painting a generation earlier, and the imitation gems in the crowns of Richard and Edward the Confessor are also reminiscent of the type of decoration found in the works of Simone, as is the Virgin's fluted, semi-transparent white veil edged with stitching. Another feature in the Wilton Diptych that evokes Simone's work is Saint John the Baptist. His spikey, tousled hair occurs, for example, in Simone's wall painting of the *Maestà* in the Palazzo Pubblico, Siena (perhaps originating in Duccio's *Maestà*) (see figs 65 and 8), in Simone's Santa Caterina Polyptych (see fig. 44), and in Lippo Memmi's *Saint John the Baptist* (National Gallery of Art, Washington DC), part of a polyptych of around 1325.[68] In the Wilton Diptych, the pose of the angel with its arm around the angel standing beside it with folded arms is similar to that of Joseph with his arm around Christ, who also has his arms folded across his chest, in the *Christ discovered in the Temple* painted in Avignon (see fig. 74), signed by Simone and dated 1342.[69]

BURGUNDY, AVIGNON AND ENGLAND

It may be that Philip the Bold (1363–1404), Duke of Burgundy, was instrumental in the commissioning of the Wilton Diptych. Like Charles IV of Bohemia, he was a frequent visitor to Avignon and likewise admired Sienese painting, again probably due to his several trips to visit successive popes.[70] Avignon was easily reached from his residence in Dijon by taking the boat down the Saône/Rhône from Chalons-sur-Saône. For example, in 1395 he took a flotilla of 17 boats accompanied by his brother John, Duke of Berry, and his nephew Louis, Duke of Orléans. They stayed in Villeneuve-lès-Avignon for a month, and in Avignon itself for a fortnight.

Philip is thought to have owned the small quadriptych by Simone Martini, known as the Orsini Polyptych after its probable commissioner Cardinal Napoleone Orsini, who died in Avignon in 1342 (see fig. 80). By at least 1791, part of this folding quadriptych was in the monastery patronised by Philip, the Chartreuse de Champmol outside Dijon[71] It is possible that the Orsini Polyptych was brought to Dijon from Avignon, either by Philip or the Duke of Berry. Philip could have acquired it at any time after 1371.[72] A small travelling polyptych of narrative panels, probably modelled on the Orsini Polyptych or something similar and now divided between Baltimore and Antwerp, is thought to have been made for Philip since it too may have come from Champmol.[73] Another Sienese painting possibly brought north by Philip or John was the *Fall of the Rebel Angels* (see also p. 226), which the Limbourg brothers seem to have drawn on, as well as the Orsini panels, in the *Très Riches Heures* for the Duke of Berry (see pp. 240–53).[74] A commission for Philip influenced by Sienese painting, particularly by Ambrogio Lorenzetti's *Presentation in the Temple* signed and dated 1342 (see fig. 41) – possibly via pattern books or derivative versions – were the wings of the Crucifixion altarpiece (fig. 186) painted by Melchior Broederlam in 1393–9 for Champmol.[75] This painting evidently imitates Italian techniques in the greenish underpainting of the flesh, and the priest's cap (fig. 187), for example, was executed in imitation *sgraffito*.[76]

Further support for Philip's involvement in the Wilton Diptych is provided by the fact that, in addition to being an admirer of Sienese painting, he was also at the nexus of negotiations for Richard II's marriage to Isabelle. Philip had always been a proponent of peace with England, and so was ideally placed to negotiate the marriage between Richard and Isabelle and the concomitant truce in the Hundred Years' War. Isabelle was formally handed over to Richard at Ardres between 27 and 30 October 1396, and they were married on 4 November in Calais.[77] Both before and after these events, Philip met frequently with Richard himself, staying in Calais at Richard's expense.[78] Before leaving for England, Richard and Isabelle dined on board Philip's boat at Saint-Omer.[79] Philip demonstrated his knowledge of Richard's devotional interests when in 1398 he sent him a New Year's gift (*étrenne*) of a gold image of Saint Edward the Confessor.[80] It was

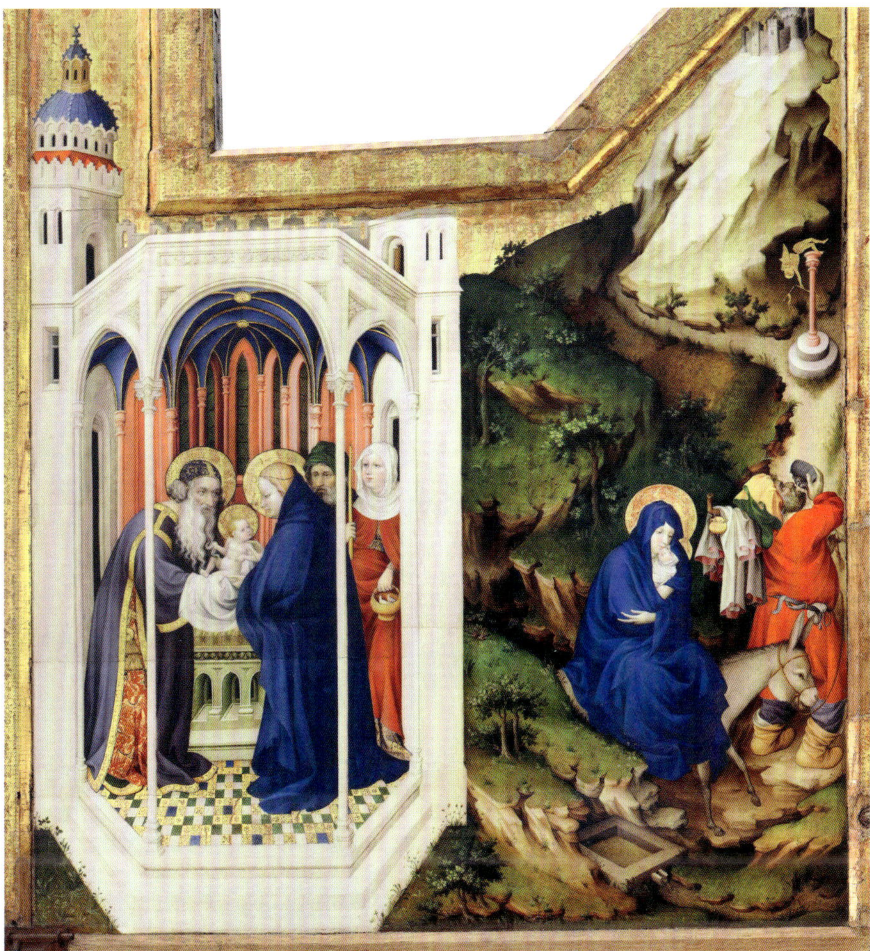

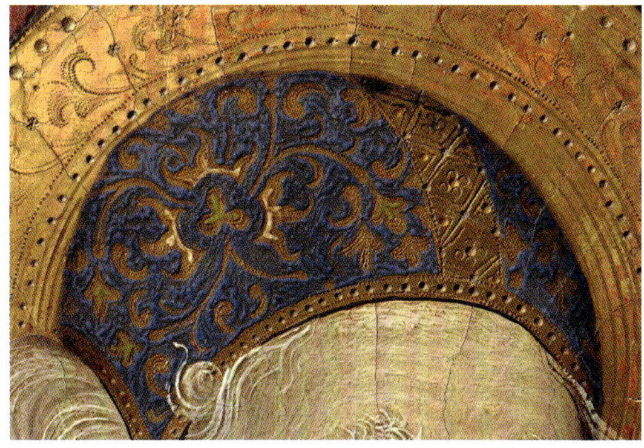

FIG. 186
Melchior Broederlam
(documented 1381–1409)
The Purification of the Virgin and the Flight into Egypt, 1393–9
(detail of the exterior of a wing of the Crucifixion Altarpiece for Champmol)
Oil on panel
Musée des Beaux-Arts, Dijon (CA1420A)

FIG. 187
Detail of the priest's cap from fig. 186, showing imitation *sgraffito*

probably Philip who ordered the matching image of Saint Edmund, given to Richard by Charles VI:[81] both saints appear in the Wilton Diptych. If the diptych is primarily by a French painter, it is possible that Philip, who was noticeably proactive in directing the lives of the painters he employed, recommended him to Richard, in the same way that a French embroiderer came to work for Richard and Isabelle on the recommendation of the Duke of Berry.[82]

Numerous features indicate that the Wilton Diptych was painted at the English court. For example, Lisa Monnas has suggested that Saint Edmund's *houppelande* (long-sleeved gown) was probably based on an actual fabric by a weaver from Lucca documented in Richard's employ.[83] Furthermore, a change was made in the pennon that symbolises both the Passion of Christ and Saint George, patron saint of England.[84] It originally terminated in a cross stippled into the gold, as commonly found in the flag held by Christ in scenes of the Resurrection.[85] However, painted over the cross is an orb that almost certainly symbolises England as the dowry of the Virgin,[86] which must have been added while the diptych was actually being painted, and several other details point to the diptych having been painted at Richard's court.

The diffusion of elements inspired by the Sienese style of painting in the courts of the north was due not only to the movements of painters, pattern books and the enthusiasm of individuals such as Charles IV of Bohemia and Philip the Bold, but also to exchanges of gifts.[87] However, the so-called International Gothic style was by no means uniform and there were deviations following regional styles.[88] The Bohemian *Virgin and Child enthroned*, the Cleveland *Annunciation* and the Wilton Diptych have very different artistic roots. Yet, all three are imbued with the refinement, technical sophistication and elegance that emanated from Italian, especially Sienese, painters of the first half of the fourteenth century, who had so much to offer to the practice and status of panel painting in northern Europe well into the fifteenth century.

I am extremely grateful to Joanna Cannon for her indefatigable encouragement and perceptive comments through the many drafts of this essay. I am also very grateful to Lorne Campbell, as well as to Susie Nash and Lisa Monnas for reading a draft of this essay and for their very helpful comments, and also to Štěpánka Chlumská, Dean Yoder, Elisabeth Ravaud, Michael Gallagher, Rachel Billinge and Helen Howard for their help.

1. The Schism ended with the election of Martin V in 1417, who returned the papacy to Rome in 1421.
2. Capron 2017, especially p. 10, with bibliography.
3. Machtelt Brüggen Israëls suggests that a *Maestà* attributable to Lippo and Tederigo in the Berenson Collection, Villa I Tatti, is identifiable with an altarpiece signed and dated 1347 once in the Orsini chapel in the Franciscan church in Avignon (see Israëls in Strehlke and Israëls 2015, pp. 452–8, pl. 69).
4. A *Virgin and Child* signed by Naddo and dated 1347 (ex-Cook Collection, sold Christie's, London, 8 December 2005, lot 22) may well have been painted in Avignon, as well as perhaps the (unconnected) signed *Man of Sorrows* of around the same date (Princely Collections, Liechtenstein, inv. GE862). See Christiansen in New York 1985–6, cat. 122, pp. 189–91.
5. Cannon 2013, pp. 219–23, especially p. 222.
6. See Gordon 2011, pp. 188–201, with bibliography.
7. Inv. DL 1967 1 A and B. See Schmidt 2005a, p. 247; Schmidt 2009, pp. 189–90.
8. Said to be from the estate of the Bishop of Tarbes, Guillaume de Rosières, who died in 1361. See Schmidt 2005a, p. 247. Inv. 1963-2-1-1, 1963-2-12.
9. For the three panels, see Thiébaut in Paris 2013, cats 27–9, pp. 200–7. They were tentatively attributed by Van Marle 1924, pp. 307–9, to Naddo Ceccarelli, and to a painter close to Naddo by De Benedictis 1974, pp. 144, 149.
10. 'tabulam seu conam de octo partibus seu tabulis divisibilibus et congiungibilibus, quam fecit fieri et pingi in Avinione' ('a panel or icon of eight parts which can be separated as well as joined together which I had made and painted in Avignon'): Campana 1951, pp. 20–3, especially p. 22 and n. 10. For the will of 16 August 1345, see Tonini 1880, p. 168.
11. The painting is associated by Christiansen 2021b, pp. 10–12, with the court of Charles IV. For Charles, see Fajt 2005–6; Boehm 2005–6b.
12. Fragments of iron (probably hinge) fixtures visible left and right in the X-radiograph (Christiansen 2021b, p. 11, fig. 2) indicate the original presence of wings. The panel, made up of two boards of a fruit wood, has been trimmed on all four edges, about 5 cm at the top (unpublished report by Michael Gallagher, Sherman Fairchild Chairman of Paintings Conservation, The Metropolitan Museum of Art, dated August 2021). Klípa 2019, p. 220, sees it as one wing of a diptych.
13. Boehm 2005–6a, p. 80.
14. Christiansen 2021b, pp. 9–10. For the royal chapels of Our Lady and of Saint Catherine, decorated 1356–7/8, see Royt 2003a, pp. 65–7; Royt 2003b.
15. Christiansen 2021b, pp. 13–17, gives a detailed analysis of the complex architecture and the throne. The biblical porch contained the throne from which Solomon issued judgement, although the throne in the painting does not overtly refer to Solomon's throne. A pentimento is in the rectangular niche directly above the Virgin's head, where a row of six slightly pointed arches was drawn spanning the full width of the niche, each arch having a trefoil design (Gallagher report cited in n. 12 above).
16. See Albrecht et al. 2022. I owe this reference to Benno Baumbauer.
17. For discussion of the display of the sole, see Grandmontagne 2005, pp. 365 ff.; for French examples of the Child also holding his toes, see especially p. 376; p. 377, fig. 118 (sculptured relief of about 1376); p. 389, fig. 122 (stained glass of 1388/90); p. 381, fig. 120 (plaster cast of statue of about 1410/20); for an Italian example, see p. 391, fig. 123 (painting signed and dated 1367 by Barnabà da Modena). I owe this reference to Susie Nash.
18. See Cannon 2010, pp. 10, 23–8, for a discussion of the adoration of the Child's foot.
19. Klípa 2019, p. 219.
20. Suckale and Fajt 2005–6, cat. 9, pp. 139–40, dating it about 1350–5; Klípa in Dáňová, Chlumská and Šefců 2017, no. 5, pp. 130–2, where it is dated about 1355–60 (i.e. in both instances after the Vyšší Brod Altarpiece). Until 1927 it was in the collection of Count Giuseppe de Campano Sanseverino, Rome.
21. Klípa in Dáňová, Chlumská and Šefců 2017, no. 3 and pp. 122–4, suggests it might have been commissioned by Charles IV. See also Grandmontagne 2005, pp. 450–4; Suckale and Fajt 2005–6, cat. 5, pp. 135–6. The two paintings belong with a group of Bohemian panels showing the Virgin and Child with a goldfinch, including the *Madonna of Most* (before 1350) and the *Madonna of Veveří* (after 1345), both in the National Gallery Prague, which Royt 2003a, p. 61, attributes to the Master of the Vyšší Brod Altarpiece, before 1350; see also Pešina 1982, pp. 90–2.
22. Pešina 1982, pp. 92–4; Royt 2003a, pp. 61–2; Grandmontagne 2005, pp. 455–9; Voigt 2008, pp. 35–6 (all dating it about 1360, i.e. well after the Vyšší Brod cycle).
23. See Pešina 1982, reconstruction p. 129, and figs 6, 7; Suckale and Fajt 2005–6, p. 37, fig. 3.2.
24. For the Vyšší Brod Altarpiece (inv. VO 13504–12; formerly DO 2089–97; O 6786–94), attributable to at least four painters, see Pešina 1982, especially pp. 21, 55; Klípa in Dáňová, Chlumská and Šefců 2017, no. 2, pp. 116–21. It consists of nine scenes from the Life of Christ, painted on maple panels (see Antušková et al. 2016, pp. 97, 101), probably for the high altar of the Cistercian monastery of Vyšší Brod. Peter I of Rožmberk moved in royal circles and was extremely powerful in the kingdom of Bohemia (Pešina 1982, pp. 19–20).
25. Klípa 2019 (before cleaning of the overpainted background and conservation of the New York panel); Christiansen 2021b (after cleaning and conservation). Klípa's attribution is doubted by Christiansen 2021b, p. 17, who sees it as of higher quality while acknowledging the affinities with the Vyšší Brod panels.
26. Klípa 2019, p. 218. For the punch marks in the Vyšší Brod Altarpiece, see Pokorný 2017.
27. Since the excellent condition of the paint surface of the New York painting precludes the taking of pigment samples, analysis of the technique was based on observation under a microscope allied to non-destructive imaging techniques: X-radiography, infrared reflectography (IRR) and macro-XR (Gallagher report cited in n. 12 above).
28. For the use of egg, and the underpainting of flesh with *terra verde* (green earth) in Italian paintings, see London 1989–90, pp. 28, 40–1.
29. Šefců et al. 2017, pp. 82–3. Although no organic analysis of the painting medium in the New York panel was undertaken, the use of oil is considered likely (Gallagher report cited in n. 12 above).
30. Samples from the *Agony in the Garden*, attributed to the Master of the Vyšší Brod Altarpiece in Šefců et al. 2017, pp. 82–3, and p. 83, fig. 6. For the slightly different and simpler underpainting for the flesh painting, lacking the red interlayer, in the other panels, see Šefců et al. 2017, pp. 83–4. See also Hamsík 1967 (1989), p. 322; Hamsík 1978, p. 530.
31. For example, in the *Virgin and Child* by the Master of the Clarisse (possibly Rinaldo da Siena), see fig. 15 in the present volume, or later the small *Maestà* attributed to Ugolino di Nerio (both in the National Gallery, London, inv. NG6571 and NG6386; see Gordon 2011, pp. 348–55, 478–85).
32. See Cannon in Boston 2022–3, cat. 1, pp. 164–93, fig. 84; Cannon 2022–3, p. 114, figs 47–50; pp. 116, 123, nn. 42, 46.
33. Jarrett 1935, pp. 78, 79, 103, 105; Gibbs 1989, p. 178.
34. Gibbs 1989, p. 181; Coletti 1963, pp. 88–9, fig. 128, suggests the Sienese painter might have been summoned to Prague by Charles IV from Avignon.
35. Gibbs 1989, pp. 183–7. Williamson 2009, p. 101, sees Charles's commissions of paintings of the Madonna of Humility as possibly prompted by his having seen Simone Martini's wall paintings in Avignon.
36. Christiansen 2021b, *passim*, considers that the painter of the New York panel may have travelled to Italy.
37. Francis 1955; Stechow 1974, pp. 21–4; Herman in

Dijon and Cleveland 2004–5, cat. 18, pp. 66–7. The earliest record of it is in the collection of the Duke of Anhalt-Dessau (1863–1925), as by Duccio.

38. Brilliant in Cleveland 2007, cat. 69, p. 195, incorrectly states that the arms are quartered with those of Bavaria.
39. Scillia 1995, especially pp. 346–8, associates it with John the Fearless's marriage to Margaret of Bavaria. Châtelet 2007a, pp. 169–73, and Châtelet 2007b, pp. 186–7, consider the punch-mark of fleurs-de-lis on the reverse (see n. 51 below) to indicate that it was commissioned by Philip on the occasion of the betrothal in 1374 of William to the eldest daughter of Charles V of France, Marie (died 1377), and given to William in 1385 on his marriage to Margaret of Burgundy. Châtelet attributes the painting to Jean d'Arbois (for whom see n. 65 below).
40. See n. 39.
41. See n. 38. For the quartered arms see, for example, the seals of William (Laurent 1993, vol. I/2, nos 65–9, pp. 377–9, and vol. II, pls 194–5) and Margaret (Laurent 1993, vol. I/2, nos 78–80, pp. 634–5, and vol. II, pls 388–9). The apparent lack of quartering in the Hainaut-Holland arms on the catafalque in the Turin-Milan Hours (cited by Scillia 1995, p. 346) is irrelevant.
42. Schmidt 1975, pp. 47–63; reprinted 2005, pp. 199–214, plus 'Nachtrag 2003', p. 213, and Schmidt 2009, pp. 197–8, both dispute Scillia's suggestion (see n. 39 above).
43. Kemperdick in Brinkmann and Kemperdick 2002, pp. 40–1, 49–51; Kemperdick 2010, pp. 94–5.
44. Wauters 1894–5, especially col. 637. See also Maillard-Luypaert 2012, pp. 327–8. I am grateful to Stephen Mossman for this reference. In view of the patronage suggested here, the direct impact of the Cleveland *Annunciation* on the Nuremberg Master analysed by Kemperdick 2010, pp. 94–5, merits further investigation.
45. Gheusi 1933, p. 44 (although male arms could also be shown in a lozenge as in the Orsini Polyptych (see fig. 80). Margaret's arms combined with those of Ludwig could have been on the reverse of the other panel, as suggested to me by Lorne Campbell.
46. Marguerite daisies were often used to refer to women whose name was Margaret. See, for example, the seals used by the two sisters-in-law, Margaret of Bavaria (Laurent 1993, vol. I/2, no. 80, p. 635; vol. II, pl. 389) and Margaret of Burgundy (Laurent 1993, vol. I/2, nos 97–8, pp. 393–4; vol. II, pls 208–9).
47. Dean Yoder, Senior Conservator of Paintings at the Cleveland Museum of Art, has kindly done X-ray fluorescence investigations that revealed the cast metal frame contains principally lead, copper, tin and iron.
48. Communication via email (9 February 2023).
49. Maillard-Luypaert 2012, p. 345; Devillers 1881, nos CCXXVII–CCXXX, pp. 363–70.
50. Wapenboek Gelre, Brussels, Bibliothèque Royale, MS Albert I, inv. 15652–6, fol. 83 (viewable online at https://uurl.kbr.be/1733715, accessed 31 August 2023), compiled between about 1370 and 1414, by which date the Hainaut-Holland arms were quartered with those of Bavaria. I owe this reference to Lorne Campbell whose help with the Cleveland *Annunciation* has been invaluable.
51. The punch-marks on the back include fleurs-de-lis that Frinta 1965, p. 264, describes as Sienese (see also Frinta 1998, p. 391, ill. Jb 75). Fleurs-de-lis are absent from the Small Bargello Diptych (Museo Nazionale del Bargello, Florence) from the same workshop, possibly by the same hand.
52. Schmidt 2009, pp. 197, 200, fig. 13; p. 203, fig. 15.
53. Dean Yoder kindly examined the *sgraffito* on my behalf.
54. Gordon et al. 2015, with bibliography.
55. For example, Constable 1929, p. 43; Rickert 1965, p. 159; Mathew 1968, p. 199; see Gordon et al. 2015, p. 109.
56. Gordon 2015. Thomas 2020 (2023), p. 162, fig. 32, sees this iconography as originating in Bohemian painting.
57. Gordon et al. 2015, p. 68, fig. 49. The outward-leaning Child may come from Bohemian sculpture (ibid., p. 112, fig. 87).
58. Muel et al. 1987, p. 18, fig. 8 (detail); no. 27 (24), pp. 150–1.
59. Inv. 1947.80; Schmidt 2005–6, p. 109, fig. 9.8, and inv. KK5003; Suckale and Fajt in New York and Prague 2005–6, cat. 117, pp. 274–6.
60. Gordon et al. 2015, pp. 94–5. *Terra verde* (or *tervert*) was used by French painters (see Nash 2010, pp. 104, 148, 150), but documentation is sparse and its use is unknown.
61. For example, Binski and Massing 2009, p. 252 (probably French, Westminster Retable, 1269); Ayers 2019, pp. 2, 52, for English (wall painting) in the 1350s; Šefců et al. 2017, for mid-fourteenth-century Bohemian; Gifford 1995, pp. 362–3, and Ravaud et al. 2017–18, p. 39, for Franco-Burgundian about 1400, etc.
62. See London 1989–90, pp. 130–5, for a full description of the technique.
63. Peggie 2014, pp. 211, 213, fig. 10.3; p. 215.
64. See Gordon et al. 2015, pp. 40–53, 61–3.
65. A French painter who could have introduced egg tempera painting to northern French painters was Jean d'Arbois (originally from the Franche Comté), who was brought to Dijon from Pavia in Lombardy and then to Paris and Bruges by Philip the Bold, returning to Pavia by June 1385 (Karet 1992, p. 9; Villela-Petit 2006). Jean d'Arbois's son, Stefano, who presumably trained with him, painted with egg; see the online catalogue entry, www.metmuseum.org/art/collection/search/770595 (accessed 31 August 2023), for the Lenbach *Crucifixion* of about 1400, The Metropolitan Museum of Art, New York (inv. 2018.87).
66. Wormald 1954, pp. 195–6.
67. For example, the reverse of the reliquary triptych in the Rijksmuseum, Amsterdam, from the former abbey of Choques (Amsterdam 1994–5, pp. 122–3, pl. 38).
68. Inv. 1939.1.291. See Boskovits 2016.
69. Although this may have been circulating in pattern books, since it is also a motif used by Giotto in frescoes in Santa Croce, Florence.
70. See Petit 1888, pp. 63–4, 484 (January 1371); pp. 129–30, 504 (August 1376); pp. 242–3, 552 (May–July 1395); also Vaughan 1962 (2002), pp. 11–14, 46–7.
71. Prochno 2002, pp. 195–8.
72. See n. 70.
73. Prochno 2002, pp. 198–9. For the Antwerp/Baltimore panels, see Nieuwdorp 1994–5, including a reconstruction; Spicer in Dijon and Cleveland 2004–5, cat. 74, pp. 206–7; Schmidt 2009, p. 204, notes that quadriptychs occur in French royal inventories predating the Antwerp/Baltimore panels.
74. Laclotte and Thiébaut 1983, no. 3, pp. 136–9; Schmidt 2005b, p. 185 and figs 12–17.
75. Jugie in Dijon and Cleveland 2004–5, cat. 70, pp. 196–7; Currie 2009.
76. Currie 2009, p. 58, fig. 27; pp. 64, 86, n. 132.
77. For an anonymous English account of the events at Ardres, see Meyer 1881; Stratford 2012, Appendix no. 2, pp. 387–91.
78. For a week from 14 August, again 11–13 October, and 31 October–5 November (Petit 1888, pp. 255, 257, 258–9).
79. Petit 1888, p. 554.
80. Dehaisnes 1886, p. 769; Vaughan 1962 (2002), p. 108; Hirschbiegel 2003, pp. 186–8, 412, and n. 974, no. 991.
81. Stratford 2012, p. 233, inv. R 970, R 971, and commentary pp. 348–50.
82. Devon 1837, p. 285.
83. Monnas 1997, pp. 171–2; Monnas (forthcoming).
84. Gordon et al. 2015, p. 74.
85. For example, in the Antwerp/Baltimore polyptych, see Nieuwdorp 1994–5; Spicer in Dijon and Cleveland 2004–5, cat. 74, pp. 206–7.
86. Gordon 1992; Gordon et al. 2015, pp. 70–3; although disputed by Madersbacher 2001, among others.
87. There were probably more gifts than are documented. A gift of a panel painting from the Duke of Burgundy (John the Fearless) in 1412 to the King of England (Henry IV) happens to be documented only because a chain for it to hang from and a 'custode' (protective case) were commissioned for it. Cited by Stroo 2016, p. 311.
88. Schmidt 2005–6, p. 105.

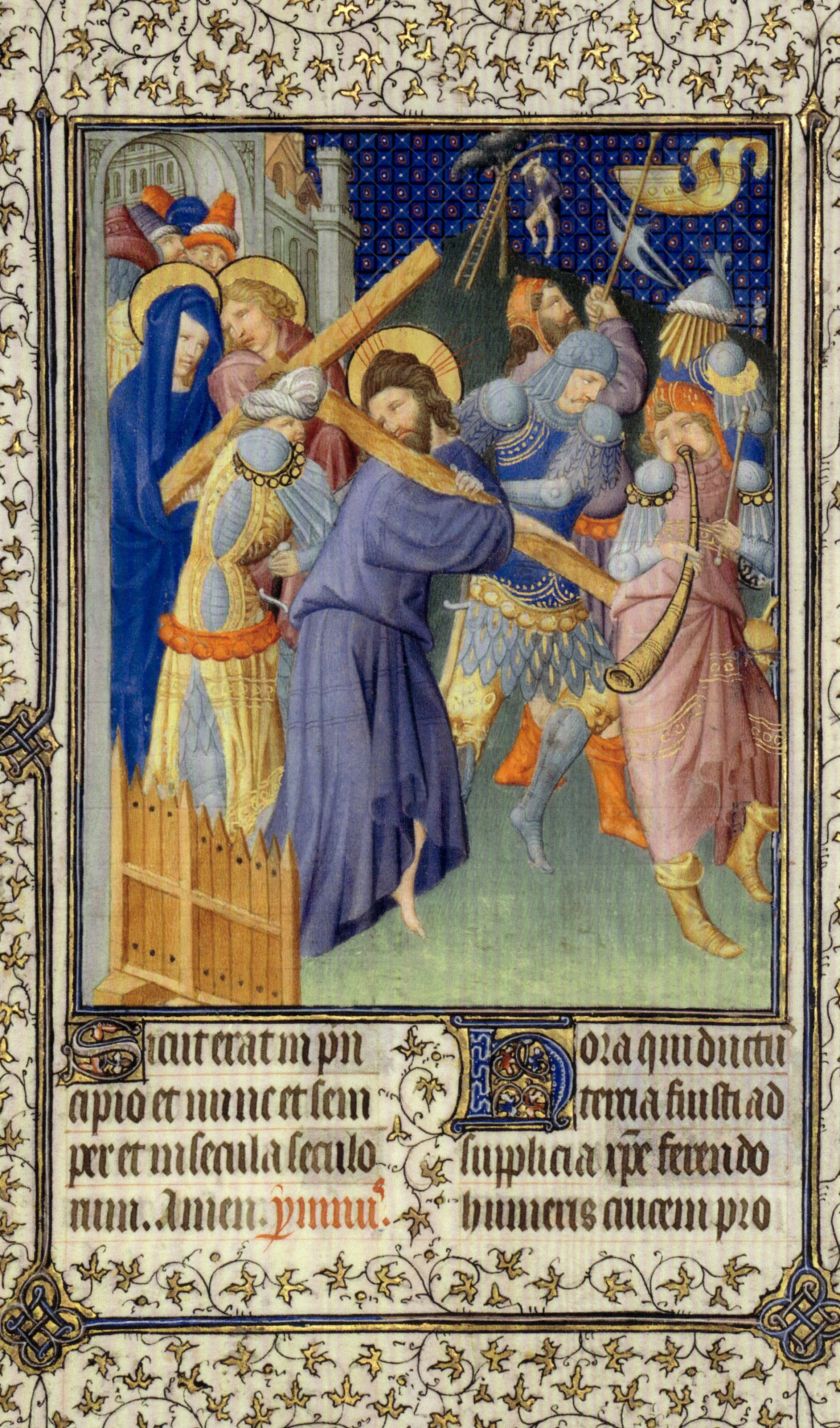
Sicut erat in prin
cipio et nunc et sem
per et in secula seculo
rum. Amen. Ymnus.
Hora qui ductu
tertia fuisti ad
supplicia xpe ferendo
humeris crucem pro

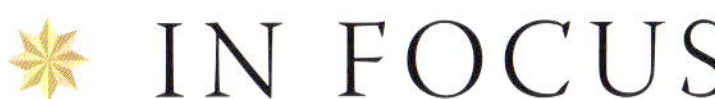

The de Limbourg Brothers and Simone Martini's Orsini Polyptych

Susie Nash

In 1791 Simone Martini's *The Way to Calvary* (fig. 189) was recorded in the prior's cell of the Chartreuse de Champmol, the Carthusian monastery founded by Philip the Bold outside Dijon in 1385.[1] The description of the painting, and the small drawing of the Orsini coat of arms on its reverse, makes its identification indisputable, and there are strong reasons to believe the entire quadriptych to which the panel belongs was in the possession of the French courts around 1400 (see also pp. 120–3).[2] Packed with invention, and on a scale that matched a manuscript page (it is in fact almost exactly the size of modern-day A4 paper),[3] this object was to be formative for the de Limbourg brothers, who worked for both Philip the Bold and John, Duke of Berry, and through them for the development of painting in northern Europe.[4]

It is well known that the illuminators looked at a wide range of Italian art, and at the Orsini ensemble in particular, but the extent and depth of this looking, and how they used what they saw, remains surprisingly little interrogated.[5] It has been noted that the brothers took entire compositional arrangements of the *Way to Calvary* and the *Deposition* (figs 191, 192, 193), as well as individual eye-catching figures from Simone's Passion scenes, like the woman tearing her hair in the *Entombment*, reused in the *Belles Heures* miniature of the same subject (figs 194, 195).[6] But their study went deeper than the lifting of isolated figures or copying the outlines of compositions: they clearly knew the surface of these works at first-hand, not just through drawings, and they returned to them more than once, in both their *Belles Heures*, completed by 1409, and their *Très Riches Heures*, left unfinished in 1416 on the death of the artists and their patron.[7] In these manuscripts the de Limbourgs took on significant elements of Simone's visual language and palette, but also his iconographic inventions, emotional intent and narrative thrust. The lessons they learnt included a delight in the complexity of fabrics, and an understanding of how these textiles could enrich the surface of a work and enliven a composition: they adopted the Sienese painter's broad, gold, decorative borders on the cloaks of figures to heighten pattern and line, the rich lampas

FIG. 188
de Limbourg Brothers
(documented 1399–1416)
The Way to Calvary, 1405–8/9
The Belles Heures of John of France, Duke of Berry, fol. 138v
Tempera and ink on parchment, 23.8 × 17 cm (single leaf)
The Metropolitan Museum of Art, New York. The Cloisters Collection, 1954 (54.1.1a,b)

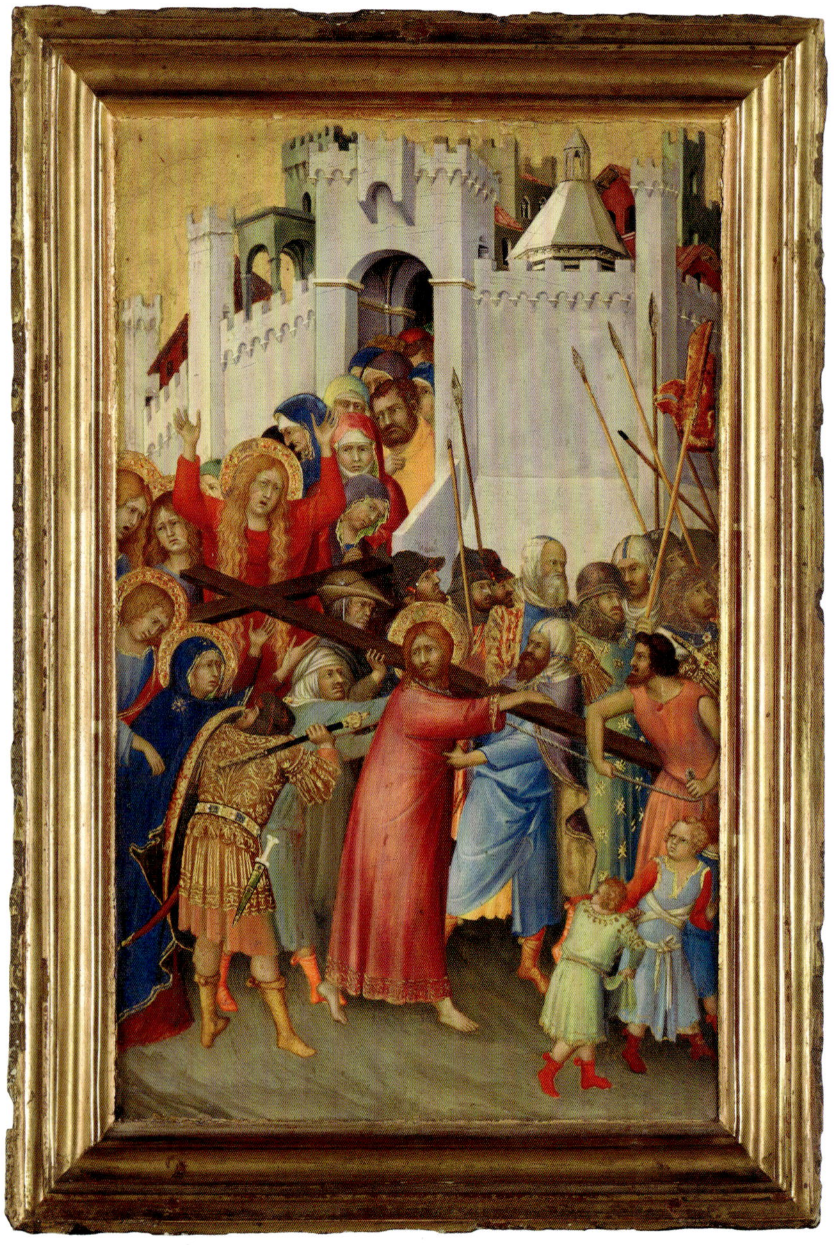

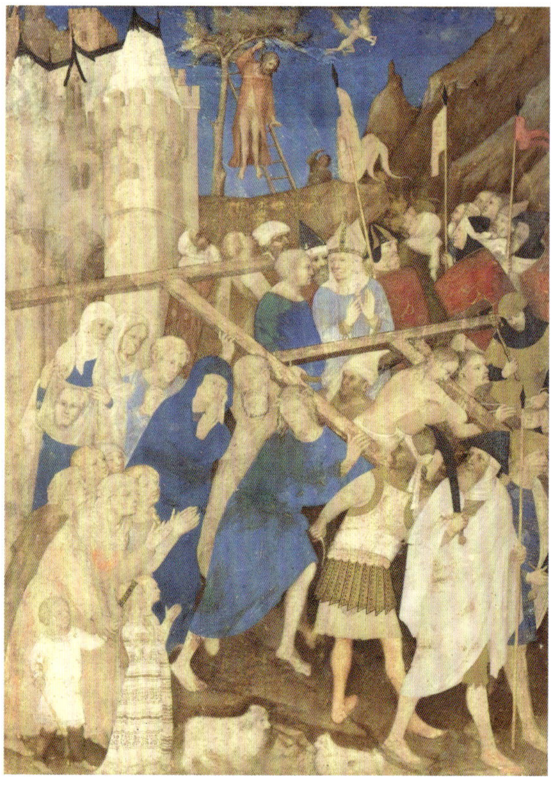

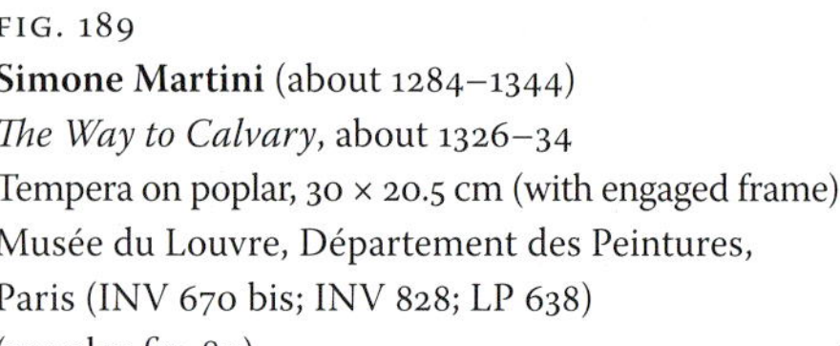

FIG. 189
Simone Martini (about 1284–1344)
The Way to Calvary, about 1326–34
Tempera on poplar, 30 × 20.5 cm (with engaged frame)
Musée du Louvre, Département des Peintures, Paris (INV 670 bis; INV 828; LP 638)
(see also fig. 80)

FIG. 190
Jacquemart de Hesdin
(about 1355–about 1414)
The Way to Calvary, about 1407–9
Parchment glued to linen, 38 × 28.3 cm
Musée du Louvre, Paris (RF 2835)

FIG. 191
de Limbourg Brothers
(documented 1399–1416)
The Way to Calvary, about 1412–16
Très Riches Heures, fol. 147r
Tempera and ink on parchment, 29 × 21 cm
Musée Condé, Chantilly (MS 65)

silks he used to pick out Roman soldiers and Jewish onlookers, and the white cloths he wrapped around heads or crossed over bodies (figs 189, 191). Simone's inventions were rarely copied by rote: the brothers reimagined his forms in different combinations, often viewed from different angles, and although they dressed their figures in more exotic outfits, inspired by Eastern dress and fabrics that filtered into French and Burgundian culture following the crusade to Nicopolis (modern-day Bulgaria) in 1396 and the presence of the Byzantine emperor Manuel Palaeologus and his retinue in Paris in 1399–1400, they nevertheless found a model for the potential of such detail in Simone's work.[8]

Simone's adroitness with revealing and concealing, and how it might heighten the drama in a narrative, was also absorbed, and at times exaggerated, by the duke's illuminators: the brims of soldiers' helmets, drawn low in Simone's works, are brought down to obscure the eyes entirely in the hands of the de Limbourgs (figs 189, 191); the possibilities of figures in the foreground, often drastically foreshortened, seen from behind and bent over, or stretching their necks to look up (figs 196, 197), are multiplied and

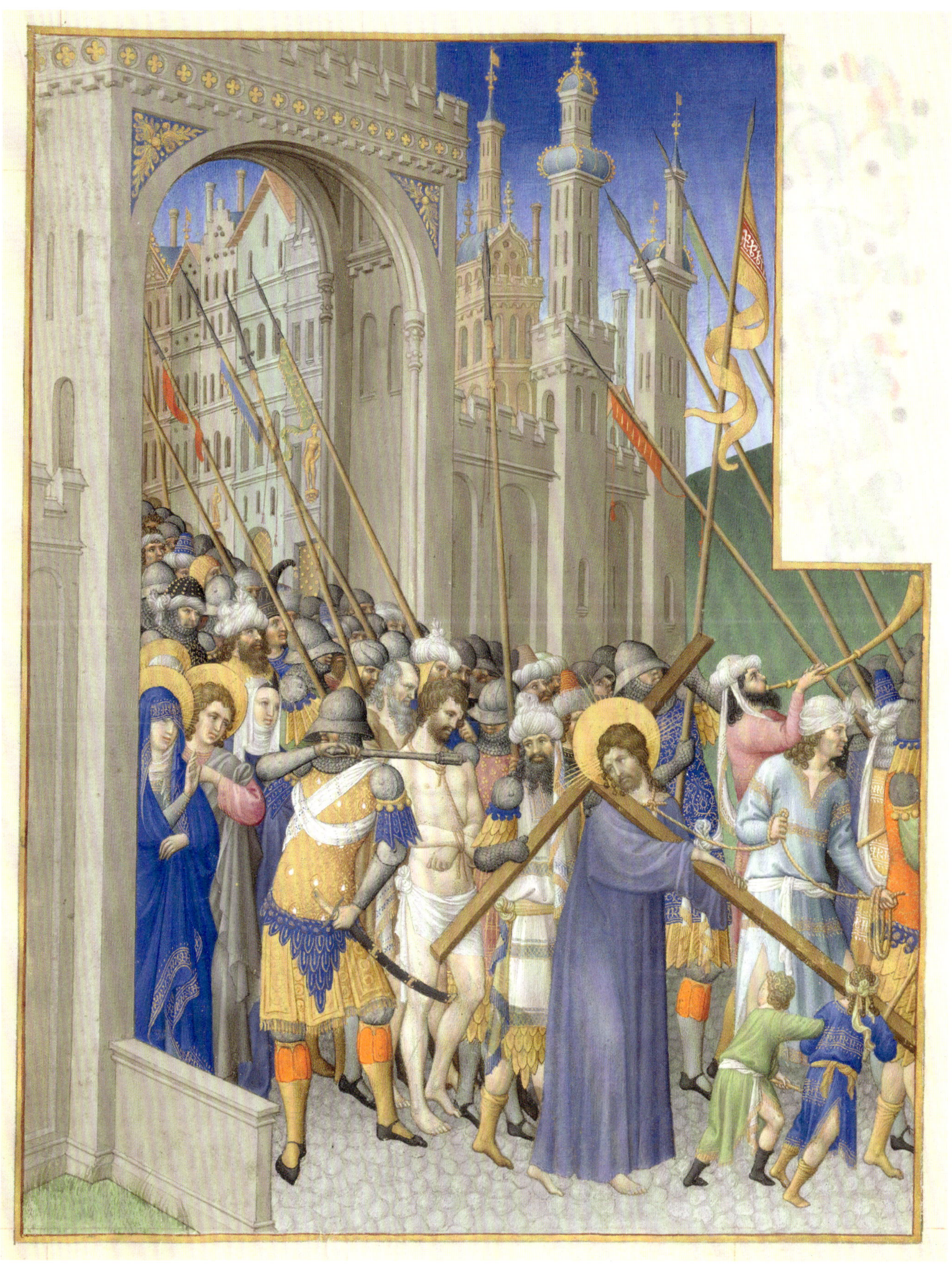

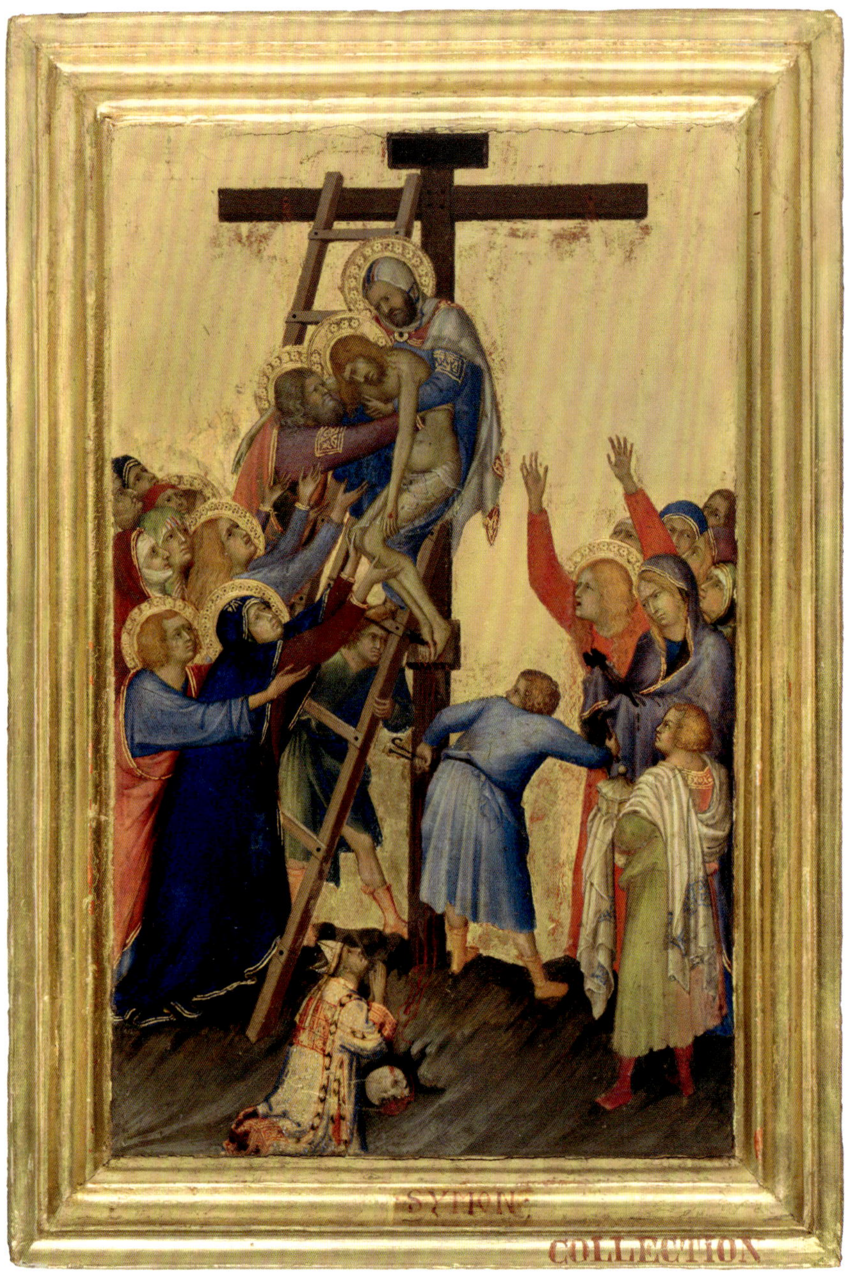

FIG. 192
Simone Martini
(about 1284–1344)
The Deposition,
about 1326–34
Tempera on poplar,
29.5 × 20.6 cm (with engaged frame)
Collection KMSKA - Flemish Community
(public domain) (260)

amplified in the *Belles Heures* and the *Très Riches Heures*, but the inspiration from Simone's panels remains tangible, and shows that they understood the relevance and purpose of certain gestures. In the *Lamentation* in the *Belles Heures*, for example, it is the idea of John covering his eyes as a gesture of extreme grief that they adopt from Simone's *Entombment*, but not, in this instance, the striking bundle of the cloak raised to his face to do so (figs 194, 200).[9] Moreover, in Simone the miniaturists found the dramatic power of crowds, a clamour of overlapping or obscured faces, strong forward movement and often violent actions, with figures cut off by, and imagined as continuing beyond, the frame (figs 189, 191). Last, but not least, the de Limbourgs' subtle and varied palette bears comparison with Simone's: they share a similar range of light blues and violets, greys set against pinks and acidic greens, with white and red used judiciously to secure particular focus or attention.

How deeply the illuminators comprehended Simone's inventions can be seen by a comparison of their *Way to Calvary* in the *Très Riches Heures* with the Orsini panel and with other renditions of it by their contemporaries, since the composition was widely known.[10] Jacquemart de Hesdin's version (fig. 190), thought to be from John of Berry's *Grandes Heures* completed in 1409, lifted the soldier seen from behind almost verbatim from Simone's panel, but he moved the figure away from the Virgin to the front of the procession instead. By contrast, the de Limbourgs did something much more sophisticated with their source material: they understood the dramatic purpose of Simone's soldier, who physically bars the Virgin from Christ, raising his mace to strike her, and they retained his role but reprised it, turning the figure round, reimagining him from the front, along with the gesture of the raised mace. Likewise, the de Limbourgs riff inventively on the two small children in the foreground of Simone's composition: this time they turn the one viewed from the front around, to be seen from the back, while the white fabric crossed over his body has been transferred to the soldier with the mace (figs 189, 191).[11]

Just as revealing is the de Limbourgs' figure of Christ in the *Way to Calvary*: alone among responses to Simone's panel, and very different from their own earlier rendition in the *Belles Heures* (fig. 188), they copy him here precisely, retaining his bulk and the tubular, unbelted robe that serves as an area of calm, standing out against the swirl of exotic draperies surrounding him (figs 189, 191). The de Limbourgs also observe and adopt from Simone the specific manner in which Christ holds the Cross, his right hand draped gently over it, the tips of the fingers of the left just visible: indeed, a tiny detail that would only be clear from very close inspection of the surface. The de Limbourgs, typically, adjust

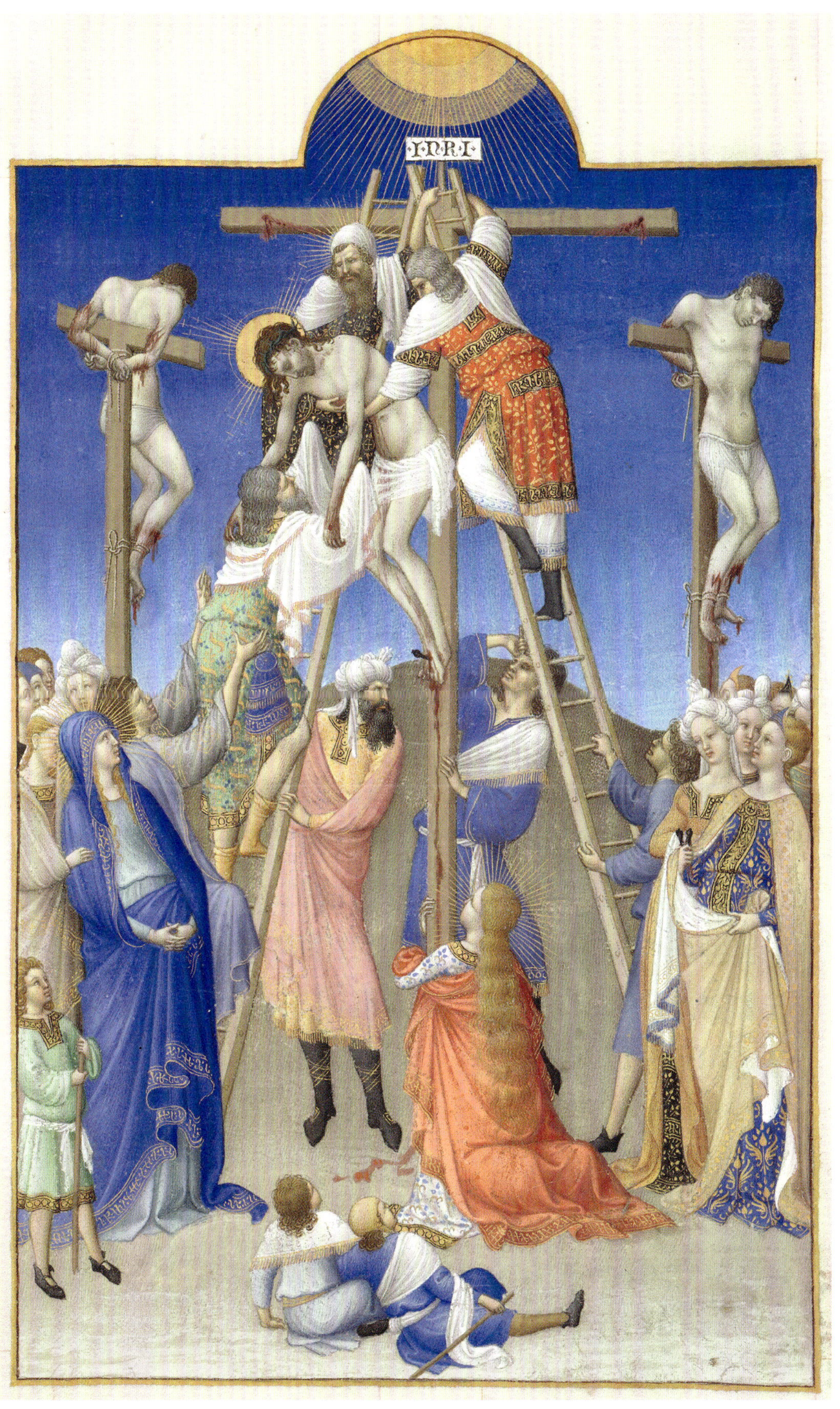

FIG. 193
The de Limbourg Brothers
(documented 1399–1416)
The Deposition, about 1412–16
Très Riches Heures, fol. 156v
Tempera and ink on parchment,
29 × 21 cm
Musée Condé, Chantilly (MS 65)

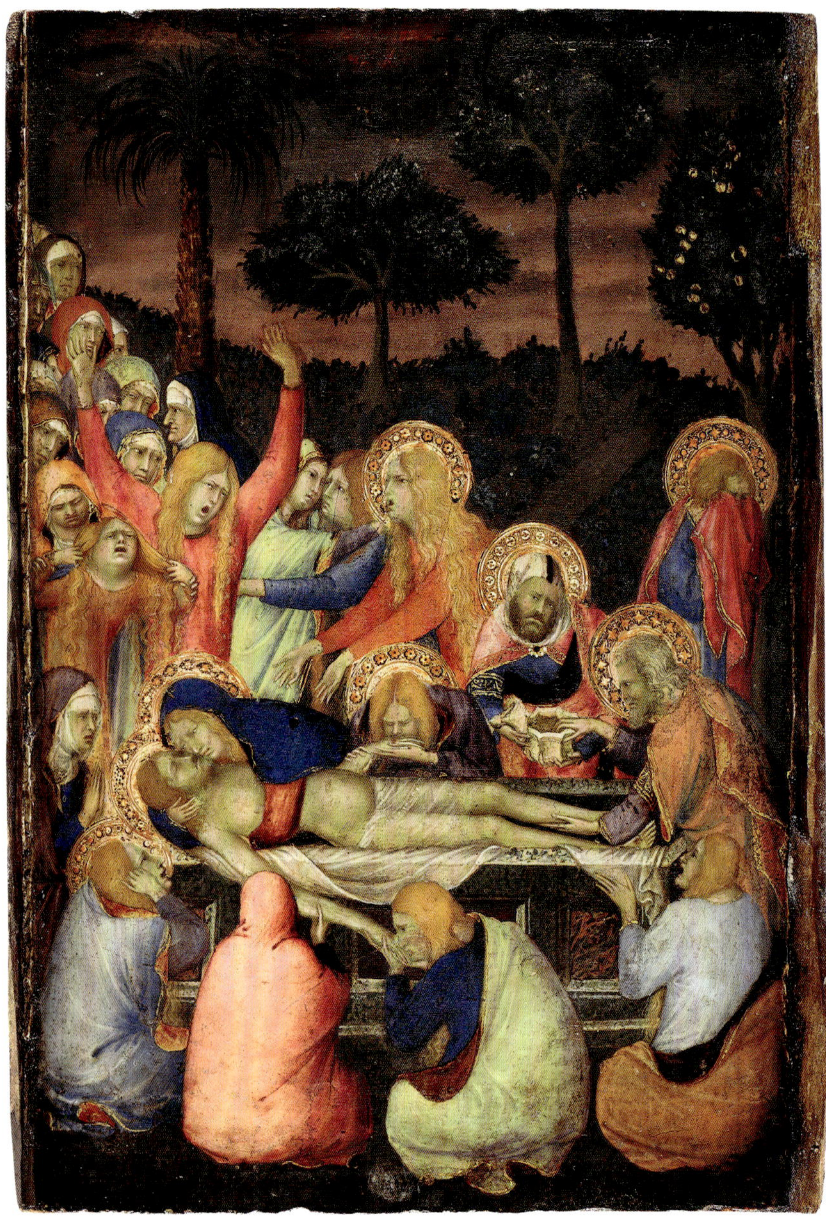

FIG. 194
Simone Martini (about 1284–1344)
The Entombment, about 1326–34
Tempera on poplar, 23.7 × 16.7 cm
Staatliche Museen zu Berlin, Gemäldegalerie (Kat. Nr. 1070A)

FIG. 195
de Limbourg Brothers
(documented 1399–1416)
The Entombment, 1405–8/9
The Belles Heures of John of France, Duke of Berry, fol. 152r

FIG. 196
de Limbourg Brothers
(documented 1399–1416)
The Stoning of Saint Stephen, 1405–8/9
The Belles Heures of John of France, Duke of Berry, fol. 162r

it subtly so that his left hand sits below his right hand, the reverse of Simone. They also follow the exact pose of Christ's feet in Simone's panel, the right firmly planted, the left slightly raised, and understand the importance of their bareness in contrast to the shod figures around him – something lost entirely in other renditions. Strikingly, again, it is they alone who copy the rope tied around Christ's neck, by which he is dragged forward, although predictably the torsion, and the moment, is changed: in the *Très Riches Heures* the figure holding the rope is about to pull it taut, whereas in Simone it is already tight – the violence of the action is in progress in one, about to happen in the other.[12]

This intense observation and deep comprehension of Simone's panels and their narrative intelligence is also evident in how the de Limbourgs responded to the Orsini *Deposition* in both the *Belles Heures* and the *Très Riches Heures*, merging it with elements of Simone's *Crucifixion* but responding to their particular patron's needs (figs 192, 193, 199). In the *Belles Heures*, the gesture of the Virgin reaching up to Christ is adopted by the de Limbourgs, as is the droop of his body (figs 192, 199); the nails received by the woman in the foreground with fabric-covered hands, emphasising their sanctity, thought to reference relics owned by Napoleone Orsini, is also retained by the de Limbourgs, but moved to the background and transferred to a male figure, replaced in the foreground by another woman with hands similarly shrouded to hold, instead, the crown of thorns, the relic owned by the French kings, of which the Duke of Berry had several complete thorns.[13] The implication here is that the de Limbourgs understood more than the surface of their source. That this source was the painting itself, not a drawing, is indicated by correspondences in the palette between the two works: the de Limbourgs have taken on the pink-red underrobe of the Virgin, and the figure holding Christ's body in light blue with a white cloth wrapped around his head. The illuminators also made use of ideas from Simone's *Deposition* in other miniatures in the *Belles Heures*: the bent-over pose of the young man in blue seen from behind holding the hammer in Simone's panel may be the source, in reverse, for the older figure leaning over Christ's body in the *Entombment* in the *Belles Heures* (fig. 195), while the figure in green holding the ointment pot with a winding cloth or shroud draped over his shoulder on the right in Simone's work seems to have been cannibalised for elements of two figures in the same miniature – the one in green with the gold pot and the figure next to him with the shroud over his shoulder.

Despite this inventive recycling, and evidence of first-hand knowledge of Simone's panels, the *Belles Heures* has a much less intimate relationship with the Orsini Polyptych than the *Très Riches Heures*. In this later manuscript, the brothers' rendition of the *Deposition*, in particular, indicates renewed observation and understanding of Simone's iconographic themes, suggesting that they returned to the surface of Simone's paintings, with some leisure, in the period after 1409. In the *Très Riches Heures* miniature, the scale and number of the figures are matched, and small details are precisely tweaked in line with their Sienese model: Christ's pose copies Simone's more exactly – the drape of his right arm over the shoulder of Nicodemus, the straighter line of his left arm and the angle of the head are directly quoted (figs 192, 193); and while the Virgin is decidedly, perhaps pointedly, different – and from a specific Florentine source[14] – the reaching gesture of the woman in light grey-blue has been retained but transferred to Saint John.[15] The Magdalen clutching the Cross in the *Deposition* in the *Très Riches Heures* and her long wavy hair are brought in from Simone's *Crucifixion* (fig. 197), along with the blood flowing down the Cross and pooling on the ground. More subtle is the reuse of the children from Simone's composition. These stand to the left of the Cross in the Orsini panel, one looking up at Christ, the other pointing to the fainting Virgin, but are moved to the right in the *Très Riches Heures*, and become three: the two sitting in the foreground solve the problem of how to fill the space left by the kneeling, diminutive figure of Orsini, their role in this respect evident in how they mimic his upwards gaze, while their small stature allows them to take this place and keep in scale with the rest of the figures.[16]

The depth of the de Limbourgs' understanding and observation is most apparent, however, in their adoption of the figure in blue seen from behind in the Orsini *Deposition*, his hammer raised to knock out, from behind, the final nail in Christ's feet.

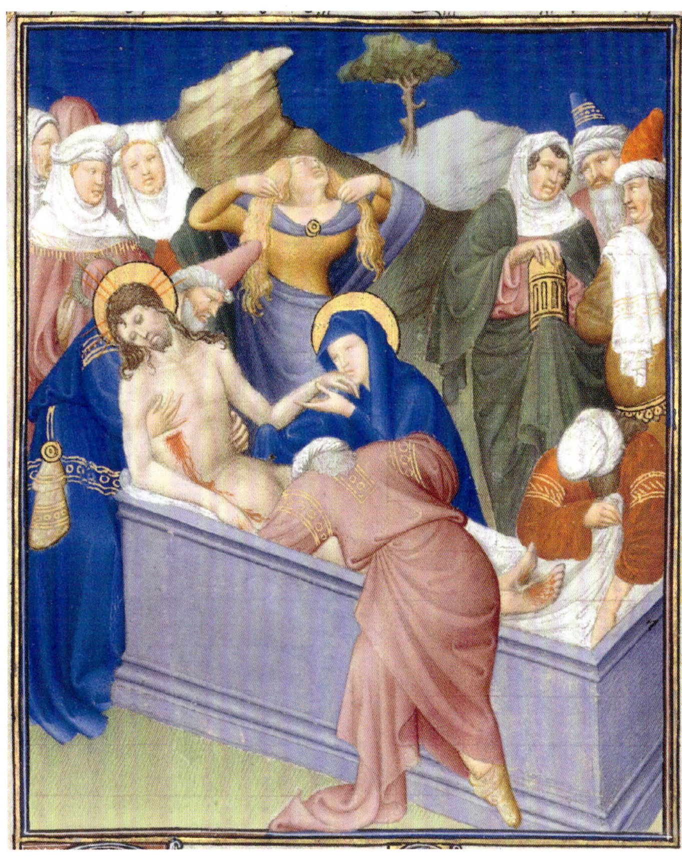

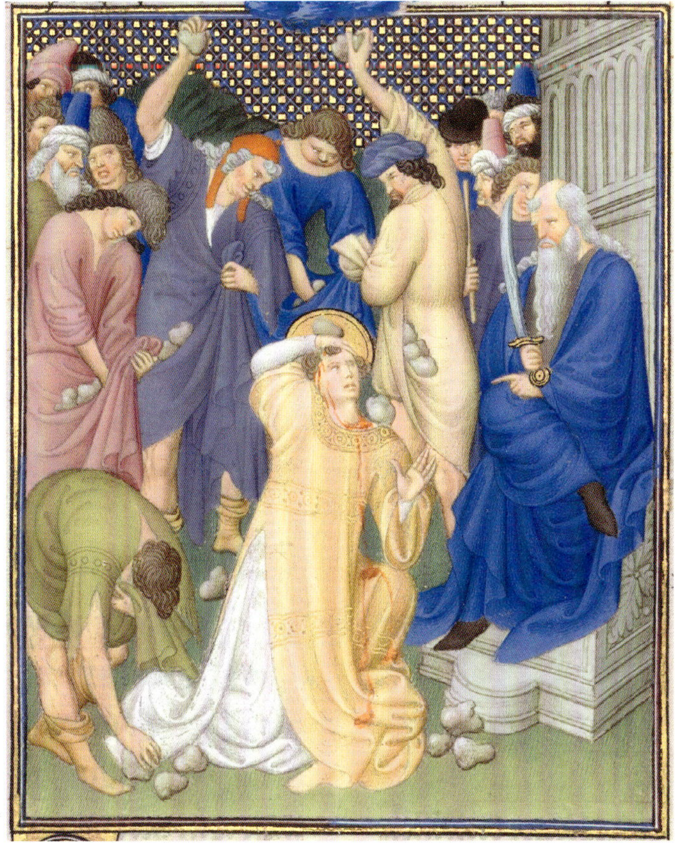

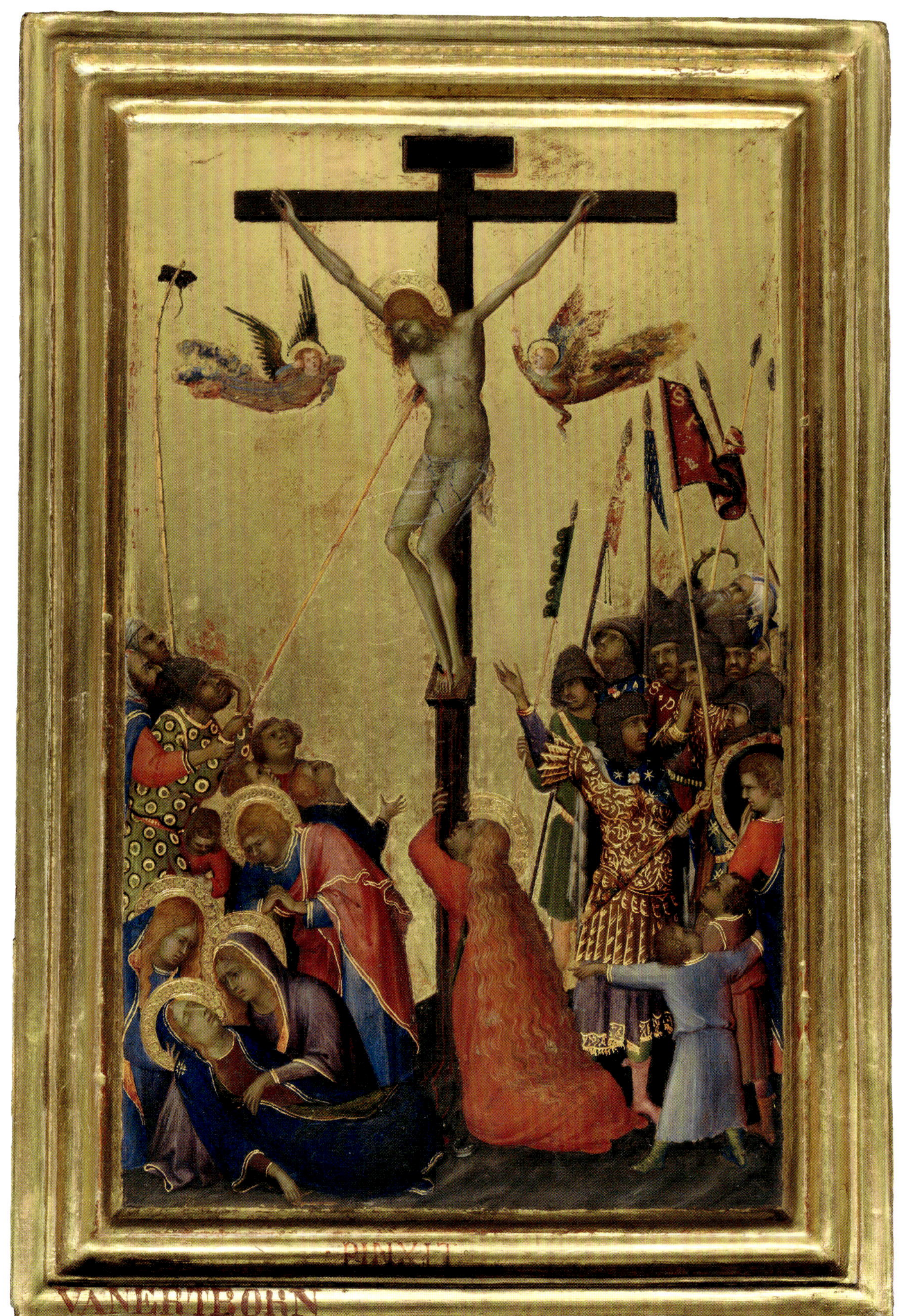

FIG. 197
Simone Martini
(about 1284–1344)
The Crucifixion,
about 1326–34
Tempera on poplar,
29.6 × 20.5 cm (with engaged frame)
Collection KMSKA - Flemish Community (public domain) (259)

FIG. 198
de Limbourg Brothers
(documented 1399–1416)
The Crucifixion, 1405–8/9
The Belles Heures of John of France, Duke of Berry,
fol. 145r

FIG. 199
de Limbourg Brothers
(documented 1399–1416)
The Deposition, 1405–8/9
The Belles Heures of John of France, Duke of Berry,
fol. 149r

Already known to them, he is not simply copied here but rethought in a manner that reveals how fully they comprehended the nature of this gesture (figs 192, 193): as with the soldier in the *Way to Calvary*, they turned the figure around, placing him in their version behind the Cross with his hand raised and holding a hammer to undertake his own swing at the nail from behind. They also reinstate to the foreground the woman holding the first two nails from Simone's composition, so she is ready to receive the third. In this narrative sequence it also then becomes clear how the exotic figure in pink who stands behind the ladder in the *Très Riches Heures*, witnessing this action, is the de Limbourgs' version of the figure in green who does the same in Simone's work, if dressed rather differently. Given all of this close looking and narrative intelligence, what the de Limbourgs were *not* interested in in Simone's work seems equally significant: the exaggerated gestures of the Virgin reaching for the Cross in the *Way to Calvary* and the dramatic, hands-in-the-air figure of the Magdalen in red who features in that panel and the *Deposition* and *Entombment* (figs 189, 192, 194) are pointedly ignored.

The access the de Limbourgs had to the Orsini ensemble, allowing such close and repeated study between 1405 and 1416 – long after they had left Philip the Bold's service – raises the question of where Simone's paintings were at that point. John of Berry was well known for asking his artists to copy works in his collection into his manuscripts, and the brothers' response to the quadriptych fits such a scenario.[17] Moreover, it was artists in Berry's employ who were most familiar with its inventions around 1400.[18] Although it is not recorded in his surviving inventories, the duke's possession of objects could be remarkably fluid, and these sources do not capture all that he owned: he exchanged numerous gifts with Philip and his heir, John the Fearless, in the years after 1404;[19] it is not inconceivable that Simone's panels passed between them more than once before coming to rest at Champmol, where Berry had endowed a chapel.[20]

Alongside the de Limbourgs' intimate study of the Orsini Polyptych, there are other moments in their miniatures that suggest the brothers also had knowledge of a more monumental Sienese work: the frescoes in the Lower Church at Assisi by Pietro

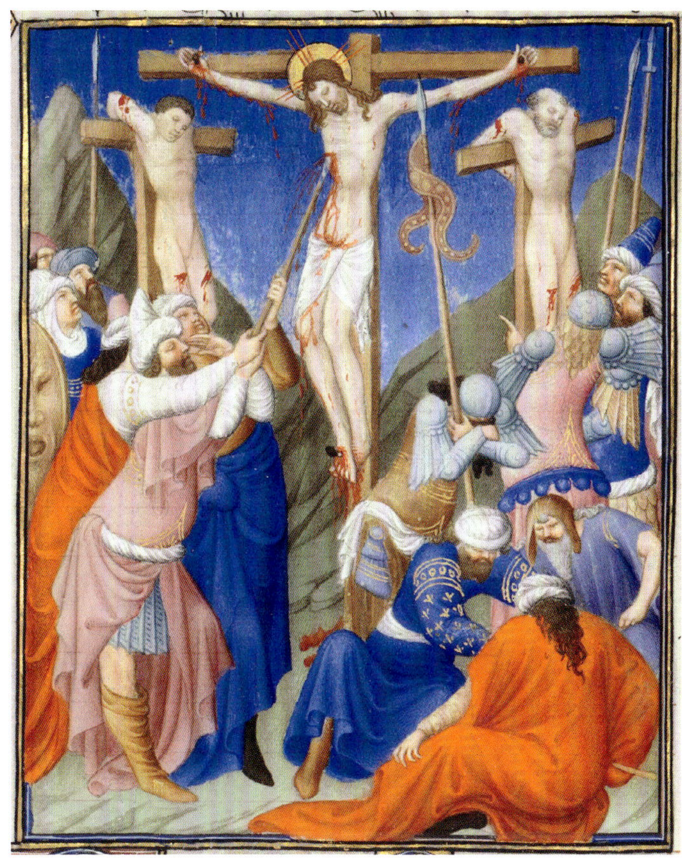

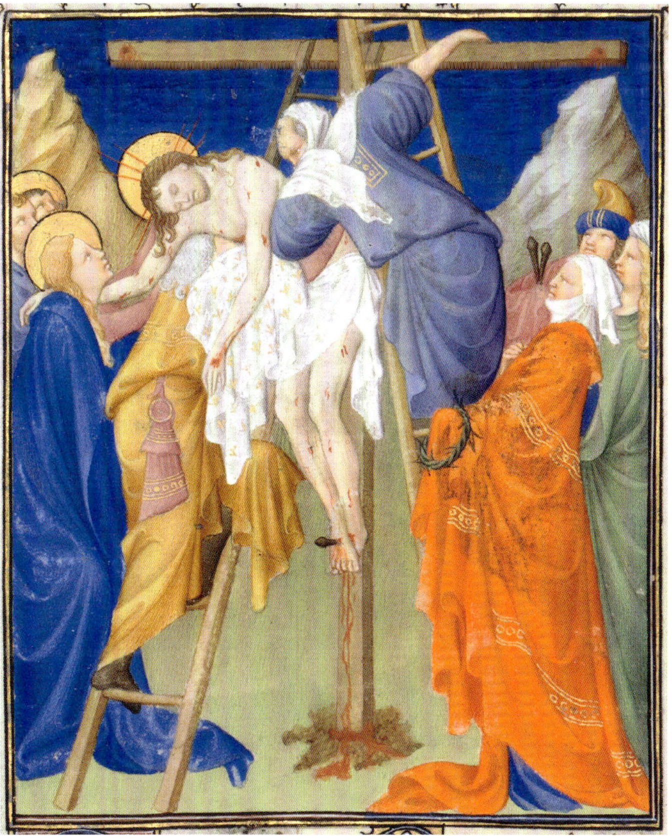

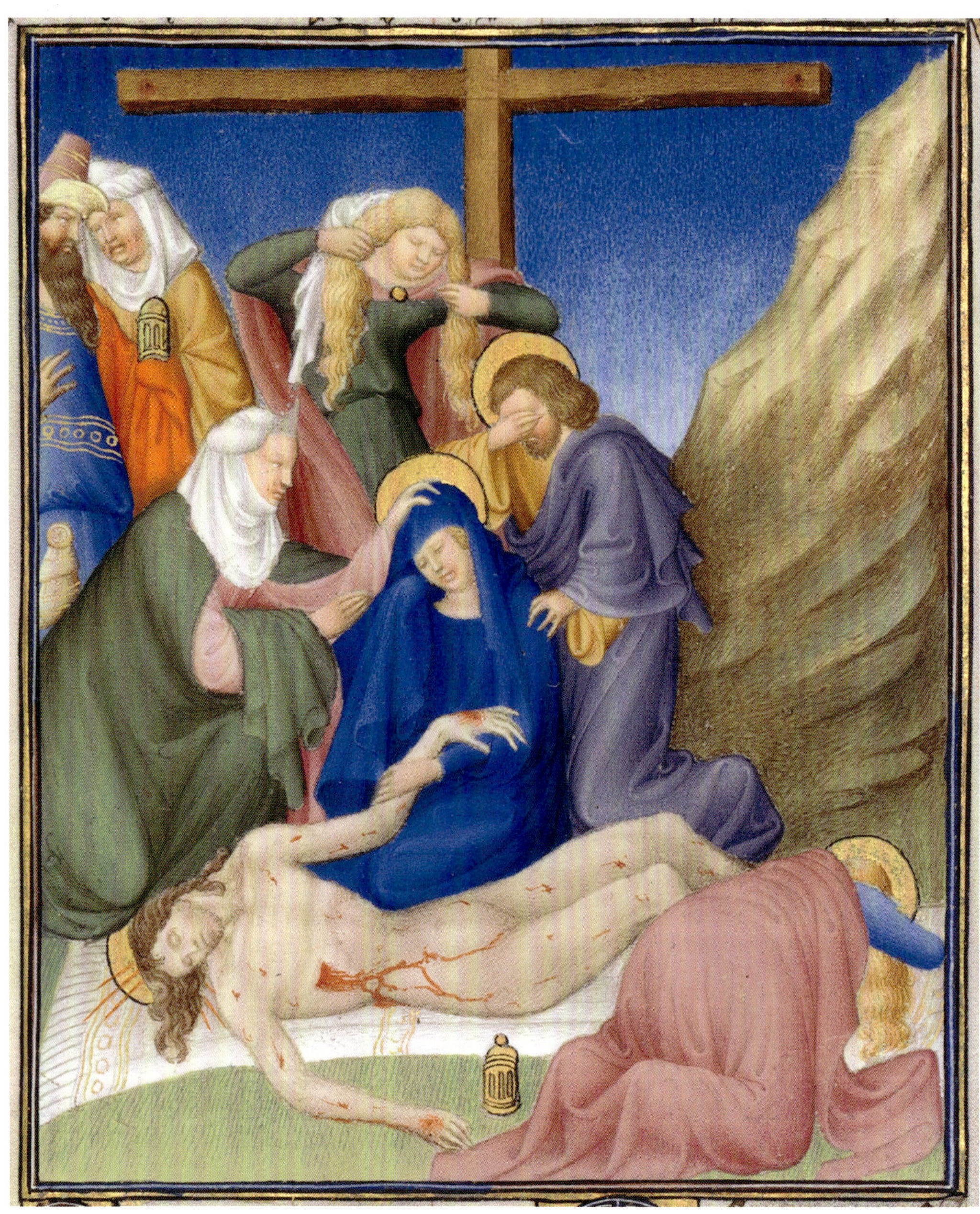

FIG. 200
de Limbourg Brothers
(documented 1399–1416)
The Lamentation, 1405–8/9
The Belles Heures of John of France, Duke of Berry, fol. 149v

Lorenzetti. In their *Lamentation* in the *Belles Heures* (fig. 200), the dramatic back-view figure of the Magdalen, her feet covered in her red robe, is drawn from the figure of the Magdalen who kneels at the foot of the Cross in Lorenzetti's *Deposition* on the wall of the south transept (fig. 201), while the woman who looks down and pulls apart her long hair in a gesture of grief in the same miniature is a direct quote from Lorenzetti's *Entombment* (fig. 202) set next to it across the arch, rather than via Simone's version, where she looks up, which comes from a distinctly different model.[21] Christ and the thieves in the *Belles Heures Crucifixion*, including the precise angle at which their crosses are set, may also have been drawn from those in Lorenzetti's *Crucifixion* in the Lower Church, although the gesture of the figure guiding Longinus's spear and the inclusion of that narrative moment in the *Belles Heures* goes back again to the Orsini panel (figs 197 and 198). Moreover, the de Limbourgs clearly knew other frescoes in Assisi, not just those by Sienese artists: the *Nativity* in the *Belles Heures* is derived in several aspects from the Lower Church fresco attributed to Giotto and his workshop, while their *Adoration of the Magi* in the *Très Riches Heures* includes the precise and unusual gesture of the Child reaching out to touch the head of the first king as he kisses his feet seen in Giotto's fresco.[22] A more painterly idea, less easily transmitted by drawings, like the night sky with its shooting stars in Pietro Lorenzetti's *Arrest of Christ* (fig. 203), seems to have inspired the same motif in their famous miniature of the *Ego Sum* in the *Très Riches Heures* (fig. 204).[23] If the de Limbourgs did see these works first-hand, their more sporadic adoption of motifs suggests restrictions on what they could see, how much light was available and how close they could get, so that what they took drawings of was necessarily selective.[24]

In recent years the thrust of scholarship has been to deny any possibility of the de Limbourgs going to Italy, but the idea deserves to be revisited.[25] The brothers were frequent travellers, and the distance to the towns of Tuscany via Avignon, and on to Assisi or Rome, some of which could be accomplished by sea, was not much farther than the trip home from Bourges to Nijmegen that they did several times in the years 1410–15, so it would not need a substantial gap in their documented history.[26] Moreover, we should not imagine their travel there need be some sort of *Wanderjahr* for artistic inspiration, but they might have been sent by their patrons for any number of reasons, given how intense diplomatic relations between the French courts, Pisa and Florence were in the years around 1405–15, with Berry, a prominent supporter of Florence, in frequent contact with the Tuscan cities, and with their bankers and purveyors of luxury items. Embassies that were sent from these cities to Paris went on a route via Avignon that took in Berry's capital at Bourges, and his agents were scouting for talented artists, 'souverains en leur art et science' (supreme in their art and science), in Siena and its environs in 1408–9.[27]

The de Limbourgs were favoured by the duke in many ways, including being given substantial (and often unexplained) financial rewards that make them plausible choices for such missions, which might have had a dual purpose.[28] These would have used their skills as artists and courtiers and taken advantage of what they might bring back for the

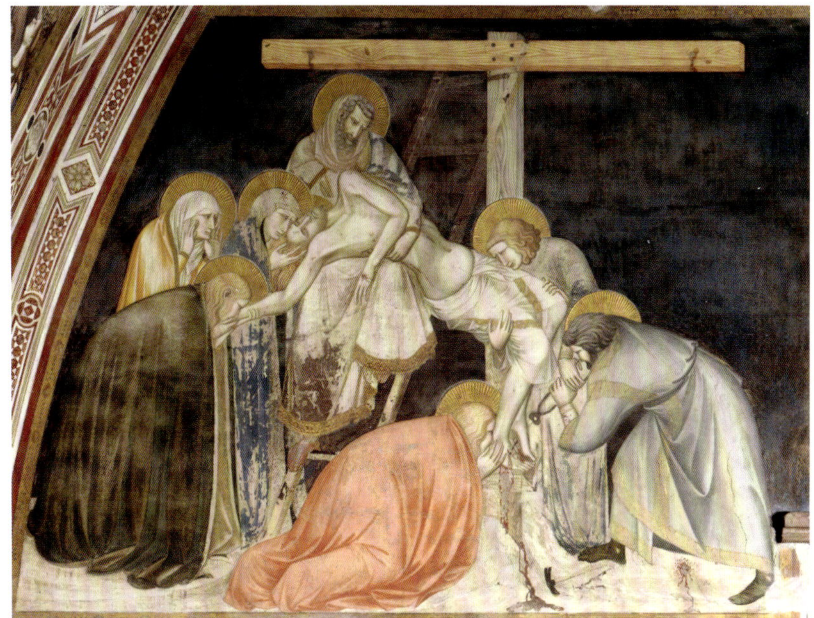

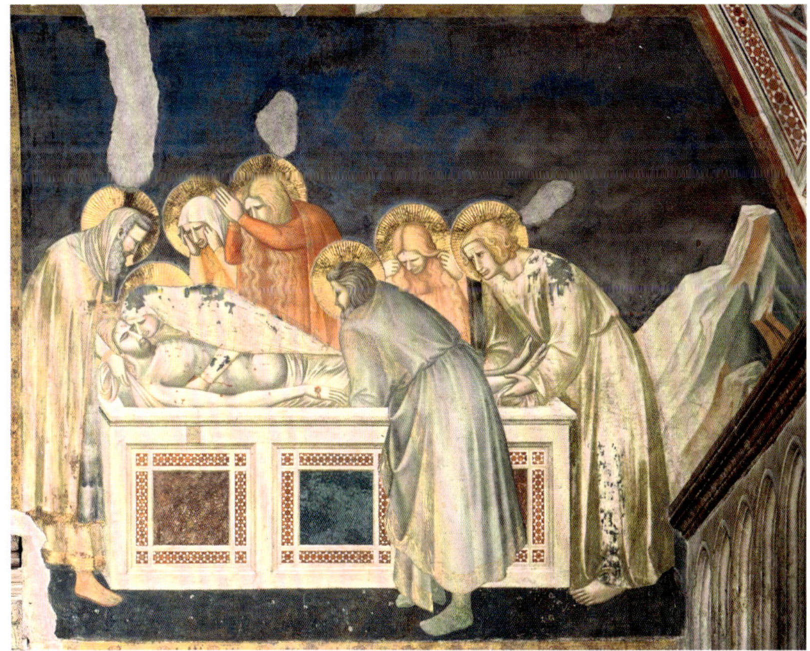

FIG. 201
Pietro Lorenzetti (documented possibly 1306; died probably 1348)
The Deposition, about 1320
Fresco
Basilica of San Francesco, Assisi

FIG. 202
Pietro Lorenzetti (documented possibly 1306; died probably 1348)
The Entombment, about 1320
Fresco
Basilica of San Francesco, Assisi

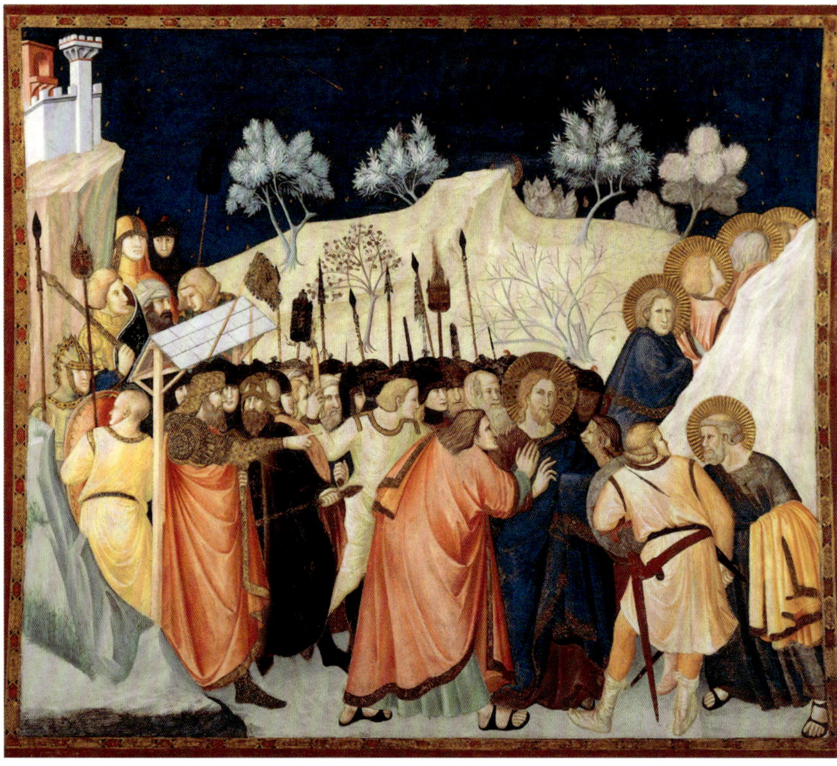

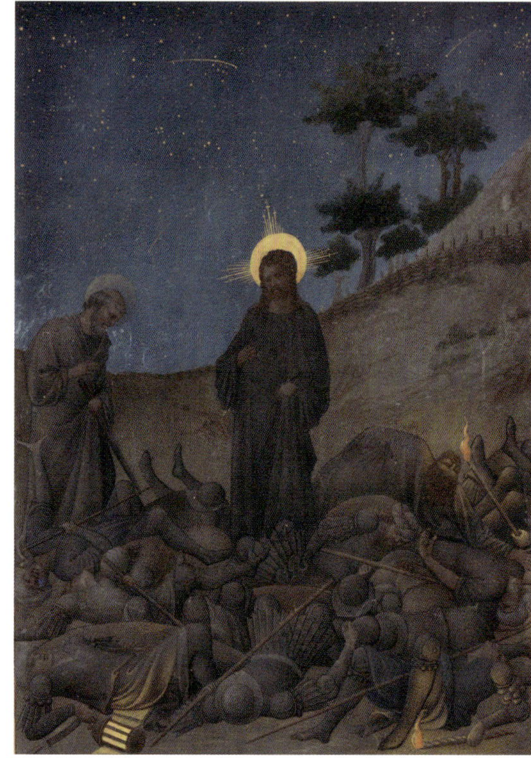

FIG. 203
Pietro Lorenzetti
(documented possibly 1306; died probably 1348)
The Arrest of Christ, about 1320
Fresco
Basilica of San Francesco, Assisi

FIG. 204
de Limbourg Brothers
(documented 1399–1416)
Ego Sum, about 1412–16
Très Riches Heures, fol. 142v
Tempera and ink on parchment, 29 × 21 cm
Musée Condé, Chantilly (MS 65)

duke, in terms of ideas and objects, the 'choses estranges' (strange things) he took pleasure in.[29]

The range of things the de Limbourgs knew from Italy, only touched on here and yet to be fully enumerated, was so wide and varied, including sculpture and antiquities, that the possibility of them all being conveyed through the circulation of drawings or imported objects seems increasingly unlikely, even given the breadth of their patrons' collections. Most tellingly, perhaps, the way the de Limbourgs handled scale, crowds, movement, architecture, landscape, light and colour in their miniatures, especially in the *Très Riches Heures*, is beyond what even their most intimate study of Simone's admittedly rich panels can account for, but the fresco cycles of Padua, Florence, Siena or Assisi would plausibly do so. In fact, it may have been the experience of Italy that made John of Berry's illuminators more receptive to all of these things in the microcosm of Simone's jewel-like, immensely intelligent work on their return.

1. For Champmol, see Monget 1898–1905; Prochno 2002; Lindquist 2008.
2. There is no earlier documented record of it at Champmol, and no trace of the three other panels once joined (?) to it, although they are reputed to have been acquired in Dijon in 1826; it is clear that all of the panels were in France by around 1400. The record of the panel at Champmol was first published in full by Reinach 1927; see also Laclotte and Thiébaut 1983, pp. 136–7; Martindale 1988, pp. 171–3; Prochno 2002, pp. 195–6.
3. The folios of the *Très Riches Heures*, at 29 × 21 cm, are almost exactly the same size as the Simone panels at 29.5 × 20.5 cm, but the painted surface of the panels, without the frame (about 23 × 15 cm), is somewhat larger than the painted area of the miniatures.
4. For the de Limbourgs and their impact, see most pertinently Meiss 1974; Nijmegen 2005; Los Angeles and New York 2008–10. I am not attempting to distinguish between the brothers in the following discussion.
5. The most extensive study of the use of Italian sources by the de Limbourgs remains Meiss 1974; Paul Durrieu and Emile Mâle had already drawn a connection between the de Limbourgs' work and the Orsini panels at the turn of the twentieth century (Durrieu 1904, p. 95; Mâle 1908, pp. 16–17); most scholars see a greater debt to Simone in the work of another of the duke's illuminators, Jacquemart de Hesdin (Panofsky 1953, p. 48; Meiss 1967, pp. 272–4; Los Angeles and New York 2008–10, p. 295); the work associated with that illuminator does not,

however, rival the close looking displayed by the de Limbourgs.

6. Meiss 1974, pp. 172, 240–51; Los Angeles and New York 2008–10, pp. 291–305; Schmidt 2005b, p. 185.
7. The *Belles Heures* was recorded in Berry's inventory in 1409 and may have been begun as early as 1405 (Meiss 1974, pp. 103–5; Los Angeles and New York 2008–10, pp. 33–45); the *Très Riches Heures* could have been begun as early as 1411 or 1412, and was recorded, unbound, in the Duke of Berry's post-mortem inventory of 1416; all three brothers were dead by August 1416. For the *Très Riches Heures*, see Cazelles and Rathofer 1988 and, most recently, Paris 2004a.
8. For orientalising costume in Parisian painting around 1400 and its sources, see Kubiski 2001.
9. Schmidt 2005b, p. 185, suggests the de Limbourgs used Simone's figure of Saint John for a figure in the *Raising of Lazarus* in the *Très Riches Heures* (fol. 171r): https://bvmm.irht.cnrs.fr/mirador/index.php?manifest=https://bvmm.irht.cnrs.fr/iiif/22470/manifest (accessed 2 September 2023). This figure, shielding his mouth and nose against the smell, raising one hand in horror, is in fact drawn directly from Giotto's *Raising of Lazarus* (about 1305) in the Arena Chapel, Padua. The grief of Simone's Saint John was not appropriate for a figure expressing another emotion entirely, and the de Limbourgs were sensitive to context in their borrowings.
10. Meiss 1967, pp. 215–18.
11. It is also worn by another child in their miniature that directly precedes it, *Christ leaving the Praetorium* (fol. 146v), with which it forms a double-page spread. For a reproduction: https://bvmm.irht.cnrs.fr/mirador/index.php?manifest=https://bvmm.irht.cnrs.fr/iiif/22470/manifest (accessed 2 September 2023).
12. The iconography of the rope, of Byzantine origin, is discussed by Derbes 1996, pp. 132–5, p. 236, n. 80; it is a motif she notes was rarely adopted by northern artists. It was also used by Ugolino di Nerio in the predella of the Santa Croce High Altarpiece in Florence (possibly 1325–8; National Gallery, London, NG1189), where the rope is also not taut and the Virgin's role and position are much closer to those adopted by the de Limbourgs, who reject the dramatic reaching gesture in Simone's panel. The de Limbourgs knew other works in Santa Croce, see n. 23 below, so this source, first-hand or through a set of drawings, is not improbable.
13. For the nail relic owned by Orsini, see Schmidt 2005a, pp. 256–60. Berry had at least four thorn relics, recorded in his 1401–3 inventory, set in an imperial crown that was subsequently broken up, see Guiffrey 1894–6, no. 10, p. 6; one of these may be that now in the reliquary in the British Museum of around 1400 (Waddesdon Bequest 67). In Simone's painting the Crown of Thorns only appears at the Crucifixion, held aloft in the background.
14. The source for this figure, as pointed out by Meiss 1974, pp. 172, 240–1, is Andrea da Firenze's *Crucifixion* in the Spanish Chapel at Santa Maria Novella of 1365–7. Schmidt 2005b, p. 185, claims the figure appears in small panels from the same circle to explain this borrowing, but none of them have the precise line of the Virgin's robe and visible strands of her hair that the de Limbourgs take from the fresco.
15. The figure of Nicodemus hooking his arm over the Cross may also be derived from Sienese models: it appears in Duccio's *Maestà* (see fig. 9), and in another of the predella panels of the Santa Croce High Altarpiece by Ugolino de Nerio (see fig. 50 and n. 12 above); my thanks to Joanna Cannon for this observation.
16. That the de Limbourgs had looked closely at them is further underlined by their presence in their miniature of the *Crucifixion in Darkness* in the *Très Riches Heures*, fol. 153r, where they follow the placement in Simone's panel, standing to the left of the Cross and pointing to the Virgin on the right: https://bvmm.irht.cnrs.fr/mirador/index.php?manifest=https://bvmm.irht.cnrs.fr/iiif/22470/manifest (accessed 2 September 2023).
17. The *Grandes Heures* is a virtual collection of miniatures copying other works Berry owned, see Paris 2004b, pp. 104–9; the de Limbourgs themselves copied medals Berry had acquired in their *Très Riches Heures*, see Villela-Petit in Amsterdam 2017–18, cat. 26, pp. 132–5.
18. Meiss 1967, pp. 215–17, 270–3.
19. For some of these, see Hirschbiegel 2003.
20. The brothers could of course have seen the work at Champmol, since their uncle Jean Malouel was working there as the ducal painter in the years 1407–14. How the work was acquired by either duke, presumably at some point in the 1390s, given when it started to be copied, is another issue. Speculation about a Burgundian connection to the Orsini through marriage seems less likely than through time spent by both dukes in Avignon in the 1390s, and their many dealings with Italian agents selling artworks old and new. Berry's foundation at Champmol, of the apse altar, is recorded in the necrology of the church, published in Prochno 2002, p. 370.
21. For these gestures and their circulation, see Cannon and Vauchez 1999, pp. 132–4. For the Lorenzetti frescos in the Lower Church, see Cooper and De Marchi, pp. 84–7, in the present volume.
22. For this gesture and its Sienese origin, see Cannon 2010, pp. 23–8; the distinctive manner of showing a partially ruined building in Giotto's fresco of the *Miracle at San Damiano* in the Upper Church seems to have been also adopted by the de Limbourgs, for their ruined temple in their *Raising of Lazarus* (fol. 171r) in the *Très Riches Heures*: https://bvmm.irht.cnrs.fr/mirador/index.php?manifest=https://bvmm.irht.cnrs.fr/iiif/22470/manifest (accessed 2 September 2023).
23. The unusual iconography of this miniature was traced to an Italian source by Alexander 1983, but the manuscript he cites does not have the starry sky. Another effect the de Limbourgs seem to have known first-hand is the depiction of a night scene through limited colour and points of illumination. This was used by Taddeo Gaddi in his *Annunciation to the Shepherds* in the Baroncelli Chapel in Santa Croce, set directly next to the *Purification of the Virgin* that the brothers copied in the *Très Riches Heures* (fol. 54v).
24. Drawing from the frescoes in the Lower Church was certainly possible, as surviving fourteenth-century sheets of entire scenes and individual motifs attest, for which see Degenhart and Schmitt 1968, part i, vol. 1, no. 52, pp. 117–18; part i, vol. 3, pl. 82b. For access and routes, see Robson 2005. Considerable light could come from the two doorways in the 'liturgical' Eastern transept arms – actually facing West (I thank Joanna Cannon for this point).
25. Schmidt 1999, pp. 28–35, Schmidt 2005b, Schmidt 2009, pp. 185–207, and Los Angeles and New York 2008–10 most firmly reject any Italian journey, arguing that drawings and paintings in the north could account for their knowledge. Those in favour of the trip include Meiss 1974 and Alexander 1983; Cazelles and Rathofer 1988 also think it probable on balance.
26. For these journeys and full details of their documented history, see Meiss 1974, pp. 71–81; Niessen, Roelofs and van Veen-Liefrink 2005, pp. 20–5. There are long periods when we cannot say where the brothers were, especially Paul.
27. Champeaux 1888; Mirot 1934. The Council of Pisa in 1409 was a moment when large foreign diplomatic contingents descended on the region. I am assuming the trip would not need to be prior to their work on the *Bible Moralisée*, Bibliothèque nationale, Paris, MS français 166, as, like Lowden 2000, pp. 270–6, and Dückers 2005, pp. 87–9, I am unsure its identity with the Bible the brothers were paid for between 1402 and 1404 is correct.
28. Niessen, Roelofs and van Veen-Liefrink 2005, pp. 21–2; Villela-Petit 2012.
29. This phrase is used by the Duke of Berry in his letter back to Pierre Salmon regarding the marquetry worker Salmon had found in Siena: 'pour ceque vous savez que nous prenons plaisir en choses estranges'; see Champeaux 1888, p. 411; Tomasi 2022, p. 117.

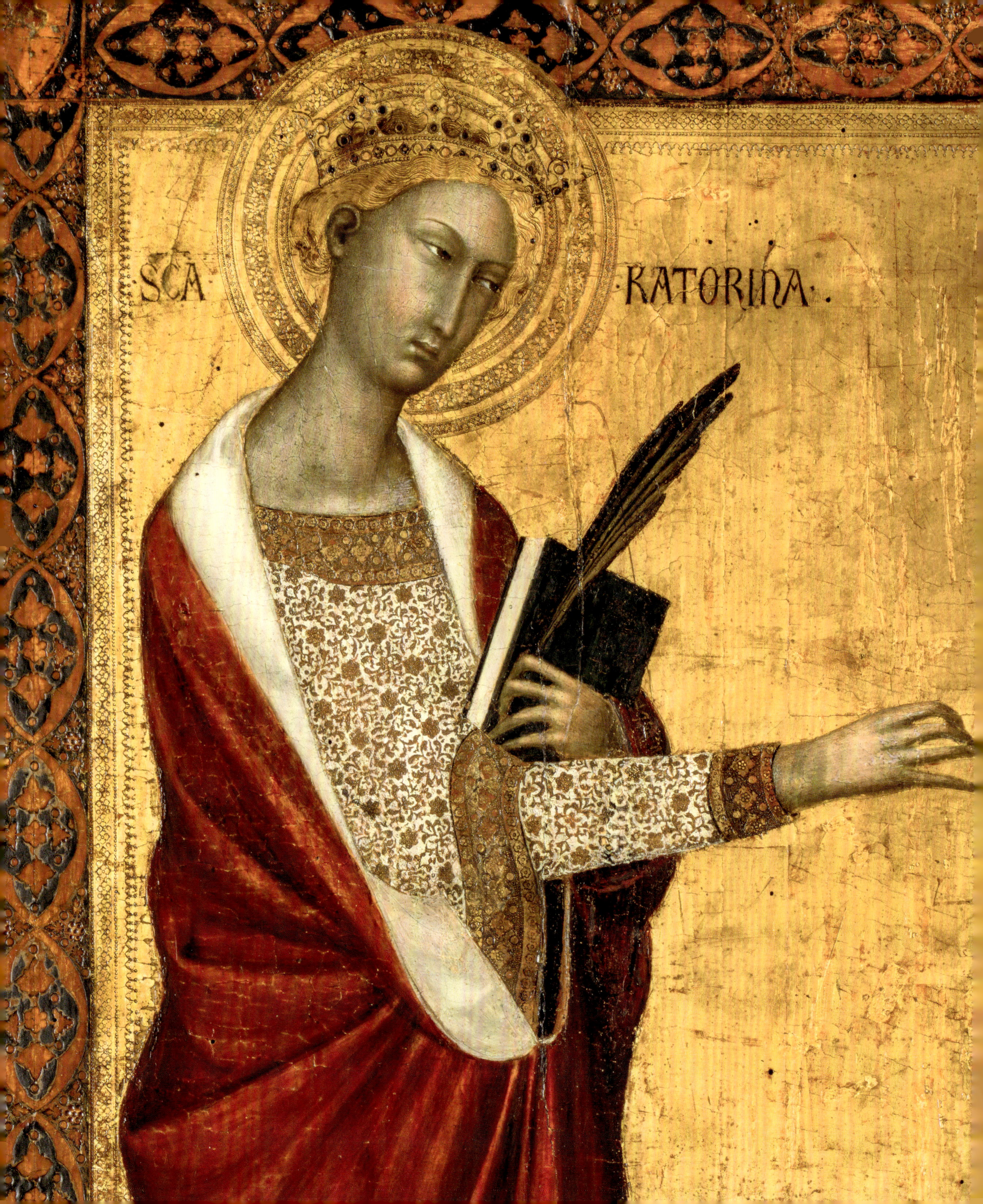
SCA
KATORINA

SIENESE PAINTINGS: DISMEMBERED, REVALUED, COLLECTED

Imogen Tedbury

In 1898 the art critic Vernon Lee proclaimed her late conversion to what she called 'the particular delightfulness of Sienese local painting':

> It was certainly mean-spirited of the Sienese to persist in being purely mediaeval right through the Renaissance, without stirring a finger to hasten the coming of Michelangelo, or Leonardo, or the Royal Academicians of today. Of course, they ought to have toiled away at anatomy, perspective, movement, and the modern spirit in general, like the Florentines. [...] But they just would not or could not; and, as I said, I am foolishly pleased they did not. There is room for many things in art, as in life. Besides progress, there is repose: the charm of the backwater.[1]

In satirising contemporary critics who judged art by the progressivist values of their own age, Lee nonetheless voiced many of the reasons that Sienese painting was somewhat neglected in the first flush of fervour for early Italian art in nineteenth-century Britain. Perceived as medieval in aesthetic and lacking a progressive trajectory towards modernity, Sienese painting was seen by some as a peripheral 'backwater' to the Florentine Renaissance. Many of the Sienese paintings transported to the British Isles were fragments from larger ensembles, dismembered during the Napoleonic occupation of Italy or earlier. Some private collectors had religious motivations for their interest in Sienese paintings, which they saw as particularly spiritual. From the mid-nineteenth century, this view also applied to Siena itself, thanks to civic efforts to restore the city's architecture to a medieval aesthetic. Algernon Charles Swinburne's poem 'Siena' (1871) captures an Anglophone view of Siena as simultaneously ancient, medieval and modern, addressing the city as the 'lady loveliest of my loves' as he weaves between the age of Christ, the age of Saint Catherine of Siena and the Risorgimento.[2] In Britain, Sienese 'primitive' paintings came to represent this sweet spirituality of medieval Siena. Explored here are some of the ways in which Sienese paintings have been valued –

p. 254
Detail of fig. 213

fig. 205
Goodhart Ducciesque Master
(active about 1310–30)
The Virgin and Child with the Annunciation and the Nativity, about 1310–15
Tempera on panel, 30.8 x 21 cm (with engaged frame)
The Metropolitan Museum of Art, New York. Marquand Fund, 1920 (20.160)

and undervalued – for their 'primitive' spirituality, their exquisite craftsmanship and their narrative import in the last two hundred years.

RISING FORTUNES

Over the centuries, Siena had retained an appreciation for masterpieces produced during the trecento, a period that its citizens continued to consider its golden age. In the eighteenth century Luigi Lanzi recorded certain painters in the city dedicated to the restoration of older paintings.[3] Nonetheless, many of the complexes that had graced the city's altars were dismantled. Some of these removals took place during the Counter-Reformation. In Florence, for example, Ugolino di Nerio's Santa Croce Altarpiece was removed from the high altar of that church, dismantled and put into storage to make way for a ciborium designed by Giorgio Vasari between 1566 and 1569.[4] Other removals took place even earlier. Duccio's *Maestà* was removed from the high altar of Siena's cathedral in 1506 and dismembered in 1771 (see p. 16). It is not known when Pietro Lorenzetti's Saint Sabinus Altarpiece was dismantled, but it had been relegated to the stairs to the Scrittoria dell'Opera by 1655 and deprived of its lateral panels and predella by 1864, when the central panel of the *Birth of the Virgin* (see fig. 40) was on display in the sacristy.[5]

During the chaos of the Napoleonic occupation of Italy, many religious orders were forced to relinquish both their homes and, in some cases, oversight of the artworks in their care. By the first decades of the nineteenth century, Sienese paintings were circulating on the British art market. Indeed, one of the first Sienese paintings to enter a British collection, Simone Martini's *Christ discovered in the Temple* (see fig. 74), was bought in May 1804 by abolitionist Sir William Roscoe, who never travelled to Italy himself but acquired this painting and two fresco fragments attributed to Giotto through an agent.[6] William Young Ottley was another early collector, whose wide-ranging art collection was partially funded by his family's plantation in Antigua, where he registered ownership of 17 enslaved people.[7] Ottley acquired some 20 panels from Ugolino di Nerio's Santa Croce Altarpiece, probably in the first decade of the nineteenth century, together with numerous other early Italian paintings, including a *Virgin and Child with the Annunciation and the Nativity* attributed to the Goodhart Ducciesque Master (fig. 205). Ottley did not record his motivations for buying these works, but a contemporary collector, the diplomat the Hon. William Thomas Fox-Strangways, explained the rationale for his own collection of primitives – now divided between Christ Church Picture Gallery and the Ashmolean Museum – as a 'most useful sort of collection … [that] might be made at no great expense and within small compasses to size and numbers'; to have a collection 'with one specimen of each school in its maturity would be [a] gallery for a king'.[8] Indeed, Prince Albert himself had a penchant for the Italian 'primitives', in part thanks to his agent Ludwig Grüner, an engraver who had studied with the Nazarenes.[9] Albert's collection, which hung in his dressing room and private quarters at Osborne House, included Duccio's *Triptych with the Crucifixion and Other Scenes* (see fig. 17), purchased through Grüner in 1845 for £190 as a work by the Florentine painter Fra Angelico.

It is unsurprising that some of the first Sienese paintings to come to Britain were acquired with attributions to Florentine artists like Giotto or Cimabue, given the tenor of contemporary discourse. Giorgio Vasari's *Lives of the Artists*,

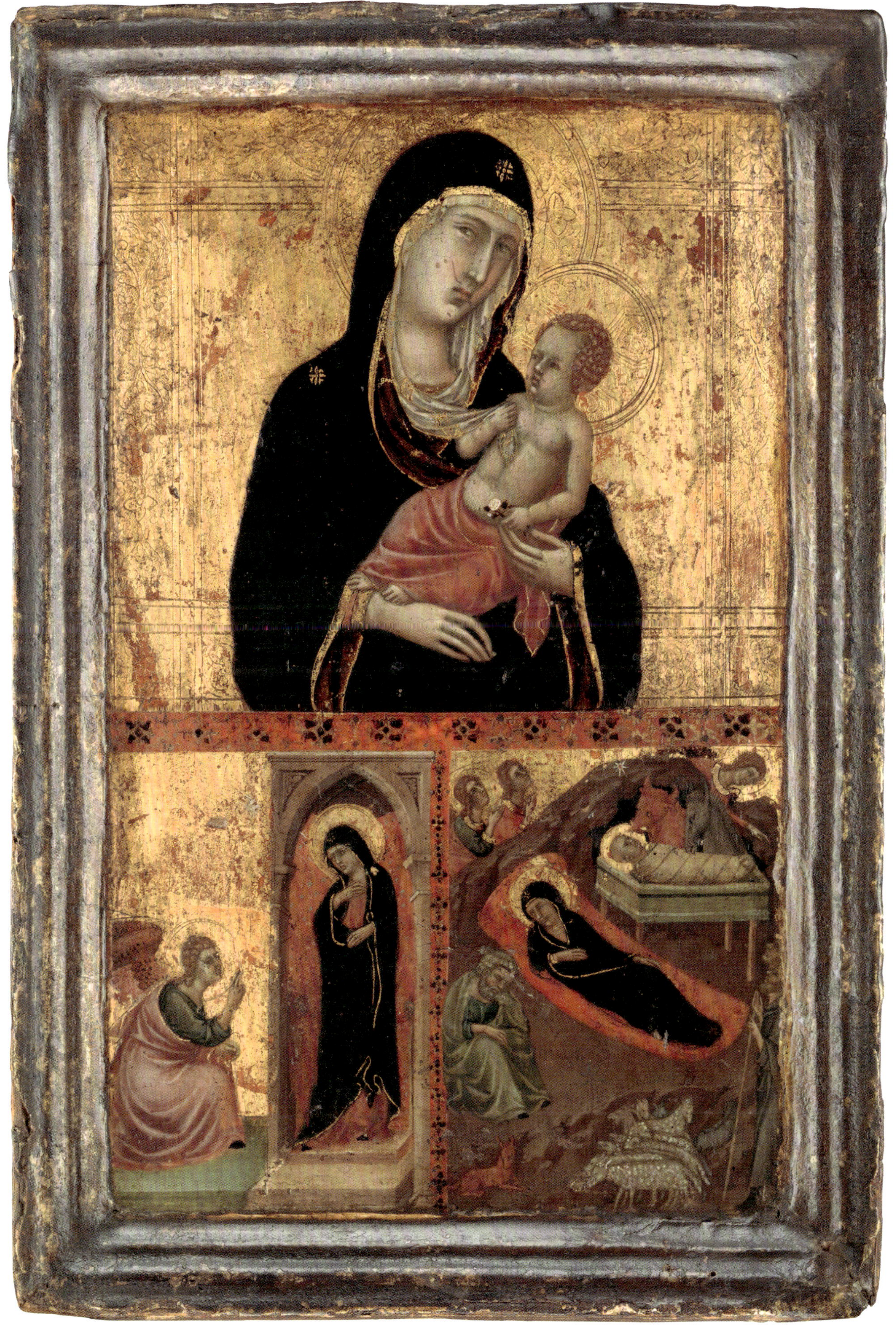

FIG. 206
Master of Città di Castello
(active about 1290–1320)
The Crucifixion, about 1315–20
Tempera on panel, 59.7 × 38 cm
Manchester City Galleries (1984.53)

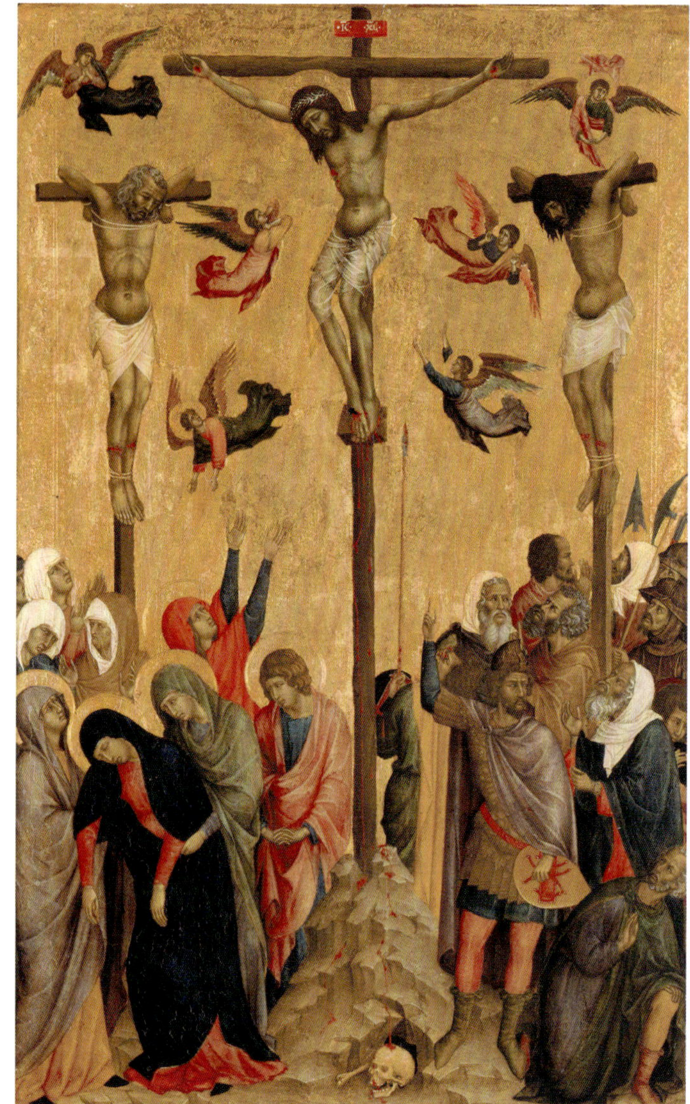

translated into English by Mrs Jonathan Foster (1850–1), was one of the most widely read art historical texts of the nineteenth century.[10] Fra Angelico remained a particular favourite, popularised by Alexis François Rio's *De la poésie Chrétienne* (1836), which offered an alternative conception of the 'primitives' in his arguments for the spiritual and moral significance of early Christian art. Rio's work was translated into English by a Miss Ward in 1854, and his ideas were also disseminated through the second volume of John Ruskin's *Modern Painters* (1846), Lord Lindsay's *Sketches of the History of Christian Art* (1847) and Anna Jameson's *Poetry of Sacred and Legendary Art* (1848).[11] These works recast Rio's Catholic appreciation of 'spiritual' art for a new Anglican audience. Lindsay had read Rio's book on his tour of Italy in 1839 and it undoubtedly shaped his personal experience of the country and its art, as well as his own art collection, which included the *Crucifixion* then attributed to Duccio (fig. 206).[12]

Such reassessments of early Italian painting were to have a long-lasting effect on the reception of early Italian art, but also on collectors like the 'spiritual aesthetes', as Susanna Avery-Quash has termed them, who were motivated by the religious subject matter of the paintings they sought to acquire.[13] By the 1850s, several of the Sienese paintings that had entered the country earlier in the century were in the possession of Anglican clergymen, such as the Revd Walter Davenport-Bromley and the Revd John Fuller Russell, who were associated with the Oxford Movement, and artist-philanthropist Thomas Gambier Parry, who wrote on the interactions of art, morality and spirituality for *The Ecclesiologist*. In his survey of British collections, Gustav Waagen described Revd Fuller Russell's home as 'so richly adorned with Italian specimens … that the spectator feels as if he was transported into a chapel at Siena or Florence'.[14] A rare watercolour, *The Rev. Walter Davenport-Bromley in his Library at Wootton Hall, Staffordshire* (fig. 207), suggests how a collector might display gold-ground altarpiece fragments in his library.

In 1857 the exhibition *Art Treasures of Great Britain* in Manchester brought many of these paintings from private collections to public display. Organised by Waagen, the exhibition was overseen by Prince Albert, who argued that the displays would provide a unique opportunity 'to illustrate the history of Art in a chronological and systematic arrangement'.[15] The exhibition remains the largest art exhibition ever held in the United Kingdom, with more than 16,000 artworks on display. Over 1.3 million visitors – about four times the population of Manchester at the time – had

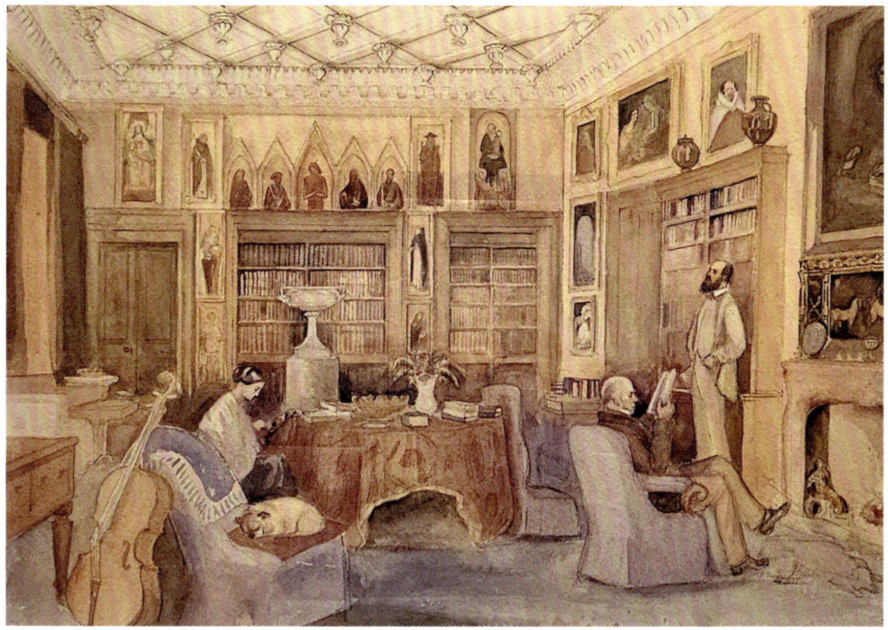

FIG. 207
Unknown artist
The Rev. Walter Davenport-Bromley in his Library at Wootton Hall, Staffordshire, about 1860
Watercolour on paper, 35 × 50 cm
Capesthorne Hall, Cheshire

the opportunity to see more than 110 early Italian paintings, among them 15 paintings of the Sienese School, including several panels from Ugolino's Santa Croce Altarpiece as well as Duccio's Crucifixion triptych, lent by Prince Albert himself and reattributed by Waagen to Duccio. The exhibition would go on to have a long-lasting impact on the reception and display of Sienese painting in Britain.

THE NATIONAL GALLERY AS TASTEMAKER

In December 1857 the National Gallery acquired 24 early Italian paintings from Francesco Lombardi and Ugo Baldi, including Duccio's triptych and Segna di Bonaventura's *Crucifix* (see fig. 53).[16] The National Gallery's Director, Sir Charles Eastlake, did not necessarily appreciate the earliest paintings himself. He described how 'the earliest Tuscan painters were selected solely for their historical importance, and as showing the rude beginnings from which, through nearly two centuries and a half, Italian art slowly advanced to the period of Raphael and his contemporaries'.[17] However, this acquisition was probably partly inspired by the *Art Treasures* exhibition, which was seen by many to epitomise the kind of displays that should be effected by a national museum, to educate and illuminate the history and development of the different artistic schools.[18] Eastlake had himself advised on the *Art Treasures* displays, and the experience probably accelerated the long negotiations for the Lombardi-Baldi paintings, which had then been known to the National Gallery Trustees for some twelve years.[19]

The National Gallery's new Sienese paintings were initially categorised together with the other works in the group as 'Tuscan or Florentine School'; Keeper Ralph Wornum explained that 'the Sienese school may be considered to have a character of its own, but as it is represented, as yet, in the National Gallery, by unimportant specimens only, it is for the present comprehended in the Florentine school'.[20] The particular 'character' of Sienese painting was then understood as a foil to Florence. Thomas Roscoe's translation of Luigi Lanzi (1828) compared the 'Dramatic' Florentine with the 'Contemplative Sienese', and Florentine skills in 'design' with the Sienese ability to express 'emotions of the heart'; Charles and Elizabeth Eastlake's translation of Franz Kugler (1874) called this a difference between Florentine 'vigour of thought' and Sienese 'depth of feeling'.[21] In 1864 Joseph Archer Crowe and Giovanni Battista Cavalcaselle's *New History of Painting in Italy* developed these contrasts of character into stylistic comparisons, comparing Florence's 'decorous simplicity' with Siena's 'fondness for ornament' and adherence to 'old technical methods' like punchwork.[22]

Siena's distinctive artistic identity became increasingly important during the years of the unification of Italy (1848–71), when the city sought to cultivate its reputation as a medieval

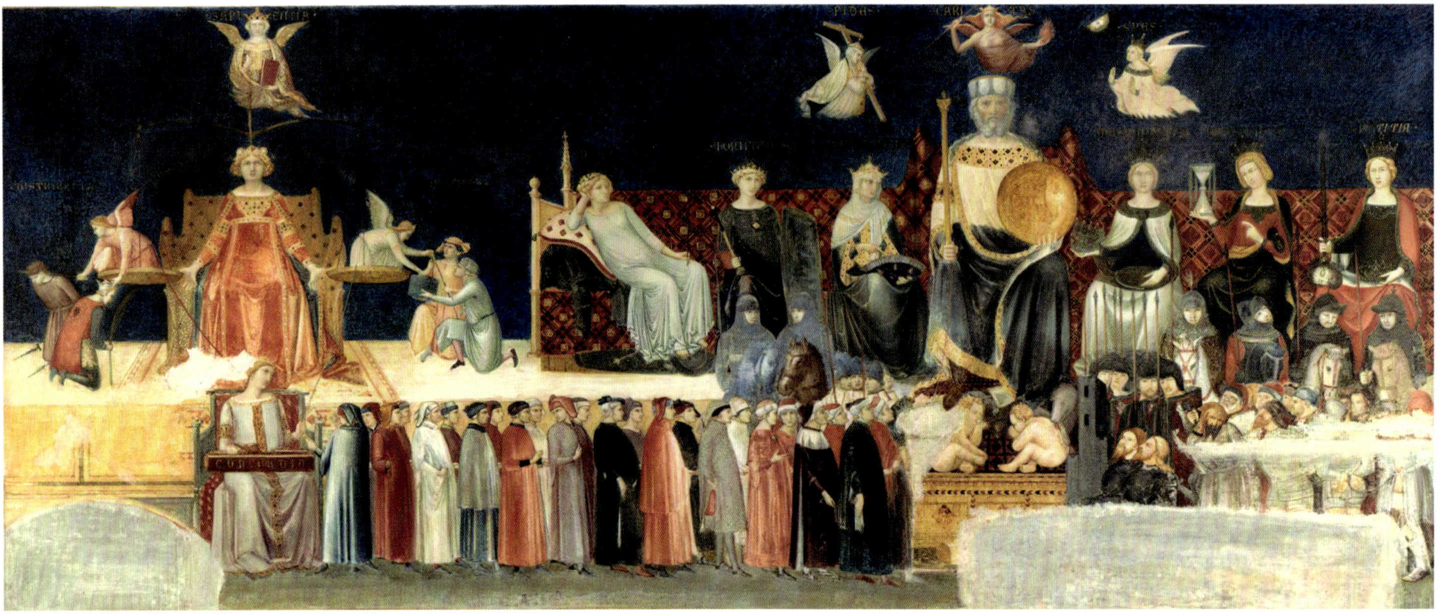

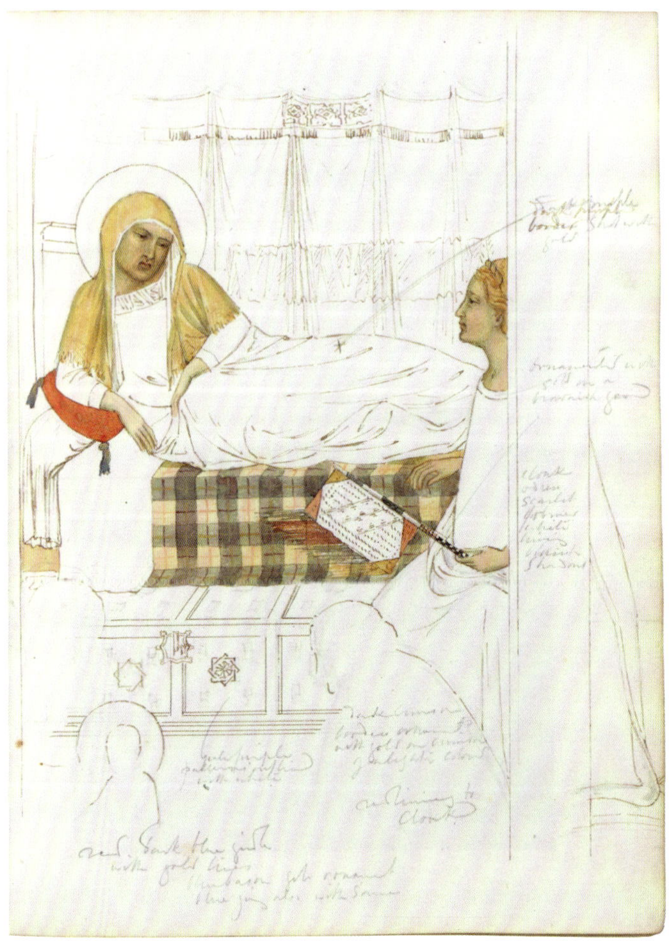

centre. Luigi Mussini, artist director of the Istituto di Belle Arti from 1852, led a programme of restoration aligned to Sienese Purismo, an artistic movement equivalent to the Nazarenes or Pre-Raphaelites.[23] Giuseppe Partini was employed to undertake large architectural restorations at the Duomo (1867–95), the Palazzo Salimbeni (1871–9) and the Palazzo Pubblico (1883), among others.[24] Not all of Partini's plans came to fruition, including the expansion of the clerestory windows of the Duomo to create an inspiring atmosphere of celestial light.[25] During these years, movable artworks were taken away for restoration and did not always return. Giovanni Pisano's *Prophet Haggai*, for example, was probably removed from the Duomo facade to the storerooms of the Opera del Duomo around this time.[26] Such was the transformation of the city during this period that in 1882 *The Liverpool Mercury* pronounced Siena 'a perfectly mediaeval city [*sic*] where the arts still live', describing in turn the 'ancient abodes' of the city's aristocracy, the 'dream of decorated Gothic' of the cathedral and even the politics of the Sienese, who had 'indignantly rejected various Republican pretenders who put forward claims as red-shirted Garibaldians and neglected patriots' in favour of 'a new noble mayor, the Marquis Chigi'. The writer described how modern Siena was so 'mediaeval' in mindset that it was 'ashamed' of its train station, and accordingly 'wraps [it] up … under her turret walls and carefully conceals it'.[27]

FIG. 208
Charles Fairfax Murray (1849–1919)
after **Ambrogio Lorenzetti**
(documented 1319; died 1348/9)
The Policy of Siena, 1873 (original, 1338)
Bodycolour on paper, 39.6 × 94 cm
Ruskin Library, Lancaster (Bem.375)

FIG. 209
Charles Fairfax Murray (1849–1919)
after **Pietro Lorenzetti** (documented possibly 1306; died probably 1348)
The Birth of the Virgin, about 1874
(original, 1342, see fig. 40)
Pencil, pen and ink, watercolour, bodycolour and gold on paper, 25 × 19 cm
The Fitzwilliam Museum, Cambridge (1402)

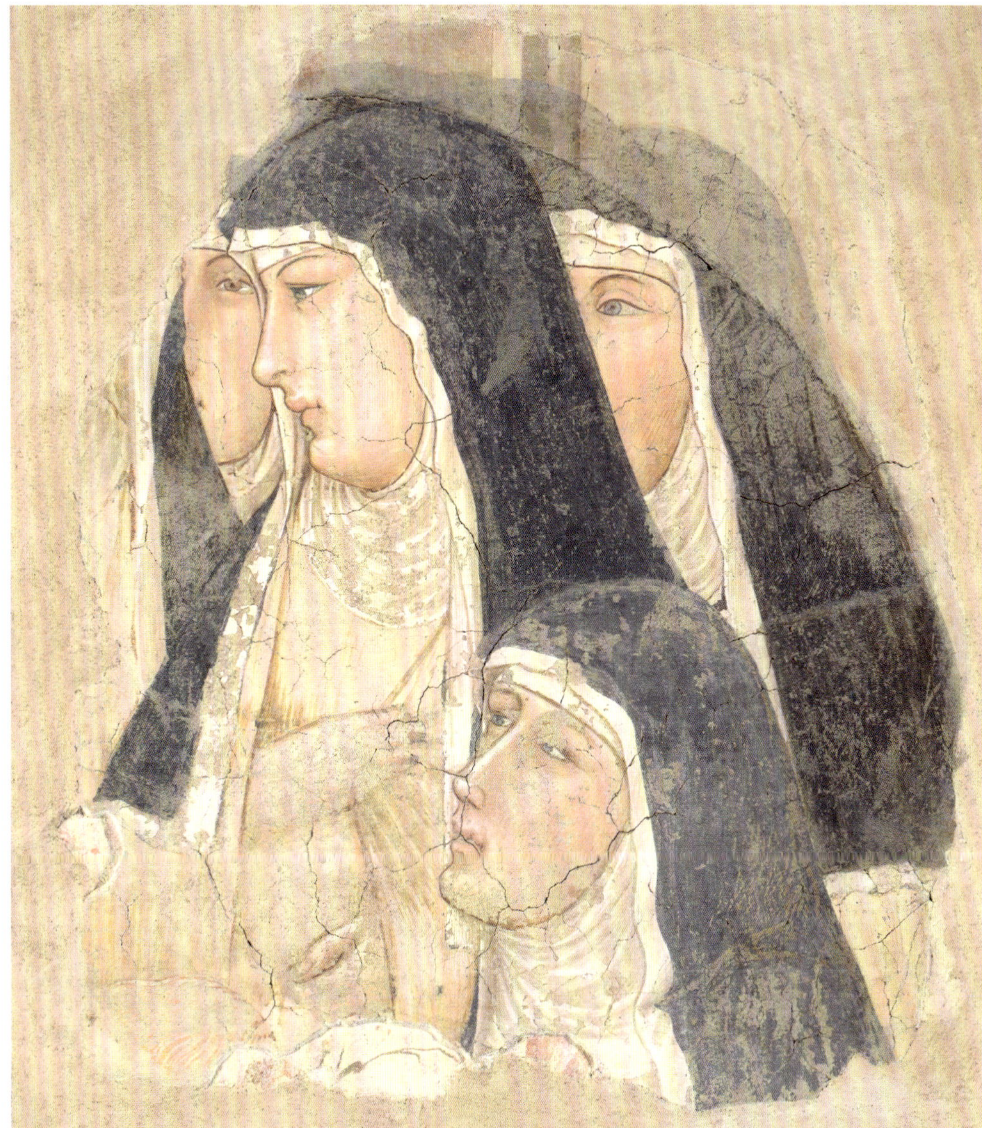

FIG. 210
Ambrogio Lorenzetti
(documented 1319; died 1348/9)
A Group of Four Poor Clares, about 1325
Fresco with areas of secco, 70.4 × 63.4 cm
The National Gallery, London. Bought, 1878 (NG1147)

The National Gallery's interests were represented in Siena by its agent Charles Fairfax Murray, a Pre-Raphaelite painter and dealer who first visited the city in 1873 as a copyist for John Ruskin. Ruskin had been distinctly underwhelmed by his initial visit to Siena in 1840, later citing his dislike of the 'over-cut, over-striped, over-crocketed, over-gabled' cathedral, 'a piece of costly confectionary, and faithless vanity.'[28] However, Ruskin had a particular interest in Ambrogio Lorenzetti's *Allegory of Good Government* fresco in the Sala della Pace of the Palazzo Pubblico, which he discussed in the first of his lectures on 'The Political Economy of Art', given at Manchester in 1857.[29] When Murray fell ill on his way to Rome, he broke his journey in Siena, where he was joined by Edward Burne-Jones.[30] Ruskin requested that Murray make a large, detailed watercolour copy of Lorenzetti's fresco (fig. 208) entitled *The Policy of Siena*. On this trip Murray met his future wife, Angelica Colivicchi, and after their marriage in 1875 the couple rented a villa from the Sienese photographer and art dealer Paolo Lombardi. Murray continued to study Sienese painting, with a particular interest in the work of Ambrogio and Pietro Lorenzetti attested by two surviving sketchbooks (fig. 209).[31] As Paul Tucker has shown, Murray shared his research with Cavalcaselle, and his discoveries were published in the Italian edition of *A New History of Painting*.[32]

On the ground in Siena, Murray was in an excellent position to identify and acquire paintings when they became

FIG. 211
Circle of Simone Martini
Christ bearing the Cross, with a Dominican Friar, about 1350
Tempera on panel, 30.5 × 21.6 cm
The Frick Collection, New York. Gift of Miss Helen Clay Frick, 1927 (1927.1.01)

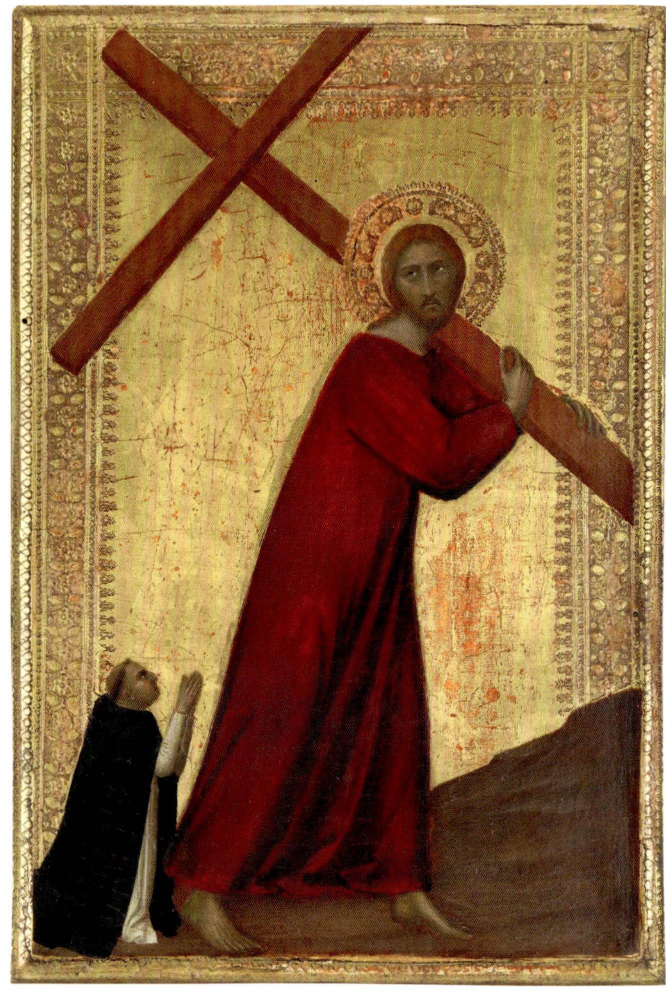

available for sale, writing regularly to Sir Frederic Burton, the National Gallery's third Director, with details of his finds. While most of these paintings were on panel, the first purchase Murray was involved in was the Gallery's fragment of *Four Poor Clares* (fig. 210) from Ambrogio Lorenzetti's frescoes for the chapter house of San Francesco, which was negotiated between 1877 and 1878.[33] At that time, the fresco had been removed from its original location and inserted into the wall of the room occupied by the head of the seminary, where it received much attention from numerous buyers. When Burton was unable to see the fresco himself on his visit to Siena early in 1877, Murray sent him a photograph of the fresco from Lombardi, on the strength of which Burton declared the fresco a 'thing of beauty' and determined to purchase it.[34] In the 1880s and 1890s, Burton oversaw the acquisition of 15 Sienese paintings, seven of which arrived at the Gallery through Murray.[35] When John Taylor's extension to the Gallery buildings was completed in 1887, the new hang was conceived by regional school, and gave the Sienese paintings their own room for the first time.[36]

LOAN EXHIBITIONS AND SIENA'S *ANNUS MIRABILIS*

Contemporary loan exhibitions provided further opportunities for the study of Sienese paintings in Britain. After the British Institution's building lease expired in 1867, the Royal Academy took over its responsibility for loan exhibitions at the instigation of Sir Frederic Leighton, then a recent Academician. At the Royal Academy's 1878 winter exhibition, the first Leighton oversaw as President, the Sienese School was represented by 16 panels of Ugolino di Nerio's Santa Croce Altarpiece. The exhibition's catalogue included an essay on the altarpiece's history and an introduction to trecento altarpiece construction and framing.[37] The rarity of this opportunity to examine Sienese paintings was noted, with *The Manchester Courier* remarking that 'the whole work is deserving of the most patient and careful study, as we have so little of the work of the Sienese school in this country, and until of late so very little of it has been known'.[38] The Royal Academy winter exhibitions continued to include Sienese paintings from private collections, such as Leighton's own panel of *Christ bearing the Cross* then attributed to Barna da Siena (fig. 211).[39]

In the winter of 1893–4, an unprecedented opportunity to view Sienese paintings from British private collections arose at the New Gallery's exhibition *Early Italian Painting, 1300–1550*. The New Gallery had been founded by defectors from the Grosvenor Gallery in 1888, and *Early Italian Painting* was the first in a series of winter loan exhibitions illustrating

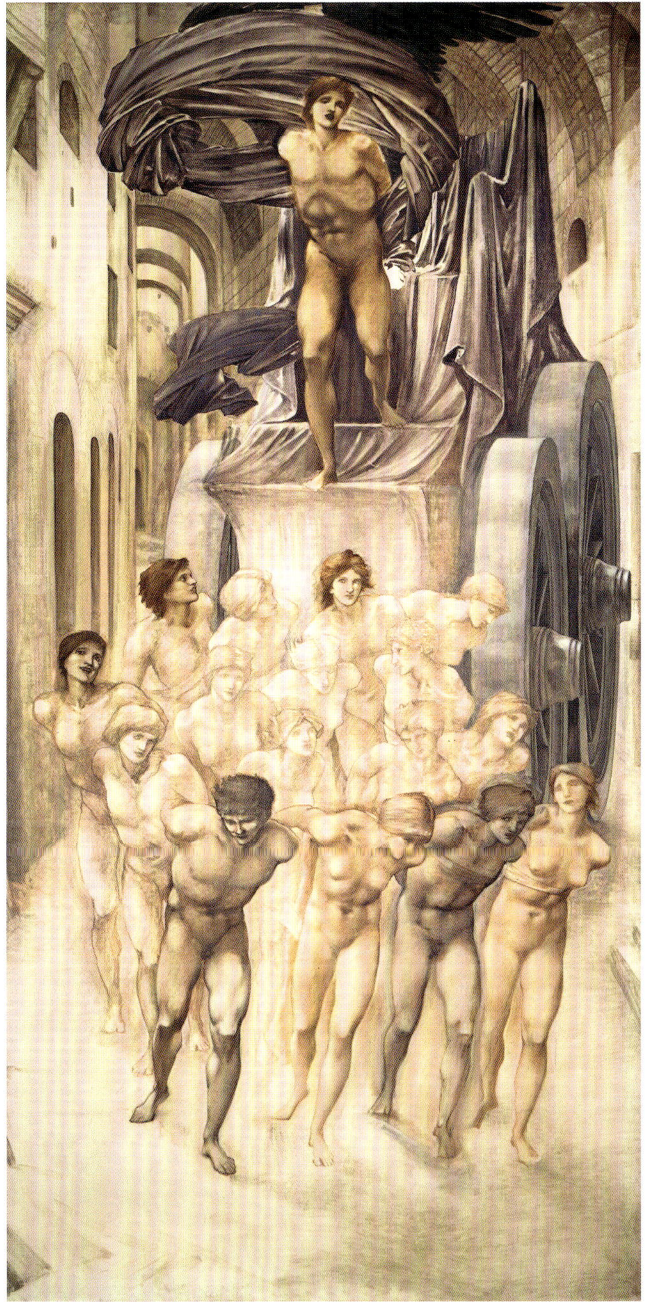

FIG. 212
Edward Burne-Jones (1833–1898)
The Car of Love, 1870–2, 1891–8
Oil on canvas, 518.2 × 273.1 cm
Victoria and Albert Museum (P.16–1909)

the 'great centres' of art that displayed paintings alongside applied arts.[40] Bringing together 28 Sienese pictures – including four panels from Duccio's *Maestà* lent by Robert Henry Benson, several panels from Ugolino's Santa Croce Altarpiece, and the Manchester *Crucifixion* lent by the new Lord Lindsay – the New Gallery's exhibition was the largest display of Sienese paintings shown together in Britain at that time. 'Are we in Italy or in England?' exclaimed one reviewer, voicing his pride that these paintings had come from English collections alone.[41] Critics with an interest in the Aesthetic Movement's celebration of beauty and 'art for art's sake', such as Robert Stevenson, argued that this was 'an exhibition to be enjoyed sensuously, like a fine day. You lounge there carelessly sunning yourself in old gold, your eyes gently caressed by mellow faded colour and richly devised intricacies of pattern', and surrendering to 'the dreamy enchantment of soulless seeing'.[42] By this date, early Italian painting was a somewhat old-fashioned subject, associated with mid-century taste. As one critic put it, 'the Siennese [*sic*] are ceasing to entrance us'.[43] The exhibition was indeed organised by an older generation, including Murray, Charles Edward Hallé, a Pre-Raphaelite artist who dated his interest in Italian art to a boyhood visit to the *Art Treasures* exhibition in 1857, and Burne-Jones, then aged 59, who was revisiting his earlier work in response to the exhibition, reworking his monumental *Car of Love* (fig. 212) to incorporate the winding streets of Siena he had recorded there decades before.[44] Loan exhibitions of this kind were an invaluable opportunity for a rising generation of connoisseurs to see Sienese paintings from private collections.

In the first years of the twentieth century, five monographs on Siena, its history, its saints and its art, were published by the 'old Sienese gang',[45] who shared an interest in the spiritual qualities of Sienese painting. An anecdote fondly recalls how the group would sit in Siena's main square, while Murray called to passers-by, 'bring out your Madonnas, two hundred lire!'[46] Robert Langton Douglas, an Anglican chaplain, art historian and later dealer, published *A History of Siena* (1902) shortly after finishing a monograph on Fra Angelico.[47] William Heywood, a British historian, and Lucy Olcott, an American art historian, collaborated to produce *Guide to Siena: History and Art* (1903).[48] In Siena, Olcott met her

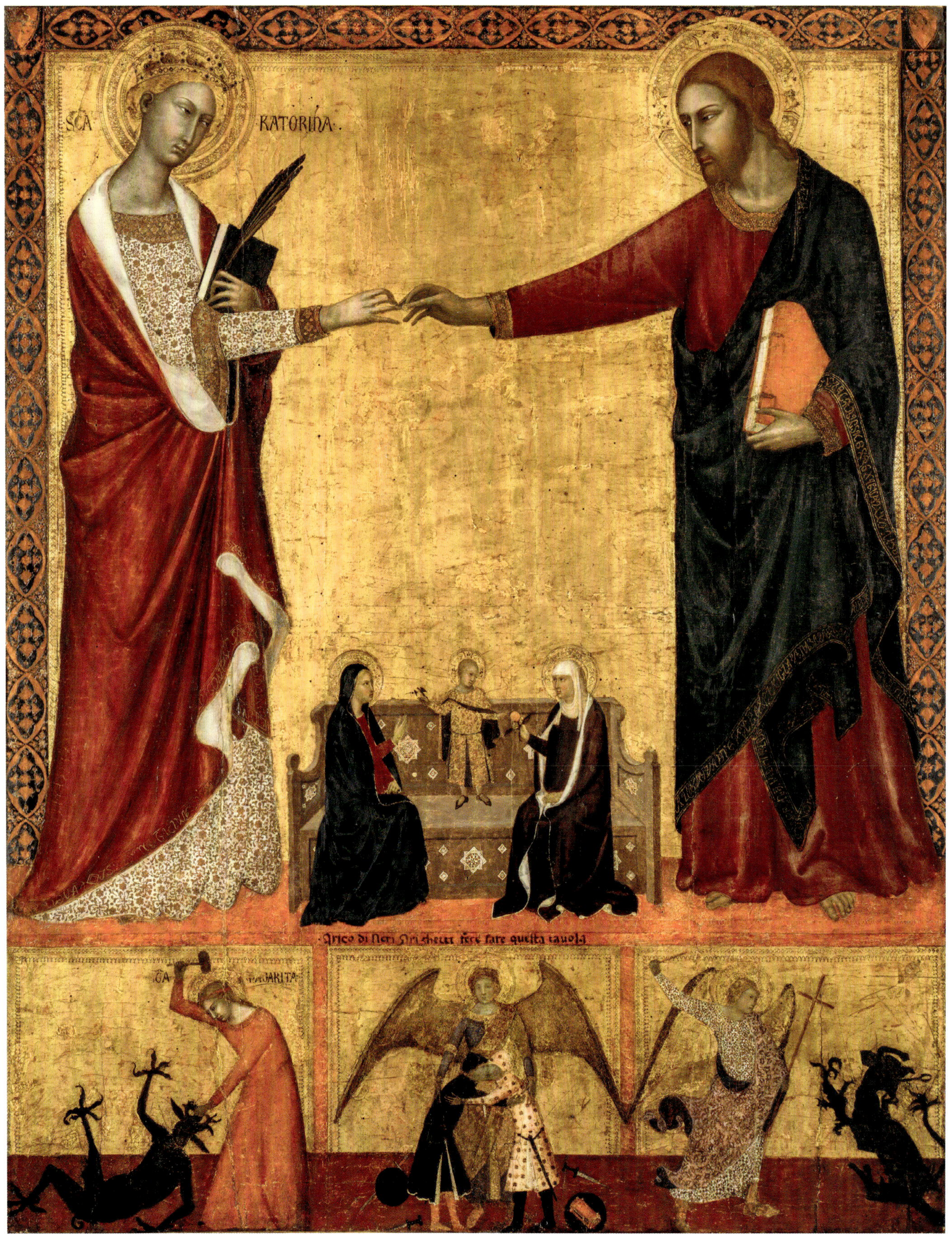
SCA KATORINA
Arico di Neri Arrighetti fece fare questa tavola

FIG. 213
Circle of Simone Martini
The Mystic Marriage of Saint Catherine, about 1340
Tempera on panel, 138.7 × 111.1 cm
Museum of Fine Arts, Boston.
Sarah Wyman Whitman Fund (15.1145)

FIG. 214
Simone Martini (about 1284–1344)
Christ on the Cross, about 1340
Tempera on panel, 25 × 13.6 cm
Harvard Art Museums/Fogg Museum,
Hervey E. Wetzel Bequest Fund (1919.51)

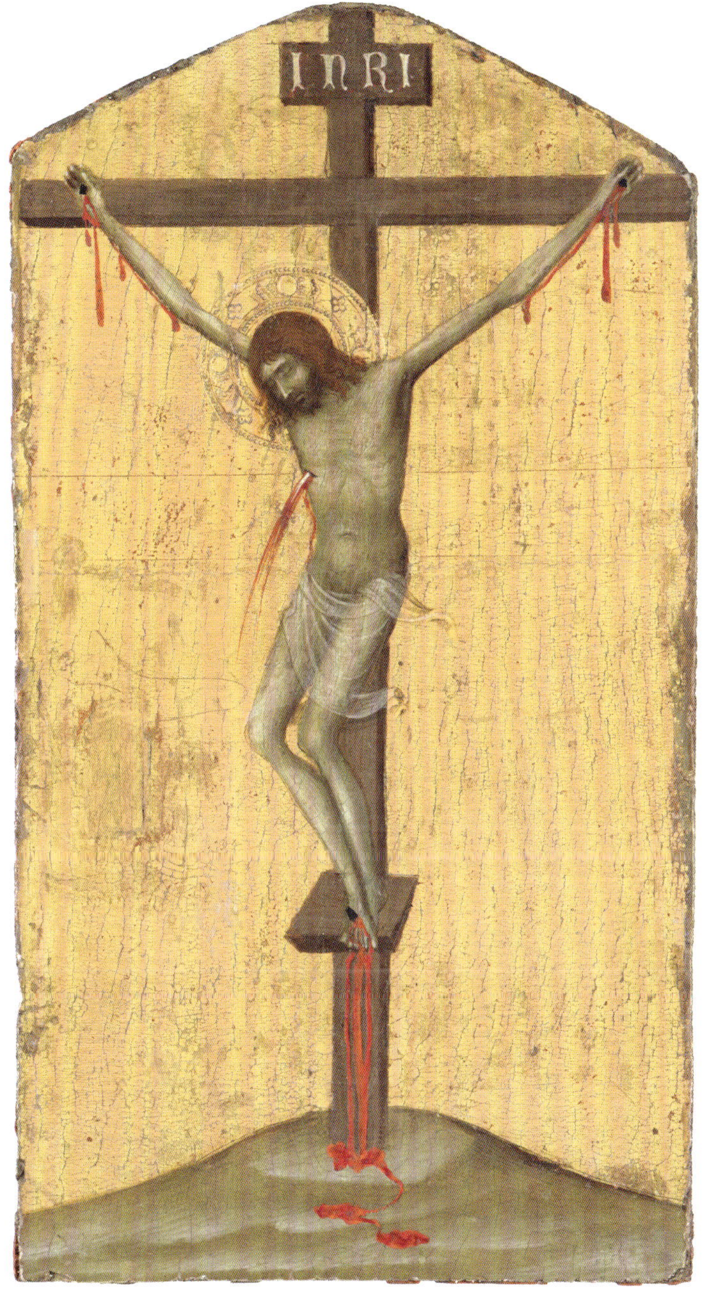

future husband, the American art historian Frederick Mason Perkins.[49] Mary and Bernard Berenson were undertaking research in this area too, sometimes in collaboration with the Perkins, who also acted as the Berensons' agents in Siena, reporting on paintings that became available for sale.[50] These scholars focused their research on the later trecento and quattrocento Sienese artists that had been neglected by earlier writers. Divisions arose between different factions, who shared relevant material and reviewed one another's work in journals like *The Nation*, *The Pilot*, *The Quarterly Review* and the newly founded *Burlington Magazine*, where Douglas, Berenson and Perkins published rival articles on Sassetta and Andrea Vanni in what has subsequently been termed the 'wars of the *Burlington*'.[51]

New art journals, together with the increasing availability of photographs, facilitated new methods of connoisseurship that had their origins in the work of Giovanni Morelli. Contemporary exhibitions began to include photographic albums and catalogues to facilitate the consultation of artworks beyond those selected for display. In 1904 the city of Siena mounted its *Mostra dell'arte antica senese*, motivated by a sense of civic pride, as curator Corrado Ricci explained: 'the Sienese always loved their city and looked after it with unresting care'.[52] Francis Haskell described this exhibition as 'probably the most important Old Master exhibition that had yet been seen anywhere in Italy'.[53] Uniting works from across the province of Siena, as well as significant works lent from abroad, the exhibition had 40,000 visitors in its six-month run, many of whom had travelled to Siena to visit the exhibition, and it was accompanied by a thorough photographic campaign by the Fratelli Alinari.[54] One significant loan from Count Stroganoff was Duccio's *Virgin and Child* (see fig. 18), published for the first time in the exhibition catalogue. A great number of visitors came from Britain, some of them, like Lady Wantage of Lockinge Park, purchasing Sienese art, ancient and modern, to take home.[55]

Lady Wantage was also among the lenders who contributed to a second Sienese art exhibition in London, which showcased Sienese paintings, drawings and 'minor arts' of the city from British collections and was timed to coincide with its monumental counterpart in Siena. Curated by Douglas, this exclusive loan exhibition was held

FIG. 215
Duccio (documented 1278; died 1319)
The Annunciation, about 1308–11
Tempera on poplar, 44.5 × 45.8 cm
The National Gallery, London. Bought, 1883 (NG1139)

FIG. 216
Duccio (documented 1278; died 1319)
The Nativity with the Prophets Isaiah and Ezekiel, about 1308–11
Tempera on poplar, 48 × 86.8 cm (with engaged frame)
National Gallery of Art, Washington, Andrew W. Mellon Collection (1937.1.8)

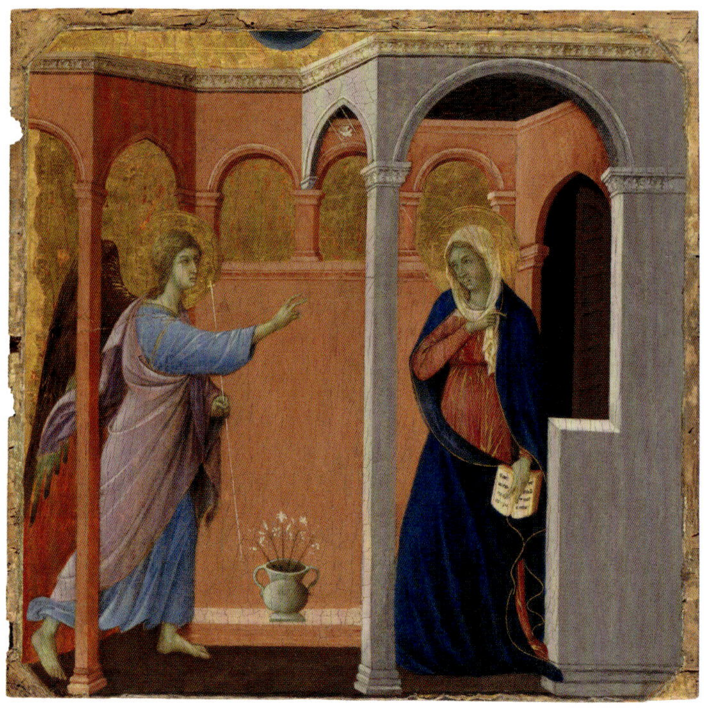

at the Burlington Fine Arts Club from May to July 1904.[56] Fundamentally a private event, open only to club members and their guests, just under half of the 79 paintings and objects in the exhibition were selected from members' collections. Benson's four panels from Duccio's *Maestà*, the Earl of Crawford's Manchester *Crucifixion* and several panels from Ugolino's Santa Croce Altarpiece – previously seen together at the New Gallery's *Early Italian Painting* exhibition – were joined by Duccio's Crucifixion triptych from the Royal Collection, *Christ bearing the Cross* then attributed to Barna da Siena, and a handful of extraordinary loans from other private collectors and museums in Britain, such as Simone Martini's *Christ discovered in the Temple*, as well as some select loans from abroad, including two panels from Simone's Orsini Polyptych, lent by the Royal Museum of Fine Arts, Antwerp. Although the exhibition was only visited by some 4,000 external visitors in its three-month run, it nonetheless marked a high point for the interest in Sienese painting in Britain.

SELLING SIENESE PAINTINGS: FROM ITALY TO BRITAIN TO THE USA

After 1904, Douglas, Berenson and Perkins began to channel their energies and expertise into dealing in, as well as the study of, Sienese art. Indeed, Douglas used the Burlington Fine Arts Club as a kind of showroom for his fledgling dealing business: before the exhibition closed, he had already sold 15 Sienese paintings, including Duccio's Crucifixion triptych (see fig. 32) and Francesco di Vannuccio's Annunciation panels (see fig. 66), to the American collector J. Pierpont Morgan.[57] Douglas later claimed that Morgan had inspired a new demand for Sienese art:

> The news went round, in Bond Street …, 'Morgan's buying Sienese pictures'. The effect can be compared to that produced in Wall Street, when, after some great slump, it began to be whispered, 'Morgan is buying Steel ordinary'. […] The great collector had, in his complex temperament, a certain mystical strain, inherited, no doubt, from some Welsh ancestor. He liked Sienese pictures.[58]

Douglas's boast that Morgan was single-handedly responsible for the interest in Sienese paintings after 1904 should be treated with caution. Isabella Stewart Gardner, for example, had already acquired her first Sienese paintings, Simone's *Virgin and Child* (see fig. 71) – then attributed to Lippo Memmi – from Stefano Bardini in 1897, and Simone's Servite Polyptych from Berenson in 1899.[59] These acquisitions inspired subsequent purchases of Sienese painting elsewhere in Boston; at the Museum of Fine Arts, which acquired the *Mystic Marriage of Saint Catherine* with an attribution to Lippo Memmi in 1915 (fig. 213), and the Fogg Art Museum, which acquired Simone Martini's *Christ on the Cross* in 1919 (fig. 214), as well as shaping taste further afield.[60] By contrast, Morgan's paintings were never shipped to the USA and they were not even included in

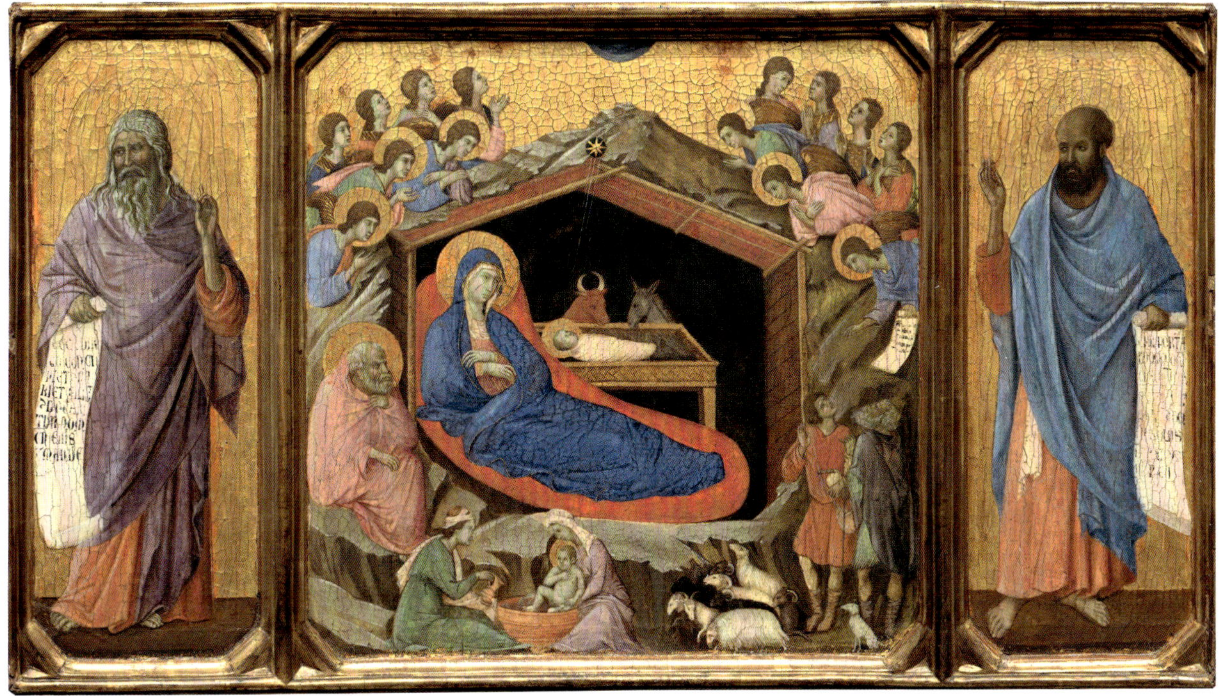

the catalogue of his collection at Prince's Gate, London, suggesting they were inaccessible to visitors.[61] However, while it is unlikely that Morgan personally affected the taste for Sienese paintings, the two exhibitions in Siena and London certainly inspired a new demand for Sienese paintings on the international art market. This taste was cultivated by Douglas and Perkins, who occasionally worked in partnership together, 'the wars of the *Burlington*' forgotten.[62] Through them, significant Sienese paintings were purchased by Philip and Robert Lehman, George Blumenthal, John G. Johnson, Helen Clay Frick and many others. Douglas and Perkins were not the only people responding to a new demand for Sienese painting after 1904. Icilio Federico Joni provided services as a dealer, framer and restorer to Berenson, Perkins and other agents in Italy while also practising as a forger. The publication of his memoirs in the 1930s contributed to the existing unease around excessive restorations as well as forgeries of early Italian paintings.[63]

The prices achieved by Sienese paintings remained relatively low until the sale of the Benson collection in 1927. The National Gallery had hoped to receive these paintings – a gift that would have meant a significant reunion of fragments from Duccio's *Maestà*. By then, there was no hope of bringing together the only two panels from the front predella outside Siena – the National Gallery's *Annunciation* (fig. 215) and the *Nativity* (fig. 216) then in the Kaiser Friedrich Museum, Berlin – but Benson's gift would have reunited six of the eight surviving panels from the back predella.[64] Benson was a Trustee of the Gallery from 1912, and he even compiled a report listing the Gallery's deficiencies in Sienese paintings, with the artists represented in his collection noted as key absences. However, as Edward Fowles's recollections reveal, Sir Joseph Duveen and Berenson were already in conversation with Benson regarding attributions and price as early as 1923.[65] After Benson's banking firm was declared insolvent, the collection was displayed at the City of Manchester Art Gallery from April until July 1927. The press expressed delight at seeing this collection exhibited as a whole in public for the first time, and it was hoped that some of these paintings would remain in Britain.[66] However, the entire collection of 115 Italian paintings was sold to Duveen for £500,000, a sum almost made back on a single sale, of Duccio's *Temptation of Christ on the Mountain* (see fig. 24), to Helen Clay Frick for $500,000, together with the 'Barna da Siena' *Christ bearing the Cross* (fig. 211) that had once been in Leighton's collection. Frick had spent several holidays driving around Italy with Perkins, who cultivated her interest in Sienese painting. She also commissioned to-scale

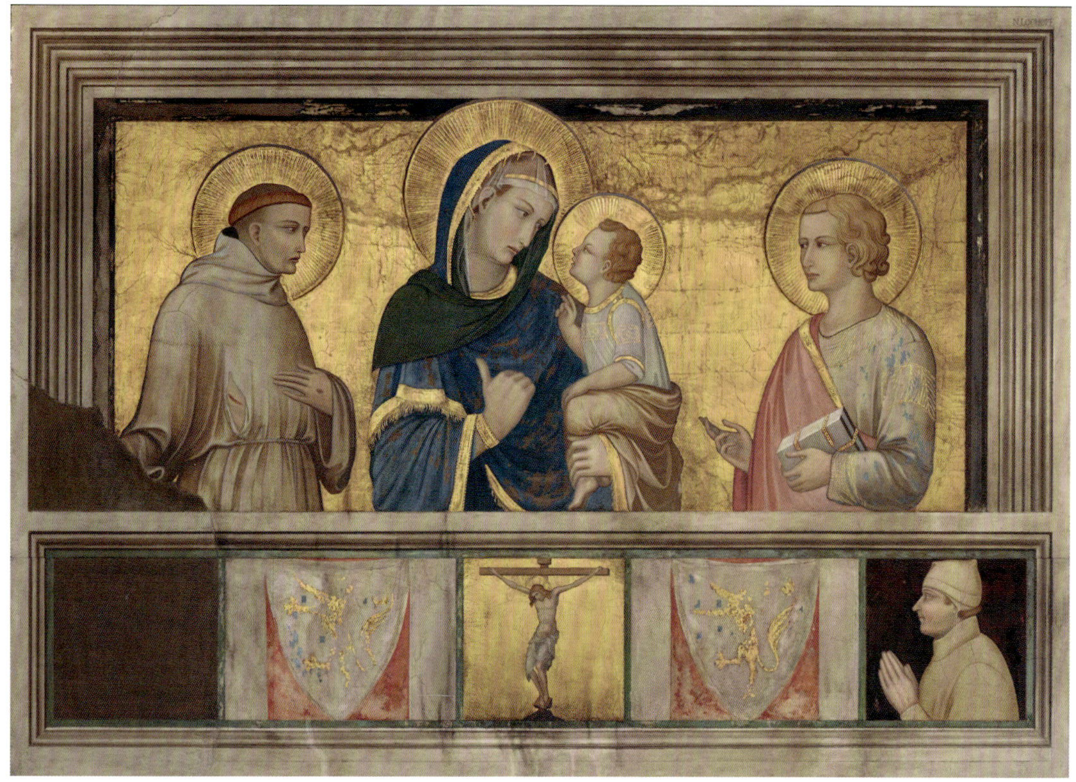

FIG. 217
Nicholas Lochoff (1872–1948)
after **Pietro Lorenzetti** (documented possibly 1306; died probably 1348)
The Virgin and Child, 1928
(original, about 1322–3, see fig. 55)
Fresco, dimensions unknown
The Frick Collection, New York

copies of important Sienese paintings from Russian copyist Nicholas Lochoff, including Pietro Lorenzetti's frescoes at Assisi (fig. 217) and Simone's *Annunciation* (see fig. 39), though her plan to commission a copy of Duccio's *Maestà* never came to fruition.[67] Duveen's involvement in the Benson sale marked the beginning of astronomical prices for gold-ground painting. After Morgan's death in 1944, his Sienese paintings were sold at Christie's, the last significant sale of Sienese paintings in Britain before the introduction in 1947 of the Waverley system to regulate the export of paintings. At the Morgan sale, Duveen secured Duccio's Crucifixion triptych, which he sold to the Museum of Fine Arts, Boston, for $250,000. The rising value placed on Duccio's work culminated in The Metropolitan Museum of Art's acquisition of Duccio's *Stoclet Madonna* for more than $45 million in 2004 (see fig. 18).

Since the very first Sienese paintings arrived in Britain, appreciation for these precious artworks followed some of the broader trends in the taste for and study of Italian art: the day of the primitives; connections between local art and Italian politics; an interest in the spiritual qualities of religious painting; the connoisseurship of understudied painters; and the rise of the international market for old master pictures. While some masterpieces remain, miraculously, in or near their original setting, like Pietro Lorenzetti's Pieve Polyptych in Arezzo, other works, including Ugolino's Santa Croce Altarpiece and Duccio's *Maestà*, have been dispersed to a greater or lesser extent, and the reconstruction of such works has been a preoccupation of scholarship in the last century (see pp. 69–77). However, the fragments of these works held in foreign museums continue to resonate with audiences around the world, inspiring enthusiasm for 'the particular delightfulness of Sienese local painting'. As Hisham Matar recently put it, 'the Sienese school is hopeful but also flattering, producing paintings that are confident of your presence, intelligence and willingness to engage'.[68] The intimate, personal relationship that individuals have had with these paintings in the past has affected the location, understanding and appreciation of these objects today.

This contribution is based on Tedbury 2018, a PhD undertaken at the Courtauld Institute of Art and the National Gallery. With especial thanks to Joanna Cannon and Caroline Campbell, and gratitude to Susanna Avery-Quash, Elisa Camporeale, Caroline Elam, Nicholas Penny, Paul Tucker, colleagues at the Courtauld Institute, the National Gallery, The Metropolitan Museum of Art, and the Getty Institute, among many other individuals and institutions.

1. Lee 1898, p. 4.
2. Swinburne 1871, pp. 191–204. The Risorgimento, or unification of Italy, was the consolidation of states in the Italian peninsula into the Kingdom of Italy. The movement took place between 1848 and 1871. The Kingdom was declared in 1861.
3. Lanzi 1792–6 (1968), vol. 1 (1792), pp. 255–6.
4. Vasari's ciborium was relegated to the Bardi di Vernio chapel in the north transept of the church when Santa Croce was renewed in the Neo-Gothic style in 1869.
5. Alfonso Landi describes the painting as 'in capo alla scala della Scrittoria dell'Opera' ('at the head of the stairs of the Scrittoria dell'Opera'); Giovanbattista Cavalcaselle saw it in the sacristy in 1864. Landi 1655 (1992); Crowe and Cavalcaselle 1864–6, vol. 2 (1864), p. 122; Volpe 1989, nos 123, 124, pp. 152–7.
6. The fresco fragments are today given to Spinello Aretino (Walker Art Gallery, Liverpool, inv. 2752 and 2753). For Roscoe, see Wilson 2008.
7. For Ottley, see Waterhouse 1962; Brigstocke, Marchand and Wright 2010.
8. Lloyd 1975, Letter 18, pp. 59–60. For Fox-Strangways's collections, see Lloyd 1983.
9. The Nazarenes were a group of nineteenth-century German artists who were inspirational to the Pre-Raphaelite Brotherhood. For Albert's early Italian paintings, see Avery-Quash 2012.
10. For Vasari and the Victorians, see Rubin 1995; Fraser 2014. For Mrs Jonathan Foster's translation, see Rubin 2010.
11. For Rio, Jameson and Ruskin, see Holcomb 1978.
12. Brigstocke 1981. Lindsay purchased this painting from Revd Walter Davenport-Bromley's sale, Christie's, 12 June 1863, lot 52. The painting is now attributed to the Master of Città di Castello.
13. Avery-Quash 2011.
14. Waagen 1854, vol. 2, p. 461.
15. Pergam 2011, Appendix 4, pp. 249–50.
16. Lombardi and Baldi had compiled these paintings between 1838 and 1844.
17. *Report of the Director of the National Gallery* (1857/8, printed 1867).
18. *The London Daily News* 1857, p. 2.
19. The paintings were first described to the Trustees by Samuel Woodburn in 1845. Avery-Quash and Sheldon 2011, pp. 167–8, pp. 210–13.
20. Wornum 1858, p. 12.
21. Lanzi 1828, vol. 1, p. 268; Kugler 1874, vol. 1, pp. 119–20.
22. Crowe and Cavalcaselle 1864–6, vol. 2 (1864), pp. 34–8.
23. For Sienese Purismo, see Siena 1988.
24. For Giuseppe Partini, see Buscioni 1981; Mariani 1921.
25. Thompson 2004.
26. When Giovanni Pisano's sculpture was purchased by the Victoria and Albert Museum in 1963 (inv. A.13-1963), the rector of the Duomo identified its attached label as the same type as that used by the Opera del Duomo in the nineteenth century.
27. *The Liverpool Mercury* 1882, p. 6.
28. Ruskin 1903–12, vol. 35 (1908), p. 270.
29. These lectures were published in *A Joy For Ever* (Ruskin 1880).
30. Burne-Jones's sketchbook from this visit is held by the Fitzwilliam Museum, Cambridge (inv. PDP, 1070(5)).
31. Elliott 2000, pp. 47–76.
32. Tucker 1998, pp. 270–6.
33. For the later lives of these frescoes, see Tedbury 2019b.
34. Murray commissioned many photographs from Lombardi, including a campaign to photograph Duccio's *Maestà* in 1886; see Tucker 2008. Letter from Burton to Murray, 30 August 1877, inv. NG 54/6.
35. Murray also gave Pietro Lorenzetti's *Saint Sabinus before the Roman Governor* to the National Gallery in 1879; accessioned in 1882 (fig. 42).
36. This room also held the National Gallery's paintings by Fra Angelico.
37. London 1878–9.
38. *The Manchester Courier* 1878, p. 6.
39. Leighton had acquired this painting, now attributed to the circle of Simone Martini, from Murray, who bought it back after Leighton's death and sold it to Robert Henry Benson.
40. Hallé 1909, p. 194.
41. *The Western Daily Express* 1894.
42. Stevenson 1894.
43. Ibid.
44. Victoria and Albert Museum (inv. P.16–1909). Hallé 1909, pp. 4–5.
45. Robert Langton Douglas's term for the group, according to Edgell 1951. For the group, see English 2005.
46. This is almost certainly a fiction. Edward Hutton's typescript autobiography, British Institute of Florence, BIF/HUT II.A.1.
47. For Douglas, see Sutton 1979; Tedbury 2020.
48. For Olcott, see Tedbury 2019a.
49. For Perkins, see Nicolai 2019; Nicolai 2016.
50. Israëls 2015b.
51. For the 'wars of the *Burlington*', see Sutton 1979; Leahy 2002; Israëls 2015b.
52. Siena 1904, p. 10; translation from Haskell 1994, p. 562.
53. Haskell 2000, p. 106. For the exhibition, see Siena 2005–6; Camporeale 2004.
54. Vigni 2005, p. 32; Haskell 1994, p. 562.
55. Export records state that in October 1904 Lady Wantage purchased two works from Icilio Federico Joni.
56. For the London exhibition, see Camporeale 2005; Camporeale 2008.
57. For Morgan's Italian paintings, see Tonkovich 2015; Camporeale 2023.
58. Douglas 1940, unpaginated.
59. Berenson and Gardner 1987, pp. 172–5, 207, 209–10, 216. See also Boston 2022–3.
60. Ilchman 2015, p. 59; Zafran 1994. For example, the *Mystic Marriage of Saint Catherine* (fig. 213), acquired by the MFA with an attribution to Lippo Memmi in 1915, or the Fogg Art Museum's acquisition of Simone Martini's *Christ on the Cross* (fig. 214) in 1919.
61. Ward and Roberts 1907.
62. Nicolai 2016.
63. Siena 2004; Mazzoni 2001.
64. For the predella of Duccio's *Maestà*, see Tedbury, pp. 46–51, in the present volume. The *Nativity with the Prophets Isaiah and Ezekiel* was acquired by the Berlin museums in 1884, probably from Charles Fairfax Murray. Duveen acquired the painting from Berlin in 1937, when the Nazi-appointed museum director de-accessioned this work and Filippo Lippi's *Madonna and Child* (about 1440; National Gallery of Art, Washington DC, inv. 1939.1.290), in exchange for Holbein's *Portrait of a Man with a Lute* (1526–7), which remains at the Staatliche Museen, Berlin (inv. 2154).
65. Fowles 1976, p. 183.
66. Douglas 1927.
67. Brazil 2002. Lochoff's copy of Simone's *Annunciation* is today at the University of Pittsburgh.
68. Matar 2019, p. 21.

ARTIST BIOGRAPHIES

Francesca Marzullo

DUCCIO

(documented 1278; died 1319)

Although little is known with certainty about Duccio's origins and formative years, he is usually assumed to have been born in Siena around 1250–5. He is first recorded as a painter in 1278 and 1279, when he received payments from the *comune* of Siena for decorating some coffers and account book covers. Other documents reveal that he owned property in the countryside and was fined on various occasions for civil misdemeanours. The earliest surviving work attributable to him is the *Crevole Madonna* (about 1280–4). In around 1284–5 he painted the diminutive *Madonna dei Francescani* and soon after this the monumental *Rucellai Madonna* (fig. 6), an altarpiece for a confraternity of Santa Maria Novella in Florence. It has been proposed on stylistic grounds that in the 1280s he had a close relationship with the Florentine Cimabue. Scholars have also speculated that he journeyed to Rome in 1280–5 and to Paris in the 1290s, although the latter hypothesis is now generally rejected. In around 1287–8 Duccio designed a stained-glass rose window in the apse of Siena Cathedral. Two small panels intended for private devotion date to the following decade: the *Virgin and Child enthroned with Angels* now in Bern (fig. 7) and the intimate *Virgin and Child* now in New York (fig. 18). Paintings from the early 1300s include a now-lost *Maestà* of about 1302 for an altar in Siena's Palazzo Pubblico, a small triptych of the Crucifixion (fig. 17) and a polyptych for San Domenico in Perugia (about 1304–8). Duccio's most ambitious project and crowning achievement came in 1308–11, when he produced the great double-sided *Maestà* for the high altar of Siena Cathedral (figs 8, 9). Among his late works are two tabernacles probably commissioned by the Dominican cardinal Niccolò da Prato (figs 31, 32), made in the years before the artist's death in 1319.

PIETRO LORENZETTI

(documented possibly 1306; died probably 1348)

Probably born in Siena around 1280, Pietro Lorenzetti first appears in the written record in 1306, when he received payment for modifications to Duccio's altarpiece of 1302 for the Cappella dei Nove in Siena's Palazzo Pubblico. In his early career he won numerous commissions outside his native city. He was present in Cortona in around 1312–16, where he painted two crucifixes, one monumental and the other a smaller, 'cut-out' cross (fig. 109), both now in the Museo Diocesano. In 1317 he went to Assisi to undertake the extremely prestigious project of completing the fresco cycle in the transept of the Lower Church of San Francesco that Giotto and his workshop had begun. His campaign at Assisi was interrupted when he was called to Arezzo to paint a polyptych for the high altar of Santa Maria della Pieve under the patronage of Bishop Guido Tarlati, for which he signed the contract in 1320 (fig. 60). It was not until the subsequent years that he finally established himself in his hometown, where he and his younger brother Ambrogio would go on to run two of the most successful painting workshops. In the 1320s the brothers collaborated on frescoes in the chapter house of the Church of San Francesco. Other Sienese commissions followed, such as the high altar for San Niccolò al Carmine completed by 1329, and now-lost murals on the facade of the hospital of Santa Maria della Scala, which Pietro and Ambrogio executed in 1335. Pietro was also active in Florence, where in around 1330–5 he painted a polyptych illustrating the life of the Beata Umiltà for San Giovanni Evangelista, now in the Gallerie degli Uffizi. Works dating to his final years include the *Birth of the Virgin*, signed and dated 1342, for the altar of Saint Sabinus in Siena Cathedral (fig. 40), and a series of devotional panels depicting the Passion of Christ, of which two are known (figs 37, 38). Another late work is a small *Virgin and Child enthroned* now in Berlin (fig. 85). This may have formed part of a diptych of which his brother painted the other half. Pietro is assumed to have died in Siena in 1348 during the plague.

SIMONE MARTINI

(about 1284–1344)

Presumably born in Siena around 1284, Simone Martini must have achieved distinction by 1315, when he signed and dated the monumental *Maestà* in the council hall of Siena's Palazzo Pubblico (fig. 65). Although the fresco is his earliest ascertained work, it was perhaps before this, in about 1313–14, that he began the murals of the chapel of Saint Martin in the Basilica of San Francesco in Assisi, which he may have completed on a return visit around 1316–17. Between 1315 and 1319 Simone painted the Saint Louis of Toulouse Altarpiece for the Angevin court in Naples (fig. 67). In the years following he produced polyptychs and other works for patrons in Pisa and Orvieto. In 1324 he married the sister of Lippo Memmi, with whom he would later collaborate on such projects as the *Annunciation* for the altar of Saint Ansanus in Siena Cathedral, signed and dated 1333 (fig. 39). His Sienese works from the 1320s include a portable polyptych commissioned in 1326 for the Palazzo Pubblico (see p. 117) and a fresco in the same building of the condottiere Guidoriccio da Fogliano, completed in 1328 or soon after. During this period he also painted the Orsini Polyptych under the patronage of a cardinal of the Orsini family (fig. 80). In about 1335 Simone left Siena for Avignon, where he was employed at the papal court. In Avignon he also befriended the poet Petrarch, for whom he illuminated the frontispiece of a volume of Virgil's poems (fig. 73) and rendered a now-lost portrait of Petrarch's love, Laura. Simone's last works in fresco were the murals in the porch of the Cathedral of Notre-Dame-des-Doms, executed in about 1341 and since ruined, although the sinopie survive. Among the late panel paintings dating to his Avignon period are a small *Christ on the Cross* of about 1340, now in the Harvard Art Museums (fig. 214), and *Christ discovered in the Temple*, signed and dated 1342, now in the Walker Art Gallery (fig. 74). Simone wrote his will on 30 June 1344 in Avignon and died there later that year.

LIPPO MEMMI

(documented 1317–50)

Lippo Memmi belonged to a family of painters and trained in the workshop of his father, Memmo di Filippuccio, who was active in San Gimignano at the beginning of the fourteenth century. Although his birth date is unknown, Lippo emerged as an independent artist by 1317, when he signed and dated his first documented commission, the *Maestà* fresco in the Palazzo del Popolo of San Gimignano. Closely recalling Simone Martini's *Maestà* in the Palazzo Pubblico of Siena, completed two years prior, the work highlights a kinship between the two painters that would shape much of Lippo's life and art. The men became brothers-in-law when Simone married Lippo's sister in 1324 and were occasional collaborators, most famously on the *Annunciation* for the altar of Saint Ansanus in Siena Cathedral in 1333 (fig. 39), which they signed jointly. In his early years, Lippo made several works in Pisa, including polyptychs for the cathedral and San Paolo a Ripa d'Arno, and, in about 1330, a polyptych for San Francesco in San Gimignano (fig. 69). Among his surviving signed paintings are the *Madonna dei Raccomandati* in Orvieto Cathedral, the *Madonna del Popolo* from Santa Maria dei Servi in Siena, a *Madonna and Child* now in the Lindenau-Museum, and the *Madonna and Child and Saint John the Baptist*, a diptych of 1333 now divided between the Gemäldegalerie, Berlin, and a private collection. Later in his career, Lippo followed Simone to the papal court in Avignon, where in 1347 he signed a now-lost panel for the Franciscan church. He subsequently returned to Siena and remained there until his death in 1356. His last known painting, signed and dated to the 1350s (the partial date once read 'MCCCL...'), is a mural of the *Maestà* in the cloister of San Domenico.

AMBROGIO LORENZETTI

(documented 1319; died 1348/9)

The younger brother of Pietro Lorenzetti, Ambrogio is thought to have been born in Siena near the end of the thirteenth century. His first dated painting, inscribed 1319, is the *Madonna di Vico l'Abate* (fig. 83). In 1321 he is documented in Florence, where in 1327 he joined the Guild of the Medici e Speziali, to which painters belonged. That he was active in Florence in the following years is confirmed by such works as the *Stories from the Life of Saint Nicholas* (about 1332–4), from the Church of San Procolo (fig. 89). Back in his native Siena, Ambrogio undertook collaborations with his brother Pietro, including frescoes in the chapter house of the Church of San Francesco in the 1320s and now-lost murals on the facade of the hospital of Santa Maria della Scala in 1335 (see pp. 17, 132–3). He also produced frescoes in the Rotunda chapel of San Galgano at Montesiepi around 1334–6 (see the sinopia for the *Annunciation*, fig. 88) and a *Maestà* for the Augustinian Hermits of Massa Marittima in about 1335–7. From 1337 to 1339 he was engaged at Siena's Palazzo Pubblico, first on now-lost episodes from Roman history on an exterior wall and then on his celebrated allegorical frescoes in the Sala dei Nove illustrating the effects of good and bad government (see figs 1 and 140). For the altar of Saint Crescentius in Siena Cathedral he painted the *Presentation in the Temple*, signed and dated 1342 (fig. 41). Around this time he also executed the *Piccola Maestà*, about 1342–4, now in the Pinacoteca nazionale di Siena (fig. 145). His *Annunciation* (1344), made for the Sienese tax office, is his last known signed and dated work (fig. 87). It is possible that the *Crucifixion* of about 1345 now in the Harvard Art Museums (fig. 86), which is attributed to him, may be one half of a diptych of which his brother painted the other panel (fig. 85). Ambrogio wrote his will in June 1348 and most likely died in Siena of the plague later that year.

TINO DI CAMAINO

(about 1280–about 1337)

Born in Siena around 1280, Tino di Camaino was the son of the architect and sculptor Camaino di Crescentino. His formative years were spent in the orbit of Giovanni Pisano, who was then master of works at Siena Cathedral. When Giovanni left this position in 1297, Tino followed him to Pisa, where he eventually succeeded the elder sculptor as master of works at Pisa Cathedral. Among Tino's Pisan projects was the tomb of Emperor Henry VII, commissioned to him around 1315, just before he returned to his native city. Back in Siena, Tino was employed at the cathedral, where he sculpted the tomb of Cardinal Riccardo Petroni in 1318 (fig. 113) and was named master of works in 1320. He was also active in Florence, completing the tomb of Gastone della Torre in Santa Croce in 1319 (see p. 165) and that of Bishop Antonio d'Orso in Florence Cathedral in 1321, as well as sculptures for the baptistery. The Tuscan phase of Tino's career came to a close in late 1323 or early 1324, when he relocated to Naples, where he remained until his death in around 1337. His first Neapolitan commission, dating to about 1324, was the free-standing tomb of the recently deceased Catherine of Austria in San Lorenzo Maggiore. Soon after this he executed the tomb of Mary of Hungary in Santa Maria Donnaregina. In the early 1330s he was hired by Abbot Philip de Haya to carve a marble altarpiece for the abbey church of Santissima Trinità at Cava dei Tirreni, near Salerno (fig. 102). A relief of the *Virgin and Child with Queen Sancia, Saints and Angels* (fig. 68) may have been commissioned to Tino by the Angevin Queen Sancia herself. Although best known for his innovative funerary monuments, Tino also produced altarpieces and small-scale reliefs intended for private devotion (fig. 105).

LANDO DI PIETRO

(about 1280–1340)

Thought to have been born in Siena or its environs in around 1280, Lando di Pietro had a successful and versatile career as a goldsmith, sculptor, architect and engineer. His first documented work was a commission of immense prestige: the crown for Emperor Henry VII's coronation as King of Italy, which took place in Milan in 1311. He then demonstrated his expertise in bell design and engineering, balancing the municipal bells of Siena in 1321, 1323 and 1332, and working on the bell of the Palazzo Vecchio in Florence in 1322. As an architect, he guided the construction of the bastions of Montemassi in 1328 and that of the walls of Paganico in 1334. Between 1336 and 1339 Lando seems to have resided in Naples, employed as a goldsmith at the court of King Robert of Anjou. Some have attributed to him the splendid arm reliquaries of Saint Louis of Toulouse and Saint Luke now in the Musée du Louvre, executed in Naples for Robert's wife, Queen Sancia of Mallorca (fig. 131). In 1338, presumably on a return visit to Siena, Lando carved the wooden crucifix of the Basilica of San Bernardino all'Osservanza (fig. 130). Reduced to fragments by a bombardment during the Second World War, the sculpture was revealed to contain two parchments inscribed with the artist's prayers, which attest to his authorship and the date (fig. 101). In December 1339 Lando was recalled from Naples by the General Council of Siena to lead the major project of expanding the cathedral, the so-called 'Duomo Nuovo'. He also collaborated with Agostino di Giovanni and Giacomo di Vanni on the difficult task of bringing waters to the fountain of the Piazza del Campo. He died not long after his return to Siena, where he was buried in the Convent of San Domenico on 3 August 1340.

LIST OF EXHIBITED WORKS

References compiled by Nicholas Flory

Works are listed chronologically under each artist. Unless otherwise stated, the works are exhibited in London and New York (all loan information correct at time of printing).

1. PAINTINGS

FIG. 143
Avignon or Naples
The Adoration of the Magi, about 1340–4
Tempera on panel, 66.4 × 46.7 cm (with engaged frame); 54.3 × 38.1 cm (painted surface)
The Metropolitan Museum of Art, New York. Robert Lehman Collection, 1975 (1975.1.9)
Selected literature:
Thiébaut in Paris 1981–2, under cat. 320, pp. 367–8; Thiébaut in Avignon 1983, under cats 61–2, pp. 184–6; Pope-Hennessy and Kanter 1987, no. 40, pp. 90–2; Schmidt 2002b, pp. 402–3; Schmidt 2005a, pp. 198, 289–90.
[London only]

FIG. 171
Bartolo di Fredi (documented 1353–1410) (triptych) and **French artist** (ivory plaques)
Reliquary Triptych with the Annunciation, Saint Ansanus, the Adoration of the Magi and the Crucifixion, about 1370 (triptych); about 1350–70 (ivory plaques)
Tempera on panel with gilded and polychromed ivory, 35.5 × 38.5 cm (open)
The Wyvern Collection, UK (0442)
Selected literature:
Freuler 1994; de Torquat 2007, Sidi in Siena 2010, cat. E.2, pp. 364–5; Mann in Cleveland, Baltimore and London 2010–11, cat. 121, pp. 204–5; Williamson 2018, pp. 23–42; Williamson 2019, no. 105, pp. 212–13.

FIG. 13
Byzantine artist
The Virgin and Child ('La Madonna del Carmine'), thirteenth century
Tempera on panel, with embossed gold and gilded silver cover (not illustrated), 28 × 22 cm (with integral frame); 21.5 × 15 cm (painted surface)
Inscription: MP ΘV (upper left and right, 'Mother of God')
From Chiesa di San Niccolò al Carmine, Siena
Kept at Museo Diocesano di San Bernardino, Siena
Owned by Ministero dell'Interno-Dipartimento per le libertà civili e l'immigrazione Direzione Centrale degli affari dei culti e per l'amministrazione del Fondo Edifici di Culto- FEC Fondo Edifici di Culto
Selected literature:
Garrison 1949, no. 126, p. 65; Bonfioli in Siena 1979, cat. 38, pp. 104–5; Cannon 1987, p. 20; Folda 2015, pp. 143–5, 262, 333–4, nn. 37, 40–2.

FIG. 7
Duccio (documented 1278; died 1319)
The Virgin and Child enthroned with Angels, about 1290–5
Tempera on poplar, 31.5 × 23.3 cm (with original frame)
Kunstmuseum Bern, Legacy of Adolf von Stürler, Versailles, 1902 (G 0873)
Selected literature:
Wagner 1974, pp. 20–5; Stubblebine 1979, vol. 1, pp. 126–7; White 1979, pp. 151–2; Freuler in Fehlmann and Freuler 2002, no. 1, pp. 46–51; Schmidt in Siena 2003–4, cat. 27, pp. 184–7.
[London only]

FIG. 18
Duccio (documented 1278; died 1319)
The Virgin and Child, about 1290–1300
Tempera on poplar, 27.9 × 21 cm (with engaged frame); 23.8 × 16.5 cm (painted surface)
The Metropolitan Museum of Art, New York. Purchase, Rogers Fund, Walter and Leonore Annenberg and The Annenberg Foundation Gift, Lila Acheson Wallace Gift, Annette de la Renta Gift, Harris Brisbane Dick, Fletcher, Louis V. Bell, and Dodge Funds, Joseph Pulitzer Bequest, several members of The Chairman's Council Gifts, Elaine L. Rosenberg and Stephenson Family Foundation Gifts, 2003 Benefit Fund, and other gifts and funds from various donors, 2004 (2004.442)
Selected literature:
Stubblebine 1979, vol. 1, pp. 27–8; White 1979, pp. 62, 160; Bellosi in Bagnoli et al. 2003, pp. 200–1; Christiansen 2007, pp. 40–7.

FIG. 17
Duccio (documented 1278; died 1319)
Triptych with the Crucifixion and Other Scenes, about 1302–8
Tempera on panel, 44.9 × 31.4 cm (central panel); 44.8 × 16.9 cm (left wing); 44.8 × 17.1 cm (right wing); 13.9 × 34.9 cm (spandrel)
The Royal Collection / HM King Charles III (RCIN 400095)
Selected literature:
Shearman 1972, no. 86, pp. 93–6; Stubblebine 1979, vol. 1, pp. 47, 122, 126–7; White 1979, pp. 153–4; Cannon and Pemberton-Pigott 2002, pp. 10–18; Bellosi in Siena 2003–4, cat. 29, pp. 192–7.
[London only]

PREDELLA PANELS FROM THE *MAESTÀ* FOR SIENA CATHEDRAL:

FIG. 215
Duccio (documented 1278; died 1319)
The Annunciation, about 1308–11
Tempera on poplar, 44.5 × 45.8 cm
Inscription: Ecce virgo concipi[et] et pa[tri] et filiu[m] [et] vocacbitur (on the Virgin's book; 'Behold, a Virgin shall conceive, and bear a son, and shall call his name [Immanuel]', Isaiah 7:14)
The National Gallery, London. Bought, 1883 (NG1139)
Selected literature:
Tarr 2000, pp. 185–213; Gordon 2011, pp. 154–63.

FIG. 25
Duccio (documented 1278; died 1319)
The Calling of the Apostles Peter and Andrew, about 1308–11
Tempera on poplar, 43.3 × 46.2 cm
National Gallery of Art, Washington, Samuel H. Kress Collection (1939.1.141)
Selected literature:
Boskovits 2016, pp. 257–93.

FIG. 27
Duccio (documented 1278; died 1319)
Christ and the Woman of Samaria, about 1308–11
Tempera on poplar, 43.5 × 46 cm
Museo Nacional Thyssen-Bornemisza,
Madrid (133 [1971.7])
Selected literature:
Boskovits and Padovani 1990, pp. 68–77.

FIG. 28
Duccio (documented 1278; died 1319)
The Healing of the Man born Blind, about 1308–11
Tempera on poplar, 45.1 × 46.7 cm
The National Gallery, London. Bought, 1883
(NG1140)
Selected literature:
Gordon 2011, pp. 164–9.

FIG. 216
Duccio (documented 1278; died 1319)
The Nativity with the Prophets Isaiah and Ezekiel,
about 1308–11
Tempera on poplar, 48 × 86.8 cm
(with engaged frame)
Inscription: ECCE VIRGO CONCIPIET [et] PARIET FILIU[M] [et] VOCABITUR NOMEN EIUS [E]MANUE[L] (on Isaiah's scroll; 'Behold, a Virgin shall conceive and bear a son, and shall call his name Immanuel', Isaiah 7:14); A[nnunti]o vobis [g]audiu[m] [m] agnu[m] (on the angel's scroll; 'Behold, I bring you good tidings of great joy', derived from Luke 2:10); VIDI PORTA[M] I[N] DOMO D[OMI]NI CLAU[SAM] [VIR NON TRANSIBIT PER EAM DOMINUS SOLUS INTRAT ET[?] IT [?] PER EAM] (on Ezekiel's scroll; 'I saw a gate in the house of the Lord which was closed and no man went through it. The Lord only enters and goes through it', derived from Ezekiel 44:2)
National Gallery of Art, Washington,
Andrew W. Mellon Collection (1937.1.8)
Selected literature:
Shapely 1979, vol. 1, pp. 168–72; Boskovits 2016, pp. 294–308.

FIG. 30
Duccio (documented 1278; died 1319)
The Raising of Lazarus, about 1308–11
Tempera on poplar, transferred to cork, 43.5 × 46.4 cm
Kimbell Art Museum, Fort Worth, Texas
(APx 1975.01)
Selected literature:
Wilkins Sullivan 1988, pp. 374–87.

FIG. 24
Duccio (documented 1278; died 1319)
The Temptation of Christ on the Mountain,
about 1308–11
Tempera on poplar, 43.2 × 46 cm
The Frick Collection, New York, Purchase 1927
Selected literature:
Frick 1968, pp. 222–7; Gordon 2009.

FIG. 23
Duccio (documented 1278; died 1319)
The Temptation of Christ on the Temple, about 1308–11
Tempera on poplar, 48 × 50 cm
Museo dell'Opera della Metropolitana, Siena

FIG. 29
Duccio (documented 1278; died 1319)
The Transfiguration, about 1308–11
Tempera on poplar, 48.5 × 51.4 cm (with engaged frame); 44 × 46.2 cm (painted surface)
The National Gallery, London. Presented by
R.H. Wilson, 1891 (NG1330)
Selected literature:
Gordon 2011, pp. 170–3.

FIG. 26
Duccio (documented 1278; died 1319)
The Wedding at Cana, about 1308–11
Tempera on poplar, 43.5 × 46.5 cm
Museo dell'Opera della Metropolitana, Siena

Maestà *selected literature:*
Stubblebine 1979, vol. 1, pp. 31–62; White 1979, pp. 80–134; Seiler 2002, pp. 251–77; Ragioneri in Siena 2003–4, cat. 32, pp. 208–31; Gordon 2011, pp. 174–82.

FIG. 32
Duccio (documented 1278; died 1319)
Triptych with the Crucifixion, Saint Nicholas, Saint Clement and the Redeemer with Angels, 1311–18
Tempera on panel, 61 × 39.4 cm (central panel, with engaged frame); 45.1 × 19.4 cm (left wing, with engaged frame); 45.1 × 20.2 cm (right wing, with engaged frame)
Inscription: S N[I]C/HOLA (left wing);
IC XC (central panel, on the titulus of the Cross, abbreviation of 'Jesus Christ'); S C[...] (right wing)
Museum of Fine Arts, Boston. Grant Walker and Charles Potter Kling Funds (45.880)
Selected literature:
Stubblebine 1979, vol. 1, pp. 11–12, 64, 68–71, 103–4; White 1973a; White 1979, pp. 46–60, *passim*; Kanter 1994, pp. 72–6; Schmidt in Bagnoli et al. 2003, pp. 202–3; Gordon 2011, pp. 197–9.

FIG. 31
Duccio (documented 1278; died 1319)
Triptych with the Virgin and Child, Saint Dominic, Saint Aurea, Patriarchs and Prophets, about 1312–15 (?)
Tempera on panel, central panel: 61.4 × 39.3 cm (with engaged frame), 43 × 34 cm (painted surface); left wing: 45.2 × 19.3 cm (with semi-integral frame), 42.3 × 16 cm (painted surface); right wing: 45.2 × 20.6 cm (with semi-integral frame), 42.5 × 16.5 cm (painted surface)
Inscription: [Da]vid (in the gable); Ecc[e] uir[go] [con]c[i]p[iet] et [pat]ri[et] filium (on the scroll of Isaiah in the gable; 'Behold, a Virgin shall concieve, and bear a son', Isaiah 7:14); In se[m]i[n]e tuo benedicentur omnes ge[n]tes (on Abraham's scroll in the gable; 'In thy seed shall all people be blessed', adapted from Genesis 22:18 or 26:4); Vide[bat] q[uod] [ru]b[us] ardebat [e]t non comburedatur' (on Moses's scroll in the gable; 'he looked, and, behold, the bush burned with fire, and the bush was not consumed', Exodus 3:2); [do]m[us] dei et porta celi (on the scroll of Jacob; '[This is] the house of God and the gate of Heaven', adapted from Genesis 28:17); [d]e mo[nt]e ad[s]cisus est lapis sine m[a]nib[us]' (on Daniel's scroll in the gable; 'the stone was cut out of the mountain without hands', Daniel 2:45); Nou[um] faciet [d?]o[minu]s teram m[u]lier circu[m]dabit [virum]' (on Jeremiah's scroll in the gable; 'For the Lord hath created a new thing in the earth. A woman shall compass [a man]', Jeremiah 31:22); S DOMINIC (left wing); S AU[REA] (right wing)
The National Gallery, London. Bought, 1857 (NG566)
Selected literature:
Stubblebine 1979, vol. 1, pp. 11–12, 63–4, 70, 169; White 1973a; White 1979, pp. 46–60, *passim*; Schmidt in Bagnoli et al. 2003, pp. 198–9; Gordon 2011, pp. 188–201.

FIG. 184
English or French artist (?)
Richard II presented by Saints John the Baptist, Edward the Confessor and Edmund; The Virgin and Child with Angels ('The Wilton Diptych'), about 1396–9
Tempera on oak, 53 × 37 cm (each wing, with integral frame)
The National Gallery, London. Bought with a special grant and contributions from Samuel Courtauld, Viscount Rothermere, C.T. Stoop and the Art Fund, 1929 (NG4451)
Selected literature:
Dunkerton et al. 1991, pp. 236–9; Gordon 1994; Gordon, Monnas and Elam 1997; Gordon 2015.
[London only]

FIG. 66
Francesco di Vannuccio (documented 1356–89)
Diptych with the Annunciation and the Assumption, about 1380
Tempera on panel, each wing 36 × 15.2 cm (with engaged frame); 30.5 × 11.7 cm (painted surface)
Inscription: [av?]e ma[ria] (in the centre of the *Annunciation*; 'Hail Mary')
The Mistress and Fellows, Girton College, Cambridge (188[a, b])
Selected literature:
Pope-Hennessy 1948; London 1983, cat. 14, p. 30; Schmidt 2005a, pp. 150–1; Fattorini in Siena 2010, cat. B.5, pp. 156–7.
[London only]

FIG. 205
Goodhart Ducciesque Master (active about 1310–30)
The Virgin and Child with the Annunciation and the Nativity, about 1310–15

Tempera on panel, 30.8 × 21 cm (with engaged frame); 26 × 16.5 cm (painted surface)
The Metropolitan Museum of Art, New York. Marquand Fund, 1920 (20.160)
Selected literature:
Brandi 1951, p. 152; Stubblebine 1979, vol. 1, p. 107; Zeri and Gardner 1986, pp. 43–4; Labriola in Boskovits 2009, pp. 106, 108.
[New York only]

FIG. 168
Probably by **Gregorio di Cecco di Luca** (documented 1389–died possibly 1428)
The Marriage of the Virgin, about 1423
Tempera on panel, 41 × 33.2 cm
The National Gallery, London. Bought, 1890 (NG1317)
Selected literature:
Bellosi in Siena 1982, pp. 294, 348; Davies 1986, pp. 470–1; Volbach 1987, vol. 2, pp. 55–6; Gordon 2003, pp. 118–21; De Marchi in Siena 2010, cat. A46b, pp. 134–7.
[London only]

FIG. 210
Ambrogio Lorenzetti (documented 1319; died 1348/9)
A Group of Four Poor Clares, about 1325
Fresco with areas of secco, 70.4 × 63.4 cm
The National Gallery, London. Bought, 1878 (NG1147)
Selected literature:
Davies 1986, pp. 298–9; Burke 2002, pp. 462–3; Frugoni 2002, pp. 196–7; Gordon 2011, pp. 284–6; Interguglielmi in Siena 2017–18, cat. 7b, pp. 132, 135.
[London only]

FIG. 84
Ambrogio Lorenzetti (documented 1319; died 1348/9)
Madonna del Latte, about 1325
Tempera on panel, 96 × 49.1 cm
Inscription: AVE MARIA GRATIA PLENA DOMINUS TECUM BENE[DICTA TU IN MULIERIBUS] (in the halo of the Virgin, 'Hail Mary, full of grace, the Lord is with thee, blessed [art thou among women]')
Arcidiocesi di Siena - Colle di Val d'Elsa - Montalcino, Museo Diocesano, Siena
Selected literature:
Rowley 1958, vol. 1, pp. 35–40; Frugoni 1988, pp. 38–9; Frugoni 2002, pp. 134–6; Buoncristiani and Caciorgna 2014; Visa Guerrero in Siena 2017–18, cat. 9, pp. 156–61.

FIG. 89
Ambrogio Lorenzetti (documented 1319; died 1348/9)
Stories from the Life of Saint Nicholas, about 1332–4
Tempera on panel, 96.2 × 52.3 and 95.8 × 52.3 cm (with partially original frames)
Gallerie degli Uffizi, Florence (inv. 1890 nn. 8348, 8349)
Selected literature:
Volpe 1951, pp. 40–1, 44, 47; Rowley 1958, vol. 1, pp. 70–3; Frugoni 2002, pp. 163–9; Amato in Siena 2017–18, cat. 13a–d, pp. 182–90; Robson 2022, pp. 133–57; Seidel and Calamai 2022, pp. 287–321.

FIG. 88
Ambrogio Lorenzetti (documented 1319; died 1348/9)
The Angel Gabriel and the Annunciate Virgin, about 1334–6
Sinopia on plaster, 241 × 173.4 and 242.4 × 172.8 cm
Arcidiocesi di Siena - Colle di Val d'Elsa - Montalcino, Eremo di San Galgano a Montesiepi, Chiusdino
Selected literature:
Borsook 1969, pp. 28–9; Norman 1993, pp. 294, 296; Dunlop 2000; Frugoni 2002, pp. 149–51; Argenziano 2014; Bartalini 2015; Seidel and Calamai in Siena 2017–18, cat. 15, pp. 198–227.

FIG. 87
Ambrogio Lorenzetti (documented 1319; died 1348/9)
The Annunciation, 1344
Tempera on panel, 130 × 152 cm (with original frame)
Inscription: 'ECCE A[N]CILLA D[OMI]NI' (spoken by the Virgin, 'Behold the handmaid of the Lord', Luke 1:38); 'AVE MARIA GRATIA PLENA DOMINU[S] TE[CUM]' (in the Virgin's halo, 'Hail Mary full of Grace, the Lord is with you', derived from Luke 1:28); 'NON EST I[M]POSSIBLE APVD DEU[M] O[MN]E V[ER]BUM' (spoken by the Angel Gabriel, 'For with God nothing shall be impossible', Luke 1:37); 'XVII DI DICE[M]BRE M CCC XLIIII FECE AMBRVOGIO LORE[N]CI QVESTA / TAVOLA ERA CAMARLE[N]GO DO[N] FRA[N]CESCO MONACO DI SA[N] GALGAMO / E ASSECVTORI BINDO PETVCCI GIOVAN[N]I DI MEO BALDINOTTI MINO DI A[N]DREOCCIO SCRITTORE A[N]GOLO LOCTI' (in the predella, '[On the] '27 day of December 1344, Ambrogio Lorenzetti made this painting for the Camerlengo (chamberlain or treasurer) Don Francesco, monk of San Galgano, and the executors Bino Petrucci, Giovanni di Meio Baldinotti, Mino d'Andreoco and the scribe Angolo Locti')
Pinacoteca nazionale di Siena, musei nazionali di Siena (88)
Selected literature:
Rowley 1958, vol. 1, pp. 8–17; Muller 1977; Torriti 1980, pp. 124–5; Caffio in Siena 2017–18, cat. 29, pp. 336–51.

FIG. 86
Ambrogio Lorenzetti (documented 1319; died 1348/9)
The Crucifixion, about 1345
Tempera on panel, 71.5 × 35.5 cm (with engaged frame); 61 × 29 cm (painted surface)
Inscription: IC XC (on the titulus of the Cross, abbreviation of 'Jesus Christ')
Harvard Art Museums/Fogg Museum, Gift of Paul J. Sachs in honor of Edward W. Forbes's thirtieth year as Director of the Fogg Museum (1939.113)
Selected literature:
Rowley 1958, vol. 1, pp. 75–7; Frinta 1971; Fahy 1978, pp. 384–5; Mortimer 1986, no. 164, p. 146; Boskovits 1988, pp. 91–3; Schmidt 2005a, p. 42.

FIG. 56
Pietro Lorenzetti (documented possibly 1306; died probably 1348)
Christ between Saints Paul and Peter, about 1315–20
Tempera on panel, 32.2 × 70.4 cm
Ferens Art Gallery: Hull Museums (2013.125)
Selected literature:
Christie's 2012, lot 28.
[London only]

FIG. 109
Pietro Lorenzetti (documented possibly 1306; died probably 1348)
Cut-out Crucifix, about 1315–20
Tempera on panel, 145 × 90 cm
Inscription: IHESVS NACARENVS REX IVDEORVM (on the titulus of the Cross; 'Jesus of Nazareth, King of the Jews')
Museo Diocesano, Cortona
Selected literature:
Volpe 1989, no. 117, pp. 149–50; Monciatti 2002, pp. 58, 60; Becchis 2012, pp. 32–5; Amato in Siena 2017–18, cat. 4, pp. 114–19.

FIG. 60
Pietro Lorenzetti (documented possibly 1306; died probably 1348)
Pieve Polyptych, about 1320
Tempera on panel, 312 × 295 × 9 cm
Inscription: S REPARATA S CATHERINA S [...] S AGATHA (upper tier, identifying the saints); S IOH[ANN]ES S PAVLVS S VINCENTIVS S LVCAS EVA[NGELISTA] S IACOBVS MAIO[R] S IACOBVS I[N] T[ER]CIS[US] S MARCELLIN[VS] S AVGVSTIN[V]S (second tier, identifying the saints); S DONATVS S IOH[ANNE]S EVANGLISTA PETRVS LAVRE[N] TII ME PI[N]XIT DEXTRA SENESIS S IOH[ANNE] S BAPTISTA S MATHEVS (main tier, identifying the saints; 'Pietro Lorenzetti of Siena painted this with his right hand'); Petrus me fecit (on Saint Reparata's sword, 'Pietro made me')
Chiesa di Santa Maria della Pieve, Arezzo
Selected literature:
Maetzke in Arezzo 1979–80, cat. 5, pp. 26–36; Guerrini 1988, pp. 3–29; Volpe 1989, pp. 37–8, no. 97, pp. 121–5; Van Os 1984, vol. 1, pp. 69–74; Freni 2000a; Monciatti in Frugoni 2002, pp. 19–24, 78; Becchis 2012, pp. 40–6.

TWO FRESCO FRAGMENTS FROM THE CHAPTER HOUSE OF SAN FRANCESCO, SIENA:

FIG. 58
Pietro Lorenzetti (documented possibly 1306; died probably 1348)
A Crowned Female Figure (Saint Elizabeth of Hungary?), about 1325
Fresco with areas of secco, 38 × 33 cm
The National Gallery, London. Layard Bequest, 1916 (NG3071)
[London only]

FIG. 59
Pietro Lorenzetti (documented possibly 1306; died probably 1348)
The Annunciate Virgin, about 1325
Fresco with areas of secco, 39 × 30 cm
The National Gallery, London. Layard Bequest, 1916 (NG3072)
[London only]

Selected literature:
Davies 1986, pp. 301–2; Volpe 1989, nos 118–19, pp. 150–1; Gordon 2011, pp. 299–304; Becchis 2012, pp. 102, 104; Interguglielmi in Siena 2017–18, cat. 7c, pp. 135, 140–1.

FIG. 40
Pietro Lorenzetti (documented possibly 1306; died probably 1348)
The Birth of the Virgin, 1335–42
Tempera on panel, 182 × 187 cm
Inscription: PETRVS LAVRENTII DE SENIS ME PINXIT A[NNO] M CCC XL II (lower centre; 'Pietro Lorenzetti of Siena painted me in the year 1342')
Museo dell'Opera della Metropolitana, Siena
Selected literature:
Van Os 1984, vol. 1, pp. 79–83; Volpe 1989, pp. 50–4, no. 123, pp. 152–4; Norman 1999b, pp. 67–85, *passim*; Monciatti 2002, pp. 91–5; De Marchi in Siena 2010, cat. B.1, pp. 148–9; Becchis 2012, pp. 127–9.
[London only]

FIG. 42
Pietro Lorenzetti (documented possibly 1306; died probably 1348)
Saint Sabinus before the Roman Governor of Tuscany, 1335–42
Tempera on poplar, 37.7 × 33.2 cm (with engaged frame)
The National Gallery, London. Presented by Charles Fairfax Murray, 1882 (NG1113)
Selected literature:
Preiser 1973, pp. 299–300; Davies 1986, pp. 300–1; Volpe 1989, p. 50, no. 124, pp. 155–6; Dunkerton et al. 1991, no. 6, pp. 226–7; Gordon 2011, pp. 288–98; Becchis 2012, pp. 120, 122.

FIG. 106
Pietro Lorenzetti (documented possibly 1306; died probably 1348)
Diptych with the Virgin and Child and the Man of Sorrows, about 1340–5
Tempera on panel, 35 × 25.9 and 35.1 × 25.9 cm (with engaged frames)
Inscription: PETRVS LAVRE[N]TII DE SENI[S] ME PI[N]XI[T] (below the *Man of Sorrows*; 'Pietro Lorenzetti of Siena painted me')
Lindenau-Museum Altenburg, Germany (Inv. 47, 48)
Selected literature:
Volpe 1989, nos 172–3, pp. 192–4; Penndorf 1998, p. 9 [*Man of Sorrows*]; Monciatti 2002, pp. 82–3; Labriola in Siena 2008, cat. 4, pp. 44–9; Paris 2009, pp. 52–5; Eclercy in Hamburg 2011–12, cat. 5, pp. 132–3.

TWO SURVIVING PANELS FROM A PORTABLE POLYPTYCH:

FIG. 37
Pietro Lorenzetti (documented possibly 1306; died probably 1348)
Christ before Pilate, 1340s
Tempera on panel, 37.8 × 27.4 cm
Vatican Museums, Vatican City (inv. 40168)
Selected literature:
Preiser 1973, pp. 300–1; Mancinelli in New York, Chicago and San Francisco 1983–4, cat. 70, pp. 137–8; Volbach 1987, no. 70, p. 55; Volpe 1989, no. 133, p. 165; Becchis 2012, pp. 120–1, 125.

FIG. 38
Pietro Lorenzetti (documented possibly 1306; died probably 1348)
The Crucifixion, 1340s
Tempera on panel, 41.9 × 31.8 cm (with engaged frame); 35.9 × 25.7 cm (painted surface)
Inscription: I N R I (on the titulus of the Cross, abbreviation of 'Iesus Nazarenus, Rex Iudaeorum', or 'Jesus of Nazareth, King of the Jews')
The Metropolitan Museum of Art, New York. Purchase, Lila Acheson Wallace Gift and Gwynne Andrews Fund, 2002 (2002.436)
Selected literature:
Christiansen 2003, pp. 8–14; Schmidt 2005a, pp. 288–9; Calley Galitz 2016, no. 99, pp. 87, 134.

FIG. 85
Pietro Lorenzetti (documented possibly 1306; died probably 1348)
The Virgin and Child enthroned, about 1345
Tempera on panel, 34.8 × 30.8 cm (with remains of original framing elements)
Staatliche Museen zu Berlin, Gemäldegalerie (Kat. Nr. 1384)
Selected literature:
Fahy 1978, pp. 385–6; Boskovits 1988, no. 35, pp. 91–3; Volpe 1989, no. 134, p. 165; Becchis 2012, pp. 113, 116–17.

FIG. 70
Simone Martini (about 1284–1344)
Saint John the Evangelist, 1320
Tempera on panel, 41.7 × 30.3 cm (with engaged frame)
Inscription: Anno d[omi]ni MCCCXX (lower centre; 'The year of Our Lord 1320')
The Henry Barber Trust, the Barber Institute of Fine Arts, University of Birmingham (38.12)
Selected literature:
Martindale 1988, pp. 32, 42, no. 8, pp. 184–5; Leone de Castris 1989, no. 27, pp. 122–3; Hemsoll 1998; Pierini 2000, pp. 120–1; Leone de Castris 2003, p. 214, no. 15, p. 353.

FIG. 71
Simone Martini (about 1284–1344)
The Virgin and Child over Saints Helen, Paul, Dominic, Stephen (?) and a Dominican Nun, about 1325
Tempera on panel, 33.4 × 25.4 cm (with engaged frame); 28.4 × 20.1 cm (painted surface)
Isabella Stewart Gardner Museum, Boston (P30w8)
Selected literature:
Martindale 1988, no. 10, p. 186; Pierini 2000, pp. 168–70; Leone de Castris 2003, no. 31, p. 361; Israëls in Boston 2022–3, cat. 5, pp. 212–23.
[New York only]

PALAZZO PUBBLICO ALTARPIECE PANELS:

FIG. 78
Simone Martini (about 1284–1344)
Saint Andrew, about 1326–7
Tempera on panel, 57.2 × 37.8 cm (with original frame)
The Metropolitan Museum of Art, New York. Gift of George Blumenthal, 1941 (41.100.23)

FIG. 76
Simone Martini (about 1284–1344)
Saint Peter, about 1326–7
Tempera on panel, 58 × 38.5 cm (with original frame)
Colección Carmen Thyssen (CTB.1997.20)

FIG. 77
Simone Martini (about 1284–1344)
The Virgin and Child, about 1326–7
Tempera on panel, 58.7 × 39.4 cm (with original frame); 57.2 × 38.4 cm (painted surface)
The Metropolitan Museum of Art, New York. Robert Lehman Collection, 1975 (1975.1.12)

FIG. 75
Simone Martini (about 1284–1344)
Saint Ansanus, about 1326–30
Tempera on panel, 57.5 × 38.1 cm (with original frame); 57.2 × 36.8 cm (painted surface)
The Metropolitan Museum of Art, New York. Robert Lehman Collection, 1975 (1975.1.13)

FIG. 79
Simone Martini (about 1284–1344)
Saint Luke, about 1326–30
Tempera on panel, 67.5 × 48.3 cm (with engaged frame)
Inscription: S LUC[AS] S EV[ANGE]LSTA (upper centre)
J. Paul Getty Museum, Los Angeles (82.PB.72)

Selected literature:
Pope-Hennessy and Kanter 1987, nos 8–9 [*Virgin and Child* and *Saint Ansanus*], pp. 18–23; Martindale 1988, no. 17(i–v), pp. 194–5; Leone de Castris 1989, no. 21, pp. 93–6, *passim*; Christiansen 1994, pp. 148–60; Bagnoli 1999, pp. 124–5, 136–42, 166; Pierini 2000, pp. 122–7; Leone de Castris 2003, pp. 242–9, no. 26a–e, p. 368.

ORSINI POLYPTYCH:

FIG. 81 (LEFT)
Simone Martini (about 1284–1344)
The Angel Gabriel, about 1326–34
Tempera on poplar, 29.7 × 20.5 cm (with engaged frame); 23 × 14 cm (painted surface)
Collection KMSKA - Flemish Community (public domain) (257)

FIG. 81 (RIGHT)
Simone Martini (about 1284–1344)
The Annunciate Virgin, about 1326–34
Tempera on poplar, 29.7 × 20.5 cm (with engaged frame); 24 × 15 cm (painted surface)
Collection KMSKA - Flemish Community (public domain) (258)

FIG. 197
Simone Martini (about 1284–1344)
The Crucifixion, about 1326–34
Tempera on poplar, 29.6 × 20.5 (with engaged frame); 23 × 14 cm (painted surface)
Inscription: PINXIT (on the frame; 'painted')
Collection KMSKA - Flemish Community (public domain) (259)

FIG. 192
Simone Martini (about 1284–1344)
The Deposition, about 1326–34
Tempera on poplar, 29.5 × 20.6 (with engaged frame); 24 × 15 cm (painted surface)
Inscription: SYMON (on the frame)
Collection KMSKA - Flemish Community (public domain) (260)

FIG. 194
Simone Martini (about 1284–1344)
The Entombment, about 1326–34
Tempera on poplar, 23.7 × 16.7 cm
Staatliche Museen zu Berlin, Gemäldegalerie (Kat. Nr. 1070A)

FIG. 189
Simone Martini (about 1284–1344)
The Way to Calvary, about 1326–34
Tempera on poplar, 30 × 20.5 cm (with engaged frame); 24.5 × 15.5 cm (painted surface)
Musée du Louvre, Département des Peintures, Paris (INV 670 bis; INV 828; LP 638)

Selected literature:
Van Os and Rinkleff-Reinders 1972; Brink 1976; Boskovits 1988, no. 64, pp. 155–9; Martindale 1988, pp. 3, 7, 51–3, 58, 67, no. 2, pp. 171–3; Leone de Castris 1989, no. 26, pp. 113–21, *passim*; Pierini 2000, pp. 212–27; Leone de Castris 2003, pp. 300–10, no. 33, pp. 362–3; Schmidt 2005a, pp. 255–60.

———

FIG. 214
Simone Martini (about 1284–1344)
Christ on the Cross, about 1340
Tempera on panel, 25 × 13.6 cm
Inscription: INRI (on the titulus of the Cross, abbreviation of 'Iesus Nazarenus, Rex Iudaeorum', or 'Jesus of Nazareth, King of the Jews')
Harvard Art Museums/Fogg Museum, Hervey E. Wetzel Bequest Fund (1919.51)
Selected literature:
Paccagnini 1955, pp. 118, 121; Fahy 1978, pp. 382–3; Mortimer 1986, no. 159, p. 141; Leone de Castris 1989, p. 18, no. 30, pp. 128–9; Leone de Castris 2003, no. 35, p. 364.

FIG. 74
Simone Martini (about 1284–1344)
Christ discovered in the Temple, 1342
Tempera on panel, 49.5 × 35.1 cm (with engaged frame)
Inscription: SYMON DE SENIS ME PINXIT SVB A[NNO] D[OMINI] M CC[C] XL II (along the lower edge; 'Simone of Siena painted me in the year of Our Lord 1342')
National Museums Liverpool, Walker Art Gallery. Presented by the Liverpool Royal Institution 1948 (2787)
Selected literature:
Martindale 1988, pp. 7–8, 22, 42, 46, 49, no. 14, pp. 190–1; Gardner 1990a; Pierini 2000, pp. 204–6; Leone de Castris 1989, no. 32, pp. 132–3; Leone de Castris 2003, no. 37, pp. 364–5; Cameron 2022.

FIG. 213
Circle of Simone Martini
The Mystic Marriage of Saint Catherine, about 1340
Tempera on panel, 138.7 × 111.1 cm (with modern engaged frame); 134.8 × 107.1 cm (painted surface)
Inscription: S[AN]C[T]A KATORINA (upper left); Arico di Neri Arighetti fece fare questa tavola (lower centre; 'Arico di Neri Arighetti had this panel made'); S[AN]C[T]A MARGARITA (lower left)
Museum of Fine Arts, Boston. Sarah Wyman Whitman Fund (15.1145)
Selected literature:
Edgell 1924, Ventroni 1972, pp. 48–9, no. 9, pp. 60–1; Kanter 1994, pp. 91–5; Jansen 2018, pp. 188–94.

FIG. 206
Master of Città di Castello (active about 1290–1320)
The Crucifixion, about 1315–20
Tempera on panel, 59.7 × 38 cm
Inscription: IC XC (on the titulus of the Cross, abbreviation of 'Jesus Christ')
Manchester City Galleries (1984.53)
Selected literature:
White 1979, pp. 154–5; Freuler 2001, pp. 36, 45; Bagnoli in Bagnoli et al. 2003, pp. 314–21, *passim*; Marquette in Lens 2015, cat. 47, pp. 168–9.
[London only]

FIG. 15
Master of the Clarisse (possibly Rinaldo da Siena [documented 1274–81])
The Virgin and Child with the Annunciation, Crucifixion and Scenes from the Last Judgement, about 1270–80
Tempera on panel (walnut?), 31.4 × 19.5 cm (with integral frame)
Inscription: YU XC (on the titulus of the Cross)
The National Gallery, London. Acquired with the assistance of the Art Fund (with a contribution from the Wolfson Foundation), 1998 (NG6571)
Selected literature:
Christie's 1998b, lot 49; Bellosi 2000, pp. 58, 60; Labriola in Labriola, De Benedictis and Freuler 2002, pp. 23, 61, n. 50; Gordon 2011, pp. 348–55; Boskovits 2021, no. 187, pp. 549–50.
[London only]

FIG. 176
Bohemian painter, here attributed to the **Master of the Vyšší Brod Altarpiece** (active about 1345–50?)
The Virgin and Child enthroned, about 1346 (?)
Oil (?) on panel, 25.8 × 20.2 cm
The Metropolitan Museum of Art, New York. Purchase, George T. Delacorte Jr. Gift, by exchange; Michel David-Weill Gift; The Lesley and Emma Sheafer Collection, Bequest of Emma A. Sheafer and Gift of Mr and Mrs Malcom P. Ripley, by exchange; The Rendl Fund; Lila Acheson Wallace Gift; and funds from various donors, by exchange, 2020 (2020.209)
Selected literature:
Klípa 2019; Christiansen 2021a; Christiansen 2021b; Christiansen 2022.
[New York only]

FIG. 69
Lippo Memmi (documented 1317–50)
Saint Paul, about 1330
Tempera on panel, 95.9 × 48.3 cm (with partially modern engaged frame); 89.2 × 41.9 cm (painted surface)
Inscription: AD A[d] A[d] AD ROMANOS pavlvs (on the letters held by the saint; 'To the Romans. Paul')
The Metropolitan Museum of Art, New York. Gift of Coudert Brothers, 1888 (88.3.99)
Selected literature:
Carli 1958, vol. 1, pp. 26–7; Coor-Achenbach 1961, pp. 129–31; Mallory 1974, pp. 187–202; Caleca 1976, pp. 53–5; Zeri and Gardner 1986, pp. 50–2; Boskovits 2016, under no. 23, pp. 203–14, *passim*.

FIG. 72
Lippo Memmi (documented 1317–50)
The Virgin and Child with Saints and Angels, about 1345
Tempera on panel, 66.7 × 33 cm (with partially modern engaged frame); 50.2 × 25.7 cm (painted surface); 3.8 × 25.4 cm (painted surface of predella)
Inscription: AVE (on the neck of the Virgin's dress; 'Hail'); GRA[TIA] (on the Virgin's cuff, 'Grace')
The Metropolitan Museum of Art, New York. Maitland F. Griggs Collection, Bequest of Maitland F. Griggs, 1943 (43.98.6)

Selected literature:
Salinger 1944; Zeri and Gardner 1986, pp. 52–3; Christiansen 1982, p. 11; Christiansen 2012.
[New York only]

FIG. 99
Lippo Vanni (documented 1344–75)
Saint Peter as Pope, about 1365
Tempera on panel, 74.1 × 32.9 cm (with modern engaged frame); 64.7 × 27.6 cm (painted surface)
Inscription: AVTORITAS DISCRETIO (on the keys, 'Authority' and 'Discernment)
The Courtauld, London (Samuel Courtauld Trust) (P.1966.GP.469)
Selected literature:
London 1961, cat. 6, n.p.; Vertova 1970, *passim*; Courtauld 1979, no. 2, p. 9; Dale 1984, no. 37, p. 202; Hanan 2001.
[London only]

FIG. 167
Niccolò di Buonaccorso (documented 1372; died 1388)
The Marriage of the Virgin, about 1380
Tempera on poplar, 50.9 × 33 cm (with engaged frame); 43 × 26.5 cm (painted surface)
Inscription: NICHOLAVS BONACHVRSI DE SENIS ME P[I]NX[I]T (lower centre, 'Niccolo di Buonacorso of Siena painted me')
The National Gallery, London. Bought, 1881 (NG1109)
Selected literature:
Davies 1986, pp. 384–5; San Diego 1997–8, pp. 47–9, 51–4, 57, 61; Schmidt 2002b, pp. 403–5, *passim*; Schmidt 2005a, p. 293; Gordon 2011, pp. 380–93.
[London only]

Segna di Buonaventura (documented 1298; died 1326/31)
Diptych with the Virgin and Child and the Crucifixion, about 1315
Tempera on panel, 38.4 × 27 cm (left wing, with engaged frame); 38.1 × 27 cm (right wing, with engaged frame)
The Metropolitan Museum of Art, New York. Robert Lehman Collection, 1975 (1975.1.1, 1975.1.2)
Selected literature:
Sterling in Paris 1957, cats 16–17, pp. 12–13; Stubblebine 1979, vol. 1, p. 96; Cole 1980, pp. 61–3; Pope-Hennessy and Kanter 1987, nos 1, 2, pp. 2–5.
[New York only, unillustrated]

2. SCULPTURE

FIG. 92
Gano di Fazio (documented 1302; died before 1318)
Old Saint, Saint John the Baptist, Saint Peter and *Young Saint with a Book*, about 1315–18
Marble with traces of polychromy, heights 73.7, 73.3, 78.6 and 75.1 cm
Museo di San Pietro all'Orto, from the Cattedrale di San Cerbone in Massa Marittima (sala II inv. 8–11)
Selected literature:
Carli 1946, pp. 46–54, *passim*; Bellosi 1984; Bartalini in Bagnoli et al. 2003, pp. 518–23; Colucci in Bartalini 2011a, pp. 43, 46, no. 17, pp. 56–7.

FIG. 96
Giovanni di Agostino (about 1310–1370)
The Virgin and Child with Saints Catherine and John the Baptist, about 1340–50
Marble with traces of polychromy and gilding, 70.5 × 52.5 × 5.9 cm
The Cleveland Museum of Art, In memory of Henry G. Dalton by his nephews, George S. Kendrick and Harry D. Kendrick (1942.1162)
Selected literature:
Kreytenberg 1993, pp. 12–15; Moskovitz in Gillerman 2001, no. 250, pp. 342–4; Brilliant in Cleveland 2007, cat. 100, pp. 266–7; Bartalini in Bartalini 2011a, p. 337, no. 33, pp. 350–1, 363.

FIG. 129
Goro di Gregorio (documented 1311–24)
Enthroned Virgin, first half of the fourteenth century
Terracotta, 44.8 × 25.4 × 24.1 cm
The Metropolitan Museum of Art, New York. The Cloisters Collection and Rogers Fund, 1998 (1998.214)
Selected literature:
Castelnuovo-Tedesco and Wixom in New York 1999, cat. 174, pp. 148–9; Barnet and Wu 2012, p. 104; Soultanian in Castelnuovo-Tedesco and Soultanian 2010, no. 40, pp. 180–5.

FIG. 108
Sienese artist (Guccio di Mannaia [documented 1295–1318]?)
The Crucifixion, about 1310–20
Marble and coloured wax, 44.8 × 28 × 3.2 cm
Arcidiocesi di Siena - Colle di Val d'Elsa - Montalcino, Siena, Palazzo Arcivescovile (from Chiesa di San Pellegrino alla Sapienza)
Selected literature:
Hueck 1969; Cioni 1979, pp. 52–4; Hueck in Siena 1982, cat. 28, pp. 96–8; Cioni 1998, pp. 80–3, 87; Cioni in Siena 2003–4, cat. 84, pp. 482–5.

FIG. 101
Lando di Pietro (about 1280–1340)
Ex-voto, 1338
Ink on parchment, 10.3 × 9.9 and 2.7 × 9.9 cm
Basilica di San Bernardino all'Osservanza, Siena. Museo Castelli
Selected literature:
Bertagna 1949; Bagnoli in Siena 1987, under cat. 12, pp. 65–8; Cooper 2006; Bartalini in Bartalini 2011a, under no. 1, pp. 304, 310.
[Smaller fragment unillustrated]

FIG. 130
Lando di Pietro (about 1280–1340)
Head of Christ (fragment of crucifix), 1338
Tempera on walnut, 31 × 22 × 18 cm
Basilica di San Bernardino all'Osservanza, Siena. Museo Castelli
Selected literature:
Bertagna 1949; Carli 1980, pp. 24–5; Bagnoli in Siena 1987, cat. 12, pp. 65–8; Bartalini in Bartalini 2011a, pp. 304–8, no. 1, pp. 310–11.

FRAGMENTS FROM THE TOMB OF GASTONE DELLA TORRE:

FIG. 115
Tino di Camaino (about 1280–about 1337)
Angel presenting a Bishop, 1318–21
Marble, 81.5 × 32 × 14 cm
Liebieghaus Skulpturensammlung, Frankfurt am Main (955)
[London only]

FIG. 116
Tino di Camaino (about 1280–about 1337)
Caryatid, 1318–21
Marble, 87 × 42 × 15 cm
Liebieghaus Skulpturensammlung, Frankfurt am Main (881)
[London only]

FIG. 117
Tino di Camaino (about 1280–about 1337)
Caryatid, 1318–21
Marble, height 80 cm
Museo Nazionale del Bargello, Florence (495)
[London only]

FIG. 114
Tino di Camaino (about 1280–about 1337)
The Virgin and Child, 1318–21
Marble, 78 × 39 cm
Later inscription: SEDES SAPIENTIAE ('Throne of Wisdom')
Museo Nazionale del Bargello, Florence (434)
[London only]

Selected literature:
Valentiner 1935, pp. 59–74, *passim*; Kreytenberg 1986, pp. 29–33, *passim*; Baldelli 2007, pp. 170–89, *passim*, no. 17, pp. 405–6; Bardelloni in Bartalini 2011a, nos 31–5, pp. 144–5.

———

TWO ANGELS FROM A TOMB MONUMENT:

FIG. 95
Tino di Camaino (about 1280–about 1337)
Angel holding a Curtain, 1319–21
Marble, 63 × 32 × 12 cm
Victoria and Albert Museum (7567–1861)
[London only]

Angel holding a Curtain, 1319–21
Marble, 64 × 43 × 12.5 cm
Victoria and Albert Museum (7566–1861)
[London only]

Selected literature:
Pope-Hennessy 1964, vol. 1, nos 29–30, pp. 32–4; Baldelli 2007, pp. 175–85, 207–9, *passim*, no. 19, p. 407; Bardelloni in Bartalini 2011a, no. 38, p. 145.

FIG. 105
Tino di Camaino (about 1280–about 1337)
Man of Sorrows, about 1329–32
Marble, 25.5 × 20 × 4 cm
Private collection
Selected literature:
Seidel 1989; Kreytenberg in New York 2002–3, pp. 14–17; Baldelli 2007, pp. 385, 388; Aceto 2011, no. 18, p. 202.

Tino di Camaino (about 1280–about 1337)
Saint John the Baptist, about 1330
Marble, 50 × 39.2 cm
Inscription: ECCE AGNUS DEI (on the scroll, 'Behold the Lamb of God')
Daniel Katz Gallery, London
Selected literature:
Bartalini 2019
[Unillustrated]

FIG. 68
Tino di Camaino (about 1280–about 1337)
The Virgin and Child with Queen Sancia, Saints and Angels, 1332–3
Marble, 51.4 × 37.8 × 8.5 cm
National Gallery of Art, Washington, Samuel H. Kress Collection (1960.5.1)
Selected literature:
Middeldorf 1976, pp. 5–6; Kreytenberg 2001, pp. 266–8; Baldelli 2007, pp. 385, 408, no. 56, pp. 424–5; Aceto 2011, pp. 187, 190, 204–5, no. 27, p. 207.

3. GOLDSMITHS' WORK

FIG. 122
English goldsmith
Triptych with Scenes from the Life of Christ, about 1325–50
Gilded silver with translucent enamel, 6.6 × 11.3 × 0.6 cm
Victoria and Albert Museum. Salting Bequest. (M.545–1910)
Selected literature:
Chamot 1930, no. 29, pp. 43–4; Gauthier 1972, no. 211, pp. 262–3, 405; Campbell 1983, no. 32, p. 41; Campbell in London 1987–8, cat. 583, pp. 459–60; Campbell 1987, pp. 1, 3.
[London only]

FIG. 127
Master of the San Galgano Crosier
Crosier, about 1315–20
Gilded copper with enamel, 193 × 14 cm
Museo dell'Opera della Metropolitana, Siena
Selected literature:
Leone de Castris 1980a, pp. 28–9; Damiani in Siena 1982, cat. 71, pp. 205–8; Damiani in Avignon 1983, cat. 48, pp. 157–9; Cioni 1998, pp. 132–462, *passim*; Cioni in Bagnoli et al. 2003, pp. 484–7.

RELIQUARY TABERNACLE:

FIG. 136
Sienese artist (?)
Frame for a portable reliquary icon, 1347
Gilded wood, modelled gesso, gilded glass, glass cabochons and relics, 66.7 × 51.3 × 25.3 cm
Inscription: HOC OPUS FACTUM FUIT SUB ANNO DOMINI [M] CCC XLVII TEMPORE DOMINI MINICINI (around the lower edge of the upper frame; 'This work was made in the year of the Lord [1]347 in the time of the Lord Minicini'); LVCAS ME FECIT (lower centre; 'Lucas made me')
The Cleveland Museum of Art, Gift of Ruth Blumka in memory of Leopold Blumka (1978.26)
Selected literature:
Gordon 1981, pp. 148–53; Preising 1995–7, pp. 19–24, *passim*, 58; Brilliant in Cleveland 2007, cat. 99, pp. 264–5, Cleveland, Baltimore and London 2010–11, cat. 117, pp. 202–3; Brilliant 2014, *passim*; Williamson 2020, pp. 32–41, *passim*, 48, 91–2, 118, 131, 140, 173.

FIG. 137
Sienese artist (?)
The Virgin and Child with Saints and the Annunciation, 1347
Gilded glass, 25.1 × 10.5 cm
The Syndics of the Fitzwilliam Museum, University of Cambridge (M.56 & A-1904)
Selected literature:
Gordon 1981, pp. 148–53; Brilliant in Cleveland 2007, pp. 264–5, under no. 99; Cleveland, Baltimore and London 2010–11, under cat. 117, pp. 202–3; Brilliant 2014, *passim*.

FIG. 123
Sienese artist
Morse with Saint Francis receiving the Stigmata, mid-fourteenth century
Gilded copper, silver, translucent enamel, parchment and glass gems, 12.9 × 12.9 × 4 cm; rock-crystal centre: 6.9 × 1 cm
The Metropolitan Museum of Art, New York. Gift of J. Pierpont Morgan, 1917 (17.190.767)
Selected literature:
Leone de Castris 1995, p. 177; Cioni 1998, p. 602.

FIG. 133
Sienese goldsmith (upper part)
Container for an Agnus Dei, about 1320–30 (lower face a fifteenth-century replacement)
Silver with translucent and champlevé enamel, 4.2 × 4.2 cm
Inscription: AGNE DEI MEISNENEMI QUI CRIMINA TOLLIS (around the border of the lid, 'Lamb of God, remember me, you who take away sins')
Musée Cluny, Paris (Cl. 11460)
Selected literature:
Taburet-Delahaye 1989, no. 64, pp. 170–1.

FIG. 94
Sienese goldsmith
Medallion with Saint Galganus in Prayer, about 1320–30
Silver and gilded copper with translucent enamel, 7.7 × 7.7 cm
Musée Cluny, Paris (Cl. 21557)
Selected literature:
Taburet-Delahaye 1988, pp. 17–29; Taburet-Delahaye 1989, no. 65, pp. 171–2; Cioni 1998, pp. 314, 317, 408.

FIG. 93
Sienese artist
Angel from the Lid of an Incense Boat, about 1325–50
Gilded copper with champlevé enamel, 9.1 × 9 × 2.6 cm
The Metropolitan Museum of Art, New York. Gift of Brimo de Laroussilhe, 2006 (2006.316)
Selected literature:
Christie's 1998a, lot 14.
[New York only]

FIG. 119
Sienese goldsmith
Reliquary-monstrance, 1331
Glass and gilded copper with translucent enamel, 45.5 × 17.7 cm
Inscription: DOMENICHO DI BENVENVTO FATORE DEL EREDE PAGHOLO DAV 1331 (on the stem, above the foot, 'Domenico di Benvenuto manager of the Pagholo estate gave [this reliquary], 1331')
Musée Cluny, Paris (Cl. 9190)
Selected literature:
Leone de Castris 1980a, pp. 37–8; Taburet-Delahaye 1989, no. 66, pp. 173–5; Cioni 1998, pp. 311, 313, 634.

FIG. 120
Sienese goldsmith
Incense Boat with the Annunciation, about 1350–75
Gilded copper, 10.2 × 9 × 21.5 cm
Musée Cluny, Paris (Cl. 11157)
Selected literature:
Taburet-Delahaye 1989, no. 69, pp. 178–9.

FIG. 124
Tondino di Guerrino (documented 1322–42) and **Andrea Riguardi** (documented 1322–1328)
Chalice, about 1320
Gilded silver with translucent and champlevé enamel, 21 × 13.8 cm
Inscription: TONDINUS E ANDREIA ME FECIT (on the stem below the knop, 'Tondino and Andrea made me')
Trustees of the British Museum, London. Purchased with a contribution from the Art Fund (as NACF) (1960,1203.1)
Selected literature:
Taburet in Avignon 1983, cat. 46, pp. 151–2; Leone de Castris 1980a, pp. 25–8; Cioni 1998, pp. 17–643, *passim*; Robinson 2008, pp. 26–7; Donato 2011–12, no. 4.S.1, pp. 45–7; Marquette in Lens 2015, cat. 84, pp. 206–7.
[London only]

FIG. 118
Attributed to Tondino di Guerrino
(documented 1322–42)
Crucifix, about 1325–30
Gilded silver with translucent enamel (re-enamelled by the Maison André, end of the nineteenth or beginning of the twentieth century), 42.6 × 22.5 cm
Musée du Louvre, Département des Objets d'art, Paris (OA 10656)
Selected literature:
Leone de Castris 1980a, p. 35; Taburet-Delahaye 1983, pp. 188–98; Taburet in Avignon 1983, cat. 51, p. 165; Cioni 1998, pp. 24–643, *passim*.

FIG. 125
Attributed to Tondino di Guerrino
(documented 1322–42)
Chalice of Peter of Sassoferrato, about 1341–2
Gilded silver with translucent enamel, 21.7 × 14.9 cm
Inscription: FRAT[R]IS PETRIS PENITENTIARII DOMINI PAPE (on the stem above the knop; 'of Brother Peter Penitentiary of the Lord Pope'); LOCI SASSIFERATI NON VENDATUR NEC DISTRATUR (on the stem below the knop; 'of the place of Sassoferrato, neither sell nor destroy')
The Metropolitan Museum of Art, New York. The Cloisters Collection, 1988 (1988.67)
Selected literature:
Cioni 1998, pp. 287–677, *passim*; Boehm in New York 1999, cat. 173, pp. 145–7; Montevecchi 2007, pp. 262–3; Barnet and Wu 2012, p. 109.
[New York only]

4. ILLUMINATED MANUSCRIPTS

FIGS 188, 195, 196, 198, 199, 200
de Limbourg Brothers (documented 1399–1416)
The Belles Heures of John of France, Duke of Berry, 1405–8/9
Tempera and ink on parchment, 23.8 × 34.1 cm (double leaf); 23.8 × 17 cm (single leaf)
The Metropolitan Museum of Art, New York. The Cloisters Collection, 1954 (54.1.1a,b)
Selected literature:
Meiss and Beatson 1974; Meiss 1974, vol. 1, pp. 102–42, 225, 331–6, 416; Husband 2005, pp. 97–111; Dückers and Roelofs in Nijmegen 2005, cats 93–102, pp. 354–73; Lorentz in Paris 2004b, cat. 188, pp. 300–1; Los Angeles and New York 2008–10.

FIG. 22
Master Honoré (documented 1289–1312)
Equity and Felony, leaf from *Laurent d'Orléans, La Somme le Roi*, about 1290–5
Tempera and ink on parchment, 15 × 10 cm
The Syndics of the Fitzwilliam Museum, University of Cambridge (MS 192)
Selected literature:
Avril in Paris 1998, under cat. 183, pp. 276–7; Stones 2013–14, vol. 1.2, no. I–45b, pp. 97–8; Panayotova in Cambridge 2016, cat. 49, pp. 210–11.
[London only]

FIG. 36
Jean Pucelle (documented 1319–34)
The Hours of Jeanne d'Evreux, Queen of France, about 1324–8
Grisaille, tempera and ink on parchment, 9.9 × 7.2 × 3.8 cm (overall with binding); 9.2 × 6.2 cm (single folio)
The Metropolitan Museum of Art, New York. The Cloisters Collection, 1954 (54.1.2)
Selected literature:
Rorimer 1957; Avril in Paris 1981–2, cat. 239, pp. 292–3; Boehm, Quandt and Wixom 2000; Boehm 2001, pp. 23–7.

FIG. 100
Lippo Vanni (documented 1344–75)
Leaf from a Gradual with King David raising his Soul to Christ, about 1350
Tempera and ink on parchment, 57 × 38.5 cm
Victoria and Albert Museum (4149)
Selected literature:
Cockerell and Harcourt Smith 1923, p. 77; Freuler 1997, p. 283, n. 56; Wainwright 1988, pp. 27–9, 31–3; De Benedictis in Labriola, De Benedictis and Freuler 2003, pp. 136, 322.
[London only]

FIG. 98
Lippo Vanni (documented 1344–75)
Cutting from a Choir Book with Saint Agatha, about 1366–70
Tempera and ink on parchment, 22 × 17.2 cm
Private collection
Selected literature:
Gore in London 1965, cat. 80, p. 46; Freuler in Lugano-Castagnola 1991, pp. 62–3; Kanter in New York 1994–5, p. 214, n. 1; Palladino in Hindman et al. 1997, pp. 134–5, n. 11; De Benedictis in Labriola, De Benedictis and Freuler 2003, pp. 138–9, 170, 319.
[London only]

5. IVORIES

Cologne, Germany
Triptych with the Coronation of the Virgin, 1325–50
Ivory with polychromy, gilt decorations and metal mounts, 39.2 × 23 × 6.1 cm (open); 39.2 × 15.2 × 6.1 cm (closed)
The Metropolitan Museum of Art, New York. Gift of J. Pierpont Morgan, 1917 (17.190.211)
Selected literature:
Koechlin 1924, vol. 1, no. 118, p. 122; vol. 2, no. 118, p. 52; Little in St Petersburg and Moscow 1990, cat. 44, pp. 94–5; Little in Cologne 2011–12, cat. 23, pp. 267–8.
[New York only, unillustrated]

Meuse Valley, France
Diptych with the Adoration of the Magi (left); *Saint Christopher, Vera Icon (True Image) of Christ held up by an Angel, and Bishop-Saint* (right), about 1325–50
Ivory with metal mounts, 7.3 × 11.3 × 0.7 cm (open); 7.3 × 5.7 × 1.3 cm (closed)
The Metropolitan Museum of Art, New York. Gift of J. Pierpont Morgan, 1917 (17.190.274)
Selected literature:
Cf. Guérin 2022, pp. 269–71; Gaborit-Chopin 2013–14, p. 124, pl. 9.
[New York only, unillustrated]

FIG. 170
Paris, France
Enthroned Virgin and Child, about 1260–80
Ivory with traces of polychromy, 18.4 × 7.6 × 7.3 cm
The Metropolitan Museum of Art, New York. Purchase, The Cloisters Collection and Michel David-Weill Gift, 1999 (1999.208)
Selected literature:
Randall 1993, no. 5, p. 36; Barnet and Wu 2012, p. 79; Guérin 2012; Guérin 2022, pp. 187, 203–6.
[New York only]

FIG. 144
Paris, France
Polyptych with the Virgin and Child and Scenes from the Infancy of Christ, 1280s
Ivory with traces of polychromy and gilding with metal hinges, 29.4 × 26.7 cm (open); 29.4 × 11.2 cm (closed)
Toledo Museum of Art, OH. Purchased with funds from the Libbey Endowment, Gift of Edward Drummond Libbey (1950.304)

Selected literature:
Little 1979, pp. 61–2; Randall 1993, no. 32, pp. 50–1; Barnet in Detroit and Baltimore 1997, cat. 17, pp. 144–6; Guérin 2013, pp. 56–71, *passim.*
[New York only]

FIG. 175
Paris, France
The Virgin and Child, 1290–1300
Ivory with polychromy, 25.3 × 15.5 × 6 cm (with original base)
Museo del Tesoro della Basilica di San Francesco, Assisi (88)
Selected literature:
Koechlin 1924, vol. 1, pp. 33, 114, 237, 252; vol. 2, no. 634, p. 238; Bemporad in Ciardi Dupré dal Poggetto 1980, no. 88, pp. 147–8; Gaborit-Chopin in Paris 1981–2, cat. 139, pp. 181–2; Guérin 2022, pp. 215, 230, n. 53, pp. 240–2, *passim.*

Paris, France
Box with Romance Scenes, about 1310–30
Ivory, 10.9 × 25.3 × 15.9 cm; 15 × 25.1 × 0.8 cm (top)
The Metropolitan Museum of Art, New York. Gift of J. Pierpont Morgan, 1917; The Cloisters Collection, 1988 (17.190.173a, b; 1988.16)
Selected literature:
Hoopes 1926; Barnes in New York 1975, cat. 10, pp. 26–7; Gaborit-Chopin in Paris 1998, cat. 101, pp. 159, 165–6; Carns 2005; Antoine in Los Angeles 2010–11, cat. 55, pp. 281–3.
[New York only, unillustrated]

Paris, France
Right Wing of a Diptych Mounted in a Book Cover, 1360–75
Ivory, champlevé enamel and copper gilt on wood support, 25.4 × 18.7 × 3.4 cm (overall); 16.7 × 10.1 cm (ivory)
The Metropolitan Museum of Art, New York. Gift of J. Pierpont Morgan, 1917 (17.190.856)
Selected literature:
Koechlin 1924, vol. 1, no. 555, pp. 195, 202, 220; vol. 2, no. 555, p. 214; Gaborit-Chopin in Paris 1981–2, p. 198.
[New York only, unillustrated]

FIG. 172
Paris, France
Diptych with the Glorification of the Virgin and the Crucifixion, about 1325–50
Ivory with later silver hinges and ebony backing, 18.1 × 22.2 × 0.8 cm (open)
The Courtauld, London (Samuel Courtauld Trust) (O.1966.GP.10)
Selected literature:
Gardner 1967, p. 143; Courtauld 1979, no. 14, p. 12; Lowden 2013, no. 8, pp. 68–71.
[London only]

FIG. 173
Paris, France or Cologne, Germany
Quadriptych with Scenes from Christ's Passion, about 1300
Ivory with traces of polychromy (with some original hinges), 23.9 × 32.1 × 1 cm (open); 23.9 × 8 × 4.2 cm (closed)
The Metropolitan Museum of Art, New York. Gift of J. Pierpont Morgan, 1917 (17.190.205)
Selected literature:
Koechlin 1924, vol. 1, pp. 155, 167, 186, 292; vol. 2, no. 282, p. 125; Little 1997, pp. 88–9; Schmidt 2005a, pp. 303–4, 314.

Probably Paris, France
Diptych with the Coronation of the Virgin and the Last Judgement, about 1260–70
Ivory with metal mounts, 12.7 × 13 × 1.9 cm (open)
The Metropolitan Museum of Art, New York. The Cloisters Collection, 1970 (1970.324.7a, b)
Selected literature:
Little 1979, pp. 64–5; Van Os in Amsterdam 1994–5, cat. 6, pp. 25–6, 176; Little in Detroit and Baltimore 1997, cat. 9, pp. 130–1; Barnet and Wu 2012, p. 80; Guérin 2022, pp. 215, 224–8.
[New York only, unillustrated]

6. TEXTILES

FIG. 154
Central Asia
Textile fragment, faded red silk with large palmette design, late thirteenth–mid-fourteenth century
Silk, with pattern weft of wrapped gold thread; weft-patterned tabby weave, 85.5 × 35 cm
The Cleveland Museum of Art, John L. Severance Fund (1993.253)
Selected literature:
Cleveland and New York 1997–8, cat. 46, p. 160; Shea 2021, p. 376, fig. 20 and pp. 411–12.

FIG. 153
Central Asia or Greater Iran
Textile fragment with small flowers and leaves (from the cope of Pope Benedict XI), late thirteenth–early fourteenth century
Silk, with pattern weft of flat gold thread; tabby-tabby lampas weave, 12.1 × 18.2 cm
The Metropolitan Museum of Art, New York. Rogers Fund, 1919 (19.191.3)
Selected literature:
Klesse 1967, p. 67, pl. 56; Cleveland 1968, cat. 301, pp. 374–5; Cleveland and New York 1997–8, cat. 37, pp. 146–7; Frattaroli in Verona 1983, pp. 172, 174–7, fig. 3; Wardwell 1988–9, p. 102, figs 22a, b; Hoeniger 1991, p. 158, fig. 8; Rosati 2016, p. 173, p. 175, fig. 4; Del Punta and Rosati 2017, p. 27, fig. 7, p. 28; Shea 2021, pp. 127–8, fig. 5.2.

FIG. 161
Central Asia or Greater Iran
Textile fragment with small leaves, late thirteenth–mid-fourteenth century
Silk, with pattern weft of flat gold thread; weft-patterned tabby weave, 14.5 × 15.5 cm
The Cleveland Museum of Art, Dudley P. Allen Fund (1985.33)
Selected literature:
Wardwell 1988–9, pp. 97, 147, fig. 3; Cleveland and New York 1997–8, cat. 38, p. 148; Shea 2021, p. 128 and pl. 29.

FIG. 159
Greater Iran, probably Tabriz
Textile fragment, crimson velvet with gold octagonal discs, late thirteenth or early fourteenth century
Silk, with pattern weft of wrapped gold thread; velvet, 58.4 × 22.9 cm
The Metropolitan Museum of Art, New York. Fletcher Fund, 1946 (46.156.72)
Selected literature:
Wardwell 1988–9, p. 111, figs 57, 77; Hoeniger 1991, p. 160, fig. 12; Sonday 1999–2000, p. 104 and *passim*; Desrosiers 2004, cats 170–1, pp. 318–22; Mackie 2015, p. 228, fig. 6.13.

FIG. 165
Lucca, Italy
Textile fragment with quadrupeds and birds, late thirteenth–early fourteenth century
Silk, with brocading weft of silk and pattern weft of wrapped gold thread; tabby-tabby lampas weave, 47.2 × 40.7 cm
The Metropolitan Museum of Art, New York. Rogers Fund, 1931 (31.69)
Selected literature:
Phillips 1931, pp. 197–8; Tietzel 1984, pp. 198–9.

FIG. 163
Lucca, Italy
Textile fragment with grapevines and birds, second quarter of the fourteenth century
Silk; tabby-tabby lampas weave, 24.1 × 25.4 cm
The Cleveland Museum of Art, Florence and Charles Abel Oriental Rug Collection by exchange (1971.75)
Selected literature:
Wardwell 1976–7, p. 183; Wardwell 1987, p. 23; Mackie 2015, pp. 237–9, fig. 6.26.

FIG. 149
Nasrid workshop, Iberia
Textile fragment with a geometric interlace design, featuring a mirrored kufic inscription (from the tomb of Don Felipe, Infante of Castile and Leon [died 1274]), 1250–75
Silk, with pattern wefts of silk and of wrapped gold thread; weft-faced compound tabby (taqueté) weave, 21 × 13 cm
The Metropolitan Museum of Art, New York. Fletcher Fund, 1946 (46.156.8)

Selected literature:
Walker and Froom in New York 1992–3, cat. 27, pp. 38–9; Feliciano 2005, pp. 113–16; Mackie 2015, pp. 183–4, figs 5.12, 5.13; Perratore 2021, p. 26.

Nasrid workshop, Iberia
Textile fragment with a geometric interlace design (part of the same textile as fig. 149, from the tomb of Don Felipe, Infante of Castile and Leon [died 1274]), 1250–75
Silk, with pattern wefts of silk and of wrapped gold thread; weft-faced compound tabby (taqueté) weave, 11.4 × 29.8 cm
The Metropolitan Museum of Art, New York. Rogers Fund, 1927 (27.58.3)
Selected literature:
See references for fig. 149.
[Unillustrated]

FIG. 146
Nasrid workshop, Iberia
Textile fragment with a geometric design, featuring naskhi and kufic inscriptions, fourteenth century
Silk; twill-tabby lampas weave, 102 × 36.3 cm
The Metropolitan Museum of Art, New York. Fletcher Fund, 1929 (29.22)
Selected literature:
Partearroyo in Granada and New York 1992, cat. 97, p. 335; Otavský and Salim 1995, no. 137, pp. 236–7; Washington and New York 2004, cat. 42, p. 139, ill. pp. 47–9; Desrosiers 2004, no. 223, pp. 392–3; Bush in Ekhtiar et al. 2011, p. 56, no. 48, pp. 81–2; Mackie 2015, p. 197, figs 5.27, 5.35.

FIG. 169
Turkey (attributed)
Rug with confronted animals, fourteenth century
Wool (warp, weft and pile); symmetrically knotted pile, 165.1 × 138.4 cm
The Metropolitan Museum of Art, New York. Purchase, Harris Brisbane Dick Fund, Joseph Pulitzer Bequest, Louis V. Bell Fund and Fletcher, Pfeiffer and Rogers Funds, 1990 (1990.61)
Selected literature:
Walker 1990, pp. 12–13; Hamburg and Stuttgart 1993, pp. 266–7; Gordon 2003, pp. 118, 120, fig. 2; Ölçer in London 2005, cat. 98, pp. 142–3, 402–3; Walker in Ekhtiar et al. 2011, p. 8, no. 234, pp. 328–30; Gordon 2011, p. 386, fig. 17; Denny 2014, p. 57.

LIST OF LENDERS

Altenburg
Lindenau-Museum

Antwerp
Koninklijk Museum voor Schone Kunsten

Arezzo
Chiesa di Santa Maria della Pieve

Assisi
Museo del Tesoro della Basilica di San Francesco

Berlin
Staatliche Museen zu Berlin, Gemäldegalerie

Bern
Kunstmuseum Bern

Birmingham
The Henry Barber Trust, the Barber Institute of Fine Arts, University of Birmingham

Boston, MA
Isabella Stewart Gardner Museum
Museum of Fine Arts, Boston

Cambridge
Girton College, University of Cambridge
The Fitzwilliam Museum

Cambridge, MA
Harvard Art Museums/Fogg Museum

Chiusdino
Chiesa di San Galgano a Montesiepi

Cleveland, OH
The Cleveland Museum of Art

Cortona
Museo Diocesano

Florence
Gallerie degli Uffizi
Museo Nazionale del Bargello

Fort Worth, TX
Kimbell Art Museum

Frankfurt
Liebieghaus Skulpturensammlung

Hull
Ferens Art Gallery

Liverpool
Walker Art Gallery

London
The British Museum
The Courtauld, London (Samuel Courtauld Trust)
Daniel Katz Gallery
His Majesty The King
The National Gallery
Victoria and Albert Museum
The Wyvern Collection

Los Angeles, CA
J. Paul Getty Museum

Madrid
Colección Carmen Thyssen
Museo Nacional Thyssen-Bornemisza

Manchester
Manchester City Galleries

Massa Marittima
Cattedrale di San Cerbone

Paris
Musée Cluny
Musée du Louvre

New York, NY
The Frick Collection
The Metropolitan Museum of Art

Siena
Arcidiocesi di Siena - Colle di Val d'Elsa - Montalcino:
- Basilica di San Bernardino all'Osservanza
- Museo Diocesano, Oratorio di San Bernardino
- Palazzo Arcivescovile

Fondo Edifici di Culto
Museo dell'Opera della Metropolitana
Pinacoteca nazionale di Siena
Soprintendenza Archeologia, Belle Arti e Paesaggio per le province di Siena, Grosseto e Arezzo

Toledo, OH
Toledo Museum of Art

Vatican City
Musei Vaticani

Washington DC
National Gallery of Art

And those lenders who wish to remain anonymous

BIBLIOGRAPHY

Aceto 1992
F. Aceto, 'Pittori e documenti della Napoli angioina: aggiunte ed espunzioni', *Prospettiva*, 67 (1992), pp. 53–65

Aceto 2010
F. Aceto, 'Spazio ecclesiale e pale di "primitivi" in San Lorenzo Maggiore a Napoli: dal "San Ludovico" di Simone Martini al "San Girolamo" di Colantonio. I', *Prospettiva*, 37 (2010), pp. 2–50

Aceto 2011
F. Aceto, 'Tino di Camaino a Napoli', in Bartalini 2011a, pp. 183–93

Albrecht et al. 2022
S. Albrecht and M. Tebel with S. Brinkmann and C. Verbeek, 'Zwei Madonnenfiguren der Lorenzkirche in Nürnberg: Objekt- und Formgeschichte im Austausch', in S. Albrecht, L.M. Ulrich and C. Forcht (eds), *Bamberger Perspektiven: Studien zur Kunst des Mittelalters*, Bamberg 2022, pp. 63–76, https://fis.uni-bamberg.de/bitstream/uniba/53978/1/fisba53978.pdf (accessed 15 October 2023)

Alessandri 1920
L. Alessandri, *Inventari della sacristia del Sacro Convento di Assisi compilati nel 1338 contenuti nel codice 337 della Comunale di Assisi*, Florence 1920

Alexander 1983
J. Alexander, 'The Limbourg Brothers and Italian Art: A New Source', *Zeitschrift für Kunstgeschichte*, 46 (1983), pp. 425–35

Allegri and Giura 2024 (forthcoming)
S. Allegri and G. Giura (eds), *Un modello in discussione. Nuove prospettive di ricerca sulla chiesa di San Francesco di Cortona*, Pisa 2024 (forthcoming)

Ames-Lewis 1997
F. Ames-Lewis, *Tuscan Marble Carving 1250–1350: Sculpture and Civic Pride*, Aldershot 1997

Amsterdam 1994–5
H.W. van Os (ed.), *The Art of Devotion in the Late Middle Ages in Europe 1300–1500*, exh. cat., Rijksmuseum, Amsterdam 1994–5

Amsterdam 2017–18
P. Roelofs, R. Dückers, E. Ravaud, V.M. Schmidt, F. Scholten, D. Thiebaut, M. Ubl (eds), *Johan Maelwael. Nijmegen, Paris, Dijon. Art around 1400*, exh. cat., Rijksmuseum, Amsterdam 2017–18

Andreuccetti 2008
P.A. Andreuccetti, *La policromia della scultura lapidea in Toscana tra XIII e XV secolo*, Florence 2008

Anheim 2015
E. Anheim, 'Simone Martini à Avignon: une histoire en négatif?', in E. Brilli, L. Fenelli and G. Wolf, *Images and Words in Exile: Avignon and Italy during the First Half of the 14th Century*, Florence 2015, pp. 365–79

Antušková et al. 2016
V. Antušková, I. Vernerová, Š. Chlumská, H. Dáňová, A. Třeštíková and R. Šefců, 'Wood as the Material of Carvings and Paintings of Bohemian and Moravian Provenance in the Years 1280–1550. Identification of Wood', *Bulletin of the National Gallery in Prague*, 26 (2016), pp. 93–111

Arezzo 1979–80
A.M. Maetzke (ed.), *Arte nell'Aretino: secondo mostra di restauri dal 1975 al 1979: dipinti e sculture restaurati dal XIII al XVIII secolo*, exh. cat., San Francesco, Arezzo 1979–80

Argenziano 2000
R. Argenziano, *Agli inizi dell'iconografia sacra a Siena: culti, riti e iconografia a Siena nel XII secolo*, Florence 2000

Argenziano 2014
R. Argenziano, 'Il ciclo do Ambrogio Lorenzetti per la cappella di San Galgano a Montesiepi: l'iconografia della Maestà e dell'Annunciazione', in A. Conti (ed.), *Speciosa Imago. L'iconografia di San Galgano dal XIII al XVII secolo*, Siena 2014, pp. 89–105

Arias 1905
G. Arias, 'Per la storia economica del secolo XIV: comunicazioni d'archivio ed osservazioni', *Archivio della R. Società Romana di Storia Patria*, 28 (1905), pp. 301–54

Ashtor 1983
E. Ashtor, *Levant Trade in the Later Middle Ages*, Princeton 1983

Athens 2000–1
M. Vassilaki (ed.), *Mother of God: Representations of the Virgin in Byzantine Art*, exh. cat., Benaki Museum, Athens 2000–1

Avery-Quash 2011
S. Avery-Quash, 'Collector Connoisseurs or Spiritual Aesthetes? The Role of Anglican Clergy in the Growth of Interest in Collecting and Displaying Early Italian Art (1830s–1880s)', in J. Sterrett and P. Thomas (eds), *Sacred Text – Sacred Space: Architectural, Spiritual and Literary Convergences in England and Wales*, Leiden and Boston, MA 2011

Avery-Quash 2012
S. Avery-Quash, '"Incessant Personal Exertions and Comprehensive Artistic Knowledge": Prince Albert's Interest in Early Italian Art', in S. Avery-Quash (ed.), *Victoria & Albert: Art and Love*, London 2012, pp. 1–22

Avery-Quash and Sheldon 2011
S. Avery-Quash and J. Sheldon, *Art for the Nation: The Eastlakes and the Victorian Art World*, London 2011

Avignon 1983
M.-C. Léonelli (ed.), *L'art gothique siennois: enluminure, peinture, orfèvrerie, sculpture*, exh. cat., Musée du Petit Palais, Avignon 1983

Avril 1978
F. Avril, *Manuscript Painting at the Court of France: The Fourteenth Century (1310–1380)*, London 1978

Ayers 2019
T. Ayers (ed.), *The Fabric Accounts of St Stephen's Chapel, Westminster 1292–1396*, trans. M. Jurkowski, Martlesham 2019, https://doi.org/10.1017/9781787446151 (accessed 25 January 2023)

Bacci 2000
M. Bacci, *'Pro remedio animae': immagini sacre e pratiche devozionali in Italia centrale (secoli XIII e XIV)*, Pisa 2000

Bacci 2009
M. Bacci, '*Imaginariae representationes*: L'iconografia evangelica e il pio esercizio della memoria', in M. Bacci (ed.), *Iconografica evangelica a Siena dalle origini al Concilio di Trento*, Siena 2009, pp. 7–25

Bacci 1944
P. Bacci, *Fonti e commenti per la storia dell'arte senese. Dipinti e sculture in Siena nel suo contado ed altrove*, Siena 1944

Bagnoli 1988
A. Bagnoli, 'I tempi della "Maestà": il restauro e le nuove evidenze', in Bellosi 1988a, pp. 109–18

Bagnoli 1994
A. Bagnoli, *La Maestà di Simone Martini*, Cinisello Balsamo 2000

Bagnoli 1999
A. Bagnoli, *La Maestà di Simone Martini*, Milan 1999

Bagnoli 2003
A. Bagnoli, 'Alle origini della pittura senese. Prime osservazioni sul ciclo dei dipinti murali', in Guerrini and Seidel 2003, pp. 107–47

Bagnoli 2018
A. Bagnoli, 'Mariano d'Agnolo Romanelli e il Reliquiario di San Marco papa', *Prospettiva*, 169–171 (2018), pp. 3–11

Bagnoli 2022
A. Bagnoli, 'Simone Martini e la Croce di San Casciano in Val di Pesa', in M. Ciatti, C. Frosinini and S. Rossi (eds), *La croce dipinta di Simone Martini a San Casciano Val di Pesa: studi, indagini e restauro*, Florence 2022, pp. 17–28

Bagnoli et al. 2003
A. Bagnoli, R. Bartalini, L. Bellosi and M. Laclotte (eds), *Duccio: Siena fra tradizione bizantina e mondo gotico*, Milan 2003

Baker 1995
P.L. Baker, *Islamic Textiles*, London 1995

Baldelli 2007
F. Baldelli, *Tino di Camaino*, Morbio Inferiore 2007

Balducci Pegolotti 1936
F. Balducci Pegolotti, *La pratica della mercatura*, ed. A. Evans, Cambridge, MA 1936

Banchi 1884
L. Banchi, *Le Prediche Volgari di San Bernardino da Siena*, Siena 1884

Bandlien 2014
B. Bandlien, 'The Armenian Embassy to King Håkon V of Norway', *Journal of the Society for Armenian Studies*, 23 (2014), pp. 49–82

Banker 1991
J.R. Banker, 'The Program for the Sassetta Altarpiece in the Church of S. Francesco in Borgo S. Sepolcro', *I Tatti Studies*, 4 (1991), pp. 11–58

Banker 2009
J.R. Banker, 'Appendix of Documents Relating to the High Altarpiece, the High Altar, and the Tomb of the Blessed Ranieri in the Church of San Francesco in Borgo San Sepolcro', in Israëls 2009, vol. 2, pp. 566–83

Banker 2010
J.R. Banker, 'Documenti relativi alla compagnia di Santa Maria della Misericordia e alla tavola di Piero della Francesca', in Betti, Frosinini and Refice 2010, pp. 15–30

Barbavara di Gravellona 2001
T. Barbavara di Gravellona, 'Tino di Camaino a Firenze e il monumento funerario del vescovo Antonio D'Orso in Duomo. I. Per una nuova lettura del sepolcro', *Annali della Scuola Normale Superiore di Pisa. Classe di Lettere e Filosofia*, series 4 and 6, 2 (2001), pp. 265–99

Barbavara di Gravellona, Samarelli and Lalli 1998
T. Barbavara di Gravellona, C. Samarelli and C. Lalli, 'Monumento al vescovo Orso: Tino di Camaino (Siena 1280 ca. – Napoli 1337) Firenze, cattedrale di Santa Maria del Fiore', *OPD Restauro*, 10 (1998), pp. 182–90

Bardelloni 2011
C. Bardelloni, 'L'attività Toscana di Tino di Camaino', in Bartalini 2011a, pp. 119–82

Barnet and Wu 2012
P. Barnet and N. Wu, *The Cloisters: Medieval Art and Architecture*, New Haven and London 2012 (2nd edn)

Barone 1886
N. Barone, 'La *Ratio Thesaurariorum* della Cancelleria Angioina', *Archivio Storico per le Province Napoletane*, 11 (1886), pp. 576–96

Barsotti 1959
R. Barsotti, *Gli antichi inventari della cattedrale di Pisa*, Pisa 1959

Bartalini 2003–4
R. Bartalini, 'Duccio di Buoninsegna e bottega: Madonna col Bambino, storie della Passione', in Siena 2003–4, pp. 244–57

Bartalini 2005
R. Bartalini, *Scultura gotica in Toscana: maestri, monumenti, cantieri del Due e Trecento*, Milan 2005

Bartalini 2011a
R. Bartalini (ed.), *Scultura gotica senese (1260–1350)*, Turin 2011

Bartalini 2011b
R. Bartalini, 'Giovanni d'Agostino', in Bartalini 2011a, pp. 329–67

Bartalini 2015
R. Bartalini, 'Ambrogio Lorenzetti a Montesiepi. Sulla committenza e la cronologia degli affreschi della cappella di San Galgano', *Prospettiva*, 157–8 (2015), pp. 2–18

Bartalini 2017–18
R. Bartalini, 'I resti del ciclo dedicato al francescano Pietro da Siena e agli altri martiri dell'India nel chisotro di San Francesco a Siena', in Siena 2017–18, pp. 268–77

Bartalini 2019
R. Bartalini, 'Tino di Camaino, un riscoperto "San Giovanni Battista" e i marmi della badia di Cava dei Tirreni', *Prospettiva*, 173 (2019), pp. 46–60

Bartalini 2023
R. Bartalini, 'Giovanni Pisano: un'attestazione in meno e una sicura attestazione in più', *La Diana*, 6 (2023), pp. 1–14

Bartalini and Cioni 2003–4
R. Bartalini and E. Cioni, 'Le vie del gotico a Siena: orafi e scultori', in Siena 2003–4, pp. 422–35

Bartoli and Parenti 2023
R. Bartoli and D. Parenti (eds), *Il polittico della Beata Umiltà di Pietro Lorenzetti: l'arte di raccontare una santa*, Livorno 2023

Baxandall 2006
M. Baxandall, *Giotto and the Orators* (1971), Oxford 2006

Beani 1906
G. Beani, *La sacrestia di S. Zeno nell'inventario del 1372*, Pistoia 1906

Beattie 2007
B.R. Beattie, *Angelus Pacis. The Legation of Cardinal Giovanni Gaetano Orsini, 1326–1334*, Boston, MA and Leiden 2007

Becchis 2012
M. Becchis, *Pietro Lorenzetti*, Milan 2012

Becchis and Pierini 2002
M. Becchis and M. Pierini, 'Appendice documentaria', in Rome 2002, pp. 60–9

Bellosi 1984
L. Bellosi, 'Gano a Massa Marittima', *Prospettiva*, 37 (1984), pp. 19–22

Bellosi 1988a
L. Bellosi (ed.), *Simone Martini: atti del convegno, Siena 27, 28, 29 marzo 1985*, Florence 1988

Bellosi 1988b
L. Bellosi, 'Il pittore oltremontano di Assisi: il gotico a Siena e la formazione di Simone Martini', in Bellosi 1988a, pp. 39–47

Bellosi 1991a
L. Bellosi, 'Per un contesto cimabuesco senese: (a) Guido da Siena e il probabile Dietisalvi', *Prospettiva*, 61 (1991), pp. 6–20

Bellosi 1991b
L. Bellosi, 'Per un contesto cimabuesco senese: (b) Rinaldo da Siena e Guido di Graziano', *Prospettiva*, 62 (1991), pp. 15–28

Bellosi 1998
L. Bellosi, *Cimabue*, Milan 1998

Bellosi 1999
L. Bellosi, *Duccio: The 'Maestà'*, London 1999

Bellosi 2000
L. Bellosi, 'Approfondimenti in margine a Cimabue', *Mitteilungen des Kunsthistorischen Institutes in Florenz*, 44 (2000), pp. 45–63

Bellosi 2002
L. Bellosi, 'The Function of the *Rucellai Madonna* in the Church of Santa Maria Novella', in Schmidt 2002c, pp. 147–60

Bellosi 2003
L. Bellosi, 'Il percorso di Duccio', in Bagnoli et al. 2003, pp. 102–29

Bellosi 2003–4a
L. Bellosi, 'Precedenti e contemporanei senesi di Duccio', in Siena 2003–4, pp. 38–49

Bellosi 2003–4b
L. Bellosi, 'Il percorso di Duccio', in Siena 2003–4, pp. 118–45

Belting 1981
H. Belting, *Das Bild und sein Publikum im Mittelalter: Form und Funktion früher Bildtalfeln der Passion*, Berlin 1981

Belting 1994
H. Belting, *Likeness and Presence: A History of the Image before the Era of Art*, trans. E. Jephcott, Chicago and London 1994

Benedetti and Cinelli 2013
M. Benedetti and L. Cinelli (eds), *Niccolò da Prato e i frati predicatori tra Roma e Avignone*, special issue of *Memorie Domenicane*, n.s. 44 (2013)

Bennett 1977
B.A. Bennett, 'Lippo Memmi, Simone Martini's "fratello in arte": The Image Revealed by his Documented Works',

PhD dissertation, University of Pittsburgh, Pittsburgh 1977

Benton 1995
T. Benton, 'The Three Cities Compared: Urbanism,' in D. Norman (ed.), *Siena, Florence and Padua: Art, Society and Religion 1280–1400. Volume II: Case Studies*, New Haven and London 1995, pp. 7–28

Berenson 1930
B. Berenson, *The Italian Painters of the Renaissance*, Oxford 1930

Berenson and Gardner 1987
B. Berenson and I.S. Gardner, *The Letters of Bernard Berenson and Isabella Stewart Gardner, 1887–1924, with Correspondence by Mary Berenson*, ed. R. van N. Hadley, Boston, MA 1987

Berlin 2005–6
S. Weppelmann (ed.), *Geschichten auf Gold: Bilderzählungen in der frühen italienischen Malerei*, exh. cat., Gemäldegalerie, Staatliche Museen zu Berlin, Berlin 2005–6

Bertagna 1949
M. Bertagna, 'Il Crocifisso di Lando Pieri,' *Studi Francescani*, 45 (1949), pp. 123–30

Betti, Frosinini and Refice 2010
M. Betti, C. Frosinini and P. Refice (eds), *Ripensando Piero della Francesca: il polittico della Misericordia di Sansepolcro: storia, studi e indagini tecnico-scientifiche*, Florence 2010

Binski 2002
P. Binski, 'How Northern was the Northern Master at Assisi?,' *Proceedings of the British Academy*, 117 (2002), pp. 73–138

Binski and Massing 2009
P. Binski and A. Massing (eds), *The Westminster Retable: History, Technique, Conservation*, Cambridge, London and Turnhout 2009

Bloch 2023
A.R. Bloch, 'Donatello's Origins: Sculpture and Goldsmithing,' in P. Motture (ed.), *Donatello: Sculpting the Renaissance*, exh. cat., Victoria and Albert Museum, London 2023, pp. 20–33

Boehm 2001
B. Drake Boehm, 'Le Mécénat de Jeanne d'Évreux,' in D. Gaborit-Chopin and F. Avril (eds), *1300: L'art au Temps de Philippe le Bel*, Paris 2001, pp. 15–31

Boehm 2005–6a
B. Drake Boehm, 'Called to Create. Luxury Artists at Work in Prague,' in New York and Prague 2005–6, pp. 75–81

Boehm 2005–6b
B. Drake Boehm, 'Charles IV. The Realm of Faith,' in New York and Prague 2005–6, pp. 23–33

Boehm, Quandt and Wixom 2000
B. Drake Boehm, A. Quandt and W.D. Wixom, *The Hours of Jeanne d'Evreux, Acc. No. 54.1.2, The Metropolitan Museum of Art, The Cloisters Collection, New York*, facsimile with commentary, New York and Lucerne 2000

Bokody 2015
P. Bokody, *Images-within-Images in Italian Painting (1250–1350): Reality and Reflexivity*, Farnham 2015

Bolgia 2022
C. Bolgia, 'Jerusalem in Rome: New Light on the Façade Mosaics of Gregory IX (1227–41) and Passion Relics in Old St Peter's,' *Gesta*, 61 (2022), pp. 153–93

Bonito Fanelli 1994
R. Bonito Fanelli, 'I doni dall'Oriente e da Champagne, Provinces et Ultramonti: commerce chiesa e moda,' in Siena 1994, pp. 50–9

Borgherini 2001
M. Borgherini, *Disegno e progetto nel cantiere medieval. Esempi toscani del XIV secolo*, Venice 2001

Borkopp-Restle 2019
B. Borkopp-Restle, *Der Schatz der Marienkirche zu Danzig: Liturgische Gewänder und textile Objekte aus dem späten Mittelalter*, Alterbach 2019

Borsook 1969
E. Borsook, *Gli affreschi di Montesiepi, con annotazioni tecniche di Leonetto Tintori*, Florence 1969

Borsook and Superbi Gioffredi 1994
E. Borsook and F. Superbi Gioffredi (eds), *Italian Altarpieces 1250–1550: Function and Design*, Oxford 1994

Boskovits 1974
M. Boskovits, 'A Dismembered Polyptych, Lippo Vanni and Simone Martini,' *The Burlington Magazine*, 116 (1974), pp. 367–76

Boskovits 1982
M. Boskovits, 'Review of Duccio di Buoninsegna and His School by J.H. Stubblebine; and Duccio di Buoninsegna by J. White,' *The Art Bulletin*, 64, no. 3 (1982), pp. 497–502

Boskovits 1986
M. Boskovits, 'Considerations on Pietro and Ambrogio Lorenzetti,' *Paragone*, 37, no. 439 (1986), pp. 3–16

Boskovits 1988
M. Boskovits, *Frühe Italienische Malerei: Gemäldegalerie Berlin, Katalog der Gemälde*, trans. E. Schleier, Berlin 1988

Boskovits 2009
M. Boskovits (ed.) *The Alana Collection: Vol. I. Italian Paintings from the 13th to 15th Century*, Florence 2009

Boskovits 2016
M. Boskovits, *Italian Paintings of the Thirteenth and Fourteenth Centuries*, NGA Online Editions, 2016, https://purl.org/nga/collection/artobject/434 (accessed 6 June 2023)

Boskovits 2021
M. Boskovits, *Mediaeval Panel Painting in Tuscany: 12th to 13th Century. A Supplement*, ed. S. Chiodo, Florence and Milan 2021

Boskovits and Fossaluzza 1998
M. Boskovits and G. Fossaluzza (eds), *La collezione Cagnola: i dipinti dal XIII al XIX secolo*, Busto Arsizio 1998

Boskovits and Padovani 1990
M. Boskovits with S. Padovani, *Early Italian Painting, 1290–1470: The Thyssen-Bornemisza Collection*, trans. F. Pouncey Chiarini, London and New York 1990

Boston 2022–3
N. Silver (ed.), *Simone Martini in Orvieto*, exh. cat., Isabella Stewart Gardner Museum, Boston, MA 2022–3

Boucheron 2018
P. Boucheron, *The Power of Images: Siena, 1338*, Cambridge 2018

Bowsky 1970
W.M. Bowsky, *The Finance of the Commune of Siena 1287–1355*, Oxford 1970

Bowsky 1981
W.M. Bowsky, *A Medieval Italian Commune: Siena under the Nine, 1287–1355*, Berkeley 1981

Boyer 2016
J.-P. Boyer, 'Un grande ufficiale, Giovanni de Haya († 1337), nella predicazione del domenicano Federico Franconi di Napoli,' in J.-M. Martin and R. Alaggio (eds), *'Quei maledetti Normanni': studi offerti a Errico Cuozzo per i suoi settant'anni da Colleghi, Allievi, Amici*, vol. 1, Ariano Irpino 2016, pp. 73–89

Brandi 1951
C. Brandi, *Duccio*, Florence 1951

Brandi 1959
C. Brandi, *Il restauro della 'Maestà' di Duccio*, Rome 1959

Brandi 1983
C. Brandi (ed.), *Palazzo Pubblico di Siena: vicende costruttive e decorazione*, Milan 1983

Brandl 1985
R. Brandl, *Die Tafelbilder des Simone Martini*, Frankfurt, Bern and New York 1985

Brazil 2002
S. Brazil, 'Nicholas Lochoff & Helen Clay Frick: Re-creating Lorenzetti's *Madonna and Child with Saint Francis and Saint John*,' *The Frick Collection Members' Magazine* (Fall 2002), pp. 10–12

Brigstocke 1981
H. Brigstocke, 'Lord Lindsay and the Sketches of the History of Christian Art,' *Bulletin of the John Rylands University Library of Manchester*, 64, no. 5 (1981), pp. 27–60

Brigstocke, Marchand and Wright 2010
H. Brigstocke, E. Marchand and A.E. Wright, *John Flaxman and William Young Ottley in Italy*, London 2010

Brilliant 2014
V. Brilliant, 'A Framework for Devotion in Trecento Siena: A Reliquary Frame in the Cleveland Museum of Art,' *Peregrinations: Journal of Medieval Art and Architecture*, 4, no. 3 (2014), pp. 66–94

Brink 1976
J.E. Brink, 'Simone Martini's "Orsini Polyptych",' *Jaarboek van het Koninklijk Museum voor Schone Kunsten Antwerpen* (1976), pp. 7–23

Brink 1977a
J.E. Brink, 'Francesco Petrarca and the Problem of Chronology in the Late Paintings of Simone Martini,' *Paragone*, 331 (1977), pp. 3–9

Brink 1977b
J.E. Brink, 'Simone Martini, Francesco Petrarca and the Humanistic Program of the Virgil Frontispiece,' *Mediaevalia*, 3 (1977), pp. 83–117

Brink 1983
J.E. Brink, 'Cardinal Napoleone Orsini and Chiara della Croce: A Note on the "Monache" in Simone Martini's Passion Altarpiece', *Zeitschrift für Kunstgeschichte*, 46 (1983), pp. 419–24

Brinkmann and Kemperdick 2002
B. Brinkmann and S. Kemperdick, *Deutsche Gemälde im Städel 1300–1500*, Städelsches Kunstinstitut, Mainz 2002

Broecke 2015
L. Broecke (ed. and trans.), *Cennino Cennini's 'Il Libro dell'Arte': A New English Translation and Commentary with Italian Transcription*, London 2015

Brucker 1962
G. Brucker, *Florentine Politics and Society, 1343–1378*, Princeton 1962

Brufani 1989
S. Brufani, 'La signoria di Muzio di Francesco in Assisi (1319–1322)', *Signorie in Umbria tra Medioevo e Rinascimento, l'esperienza dei Trinci*, vol. 2, Perugia 1989, pp. 447–51

Budapest and Luxembourg 2006
I. Takács (ed.), *Sigismundus: Rex et Imperator. Kunst und Kultur zur Zeit Sigismunds von Luxemburg 1387–1437*, exh. cat., Szépmüvészeti Museum, Budapest 2006; Musée national d'histoire et d'art, Luxembourg 2006

Bullard 1977
C.F. Bullard, 'The Development of Pictorial Space in Italian Gothic Sculptural Relief', PhD dissertation, Syracuse University, Ann Arbor 1977

Buoncristiani and Caciorgna 2014
A. Buoncristiani and M. Caciorgna, *La Madonna del Latte Ambrogio Lorenzetti*, Livorno 2014

Buoninsegni 1581
M.P. Buoninsegni, *Historia fiorentina*, Florence 1581

Burkart 2006
L. Burkart, 'Das Verzeichnis als Schatz. Überlegungen zu einem Inuentarium Thesauri Romane Ecclesie der Biblioteca Apostolica Vaticana (Cod. Ottob. lat. 2516, fol. 126r–132r)', *Quellen und Forschungen aus italienischen Archiven und Bibliotheken*, 86 (2006), pp. 144–207

Burke 2002
S.M. Burke, 'The *Martyrdom of the Franciscans* by Ambrogio Lorenzetti', *Zeitschrift für Kunstgeschichte*, 65 (2002), pp. 460–92

Burresi 2001
M. Burresi (ed.), *Scultura lignea pisana: percorsi nel territorio tra Medioevo e Rinascimento*, Milan 2001

Buscioni 1981
C. Buscioni, *Giuseppe Partini 1842–1895: architetto del purismo senese*, Florence 1981

Butterfield 1994
A. Butterfield, 'Social Structure and the Typology of Funerary Monuments in Early Renaissance Florence', *Res: Anthropology and Aesthetics*, 26 (1994), pp. 47–67

Butzek 2001a
M. Butzek, 'Le pale di Sant'Ansano e degli altri protettori della città nel Duomo di Siena: una storia documentaria', in Cecchi 2001a, pp. 35–59

Butzek 2001b
M. Butzek, 'Per la storia delle due "Madonna delle Grazie" nel Duomo di Siena', *Prospettiva*, 103–4 (2001), pp. 97–109

Butzek 2006
M. Butzek, 'Chronologie', in Haas and von Winterfeld 2006, pp. 1–262

Butzek and Cecchi 2001
M. Butzek and A. Cecchi, 'Appendice documentaria', in Cecchi 2001a, pp. 129–34

Cadili 2013
A. Cadili, 'La diplomazia e le missioni legatizie', in Benedetti and Cinelli 2013, pp. 85–139

Caffio 2017–18
A. Caffio, 'I perduti affreschi della facciata dell'ospedale di Santa Maria della Scala a Siena', in Siena 2017–18, pp. 363–73

Caglioti 2005
F. Caglioti, 'Giovanni di Balduccio a Bologna: l'"Annunciazione" per la rocca papale di Porta Galliera (con una digressione sulla cronologia napoletana e bolognese di Giotto)', *Prospettiva*, 117–18 (2005), pp. 21–62

Caleca 1976
A. Caleca, 'Tre polittici di Lippo Memmi: un'ipotesi sul Barna e la bottega di Simone e Lippo, 1', *Critica d'arte*, 41 (1976), pp. 49–59

Caleca 1977
A. Caleca, 'Tre polittici di Lippo Memmi, un'ipotesi sul Barna, e la bottega di Simone e Lippo, 2', *Critica d'Arte*, 42 (1977), pp. 55–80

Calley Galitz 2016
K. Calley Galitz, *The Metropolitan Museum of Art: Masterpiece Paintings*, New York 2016

Callori di Vignale and Santamaria 2014
F. Callori di Vignale and U. Santamaria (eds), *Il calice di Guccio di Mannaia nel Tesoro della Basilica di San Francesco ad Assisi. Storia e restauro*, Vatican City 2014

Cambridge 2016
S. Panayotova (ed.), *Colour: The Art & Science of Illuminated Manuscripts*, exh. cat., Fitzwilliam Museum, Cambridge 2016

Cameron 2022
J.A. Cameron, 'A New Angle on Simone Martini's "Holy Family"', in Cooper and Williamson 2022, pp. 229–47

Campana 1951
A. Campana, 'Per la storia delle cappelle trecentesche della chiesa malatestiana di San Francesco', *Studi Romagnoli*, 2 (1951), pp. 17–37

Campbell 2005
A. Campbell, 'A Spectacular Celebration of the Assumption in Siena', *Renaissance Quarterly*, 58 (2005), pp. 435–63

Campbell 2001
C.J. Campbell, 'The City's New Clothes: Ambrogio Lorenzetti and the Poetics of Peace', *The Art Bulletin*, 83, no. 2 (2001), pp. 240–58

Campbell 2004
C.J. Campbell, '"Symone nostro senensi iocundissima": The Court Artist, Heart, Mind, and Hand', in S.J. Campbell (ed.), *Artists at Court: Image-making and Identity, 1300–1550*, Boston, MA 2004, pp. 33–45

Campbell 1983
M. Campbell, *An Introduction to Medieval Enamels*, London 1983

Campbell 1987
M. Campbell, 'L'oreficeria italiana nell'Inghilterra medievale, con una nota sugli smalti medievali italiani del Victoria and Albert Museum', *Bollettino d'Arte*, 43 (1987), pp. 1–16

Camporeale 2004
E. Camporeale, 'La mostra del 1904 dell'antica arte senese a distanza di un secolo', in *Atti e memorie (Accademia toscana di scienze e lettere La Colombaria)*, 69 (n.s. 55), Florence 2004, pp. 47–126

Camporeale 2005
E. Camporeale, 'L'esposizione di arte senese del 1904 al Burlington Fine Arts Club di Londra', in Siena 2005–6, pp. 484–517

Camporeale 2008
E. Camporeale '1904, "annus mirabilis" per l'antica arte senese', in E. Castelnuovo and A. Monciatti, *Medioevo/Medioevi: un secolo di esposizioni d'arte medievale*, Pisa 2008, pp. 109–40

Camporeale 2023
E. Camporeale, 'On the Early Italian Pictures of John Pierpont Morgan (1837–1913)', *Colnaghi Studies*, 12 (2003), pp. 26–41

Cannon 1980
J. Cannon, 'Dominican Patronage of the Arts in Central Italy: The *Provincia Romana*, c.1220–c.1320', PhD dissertation, The Courtauld Institute of Art, London 1980

Cannon 1982
J. Cannon, 'Simone Martini, the Dominicans and the Early Sienese Polyptych', *Journal of the Warburg and Courtauld Institutes*, 45 (1982), pp. 69–93

Cannon 1987
J. Cannon, 'Pietro Lorenzetti and the History of the Carmelite Order', *Journal of the Warburg and Courtauld Institutes*, 50 (1987), pp. 18–28

Cannon 1994
J. Cannon, 'The Creation, Meaning, and Audience of the Early Sienese Polyptych: Evidence from the Friars', in Borsook and Superbi Gioffredi 1994, pp. 41–79

Cannon 2000a
J. Cannon, 'Introduction: Secular Power and the Sacred in the Art of the Central Italian City-State', in Cannon and Williamson 2000, pp. 1–17

Cannon 2000b
J. Cannon, 'Popular Saints and Private Chantries: The Sienese Tomb-Altar of Margherita of Cortona and Questions of Liturgical Use', in N. Bock, S. de Blaauw, C. Luitpold Frommel and H. Kessler (eds), *Kunst und Liturgie im Mittelalter. Akten des internationalen Kongresses der Bibliotheca Hertziana und des Nederlands Instituut te Rome, Rom, 28–30 September 1997*, Munich 2000, pp. 149–62

Cannon 2010
J. Cannon, 'Kissing the Virgin's Foot: *Adoratio* before the Madonna and Child Enacted, Depicted, Imagined', *Studies in Iconography*, 31 (2010), pp. 1–50
Cannon 2013
J. Cannon, *Religious Poverty, Visual Riches: Art in the Dominican Churches of Central Italy in the Thirteenth and Fourteenth Centuries*, New Haven and London 2013
Cannon 2021
J. Cannon, 'The Writer as Viewer: Recollecting Art in the Text of the *Meditationes Vitae Christi*', in Flora and Tóth 2021, pp. 199–223
Cannon 2022–3
J. Cannon, 'Simone Martini and the Possibilities of the Polyptych', in Boston 2022–3, pp. 104–23
Cannon and Pemberton-Pigott 2002
J. Cannon and V. Pemberton-Pigott, 'The Royal Collection Duccio: A Triptych Reconsidered', *Apollo*, 156, no. 486 (2002), pp. 10–18
Cannon and Vauchez 1999
J. Cannon and A. Vauchez, *Margherita of Cortona and the Lorenzetti: Sienese Art and the Cult of a Holy Woman in Medieval Tuscany*, University Park, PA 1999
Cannon and Williamson 2000
J. Cannon and B. Williamson (eds), *Art, Politics, and Civic Religion in Central Italy 1261–1352*, Courtauld Research Papers No. 1, Aldershot 2000
Capron 2017
E. Capron, 'Simone Martini's Last Documented Work', *The Burlington Magazine*, 159 (2017), pp. 4–13
Capron 2019
E. Capron, 'Altarpieces in Late Medieval Avignon: Case Studies in Patronage and Reception', PhD dissertation, The Courtauld Institute of Art, London 2019
Carli 1946
E. Carli, *Goro di Gregorio*, Florence 1946
Carli 1958
E. Carli, *Pittura pisana del trecento*, 2 vols, Milan 1958
Carli 1961
E. Carli, *Duccio di Buoninsegna*, Milan 1961
Carli 1979
E. Carli, *Il Duomo di Siena*, Genoa 1979
Carli 1980
E. Carli, *Gli scultori senese*, Milan 1980
Carmi and Felicetti 2007
C. Carmi and S. Felicetti, 'Camaino di Crescentino e Tino di Camaino da Siena: repertorio delle fonti documentarie (1298–1348)', in Baldelli 2007, pp. 427–52
Carns 2005
P.M. Carns, 'Compilatio in Ivory: The Composite Casket in the Metropolitan Museum', *Gesta*, 44, no. 2 (2005), pp. 69–88
Carruthers 2010
M. Carruthers, 'The Concept of *ductus*, or Journeying through a Work of Art', in M. Carruthers (ed.), *Rhetoric beyond Words: Delight and Persuasion in the Arts of the Middle Ages*, Cambridge 2010, pp. 190–213
Carter Southard 1988
E. Carter Southard, 'Reflections on the Documented Work by Simone Martini in the Palazzo Pubblico', in Bellosi 1988a, pp. 103–8
Casole d'Elsa 2010
A. Bagnoli (ed.), *Marco Romano e il contesto artistico senese fra la fine del Duecento e gli inizi del Trecento*, exh. cat., Museo Archeologico e della Collegiata, Casole d'Elsa 2010
Castelli 2009
C. Castelli, 'The Construction of Wooden Supports of Late-Medieval Altarpieces', in Israëls 2009, vol. 1, pp. 319–35
Castelli 2016
C. Castelli, 'Techniques of Construction of Wooden Supports for Painting', in M. Ciatti and C. Frosinini (eds), *Structural Conservation of Panel Paintings at the Opificio Delle Pietre Dure in Florence: Method, Theory, and Practice*, Florence 2016, pp. 285–349
Castelnuovo 1962
E. Castelnuovo, *Un pittore italiano alla corte di Avignone: Matteo Giovannetti e la pittura in Provenza nel secolo XIV*, Turin 1962
Castelnuovo-Tedesco and Soultanian 2010
L. Castelnuovo-Tedesco and J. Soultanian, *Italian Medieval Sculpture in The Metropolitan Museum of Art and The Cloisters*, New Haven and London 2010
Cazelles and Rathofer 1988
R. Cazelles and J. Rathofer, *Illuminations of Heaven and Earth. The Glories of the Très Riches Heures du Duc de Berry*, New York 1988
Cecchi 2001a
A. Cecchi (ed.), *Simone Martini e 'l'Annunciazione' degli Uffizi*, Milan 2001
Cecchi 2001b
A. Cecchi, 'L'*Annunciazione* dimenticata: dal Duomo di Siena alla Galleria degli Uffizi', in Cecchi 2001a, pp. 61–75
Cecchini 1983
G. Cecchini, 'Palio and Contrade: Historical Evolution', in A. Falassi and G. Catoni (eds), *Palio*, Milan 1983, pp. 309–58
Cenci 1985
C. Cenci, 'Fra Guglielmo de Falgar o Fra Guglielmo Farinier', *Archivum Franciscanum Historicum*, 78 (1985), pp. 481–9
Cennini 2015
C. Cennini, *Il libro dell'arte*, trans. L. Broecke, London 2015
Ceppari Ridolfi and Turrini 1993
M.A. Ceppari Ridolfi and P. Turrini, *Il Mulino delle Vanita: lusso e ceremonie nella Siena medievale: con l'edizione dello Statuto del Donnaio, 1343*, Siena 1993
Chamot 1930
M. Chamot, *English Medieval Enamels*, London 1930
Champeaux 1888
A. de Champeaux, 'Les relations du duc Jean de Berry avec l'art italien', *Gazette des Beaux-Arts*, 38 (1888), pp. 409–15
Châtelet 2007a
A. Châtelet, 'Les commandes artistiques parisiennes des deux premiers ducs de Bourgogne de la maison Valois', in W. Paravicini and B. Schnerb (eds), *Paris, Capitale des Ducs de Bourgogne*, Ostfildern 2007, pp. 165–81
Châtelet 2007b
A. Châtelet, 'Robert Campin et le Hainaut', in L. Nys and D. Vanwijnsberghe, with the collaboration of X. Fontaine and J. Debergh, *Campin in Context, Peinture et société dans le Vallée de l'Escaut à l'époque de Robert Campin 1375–1445. Actes du colloque international organisé par l'Université de Valenciennes et du Hainaut-Cambrésis, l'Institut royal du Patrimoine artistique/ Koninklijk Instituut voor het Kunstpatrimonium et l'Association des Guides de Tournai, Tournai, Maison de la Culture, 30 March – 1 April 2006*, Valenciennes and Brussels 2007, pp. 183–90
Christiansen 1982
K. Christiansen, 'Fourteenth-century Italian Altarpieces', *The Metropolitan Museum of Art Bulletin*, 40, no. 1 (1982), pp. 14–56
Christiansen 1994
K. Christiansen, 'Simone Martini's Altar-piece for the Commune of Siena', *The Burlington Magazine*, 136 (1994), pp. 148–60
Christiansen 2003
K. Christiansen, 'Paul Delaroche's *Crucifixion* by Pietro Lorenzetti', *Apollo*, 157, no. 492 (2003), pp. 8–14
Christiansen 2007
K. Christiansen, 'The Metropolitan's Duccio', *Apollo*, 165, no. 540 (2007), pp. 40–7
Christiansen 2008
K. Christiansen, *Duccio and the Origins of Western Painting*, New York, New Haven and London 2008
Christiansen 2012
K. Christiansen, 'Madonna and Child with Saints and Angels', 2012, *The Met Collection Online*, www.metmuseum.org/art/collection/search/437063 (accessed 1 February 2024)
Christiansen 2021a
K. Christiansen, 'The Architecture in a Bohemian Panel in The Metropolitan Museum of Art', *Prospettiva*, 181–2 (2021), pp. 31–5
Christiansen 2021b
K. Christiansen, 'Un tableau bohémien et la cour de Charles IV à Prague', *Revue de l'Art*, 213 (2021), pp. 8–19
Christiansen 2022
K. Christiansen, 'The Fourteenth-Century Bohemian "Virgin and Child Enthroned" at The Met: Some Preliminary Thoughts', in A. Koopstra, C. Seidel and J.P. Waterman (eds), *Tributes to Maryan W. Ainsworth. Collaborative Spirit: Essays on Northern European Art, 1350–1650*, Turnhout 2022, pp. 32–51
Christie's 1998a
Christie's, New York, *Important European Works of Art, Furniture & Tapestries*, 28 January 1998

Christie's 1998b
Christie's, London, *Important Old Master Pictures*, 10 July 1998

Christie's 2012
Christie's, London, *Old Master and British Paintings Evening Sale*, 3 July 2012

Ciardi Dupré dal Poggetto 1980
M.G. Ciardi Dupré dal Poggetto (ed.), *Il tesoro della basilica di San Francesco ad Assisi: saggi e catalogo*, Florence 1980

Ciatti 2002
M. Ciatti, 'The Restoration and Study of the Crucifix', in Ciatti and Seidel 2002, pp. 25–64

Ciatti and Seidel 2002
M. Ciatti and M. Seidel (eds), *Giotto: The Santa Maria Novella Crucifix*, Florence 2002

Cioni 1979
E. Cioni Liserani, 'Alcune ipotesi per Guccio di Mannaia', *Prospettiva*, 17 (1979), pp. 47–58

Cioni 1998
E. Cioni, *Scultura e smalto nell'oreficeria senese dei secoli XIII e XIV*, Florence 1998

Cioni 2005
E. Cioni, *Il reliquiario di San Galgano*, Florence 2005

Cioni 2010
E. Cioni, 'Nuove acquisizioni sulla bottega "dei Tondi": un document e alcuni smalti', *Opera. Nomina. Historiae*, 2–3 (2010), pp. 151–218

Cioni 2018
E. Cioni, 'Per Matteo di Mino di Pagliaio. Nuove considerazioni sull'oreficeria senese della seconda metà del Trecento', *Prospettiva*, 169–71 (2018), pp. 12–46

Cioni and Fattorini 2021
E. Cioni and G. Fattorini, *Francesco d'Antonio. Il reliquiario del braccio destro di San Giovanni Battista. Oreficeria a Siena al tempo di Pio II*, Milan 2021

Cleveland 1968
S. Lee and W.-K. Ho (eds), *Chinese Art under the Mongols: The Yuan Dynasty (1279–1368)*, exh. cat., The Cleveland Museum of Art, Cleveland 1968

Cleveland 2007
H.A. Klein (ed.), *Sacred Gifts and Worldly Treasures. Medieval Masterworks from the Cleveland Museum of Art*, exh. cat., The Cleveland Museum of Art, Cleveland 2007

Cleveland, Baltimore and London 2010–11
M. Bagnoli, H.A. Klein, C. Griffith Mann and J. Robinson (eds), *Treasures of Heaven: Saints, Relics, and Devotion in Medieval Europe*, exh. cat., The Cleveland Museum of Art, Cleveland 2010–11; Walters Art Museum, Baltimore 2011; British Museum, London 2011

Cleveland and New York 1997–8
J.C.Y. Watt and A.E. Wardwell (eds), with an essay by M. Rossabi, *When Silk Was Gold: Central Asian and Chinese Textiles*, exh. cat. The Cleveland Museum of Art, Cleveland 1997–8; The Metropolitan Museum of Art, New York 1998

Cockerell and Harcourt Smith 1923
S.C. Cockerell and C. Harcourt Smith, *Catalogue of Miniatures, Leaves, and Cuttings from Illuminated Manuscripts. Victoria and Albert Museum. Department of Engraving, Illustration and Design*, London 1923

Cole 1973
B. Cole, 'Old in New in the Early Trecento', *Mitteilungen Des Kunsthistorischen Institutes in Florenz*, 17 (1973), pp. 229–48

Cole 1980
B. Cole, *Sienese Painting: From Its Origins to the Fifteenth Century*, New York 1980

Coletti 1963
L. Coletti, *Tommaso da Modena*, Venice 1963

Collareta 1983
M. Collareta, *Calici Italiani*, Florence 1983

Cologne 2011–12
D. Täube and M.V. Fleck (eds), *Glanz und Grösse des Mittelalters: Kölner Meisterwerke aus den grossen Sammlungen der Welt*, exh. cat., Museum Schnütgen, Cologne 2011–12

Concioni, Ghilarducci and Ferri 1991
G. Concioni, G. Ghilarducci and C. Ferri, *Orafi medioevali*, Lucca 1991

Constable 1929
W.G. Constable, 'The Date and Nationality of the Wilton Diptych', *The Burlington Magazine*, 55 (1929), pp. 36–45

Cook 2005
W.R. Cook (ed.), *The Art of the Franciscan Order in Italy*, Leiden 2005

Cooper 2005
D. Cooper, '"In loco tutissimo e firmissimo": The Tomb of St Francis in History, Legend and Art', in Cook 2005, pp. 1–37

Cooper 2006
D. Cooper, 'Projecting Presence: The Monumental Cross in the Italian Church Interior', in R. Maniura and R. Shepherd (eds), *Presence: The Inherence of the Prototype within Images and Other Objects*, Aldershot and Burlington, VT 2006, pp. 47–69

Cooper 2013
D. Cooper, 'Redefining the Altarpiece in Early Renaissance Italy: Giotto's *Stigmatization of Saint Francis* and its Pisan Context', *Art History*, 36 (2013), pp. 686–713

Cooper 2018
D. Cooper, 'Windows, Light and Worldly Space in Italian Annunciation Imagery around 1300', in S. Panayotova and P. Ricciardi (eds), *Manuscripts in the Making: Art and Science*, vol. 2, London 2018, pp. 15–22

Cooper 2021
D. Cooper, 'Fra Jacopo in the Archives: San Gimignano as a Context for the *Meditations on the Life of Christ*', in Flora and Tóth 2021, pp. 17–42

Cooper 2022
D. Cooper, 'The Siena Connection: A Franciscan Provincial Minister between Tuscany and Assisi at the Dawn of the Trecento', in Cooper and Williamson 2022, pp. 89–110

Cooper 2024 (forthcoming)
D. Cooper, 'Reconstructing San Francesco, Cortona: Archival Archaeology and the Medieval Church Interior', in Allegri and Giura 2024 (forthcoming)

Cooper and Robson 2013
D. Cooper and J. Robson, *The Making of Assisi: The Pope, the Franciscans, and the Painting of the Basilica*, New Haven and London 2013

Cooper and Williamson 2022
D. Cooper and B. Williamson (eds), *Late Medieval Italian Art and Its Contexts: Essays in Honour of Professor Joanna Cannon*, Woodbridge 2022

Coor-Achenbach 1961
G. Coor-Achenbach, 'Two Unknown Paintings by the Master of the Glorification of St Thomas and Some Closely Related Works', *Pantheon*, 19 (1961), pp. 126–35

Cormack 2000–1
R. Cormack, 'The Mother of God in the Mosaics of Hagia Sophia at Constantinople', in Athens 2000–1, pp. 107–23

Cornelison 1998
S.J. Cornelison, 'Art and Devotion in Late Medieval and Renaissance Florence: The Relics and Reliquaries of Saints Zenobius and John the Baptist', PhD dissertation, The Courtauld Institute of Art, London 1998

Cornelison 2021
S.J. Cornelison, 'Art and Religion in Late Renaissance Arezzo: Reconsidering Vasari's Church Renovations', in P. Howard, N. Terpstra and R. Saccenti (eds), *Renaissance Religions: Modes and Meanings in History*, Turnhout 2021, pp. 301–23

Corrie 1990
R. Corrie, 'The Political Meaning of Coppo di Marcovaldo's Madonna and Child in Siena', *Gesta*, 29 (1990), pp. 61–75

Corrie 1996
R. Corrie, 'Coppo di Marcovaldo's *Madonna del Bordone* and the Meaning of the Bare-Legged Christ Child in Siena and the East', *Gesta*, 35 (1996), pp. 43–65

Courtauld 1979
General Catalogue of the Courtauld Institute Galleries, with an introduction by A. Blunt, London 1979

Cros Gutiérrez 2008
A. Cros Gutiérrez, 'The Artistic Patronage of Gil de Albornoz (1302–1367), A Cardinal In Context', PhD thesis, University of Warwick, 2008, 2 vols, vol. 1

Crowe and Cavalcaselle 1864–6
J.A. Crowe and G.B. Cavalcaselle, *A New History of Painting in Italy, from the Second to the Sixteenth Century*, 3 vols, London 1864–6

Crowe and Cavalcaselle 1885
J.A. Crowe and G.B. Cavalcaselle, *Storia della pittura in Italia. Dal secolo II al secolo XVI*, vol. 3, *I pittori della scuola senese nel secolo XIV e ne' primi anni del seguente, ed alcuni altri di Pisa e di Lucca seguaci di quella maniera*, Florence 1885

Currie 2009
C. Currie, 'Genesis of a Pre-Eyckian Masterpiece: Melchior Broederlam's Painted Wings for the *Crucifixion Altarpiece*', in Stroo 2009, vol. 2, *Essays*, pp. 23–86

D'Accone 1997
F.A. D'Accone, *The Civic Muse: Music and Musicians in Siena during the Middle Ages and the Renaissance*, Chicago and London 1997

Dale 1984
S. Dale, 'Lippo Vanni: Style and Iconography', PhD dissertation, Rutgers University, New Jersey 1984

Dalton 1912
O.M. Dalton, *Catalogue of the McClean Bequest: The Fitzwilliam Museum*, Cambridge 1912

Dáňová, Chlumská and Šefců 2017
H. Dáňová, Š. Chlumská and R. Šefců (eds), *For the Eyes to Admire: Decorative Techniques in Painting and Sculpture, 14th–16th Century*, Prague 2017

Davies 2009
G. Davies, '"Omnes et singuli aurifices": Guild Regulations and the Chalice Trade in Central Italy c. 1250–1500', in H. Maginnis and S. Zuraw (eds), *The Historian's Eye: Essays on Italian Art in Honor of Andrew Ladis*, Athens, GA 2009, pp. 33–44

Davies 2014
G. Davies, 'The Chalice in Central Italy 1250–1500: Making, Ownership, Use', PhD dissertation, The Courtauld Institute of Art, London 2014

Davies 2022
G. Davies, 'Guccio di Mannaia and the Concept of a "Franciscan" Chalice', in Cooper and Williamson 2022, pp. 51–68

Davies 1986
M. Davies, *National Gallery Catalogues: The Earlier Italian Schools*, London 1986

De Benedictis 1974
C. De Benedictis, 'Naddo Ceccarelli', *Commentari*, 25 (1974), pp. 139–54

De Benedictis 1976
C. De Benedictis, 'Il polittico della passione di Simone Martini e una proposta per Donato', *Antichità Viva*, 15 (1976), pp. 3–11

De Benedictis 1979
C. De Benedictis, *La pittura senese 1330–1370*, Florence 1979

De Dalmases 1992
N. de Dalmases, *Orfebreria catalane medieval: Barcelona 1300–1500 (aproximació a l'estudi)*, Barcelona 1992

Degenhart and Schmitt 1968
B. Degenhart and A. Schmitt, *Corpus der italienischen Zeichnungen, 1300–1450*, vol. 1, Berlin 1968

De Giorgio 2021
T. De Giorgio, 'Una scultura seriale della bottega di Tino di Camaino appartenuta all'Infanta Maria Apollonia di Savoia: la Madonna delle grazie del Museo Diocesano di Torino', *Napoli Nobilissima*, 7, no. 1 (2021), pp. 5–13

Dehaisnes 1886
M. le Chanoine Dehaisnes, *Documents et extraits divers concernant l'histoire de l'art dans la Flandre, l'Artois et le Hainaut avant le XV siècle, II, 1374–1401*, Lille 1886

DeLancey 2010
J.A. DeLancey, 'Shipping Colour: *Valute*, Pigments, Trade and Francesco di Marco Datini', in Kirby, Nash and Cannon 2010, pp. 74–85

Della Valle 1785
G. della Valle, *Lettere senesi sopra le belle arti*, Siena 1785

Del Punta and Rosati 2017
I. Del Punta and M.L. Rosati, *Lucca, una città di seta: produzione, commercio e diffusione dei tessuti lucchesi nel tardo medioevo*, Lucca 2017

De Marchi 2004
A. De Marchi, 'La tavola d'altare', in M. Seidel (ed.), *Storia delle arti in Toscana: il Trecento*, Florence 2004, pp. 15–44

De Marchi 2006
A. De Marchi, 'La parte di Simone e la parte di Lippo', *Nuovi Studi. Rivista di arte antica e moderna*, 11 (2006), pp. 5–24

De Marchi 2009
A. De Marchi, '"Cum dictum opus sit magnum": il documento pistoiese del 1274 e l'allestimento trionfale dei tramezzi in Umbria e Toscana fra Due e Trecento', in A.C. Quintavalle (ed.), *Medioevo: immagine e memoria*, Milan 2009, pp. 603–21

De Marchi 2010
A. De Marchi, 'Partimenti assisati: il Maestro di Figline e la sua bottega', in A.C. Quintavalle (ed.), *Medioevo: le officine*, Milan 2010, pp. 623–34

De Marchi 2016
A. De Marchi, 'Una rilettura del ciclo duecentesco nella chiesa inferiore del Duomo di Siena nella prospettiva della Maestà di Duccio', *Ricerche di storia dell'arte*, 120 (2016), pp. 33–46

De Marchi 2021
A. De Marchi, 'L'eredità della "Maestà" di Duccio nel polittico pisano di Simone', *Bollettino d'arte*, 49 (2021), pp. 15–32

De Marchi 2024 (forthcoming)
A. De Marchi, 'Pietro Lorenzetti a Cortona, sulla strada di Assisi', in Allegri and Giura 2024 (forthcoming)

Demaria 2021
C. Demaria, 'Un contesto per la pala di Umiltà da Faenza di Pietro Lorenzetti', *Arte Cristiana*, 109, no. 924 (2021), pp. 166–77

De Nicola 1906
G. de Nicola, 'L'affresco di Simone Martini ad Avignone', *L'Arte*, 9 (1906), pp. 336–44

Denny 1967
D. Denny, 'Simone Martini's "The Holy Family"', *Journal of the Warburg and Courtauld Institutes*, 30 (1967), pp. 138–49

Denny 2014
W.B. Denny, *How to Read Islamic Carpets*, New Haven and London 2014

Dent 2005
P. Dent, 'The Body of Christ in Fourteenth-century Tuscan Sculpture', PhD dissertation, The Courtauld Institute of Art, London 2005

Dent 2007
P. Dent, 'Contemplative Relief: Meditating on Christ through Sculptural Form in Early Trecento Italy', in D. Cooper and M. Leino (eds), *Depth of Field: Relief Sculpture in Renaissance Italy*, Oxford 2007, pp. 41–69

Dent 2008
P. Dent, '"Laude Dei Trini": Observations towards a Reconstruction of Giovanni Pisano's Pistoia Pulpit', *Journal of the Warburg and Courtauld Institutes*, 71 (2008), pp. 121–38

Dent 2011
P. Dent, '"[P]er concorrenza d'uno [...] da un Tedesco": Giovanni Pisano, Vasari, and the Competitive Motive at Pistoia, c. 1301', *Zeitschrift für Kunstgeschichte*, 74, no. 1 (2011), pp. 29–44

Dent 2017
P. Dent, '"A window for the pain": Surface, Interiority and Christ's Flagellated Skin in Late Medieval Sculpture', in L. Tracy (ed.), *Flaying in the Pre-Modern World: Practice and Representation*, Cambridge 2017, pp. 208–39

Derbes 1989
A. Derbes, 'Siena and the Levant in the Later Dugento', *Gesta*, 28 (1989), pp. 190–204

Derbes 1996
A. Derbes, *Picturing the Passion in Late Medieval Italy: Narrative Painting, Franciscan Ideologies, and the Levant*, New York and Cambridge 1996

Derbes and Neff 2023
A. Derbes and A. Neff, 'The Santa Clara Passion Panel and the Poor Clares of Palma de Mallorca: A Preliminary Report', *Specula*, 5 (2023), pp. 95–120, https://doi.org/10.46583/specula_2023.1.1096 (accessed 29 November 2023)

Desrosiers et al. 2004
S. Desrosiers, with G. Cornu, V. Huchard, F. Valantin and T. Bouzid, *Soieries et autres textiles de l'antiquité au XVIe siècle, Musée de Cluny, Musée National du Moyen Âge, Catalogue*, Paris 2004

De Torquat 2007
A. de Torquat, 'A Fourteenth-Century Painted Reliquary Attributed to Bartolo di Fredi with Two Inserted Ivories', MA dissertation, The Courtauld Institute of Art, London 2007

Detroit and Baltimore 2007
P. Barnet (ed.), *Images in Ivory: Precious Objects of the Gothic Age*, exh. cat., Detroit Institute of Arts, Detroit; Walters Art Museum, Baltimore 1997

Deuchler 1984
F. Deuchler, *Duccio*, Milan 1984

Devillers 1881
L. Devillers, *Cartulaire des comtes de Hainaut*, vol. 1, Brussels 1881

Devon 1837
F. Devon, *Issues of the Exchequer. A Collection of Payments Made Out of His Majesty's Revenue from King Henry III to King Henry VI Inclusive*, London 1837

De Voragine 2012
J. de Voragine, *The Golden Legend: Readings on the Saints*, trans. W.G. Ryan, Princeton 2012

DeWald 1955
E. DeWald, 'Observations on Duccio's Maestà', in K. Weitzmann (ed.), *Late Classical and Mediaeval Studies in Honor of Albert Mathias Friend, Jr.*, Princeton 1955, pp. 363–86

De Wesselow 2000
T. De Wesselow, 'Ambrogio Lorenzetti's "Mappamondo": A Fourteenth-Century Picture of the World Painted on Cloth', in C. Villers (ed.), *The Fabric of Images: European Paintings on Textile Supports in the Fourteenth and Fifteenth Centuries*, London 2000, pp. 55–65

De Wesselow 2004
T. De Wesselow, 'The "Guidoriccio" Fresco: A New Attribution', *Apollo*, 159, no. 505 (2004), pp. 3–12

De Wesselow 2022
T. De Wesselow, 'Simone Martini's "Treaty with the House of Santa Fiora" in Siena's Palazzo Pubblico: Its Date and Significance', in Cooper and Williamson 2022, pp. 111–31

Dietl 2009
A. Dietl, *Die Sprache der Signatur: Die mittelalterlichen Künstlerinschriften Italiens*, Berlin 2009

Dijon and Cleveland 2004–5
S. Fliegel, S. Jugie and V. Barthélémy (eds), *Art from the Court of Burgundy: The Patronage of Philip the Bold and John the Fearless, 1364–1419*, exh. cat., Musée des Beaux-Arts, Dijon 2004; The Cleveland Museum of Art, Cleveland 2004–5

Di Simone 2017
P. Di Simone, 'La "Maestà con i Santi Quattro Coronati" di Simone Martini ritrovata: un disegno per Seroux d'Agincourt', *Nuovi Studi. Rivista di arte antica e moderna*, 23 (2017), pp. 39–60

Distefano 2021
G. Distefano, *Esmaltis viridibus. Lo smalto de plique tra XIII e XIV secolo*, Savigliano 2021

Donato 2003
M.M. Donato, '*Kunstlerliteratur* monumentale: qualche riflessione e un progetto per la firma d'artista, dal medioevo al rinascimento', *Letteratura & arte*, 1 (2003), pp. 23–47

Donato 2011–12
M.M. Donato (ed.), 'Opera firmate nell'arte italiana/Medioevo: Siena e artisti senesi. Maestri orafi', special issue of *Opera. Nomina. Historiae: Giornale di cultura artisticai*, 5–6 (2011–12), pp. 1–399

Dorini 1942
U. Dorini (ed.), *Statuti dell'arte di Por Santa Maria del tempo della Repubblica*, Florence 1942

Douglas 1927
R.L. Douglas, 'I dipinti senesi della collezione Benson passati da Londra in America', *La Balzana: Bollettino di statistica e di attività municipale*, 1, no. 3 (1927), pp. 3–9

Douglas 1940
R.L. Douglas, *The Collection of Frank Channing Smith, Jr.*, Worcester, MA 1940

Droandi 2005
I. Droandi, 'Pittori "forestieri" ad Arezzo', in A. Galli and P. Refice (eds), *Arte in terra d'Arezzo. Il Trecento*, Florence 2005, pp. 41–56

Dückers 2005
R. Dückers, 'In the Beginning ... The Bible Moralisée and the Work of the Limbourg Brothers', in Nijmegen 2005, pp. 85–96

Dumoutet 1926
É. Dumoutet, *Le Désir de voir l'hostie: et les origines de la devotion au Saint-Sacrement*, Paris 1926

Dunkerton et al. 1991
J. Dunkerton, S. Foister, D. Gordon and N. Penny, *Giotto to Dürer: Early Renaissance Painting in The National Gallery*, London 1991

Dunlop 2000
A. Dunlop, 'Once more on the Patronage of Ambrogio Lorenzetti's Frescoes at S. Galagano, Montesiepi', *Zeitschrift fur Kunstgeschichte*, 63 (2000), pp. 387–403

Durand 2004
J. Durand, 'Precious-Metal Icon Revetments', in New York 2004, pp. 243–51

Durrieu 1904
P. Durrieu, *Les Très Riches Heures de Jean de France, duc de Berry*, Paris 1904

D'Urso 1991
G. D'Urso, 'Simone Martini, il polittico Orsini e il suo committente', *Prospettiva*, 63 (1991), pp. 48–50

Edgell 1924
G.H. Edgell, 'The Boston Mystic Marriage of St Catherine and Five More Panels by Barna Senese', *Art in America*, 12 (1924), pp. 49–52

Edgell 1951
G.H. Edgell, 'R. Langton Douglas', *College Arts Association*, 11, no. 2 (1951), p. 134

Egidi 1908
P. Egidi, *Necrologi e libri affini della provincia romana. Fonti per la Storia d'Italia*, vol. 1, Rome 1908

Ehrle 1885
F. Ehrle, 'Zur Geschichte des Schatzes, der Bibliothek und der Archivs der Päpste in vierzehnten Jahrundert. Die ghibellinische Schilderhebung in Assisi und Beraubung des päpstlichen Schatzes, 1319', *Archiv für Literatur- und Kirchengeschichte des Mittelalters*, 1 (1885), pp. 228–364

Ehrle 1889
F. Ehrle, 'Zur Geschichte des päpstlichen Hofceremoniells im 14. Jahrhundert', *Archiv für Literatur- und Kirchengeschichte des Mittelalters*, 5 (1889), pp. 565–602

Eisenberg 1981
M. Eisenberg. 'The First Altar-piece for the "Cappella de'Signori" of the Palazzo Pubblico in Siena: "... tales figure sunt adeo pulcre ..."', *The Burlington Magazine*, 123 (1981), pp. 134–48

Ekhtiar et al. 2011
M. Ekhtiar, P.P. Soucek, S.R. Canby and N. Haidar (eds), *Masterpieces from the Department of Islamic Art in The Metropolitan Museum of Art*, New York 2011

Elliott 2000
D.B. Elliott, *Charles Fairfax Murray: The Unknown Pre-Raphaelite*, Lewes 2000

Enaud 1963
F. Enaud, 'Les fresques de Simone Martini à Avignon', *Les Monuments historiques de la France*, 9 (1963), pp. 115–80

English 2005
E.D. English, 'Medieval and Renaissance Siena and Tuscany c.1900. Civic Life, Religion and the Countryside', in J.E. Law and L. Ostermark-Johansen (eds), *Victorian and Edwardian Responses to the Italian Renaissance*, Aldershot 2005, pp. 281–96

Ercoli 1980
G. Ercoli, 'Il Trecento senese nei Commentari di Lorenzo Ghiberti', in *Lorenzo Ghiberti nel suo tempo. Atti del Convegno internazionale di studi (Firenze 18–21 ottobre 1978)*, Florence 1980, vol. 1, pp. 317–41

Ermini 2016
G. Ermini, '"In mano di Mario". Notizie inedite e nuovi argomenti per Ambrogio Lorenzetti e gli orafi senesi del Trecento', *Prospettiva*, 161–2 (2016), pp. 104–21

Fabretti 1850
A. Fabretti (ed.), 'Brevi annali della Città di Perugia (1194–1352)', *Archivio storico italiano*, 16 (1850), pp. 53–68

Fahy 1978
E. Fahy, 'Italian Painting before 1500', *Apollo*, 107, no. 195 (1978), pp. 377–88

Fajt 2005–6
J. Fajt, 'Towards a New Imperial Style', in New York and Prague 2005–6, pp. 3–21

Fattorini 2010
G. Fattorini, 'La lezione trecentesca e le immagini dell'indentità civica', in Siena 2010, pp. 142–7

Fehlmann and Freuler 2002
M. Fehlmann and G. Freuler, *Die Sammlung Adolf von Stürler*, Bern 2002

Fehrenbach 2020a
F. Fehrenbach, 'The Colors of Monochrome Sculpture', in A.R. Bloch and D.M. Zolli (eds), *The Art of Sculpture in Fifteenth-century Italy*, Cambridge 2020, pp. 64–82

Fehrenbach 2020b
F. Fehrenbach, 'The Most Difficult of All: The Life and Death of Italian Tomb Sculpture, c. 1280–1490', in G. Borggreen, M.F. Hansen and R. Tindbæk (eds), *Dead or Alive! Tracing the Animation of Matter in Art and Visual Culture*, Aarhus 2020, pp. 65–94

Feliciano 2005
M.J. Feliciano, 'Muslim Shrouds for Christian Kings? A Reassessment of Andalusī Textiles in Thirteenth-century Castilian Life and Ritual', in C. Robinson and L. Rouhi (eds),

Under the Influence: Questioning the Comparative in Medieval Castile, Leiden 2005, pp. 101–31

Feltman and Thompson 2019
J. Feltman and S. Thompson (eds), *The Long Lives of Medieval Art and Architecture*, London 2019

Ferber 1984
S.H. Ferber, 'Jean Pucelle and Giovanni Pisano', *The Art Bulletin*, 66, no. 1 (1984), pp. 65–72

Ferguson 1954 (1961)
G. Ferguson, *Signs & Symbols in Christian Art*, New York 1954 (1961)

Ferrante 2018
D. Ferrante, 'Reopening the Boston Duccio: The Triptych in the Museum of Fine Arts', MA dissertation, The Courtauld Institute of Art, London 2018

Ferrante 2016
G. Ferrante, *Il libro di Luigi di Ridolfo Peruzzi*, Bologna 2016

Fleck 2008
C. Fleck, 'The Rise of the Court Artist: Cavallini and Giotto in Fourteenth-century Naples', *Art History*, 31 (2008), pp. 460–83

Flora 2018
H. Flora, *Cimabue and the Franciscans*, Turnhout 2018

Flora and Tóth 2021
H. Flora and P. Tóth (eds), *The 'Meditationes Vitae Christi' Reconsidered: New Perspectives on Text and Image*, Turnhout 2021

Florence 2015
B. Chiesi, I. Ciseri and B. Paolozzi Strozzi (eds), *Il medioevo in viaggio*, exh. cat., Museo Nazionale del Bargello, Florence 2015

Florence 2017
C. Hollberg (ed.), *Textiles and Wealth in 14th-century Florence: Wool, Silk, Painting*, exh. cat., Galleria dell'Accademia, Florence 2017

Folda 2015
J. Folda, *Byzantine Art and Italian Panel Painting: The Virgin and Child Hodegetria and the Art of Chrysography*, New York 2015

Fontana 2002
V.M. Fontana, 'The Pseudo-epigraphic Characters', in Ciatti and Seidel 2002, pp. 217–25

Forte 1967
S.L. Forte, 'Il card. Matteo Orsini O.P. e il suo testamento', *Archivum Fratrum Praedicatorum*, 37 (1967), pp. 181–262

Fowles 1976
E. Fowles, *Memories of Duveen Brothers*, London 1976

Fozi 2021
S. Fozi, *Romanesque Tomb Effigies: Death and Redemption in Medieval Europe, 1000–1200*, University Park, PA 2021

Francis 1955
H.S. Francis, 'A Fourteen-century "Annunciation"', *Bulletin of the Cleveland Museum of Art*, 42, no. 10 (1955), pp. 215–19

Franco 2021
B. Franco, 'The Significance of Montaperti', in S. Casciani and H. Richardson Hayton, *A Companion to Late Medieval and Early Modern Siena*, Leiden 2021, pp. 31–50

Fraser 2014
H. Fraser, 'Vasari's Lives and the Victorians', in D. Cast (ed.), *The Ashgate Research Companion to Giorgio Vasari*, Burlington, VT 2014, pp. 277–94

Frattaroli 2009–10
P. Frattaroli, 'The Textile Decorations of Giotto, Simone Martini and Their Schools', *Text*, 37 (2009–10), pp. 35–48

Freni 2000a
G. Freni, 'The Arentine Polyptych by Pietro Lorenzetti: Patronage, Iconography and Original Setting', *Journal of the Warburg and Courtauld Institutes*, 63 (2000), pp. 59–110

Freni 2000b
G. Freni, 'The Reliquary of the Holy Corporal in the Cathedral of Orvieto: Patronage and Politics', in Cannon and Williamson 2000, pp. 117–78

Freni 2001
G. Freni, 'The Aretine Polyptych by Pietro Lorenzetti: Patronage, Iconography and Original Setting', *Journal of the Warburg and Courtauld Institutes*, 63 (2000), pp. 59–110

Freuler 1981
G. Freuler, 'Die Fresken des Biagio di Goro Ghezzi in S. Michele in Paganico', *Mitteilungen des Kunsthistorischen Institutes in Florenz*, 25 (1981), pp. 31–58

Freuler 1994
G. Freuler, *Bartolo di Fredi Cini: ein Beitrag zur sienesischen Malerei des 14. Jahrhunderts*, Disentis 1994

Freuler 1997
G. Freuler, *Corpus of Florentine Painting: Tendencies of Gothic in Florence: Don Silvestro dei Gherarducci*, ed. M. Boskovits, Florence 1997

Freuler 2001
G. Freuler, 'Duccio et ses contemporains. La Maître de Città di Castello', *Revue de l'Art*, no. 134 (2001), pp. 27–50

Frick 1968
The Frick Collection: An Illustrated Catalogue, New York 1968

Frinta 1965
M. Frinta, 'An Investigation of the Punched Decoration of Mediaeval Italian and Non-Italian Panel Paintings', *The Art Bulletin*, 47, no. 2 (1965), pp. 261–5

Frinta 1971
M.S. Frinta, 'Note on the Punched Decoration of Two Early Painted Panels at the Fogg Art Museum: *St Dominic* and the *Crucifixion*', *The Art Bulletin*, 53, no. 3 (1971), pp. 306–9

Frinta 1998
M.S. Frinta, *Punched Decoration on Late Medieval Panel and Miniature Painting*, Prague 1998

Frugoni 1988
C. Frugoni, *Pietro and Ambrogio Lorenzetti*, New York 1988

Frugoni 2002
C. Frugoni (ed.), *Pietro e Ambrogio Lorenzetti*, Florence 2002

Gaborit-Chopin 1996
D. Gaborit-Chopin, 'Guillaume Julien et Compagnie', in A. Calderoni-Masetti (ed.), *Studi di oreficeria*, supplement to *Bollettino d'Arte*, series 6, 81, no. 95 (1996), pp. 71–83

Gaborit-Chopin 1999
D. Gaborit-Chopin, 'L'orfèvrerie émaillée à Paris vers 1300', *Bulletin archéologique du Comité des Travaux Historiques et Scientifiques. Moyen Âge, renaissance, temps modernes*, 27 (1999), pp. 81–101

Gaborit-Chopin 2013–14
D. Gaborit-Chopin, 'Documents et oeuvres d'art. Remarques sur quelques ivoires gothiques français', *Cahiers archéologiques*, 55 (2013–14), pp. 119–30

Gardner 1967
J. Gardner, 'The Ivories in the Gambier-Parry Collection', *The Burlington Magazine*, 109 (1967), pp. 139–44

Gardner 1976
J. Gardner, 'Saint Louis of Toulouse, Robert of Anjou and Simone Martini', *Zeitschrift für Kunstgeschichte*, 39, no. 1 (1976), pp. 12–33

Gardner 1981
J. Gardner, 'Some Franciscan Altars of the 13th and 14th Centuries', in A. Borg and A. Martindale (eds), *The Vanishing Past: Studies of Medieval Art, Liturgy and Metrology Presented to Christopher Hohler*, Oxford 1981, pp. 29–38

Gardner 1990a
J. Gardner, 'The Back of the Panel of Christ Discovered in the Temple by Simone Martini', *Arte Cristiana*, 78 (1990), pp. 389–98

Gardner 1990b
J. Gardner, 'The French Connection: Thoughts about French Patrons and Italian Art, c. 1250–1300', in C.M. Rosenberg (ed.), *Art and Politics in Late Medieval and Early Renaissance Italy: 1250–1500*, Notre Dame, IN 1990, pp. 81–102

Gardner 1994
J. Gardner, 'Altars, Altarpieces, and Art History: Legislation and Usage', in Borsook and Superbi Gioffredi 1994, pp. 5–39

Gardner 2001–2
J. Gardner, 'The Artistic Patronage of Boniface VIII: The Perugian Inventory of the Papal Treasure of 1311', *Römisches Jahrbuch der Bibliotheca Hertziana*, 34 (2001–2), pp. 69–86

Gardner 2008
J. Gardner, 'Thirteenth-century Gothic Façades in Italy', in A. Quintavalle (ed.), *Medioevo: arte e storia. Atti del convegno internazionale di studi Parma 2007*, Milan 2008, pp. 669–80

Gardner von Teuffel 1979
C. Gardner von Teuffel, 'The Buttressed Altarpiece: A Forgotten Aspect of Tuscan Fourteenth Century Altarpiece Design', *Jahrbuch der Berliner Museen*, 21 (1979), pp. 21–65

Gardner von Teuffel 1985
C. Gardner von Teuffel, 'Review of H. van Os, *Sienese Altarpieces 1215–1460*, vol. I, Groningen 1984', *The Burlington Magazine*, 127 (1985), p. 391

Gardner von Teuffel 2004
C. Gardner von Teuffel, 'Carpenteria e macchine d'altare: per la storia della ricostruzione delle pale di San Pietro e di Sant'Agostino a Perugia', in V. Garibaldi and F.F. Mancini (eds), *Perugino: il divin pittore*, exh. cat., Galleria Nazionale dell'Umbria, Perugia 2004, pp. 141–53

Gardner von Teuffel 2005
C. Gardner von Teuffel, *From Duccio's Maestà to Raphael's Transfiguration: Italian Altarpieces and Their Settings*, London 2005

Gardner von Teuffel 2006
C. Gardner von Teuffel, 'Review of S. Weppelmann (ed.), *Geschichten auf Gold: Bilderzählungen in der frühen italienischen Malerei*, Gemäldegalerie, Berlin 2005', *The Burlington Magazine*, 148 (2006), pp. 217–20

Gardner von Teuffel 2009
C. Gardner von Teuffel, 'Sassetta's Franciscan Altarpiece at Borgo San Sepolcro: Precedents and Context', in Israëls 2009, vol. 1, pp. 210–29

Gardner von Teuffel 2010
C. Gardner von Teuffel, 'Piero della Francesca. La Madonna della Misericordia: i contratti artistici: esame e contestualizzazione', in Betti, Frosinini and Refice 2010, pp. 71–84

Gardner von Teuffel 2015
C. Gardner von Teuffel, 'The Carmelite Altarpiece (circa 1290–1550): The Self-identification of an Order', *Mitteilungen des Kunsthistorischen Institutes in Florenz*, 57 (2015), pp. 3–41

Gardner von Teuffel 2021
C. Gardner von Teuffel, 'Reconstruction, Construction, and Deconstruction of Late Medieval Sienese Altarpieces from Ugolino di Nerio to Sassetta: A Reassessment', *Jahrbuch der Berliner Museen*, NF 62 (2021), pp. 7–26

Gardner von Teuffel (forthcoming)
C. Gardner von Teuffel, 'Botticelli, Ugolino di Nerio and a Sassetti Memorial Portrait' (forthcoming)

Garibaldi 2015
V. Garibaldi, *Galleria Nazionale dell'Umbria: dipinti e sculture dal XIII al XV secolo, catalogo generale I*, Perugia 2015

Garrison 1949
E.B. Garrison, *Italian Romanesque Panel Painting: An Illustrated Index*, Florence 1949

Gauthier 1972
M.-M. Gauthier, *Émaux du Moyen Age occidental*, Paris 1972

Gauthier 1983
M.-M. Gauthier, 'Il tesoro di Bonifacio VIII', in Romanini 1983, pp. 529–35

Gérard-Marchant 2013
L. Gérard-Marchant, *Draghi rossi e querce azzurre: elenchi descritivi di abito di lusso (Firenze 1343–1345)*, Florence 2013

Gerevini 2022
S. Gerevini, 'Artistic Appropriation, Institutional Identity, and Civic Religion in Fourteenth-century Siena: The Byzantine Treasury of the Hospital of Santa Maria della Scala', in Cooper and Williamson 2022, pp. 249–69

Gheusi 1933
P.-B. Gheusi, *Le Blason. Théorie nouvelle de l'art héraldique. Traité complet de la science des armoiries d'après les règles et les figures du moyen âge, avec les dessins de l'auteur*, Paris 1933

Ghiberti before 1455 (1998)
L. Ghiberti, *I commentarii (Biblioteca Nazionale Centrale di Firenze, II, I, 333)*, ed. L. Bartoli, Florence 1998

Gibbs 1989
R. Gibbs, *Tomaso da Modena*, Cambridge 1989

Gifford 1995
E.M. Gifford, 'A Pre-Eyckian Altarpiece in the Context of European Painting Materials and Technique around 1400', in Smeyers and Cardon 1995, pp. 357–70

Gillerman 2001
D. Gillerman (ed.), *Gothic Sculpture in America: II. Museums in the Midwest*, Turnhout 2001

Giorgi 2003–4
S. Giorgi, 'Guido da Siena', in Siena 2003–4, pp. 60–1

Giorgi and Moscadelli 2005
A. Giorgi and S. Moscadelli, *Costruire una cattedrale. L'Opera di Santa Maria di Siena tra XII e XIV secolo*, Munich 2005

Giorgi and Moscadelli 2017–18
A. Giorgi and S. Moscadelli, '"Dixit sua sapientia verba": Documenti per una biografia di Ambrogio Lorenzetti', in Siena 2017–18, pp. 473–83

Giura 2018
G. Giura, *San Francesco di Asciano: opere, fonti e contesti per la storia della Toscana francescana*, Florence 2018

Giura 2024 (forthcoming)
G. Giura, 'La chiesa e le fonti. La topografia storico-artistica di San Francesco e la sua decorazione fino alla Controriforma', in Allegri and Giura 2024 (forthcoming)

Gnudi 1956
C. Gnudi, 'Grandezza di Simone', in M. Natale (ed.), *Scritti di storia dell'arte in onore di Lionello Venturi*, 2 vols, Rome 1956, vol. 1, pp. 87–100

Gordon 1981
D. Gordon, 'A Sienese Verre Églomisé and Its Setting', *The Burlington Magazine*, 123 (1981), pp. 132–53

Gordon 1992
D. Gordon, 'A New Discovery in the Wilton Diptych', *The Burlington Magazine*, 134 (1992), pp. 662–7

Gordon 1994
D. Gordon (ed.), *The Wilton Diptych: Making and Meaning*, London 1994

Gordon 2003
D. Gordon, *National Gallery Catalogues: The Fifteenth Century Italian Paintings, 1400–1460*, vol. 1, London 2003

Gordon 2009
D. Gordon, 'Duccio's Adjustment to "The Temptation of Christ on the Mountain" from His "Maestà"', *The Burlington Magazine*, 151 (2009), pp. 19–21

Gordon 2011
D. Gordon, *National Gallery Catalogues: The Italian Paintings before 1400*, London 2011

Gordon 2015
D. Gordon, 'A Possible French Source for the Left Wing of the Wilton Diptych', *The Burlington Magazine*, 157 (2015), pp. 821–6

Gordon et al. 2015
D. Gordon with an essay by C. Barron and contributions by A. Roy, R. Billinge and M. Wyld, *The Wilton Diptych*, London 2015

Gordon, Monnas and Elam 1997
D. Gordon, L. Monnas and C. Elam (eds), *The Regal Image of Richard II and the Wilton Diptych*, London 1997

Gordon and Reeve 1984
D. Gordon and A. Reeve, 'Three Newly-acquired Panels from the Altarpiece for Santa Croce by Ugolino di Nerio: Evidence for the Reconstruction of the Altarpiece', *National Gallery Technical Bulletin*, 8 (1984), pp. 36–45

Gosche 1899
A. Gosche, *Simone Martini*, Leipzig 1899

Gozzoli 1970
M.C. Gozzoli, *L'opera completa di Simone Martini*, Milan 1970

Grabar 1975
A. Grabar, *Les revêtements en or et en argent des icônes byzantines du moyen âge*, Venice 1975

Graham 2013
E.E. Graham, 'Reconsidering Reputation through Patronage: Cardinal Napoleone Orsini and Angelo Clareno at the Avignonese papal court', *Journal of Medieval History*, 39 (2013), pp. 357–75

Granada and New York 1992
J.D. Dodds (ed.), *Al-Andalus: The Art of Islamic Spain*, exh. cat., Alhambra, Granada; The Metropolitan Museum of Art, New York 1992

Grandjean 1905
C. Grandjean (ed.), *Les Registres de Benoît XI: recueil des bulles de ce pape*, Paris 1905

Grandmontagne 2005
M. Grandmontagne, *Claus Sluter und die Lesbarkeit mittelalterlicher Skulptur: das Portal der Kartause von Champmol*, Worms 2005

Gubbio 2018
G. Benazzi, E. Lunghi and E. Neri Lusanna (eds), *Gubbio al tempo di Giotto: tesori d'arte nella terra di Oderisi*, exh. cat., Palazzo dei Consoli, Museo diocesano, Palazzo ducale, Gubbio 2018

Guérin 2010
S.M. Guérin, '*Avorio d'ogni ragione*: The Supply of Elephant Ivory to Northern Europe in the Gothic Era', *Journal of Medieval History*, 36 (2010), pp. 156–74

Guérin 2012
S.M. Guérin, 'An Ivory Virgin at the Metropolitan Museum, New York, in a Gothic Sculptor's Oeuvre', *The Burlington Magazine*, 154 (2012), pp. 394–402

Guérin 2013
S.M. Guérin, 'Meaningful Spectacles: Gothic Ivories Staging

the Divine', *The Art Bulletin*, 95, no. 1 (2013), pp. 53–77

Guérin 2019
S.M. Guérin, 'Gold, Ivory, and Copper: Materials and Arts of Trans-Saharan Trade', in K.B. Berzock (ed.), *Caravans of Gold, Fragments in Time: Art, Culture, and Exchange across Medieval Saharan Africa*, exh. cat., Block Museum of Art, Northwestern University, Evanston, Princeton 2019, pp. 175–201

Guérin 2022
S.M. Guérin, *French Gothic Ivories: Material Theologies and the Sculptor's Craft*, Cambridge and New York 2022

Guérin (forthcoming)
S.M. Guérin, 'Reaching for the Stars: Failed Enamels c. 1300', in *Process of Failure: The Importance of Making Mistakes in Early Modern Art*, special issue of *Oxford Art Journal* (forthcoming)

Guerrini 1988
A. Guerrini, 'Intorno al polittico di Pietro Lorenzetti per la pieve di Arezzo', *Rivista d'Arte: studi documentari per la storia delle arti in Toscana*, 40 (1988), pp. 3–29

Guerrini and Seidel 2003
R. Guerrini and M. Seidel (eds), *Sotto il duomo di Siena: Scoperte archeologiche, architettoniche e figurative*, Siena and Milan 2003

Guiffrey 1894–6
J. Guiffrey, *Inventaires de Jean Duc de Berry (1401–1416)*, Paris 1894–6

Guillemain 1979
B. Guillemain, 'Une grande ville d'Occident au XIVe siècle', in S. Gagnière et al., *Histoire d'Avignon*, Aix-en-Provence 1979, pp. 215–32

Guillouët and Vilain 2018
J.-M. Guillouët and A.Vilain (eds), *Microarchitectures médiévales: l'échelle à l'épreuve de la matière*, Paris 2018

Haas and von Winterfeld 2006
W. Haas and D. von Winterfeld (eds), *Die Kirchen von Siena, 3: Der Dom S. Maria Assunta, 1: Architektur, pt. 1*, Munich 2006

Hager 1962
H. Hager, *Die Anfänge des italienischen Altarbildes: Untersuchungen zur Enstehungsgeschichte des toskanischen Hochaltarretabels*, Munich 1962

Hallé 1909
C.E. Hallé, *Notes from a Painter's Life*, London 1909

Hamburg 2011–12
M. Philipp (ed.), *Die Erfindung des Bildes: Frühe italienische Meister bis Botticelli*, exh. cat., Bucerius Kunst Forum, Hamburg 2011–12

Hamburg and Stuttgart 1993
H. Kirchheim, M. Franses, F. Spuhler, G. Muse, J. Rageth and E. Herrmann, *Orient stars: A Carpet Collection*, exh. cat., Deichtorhallen, Hamburg; Linden-Museum, Stuttgart, 1993

Hamburger (forthcoming)
J.F. Hamburger, *Flesh and Fabric: The Raiment of the Passion in a Crucifixion by Pietro Lorenzetti*, with a technical examination by C. Morilla, A. Miller and K. Holder, Cambridge, MA and Florence (forthcoming)

Hamsík 1967 (1989)
M. Hamsík, 'Die Technik der böhmischen Tafelmaleri des 14. Jarhunderts', in E. Hütter, H. Magirius and F. Löffler (eds), *Kunst des Mittelalters in Sachsen. Festschrift Wolf Schubert. Dargebracht zum 60 Geburtstag am 28 Januar 1963*, Weimar 1967, pp. 321–6 (revised and supplemented in *Technologia Artis*, 1989, https://technologiaartis.org/1malba-drevo-ktech.html, accessed 15 October 2023)

Hamsík 1978
M. Hamsík, 'Die Technik der böhmischen Madonnenbilder um 1350–1360', *Umění*, 25 (1978), pp. 529–34

Hanan 2001
M. Hanan, 'A Reassessment of the Courtauld Gallery's "St Peter as Pope" in the Context of Mid-Trecento Sienese Painting', MA dissertation, The Courtauld Institute of Art, London 2001

Hansen 1993
S. Hansen, *La Loggia della Mercanzia in Siena*, Siena 1993

Haskell 1994
F. Haskell, 'Old Master Exhibitions and the Second "Rediscovery of the Primitives"', in P. Rosenberg, C. Scailliérez and D. Thiébaut (eds), *Hommage à Michel Laclotte: études sur la peinture du Moyen Âge et de la Renaissance*, Milan and Paris 1994, pp. 552–64

Haskell 2000
F. Haskell, *The Ephemeral Museum: Old Master Paintings and the Rise of the Art Exhibition*, New Haven and London 2000

Hayez 1994
J. Hayez, 'La gestion d'une relation épistolaire dans les milieux d'affaires toscans à la fin du Moyen Age', in *La circulation des nouvelles au Moyen Age (Actes des congrès de la Société des historiens médiévistes de l'enseignement supérieur public. 24e congrès, Avignon, 1993)*, Paris 1994, pp. 63–84

Hayez 2012
J. Hayez, 'Il migrante e il padrone. Il palazzo nella vita di Francesco Datini', in J. Hayez and D. Toccafondi (eds), *Palazzo Datini a Prato. Una casa fatta per durare mille anni*, Florence 2012, vol. 1, pp. 168–207

Hemsoll 1998
D. Hemsoll, 'Simone Martini's *St John the Evangelist* Re-examined', *Apollo*, 147, no. 432 (1998), pp. 3–10

Hills 1987
P. Hills, *The Light of Early Italian Painting*, New Haven and London 1987

Hills 2018
P. Hills, *Veiled Presence: Body and Drapery from Giotto to Titian*, New Haven and London 2018

Hindman et al. 1997
S. Hindman, M. Levi d'Ancona, P. Palladino, and M.F. Saffioti, *The Robert Lehman Collection: IV Illuminations*, New York 1997

Hirschbiegel 2003
J. Hirschbiegel, *Étrennes. Untersuchungen zum höfischen Geschenkverkehr im spätmittelalterlichen Frankreich der Zeit König Karls VI (1380–1422)*, Munich 2003

Hoch 1995
A. Hoch, 'The Franciscan Provenance of Simone Martini's Angevin St Louis in Naples', *Zeitschrift für Kunstgeschichte*, 58 (1995), pp. 22–38

Hoeniger 1991
C.S. Hoeniger, 'Cloth of Gold and Silver: Simone Martini's Techniques for Representing Luxury Textiles', *Gesta*, 30, no. 2 (1991), pp. 154–62

Hoeniger 1995
C.S. Hoeniger, *The Renovation of Paintings in Tuscany, 1250–1500*, Cambridge and New York 1995

Hohenfeld 2014
K. Hohenfeld, *Die Madonnenskulpturen des Giovanni Pisano: Stilkritik, Kulturtransfer und Materialimitation*, Weimar 2014

Holcomb 1978
A.M. Holcomb, 'A.-F. Rio, Anna Jameson and Some Sources of the Second Volume of Modern Painters by Ruskin (1846)', *Gazette des Beaux-Arts*, 91 (1978), pp. 35–8

Hook 1979
J. Hook, *Siena: A City and Its History*, London 1979

Hoopes 1926
T.T. Hoopes, 'An Ivory Casket in the Metropolitan Museum of Art', *The Art Bulletin*, 8, no. 3 (1926), pp. 127–39

Hueck 1969
I. Hueck, 'Una crocifissione su marmo del primo Trecento e alcuni smalti senesi', *Antichità viva*, 8, no. 1 (1969), pp. 22–34

Hueck 1982
I. Hueck, 'Pace di Valentino und die Entwicklung des Kelches im Duecento', *Mitteilungen des Kunsthistorischen Institutes in Florenz*, 16, no. 3 (1982), pp. 259–78

Hueck 1983
I. Hueck, 'Il cardinale N. Orsini e la cappella de S. Nicola nella basilica francescana ad Assisi', in Romanini 1983, pp. 187–98

Hueck 1990
I. Hueck, 'La tavola di Duccio e la Compagnia della Laudi di Santa Maria Novella', in *La Maestà di Duccio restaurata*, Florence 1990, pp. 33–46

Hueck 2001
I. Hueck, 'L'Annunciazione e Santi' di Simone Martini e Lippo Memmi', in Cecchi 2001a, pp. 11–33

Hueck 2007
I. Hueck, 'Die Entwicklung des gotischen Messkelchs in Italien und seine Darstellungen in der Malerei', in S. Weppelmann (ed.), *Zeremoniell und Raum in der frühen italienischen Malerei*, Petersberg 2007, pp. 52–9

Husband 2005
T.B. Husband, 'The *Belles Heures* of Jean, duc de Berry. A Visual Analysis', in Nijmegen 2005, pp. 96–111

Hyman 2022
T. Hyman, *Sienese Painting: The Art of a City-Republic (1278–1477)*, London 2022 (2nd edn)
Ilchman 2015
F. Ilchman, 'Boston Collectors in the Wake of "Mrs Jack"', in Reist 2015, pp. 50–9
Inventarium 1892
'Inventarium thesauri Ecclesiae Romanae apud Perusium Asservati issu Clementis Papae V, factum anno MCCCXI', in *Regestum Clementis papae V: ex vaticanis archetypis sanctissimi domini nostri Leonis XIII: Appendices*, vol. 1, Rome 1892, pp. 369–464
Israëls 2006
M. Israëls, 'Altars on the Street: The Wool Guild, the Carmelites and the Feast of Corpus Domini in Siena (1356–1456)', *Renaissance Studies*, 20, no. 2 (2006), pp. 180–200
Israëls 2008
M. Israëls, 'An Angel at Huis Bergh. Clues to the Structure and Function of Duccio's *Maestà*', in A. de Vries (ed.), *Voyages of Discovery in the Collections of Huis Bergh*, 's-Heerenberg 2008, pp. 122–33
Israëls 2009
M. Israëls (ed.), *Sassetta: The Borgo San Sepolcro Altarpiece*, 2 vols, Florence and Leiden 2009
Israëls 2012
M. Israëls, 'La decorazione pittorica dell'Antiporto di Camollia, di Porta Romana e di Porta Pispini a Siena', in E. Pellegrini (ed.), *Fortificare con arte: mura, porte e fortezze nella storia*, Siena 2012, pp. 201–19
Israëls 2015a
M. Brüggen Israëls, 'Attributed to Pietro Lorenzetti: Pinnacle Panel of an Altarpiece: *Saint Mark* (Reconfigured as *Christ the Redeemer* for the Toscanelli Altarpiece)', in Strehlke and Israëls 2015, pp. 379–83
Israëls 2015b
M. Brüggen Israëls, 'The Berensons "Connosh" and Collect Sienese Painting', in Strehlke and Israëls 2015, pp. 47–69
Israëls 2015c
M. Brüggen Israëls, 'The Memmi-Martini Compagnia', in Strehlke and Israëls 2015, pp. 441–3
Israëls 2020
M. Brüggen Israëls, 'Fabbrica e funzionamento delle pale bifronti tra Duecento e Quattrocento', in Perugia 2020, pp. 89–101
Israëls 2022–3
M. Brüggen Israëls, 'A Patron's Painter: Simone Martini at Orvieto', in Boston 2022–3, pp. 124–61
Israëls 2024 (forthcoming)
M. Brüggen Israëls, 'The Stage for Simone Martini's *Saint Louis of Toulouse*', in T. Kennedy and T. Flanigan (eds), *Acts of the Andrew Ladis Memorial Trecento Conference*, Turnhout 2024 (forthcoming)
Israëls et al. 2009
M. Israëls, with contributions from J.R. Banker, R. Bellucci, R. Billinge, G. Bisacca, C. Castelli, C. Frosinini, C. Gardner von Teuffel, B. Hartwieg, E. Ravaud, A. Santacesaria, C.B. Strehlke, D. Thiébaut, S. Urry, 'The Reconstruction of Sassetta's Borgo San Sepolcro Altarpiece', in Israëls 2009, vol. 1, pp. 160–209
Jacobus 2019
L. Jacobus, 'Flying Pigs, Fiery Whirlwinds and a 300-year-old Virgin: Costume and Continuity in a Sacred Performance', in Feltman and Thompson 2019, pp. 47–62
Jacoby 2016
D. Jacoby, 'Oriental Silks at the Time of the Mongols: Patterns of Trade and Distribution in the West', in Von Fircks and Schorta 2016, pp. 92–123
Jansen 2018
K.L. Jansen, *Peace and Penance in Late Medieval Italy*, Princeton and Oxford 2018
Jarrett 1935
B. Jarrett, *The Emperor Charles IV*, London 1935
Kanter 1994
L.B. Kanter, *Italian Paintings in the Museum of Fine Arts, Boston, Volume I, 13th–15th Century*, Boston, MA 1994
Karet 1992
E. Karet, 'The Pavian Origins of Stefano da Verona', *Arte Lombarda*, 100, no. 1 (1992), pp. 8–19
Karnes 2011
M. Karnes, *Imagination, Meditation, and Cognition in the Middle Ages*, Chicago 2011
Kemp 1990
M. Kemp, *The Science of Art: Optical Themes in Western Art from Brunelleschi to Seurat*, New Haven and London 1990
Kemperdick 2010
S. Kemperdick, *Deutsche and böhmische Gemälde 1230–1430*, Staatliche Museen zu Berlin, Berlin 2010
Kim 2022
D.Y. Kim, *Groundwork: A History of the Renaissance Picture*, Princeton 2022
King 1960
D. King, 'Sur la Signification de "Diasprum"', *Bulletin de Liaison du Centre International d'Étude des Textiles Anciens*, 11 (1960), pp. 42–7
King and King 1988
D. and M. King, 'Silk Weaves of Lucca in 1376', in I. Estham and M. Nockert (eds), *Opera Textilia Variorum Temporum: To Honour Agnes Geijer on Her Ninetieth Birthday 26th October 1988*, Stockholm 1988, pp. 67–76
Kirby, Nash and Cannon 2010
J. Kirby, S. Nash and J. Cannon (eds), *Trade in Artists' Materials: Markets and Commerce in Europe to 1700*, London 2010
Kleinschmidt 1928
B. Kleinschmidt, *Die Basilika San Francesco in Assisi*, Berlin 1928
Klesse 1967
B. Klesse, *Seidenstoffe der italienischen Malerei des 14 Jahrhunderts*, Bern 1967
Klípa 2019
J. Klípa, 'The Enthroned Madonna from Dijon: A Recently Discovered Painting from the Workshop of the Master of the Vyšší Brod Altarpiece', *Umění*, 67, no. 3 (2019), pp. 215–25
Koechlin 1924
R. Koechlin, *Les ivoires gothique français*, 3 vols, Paris 1924
Kozlowski 2015
S.K. Kozlowski, 'Circulation, Convergence, and the Worlds of Trecento Panel Painting: Simone Martini in Naples', *Zeitschrift für Kunstgeschichte*, 78 (2015), pp. 205–38
Kozlowski 2022
S.K. Kozlowski, *Portable Panel Paintings at the Angevin Court of Naples: Mobility and Materiality in the Trecento Mediterranean*, Turnhout 2022
Kreytenberg 1979
G. Kreytenberg 'Tino di Camainos Grabmäler in Florenz', *Städel-Jahrbuch*, 7 (1979), pp. 33–60
Kreytenberg 1986
G. Kreytenberg, *Tino di Camaino*, Florence 1986
Kreytenberg 1988
G. Kreytenberg, 'Tino di Camaino e Simone Martini', in Bellosi 1988a, pp. 203–9
Kreytenberg 1993
G. Kreytenberg, 'Der heilige Galganus und der Bildhauer Agostino di Giovanni', *Pantheon*, 51 (1993), pp. 4–17
Kreytenberg 1995
G. Kreytenberg, 'L'Arca di San Ranieri di Tino di Camaino: questioni di tipologia ed iconografia', in M. Burresi (ed.), *Storia ed arte nella Piazza del Duomo: conferenze 1992–1993*, Pisa 1995, pp. 25–52
Kreytenberg 2001
G. Kreytenberg, 'Ein dopplseitiges Triptychon in Marmor von Tino di Camaino aus de Zeit um 1334', in T. Michalsky (ed.), *Medien der Macht. Kunst zur Zeit der Anjous in Italien*, Berlin 2001, pp. 261–74
Kreytenberg 2013
G. Kreytenberg, 'Original und Replik: zum Werk von Tino di Camaino in Neapel, als auch Giotto dort 1328–1333 tätig war', *Commentari d'arte*, 19, no. 54–5 (2013), pp. 39–44
Kubiski 2001
J. Kubiski, 'Orientalizing Costume in Early Fifteenth-century French Manuscript Painting (Cité des Dames Master, Limbourg Brothers, Boucicaut Master, and Bedford Master)', *Gesta*, 40 (2001), pp. 161–80
Kugler 1874
F. Kugler, *Handbook of Painting: The Italian Schools. Based on the Handbook of Kugler*, trans. C.L. Eastlake and E.R. Eastlake, 2 vols, London 1874
Kupfer 1996
M. Kupfer, 'The Lost Wheel Map of Ambrogio Lorenzetti', *The Art Bulletin*, 78, no. 2 (1996), pp. 286–310
Labande and Requin 1910
L.-H. Labande and H. Requin, 'L'ancien couvent des Dominicains d'Avignon', *Congrès archéologique de France*, 2, no. 76 (1910), pp. 299–331

Labriola, De Benedictis and Freuler 2002
A. Labriola, C. De Benedictis and G. Freuler (eds), *La miniatura senese 1270–1420*, Milan 2002

Laclotte 2015
M. Laclotte, 'Pietro Lorenzetti: First Documented Siena, 1306; Last Documented, 1345, Castiglione del Bosco (Siena)', in Strehlke and Israëls 2015, pp. 373–4

Laclotte and Thiébaut 1983
M. Laclotte and D. Thiébaut, *L'école d'Avignon*, Paris 1983

La Maestà di Duccio restaurata 1990
La Maestà di Duccio restaurata, Gli Uffizi, Studi e ricerche 6, Florence 1990

Lamy 2000
M. Lamy, *L'Immaculée Conception: étapes et enjeux d'une controverse au Moyen-Âge (XIIe–XVe siècles)*, Paris 2000

Landi 1655 (1992)
A. Landi, *'Racconto' del Duomo di Siena*, ed. E Carli, Florence 1992

Lanzi 1792–6 (1968)
L. Lanzi, *Storia pittorica della Italia dal risorgimento delle belle arti fin presso al fine del XVIII secolo* (1792–6), ed. M. Capucci, 3 vols, Florence 1968

Lanzi 1828
L. Lanzi, *The History of Painting in Italy: From the Period of the Revival of the Fine Arts to the End of the Eighteenth Century*, trans. T. Roscoe, 6 vols, London 1828

Laurent 1993
R. Laurent, *Les sceaux des princes territoriaux belges du Xe siècle à 1482*, vols I/2 and II, Brussels 1993

Leahy 2002
H.R. Leahy, '"For Connoisseurs": The Burlington Magazine 1903–11', in E. Mansfield (ed.), *Art History and Its Institutions: Foundations of a Discipline*, London 2002, pp. 231–45

Lee 1898
V. Lee, 'The Wares of Autolycus. Siena and Simon Martini', *The Pall Mall Gazette*, 19 July 1898, p. 4

Lenoble 2013
C. Lenoble, *L'exercice de la pauvreté: Économie et religion chez les franciscains d'Avignon (XIIIe–XVe siècle)*, Rennes 2013

Lens 2015
M.-L. Marguerite and X. Dectot (eds), *D'or et d'ivoire: Paris, Pise, Florence, Sienne, 1250–1320*, exh. cat., Musée du Louvre-Lens, Lens 2015

Leoncini 1994
A. Leoncini, *I tabernacoli di Siena: arte e devozione popolare*, Siena 1994

Leone de Castris 1980a
P. Leone de Castris, 'Tondino di Guerrino e Andrea Riguardi: orafi e smaltisti a Siena, 1308–1338', *Prospettiva*, 21 (1980), pp. 24–44

Leone de Castris 1980b
P. Leone de Castris, 'Une attribution à Lando di Pietro: le bras-reliquaire de saint Louis de Toulouse', *Revue du Louvre*, 30 (1980), pp. 71–6

Leone de Castris 1988
P. Leone de Castris, 'Oreficerie e smalti primo-trecenteschi nella Napoli angioina: evidenza documentarie e materiali', in A.R.C. Masetti (ed.), *Atti della seconda giornata di studio sugli smalti traslucidi Italiani (Pisa, Scuola Normale Superiore, 11 November 1986), classe di lettere e filosofia*, series 3, 18, no. 1 (1988), pp. 115–36

Leone de Castris 1989
P. Leone de Castris, *Simone Martini: catalogo completo dei dipinti*, Florence 1989

Leone de Castris 1991
P. Leone de Castris, 'L'area di diffusione commerciale del prodotto traslucido senese 1290–1350; lo stato della questione', *Annali della Scuola Normale Superiore di Pisa, classe di lettere e filosofia*, series 3, 21, no. 1 (1991), pp. 329–57

Leone de Castris 1995
P. Leone de Castris, 'Il reliquiario del Corporale e l'oreficeria senese del primo Trecento', in G. Barlozzetti (ed.), *Il Duomo di Orvieto e le grandi cattedrali del duecento: atti del convegno internazionale di studi (Orvieto, 12–14 novembre 1990)*, Turin 1995, pp. 169–91

Leone de Castris 2003
P. Leone de Castris, *Simone Martini*, Milan 2003

Leone de Castris 2006
P. Leone de Castris, *Giotto a Napoli*, Naples 2006

Le Pogam 2004
P-Y. Le Pogam, *Les maîtres d'oeuvre au service de la papauté dans la seconde moitié du XIIIe siècle*, Rome 2004

Liberati 2023
R. Liberati, 'Forging Bonds across Continents: Italian Merchants and Īl-Khānid Diplomacy', *Crossroads*, 22 (2023), pp. 1–28, doi: 10.1163/26662523-bja10016 (accessed 13 February 2024)

Lindquist 2008
S. Lindquist, *Agency, Visuality and Society at the Chartreuse de Champmol*, Aldershot 2008

Lisini 1904
A. Lisini, 'Notizie di orafi e di oggetti di oreficeria senese', *Bullettino Senese di Storia Patria*, 11 (1904), pp. 645–78

Lisini 1930
A. Lisini, 'Le leggi prammatiche durante il governo dei Nove (1287–1355)', *Bullettino Senese di Storia Patria*, n.s. 1, pp. 40–70

Little 1979
C.T. Little, 'Ivoires et art gothique', *Revue de l'art*, 46 (1979), pp. 58–67

Little 1997
C.T. Little, 'Gothic Ivory Carving in Germany', in Detroit and Baltimore 1997, pp. 80–93

Lloyd 1975
C. Lloyd, 'Picture-Hunting in Italy: Some Unpublished Letters (1824–1829)', *Italian Studies*, 30 (1975), pp. 42–68

Lloyd 1983
C. Lloyd, 'Fox-Strangways and Fortnum: Two Collectors of Italian Art', *Apollo*, 118, no. 254 (1983), pp. 280–7

Loenertz 1937
R. Loenertz O.P., *La Société des Frères Pérégrinants. Étude sur l'Orient dominicain*, Rome 1937

London 1878–9
Exhibition of Works by the Old Masters, and by Deceased Masters of the British School. [...] Winter Exhibition. Ninth Year. MDCCCLXXVIII, exh. cat., Royal Academy of Arts, London 1878–9

London 1961
An Exhibition of Paintings from the Gambier Parry Collection, exh. cat., The Courtauld Institute of Art, London 1961

London 1965
D. Sutton and P. Murray (eds), *A Loan Exhibition: The Art of Painting in Florence and Siena from 1250 to 1500*, exh. cat., Wildenstein, London 1965

London 1983
D. Gordon (ed.), *Early Italian Paintings and Works of Art 1300–1480*, exh. cat., Matthiesen Gallery, London 1983

London 1987–8
J. Alexander and P. Binski (eds), *Age of Chivalry: Art in Plantagenet England 1200–1400*, exh. cat., Royal Academy of Arts, London 1987–8

London 1989–90
D. Bomford, J. Dunkerton, D. Gordon and A. Roy, with contributions from J. Kirby, *Art in the Making: Italian Painting before 1400*, exh. cat., The National Gallery, London 1989–90

London 2005
D.J. Roxburgh (ed.), *Turks: A Journey of a Thousand Years, 600–1600*, exh. cat., Royal Academy of Arts, London 2005

London 2008–9
R. Cormack and M. Vassilaki (eds), *Byzantium 330–1453*, exh. cat., Royal Academy of Arts, London 2008–9

London 2016
C. Browne, G. Davies and M. Michael, with the assistance of M. Zöschg (eds), *Opus Anglicanum: English Medieval Embroidery*, exh. cat., Victoria and Albert Museum, London 2016

Lorenzini 2013
F. Lorenzini, 'Niccolò da Prato e la sua famiglia: tra erudizione e biografia', in Benedetti and Cinelli 2013, pp. 39–57

Los Angeles 2010–11
E. Morrison and A.D. Hedeman (eds), *Imagining the Past in France: History in Manuscript Painting, 1250–1500*, exh. cat., J. Paul Getty Museum, Los Angeles 2010–11

Los Angeles and New York 2008–10
T.B. Husband, *The Art of Illumination: The Limbourg Brothers and the Belles Heures of Jean de France, Duc de Berry*, exh. cat., J. Paul Getty Museum, Los Angeles, 2008–9; The Metropolitan Museum of Art, New York 2009–10

Lowden 1997
J. Lowden, *Early Christian and Byzantine Art*, London 1997

Lowden 2000
J. Lowden, *The Making of the Bibles Moralisées*, Philadelphia 2000

Lowden 2013
J. Lowden, *Medieval and Later Ivories in the Courtauld Gallery: Complete Catalogue*, London 2013

Loyrette 1978
H. Loyrette, 'Une source pour la reconstruction du polyptyque d'Ugolino da Siena à Santa Croce', *Paragone*, 29 (1978), pp. 15–23

Lucca 1990
C. Baracchini (ed.), *Oreficeria Sacra a Lucca dal XIII al XV secolo*, 2 vols, exh. cat., National Museum of Palazzo Mansi, Lucca 1990

Lugano-Castagnola 1991
G. Freuler (ed.), *'Manifestatori delle cose miracolose': arte italiana del '300 e '400 da collezioni in Svizzera e nel Liechtenstein*, exh. cat., Fondazione Thyssen-Bornemisza, Lugano-Castagnola 1991

Lunghi 2012
E. Lunghi, *Giotto e i pittori giotteschi ad Assisi: guida alle opere di Giotto e dei pittori umbri del Trecento nelle chiese e nei musei di Assisi*, Marsciano 2012

Lusini 1912
V. Lusini, 'Di Duccio di Buoninsegna', *Rassegna d'arte senese*, 8 (1912), pp. 60–98

Luzi 1866
L. Luzi, *Il Duomo di Orvieto*, Florence 1866

Machetti 1929
I. Machetti, 'Orafi Senesi', *La Diana*, 4 (1929), pp. 5–109

Mack 2002
R. Mack, *From Bazaar to Piazza: Islamic Trade and Italian Art 1300–1600*, Berkeley and Los Angeles 2002

Mackie 2015
L.W. Mackie, *Symbols of Power: Luxury Textiles from Islamic Lands, 7th–21st Century*, New Haven and London 2015

MacLennan et al. 2019
D. MacLennan, L. Llewellyn, J.K. Delaney, K.A. Dooley, C. Schmidt Patterson, Y. Szafran and K. Trentelman, 'Visualizing and Measuring Gold Leaf in Fourteenth- and Fifteenth-century Italian Gold Ground Paintings Using Scanning Macro X-ray Fluorescence Spectroscopy: A New Tool for Advancing Art Historical Research', *Heritage Science*, 7, no. 25 (2019), pp. 1–9

Madersbacher 2001
L. Madersbacher, 'Land in der gläsernen Kugel. Das "Weltbild" des Wilton-Diptychons in Kontext christlicher Weltsymbolik', in P. Naredi-Rainer and L. Madersbacher (eds), *Imitatio. Von der Produktivität künstlerischer Anspielungen und Missverständnisse*, Berlin 2001, pp. 71–93

Maginnis 1976
H.B.J. Maginnis, 'The Passion Cycle in the Lower Church of San Francesco, Assisi: The Technical Evidence', *Zeitschrift für Kunstgeschichte*, 39 (1976), pp. 193–208

Maginnis 1980
H.B.J. Maginnis, 'A Lorenzettian Crucifix in Cortona', *Racar*, 7, no. 1–2 (1980), pp. 59–61

Maginnis 1988
H.B.J. Maginnis, 'The Lost Facade Frescoes from Siena's Ospedale di S. Maria della Scala', *Zeitschrift für Kunstgeschichte*, 51 (1988), pp. 180–94

Maginnis 1997
H.B.J. Maginnis, *Painting in the Age of Giotto: A Historical Reevaluation*, University Park, PA 1997

Maginnis 2000
H.B.J. Maginnis, 'Introduction' and 'Appendix 2: The Rucellai Madonna', in Satkowski 2000, pp. 13–29 and 233–4

Maginnis 2001
H.B.J. Maginnis with G. Erasmi, *The World of the Early Sienese Painter*, University Park, PA 2001

Maginnis 2002
H.B.J. Maginnis, 'Everything in a Name? or The Classification of Sienese Duecento Painting', in Schmidt 2002c, pp. 470–85

Maillard-Luypaert 2012
M. Maillard-Luypaert, 'Marguerite d'Avesnes, madame de Hainaut (1346–1356): "Faible femme" ou femme affaible?', in É. Bousmar, J. Dumont, A. Marchandisse and B. Schnerb (eds), *Femmes de pouvoir, femmes politiques durant les derniers siècles du Moyen Âge et au cours de la première Renaissance*, Brussels 2012, pp. 325–48

Mâle 1908
E. Mâle, *L'Art religieux de la fin du moyen âge en France. Etude sur l'iconographie du moyen âge et sur les sources d'inspiration*, Paris 1908

Mallory 1969
M. Mallory, 'A Lost *Madonna Del Latte* by Ambrogio Lorenzetti', *The Art Bulletin*, 51 (1969), pp. 41–7

Mallory 1974
M. Mallory, 'An Altarpiece by Lippo Memmi Reconsidered', *The Metropolitan Museum Journal*, 9 (1974), pp. 187–202

Mallory and Moran 1981–2
M. Mallory and G. Moran, 'Guido Riccio da Fogliano: A Challenge to the Famous Fresco Long Ascribed to Simone Martini and the Discovery of a New One in the Palazzo Publico in Siena', *Studies in Iconography*, 7–8 (1981–2), pp. 1–13

Mariani 1921
V. Mariani, *L'architetto Giuseppe Partini*, Siena 1921

Markowsky 1976
B. Markowsky, *Europaïsche Seidengewebe des 13–18 Jahrhunderts*, Cologne 1976

Martindale 1972
A. Martindale, *The Rise of the Artist in the Middle Ages and Early Renaissance*, New York 1972

Martindale 1988
A. Martindale, *Simone Martini: Complete Edition*, Oxford 1988

Martindale 1990
A. Martindale, 'Simone Martini and the Problem of Retirement', in E. Fernie and P. Crossley (eds), *Medieval Architecture and Its Intellectual Context: Studies in Honour of Peter Kidson*, London 1990, pp. 283–8

Matar 2019
H. Matar, *A Month in Siena*, London 2019

Mathew 1968
G. Mathew, *The Court of Richard II*, London 1968

Mazzoni 2001
G. Mazzoni, *Quadri antichi del Novecento*, Vicenza 2001

McHam 2013
S.B. McHam, *Pliny and the Artistic Culture of the Italian Renaissance: The Legacy of the 'Natural History'*, New Haven and London 2013

Meiss 1967
M. Meiss, *French Painting in the Time of Jean de Berry: The Late Fourteenth Century and the Patronage of the Duke*, 2 vols, London and New York 1967

Meiss 1974
M. Meiss, *French Painting in the Time of Jean de Berry: The Limbourgs and Their Contemporaries*, 2 vols, London 1974

Meiss and Beatson 1974
M. Meiss and E.H. Beatson, *The Belles Heures of Jean de Berry*, New York 1974

Meyer 1881
P. Meyer, 'L'entrevue de Ardres 1396', *Annuaire-Bulletin de la Société de l'Histoire de France*, 18 (1881), pp. 209–24

Michael 2009
M.A. Michael, 'Reorienting the Westminster Retable: Islam, Byzantium and the West', in Binski and Massing 2009, pp. 97–103

Middeldorf 1976
U. Middeldorf, *Sculptures from the Samuel H. Kress Collection: European Schools, XIV–XIX Century*, London 1976

Middeldorf Kosegarten 1966
A. Middeldorf Kosegarten, 'Beiträge zur sienesischen Reliefkunst des Trecento', *Mitteilungen des Kunsthistorischen Institutes in Florenz*, 12, no. 3–4 (1966), pp. 207–24

Middeldorf Kosegarten 1988
A. Middeldorf Kosegarten, 'Simone Martini e la scultura senese contemporanea', in Bellosi 1988a, pp. 193–202

Mihalik 1926–7
A. Mihalik, 'I maestri orafi Pietro e Niccolò Gallicus di Siena, in Ungheria', *Bullettino Senese di Storia Patria*, 33–4 (1926–7), pp. 87–101

Milanesi 1854
G. Milanesi, *Documenti per la storia dell'arte senese*, 2 vols, Florence 1854

Mills 1975 (1983)
J. Mills, *Carpets in Pictures*, Themes and Painters in the National Gallery, series 2, no. 1, London 1975; reprinted as *Carpets in Paintings*, London 1983

Mina 2000
G. Mina, 'Coppo di Marcovaldo's Madonna del Bordone: Political Statement or Profession of Faith?', in Cannon and Williamson 2000, pp. 237–93

Minerbeti 1770 (1900)
P. Minerbeti, 'Cronica Volgare di Anonimo Fiorentino dall'anno

1385 al 1409' (1770), in E. Bellondi (ed.), *Rerum Italicarum Scriptores: Raccolta degli Storici Italiani dal cinquecento al millecinquecento*, vol. 27.2, Città di Castello 1900, pp. 3–404

Mirot 1934
L. Mirot, 'Un conflit diplomatique au XVe siècle. L'arrestation des ambassadeurs florentins en France (1406–1408)', *Bibliothèque de l'école des chartes*, 95 (1934), pp. 74–115

Molinier 1888
É. Molinier, *Inventaire du trésor du Saint Siège sous Boniface VIII (1295)*, Paris 1888

Monciatti 2002
A. Monciatti, 'Pietro Lorenzetti', in Frugoni 2002, pp. 13–115

Monget 1898–1905
C. Monget, *La chartreuse de Dijon*, 3 vols, Tournai 1898–1905

Monnas 1993a
L. Monnas, 'The Price of Camacas Purchased for the English Court during the Fourteenth Century', in S. Cavaciocchi (ed.), *La seta in Europa secc. XIII–XX, Istituto Internazionale di Storia Economica, 'F. Datini', Serie II – Atti delle 'Settimane di Studi', e altri Convegni*, Florence 1993, pp. 741–53

Monnas 1993b
L. Monnas, 'Dress and Textiles in the St Louis Altarpiece: New Light on Simone Martini's Working Practice', *Apollo*, 137, no. 373 (1993), pp. 166–74

Monnas 1997
L. Monnas, 'Fit for a King: Figured Silks Shown in the Wilton Diptych', in Gordon, Monnas and Elam 1997, pp. 165–77

Monnas 2001
L. Monnas, 'Textiles for the Coronation of Edward III', *Textile History*, 32, no. 1 (2001), pp. 2–35

Monnas 2008
L. Monnas, *Merchants, Princes and Painters: Silk Fabrics in Italian and Northern Paintings, 1300–1550*, New Haven and London 2008

Monnas 2010
L. Monnas, 'The Impact of Oriental Silks on Italian Silk-weaving in the Fourteenth Century', in L.E. Saurma-Jetsch and A. Eisenbeiss (eds), *The Power of Things and the Flow of Cultural Transformation*, Berlin and Munich 2010

Monnas 2019
L. Monnas, 'All that Glitters: Cloth of Gold as a Vehicle for Display', in C. Brachmann (ed.), *Arrayed in Splendour: Art, Fashion, and Textiles in Medieval and Early Modern Europe*, Turnhout 2019, pp. 95–133

Monnas 2024 (forthcoming a)
L. Monnas, 'Lucchese Silks with Grapevines and Small Patterns from the First Half of the Fourteenth Century', in *Le arti del tessuto: filati, disegni, colori, Atti del VII convegno internazionale, Il colore nel medioevo (Lucca, 1–3 dicembre 2022)*, Lucca 2024 (forthcoming)

Monnas 2024 (forthcoming b)
L. Monnas, 'Maphoria, Veils, Wimples and Gorgets Worn by the Virgin in Tuscan Painting 1250–1400: Tradition and Innovation', in J. Brack, J. Glodt and N. Sarzeaud (eds), *Textiles, rituels, images (Europe occidentale XIIIe–XVIIe siècles), actes des journées d'étude tenues à Paris les 6 et 7 mai 2021, à l'institut national d'histoire et de l'art, Paris, site de l'HiCSA*, Paris 2024 (forthcoming), pp. 266–92

Monnas (forthcoming)
L. Monnas, 'From Martial Sign to Mark of Distinction: The Costly Display of Heraldic Clothing and Furnishing', in N. Ramsay (ed.), *Heralds and Heraldry in Medieval England*, Donington (forthcoming)

Montevecchi 2007
B. Montevecchi, 'Oreficeria Toscana belle Marche', in S. Blasio (ed.), *Marche e Toscana: terre di grandi maestri tra Quattro e Seicento*, Pisa 2007, pp. 261–76

Morandi and Cairola 1975
U. Morandi and A. Cairola, *Lo Spedale di Santa Maria della Scala in Siena*, Siena 1975

Moretti 2004
S. Moretti, 'Lando di Pietro', in M. Caravale (ed.), *Dizionario biografico degli Italiani*, vol. 63, Rome 2004, pp. 438–40

Moretti 2007
S. Moretti, 'Manno di Bandino', in M. Caravale (ed.), *Dizionario biografico degli Italiani*, vol. 69, Rome 2007, pp. 109–10

Morgan 1988
N.J. Morgan, *Early Gothic Manuscripts (II) 1250–1285*, London 1988

Morgan 2016
N.J. Morgan, 'Modelling in Manuscript Painting *c.*1050–*c.*1500', in Cambridge 2016, pp. 220–8

Mortimer 1986
K.A. Mortimer, with contributions from W.G. Klingelhofer, *Harvard University Art Museums: A Guide to the Collections*, New York 1986

Moskowitz 2001
A.F. Moskowitz, *Italian Gothic Sculpture, c. 1250–c. 1400*, Cambridge 2001

Muel et al. 1987
F. Muel, A. Ruais, C. Mérindol and F. Salet, *La Tenture de l'Apocalypse d'Angers*, Paris 1987

Muller 1977
N.E. Muller, 'Ambrogio Lorenzetti's Annunciation. A Re-Examination', *Mitteilungen des Kunsthistorischen Institutes in Florenz*, 21 (1977), pp. 1–12

Muller 1988
N.E. Muller, 'The Development of Sgraffito in Sienese Painting', in Bellosi 1988a, pp. 147–51

Muller 1994
N.E. Muller, 'Reflections on Ugolino di Nerio's Santa Croce Polyptych', *Zeitschrift für Kunstgeschichte*, 57, no. 1 (1994), pp. 45–74

Muller 2012
N.E. Muller, 'In a New Light: The Origins of Reflective Halo Tooling in Siena', *Zeitschrift für Kunstgeschichte*, 75 (2012), pp. 153–78

Nagel and Wood 2010
A. Nagel and C.S. Wood, *Anachronic Renaissance*, New York and Cambridge, MA 2010

Napione 2013
E. Napione, 'Il cardinale mecenate e la sua memoria figurativa. La "modernità" di Duccio di Boninsegna', in Benedetti and Cinelli 2013, pp. 283–300

Naples 1960
R. Causa (ed.), *Mostra di restauri, soprintendenze alle Gallerie della Campania IV, Laboratorio di conservazione*, exh. cat., Palazzo Reale, Naples 1960

Napolitano 2016
E.G. Napolitano, 'The Transfer of Arabic Inscriptions in Italian Gothic and Renaissance Painting. A New Approach. The Words *al-mulk*, *baraka* and *al-yumn* in the 14th and 15th Centuries Italian Paintings', in A. Peliterri, M.G. Sciortino, D. Sicari and N. Elsakaan (eds), *Redefining a Space of Encounter. Islam and Mediterranean: Identity, Alterity and Interactions. Proceedings of the 28th Congress of the Union Européene des Arabisants et Islamisants*, Palermo 2016, pp. 337–56

Nash 2010
S. Nash, '"Pour couleurs et autres choses prise de lui…". The Supply, Acquisition, Cost and Employment of Painters' Materials at the Burgundian Court *c.*1375–1419', in Kirby, Nash and Cannon 2010, pp. 97–182

Neff 1998
A. Neff, 'The Pain of *Compassio*: Mary's Labor at the Foot of the Cross', *The Art Bulletin*, 80, no. 2 (1998), pp. 254–73

Neff 2019
A. Neff, *A Soul's Journey: Franciscan Art, Theology, and Devotion in the Supplicationes variae*, Toronto 2019

Nethersole 2018
S. Nethersole, 'Traditional Rivals? Artistic Dialogues between Florence and Siena in the Second Quarter of the Fifteenth Century', in A. Schumacher (ed.), *Florence and Its Painters: From Giotto to Leonardo da Vinci*, exh. cat., Alte Pinakothek, Munich 2018, pp. 115–23

Nevola 2000
F. Nevola, '"Per Ornato Della Città": Siena's Strada Romana and Fifteenth-century Urban Renewal', *The Art Bulletin*, 82, no. 1 (2000), pp. 26–50

Newbery 2007
T.J. Newbery, *The Robert Lehman Collection, Vol. 13, Frames*, New York 2007

Newton 1981
S.M. Newton, 'Queen Philippa's Squirrel Suit', in M. Flury-Lemburg and K. Stolleis (eds), *Documenta Textilia: Festschrift für Sigrid Müller-Christensen*, Munich 1981, pp. 342–8

New York 1975
T.B. Husband and J. Hayward (eds), *The Secular Spirit: Life and Art at the End of the Middle*

Ages, exh. cat., The Cloisters, The Metropolitan Museum of Art, New York 1975

New York 1985–6
J.P. O'Neill (ed.), *Liechtenstein. The Princely Collections*, exh. cat., The Metropolitan Museum of Art, New York 1985–6

New York 1990
T.J. Newbery, G. Bisacca and L.B. Kanter, *Italian Renaissance Frames*, exh. cat., The Metropolitan Museum of Art, New York 1990

New York 1994–5
L.B. Kanter, B. Drake Boehm, C.B. Strehlke, G. Freuler, C.C. Mayer Thurman and P. Palladino, *Painting and Illumination in Early Renaissance Florence 1300–1450*, exh. cat., The Metropolitan Museum of Art, New York 1994–5

New York 1999
W.D. Wixom (ed.), *Mirror of the Medieval World*, exh. cat., The Metropolitan Museum of Art, New York 1999

New York 2002–3
A. Butterfield and A. Radcliffe (eds), *Italian Sculpture from the Gothic to the Baroque*, exh. cat., Salander-O'Reilly Galleries, New York 2002–3

New York 2004
H.C. Evans (ed.), *Byzantium: Faith and Power (1261–-1557)*, exh. cat., The Metropolitan Museum of Art, New York 2004

New York 2006–7
C.T. Little (ed.), *Set in Stone: The Face in Medieval Sculpture*, exh. cat., The Metropolitan Museum of Art, New York 2006–7

New York, Chicago and San Francisco 1983–4
C. Pietrangeli, P. de Montebello, O. Raggio and M.E. Frazer (eds), *The Vatican Collections: The Papacy and Art*, exh. cat., The Metropolitan Museum of Art, New York 1983; The Art Institute of Chicago, Chicago 1983; The Fine Arts Museums, San Francisco 1983–4

New York and Los Angeles 2002–3
L. Komaroff and S. Carboni (eds), *The Legacy of Genghis Khan: Courtly Art and Culture in Western Asia, 1256–1353*, exh. cat., The Metropolitan Museum of Art, New York 2002–3; Los Angeles County Museum of Art, Los Angeles 2003

New York and Prague 2005– 6
B. Drake Boehm and J. Fajt (eds), *Prague. The Crown of Bohemia 1347–1437*, exh. cat., The Metropolitan Museum of Art, New York 2005–6; Prague Castle, Prague 2006

Nicolai 2016
F. Nicolai, 'More than an Expatriate Scholar: Frederick Mason Perkins as Art Adviser, Agent and Intermediary for American Collectors of the Twentieth Century', *Journal of the History of Collections*, 28, no. 2 (2016), pp. 311–25

Nicolai 2019
F. Nicolai, '"Primitives" in America: Frederick Mason Perkins and the Early Renaissance Italian Paintings in the Lehman and Blumenthal Collections', *Journal of the History of Collections*, 31, no. 1 (2019), pp. 131–50

Nico Ottaviani 2005
M.G. Nico Ottaviani (ed.), *La legislazione suntuaria secoli XIII–XVI: Umbria*, Rome 2005

Nieri 2022
P. Nieri, 'Il restauro del polittico pisano di Simone Martini: conferme e novità emerse dai dati diagnostici e tecnico-materici', *Bollettino d'Arte*, 39 (2022), pp. 71–88

Niessen, Roelofs and van Veen-Liefrink 2005
W. Niessen, P. Roelofs and M. van Veen-Liefrink, 'The Limbourg Brothers in Nijmegen, Bourges, and Paris', in Nijmegen 2005, pp. 13–27

Nieuwdorp 1994–5
H. Nieuwdorp, 'The Antwerp-Baltimore Polyptych. A Portable Altarpiece Belonging to Philip the Bold, Duke of Burgundy', in Amsterdam 1994–5, pp. 137–50

Nijmegen 2005
R. Dückers and P. Roelofs (eds), *The Limbourg Brothers: Nijmegen Masters at the French Court, 1400–1416*, exh. cat., Museum Het Valkhof, Nijmegen, 2005

Norman 1993
D. Norman, 'The Commission for the Frescoes at Montesiepi', *Zeitschrift für Kunstgeschichte*, 56 (1993), pp. 289–300

Norman 1995a
D. Norman, '"A noble panel": Duccio's *Maestà*', in D. Norman (ed.), *Siena, Florence and Padua: Art, Society and Religion 1280–1400*, New Haven and London 1995, vol. 2, pp. 55–81

Norman 1995b
D. Norman, '"In the Beginning Was the Word": An Altarpiece by Ambrogio Lorenzetti for the Augustinian Hermits of Massa Marittima', *Zeitschrift für Kunstgeschichte*, 58 (1995), pp. 478–503

Norman 1997
D. Norman, 'Pisa, Siena and the Maremma: A Neglected Aspect of Ambrogio Lorenzetti's Paintings in the Sala dei Nove', *Renaissance Studies*, 11, no. 4 (1997), pp. 310–42

Norman 1999a
D. Norman, '"Little desire for glory": The Case of Ambrogio and Pietro Lorenzetti', in E. Barker, N. Webb and K. Woods (eds), *The Changing Status of the Artist*, New Haven and London 1999, pp. 32–55

Norman 1999b
D. Norman, *Siena and the Virgin: Art and Politics in a Late Medieval City State*, New Haven and London 1999

Norman 2003
D. Norman, *Painting in Late Medieval and Renaissance Siena (1260–1555)*, New Haven and London 2003

Norman 2006
D. Norman, '"Sotto uno baldacchino trionfale": The Ritual Significance of the Painted Canopy in Simone Martini's *Maestà*', *Renaissance Studies*, 20, no. 2 (2006), pp. 147–60

Norman 2010a
D. Norman, 'Politics and Piety: Locating Simone Martini's "Saint Louis of Toulouse" Altarpiece', *Art History*, 33 (2010), pp. 596–619

Norman 2010b
D. Norman, 'Sanctity, Kingship and Succession: Art and Dynastic Politics in the Lower Church at Assisi', *Zeitschrift für Kunstgeschichte*, 73, no. 3 (2010), pp. 297–334

Norman 2014
D. Norman, 'The Sicilian Connection: Imperial Themes in Simone Martini's St. Louis of Toulouse Altarpiece', *Gesta*, 53 (2014), pp. 25–45

Norman 2018
D. Norman, *Siena and the Angevins, 1300–1350: Art, Diplomacy, and Dynastic Ambition*, Turnhout 2018

Norman 2024 (forthcoming)
D. Norman, 'Between Siena and Avignon. Simone Martini, the Paparoni and the Orsini Cardinals', *Bullettino Senese di Storia Patria*, 130 (2024), pp. 11–48 (forthcoming)

Novelli 2011
S. Novelli, 'Sulla committenza e il contesto del monumento funebre per Gastone della Torre di Tino di Camaino', *Prospettiva*, 141–2 (2011), pp. 132–44

Oertel 1968
R. Oertel, *Early Italian Painting to 1400*, London 1968

Opitz 2017
C.N. Opitz, 'Buying, Gifting, Storing: Ivory Virgins in Documentary Sources from Late Medieval Central Europe', in C. Yvard (ed.), *Gothic Ivory Sculpture: Content and Context*, London 2017, pp. 46–55, courtauld.ac.uk/research/research-resources/publications/courtauld-books-online/gothic-ivory-sculpture-content-and-context/ (accessed 26 September 2023)

Origo 1955
I. Origo, 'The Domestic Enemy: The Eastern Slaves in Tuscany in the Fourteenth and Fifteenth Centuries', *Speculum*, 30 (1955), pp. 321–66

Orsi Landini 2019
R. Orsi Landini, *Moda a Firenze e in Toscana nel Trecento*, Florence 2019

Ortenberg 1990
V. Ortenberg, 'Archbishop Sigeric's Journey to Rome in 990', *Anglo-Saxon England*, 19 (1990), pp. 197–246

Orvieto 2006–7
A. Cannistrà (ed.), *Le stanze delle meraviglie: da Simone Martini a Francesco Mochi: verso il nuovo museo dell'Opera del Duomo di Orvieto*, exh. cat., Palazzi Papali e chiesa di Sant'Agostino, Orvieto 2006–7

Otavský and Salim 1995
K. Otavský and M.A.M. Salim, *Mittelalterliche Textilien I. Ägypten, Persien und*

Mesopotamien, Spanien und Nordafrica, Riggisberg 1995

Otavský and Wardwell 2011
K. Otavský and A.E. Wardwell, *Mittelalterlichen Textilien II: Zwischen Europa und China*, Riggisberg 2011

Paccagnini 1955
G. Paccagnini, *Simone Martini*, Milan 1955

Padovani 1979
S. Padovani, 'Una tavola di Castiglione d'Orcia restaurata di recente', *Prospettiva*, 17 (1979), pp. 82–8

Panayotova 2016a
S. Panayotova, 'Colour in Illuminated Manuscripts', in Cambridge 2016, pp. 15–23

Panayotova 2016b
S. Panayotova, 'Colour Theory, Optics and Manuscript Illumination', in Cambridge 2016, pp. 305–15

Panofsky 1953
E. Panofsky, *Early Netherlandish Painting. Its Origin and Character*, 2 vols, Cambridge, MA 1953

Paravicini Bagliani 1980
A. Paravicini Bagliani, *I testamenti dei cardinali del Duecento*, Rome 1980

Paris 1957
C. Sterling (ed.), *Exposition de la collection Lehman de New York*, exh. cat., Musée de l'Orangerie, Paris 1957

Paris 1981–2
F. Baron, F. Avril, P. Chapu, D. Gaborit-Chopin and F. Perrot (eds), *Les Fastes du Gothique: Le siècle de Charles V*, exh. cat., Galeries nationales du Grand Palais, Paris 1981–2

Paris 1990
M. Laclotte, 'Polyptyques anciens et modernes, sur le mot polyptyque', in *Polyptyques. Le tableau multiple du moyen âge au vingtième siècle*, exh. cat., Musée du Louvre, Paris 1990, pp. 11–15

Paris 1998
D. Gaborit-Chopin (ed.), *L'Art au temps des rois maudits: Philippe le Bel et ses fils 1285–1328*, exh. cat., Galeries nationales du Grand Palais, Paris 1998

Paris 2004a
P. Stirnemann, I. Villela-Petit and E. Toulet, A.M. González Díaz and F. Autrand, *Les Très Riches Heures du duc de Berry et l'enluminure en France au début de xve siècle*, exh. cat., Musée Condé, Paris 2004

Paris 2004b
E. Taburet-Delahaye and F. Avril (eds), *Paris 1400: les arts sous Charles VI*, exh. cat., Musée du Louvre, Paris 2004

Paris 2009
P.-N. Sainte-Fare-Garnot (ed.), *De Sienne à Florence, les primitifs italiens: la collection du Musée d'Altenbourg*, exh. cat., Musée Jacquemart-André, Paris 2009

Paris 2013
D. Thiébaut (ed.), *Giotto e Compagni*, exh. cat., Musée du Louvre, Paris 2013

Partner 1965
P. Partner, 'Florence and the Papacy, 1300–1375', in J.R. Hale, J.R.L. Highfield and B. Smalley (eds), *Europe in the Late Middle Ages*, London 1965, pp. 76–121

Pasztor 1955
E. Pasztor, 'Il processo di Andrea da Gagliano (1337–1339)', *Archivum Franciscanum Historicum*, 48 (1955), pp. 3–48

Peggie 2014
D. Peggie, 'The Chemistry and Chemical Investigation of the Transition from Egg Tempera Painting to Oil in Italy in the 15th Century', in A. Sgamellotti, B.G. Brunetti and C. Miliani (eds), *Science and Art: The Painted Surface*, London 2014, pp. 209–29

Pelikan 1996
J. Pelikan, *Mary through the Centuries: Her Place in the History of Culture*, New Haven and London 1996

Penndorf 1998
J. Penndorf, *Frühe italienische Malerei im Lindenau-Museum, Altenburg*, Leipzig 1998

Pergam 2011
E.A. Pergam, *The Manchester Art Treasures Exhibition of 1857: Entrepreneurs, Connoisseurs and the Public*, Farnham 2011

Perratore 2021
J. Perratore, 'Spain 1000–1200: Art at the Frontiers of Faith', *The Metropolitan Museum of Art Bulletin*, 79, no. 2 (2021), pp. 5–47

Perugia 2020
G.E. Solberg (ed.), *Taddeo di Bartolo*, exh. cat., Galleria Nazionale dell'Umbria, Perugia 2020

Peruzzi 1583 (2012)
A. Peruzzi, *Visita Apostolica alle diocesi di Cortona e Sansepolcro 1583 e decreti generali* (1583), ed. S. Pieri and C. Volpi, Arezzo 2012

Pešina 1982
J. Pešina, *The Master of the Hohenfurth Altarpiece and Bohemian Gothic Panel Painting*, Prague 1982

Peter 1939
A. Peter, 'Quand Simone Martini est'il venu en Avignon?', *Gazette des Beaux-Arts*, 21 (1939), pp. 153–75

Petit 1888
E. Petit, *Itinéraires de Philippe le Hardi et de Jean Sans Peur, ducs de Bourgogne (1363–1419) d'après les comptes de dépenses de leur hôtel*, Paris 1888

Petrarca (2001)
F. Petrarca, *Canzoniere*, Milan 2001

Phillips 1931
J.G. Phillips, 'A Diasper Silk from Lucca', *The Metropolitan Museum of Art Bulletin* (1931), pp. 197–8

Piccinni 2022
G. Piccinni, *Operazione Buon governo: un laboratorio di comunicazione politica nell'Italia del Trecento*, Turin 2022

Pichi 2003
S. Pichi, *Sansepolcro. Oreficeria dal medioevo al Cinquecento*, Arezzo 2003

Pierini 2000
M. Pierini, *Simone Martini*, Milan 2000

Pietralunga before 1580 (1982)
L. Pietralunga, *Descrizione della Basilica di S. Francesco e di altri santuari di Assisi* (before 1580), ed. P. Scarpellini, Treviso 1982

Pietramellara 1980
C. Pietramellara, *Il Duomo di Siena: evoluzione della forma dalle origini alla fine del Trecento*, Florence 1980

Pini 2006
R. Pini, 'La statua di Bonifacio VIII, Manno da Siena e gli orefici a Bologna', in M. Miglio (ed.), *Le culture di Bonifacio VIII. Atti del convegno organizzato nell'ambito delle celebrazioni per il VII centenario della morte. Bologna, 13–15 dicembre 2004*, Rome 2006, pp. 230–40

Pippal 1993–4
M. Pippal, 'Die Maestà von Massa Marittima und Pucelles "italienische reise": Zur Frage des künstlerischen Austausches zwischen Paris und Siena im zweiten Jahrzehnt des 14. Jahrhunderts', *Wiener Jahrbuch für Kunstgeschichte*, 46–7 (1993–4), pp. 557–68

Platts 2024 (forthcoming)
C. Platts, '"With His Right Hand": Signatures, Gestures, and Artistic Self-Awareness in Pietro Lorenzetti's Arezzo Altarpiece', in T. Kennedy and T. Flanigan (eds), *Acts of the Andrew Ladis Memorial Trecento Conference*, Turnhout 2024 (forthcoming)

Plesters and Roy 1986
J. Plesters and A. Roy, 'The Material and Techniques of Cennino Cennini Illustrated', *National Gallery Technical Bulletin*, 9 (1986), pp. 26–37

Pliny (1938)
Pliny the Elder, *Natural History*, trans. H. Rackham, 10 vols, London 1938

Poeschke 1985
J. Poeschke, *Die Kirche San Francesco in Assisi und ihre Wandmalereien*, Munich 1985

Pokorný 2017
A. Pokorný, 'Punched Decoration in Bohemian Medieval Panel Paintings', in Dáňová, Chlumská and Šefců 2017, pp. 30–59

Polzer 2010
J. Polzer, 'Simone Martini's Orsini Folding Polyptych: Place of Origin and Date and Its Relation to the 1333 Uffizi Annunciation', *Arte Cristiana*, 98 (2010), pp. 321–30, 401–8

Pope-Hennessy 1939
J. Pope-Hennessy, 'Recent Research', *The Burlington Magazine*, 75 (1939), pp. 128–30

Pope-Hennessy 1948
J. Pope-Hennessy, 'A Diptych by Francesco di Vannuccio', *The Burlington Magazine*, 90 (1948), pp. 136–9, 141

Pope-Hennessy 1964
J. Pope-Hennessy, *Catalogue of Italian Sculpture in the Victoria and Albert Museum. Volume I: Text. Eighth to Fifteenth Century*, 3 vols, London 1964

Pope-Hennessy and Kanter 1987
J. Pope-Hennessy, assisted by L.B. Kanter, *The Robert Lehman Collection. Vol. 1, Italian Paintings*, New York 1987

Prazniak 2010
R. Prazniak, ‘Siena on the Silk Roads: Ambrogio Lorenzetti and the Mongol Global Century, 1250–1350’, *Journal of World History*, 21, no. 2 (2010), pp. 177–217

Prazniak 2019
R. Prazniak, *Sudden Appearances: The Mongol Turn in Commerce, Belief, and Art*, Honolulu 2019

Preiser 1973
A. Preiser, *Das Entstehen und die Entwicklung der Predella in der italienischen Malerei*, Hildesheim and New York 1973

Preising 1995–7
D. Preising, ‘Bild und Reliquie. Gestalt und Funktion gotischer Reliquientafeln und altärchen’, *Aachener Kunstblätter*, 61 (1995–7), pp. 13–84

Prochno 2002
R. Prochno, *Die Kartause von Champmol. Grablege der burgündischen Herzöge 1364–1477*, Berlin 2002

Prou 1885
M. Prou, ‘Inventaire des meubles du cardinal Geoffroi d'Altari (1287)’, *Mélanges d'archéologie et d'histoire*, 5 (1885), pp. 382–411

Ragionieri 2003–4
G. Ragionieri, ‘Duccio di Buoninsegna’, in Siena 2003–4, pp. 150–1

Ragusa and Green 1961
I. Ragusa and R.B. Green, *Meditations on the Life of Christ: An Illustrated Manuscript of the Fourteenth Century*, Princeton 1961

Randall 1993
R.H. Randall Jr, *The Golden Age of Ivory: Gothic Carvings in Northern America Collections*, New York 1993

Ransom 2021
L. Ransom, ‘Mixed Media: Questioning Format in Late Medieval Pictorial *Vita Christi* Cycles’, in Flora and Tóth 2021, pp. 225–47

Ravaud et al. 2017–18
E. Ravaud, M. Eveno, G. Bastian and W. Nowik, ‘Painting in the Circle of Johan Maelwael. A Material Analysis of Panel Paintings in France around 1400’, in Amsterdam 2017–18, pp. 35– 41

Recht 2008
R. Recht, *Believing and Seeing: The Art of Gothic Cathedrals*, Chicago 2008

Redigonda 1960
A.L. Redigonda, ‘Albertini, Niccolò (Niccolò da Prato)’, in M. Caravale (ed.), *Dizionario biografico degli italiani*, vol. 1, Rome 1960, pp. 734–6

Reinach 1927
S. Reinach, ‘Three Early Panels from the Ducal Residence at Dijon’, *The Burlington Magazine*, 50, no. 290 (1927), pp. 234–45

Reist 2015
I. Reist (ed.), *A Market for Merchant Princes: Collecting Italian Renaissance Paintings in America*, University Park, PA 2015

Renouard 1941
Y. Renouard, *Les relations des papes d'Avignon et des compagnies commerciales et bancaires de 1316 à 1378*, Paris 1941

Rickert 1965
M. Rickert, *Painting in Britain: The Middle Ages*, Harmondsworth and Baltimore, 1965

Robinson 1975
D. Robinson, ‘Burne-Jones, Fairfax Murray and Siena’, *Apollo*, 102, no. 165 (1975), pp. 348–51

Robinson 2008
J. Robinson, *Masterpieces: Medieval Art*, London 2008

Robson 2004
J. Robson, ‘Judas and the Franciscans: Perfidy Pictured in Lorenzetti's Passion Cycle at Assisi’, *The Art Bulletin*, 86, no. 1 (2004), pp. 31–57

Robson 2005
J. Robson, ‘The Pilgrim's Progress: Reinterpreting the Trecento Fresco Programme in the Lower Church at Assisi’, in Cook 2005, pp. 39–70

Robson 2022
J. Robson, ‘Crisis and Charity in Fourteenth-century Florence: Ambrogio Lorenzetti's Saint Nicholas Panels for San Procolo’, in Cooper and Williamson 2022, pp. 133–57

Rollo-Koster 2015
J. Rollo-Koster, *Avignon and Its Papacy, 1309–1417: Popes, Institutions and Society*, Lanham, Boulder, New York and London 2015

Romagnoli 1976
E. Romagnoli, *Biografia cronologica de'bellartisti senesi: 1200–1800* (MS 1835), 12 vols, Florence 1976

Romanini 1983
A.M. Romanini (ed.), *Roma anno 1300: atti della IV Settimana di studi di storia dell'arte medievale dell'Università di Roma ‘La Sapienza’ (19–24 maggio 1980)*, Rome 1983

Romano 2001
S. Romano, *La basilica di San Francesco ad Assisi: pittori, botteghe, strategie narrative*, Rome 2001

Romano 2015
S. Romano, ‘Per la data della Crocifissione nel transetto nord della chiesa inferiore di Assisi’, *Zeitschrift für Kunstgeschichte*, 78, no. 3–4 (2015), pp. 345–55

Rome 2002
A. Tomei (ed.), *Le biccherne di Siena: arte e finanza all'alba dell'economia moderna*, exh. cat., Palazzo del Quirinale, Rome 2002

Rorimer 1957
J.J. Rorimer (ed.), *The House of Jeanne d'Évreux, Queen of France, at the Cloisters, the Metropolitan Museum of Art*, New York 1957

Rosati 2016
M.L. Rosati, ‘“De opere curioso minute”: The Vestments of Benedict XI in Perugia, and the Fourteenth-century Perceptions of “Panni Tartarici”’, in Von Fircks and Schorta 2016, pp. 172–83

Rosati 2020
M.L. Rosati, ‘*Panni tartarici*: Fortune, Use and the Cultural Reception of Oriental Silks in the Thirteenth and Fourteenth-century European Mindset’, in D. Schäfer and L. Molà (eds), *Seri-Technics: Historical Silk Technologies*, Berlin 2020, pp. 73–88

Rosser 2012
G. Rosser, ‘Beyond Naturalism in Art and Poetry: Duccio and Dante on the Road to Emmaus’, *Art History*, 35 (2012), pp. 474–97

Rowlands 1965
J. Rowlands, ‘The Date of Simone Martini's Arrival in Avignon’, *The Burlington Magazine*, 107 (1965), pp. 25–6

Rowley 1958
G. Rowley, *Ambrogio Lorenzetti*, 2 vols, Princeton 1958

Royt 2003a
J. Royt, *Medieval Painting in Bohemia*, Prague 2003

Royt 2003b
J. Royt, ‘The Dating and Iconography of the So-called Relics Scenes in the Chapel of Our Lady at Karlštejn Castle’, in J. Fajt (ed.), *Court Chapels of the High and Late Middle Ages and Their Artistic Decoration. Proceedings from the International Symposium. Convent of St Agnes of Bohemia, 23–25 September 1998*, Prague 2003, pp. 64–7

Rubin 1995
P. Rubin, *Giorgio Vasari: Art and History*, New Haven and London 1995

Rubin 2010
P. Rubin, ‘“Not … What I Would Fain Offer, but … What I Am Able to Present”: Mrs. Jonathan Foster's Translation of Vasari's Lives’, in K. Burzer, C. Davis, S. Feser and A. Nova (eds), *Le Vite del Vasari: Genesi, topoi, ricezione/ Die Vite Vasaris: Entstehung, Topoi, Rezeption*, Florence 2010, pp. 317–31

Ruskin 1880
J. Ruskin, *A Joy For Ever*, London 1880

Ruskin 1903–12
J. Ruskin, *The Complete Works of John Ruskin*, ed. E.T. Cook and A. Wedderburn, 39 vols, London 1903–12

Salinger 1944
M. Sallinger, ‘An Early Sienese Panel in the Griggs Collection’, *The Metropolitan Museum of Art Bulletin*, 2, no. 6 (1944), pp. 181–3

Salmi 1912
M. Salmi, ‘Il crocifisso di Segna di Bonaventura ad Arezzo’, *L'arte*, 15 (1912), pp. 33–5

San Diego 1997–8
P. Palladino (ed.), *Art and Devotion in Siena after 1350. Luca di Tommè and Niccolò di Buonaccorso*, exh. cat., Timken Museum of Art, San Diego 1997–8

Santi 2013
F. Santi, ‘Niccolò di Martino da Prato. Vescovo di Spoleto e cardinale d'Ostia (Prato, ca. 1250 – Avignone, 27 aprile 1321)’, in Benedetti and Cinelli 2013, pp. 59–71

Sapori 1943
A. Sapori, *I libri della ragione bancaria dei Gianfigliazzi*, Milan 1943

Satkowski 2000
J.I. Satkowski, *Duccio di*

Buoninsegna: The Documents and Early Sources, ed. and with an introduction by H.B.J. Maginnis, Athens, GA 2000

Scarpelli 2012
S. Scarpelli, 'Restoration in Relation to the Polyptych's State of Preservation and Execution Techniques', in A. Tartuferi (ed.), *Giotto: il restauro del polittico di Badia/The Restoration of the Badia Polyptych*, Florence 2012, pp. 103–49

Schimmelpfennig 1990
B. Schimmelpfennig, 'Papal Coronations in Avignon', in J.M. Bak (ed.), *Coronations: Medieval and Early Modern Monarchic Ritual*, Berkeley and Los Angeles 1990, pp. 179–96

Schmidt 1975
G. Schmidt, 'Zur Datierung des "kleinen Bargello-Diptychons" und der Verkündigungstafel in Cleveland', in A. Châtelet and N. Reynaud (eds), *Études d'art français offertes à Charles Sterling*, Paris 1975, pp. 47–63; reprinted in *Malerei der Gotik, Fixpunkte und Ausblicke*, vol. 2, *Malerei der Gotik in Süd- und Westeuropa. Studien zum Herrscherporträt*, Graz 2005, pp. 199–214

Schmidt 2005–6
G. Schmidt, 'The Beautiful Style', in New York and Prague 2005–6, pp. 105–11

Schmidt 1984
T. Schmidt, *Libri Rationum Camerae Bonifatii Papae VIII*, Vatican 1984

Schmidt 1996
V.M. Schmidt, 'Il trittico di Duccio alla National Gallery di Londra: la datazione, l'iconografia e il committente', *Prospettiva*, 81 (1996), pp. 19–30

Schmidt 1999
V.M. Schmidt, 'Northern Artists and Italian Art during the late Middle Ages. Jean Pucelle and the de Limbourg Brothers Reconsidered', in V.M. Schmidt, G.-J. van der Sman, M. Vecchi and J. van Waadenoijen (eds), *Italy and the Low Countries – Artistic Relations. The Fifteenth Century. Proceedings of the Symposium held at the Museum Catharijneconvent, Utrecht, 14 March 1994*, Florence 1999, pp. 21–38

Schmidt 2000
V.M. Schmidt, 'La "Madonna dei francescani" di Duccio: forma, contenuti, funzione', *Prospettiva*, 97 (2000), pp. 30–44

Schmidt 2002a
V.M. Schmidt, 'A Duccesque Painting Representing St John the Baptist Bearing Witness in the Museum of Fine Arts', *Bulletin du Musée Hongrois des Beaux-Arts*, 96 (2002), pp. 51–66

Schmidt 2002b
V.M. Schmidt, 'Portable Polyptychs with Narrative Scenes: Fourteenth-century *De luxe* Objects between Italian Panel Painting and French *Ars somptuaires*', in Schmidt 2002c, pp. 395–425

Schmidt 2002c
V.M. Schmidt (ed.), *Studies in the History of Art, 2002, Vol. 61, Symposium Papers XXXVIII: Italian Panel Painting of the Duecento and Trecento*, New Haven and London, 2002

Schmidt 2003a
V.M. Schmidt, 'Duccio di Buoninsegna: *Crocifissione e Cristo in gloria; san Nicola da Bari; San Clemente (?)*', in Bagnoli et al. 2003, pp. 202–3

Schmidt 2003b
V.M. Schmidt, 'Duccio di Buoninsegna: *Madonna col Bambino e quattro angeli; sette profeti e patriarchi; San Domenico; Sant'Aurea di Ostia*', in Bagnoli et al. 2003, pp. 198–9

Schmidt 2005a
V.M. Schmidt, *Painted Piety: Panel Paintings for Personal Devotion in Tuscany 1250–1400*, Florence 2005

Schmidt 2005b
V.M. Schmidt, 'The Limbourgs and Italian Art', in Nijmegen 2005, pp. 179–88

Schmidt 2009
V.M. Schmidt, 'Panel Paintings in France and the Southern Netherlands and the Influence of Italy', in Stroo 2009, vol. 2, *Essays*, pp. 183–216

Schmitt 1959
C. Schmitt, *Un pape réformateur et un défenseur de l'unité de l'Église: Benoît XII et l'Ordre des frères mineurs (1334–1342)*, Florence 1959

Scillia 1995
D. Scillia, 'The Cleveland Annunciation and the Origins of Flemish Painting', in Smeyers and Cardon 1995, pp. 345–56

Šefců et al. 2017
R. Šefců, V. Pitthard, Š. Chlumská and I. Turková, 'A Multianalytical Study of Binding Media and Pigments on Bohemian Panel Paintings from the First Half of the 14th Century', *Journal of Cultural Heritage*, 23 (2017), pp. 77–86

Seidel 1976
M. Seidel, 'Ein verkanntes Meisterwerk des Giovanni Pisano: Das Kreuz aus S. Maria a Ripalta in Pistoia', *Pantheon*, 34 (1976), pp. 3–13

Seidel 1981
M. Seidel, 'Das Frühwerk von Pietro Lorenzetti', *Städel Jahrbuch*, 8 (1981), pp. 79–158

Seidel 1985
M. Seidel, 'Ikonographie und Historiographie: "conversation angelorum in silvis" Eremiten-Bilder von Simone Martini und Pietro Lorenzetti', *Städel Jahrbuch*, 10 (1985), pp. 77–142

Seidel 1988
M. Seidel, 'Condizionamento iconografico e scelta semantica: Simone Martini e la tavola del Beato Agostino Novello', in Bellosi 1988a, pp. 75–80

Seidel 1989
M. Seidel, 'Das "gemeißelte Bild" im Trecento: Ein neu entdecktes Meisterwerk von Tino di Camaino', *Pantheon*, 47 (1989), pp. 4–13

Seidel 1991
M. Seidel, 'Un "Crocifisso" di Giovanni Pisano a Massa Marittima', *Prospettiva*, 62 (1991), pp. 67–77

Seidel 2000
M. Seidel, '"Sculpens in ligno splendida": sculture lignee giovanili di Giovanni Pisano', in M. Burresi (ed.), *Sacre Passioni: scultura lignea a Pisa dal XII al XV secolo*, exh. cat., Museo Nazionale e Civico di San Matteo, Pisa 2000, pp. 79–94

Seidel 2005a
M. Seidel, *Italian Art of the Middle Ages and the Renaissance*, 2 vols, Venice 2005

Seidel 2005b
M. Seidel, 'The Ivory Madonna in the Treasury of Pisa Cathedral', in Seidel 2005a, vol. 2, pp. 345–88

Seidel 2005c
M. Seidel, 'The Sculpted Image: Tino di Camaino Measures Up to Simone Martini', in Seidel 2005a, vol. 2, pp. 627–38

Seidel 2007
M. Seidel, 'La scoperta del sorriso. Vie di diffusione del gotico francese (Italia centrale, 1315–25), *Mitteilungen des Kunsthisorischen Institutes in Florenz*, 51 (2007), pp. 45–158

Seidel 2012
M. Seidel, *Father and Son: Nicola and Giovanni Pisano*, 2 vols, Munich 2012

Seidel and Calamai 2017–18a
M. Seidel and S. Calamai, 'La Maestà di Massa Marittima', in Siena 2017–18, pp. 232–61

Seidel and Calamai 2017–18b
M. Seidel and S. Calamai, 'La metafisica della luce: Ambrogio Lorenzetti come iconografo', in Siena 2017–18, pp. 37–77

Seidel and Calamai 2022
M. Seidel and S. Calamai, *Ambrogio Lorenzetti: i capolavori delle Gallerie degli Uffizi*, Florence 2022

Seiler 2002
P. Seiler, 'Duccio's *Maestà*: The Function of the Scenes from the Life of Christ on the Reverse of the Altarpiece: A New Hypothesis', in Schmidt 2002c, pp. 250–77

Ševčenko 1991
N.P. Ševčenko, 'Virgin Hodegetria', in A.P. Kazhdan, A.-M. Talbot, A. Cutler, T.E. Gregory and N.P. Ševčenko (eds), *The Oxford Dictionary of Byzantium*, 3 vols, Oxford 1991, vol. 3, pp. 2172–3

Shapely 1979
F.R. Shapely, *Catalogue of the Italian Paintings*, 2 vols, Washington DC 1979

Shea 2020
E.L. Shea, *Mongol Court Dress, Identity Formation, and Global Exchange*, London 2020

Shea 2021
E.L. Shea, 'The Spread of Gold Thread Production in the Mongol Period: A Study of Gold Textiles in the China National Silk Museum, Hangzhou', *Journal of Song-Yuan Studies*, 50 (2021), pp. 381–415

Shearman 1972
J. Shearman, *The Early Italian Pictures in the Collection of Her Majesty the Queen*, Cambridge 1972

Shorr 1954
D. Shorr, *The Christ Child in*

Devotional Images in Italy during the XIV Century, New York 1954

Siena 1904
C. Ricci, *Mostra dell'antica arte senese*, exh. cat., Palazzo Pubblico, Siena 1904

Siena 1979
P. Torriti (ed.), *Mostra di opera d'arte restaurate nelle province di Siena e Grosseto*, exh. cat., Pinacoteca Nazionale, Siena 1979

Siena 1982
G. Chelazzi Dini (ed.), *Il gotico a Siena: miniature, pitture, oreficerie, oggeti d'arte*, exh. cat., Palazzo Pubblico, Siena 1982

Siena 1987
A. Bagnoli and R. Bartalini (eds), *Scultura dipinta: maestri di legname e pittori a Siena, 1250–1450*, exh. cat., Pinacoteca Nazionale, Siena 1987

Siena 1988
M. Batazzi, G. Marziali and L. Sensini, *Siena tra purismo e liberty*, exh. cat., Palazzo Pubblico, Siena 1988

Siena 1994
M. Ciatti (ed.), *'Drappi, velluti, taffeta ed altre cose': antichi tessuti a Siena e nel suo territorio*, exh. cat., Church of Sant'Agostino, Siena 1994

Siena 2003–4
A. Bagnoli, R. Bartalini, L. Bellosi and M. Laclotte (eds), *Duccio: alle origine della pittura senese*, exh. cat., Santa Maria della Scala and Museo dell'Opera del Duomo, Siena 2003–4

Siena 2004
G. Mazzoni, *Falsi d'autore: Ilicio Federico Ioni e la cultura del falso fra otto e novecento*, exh. cat., Santa Maria della Scala, Siena 2004

Siena 2005–6
G. Cantelli, L.S. Pacchierotti and B. Pulcinelli, *Il segreto della civiltà: la mostra dell'antica arte senese del 1904, cento anni dopo*, exh. cat., Palazzo Pubblico, Siena 2005–6

Siena 2008
M. Boskovits (ed.), *Maestri senesi e toscani nel Lindenau-Museum di Altenburg*, exh. cat., Pinacoteca Nazionale, Siena 2008

Siena 2010
M. Seidel (ed.), *Le arti a Siena nel primo Rinascimento: Da Jacopo della Quercia a Donatello*, exh. cat., Santa Maria della Scala, Opera della Metropolitana and Pinacoteca Nazionale, Siena 2010

Siena 2017–18
A. Bagnoli, R. Bartalini and M. Seidel (eds), *Ambrogio Lorenzetti*, exh. cat., Santa Maria della Scala, Siena 2017–18

Sirocco 2014
E. Sirocco, 'L'altare maggiore angioino della basilica napoletana di S. Chiara', in F. Aceto, S. d'Ovidio and E. Sirocco (eds), *La chiesa e il convento di Santa Chiara: artistica, vita religiosa e progettualità politica nella Napoli di Roberto d'Angiò e Sancia di Maiorca*, Battipaglia 2014, pp. 313–59

Skaug 1994
E.S. Skaug, *Punch Marks from Giotto to Fra Angelico: Attribution, Chronology, and Workshop Relationships in Tuscan Panel Painting: With Particular Consideration to Florence, c.1330–1430*, 2 vols, Oslo 1994

Smeyers and Cardon 1995
M. Smeyers and B. Cardon (eds), *Flanders in a European Perspective. Manuscript Illumination around 1400 in Flanders and Abroad. Proceedings of the International Colloquium, Leuven, 7–10 September 1993*, Leuven 1995

Snyder 2014
J. Snyder, 'Vestiary Signs of Pilgrimage in Twelfth-century Europe', in J. Robinson, L. de Beer and A. Harnden (eds), *Matter of Faith: An Interdisciplinary Study of Relics and Relic Veneration in the Medieval Period*, London 2014, pp. 8–14

Solberg 2020
G.E. Solberg, 'Dedicato a Taddeo di Bartolo: la mostra', in Perugia 2020, pp. 15–33

Sonday 1999–2000
M. Sonday, 'A Group of Possibly Thirteenth-century Velvets with Gold Disks in Offset Rows', *The Textile Museum Journal*, 38–9 (1999–2000), pp. 101–51

Spallanzani 2014
M. Spallanzani, *Rugs in Late Medieval Siena, The Bruschettini Foundation for Islamic and Asian Art: Textile Studies III*, Florence 2014

Spannocchi 2003–4
S. Spannocchi, 'Simone Martini', in Siena 2003–4, pp. 394–5

Spufford 1986
P. Spufford, *Handbook of Medieval Exchange*, London 1986

Spufford 2002
P. Spufford, *Power and Profit: The Merchant in Medieval Europe*, London 2002

Spufford 2010
P. Spufford, 'Lapis, Indigo, Woad: Artists' Materials in the Context of International Trade before 1700', in Kirby, Nash and Cannon 2010, pp. 10–25

Starn 1987
R. Starn, 'The Republican Regime of the "Room of Peace" in Siena, 1338–40', *Representations*, 18 (Spring 1987), pp. 1–32

Starn and Partridge 1993
R. Starn and L. Partridge, *Arts of Power: Three Halls of State in Italy, 1300–1600*, Berkeley 1993

Stechow 1974
W. Stechow, *The Cleveland Museum of Art. European Paintings before 1500. Catalogue of Paintings: Part One*, Cleveland 1974

Stehlikova 1994
D. Stehlikova, 'Some Enamels of the XIV Century from Czech Collections', in A.R.C. Masetti (ed.), *Atti della quarta giornata di studio sugli smalti traslucidi Italiani, Annali della Scuola Normale Superiore di Pisa, classe di lettere e filosofia*, supplement 3, 24, no. 2–3 (1994), pp. 643–60

Stevenson 1894
R. Stevenson, 'Early Italian Art at the New Gallery', *The Standard*, 1 January 1894, p. 2

Stones 2013–14
A. Stones, *Gothic Manuscripts 1260–1320: A Survey of Manuscripts Illuminated in France, II*, 2 vols, London and Turnhout 2013–14

St Petersburg and Moscow 1990
E.R. Kankovskaia (ed.), *Dekorativno-Prikladnoe Iskusstvo ot Pozdnei Antichnosti do Pozdnei Gotiki*, exh. cat., State Hermitage Museum, St Petersburg; Pushkin Museum, Moscow 1990

Stratford 2012
J. Stratford, *Richard II and the English Royal Treasure*, Woodbridge 2012

Strehlke 2004
C.B. Strehlke, *Italian Paintings, 1250–1450, in the John G. Johnson Collection and the Philadelphia Museum of Art*, Philadelphia 2004

Strehlke 2022–3
C.B. Strehlke, 'The "bed on which they lay": Simone Martini's Family, Art, and Places', in Boston 2022–3, pp. 60–103

Strehlke and Israëls 2015
C.B. Strehlke and M. Brüggen Israëls (eds), *The Bernard and Mary Berenson Collection of European Paintings at I Tatti*, Florence 2015

Stroo 2009
C. Stroo (ed.), *Pre-Eyckian Panel Painting in the Low Countries*: vol. 1, *Catalogue*; vol. 2, *Essays*, Brussels 2009

Stroo 2016
C. Stroo, 'The Enigmatic Carrand Diptych. Between Tradition and Innovation: Pictorial and Iconographic Peculiarities of a Pre-Eyckian Panel Painting', in P. Charron, M. Gil and A. Vilain (eds), *La Pensée du Regard: études de l'histoire de l'art du Moyen Age offertes à Christian Heck*, Turnhout 2016, pp. 311–22

Struchholz 1995
E. Struchholz, *Die Choranlagen und Chorgestühle des Sieneser Domes*, Münster and New York 1995

Stubblebine 1964
J.H. Stubblebine, *Guido da Siena*, Princeton 1964

Stubblebine 1972
J.H. Stubblebine, 'Duccio's *Maestà* of 1302 for the Chapel of the Nove', *Art Quarterly*, 35 (1972), pp. 239–68

Stubblebine 1973
J.H. Stubblebine, 'Cimabue and Duccio in Santa Maria Novella', *Pantheon*, 31 (1973), pp. 15–21

Stubblebine 1979
J.H. Stubblebine, *Duccio di Buoninsegna and His School*, 2 vols, Princeton 1979

Suckale and Fajt 2005–6
R. Suckale and J. Fajt, 'The Circle of Charles IV', in New York and Prague 2005–6, pp. 35–45

Sutton 1979
D. Sutton, 'V. The Discovery of Sassetta', *Apollo*, 109, no. 206 (1979), pp. 288–93

Swinburne 1871
A.C. Swinburne, *Songs before Sunrise*, London 1871

Syson 2007–8
L. Syson, 'The City and its Saints', in L. Syson (ed.), *Renaissance Siena: Art for a City*, exh. cat.,

The National Gallery, London, 2007–8, pp. 80–1

Taburet-Delahaye 1983
E. Taburet-Delahaye, 'Acquisitions. Une croix siennoise', *La Revue du Louvre et des musées de France* (1983), pp. 188–98

Taburet-Delahaye 1988
E. Taburet-Delahaye, 'Il san Galgano del museo di Cluny e il calice dell'abbazia di San Michele a Siena: proposte per il "maestro de Frosini"', *Bollettino d'arte*, supplement to vol. 43 (1988), pp. 17–30

Taburet-Delahaye 1989
E. Taburet-Delahaye, *L'orfèvrerie gothique (XIIIe–début Xve siècle) au Musée de Cluny: Catalogue*, Paris 1989

Taburet-Delahaye 1994
E. Taburet-Delahaye, 'Lo smalto traslucido a Siena e a Parigi nella prima meta del Trecento', in V. Pace and M. Bagnoli (eds), *Il gotico europeo in Italia*, Naples 1994, pp. 325–41

Taburet-Delahaye 1995
E. Taburet-Delahaye, 'L'orfèvrerie au poinçon d'Avignon au XIVe siècle', *Revue de l'Art*, 108 (1995), pp. 11–22

Taney, Miller and Stallings-Taney 2000
F.X. Taney, A. Miller and C.M. Stallings-Taney (eds and trans.), *John of Caulibus, Meditations on the Life of Christ*, Asheville, NC 2000

Tanfani Centofani 1897
L. Tanfani Centofani, *Notizie di artisti tratte dai documenti pisani*, Pisa 1897

Tangheroni 1987
M. Tangheroni, 'Siena e il commercio internazionale del Duecento e nel Trecento', in F. Cardini, M. Cassandro, G. Cherubini, G. Pinto, M. Tangheroni, C.M. Cipolla (eds), *Banchieri e mercanti di Siena*, Rome 1987, pp. 21–105

Tarr 2000
R. Tarr, '"Ecce virgo concipiet": The Iconography and Context of Duccio's London Annunciation', *Viator*, 31 (2000), pp. 185–233

Tedbury 2018
I. Tedbury, '"Each School Has Its Day": The Collecting, Reception and Display of Trecento and Quattrocento Sienese Painting in Britain, 1850–1950', PhD dissertation, The Courtauld Institute of Art, London 2018

Tedbury 2019a
I. Tedbury, 'Collaboration and Correction: Re-examining the Writings of Lucy Olcott, "a lady resident in Siena"', *19: Interdisciplinary Studies in the Long 19th Century*, 29 (2019), https://doi.org/10.16995/ntn.838 (accessed 1 September 2023)

Tedbury 2019b
I. Tedbury, 'Restoration, Revival, Remembrance: The Nineteenth-century Lives of the Lorenzetti Chapter House Frescoes from San Francesco, Siena', in Feltman and Thompson 2019, pp. 189–207

Tedbury 2020
I. Tedbury, 'Scholar, Dealer and Museum Man: Robert Langton Douglas in the International Old Master Market', in S. Avery-Quash and B. Pezzini (eds), *A Worldwide Market for Old Masters between the Napoleonic Era and the Great Depression*, London 2020, pp. 161–78

Tenneroni 1888
A. Tenneroni, 'Inventario di sacri arredi appartenuti ai Cardinali Bentivenga e Matteo Bentivegna d'Acquasparta', *Archivio Storico Italiano*, 5, no. 2 (1888), pp. 260–6

Testa and Interguglielmi 2017–18
F. Testa and F. Interguglielmi, 'Il ciclo di affreschi della sala capitolare di San Francesco a Siena', in Siena 2017–18, pp. 132–51

Testi Cristiani 1987
M.L. Testi Cristiani, *Nicola Pisano: architetto scultore*, Pisa 1987

Testi Cristiani 1990
M.L. Testi Cristiani, '"Circostanze avignonesi": il crocifisso double-face del cardinale Godin a Tolosa', *Critica d'arte*, 55, no. 4 (1990), pp. 42–61

***The Liverpool Mercury* 1882**
'An Appenine City', *The Liverpool Mercury*, 26 December 1882, p. 6

***The London Daily News* 1857**
'The Art Treasures Exhibition, Manchester', *The London Daily News*, 1 June 1857, p. 2

***The Manchester Courier* 1878**
'The Winter Art Season. No. VI. The Old Masters. Second Notice [From our special correspondent.] London, Tuesday', *The Manchester Courier*, 16 January 1878, p. 6

***The Western Daily Express* 1894**
'Italian Art at the New Gallery', *The Western Daily Express*, 1 January 1894, p. 3

Thode 1885
H. Thode, *Franz von Assisi und die Anfange der Kunst der Renaissance in Italie*, Berlin 1885

Thomas 2020 (2023)
A. Thomas, *The Court of Richard II and Bohemian Culture: Literature and Art in the Age of Chaucer and the Gawain Poet*, Woodbridge 2020, online publication January 2023, doi.org/10.1017/9781787449190 (accessed 26 May 2023)

Thompson 2004
N.M. Thompson, 'Architectural Restoration and Stained Glass in Nineteenth-century Siena: The Place of Light in Giuseppe Partini's Purismo', in G. Morgan (ed.), *The Year's Work in Medievalism*, vol. 19, Eugene, OR 2004, pp. 41–53

Tietzel 1984
B. Tietzel, *Italienisches Seidengewebe des 13., 14. and 15. Jahrhunderts. Deutsches Textilmuseum Krefeld*, Cologne 1984

Tigler 2004
G. Tigler, 'Tipologie di monumenti funebri', in M. Seidel (ed.), *Storie delle arti in Toscana. Il Trecento*, Florence 2004, pp. 45–74

Tigler 2007
G. Tigler, 'Giovanni Pisano e le sculture della parte bassa della facciata', in M. Lorenzoni (ed.), *La facciata del duomo di Siena*, Cinisello Balsamo 2007, pp. 131–45

Tintori and Fehm 1983
L. Tintori and S.A. Fehm, 'Observations on Simone Martini's Frescoes in the Montefiore Chapel at Assisi', in H.W. van Os (ed.), *La pittura nel XIV e XV secolo: atti del XXIV Congresso Internazionale di Storia dell'Arte, Bologna 1979*, Bologna 1983, pp. 175–87

Tomasi 2022
M. Tomasi, *Ecrire l'art en France au temps de Charles V et Charles VI (1360–1420). Le témoignage des chroniqueurs*, Turnhout 2022

Tonini 1880
L. Tonini, *Storia civile e sacra riminese. Appendice di Documenti al Volume IV della Storia di Rimini*, Rimini 1880

Tonkovich 2015
J. Tonkovich, 'Discovering the Renaissance: Pierpont Morgan's Shift to Collecting Italian Old Masters', in Reist 2015, pp. 38–47

Torriti 1980
P. Torriti, *La Pinacoteca nazionale di Siena: i dipinti dal XII al XV secolo*, Genoa 1980

Tóth 2021
P. Tóth, 'The Earliest Reference to the *Meditationes Vitae Christi*: New Evidence for Its Date, Authorship, and Language', in Flora and Tóth 2021, pp. 43–74

Toynbee 1929
M.R. Toynbee, *St Louis of Toulouse and the Process of Canonisation in the Fourteenth Century*, Manchester 1929

Tucker 1998
P. Tucker, 'Giovanni Battista Cavalcaselle, John Ruskin e Charles Fairfax Murray: interlocutori e antagonisti', in A.C. Tommasi (ed.), *Giovanni Battista Cavalcaselle conoscitore e conservatore: atti del convegno*, Venice 1998, pp. 257–76

Tucker 2008
P. Tucker, *Charles Fairfax Murray and Duccio's Maestà: Photography, Art History and the Market in Early Paintings in Late Nineteenth-century Siena*, Bembridge 2008

Tura del Grasso 1933
A. di Tura del Grasso, 'Chronaca senese', in A. Lisini and F. Iacometti (eds), *Rerum Italicarum Scriptores*, 26 vols, vol. 15, pt 6, Bologna 1933

Valentiner 1935
W.R. Valentiner, *Tino Di Camaino: A Sienese Sculptor of the Fourteenth Century*, Paris 1935

Valentiner 1954
W.R. Valentiner, 'Tino di Camaino in Florence', *The Art Quarterly*, 17 (1954), pp. 117–32

Van der Ploeg 1993
K. van der Ploeg, *Art, Architecture and Liturgy: Siena Cathedral in the Middle Ages*, Groningen 1993

Van Marle 1924
R. Van Marle, *The Development of the Italian Schools of Painting. II The Sienese School*, The Hague 1924

Van Os 1969
H.W. van Os, *Maris Demut und Verherrlichung in der sienesischen Malerei 1300–1450*, The Hague 1969

Van Os 1978
H.W. van Os, 'The Discovery of

an Early Man of Sorrows on a Dominican Triptych', *Journal of the Warburg and Courtauld Institutes*, 41 (1978), 65–75

Van Os 1984
H.W. van Os, *Sienese Altarpieces, 1215–1460: form, content, function*, with a contribution by K. van der Ploeg, 2 vols, Groningen 1984

Van Os 1990
H.W. van Os with a contribution by G. Aronow, *Sienese Altarpieces 1215–1460: Form, Content, Function, vol. II 1344–1460*, Groningen 1990

Van Os and Rinkleff-Reinders 1972
H.W. van Os and M. Rinkleff-Reinders, 'De Reconstructie van Simone Martini's zgn. Polyptiek van de Passie', *Nederlands Kunsthistorisch Jaarboek (NKJ)/ Netherlands Yearbook for History of Art*, 23 (1972), pp. 13–26

Vasari 1550 (1967)
G. Vasari, *Le vite de' più eccellenti pittori, scultori e architettori nelle redazioni del 1550 e 1568* (1550), ed. R. Bettarini and P. Barocchi, vol. 2 (Testo), Verona 1967

Vasari 1568 (1996)
G. Vasari, *Lives of the Painters, Sculptors and Architects* (1568), trans. G. du C. de Vere, intro. and notes D. Ekserdjian, vol. 1, London 1996

Vassilaki and Tsironis 2000–1
M. Vassilaki and N. Tsironis, 'Representations of the Virgin and Their Association with the Passion of Christ', in Athens 2000–1, pp. 452–63

Vauchez 1977
A. Vauchez, 'La commune de Sienne, les Ordres Mendiants et le culte des saints. Histoire et enseignements d'une crise (novembre 1328, avril 1329)', *Mélanges de l'Ecole française de Rome. Moyen-Age, Temps modernes*, 89, no. 2 (1977), pp. 757–67

Vaughan 1962 (2002)
R. Vaughan, *Philip the Bold. The Formation of the Burgundian State*, London and New York 1962 (reprinted paperback edn, Woodbridge 2002)

Ventroni 1972
S. Delogu Ventroni, *Barna da Siena*, Pisa 1972

Verona 1983
L. Magagnato (ed.), *Le stoffe di Cangrande: ritrovamenti e ricerche sul 300 veronese*, exh. cat., Museo di Castelvecchio, Verona 1983

Verona 2004–5
P. Marini, E. Napione and G.M. Varanini (eds), *Cangrande della Scala: la morte e il corredo di un principe nel medioevo europeo*, exh. cat., Museo di Castelvecchio, Verona 2004–5

Vertova 1970
L. Vertova, 'Lippo Vanni versus Lippo Memmi', *The Burlington Magazine*, 112 (1970), pp. 437–41

Vigni 2005
L. Vigni, 'Economia, politica e società a Siena dall fine dell'Ottocento ai primi anni del Novecento', in Siena 2005–6, pp. 19–39

Villela-Petit 2006
I. Villela-Petit, 'Propositions pour Jean d'Arbois', in E. Taburet-Delahaye (ed.), *La Création Artistique en France autour de 1400: actes du colloque international, Ecole du Louvre, Musée des Beaux-Arts de Dijon, Université de Bourgogne*, Paris 2006, pp. 315–44

Villela-Petit 2012
I. Villela-Petit, 'La banque Limbourg Frères', *Bulletin de la Société française de numismatique*, 67 (2012), pp. 172–7

Voigt 2008
K.C. Voigt, *Staatliche Kunsthalle Karlsruhe*, Munich and Berlin 2008

Volbach 1987
W.F. Volbach, *Catalogo della Pinacoteca Vaticana: il Trecento, Firenze e Siena*, Vatican City 1987

Volpe 1951
C. Volpe, 'Ambrogio Lorenzetti e le congiunzioni fiorentine-senesi nel quatro decennio del Trecento', *Paragone* (1951), pp. 40–52

Volpe 1989
C. Volpe, *Pietro Lorenzetti*, Milan 1989

Von Fircks and Schorta 2016
J. von Fircks and R. Schorta (eds), *Oriental Silks in Medieval Europe*, Riggisberger Berichte 21, Riggisberg 2016

Waagen 1854
G.F. Waagen, *Treasures of Art in Great Britain: Being an Account of the Chief Collections of Paintings, Drawings, Sculptures, Illuminated MSS*, trans. E.R. Eastlake, 3 vols, London 1854

Wagner 1974
H. Wagner, *Italienische Malerei 13. Bus 16, Jahrundert*, Bern 1974

Wainwright 1975
V. Wainwright, 'The Will of Ambrogio Lorenzetti', *The Burlington Magazine* 117 (1975), pp. 543–4

Wainwright 1988
V. Wainwright, 'Late Illuminations by Lippo Vanni and His Workshop', *Pantheon*, 46 (1988), pp. 26–36

Waley 1991
D.P. Waley, *Siena & the Sienese in the Thirteenth Century*, Cambridge 1991

Walker 2012
A. Walker, 'Globalism', *Medieval Art History Today – Critical Terms, Studies in Iconography*, 33 (2012), pp. 183–96

Walker 1990
D. Walker, 'Recent Acquisitions. Islamic Art: Animal Rug', *The Metropolitan Museum of Art Bulletin*, 48, no. 2 (1990), pp. 12–15

Ward and Roberts 1907
T.H. Ward and W. Roberts, *Pictures in the Collection of J. Pierpont Morgan at Prince's Gate and Dover House, London*, 3 vols, London 1907

Wardwell 1976–7
A.E. Wardwell, 'The Stylistic Development of 14th and 15th-century Italian Silk Design', *Aachener Kunstblatter*, 47 (1976–7), pp. 177–225

Wardwell 1987
A.E. Wardwell, 'Flight of the Phoenix: Crosscurrents in Late Thirteenth- to Fourteenth-century Silk Patterns and Motifs', *The Bulletin of the Cleveland Museum of Art*, 74, no. 1 (1987), pp. 2–35

Wardwell 1988–9
A.E. Wardwell, '*Panni Tartarici*: Eastern Islamic Silks Woven with Gold and Silver (13th and 14th Centuries)', *Islamic Art: An Annual Dedicated to the Art and Culture of the Muslim World*, 3 (1988–9), pp. 95–173

Warnke 1993
M. Warnke, *The Court Artist: On the Ancestry of the Modern Artist*, Cambridge 1993

Washington and New York 2004
H. Ecker, *Caliphs and Kings: The Art and Influence of Islamic Spain*, exh. cat., Arthur M. Sackler Gallery, Smithsonian Institute, Washington DC; Hispanic Society of America, New York 2004

Waterhouse 1962
E.K. Waterhouse, 'Some Notes on William Young Ottley's Collection of Italian Primitives', *Italian Studies*, 17 (1962), pp. 272–80

Wauters 1894–5
A. Wauters, 'Marguerite de Hainaut', in *Biographie Nationale. Academie royale des sciences, des lettres et des beaux-arts de Belge*, Brussels 1894–5, vol. 13, columns 636–46, https://academieroyale.be/Academie/documents/FichierPDFBiographieNationaleTome2055.pdf (accessed 27 November 2023)

Weigelt 1911
C. Weigelt, *Duccio di Buoninsegna: Studien zur Geschichte der frühsienesischen Tafelmalerei*, Leipzig 1911

Weppelmann 2005–6
S. Weppelmann, 'Geschichten auf Gold in neuem Licht: Das Hochaltarretabel aus der Franziskanerkirche Santa Croce', in Berlin 2005–6, pp. 26–50

Weppelmann and Winkler 2005–6
S. Weppelmann and S. Winkler, 'Digitale Kunstgeschichte? Eine Fallstudie an Ugolinos Altarwerk aus Santa Croce', in Berlin 2005–6, pp. 118–25

White 1966
J. White, *Art and Architecture in Italy, 1250 to 1400*, Harmondsworth, Baltimore and Victoria 1966

White 1967
J. White, *The Birth and Rebirth of Pictorial Space*, London 1967 (2nd edn)

White 1973a
J. White, 'Carpentry and Design in Duccio's Workshop: The London and Boston Triptychs', *The Journal of the Warburg and Courtauld Institutes*, 36 (1973), pp. 92–105

White 1973b
J. White, 'Measurement, Design and Carpentry in Duccio's *Maestà*', *The Art Bulletin*, Part I, 55, no. 3 (1973), pp. 334–66; Part II, 55, no. 4 (1973), pp. 547–69

White 1979
J. White, *Duccio: Tuscan Art and the Medieval Workshop*, New York 1979

Whittington 2022
K. Whittington, 'Painting the Sculptural Body in Lucca and Florence: Intermediality in Croci

Dipinte', *Gesta*, 61, no. 1 (2022), pp. 81–107
Wilckens 1992
L. von Wilckens, *Mittelalterliche Seidenstoffe*, Staatliche Museen zu Berlin, Kunstgewerbemuseum, Berlin 1992
Wilkins Sullivan 1985
R. Wilkins Sullivan, 'The Anointing in Bethany and Other Affirmations of Christ's Divinity on Duccio's Back Predella', *The Art Bulletin*, 67, no. 1 (1985), pp. 32–50
Wilkins Sullivan 1988
R. Wilkins Sullivan, 'Duccio's *Raising of Lazarus* Reexamined', *The Art Bulletin*, 70, no. 3 (1988), pp. 374–87
Williamson 2007
B. Williamson, 'Site, Seeing, and Salvation in Fourteenth-century Avignon', *Art History*, 30 (2007), pp. 1–25
Williamson 2009
B. Williamson, *The Madonna of Humility: Development, Dissemination and Reception, c.1340–1400*, Woodbridge 2009
Williamson 2018
B. Williamson, 'Matter and Materiality in an Italian Reliquary Triptych', *Gesta*, 57, no. 1 (2018), pp. 23–42
Williamson 2020
B. Williamson, *Reliquary Tabernacles in Fourteenth-century Italy: Image, Relic and Material Culture*, Woodbridge 2020
Williamson 2019
P. Williamson, *The Wyvern Collection: Medieval and Later Ivory Carvings and Small Sculpture*, London 2019
Williamson and Davies 2014
P. Williamson and G. Davies, *Medieval Ivory Carvings, 1200–1550*, 2 vols, London 2014
Wilson 2008
A. Wilson, *William Roscoe: Commerce and Culture*, Liverpool 2008
Wixom 1979
W.D. Wixom, 'Eleven Additions to the Medieval Collection', *The Bulletin of the Cleveland Museum of Art*, 46 (1979), pp. 87–151
Wormald 1954
F. Wormald, 'The Wilton Diptych', *Journal of the Warburg and Courtauld Institutes*, 17, no. 3–4 (1954), pp. 191–203
Wornum 1858
R.N. Wornum, *Descriptive and Historical Catalogue of the Pictures in the National Gallery with Short Biographical Notices of the Painters. Foreign Schools*, London 1858 (23rd edn)
Wright 2022–3
A. Wright, 'The Transformation of Gold', in Boston 2022–3, pp. 39–59
Zafran 1994
E.M. Zafran, 'On the Collecting of Early Italian Paintings in Boston', in Kanter 1994, pp. 11–49
Zappasodi 2010
E. Zappasodi, 'La più antica decorazione della sagrestia-capitolo di Santa Croce', *Ricerche di storia dell'arte*, 102 (2010), pp. 49–64
Zappasodi 2018
E. Zappasodi, *'Sorores reclusae': spazi di clausura e immagini dipinte in Umbria fra XIII e XIV secolo*, Florence 2018
Zeri 1971
F. Zeri, *Diari di lavoro*, vol. 1, Bergamo 1971
Zeri and Gardner 1980
F. Zeri and E.E. Gardner, *Italian Paintings: A Catalogue of the Collection of The Metropolitan Museum of Art*, Greenwich, CT 1980
Zeri and Gardner 1986
F. Zeri and E.E. Gardner, *Italian Paintings: A Catalogue of the Collection of The Metropolitan Museum of Art: Sienese and Central Italian Schools*, New York 1986
Zöschg 2022
M. Zöschg, '"Speculum sine macula": The *Trittico di Santa Chiara* in Trieste as an Object of Clarissan Devotion', in Cooper and Williamson 2022, pp. 69–87

PICTURE CREDITS

Altenburg/Thüringen
Lindenau-Museum, Altenburg © Lindenau-Museum Altenburg / Photo: Bertram Kober/Punctum: 106.

Antwerp
Koninklijk Museum voor Schone Kunsten, Antwerp, Belgium © photo: Hugo Maertens, Collection KMSKA - Flemish Community: 81, 192, 197.

Arezzo
Santa Maria della Pieve © Gentile concessione dell'Ufficio Beni Culturali della Diocesi di Arezzo-Cortona-Sansepolcro / L.A.D. Photographic di Angelo Latronico: 60; © Photo Scala, Florence: 61, 62, 63.

Assisi
Basilica of San Francesco © akg-images / Stefan Diller: 201, 202; © akg-images / De Agostini Picture Lib. / G. Dagli Orti: 55, 203; © Photo Scala, Florence: 54, 148. Museo Tesoro Basilica di San Francesco © Museo Tesoro Basilica di San Francesco: 175; © Photo Scala, Florence: 121.

Baltimore, MD
© The Walters Art Museum, Baltimore, Maryland: 138.

Berlin
Gemäldegalerie, Staatliche Museen zu Berlin-Preussischer Kulturbesitz © Photo Scala, Florence/bpk, Bildagentur für Kunst, Kultur und Geschichte, Berlin / Christoph Schmidt: 85 © Photo Scala, Florence/bpk, Bildagentur für Kunst, Kultur und Geschichte, Berlin / Jörg P. Anders: 10, 194.

Bern
© Kunstmuseum Bern: 7.

Birmingham
© The Henry Barber Trust, The Barber Institute of Fine Arts, University of Birmingham: 70.

Boston, MA
© Museum of Fine Arts, Boston, Massachusetts: 32, 213.
© Isabella Stewart Gardner Museum, Boston, Massachusetts: 71.

Cambridge
© Fitzwilliam Museum, Cambridge: 22, 137, 139, 209.
Girton College Cambridge © The Mistress and Fellows, Girton College, Cambridge: 66.

Cambridge, MA
© President and Fellows of Harvard College, Cambridge, Massachusetts: 86, 214.

Castello di Gallico
Salini Collection © Foto Studio Lensini Siena: 104.

Cava dei Tirreni
Abbazia della Santissima Trinità © Penta Springs Limited / Alamy Stock Photo: 102.

Chantilly
Musée Condé, Chantilly © RMN-Grand Palais (domaine de Chantilly) / Michel Urtado: 191, 193, 204.

Chiusdino
San Galgano a Montesiepi,

Chiusdino © Foto Studio Lensini Siena: 88.
Città di Castello
© Diocesi di Città di Castello - Museo del Duomo - Archivio fotografico: 128.
Cleveland, OH
© The Cleveland Museum of Art, Cleveland, Ohio: 96, 136, 154, 161, 163, 181, 182, 183.
Cortona
Museo Diocesano, Cortona © Foto Studio Lensini Siena, 51, 52, 109.
Dijon
Musée des Beaux-Arts de Dijon © Manuel Cohen/Scala, Florence: 186; © DeAgostini Picture Library/Scala, Florence: 187.
Florence
Biblioteca Medicea Laurenziana, Florence © Su concessione del Ministero per i Beni e le Attività Culturali: 110.
Gallerie degli Uffizi, Florence © Gabinetto Fotografico delle Gallerie degli Uffizi: 89, 141; © Photo Scala, Florence - courtesy of the Ministero Beni e Alt. Culturali e del Turismo: 6, 39, 41, 91, 147, 160.
Museo dell'Opera di Santa Croce, Florence © Ghigo Roli / Bridgeman Images: 111.
Museo Nazionale del Bargello, Florence © Photo Scala, Florence - courtesy of the Ministero Beni e Alt. Culturali e del Turismo: 114; © Soprintendenza Speciale per il Polo Museale Fiorentino, Gabinetto Fotografico, Ministero per i Beni e le Attività Culturali: 117.
Fort Worth, TX
© Kimbell Art Museum, Fort Worth, Texas: 30.
Frankfurt am Main
Liebieghaus Skulpturensammlung, Frankfurt am Main: 115, 116.
Hull
© Ferens Art Gallery: 56.
Istanbul
Hagia Sofia © akg-images / Erich Lessing: 20.
Karlsruhe
© Staatliche Kunsthalle Karlsruhe: 178.
Lancaster
Ruskin Library © akg-images: 208.
Liverpool
Walker Art Gallery, National Museums Liverpool © National Museums Liverpool: 74.
London
© The National Gallery, London: 8, 9, 15, 28, 29, 31, 42, 49, 50, 53, 58, 59, 167, 184, 185, 210, 215.
© The Samuel Courtauld Trust, The Courtauld Gallery, London: 99, 172.
Victoria and Albert Museum, London © V&A Images / Victoria and Albert Museum, London: 95, 100, 122, 212.
The Royal Collection / HM King Charles III. Royal Collection Trust / © His Majesty King Charles III 2024: 17, 150.
The British Museum, London © The Trustees of the British Museum: 124.
Los Angeles, CA
The J. Paul Getty Museum, Los Angeles, California. Digital image courtesy of the Getty's Open Content Program: 79.
Macclesfield
© courtesy Capesthorne Hall: 207.
Madrid
© Museo Thyssen-Bornemisza, Madrid: 27, 76.
Manchester
Manchester Art Gallery © Manchester City Galleries: 206.
Massa Marittima
Cattedrale di San Cerbone © Foto Studio Lensini Siena: 92.
Milan
Biblioteca-Pinacoteca Ambrosiana, Milan © Photo Scala, Florence: 73.
Naples
Museo Nazionale di Capodimonte, Naples © Photo Scala, Florence: 67, 157.
New York, NY
The Frick Collection, New York © The Frick Collection, New York: 211, 217; © The Frick Collection / photo Michael Bodycomb: 24.
© The Metropolitan Museum of Art, New York: 18, 19, 36, 38, 69, 72, 75, 77, 78, 93, 123, 125, 129, 143, 146, 149, 153, 159, 165, 169, 170, 173, 176, 188, 195, 196, 198, 199, 200, 205.
© James Stevenson / The New Yorker Collection/The Cartoon Bank: 64.
Orvieto
Museo dell'Opera del Duomo © Ghigo Roli / Bridgeman Images: 97, 126; © Photo Scala, Florence: 47.
Paris
Musée de Cluny - musée national du Moyen Âge © RMN-Grand Palais (musée de Cluny - musée national du Moyen Âge) / image RMN-GP: 94; © RMN-Grand Palais (musée de Cluny - musée national du Moyen Âge) / Jean-Gilles Berizzi: 134; © RMN-Grand Palais (musée de Cluny - musée national du Moyen Âge) / René-Gabriel Ojeda: 166; © RMN-Grand Palais (musée de Cluny - musée national du Moyen Âge) / Michel Urtado: 119, 133, 174; © RMN-Grand Palais (musée de Cluny - musée national du Moyen Âge) / Franck Raux: 120.
Musée du Louvre, Paris © RMN-Grand Palais (musée du Louvre) / image RMN-GP: 118; © RMN-Grand Palais (musée du Louvre) / Gérard Blot: 189, 190; © RMN-Grand Palais/Jean-Gilles Berizzi: 131; © RMN-Grand Palais (musée du Louvre) / Franck Raux: 82.
Perugia
Museo Beato Benedetto XI, Perugia © photo Fondazione Bruschettini per l'Arte Asiatica e Islamica, Genova / Bruschettini Foundation for Islamic and Asian Art, Genoa: 156.
Pisa
Museo Nazionale di S. Matteo, Pisa © Soprintendenza per i Beni Ambientali, Architettonici e Storici per le provincie Pisa, Livorno, Lucca e Massa Carrarra: 45; © Photo Scala, Florence - courtesy of the Ministero Beni e Att. Culturali e del Turismo: 44.
Pistoia
Church of Sant'Andrea © Photo Scala, Florence: 34.
Prague
© Museum of Decorative Arts, Prague: 135.
National Gallery of Prague © photo National Gallery Prague 2024: 177; © akg-images / Erich Lessing: 179.
Princeton
© Princeton University Art Museum: 14.
Private collections
© Matilde Grimaldi: 80.
© Photo courtesy of the owners: 98, 105, 171.
San Casciano Val di Pesa
Museo di Arte Sacra © Scala, Florence: 83.
Siena
© Foto Studio Lensini Siena: 3, 14, 16.
Banca Monte dei Paschi di Siena © Foto Studio Lensini Siena: 103.
Basilica di San Domenico, Siena © Foto Studio Lensini Siena: 12.
Museo dell'Opera della Metropolitana, Siena © Foto Studio Lensini Siena: 2, 5, 11, 21, 23, 26, 35, 40, 46, 127, 151.
Palazzo Pubblico, Siena © Bridgeman Images: 1; © Foto Studio Lensini Siena: 65, 152, 155; © Photo Scala, Florence: 140; © Mark Edward Smith / Bridgeman Images: 4.
Pinacoteca nazionale di Siena © Foto Studio Lensini Siena: 87, 108, 162; © courtesy of Ministero per i Beni e le Attività Culturali, Soprintendenza PSAE di Siena & Grosseto: 164; © Photo Scala, Florence - courtesy of the Ministero Beni e Alt. Culturali e del Turismo: 90; © Photo Scala / courtesy of Ministero per i Beni e le Attività Culturali, Soprintendenza PSAE di Siena & Grosseto: 145.
San Bernardino all'Osservanza, Siena © Foto Studio Lensini Siena: 84, 101, 130.
San Francesco, Siena © Foto Studio Lensini Siena: 43; © Photo Scala, Florence - courtesy of the Ministero Beni e Att. Culturali e del Turismo: 57, 142.
Siena Cathedral © Foto Studio Lensini Siena: 33; © DeAgostini Picture Library/Scala, Florence: 113.
St Petersburg
The State Hermitage Museum, St Petersburg © Album / Alamy Stock Photo: 107.
Toledo
Cathedral, Toledo © Album / Alamy Stock Photo: 132.
Toledo, OH
© Toledo Museum of Art, Toledo, Ohio: 144.
Urbino
Museo Diocesano Albani, Urbino © photo Ludovica Rosati: 158.
Vatican City, Rome
© Biblioteca Apostolica Vaticana, Archivio Fotografico: 48.
© Governorate of the Vatican City State - Directorate of the Vatican Museums: 37.
Washington, DC
National Gallery of Art, Washington, DC. Courtesy National Gallery of Art, Washington: 25, 68, 216.

INDEX

Page numbers in *italics* refer to the illustrations.

AUTHORS

Caroline Campbell is Director of the National Gallery of Ireland, Dublin.

Joanna Cannon is Professor Emerita at the Courtauld Institute of Art, London.

Emma Capron is Acting Curator of Early Netherlandish and German Paintings at the National Gallery, London.

Donal Cooper is Professor of Italian and Mediterranean Art at the University of Cambridge and Fellow of Jesus College.

Glyn Davies is Head of Curatorial at the London Museum.

Peter Dent is a Senior Lecturer in History of Art at the University of Bristol.

Nicholas Flory is the Simon Sainsbury Curatorial Fellow at the National Gallery, London.

Christa Gardner von Teuffel is an art historian with special interests in Italian religious art.

Dillian Gordon is an art historian, formerly Curator of Italian Paintings before 1460 at the National Gallery, London.

Sarah M. Guérin is an Associate Professor in the History of Art Department at the University of Pennsylvania.

Laura Llewellyn is Curator of Italian Paintings before 1500 at the National Gallery, London.

Andrea De Marchi is Professor of the History of Medieval Art at the University of Florence.

Francesca Marzullo is Senior Research Associate in European Paintings at The Metropolitan Museum of Art, New York.

Lisa Monnas is an independent scholar, specialising in late medieval and Renaissance textiles.

Susie Nash is the Deborah Loeb Brice Professor of Renaissance Art at the Courtauld Institute of Art, London.

Imogen Tedbury is Curator of Italian Paintings before 1500 at the National Gallery, London (maternity cover).

Beth Williamson is Professor of Medieval Culture and Chair in the History of Art at the University of Bristol.

Stephan Wolohojian is John Pope-Hennessy Curator in Charge of European Paintings at The Metropolitan Museum of Art, New York.

ACKNOWLEDGEMENTS

Cassandra Albinson, John D. Alexander, Angeliki Alexandri, Scott Allan, Sébastien Allard, Elisabeth Antoine-Konig, Marian Aparicio, Christopher Apostle, Victoria Avery, Susanna Avery-Quash, Jane Avison, Sussan Babaie, Michele Bacci, Alessandro Bagnoli, Colin Bailey, Paola Baldetti, Sophie Ballinger, Geanna Barlaam, Claire Barry, Yves Baury, Rachel Beaujean-Deschamps, Lloyd de Beer, Candace K. Beinecke, Alex Bell, Luca Benedetto, Marzia Benini, Paul Binski, Rebecca Birrer, Beatriz Blanco, Sonia Boccia, Barbara Drake Boehm, Thomas Bohl, John Booth, Laura Bonelli, Mar Borobía, Suzanne Bosman, Antonia Bostrom, Alixe Bovey, Aoife Brady, Claire Breay, Adele Breda, Xanthe Brooke, David Alan Brown, John Browne, Kathleen Buehler, Godfrey Burke, Rickie Burman, Aviva Burnstock, Fiona Campbell, Laurence des Cars, Harrison Carter, Isacco Cecconi, Davina Cheung, Alan Chong, Nicola Christie, Mons. Carlo Ciattini, Lorenzo Cinatti, Fra Mario Cisotto, Megan Convery, Jill Cook, Guido Cornini (+), David Crombie, Alan Crookham, Nicholas Cullinan, Paola D'Agostino, Nathan Daly, Richard Dark, Peter and Katharine Darrow, Hélène David-Weill, Michel David-Weill (+), Tom Davies, Alexandra Davis, Xavier Dectot, Giovanni Luca Delogu, Philipp Demandt, Veerle De Meester, Anne Derbes, Sarah Derry, Christine Descatoire, Anna Detheridge, Richard Deutsch, CD Dickerson, Jo Dillon, Cardinal Archbishop Timothy Dolan, Jannic Durand, Antony Eastmond, Michael Eissenhauer, Taylor Elyea, Karen Eslea, Helen Evans, Gabriele Fattorini, Anne Fay, Kaywin Feldman, Dominic Ferrante, Julie Firth, Andrew Fletcher, Peggy Fogelman, Sam Fogg, Susan Foister, Jenny Foot, Fra Thomas Freidel, Olivier Gabet, Julien Gallon, Fra Mauro Gambetti, Jennifer Garpner, Davide Gasparotto, Stefania Gerevini, Alexandra Gerstein, Cristina Gnoni (+), Juraj Grac, Jan Green, Simon Green, Diana Greenwald, Matilde Grimaldi, William Griswold, Emily Guerry, Natasha Halford, Claire Hallinan, Jessica Harrison-Hall, Babette Hartwieg, Maria Harvey, Anne Hawley, Tom Hemming, Katrin Henkel, Nicholas Herman, Erma Hermans, Jason Herrick, Patrick Herron, Mary Hersov, Paul Hills, Gretchen Hirschauer, Dagmar Hirschfelder, Adrian Hunt, Tristram Hunt, Graham and Amanda Hutton, Jane Hyne, Frederick Ilchman, Alessandra Isolan, Hamilton E. James, Barbara Jatta, Mark Jones, Nicola Kalinsky, Danny Katz, Guillaume Kientz, Susannah Kingwill, Tim Knox, Sarah Kozlowski, Roland Krischke, Olivier Laville, Eric Lee, Heather Lemonides-Brown, Cristiano Leone, Isabella Leone, Séverine Lepape, Adam Levine, Naomi Lewis, Nicole Linderman, Laura Lindsay, Inbal Livne, Archbishop Paolo Lojudice, Anna Lutz, Gerhard Lutz, Rhona MacBeth, Olivia Maguire, Giovanni Malpelo, Griffith Mann, Mayor Marie Mayot, Gianni Mazzoni, Florian Meunier, Janet Moore, Fra Marco Moroni, Jane Munroe, Rebecca Myles, Letizia Nesi, Scott Nethersole, Austin Nevin, Cardinal Archbishop Vincent Nichols, Tom Nickson, Christina Nielsen, Diana Norman, Anh Nyguen, Chris Oberon, Kate O'Donoghue, Kerri Offord, Miriam Orlando, Patrick O'Sullivan, Stella Panayotova, Amy Passiak, Maria Vittoria Pellini, Sandra Penketh, Nicholas Penny, Nathalie Petitdidier, Roberta Pieraccioli, Anna Pizzamano, Belinda Philpot, Gianfranco Pocobene, Timothy Potts, Jennifer Powell, Laura Pye, Carmen Ramos, Richard Rand, Matthew Reeves, Paola Refice, John Renner, Anna Reynolds, Suzanne Reynolds, Eleanor Richards, Purificacion Ripio, James Robinson, Mons. Alberto Rocca, Cristina Roccaforte, Pierrick Rodriguez, Gianni Rogialli, Stefan Roller, Ursola Romalli, Sandra Romito, Gervase Rosser, Gianni Rossi, Elena Rossoni, Hannah Rothschild, Neville Rowley, Julie Rowlins, Sir Paul and Lady Ruddock, Per Rumberg, Francis Russell, Benjamin Rux, Xavier Salomon, Giovanni Santinucci, Peter Schade, Robert Schindler, Eike Schmidt, Linda Schofield, Vera-Simone Schulz, Karen Serres, George Shackelford, Desmond Shawe-Taylor, Gretchen Shie Miller, Dominique Shweky, Nathaniel Silver, Kirsten Simster, Hannah Sisk, Samantha Sizemore, Vicky Skelding-Bloor, Guillermo Solana, Naomi Speakman, Eve Straussman-Pflanzer, Carl Strehlke, Luke Syson, Patrizia Tarchi, Federica Tarducci, Angelo Tartuferi, Martha Tedeschi, Matthew Teitelbaum, Dominique Thiébaut, James Thompson, Sue Thompson, Dora Thornton, Cecilia Treves, Letizia Treves, Chiara Valdambrini, Nico Van Hout, Fleur Van Paassen, Ernst Vegelin van Claerbergen, Amanda Venezia, Simone Verde, Dominique Vingtain, Ian Wardropper, Robert Wenley, Hannah Westall, Lucy Whitaker, Roger Wieck, Carmen Willems, Hannah Williamson, Matthias Wivel, Lucy Wrapson, Nina Zimmer, Michaela Zöschg.

Finally, the curators would like to acknowledge the patience, love and support of their families and friends during the decade-long course of this project.

PUBLISHED TO ACCOMPANY THE EXHIBITION

Siena: The Rise of Painting, 1300–1350
The Metropolitan Museum of Art, New York, 13 October 2024 – 26 January 2025
The National Gallery, London, 8 March – 22 June 2025

Curated by Caroline Campbell, Laura Llewellyn, Imogen Tedbury and Stephan Wolohojian in collaboration with Joanna Cannon

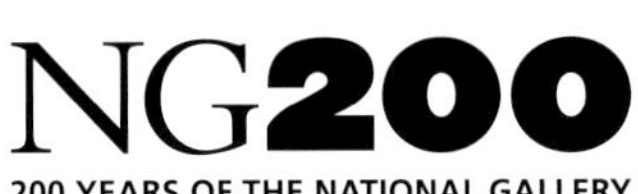

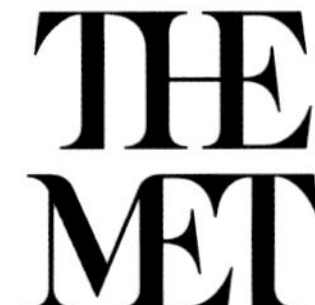

EXHIBITION SUPPORTED BY

Lead Philanthropic Supporter

the HUO FAMILY FOUNDATION

Lead Exhibition Sponsor

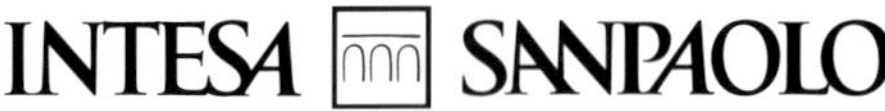

Gregory Annenberg Weingarten

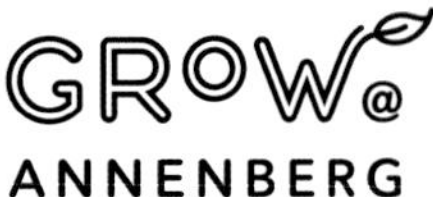

The London Community Foundation

COCKAYNE

PEGGY CZYZAK-DANNENBAUM

THE VASEPPI TRUST

LAURA LINDSAY

With additional support from

Sam Fogg
The Hutton Foundation
Fabrizio Moretti
Elizabeth and Daniel Peltz OBE
Marco Voena
Count and Countess Emilio Voli
And other donors

This exhibition has been made possible by the provision of insurance through the Government Indemnity Scheme. The National Gallery would like to thank HM Government for providing Government Indemnity and the Department for Culture, Media and Sport and Arts Council England for arranging the indemnity.

Authorised Representative in the EU Details:
Easy Access System, Europe, Mustamäe tee 50,
10621 Tallinn, Estonia, gpsr.requests@easproject.com

First published in 2024 by National Gallery Global Limited
Trafalgar Square, London WC2N 5DN
www.shop.nationalgallery.org.uk

Reprinted twice 2025

ISBN: 9781857097160
1053024

British Library Cataloguing-in-Publication Data
A catalogue record is available from the British Library
Library of Congress Control Number: 2024934831

Publisher: Laura Lappin | Senior Project Editor: Flora Allen
Managing Editor: Diana Adell | Copy-editor: Linda Schofield
Production: Jane Hyne | Picture Researcher: Suzanne Bosman
Designed and typeset in Warnock by Adrian Hunt
Origination by ALTA, London | Printed in Italy by Conti Tipocolor
Paper: GardaMatt Art 150gsm

All measurements give height before width.

FRONT COVER: Simone Martini, *The Angel Gabriel* (detail of fig. 81)
BACK COVER: Nasrid workshop, Iberia, *Textile fragment* (detail of fig. 146)

p. 2, detail of fig. 215; p. 7, detail of fig. 87;
pp. 18–19, detail of fig. 31; pp. 60–1, detail of fig. 40;
pp. 142–3, detail of fig. 95; pp. 190–1, detail of fig. 173.